Oracle Press™

Oracle WebCenter 11*g* Handbook

ORACLE®

Oracle Press™

Oracle WebCenter 11*g* Handbook: Build Rich, Customizable Enterprise 2.0 Applications

Frédéric Desbiens
Peter Moskovits
Philipp Weckerle

New York Chicago San Francisco
Lisbon London Madrid Mexico City Milan
New Delhi San Juan Seoul Singapore Sydney Toronto

The McGraw-Hill Companies

Cataloging-in-Publication Data is on file with the Library of Congress

McGraw-Hill books are available at special quantity discounts to use as premiums and sales promotions, or for use in corporate training programs. To contact a representative, please e-mail us at bulksales@mcgraw-hill.com.

Oracle WebCenter 11*g* Handbook: Build Rich, Customizable Enterprise 2.0 Applications

2 3 4 5 6 7 8 9 0 WFR WFR 0 1

ISBN 978-0-07-162932-4
MHID 0-07-162932-7

Sponsoring Editor
Lisa McClain

Editorial Supervisor
Patty Mon

Project Editor
Emilia Thiuri

Acquisitions Coordinator
Meghan Riley

Technical Editors
Vanessa Wang, Sachin Agarwal, Chris Broadbent, Vince Casarez, Robin Fisher, Christian Hauser, Soy Joseph, Sanjay Khanna, Istvan Kiss, Christina Kolotouros, Gangadhar Konduri, Olivier Lafontaine, Simon Lessard, Alison MacMillan, Duncan Mills, Lynn Munsinger, Frank Nimphius, Nicolas Pombourcq, Stewart Wilson

Copy Editor
Mandy Erickson

Proofreader
Paul Tyler

Indexer
Karin Arrigoni

Production Supervisor
Jean Bodeaux

Composition
Apollo Publishing Service

Illustration
Apollo Publishing Service

Art Director, Cover
Jeff Weeks

Cover Designer
Pattie Lee

To Roxanne, my love, who will not understand this book and yet understands me so well. To our children, Emmanuelle and Michel, because I found the strength to write each word in their smiles.

—Frédéric

To my kids: Danka for being the sweetest little boy and Lea for being such a patient baby.
To my wife, Anna, for bringing Lea to this world in the middle of Chapter 4.

—Peter

To the most important things in life, friends and family. Without their support, those long nights and exhausting stretches of work would have been much harder.

—Philipp

About the Authors

Frédéric Desbiens is a senior technical architect and trainer for Fujitsu America. He has over twelve years of software development experience, and was involved in the development of several enterprise-level web applications using Java Enterprise Edition and the Microsoft .NET framework. In the last few years, he has strived to achieve balance between business and technology concerns, with his current focus areas being SOA, web portals, and content management systems. He holds an MBA in eCommerce, a BS in computer science, and a BA in education.

Peter Moskovits is a senior principal product manager for Oracle WebCenter and leads the product management efforts for the WebCenter Framework and social computing services. He joined Oracle in Hungary in 1998 as an Oracle University instructor. Later, he authored several training classes on portals and portlet development. After playing an active role in architecting and building the Oracle WebCenter product, Peter now focuses on the overall strategy of the Oracle WebCenter development experience and custom application development, as well as portlet development tools and technologies. He is a frequent speaker at conferences, such as JavaOne, ODTUG, and Oracle OpenWorld. Peter is an Oracle Certified Professional and holds an MS degree in computer science.

Philipp Weckerle started his career in IT in 1992 as a developer and DBA at a small consulting firm in Vienna. In 1999, he moved to Oracle Austria as a support analyst, and in 2001, he transferred to Oracle headquarters in Redwood Shores. There he joined the product management team and was initially responsible for Oracle Reports. In 2004, Philipp joined the first design team for the product that is today called Oracle WebCenter. After that, Philipp became lead product manager for the content integration aspects of Oracle WebCenter, closely working with Development on the design of features such as the document library and the Java Content Repository. Today, Philipp is back in Austria acting as a solution architect for Enterprise 2.0 with Oracle Austria.

About the Technical Editors

Vanessa Wang is a principal technical writer who has spent more than a decade producing a wide variety of documentation, instructional materials, and white papers for Oracle products and services. She currently leads the documentation effort for custom application development with Oracle WebCenter and is a frequent contributor to Oracle OpenWorld. She holds an MA degree in instructional technologies and education.

Sachin Agarwal is the director for product management and strategy for Oracle's Enterprise 2.0 and Portal products and focuses on how Oracle's next-generation collaboration and user interaction technologies can be leveraged by businesses. He has been with Oracle since 2005, holding key positions within Oracle's Fusion Middleware Division, including platform product management and development.

Sachin has over 15 years of enterprise software industry experience. Prior to joining Oracle, he held key positions at Oblix, BMC Software, and Infosys.

Chris Broadbent is a consulting member of technical staff at Oracle where he has worked on the Portal and WebCenter platforms for nine years. He has almost 20 years of experience designing and building enterprise class applications, tools, and frameworks.

Vince Casarez, vice president of Oracle Corporation, focuses on Web 2.0 technology development, Enterprise 2.0, and portal products. Over the past 14 years, Vince has held many key positions at Oracle. Currently, he is vice president of product management for Enterprise 2.0 and Portal products. He has recently coauthored a book entitled *Reshaping Your Business with Web 2.0* that remains on the Amazon Technology best-seller list since its introduction in September 2008. He also has responsibility for managing the WebCenter development team handling Web 2.0 and social computing services.

Previously, he focused on hosted portal development and operations, which included Oracle Portal Online for external customers, Portal Center for building a portal community, and My Oracle for the employee intranet. Before that, he was vice president of tools marketing where he handled all tools products including development tools and business intelligence tools. He also held the position of director of product management for Oracle's JDeveloper. Before joining Oracle, Vince spent seven years at Borland International, where he was group product manager of Paradox for Windows and dBASE for Windows. He holds a bachelor's degree in biochemistry from the University of California, Los Angeles.

Robin Fisher is a senior manager in the WebCenter team at Oracle. He is responsible for various aspects of the WebCenter framework, including the JSF Portlet Bridge, contextual framework, and taxonomy. Robin has been involved in the development efforts for Oracle Portal, Oracle JDeveloper, and Oracle Reports.

Christian Hauser is principal product manager, Enterprise 2.0 and Portals. He joined Oracle in September 1997 as a support analyst for tools. While he was a part of the Oracle support services organization, he supported various products like Reports, Forms, and Designer before moving to the Internet products group to support WebDB, Portal, and JDeveloper. Christian took on the role of EMEA portal team leader in 2001, and in April 2002, he joined the portal and reports product management team. Currently, Christian is responsible for driving the social networking aspects of Oracle WebCenter. In addition, Christian oversees Global Outbound activities such as field enablement, customer visits, support interactions, and the evangelization of WebCenter Suite at conferences. Christian is based in Austria, Europe.

Soy Joseph is software development manager at Oracle where he manages the various implementations of Oracle WebCenter and Oracle Portal within the company. He has over 14 years of experience in the software industry focusing on implementation and management of Oracle Database, Oracle Application Server, and the new Fusion Middleware 11*g*. Prior to joining Oracle in 2002, he worked for two startup companies in the U.S. and spent four years at a major finance company in Muscat, Oman. Soy holds a degree in computer science from the University of Madras, India. He has been involved in the WebCenter project from its inception. He was instrumental in facilitating the successful implementation of the WebCenter Suite within Oracle and for the selected customers who chose to be early adopters of the product. His extensive knowledge and work experience with the product has been utilized in the review of the install and administration chapters of this book.

Sanjay Khanna is a product manager for Oracle WebCenter. He has a long-standing interest in and has made extensive contribution to portals and Web 2.0 technologies. During his ten-year relationship with Oracle, he has played a major role in shaping several generations of Oracle's user interaction products, ranging from Oracle WebDB to Oracle WebCenter. Prior to working with Oracle, he was a consultant for software implementation to several large corporations. Sanjay has a BE degree in computer science from the University of Pune, India and an MBA from California State University.

Istvan Kiss is a curriculum developer working for the WebCenter team that develops courses about Oracle WebCenter 11*g*. He has been with Oracle since 1996, working first as an Oracle University instructor, where he taught Java at all levels, from beginner Java courses up to JEE and ADF development and XML. He has also taught middle-tier courses such as application server administration and various portal courses all over Europe.

Istvan graduated from Technical University of Budapest in 1979 as an electronic engineer and worked at the university as an assistant lecturer. During the next 17 years, he gradually became more involved with teaching computer science courses and was one of the first instructors to teach Java at the university level in Hungary. Istvan currently lives in Hungary's capital, Budapest.

Christina (Gibb) Kolotouros is a director of product management for Oracle WebCenter. She has been with Oracle since 1994, starting as a product manager for Oracle (Data) Browser and Oracle Data Query. Over a decade later, Christina was managing product management, documentation, and curriculum development for business intelligence tools and some data warehousing. About 18 months ago, Christina moved over to the world of portals and building Enterprise 2.0 applications as part of the WebCenter team. In addition to product management responsibilities, she also manages the curriculum development. She has a BSEE in electrical engineering and computer science from the Massachusetts Institute of Technology.

Gangadhar Konduri is director of product management in the Fusion Middleware division of Oracle. Gangadhar has been with Oracle since 1999, holding various product management and development positions. He is a key architect of metadata management services for the Middleware platform. He made key contributions to the architecture of several areas of WebCenter, including WebCenter Composer and WebCenter Spaces. He holds product management responsibilities for various products in Fusion Middleware, including metadata services, several areas of WebCenter, and the core components of Oracle's Fusion applications architecture. Gangadhar has a B.Tech in computer sciences and engineering from Indian Institute of Technology (I.I.T), Kharagpur, where he graduated *summa cum laude*. He has an MS in electrical engineering and computer sciences from Massachusetts Institute of Technology (M.I.T).

Olivier Lafontaine is a senior software developer with a strong interest in data persistence. He has over seven years of experience developing Java and Java EE applications and frameworks. For the past three years, with Fujitsu Consulting, he has successfully helped customers develop applications using Oracle ADF.

Simon Lessard is a member of the JSR-314 expert group in charge of Java Server Faces evolution. He is also member of the Apache MyFaces PMC with a strong focus on MyFaces 2.0 and Trinidad. He has been using Java since 2000 and is a software engineering graduate from University Laval.

Alison MacMillan is a consulting member of technical staff with Oracle Corporation, and is a developer and architect for Oracle WebCenter's content integration team. She is a member of the JSR-283 (JCR 2.0) expert group and Oasis Content Management Interoperability Specification (CMIS) Technical Committee. She has over 20 years of experience in software development, including the last 11 years with Oracle.

Duncan Mills is senior director of product management for Oracle's application development Tools, including Oracle JDeveloper, Forms, and the ADF Framework. Duncan is currently responsible for product direction, evangelism, and courseware development around the development tools products. He has worked with Oracle in a variety of applications development and DBA roles since 1988. For the past 14 years, he has worked in both support and product development, with the past eight years in product management. Duncan is the coauthor of the Oracle Press books *Oracle JDeveloper 10*g *for Forms and PL/SQL Developers: A Guide to Web Development with Oracle ADF* and *Oracle JDeveloper 11*g *Handbook: A Guide to Fusion Web Development.*

Lynn Munsinger is a principal product manager for the Java Tools development group at Oracle, specializing in JDeveloper and ADF. Her career at Oracle began in 1998, and she has been responsible for the support, education, and technical evangelism of Oracle's application development tools ever since. She is coauthor of *Oracle Fusion Developer Guide: Building Rich Internet Applications with Oracle ADF, Business Components, and ADF Faces,* available in late 2009. Lynn is also the primary developer of the Fusion Order Demo sample application for Fusion Middleware, and is a frequent presenter at user group and industry conferences.

Frank Nimphius is a principal product manager for application development tools at Oracle Corporation. In his current role, Frank contributes to the development of Oracle JDeveloper and the Oracle Application Development Framework, with a special interest in JavaServer Faces, ADF Faces and AJAX technologies, as well as application security.

Nicolas Pombourcq is a software development manager at Oracle where he has been working on content integration in WebCenter for the last four years.

Stewart Wilson is a director of development in the WebCenter team at Oracle. He is responsible for various parts of the WebCenter framework and services, including portlets and the JDeveloper extension. Stewart has held various development positions at Oracle since 1994. He's been involved in the development efforts for Oracle Portal, Oracle JDeveloper, and Oracle Reports.

Contents at a Glance

PART I
Introduction to Oracle WebCenter and the Application Development Framework

PART II
Building WebCenter Applications

PART III
Tailoring Your Applications

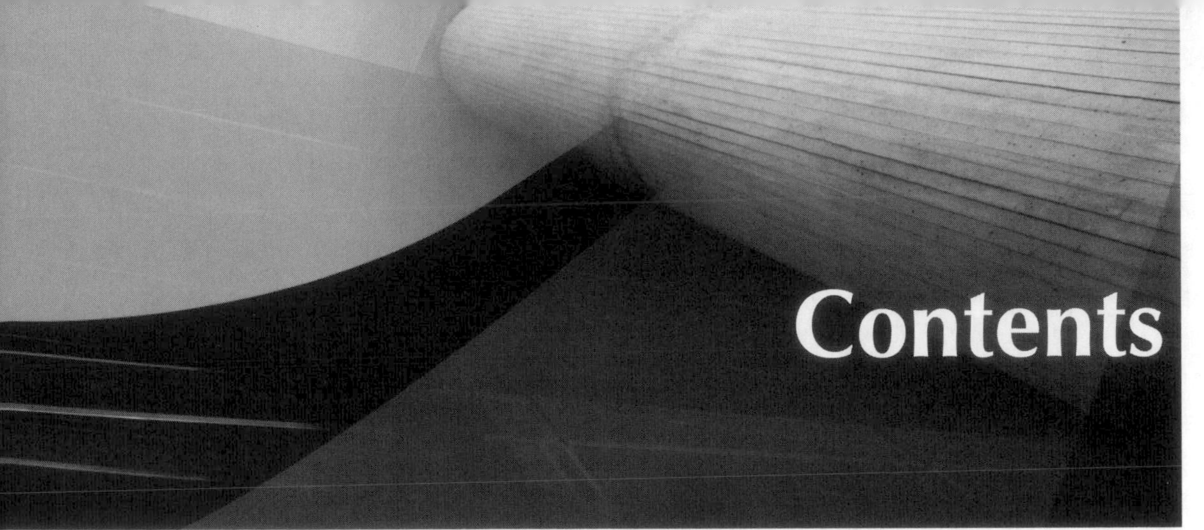

Contents

PART III
Tailoring Your Applications

PART IV

Administering Your Applications

PART V

Oracle Applications Integration

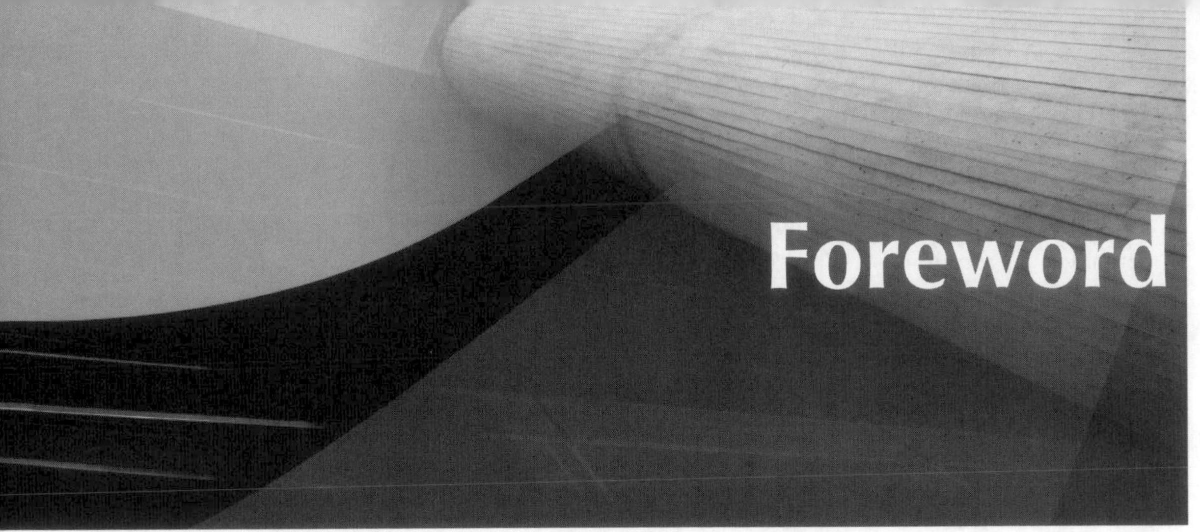

Foreword

Oracle Fusion Middleware 11*g* is an extraordinary release in Oracle's history. Oracle Fusion Middleware 11*g* provides the foundation for Fusion Applications and how our customers develop, deploy, and manage enterprise applications.

As the user interaction layer of Oracle Fusion Middleware, Oracle WebCenter plays a key role in this release. In a single framework, it supports the development of all styles of web sites, portals, and composite applications. It provides the ability for users and site administrators to highly personalize the behavior and look and feel of the portal to meet user requirements while insulating them from future upgrades. Also, it delivers an adaptable service model that follows what the SOA world has done for enterprise applications, and enables delivery of reusable, customizable, and personalizable social computing services.

Oracle WebCenter 11*g* introduces the Enterprise Business Dictionary and Integration Framework. Users need to interact through the portal with all the resources in the enterprise; therefore they must integrate a business dictionary and provide prepackaged integration with enterprise applications, content, rich media, business processes, and business intelligence in a role-specific way in order to speed user awareness of these critical resources.

Built on top of the WebCenter Framework and Services in WebCenter 11*g*, we introduce the concept of dynamic online communities, called WebCenter Spaces. Since much of the work of dynamically changing business applications and processes is done by groups of people working with each other, enterprise portals must host dynamic online business communities that users can interact with using their familiar personal productivity tools.

Enterprise communities must also provide social computing services to allow online users to find others in the organization and to exploit the tools to communicate and share information with them quickly and easily. Users also need to access information from the enterprise portal pervasively; therefore, modern portals need to provide the ability to deliver this information to users whenever it's required.

This book, written by experts who were deeply involved in the design, implementation, and early adoption of Oracle Fusion Middleware 11*g*, guides you through the concepts of Oracle WebCenter, and provides practical steps for architecting, building, and managing rich, customizable Enterprise 2.0 portals and applications. As the most comprehensive book covering Oracle WebCenter 11*g*, it should be invaluable help to you as you use the product.

Thomas Kurian
Executive Vice President
Oracle Product Development

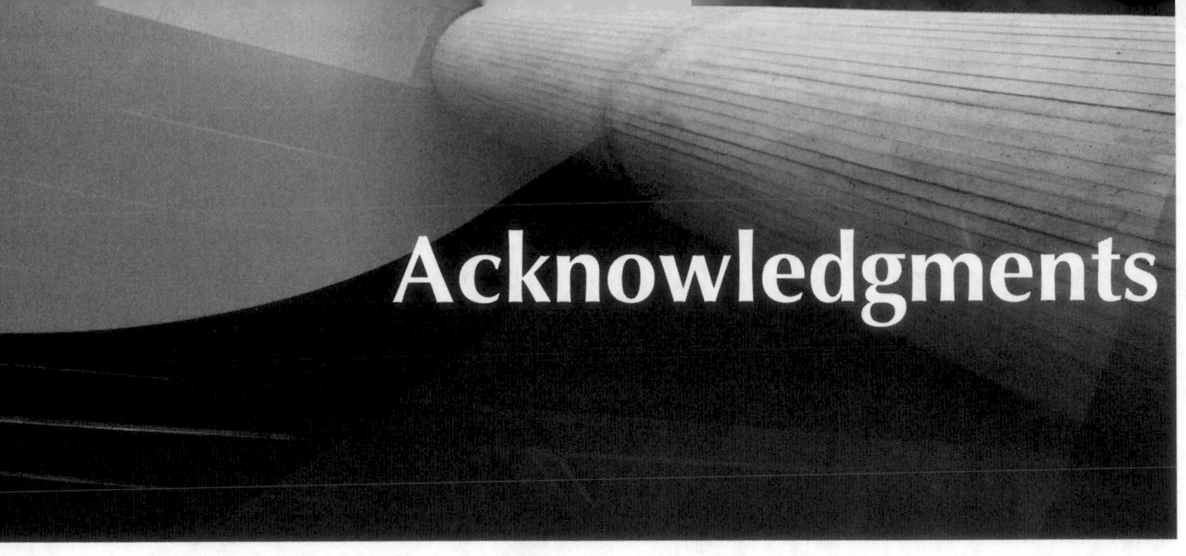

Acknowledgments

A warm thank you to Simon Lessard and Olivier Lafontaine, fellow colleagues from Fujitsu America. I keep great memories of the long, rambling exchanges about WebCenter, Web 2.0, and Java architecture that we've had over the years. They supported me through maybe the greatest challenge of my life, all the while I was writing this book.

I also want to express my gratitude to Gilles Belley, director of the Oracle Solutions and Expertise Center for Fujitsu's Quebec City office. He believed in my capacities and gave me many opportunities to put them to good use.

Special thanks to Éric Marcoux, Oracle Ace Director. It is Éric who introduced me to Peter and Philipp, thus enabling me to contribute to this book.

Finally, how could I forget to mention my parents here? I gave them much trouble early on, so much in fact that they weren't able to find babysitters for me. It took me a while, but I finally put my surplus energy to good use. They always wanted the best for me, and I am grateful for all the sacrifices they have made.

—Frédéric

First and foremost, I'd like to express my appreciation to Vanessa Wang, principal technical writer at Oracle, who assisted us through the entire life cycle of the book, from helping us with the proposal to managing the entire review process with a large number of technical reviewers. Thank you, Vanessa!

This book could not have happened without the input and thorough feedback of our technical reviewers who are the most prominent experts in the field. Their biographies are in this book—please read them.

I'd like to thank the exceptionally professional team of our publisher: Lisa McClain, senior acquisitions editor and Meghan Riley, acquisitions coordinator. Lisa and Meghan helped us stay focused and on schedule. Their experience and assistance helped us through tough times.

Thanks to the copy editing team, Emilia Thiuri, project editor, and Mandy Erickson, copy editor, for ensuring that a book written by three non-native speakers reads well.

I would also like to thank my management team at Oracle for their continued support: Josh Lannin, director of product management, Vince Casarez, vice president of product management, and Rahul Patel, vice president of product development.

At Oracle, I am especially inspired by four people who started out as colleagues and quickly became close family friends. Istvan Kiss, first my college professor, then my mentor and fellow instructor at Oracle, never fails to challenge me to think harder and do better. Ellen Gravina, senior principal curriculum developer, the cake wizard from the Right Coast, supplies us with cookies and cakes for every thinkable and unthinkable occasion. Her sweets always cheered me up even in the toughest book-writing times. Julie Tower, the unforgettable office mate, is always ready to improve and correct my English. Julie's words about the hardships of writing a book echoed so many times during my own writing. And last but not least, Sue Vickers, a close colleague and former manager, always knows how to stay calm and bright.

I'd like to thank Éric Marcoux, chief architect of University Laval, who recognized the need and importance of a book on this subject.

Thanks also to my extended family for their patience and encouragement during this busy period.

And, finally, many special thanks to my fellow authors: Philipp, who joined the team without hesitation and played such a great host while I was visiting Vienna to finish up the writing phase; and Frédéric, who despite not knowing the other two authors personally, proved to be an excellent partner and fellow author.

—Peter

I would like to thank the whole Oracle WebCenter development team who have created an exciting product. I would also like to thank Stewart Wilson who has spent numerous hours on the phone and instant messaging to help me through various oddities—the perks of writing a book on the leading edge of technology development.

—Philipp

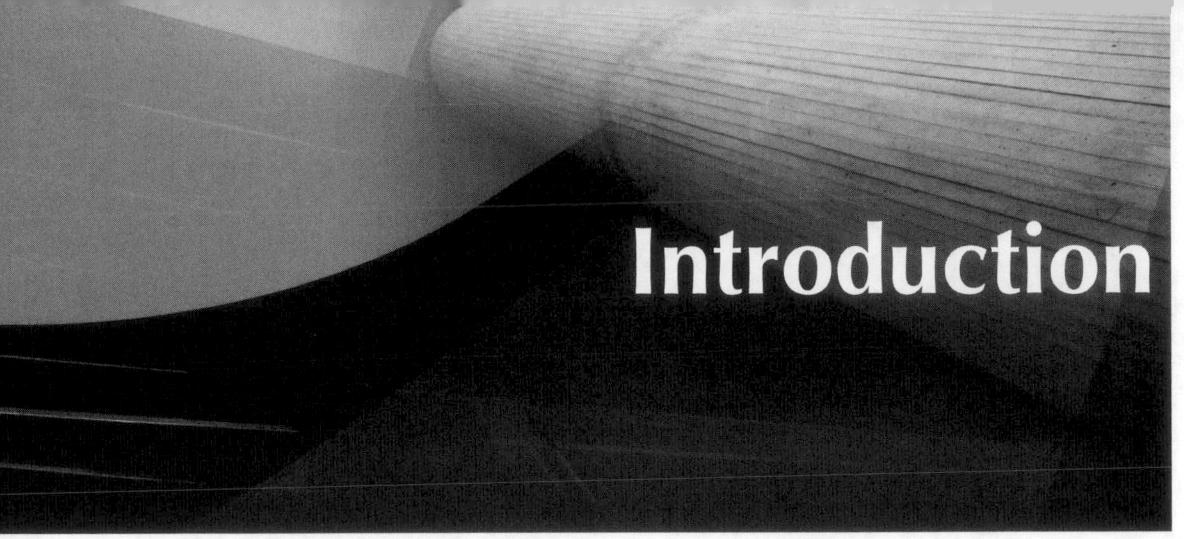

Oracle WebCenter is the leading-edge product for developing next-generation enterprise portals and composite applications with Web 2.0 in mind. This book introduces you to the aspects of developing WebCenter applications and enriching those applications with social computing services, including discussions, documents, blogs, wikis, tags, and links. It gives you an overview of the architecture behind Oracle WebCenter and the Oracle Fusion platform, and it guides you through the complete cycle from development and testing in Oracle JDeveloper all the way to deploying your application to the Oracle WebLogic Server.

This book can be used to get a first glance at Oracle WebCenter, and it can be a guide during later phases of development as well, by providing hints and tips for developers. You can pick and choose the chapters to read based upon the particular phase you are in.

PART I

Introduction to Oracle WebCenter and the Application Development Framework

CHAPTER 1

Business Application Development: The Journey to WebCenter

Keeping Up with Requirements

Business application requirements have typically been driven by user, business, or technology needs—and sometimes current fads. The range of requirements has spanned from immediate technical needs, like tracking Social Security numbers and vaccinations for government agencies, to incorporating animated images (in some cases, as many as possible) into web page banners. In the past, business applications may have been built because a user needed a specific data-entry application, or a business required a large-scale reporting application to track internal production and sales. When the Web and portals became more popular, many companies wanted to have more of a presence on the Web, and they quickly created web sites and web applications, sometimes using trendy software and design tools with little consideration for long-term impact.

Regardless of the motivations behind the requirements, one need has remained: business applications must be available as soon as possible, and at as little cost as possible. Historically, the application development life cycle has been measured in months and sometimes years. As companies and consumers become increasingly accustomed to personalized, on-demand computing and "instant information," business application developers must also keep pace with their audience's needs while minimizing the impact on existing systems.

The Losing Battle

To address the wide array of requirements, application developers have had to endure the age-old question: Should we customize or not—and if we customize, how much? Customizing applications to address business requirements is ideal for the end user. Developers can create rich applications that are tailored to any type of user. These applications, however, have traditionally been complex, requiring a high level of technical knowledge to build and maintain. Alternatively, with standard, off-the-shelf applications, the initial investment is low: the cost is generally lower than a custom-built application, and the applications usually require less technical knowledge to implement. However, these standard applications do not always satisfy all users, nor do they necessarily adequately address the requirements of the business.

As the 20th century came to a close, many application developers resorted to using myriad different technologies and services—some custom-built, and some not—to balance their various business and end user requirements, all while keeping costs down. In doing so, their applications have become extremely complex. The level of expertise required to maintain these applications skyrocketed, while the number of people who have the expertise has dwindled. This shortage has led to an artificial expansion of project teams to cover business information technology (IT) requirements, which has, in turn, increased cost, negating the initial intention to reduce cost of development.

At this point, developers faced a losing battle: with standard applications, the end users were dissatisfied because the applications only partially fulfill their requirements; with customized, or even partially customized applications, upper managers were stuck with an ever-growing information technology bill. This situation could only lead to one thing: a technical revolution.

The First Revolution: Enterprise Portals

Around the turn of the century, the concept of *enterprise portals* was born. The purpose of these portals was to provide a component (namely, a portlet)–based environment that would allow both the components, as well as the overall application, to be customized specifically to a user's requirements with minimal development and maintenance, thus resolving the long-fought battle.

Initially, portals were used to create dashboards, which are single-entry points that present only vital, user-defined information. Users could assemble and arrange portlets on their individualized pages without affecting other users of the same portal application. They could also contextually wire these components and portlets together so the information they viewed in a single snapshot was always customized for them and could be catered to their daily work. Portals quickly gained momentum as, for the first time, users could directly influence the applications they had to work with every day.

With enterprise portals, users could essentially custom build their own applications out of components created by the application developers. The developers could focus on creating the small, easily maintained components with defined functionality and provide those to their users. Users were then able to build a virtually infinite number of applications, each made specifically for the user—something traditional application development could not achieve. Even now, with other technologies available, enterprise portals remain popular for certain purposes. However, while this was a step in the right direction, users and businesses soon found themselves wanting more, especially as the line between personal and business online tasks blurred, and demand for interactivity and transactions increased.

IT departments took advantage of what was available at the time to create portlets out of applications and let users have more control over their workspaces, or dashboards. Unfortunately, the component frameworks that were used to build portlets and their standardized successors (JSR 168 and WSRP) were never intended for building applications; they were designed to expose information in a reusable way. That is to say, these portlets were meant to be informational in nature, not transactional. As a result, these portlets were clunky, complex, and difficult to maintain, recalling the pre-revolution days when many applications were partially customized behind the scenes, leading to intricate and overly complicated maintenance and upgrade processes. Furthermore, enterprise portals were designed to accommodate two categories of components: portlets and content. So if a component did not fall in one of those two categories, it had to somehow be conformed to one or the other.

At the same time, another major problem arose: now that different sources within and outside the enterprise could be integrated into a single experience for the user, the next hurdle was to figure out how information could be secured and, more specifically, how the security information across all those information stores could be combined. The first and most obvious solution was to centralize the user and rights management into one identity store and integrate those information sources with this identity store. In some cases that was a valid option, but in most cases, centralizing the user and rights managements stores was a big problem because of organizational or technical limitations. The need arose for a supporting framework that would allow a way to automatically sign in users across disparate systems, each requiring specific credentials. And so was born Single Sign-On, which provides the ability to log into an application once and access all the supporting and integrated applications without having to reenter credentials. This was a boon for users and developers alike.

The Second Revolution: Composite Applications

As user requirements surpassed enterprise portal capabilities, a new concept evolved: *composite applications*. The notion behind composite applications was to combine the customizability and flexibility of enterprise portals with the productivity and interactivity of traditional enterprise applications in a single, new framework. Single Sign-On enabled such frameworks to exist by streamlining the authentication process. However, for developers to effectively build composite applications, they needed an open and standardized development environment that would allow an application to transform from a traditional, transactional application to a fully composite application without the need for reengineering.

The key to composite applications centers on building application *components*—creating reusable modules that can be used (and reused) in traditional and composite applications alike but also be flexible enough to accommodate existing technologies like portlets, as well as new concepts, such as rich desktop-like interaction. By building reusable components and then assembling them together, developers would be able to implement new requirements quickly and efficiently by reusing existing functionalities or enhancing existing ones. Also, vendors of these applications could create their own components to integrate with the original application, thus customizing the user experience and reducing IT costs.

Composite applications may sound awfully similar to the idea behind enterprise portals, but there was one major difference: the components in composite applications were *designed* to be modularized and reused. Rather than reverse engineer an application to fit it into an enterprise portal by stretching portlets, developers deliberately designed and built reusable components for these applications. By using new technology that enabled fresh component creation and by planning ahead, application developers not only reduced their initial development time, but they were able to significantly decrease the amount of effort and resources spent on maintenance and upgrades; in some cases, they eliminated reverse-engineering entirely.

...And Then Came Web 2.0

Originally, the World Wide Web was conceived as a mechanism for presenting text- and image-rich pages connected together by hyperlinks that anyone could access as long as he or she had a computer and online access. This essentially was Web 1.0.

As the Web developed, it became clear that, in enterprise environments, a lot of information was held as structured information within business applications. Enterprise portals could link information from these sources; these portals became Web 1.5.

As enterprise portals became more popular, the Web transformed from a pure information source to one that provides a variety of services, which have now become a vital part of a user's day-to-day toolbox, both for personal and business use. As these new service concepts have emerged, users' expectations of the interaction level have changed as well. In the Web 1.0 era, plain information pages were sufficient. However, today's users expect highly interactive web experiences, conceptually and technically. The IT response to these expectations has given rise to "the next generation Web" or Web 2.0.

This modern-day Internet has evolved from the more personal areas of the Web to where individuals use online technologies to communicate, collaborate, and socialize. At first, these technologies were mainly used for personal purposes, but it didn't take long for businesses to realize that the concepts behind these services could be leveraged to produce effective enterprise solutions for business applications. However, the fast-paced development of these services in both industries has led to an explosion in the production of online content, creating a new challenge in terms of management and maintenance.

Modern web users are bombarded with an incredible volume of information every day, so to avoid losing the most salient and important information in the noise, application developers must ensure that content is presented in context as much as possible. Doing so will help users understand and digest the necessary and relevant information. By coupling this with rich user interaction and highly interactive user interfaces, users' productivity and interaction with the application can be vastly streamlined and improved. By further enhancing applications with social and collaborative services, a richer and more effective experience can be created for larger groups working together, creating a whole new paradigm of interpersonal interaction and information sharing.

Getting There with Java

Now that we know where we're headed, let's get back to the real work: development. In the early days, web application developers started using Java to build composite applications. Java was originally conceived as an open, portable programming language that would allow the creation of applications, independent of the platform they ran on; this was achieved by running all applications inside a virtual machine (JVM) on the desired platforms. Java enabled web application developers to build the components, or servlets, they needed for the composite applications. Only one part of the problem was solved, however. While developers could build well-designed modular components, they still found themselves hand coding user interfaces (UIs) in HTML. These were basic and did not necessarily fulfill their user requirements.

With web applications becoming increasingly massive and complex, hand coding UIs soon became unwieldy and obsolete. Another concept was then born: JavaServer Pages (JSPs). JSPs enabled developers to embed Java code directly into HTML pages, making it much easier to build rich, interactive web application UIs while still providing the necessary scripting capabilities to create rich application UIs, not just basic HTML forms.

By combining the platform-independent Java servlets with JSPs, web application development became more than simply making web pages dynamic; they became a viable alternative for creating enterprise applications, with one advantage: once the application was available on a server, no additional work was needed for a user to access the application. That is to say, users did not have to install any client-side software, nor did developers have to go through the hassle of shipping application updates. The users' software access and the developers' application maintenance could all be done in a centralized manner via the Web, with minimal impact on users.

Rethinking Application Development

The ability to build JSPs on top of Java servlets was a huge benefit to web application developers, and it resulted in an explosion of web application development. User and business requirements also increased as developers realized the potential of the new technology, and new functionality and components were in high demand. Developers were now able to build the interactive, efficient, composite applications that everyone wanted. At the same time, there was a convergence of technologies—as businesses moved toward building single-enterprise applications to encompass the different parts of their organizations, they also faced an integration issue. As web application developers struggled to assemble various types of portals, applications, portlets, and content management systems—everything but the kitchen sink—into a single, viable composite application, they realized that they faced a new challenge. The disparate technologies were also built on different processes and platforms, and from different approaches, which led to an extremely complicated development process.

To address this problem and streamline the process, developers needed to rethink the way they architected their applications. They discovered that, at its core, an application was generally comprised of three major areas: the *model*, which consists of business objects encapsulating the data used in the application; the *user interface*, which presents the data and any tasks or behavior associated with it; and the *control layer*, which lies between the model and user interface and is essentially a mechanism that orchestrates the interaction between the application components and implements user actions.

These three areas can be distilled into a single design pattern, which divides the application into the three layers. This design pattern is implemented in application development frameworks as the model-view-controller (MVC). The MVC contains the *model*, which is responsible for accessing and managing the application data or more generic business objects; the *controller*, which looks after the page flow and navigation in the application; and the *view*, which renders the user interface. While each of these concepts has been around for a long time, the implementation of three layers into application development frameworks is a relatively new phenomenon.

Currently, many frameworks expose one or two of the MVC layers, leaving the third layer to be addressed by the application developer, and frequently requiring additional coding to make them work. For example, some view frameworks can be used to build sophisticated user interfaces, but because they usually rely on services to manage data that need to be made available by the developer, they do not support easy flow or access to data.

Implementing MVC into application development frameworks has helped solve some of the process issues that application developers were contending with. However, even with the view layer, the user interfaces they could create with JSPs just did not suffice. This sparked the birth of a new user interface development framework: JavaServer Faces (JSF), which provides a wide array of user interface components that can be directly bound to the data sources. In doing so, JSF supports the creation of sophisticated UIs based on a wide range of view technologies, including HTML, XML, JavaScript, and Flash.

Making It All Easier: Oracle Application Development Framework

While MVC helped streamline the development process, it still required a high level of expertise and knowledge of the technology to build the applications. There weren't many tools available to help developers organize their application development environments, or to keep track of the myriad data sources, components, and pages in their applications.

To solve this problem, Oracle has combined the MVC into one development framework (Oracle Application Development Framework, or Oracle ADF) to significantly enhance the productivity. This framework has been integrated into Oracle's Java development tool, Oracle JDeveloper. To further assist application developers, Oracle has bolstered JSF in its framework with an extensible and unified connection architecture, which in turn removes the need for the developer to keep track of different data sources used with the application. The developer can instead use Oracle ADF's standardized data binding architecture to manage the communication between the application and its data sources.

Oracle ADF has undergone several revisions since its initial release and has become a sophisticated framework that covers all three MVC concepts. Oracle Business Components, for example, illustrates how Oracle ADF implements data access mechanisms, which are abstracted via a data binding mechanism following JSR 227 (a standard data binding and data access facility for Java EE). In Oracle Business Components, ADFc, the controller, allows a developer to visually define the flow within the application, and ADF Faces, a collection of more than 150 components, facilitates the view, or the user interface. Oracle ADF also supports the creation of JSFs, thus tying together both the development framework and rich UI tools that web application developers need to simplify the composite application development process.

The Underlying Layer: SOA

To further standardize application development, Oracle bundled business logic and data into business services using a service-oriented architecture, or SOA. Based on SOA, these services are exposed through different kinds of technologies such as web services, and can be consumed by other applications. For example, a web service can be created to show stock information based on the ticker symbol, which multiple applications can then consume. The developer can modify this web service without disrupting the development of the consuming applications. This concept takes the notion of the composite applications to a new level: not only can developers provide on-demand application development with little to no application downtime, their jobs are simplified as they can build and replace web services for applications by simply referencing web service endpoint URLs.

Bringing Us to…Enterprise 2.0

Now that developers have the framework to build their applications and the architecture to build true composite applications, we've arrived at Enterprise 2.0. For users, Enterprise 2.0 is about transforming how people work and interact with applications and with each other—to become more collaborative and interactive and to keep desired and vital information available at their fingertips. For businesses, it's about giving companies the ability to keep up with trends and daily requirements without disrupting business processes or increasing IT costs. For developers, it's about making it easy to develop rich, customized applications to serve their users, integrate with existing business applications, and keep maintenance to a minimum. Both Oracle ADF and SOA enable developers to achieve some of these goals, and the methodology of coupling these has resulted in Enterprise 2.0.

Oracle is spearheading Enterprise 2.0 development with ADF, which combines the capabilities of traditional transactional applications with the capabilities of composite applications to enable the creation of next-generation applications and portals. However, while Oracle ADF provides a standardized, organized, and extremely feature-rich approach to application development, there still remains a gap: how do developers pull together the myriad Web 2.0 features their users and businesses have come to rely on in their day-to-day environments and integrate these into their Enterprise 2.0 applications? How do they provide enterprise portal capabilities that their users are so accustomed to enjoying in their daily workspaces? This is where Oracle WebCenter enters the picture.

Which Leads Us to Oracle WebCenter

Oracle WebCenter provides the first *complete* Enterprise 2.0 development platform on the market. It is a comprehensive suite of components and services, and provides all necessary building blocks to create next-generation Enterprise 2.0 applications and portals. Oracle WebCenter Framework extends the capabilities of the Oracle Application Development Framework with enterprise portal capabilities, including run-time personalization and customization.

Oracle WebCenter provides a single development environment where web application developers can provide their users with the ability to perform all the tasks they've come to expect from their online experience: to manage content, create their own online communities and online presence, collaborate and instantly communicate with others, and personalize their applications. That is, developers can now efficiently build true composite applications all from within a single, organized environment. Oracle WebCenter empowers users and developers alike, by enabling developers to leverage a powerful and solid application development framework and build feature-rich, effective, and *fully customized* applications and portals for their users.

Oracle WebCenter includes a variety of Web 2.0 features, such as wikis and blogs, instant messaging, online presence, tagging, linking or bookmarking, browser-based page editing, and different levels of customization for any type of user, whether an administrator, an end user, or anything in between. It also includes services that are high in demand, such as discussion forums, online document sharing, and application-wide search tools. Not only are all these features available for you, as an application developer, to expose to your users, WebCenter makes it easy for you to integrate these services into existing or new applications. By harnessing all the technologies that have been built to make coding and maintenance easier, WebCenter also streamlines the maintenance and upgrade processes and reduces IT costs.

In the subsequent chapters, we will show you how you can leverage the power of Oracle WebCenter to create true next-generation applications as well as how you can integrate the services to unleash the power of Enterprise 2.0 in your environment. We will show you how to use Oracle WebCenter and its auxiliary services, such as Oracle Content Server and Oracle Secure Enterprise Search. We'll also show you a few tricks and tips to simplify development and explain how to best use Oracle WebCenter in your environment to create exciting next-generation applications that will take your enterprise to a new level.

CHAPTER 2

The WebCenter Development Environment

Oracle JDeveloper is a strategic development tool that Oracle's own developers heavily rely on to build Oracle's next-generation enterprise application: Fusion Application. The main objective of Oracle JDeveloper is to simplify enterprise developers' lives when they're building rich Internet applications. By integrating the database, web services, SOA, portlets, and an XML development tool, JDeveloper provides a complete development environment and supports the full development and deployment life cycle of your application. JDeveloper provides a declarative visual development, offering many different ways to add functionality to your Enterprise 2.0 applications. It presents several views of the same artifact: a *design* view giving you a good idea what your application will look like at run time, a *source* view that enables you to directly interact with your application, a *history* view to track changes in your application, and an *overview* that helps you view your application as a whole.

Using JDeveloper

Oracle WebCenter extends the JDeveloper environment by enabling you to incorporate Enterprise 2.0 capabilities into your applications, such as run-time customization and online social collaboration services.

Installing JDeveloper

You must follow two key steps to successfully set up your development environment:

1. Install Oracle JDeveloper.
2. Install the WebCenter Extension, which provides you the WebCenter-specific connectors and view components, including JSF view components and the Oracle ADF reusable components, called task flows.

JDeveloper comes in two flavors: a stripped-down, lean version, designed for Java developers, called the Java Edition, and a complete, full-blown version with all the bells and whistles called the Studio Edition. The Java Edition contains the core Java and XML capabilities, and does not contain Java EE, Oracle ADF, database, SOA, or WebCenter. Throughout this book, we use the Studio Edition for Oracle ADF and WebCenter development.

Oracle recommends the following minimum software and hardware configuration: 2GB RAM, 2.5GB disk space, and JDK 6.0 Update 11 (available for download at http://java.sun.com/javase/downloads/index.jsp). Supported operating systems include Windows Vista, Windows Server 2003 R2, Windows XP Service Pack 2, Red Hat Enterprise Linux 4.0 and 5.0, Oracle Enterprise Linux 4.0 and 5.0, SUSE Linux Enterprise Server 10, and Apple Mac OS X Version 10.5.2 or later.

Interestingly, the documentation lists 1024x768 as the display resolution requirement, which clearly is unusable for any kind of productive work. High-display resolution is just as important as sufficient RAM. As you delve deeper into development and start building more complex applications, 3 or 4GB RAM is optimal. Based on our experience, using a 22- or 24-inch monitor is no luxury by any means.

To install the JDeveloper Studio Edition, download from Oracle Technology Network (http://oracle.com/technology) the EXE file for Windows or the BIN file for Linux. You can use the JAR version on all other platforms. The files are called jdevstudio11110install.exe, jdevstudio11110install.bin, and jdevstudio11110install.jar. These versions include JDeveloper Studio 11.1.1.0, the Oracle ADF run-time libraries, and an integrated WebLogic Server 10*g* (10.1.3).

The EXE and BIN versions include the JDK; if you are using the JAR version, you must download the JDK separately and install it yourself. To make sure that you have the right version of the JDK installed and that it's in the correct path, check your JDK version by typing the following:

```
C:\>java -version
java version "1.6.0_11"
Java(TM) SE Runtime Environment (build 1.6.0_11-b03)
Java HotSpot(TM) Client VM (build 11.3-b02, mixed mode, sharing)
```

If you need to automate or script the installation of JDeveloper, you can run the installer in silent mode. During silent installation, the configuration settings are read from an XML file that you create before beginning the installation. Refer to the documentation for more information about the silent installation option.

Starting JDeveloper

After a successful installation, on Windows you can start JDeveloper from your Start menu: Start | All Programs | Oracle Middleware | Oracle JDeveloper. Alternatively, you can start it from the following location in your file system: <MIDDLEWARE_HOME>\jdeveloper\jdeveloper.exe, where <MIDDLEWARE_HOME> is the root directory where JDeveloper was installed.

When you're starting JDeveloper the first time, you are prompted to select the role you want JDeveloper to use. Since the Studio Edition can be overwhelming at times, you have a series of options to restrict the features and functions exposed to you. Picking the right role, demonstrated in Figure 2-1, is the first in this series.

FIGURE 2-1 *The Select Role dialog*

This dialog is a powerful way of controlling what you see on the UI; JDeveloper calls it shaping. It removes unneeded menu items and preferences from JDeveloper's New Gallery, dialogs, and even individual fields from dialogs. Later, you will learn about technology scopes that serve a similar purpose on the project level.

The roles offered are

- **Default Role** In this role, JDeveloper is not restricted; all technologies are available to you in the UI. If you're unsure about your selection, pick this option.
- **Customization Developer** This role enables you to edit the metadata in JDeveloper. The ability to store application customization as metadata plays a key role in WebCenter applications.
- **Database Edition** If your main objective is to interact with databases, select this option. For example, if you intend to browse databases, import and export data, use SQL Worksheet or SQL*Plus, or build and debug PL/SQL and Java stored procedures, you may want to choose this role. The Studio Edition of JDeveloper includes all the features of Oracle SQL Developer, so there is no need for you to install both products.
- **Java EE Edition** This option is for you if you are building and deploying core Java EE applications using servlets, JSPs, Struts, Enterprise JavaBeans (EJBs), and TopLink.

- **Java Edition** If you are building Java programs, for example stand-alone desktop applications with Swing, this option is your best bet.

The next question prompts you to decide whether you want to migrate your settings from an earlier version of JDeveloper to this new version. By selecting Yes, settings such as your web browser proxy and default browser settings will be migrated over to the new environment.

If you missed it the first time you started JDeveloper, you can invoke the system setting migration utility by starting JDeveloper with the command-line argument –migrate.

NOTE

Migration is supported only from the latest production version of JDeveloper 10g (10.1.3.4). Migration from technology preview versions of JDeveloper and WebCenter are not supported. For more information about system setting migration, refer to the JDeveloper documentation.

Wandering Around in JDeveloper

After JDeveloper opens, you can confirm its version by opening Help | About from the menu, shown in Figure 2-2.

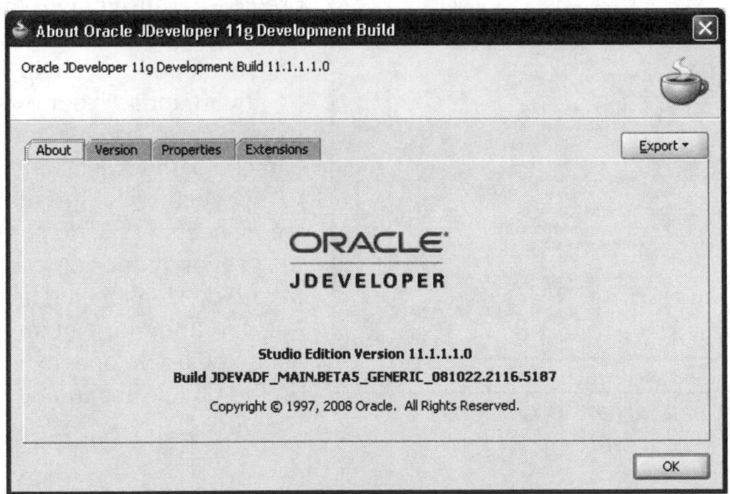

FIGURE 2-2 *The About dialog*

You can use this dialog to confirm that you have installed the Studio Edition of JDeveloper. This information can be helpful to you when you're calling Oracle Support, as they will most likely ask the version and build number of JDeveloper you're using.

You can find out more details about your environment by clicking the Version tab. Here, you can find the version details of the IDE, the JDK being used by JDeveloper, and the version of Oracle ADF.

JDeveloper provides an Extension SDK, which is a public API that developers can use to build plug-ins or extensions to enhance and customize the environment. Some of these extensions are pre-packaged with JDeveloper's IDE, while others are available online. You can access online extensions by clicking the Help | Check for Updates for an easy, one-click installation.

In JDeveloper 11*g*, most of the IDE functionality is implemented as an extension to JDeveloper. This allows a modular installation and upgrade model, and makes JDeveloper very flexible. The WebCenter design-time functionality is packaged as a JDeveloper Extension. You must install the WebCenter Extension to build WebCenter applications. The WebCenter Extension is made available online through the Help | Check for Updates mechanism. To confirm that the WebCenter Extension is installed in your environment, invoke Help | About. The Extensions tab shows all the extensions installed. It also provides an insight into the level of complexity and completeness of JDeveloper as an IDE.

If you update your existing extensions or add new ones, you can check the Extensions tab to verify whether the installation was successful and to confirm the version number of the newly installed extension (Figure 2-3). You can find more information about the JDeveloper extensions on the Oracle Technology Network (OTN).

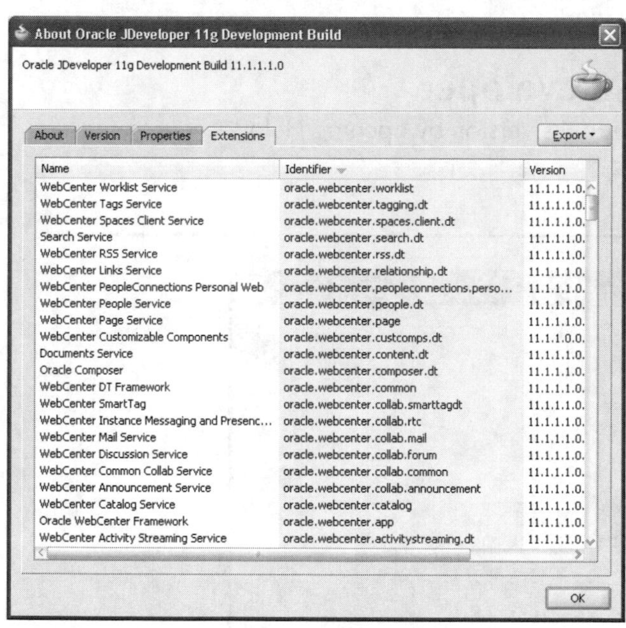

FIGURE 2-3 *WebCenter extensions listed in JDeveloper*

The Help | Check for Updates menu option allows you to add new extensions and updates directly from a hosted location, or from your local hard drive. Extensions that you install from your local hard drive are in ZIP format. If you install from a ZIP file, be sure you don't unzip your extension before installing the extension; simply point JDeveloper to the ZIP file in your file system.

Tools to Build WebCenter Applications

To familiarize yourself with JDeveloper and the tools it provides to build WebCenter applications, let's open an existing application, shown in Figure 2-4, and walk through it step by step. We'll refer to these tools in their default locations, but note that they can be moved, hidden, or turned off.

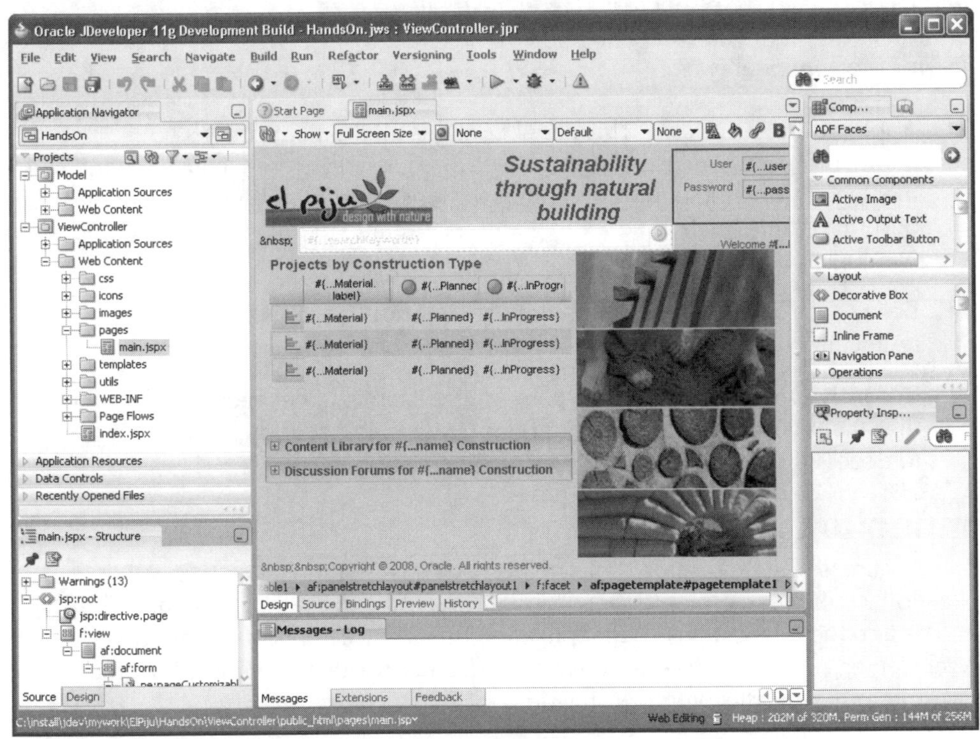

FIGURE 2-4 *A WebCenter application opened in JDeveloper*

Let's start with the Application Navigator, on the left. Here, we find all the artifacts that make up an application.

The building blocks of every application are grouped into four accordion panels:

- **Projects** Every application consists of one or more projects. Applications can be created from scratch or based on application templates. One of the application templates you can use is the WebCenter Application template, offering a great starting point for beginner and intermediate WebCenter developers. JDeveloper allows developers to define their own templates as well. This is especially useful in large development organizations, as it supports the standardization of development processes and procedures.

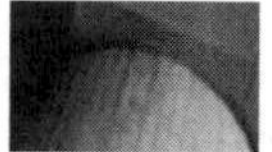

NOTE
Applications generally contain two projects: a Model and a ViewController project. After the application and its projects have been created, you have full control over them: you can rename them, delete them, or create new ones.

- **Application Resources** This panel contains all the connections your application uses (such as the database, web service, presence and instant messaging, or content repository connections) as well as your application's descriptor files (such as adf-config.xml, jazn-data.xml, jps-config.xml, and weblogic-application.xml).

- **Data Controls** This panel lists the data controls you used in this application.

- **Recently Opened Files** As its name suggests, this panel keeps track of the files that you have edited lately, and provides a quick and easy way to access them.

Connections

Of all the panels, the most important one from a WebCenter perspective is the Application Resources | Connections section. Here, you can create new connections, as well as find the connections your application uses. These connections are used by the WebCenter Web 2.0 services, such as threaded discussions, presence, document library, and remote portlet producers (Figure 2-5).

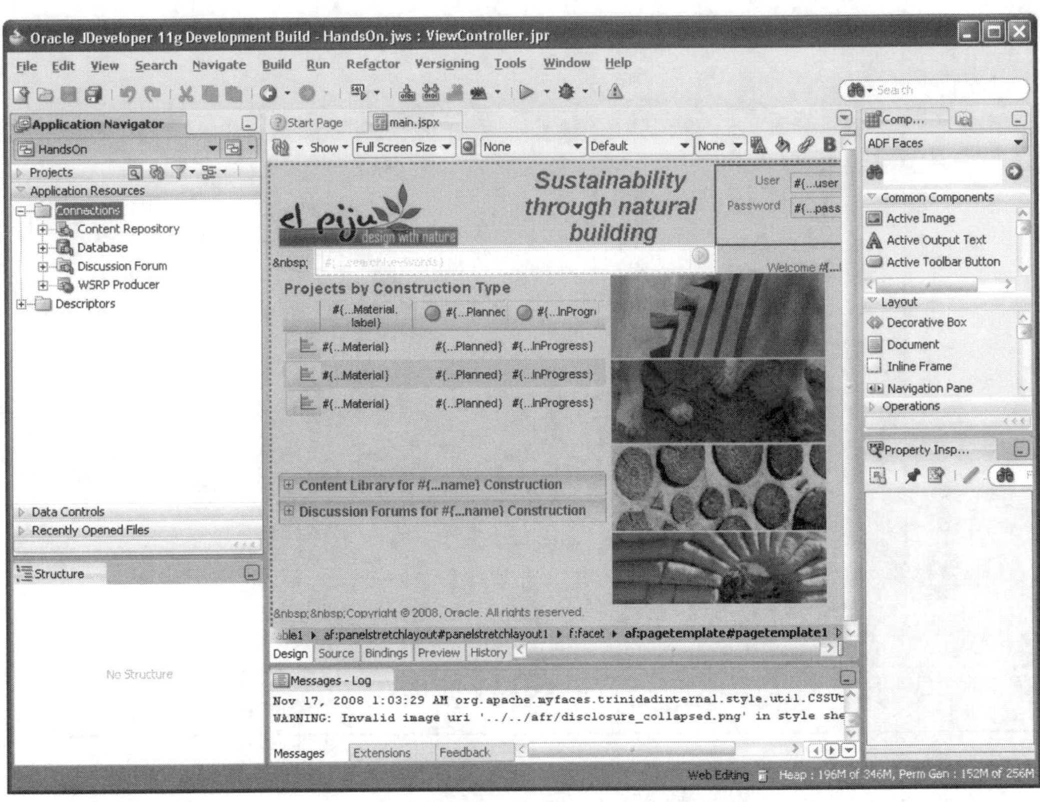

FIGURE 2-5 *Connections of a WebCenter application*

Our sample application contains four connections (Content Repository, Database, Discussions, and WSRP Producer), shown in Figure 2-6, but the JDeveloper Studio Edition offers many more connection options.

Another way of creating connections is through the context menu of the Connections node, shown in Figure 2-7.

Table 2-1 lists some WebCenter connections and descriptions for each.

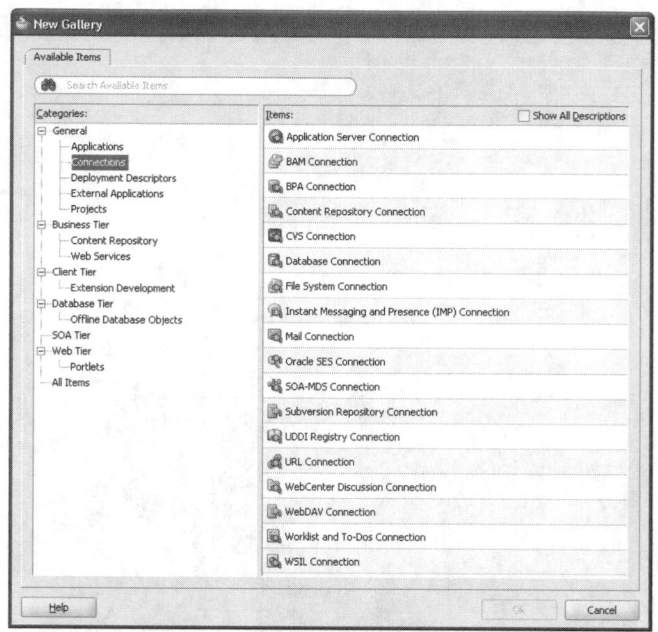

FIGURE 2-6 *Creating new connections using the New Gallery*

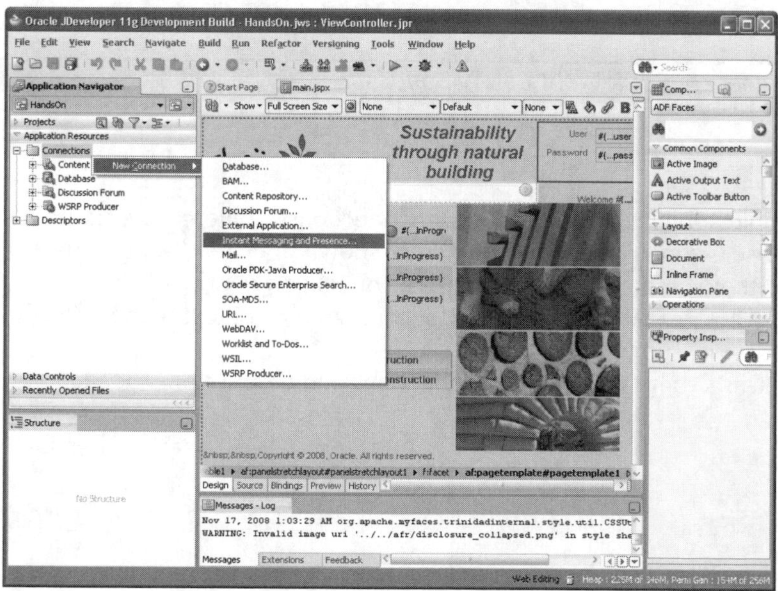

FIGURE 2-7 *Creating connections through the context menu of the Connections node*

WebCenter Connection Name	Description
Content Repository Connection	The Content Repository Connection lets you establish a connection to your document management system. You can connect to Oracle Content Server, Universal Content Management, Oracle Portal, or your file system. This connection is used by the Documents service task flows and the content integration data control.
Instant Messaging and Presence Connection	The Instant Messaging and Presence (IMP) Connection lets you create a connection to your presence server. You can use Microsoft Live Communication Server (LCS) as a back-end server. This connection is used by the Buddies task flow and the Presence JSF view components.
External Application Connection	The External Application Connection lets you specify a connection to an application that you do not control (for example mail.yahoo.com or gmail.com) but want to allow your end users to access without providing their credentials a second time after authenticating with your WebCenter application. This is a simple but often used technique to implement identity mapping between web applications using different identity management infrastructure. The External Application Connection is used by the External Application Change Password task flow and many other connections, including the Content Repository and Mail connections.
Mail Connection	The Mail Connection lets you create a connection to your IMAP or Microsoft Exchange Server. This connection is used by the Mail Service task flows.
Oracle PDK-Java Producer Connection	The Oracle PDK-Java Producer Connection lets you connect to an Oracle proprietary portlet producer, such as OmniPortlet or Web Clipping.
Oracle Secure Enterprise Search Connection	The Oracle Secure Enterprise Search Connection lets you create a connection to SES, thus expanding the scope WebCenter search provides. The Oracle Secure Enterprise Search Connection is used by the Search task flows.

TABLE 2-1 *WebCenter Connections*

WebCenter Connection Name	Description
WebCenter Discussion Connection	The WebCenter Discussion Connection lets you create a connection to a Jive discussion forum server. This connection is used by the Discussions service task flows.
Worklist Connection	The Worklist Connection lets you create a connection to a Business Process Execution Language (BPEL) server. This connection is used by the Worklist service task flow.
WSRP Producer Connection	The WSRP Producer Connection lets you create a connection to a WSRP 1.0 or WSRP 2.0 portlet producer.

TABLE 2-1 *WebCenter Connections* (continued)

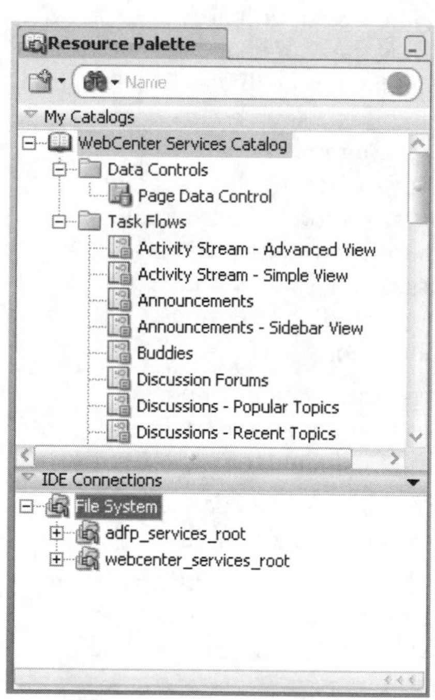

FIGURE 2-8 *Resource Palette*

The Resource Palette

Another key functional area in JDeveloper is the Resource Palette. By default, the Resource Palette resides on the right side of JDeveloper. The Resource Palette is organized into two accordion panels containing resource catalogs and connections (Figure 2-8).

The connections in the IDE Connection panel can be of the same types as the connections previously mentioned in Table 2-1, in the Application Resources panel. The connections defined in the Resource Palette are IDE-level connections: that is, they stay in the IDE as you navigate from application to application. The IDE connections are not scoped to the applications; they are fixed for your development environment. This feature allows you to reuse your connections not only within a single application, but across your applications as well. When you create a new application, you can simply drag your IDE connection over to your application and use it as an application-level connection. Connections defined under the Resource Palette are not

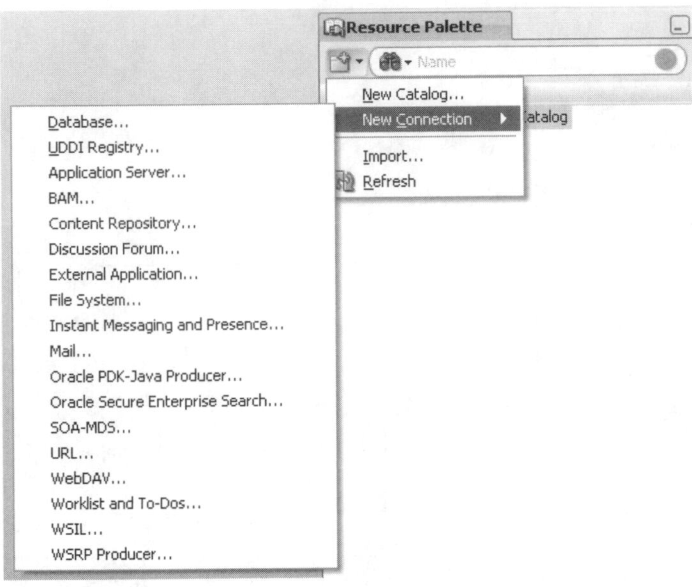

FIGURE 2-9 *Creating IDE connections in the Resource Palette*

deployed as part of your applications (Figure 2-9), only connections that you find under the Application Navigator.

To create a new connection under the Resource Palette, click the New icon next to the search box at the top of the Resource Palette.

In addition to the connections, the Resource Palette provides you with a way to organize and group all your resources. Under My Catalogs, you see a WebCenter Services Catalog. This is a resource catalog defined by and packed with the WebCenter Extension for JDeveloper, and it contains the WebCenter Web 2.0 task flows and data controls. We'll discuss this more in the next section.

The resource catalog, shown in Figure 2-10, provides a read-only view of one or more otherwise unrelated repositories and resources that developers can use in their applications. Examples for resource repositories include databases, Universal Description, Discovery and Integration (UDDI) registries, and Metadata Services (MDS) repositories. The Resource Catalog Service federates these repositories, and the Resource Palette surfaces them.

NOTE

Applications at run time use the same underlying infrastructure, the resource catalog, when offering resources to be added to pages in Oracle Composer.

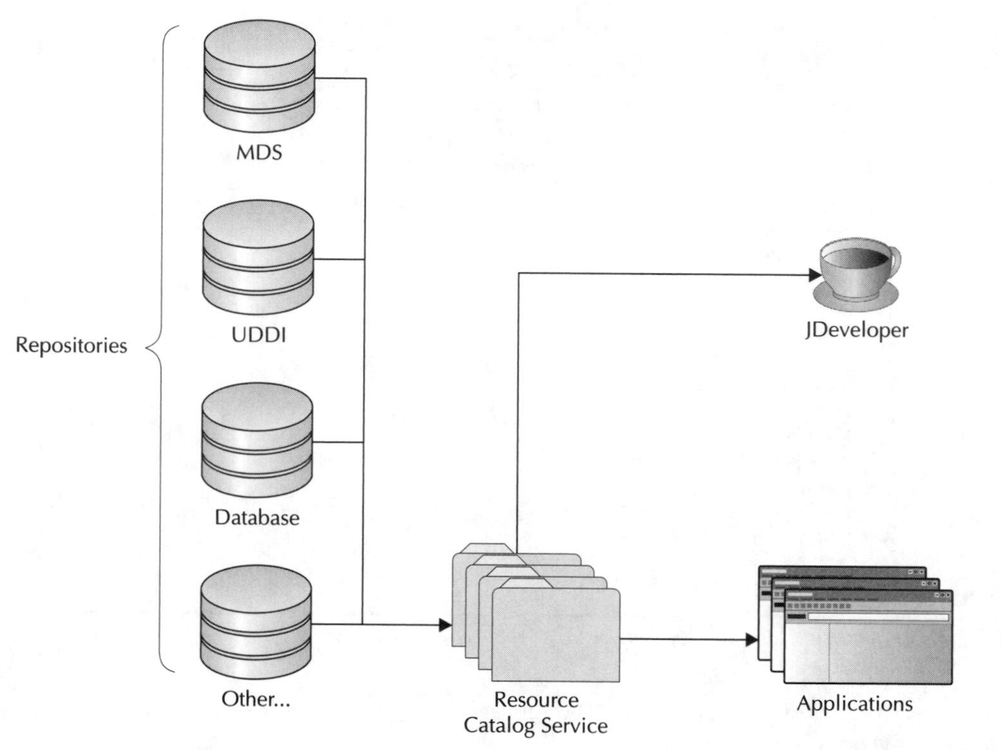

FIGURE 2-10 *The Resource Catalog Service*

Resource catalogs can include a wide variety of resource types, including:

- JSF view components
- ADF task flows
- Connections
- Resources made available through connections (for example, portlets, documents, and so on)
- Data controls

The WebCenter Services Resource Catalog

The JDeveloper WebCenter extension provides a pre-defined resource catalog containing the task flows and web services that you need to build WebCenter applications. As shown in Figure 2-8, it contains the Page Service's Page Data Control, as well as the more than 40 task flows that represent the different WebCenter Web 2.0 Services, sometimes referred to as WebCenter Social Computing Services. For example, the Discussions service provides six task flows: a generic purpose main view, called Discussion Forums, to view, create, and manage discussions; a sidebar view that you can consume when you want to provide a quick summary of the discussions and the real estate is limited on your page; and four smaller ones, to access popular, recent, and watched topics, as well as watched forums.

You can learn more about the WebCenter Web 2.0 Services and the role of the various task flows in Chapter 8.

Build Your Own Resource Catalog

Best of all, you can modify existing resource catalogs. Even better: you can build your own. The real benefit of building your own resource catalog is that all your frequently used components are grouped together and organized the way it makes sense to you.

In large development organizations, developers very often use one or more centrally managed resource catalogs. To share a resource catalog you can easily export and import it.

To create a new resource catalog, click the New icon on the Resource Palette, right next to the Search field. Select New Catalog from the menu (Figure 2-11).

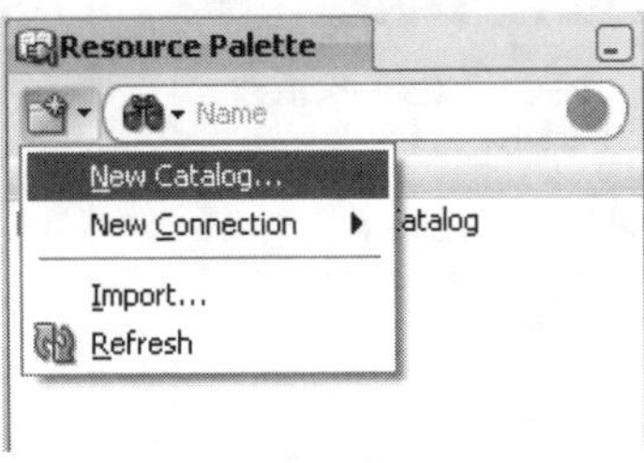

FIGURE 2-11 *Creating a new resource catalog*

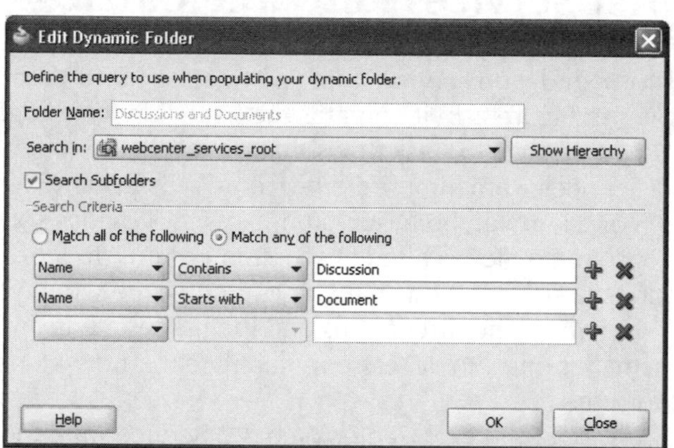

FIGURE 2-12 *Defining a dynamic folder*

You can populate your new catalog by dropping resources onto it from other catalogs. You can organize your resources into folders. Besides allowing you to create new connections, the New icon on the Resource Palette next to the Search field lets you create new folders.

You can also create folders based on search conditions (Figure 2-12). These folders are called *dynamic folders*. Any resource matching the condition will be listed under the dynamic folder (Figure 2-13).

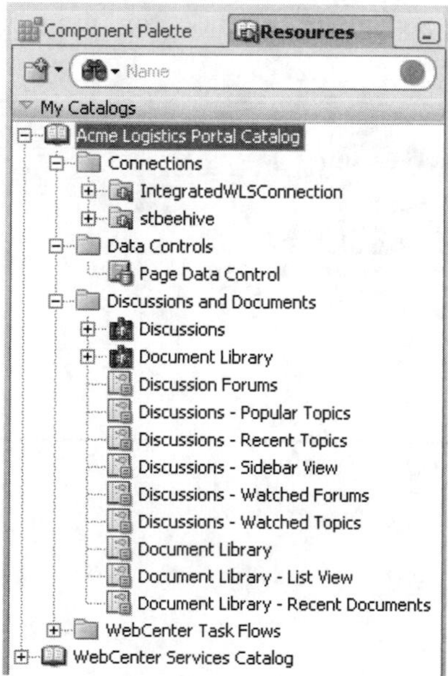

FIGURE 2-13 *A custom resource catalog*

Property Inspector and Structure Panel

While not WebCenter-specific, the Property Inspector is the JSF and ADF developer's very good friend. The visual and functional appearance and behavior of JSF view components and task flows are controlled through their properties.

One way of specifying the properties of these components is by editing the actual source code of the applications. This is not as hard as you'd think, thanks to JDeveloper's code insight feature, which suggests property names and sometimes values for these properties, as shown in Figure 2-14.

In general, it's easier to use the Property Inspector than to modify the source code. By default, the Property Inspector is located at the bottom right of your JDeveloper interface; it displays the properties of the currently selected objects (Figure 2-15).

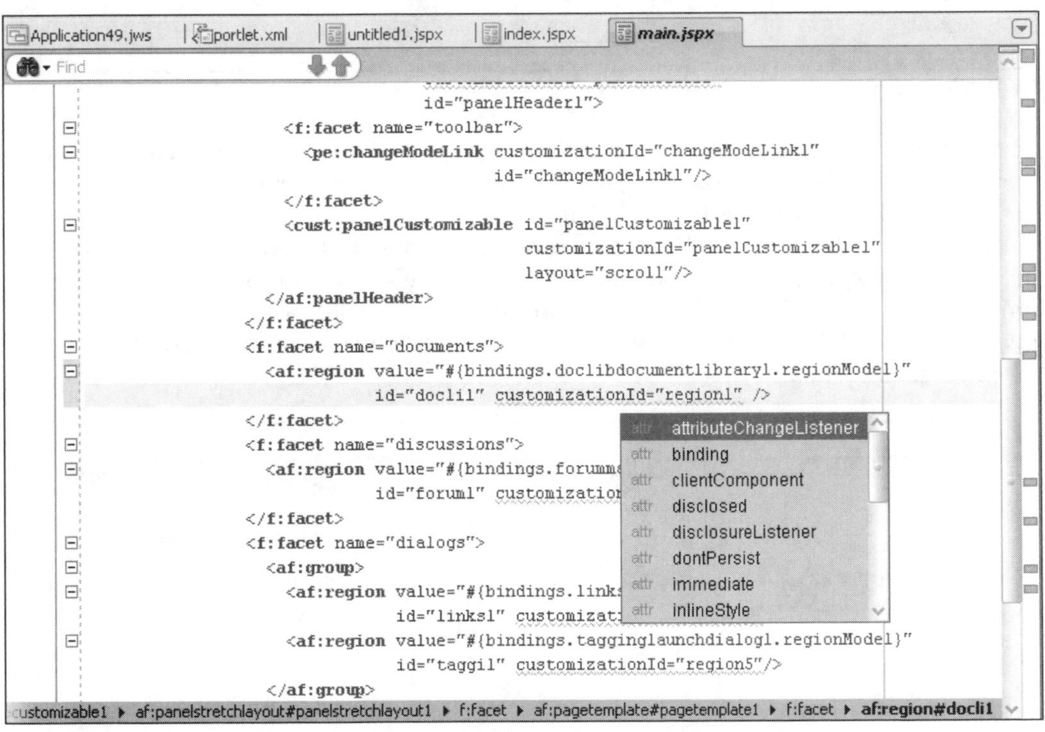

FIGURE 2-14 *JDeveloper's source editor with code insight*

FIGURE 2-15 *The Property Inspector*

Many developers find it more convenient to position the Property Inspector in horizontal view, right next to the log window. In this view, the property families are presented as horizontal tabs (Figure 2-16).

We discussed earlier that JDeveloper provides a number of views of your pages, including the design, source, bindings, and history views. You will spend a lot of time in these views while building your applications. However, no developer can live without the "X-ray" view of the selected pages and objects that are presented in the Structure panel.

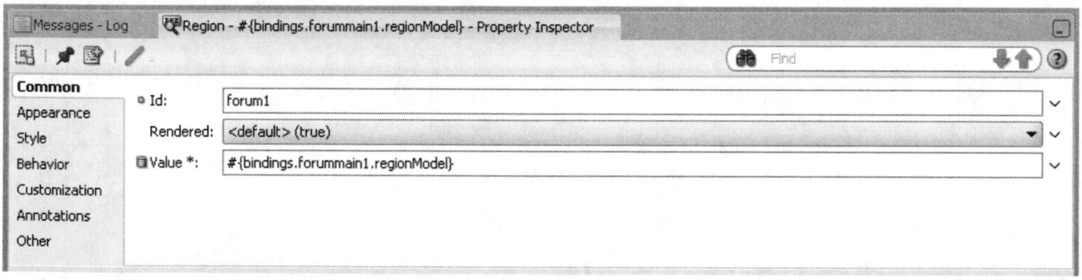

FIGURE 2-16 *Property Inspector in horizontal view*

The Structure panel is almost like an X-ray view of your application, because it gives you very precise and detailed information about certain aspects of your pages. You can see how the view components are nested, making it easy for you to rearrange them. You can use the Structure panel, shown in Figure 2-17, to identify the actual drop target for your task flows or JSF view components. It lets you easily identify the area or component of the page where you want to drop it.

The panes that show information about your selection, such as the Property Inspector, the Structure panel, and the Source or Design view of your page, are dynamic—which means that they update according to the area you've selected. This synchronization of the windows can be a huge help to you. You can also freeze the views, if needed. The Freeze icon, represented by a red pin in both the Structure panel and Property Inspector, lets you do just that. You can open multiple windows by clicking on the New View icon, then freeze the contents of any number of them so you can compare the structures and properties of different files and objects.

The WebCenter JSF View Components

In addition to the connections and rich set of task flows, the WebCenter Extension contains many useful JSF view components. Some of them work by themselves; some others play well with the WebCenter task flows.

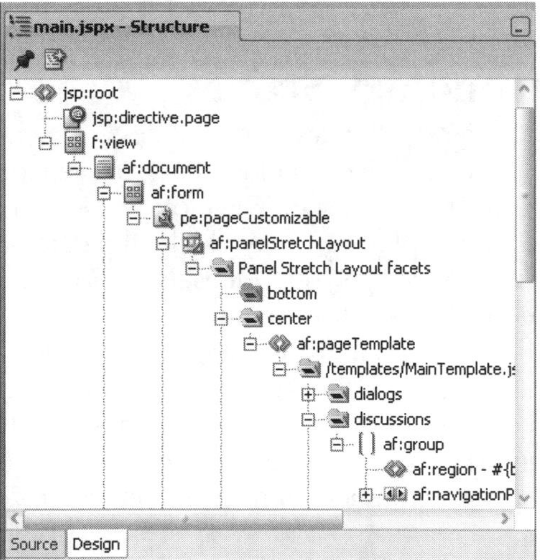

FIGURE 2-17 *The Structure panel*

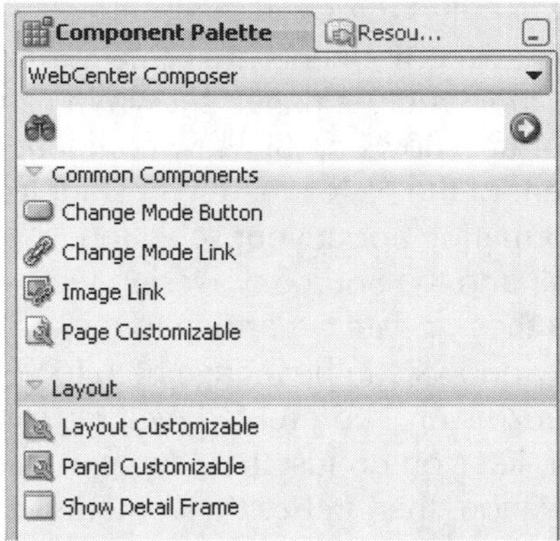

FIGURE 2-18 *JSF view components offered by Oracle Composer*

For example, Oracle Composer, responsible for providing the run-time customization capabilities, offers seven JSF view components (Figure 2-18). You can learn more about Composer and run-time customization in Part III of this book.

Some of the WebCenter Web 2.0 Services, such as Tags and Links, provide JSF view components as well. The JSF view components are accessible through the Component Palette.

Shaping and Technology Scopes

Shaping specifies certain aspects of the development environment in order to provide a more natural and streamlined development experience. As mentioned earlier in this chapter, the first time you start JDeveloper, you can specify which hat you are wearing: whether you're playing, for example, the database, the Swing, or the Java EE developer's role. To change your role, select Tools | Preferences | Roles from the menu. This functionality is called shaping.

Another way of tailoring JDeveloper is by using technology scopes. Technology scopes, shown in Figure 2-19, specify the technologies your projects use. When you are creating new objects and resources, technology scopes filter the items that are offered in the New Gallery. They also filter menus and palettes. While the technology scope affects the JDeveloper environment, it does not affect the contents of your projects and applications.

The New Gallery for a project with the above technology scope looks as shown in Figure 2-20. For an unfiltered view of the New Gallery, click the All Technologies tab in the New Gallery.

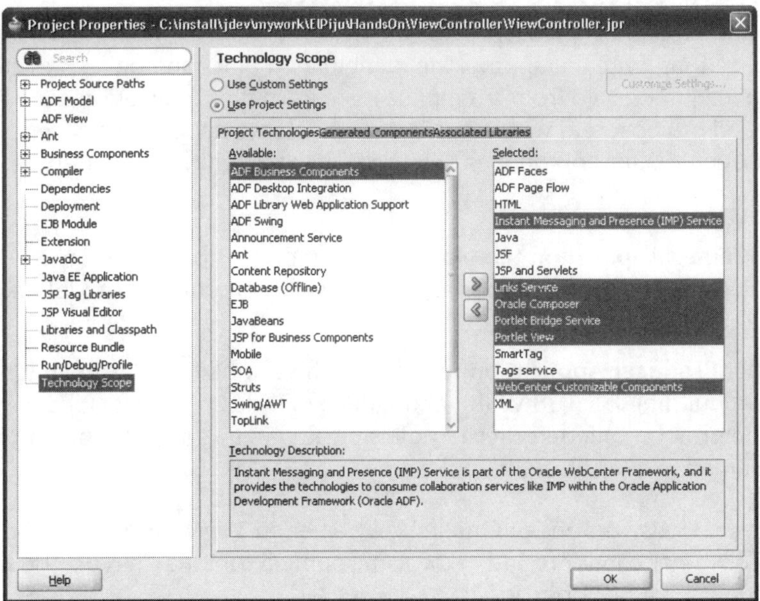

FIGURE 2-19 *Technology scopes*

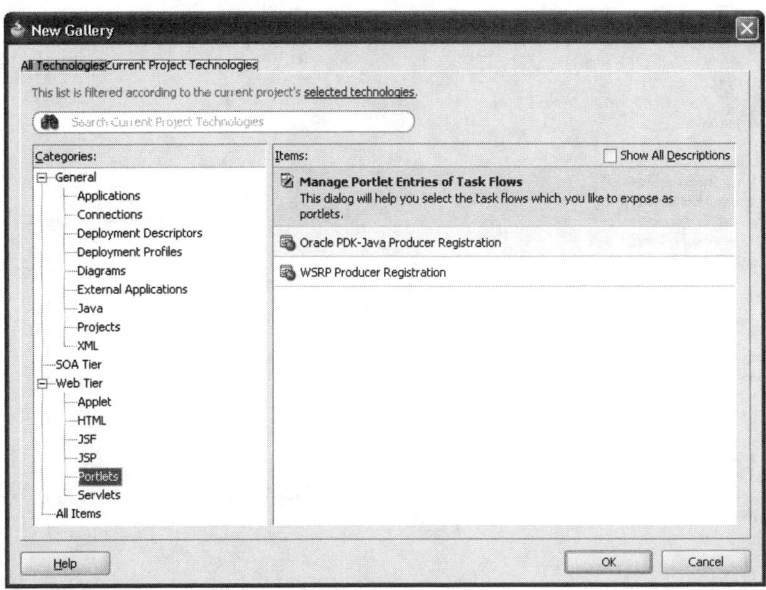

FIGURE 2-20 *New Gallery filtered according to the technology scope specified for the project*

Application and Project Templates

Application and project templates provide a quick way to create the project structure for your applications, with the appropriate combination of technologies predefined. The new application created from a template appears in the Application Navigator with pre-seeded projects, and with associated technology scopes already set.

The WebCenter Extension defines two WebCenter-specific application templates:

- **WebCenter Application template** This template is configured to build WebCenter applications and consists of two projects: Model and ViewController.
- **Portlet Producer Application template** This template is designed to assist you in building JSR 168/WSRP and Oracle PDK-Java portlets. It consists of one project, called Portlets. Portlets created in this application can be consumed in a WebCenter application.

Unlike in previous versions of Oracle WebCenter, in 11*g* your portlet producer and portlet consumer cannot reside in the same application; they have to be built and deployed in separate applications.

JDeveloper also lets you create new application and project templates to standardize and speed up the creation of your new applications (Figure 2-21).

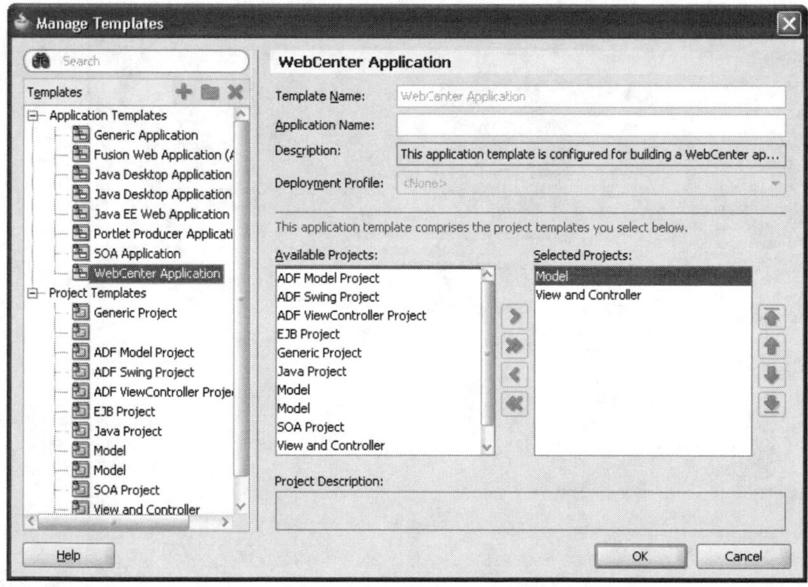

FIGURE 2-21 *Managing application and project templates*

Running and Managing Your Applications

JDeveloper ships with a Java EE container integrated with the IDE, called the Integrated WebLogic Server. In Release 11, WebLogic Server is used as the default integrated server. In addition to running your Java EE applications, this container serves as a preconfigured environment, hosting a variety of useful and several sample portlets. The portlets are deployed to the Oracle portlet container, running on top of the WebLogic Server. The Resource Palette contains an IDE-level connection pointing to the Integrated WebLogic Server.

Managing the WebLogic Server and your applications is straightforward once you understand the logic behind how JDeveloper handles them.

You can start up WebLogic Server explicitly, by selecting Run | Start Server Instance from the menu.

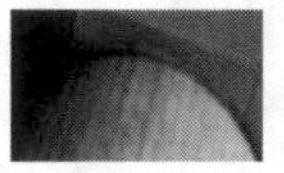

NOTE
To run the server, you must have an active project open in JDeveloper; otherwise the Run menu is disabled.

The Integrated WebLogic Server runs on port 7101, by default. You can change the default port through the Tools | Preferences | Run | Edit Server Instances | Server Instances | Default Server | Startup menu item (Figure 2-22).

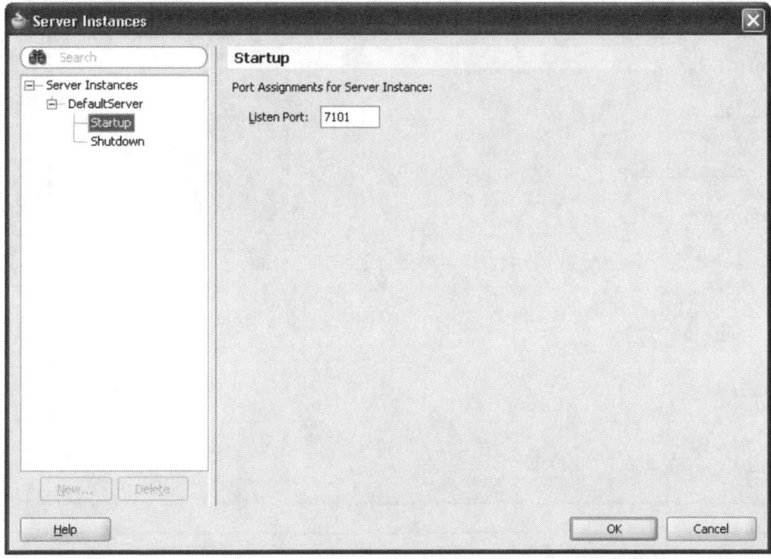

FIGURE 2-22 *Changing the port number on which the Integrated WebLogic Server is listening*

Accessing the Preconfigured Portlets

Once the server is running, all the previously deployed applications are accessible. For example, to access the producer test page of the WSRP sample portlets provided by Oracle, enter the following address in your browser (Figure 2-23): http://localhost:7101/portletapp/info.

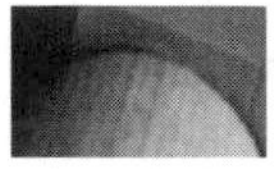

NOTE

WSRP stands for Web Services for Remote Portlets. WSRP is an OASIS web services standard and is the protocol used to access remote portlets. Oracle WebCenter supports two versions of WSRP: 1.0 and 2.0. You can learn more about WSRP and portlets in general in Chapter 5.

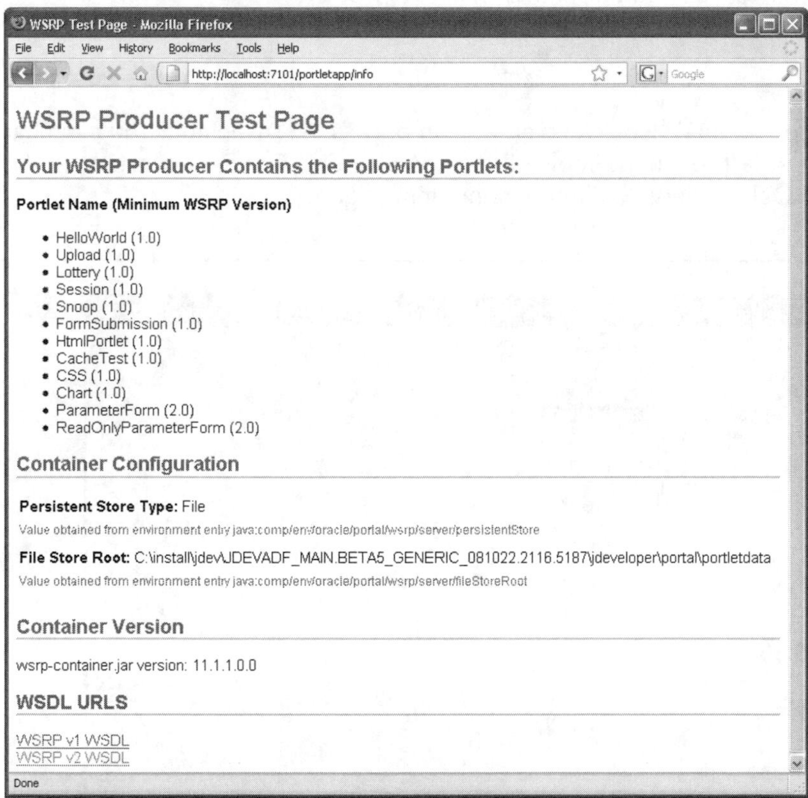

FIGURE 2-23 *The sample portlet producer test page*

In the above URL, portletapp is the context root of the deployed portlet application, pointing to the portlet producer test page. Every WSRP portlet producer, including any you build yourself, has a test page under <context-root>.

To access the WSRP registration endpoint URL, simply click on the WSDL URL links on the bottom of the portlet producer test page. Oracle PDK-Java portlet producers are accessible under the <context-root>/providers URL pattern.

The Integrated WebLogic Server provides you with the predeployed portlet applications that are listed in Table 2-2:

Another way of starting up the Integrated WebLogic Server is by simply running an application page. When you run a page, the assumption is that you are testing the application, and it's not something you'd like to have permanently deployed to your Java EE container. Therefore, when you stop the Integrated Server, your application will be undeployed.

Portlet	Portlet Producer Test Page
Rich Text Portlet	http://<host>:<port>/richtextportlet http://localhost:7101/richtextportlet
WSRP 2.0 Parameter Form and Parameter Display portlets	http://<host>:<port>/wsrp-tools http://localhost:7101/wsrp-tools
JSR 168 Sample Portlets	http://<host>:<port>/portletapp http://localhost:7101/portletapp
OmniPortlet	http://<host>:<port>/portalTools/omniPortlet/providers http://localhost:7101/portalTools/omniPortlet/providers
Web Clipping Portlet	http://<host>:<port>/portalTools/webClipping/providers http://localhost:7101/portalTools/webClipping/providers
PDK-Java Sample Portlet	http://<host>:<port>/jpdk/providers http://localhost:7101/jpdk/providers

TABLE 2-2 *Portlet Applications Predeployed to the Integrated WebLogic Server*

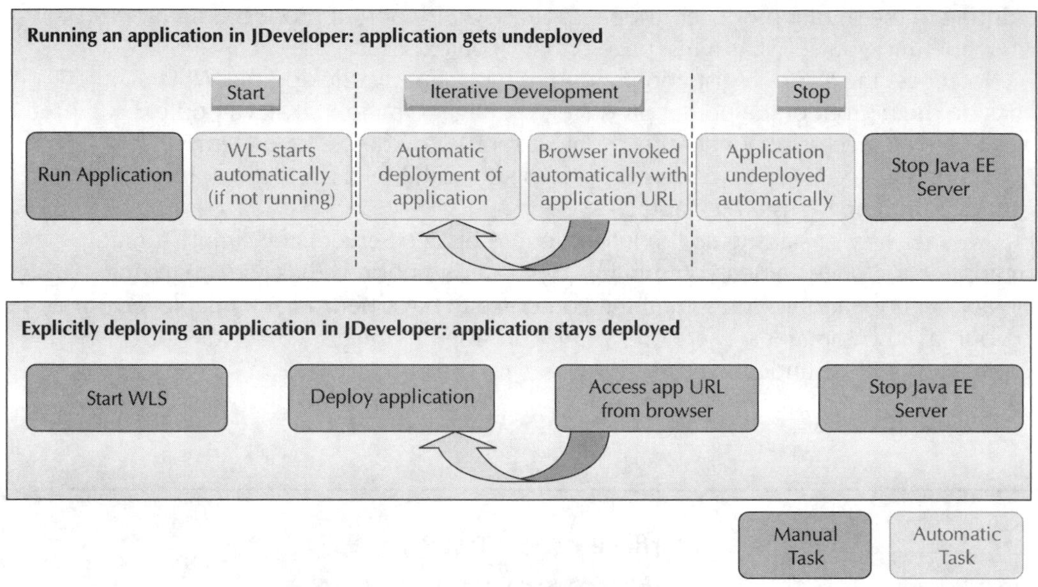

FIGURE 2-24 *Running versus deploying applications*

If you want to prevent the Integrated Server from undeploying your application when it stops, you have to explicitly deploy your application. This is demonstrated in Figure 2-24.

You can use the Run Manager to monitor and manage the applications you are currently running. You can bring up the Run Manager through the View | Run Manager menu option (Figure 2-25).

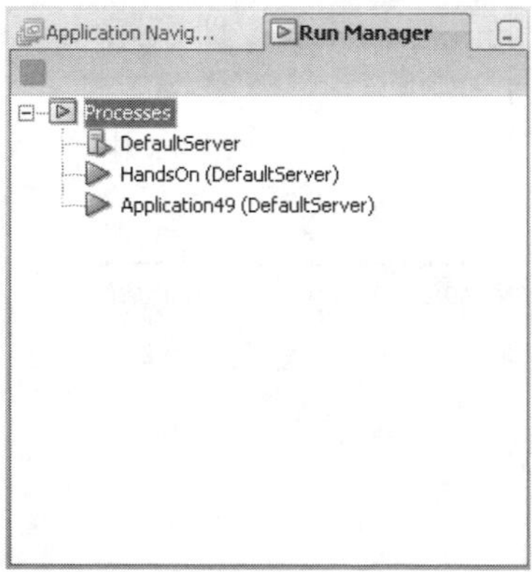

FIGURE 2-25 *The Run Manager*

Application Server Navigator and WebLogic Server (WLS) Administration Console

Another useful tool you can use in JDeveloper is the Application Server Navigator. The Application Server Navigator allows you to connect to your Java EE container and provides a high-level overview of it. It also allows you to undeploy applications from your Integrated Server directly from JDeveloper; this is demonstrated in Figure 2-26.

A more sophisticated tool to manage the Integrated WebLogic Server is the WebLogic Server Administration Console. You can access this through the following URL:

http://localhost:7101/console

The default username and password for the console is weblogic/weblogic1. To learn more about the WebLogic Server Administration Console, shown in Figure 2-27, refer to its documentation.

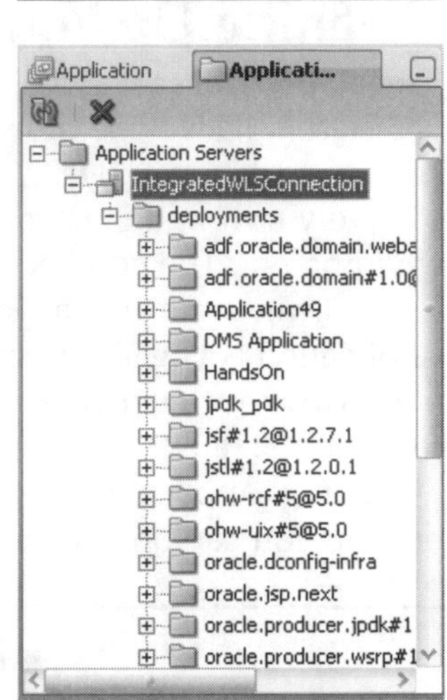

FIGURE 2-26 *The Application Server Navigator*

FIGURE 2-27 *The WebLogic Server Administration Console*

Cleaning Up Your Development Environment

JDeveloper allows you to work with multiple applications at the same time. When you start it, JDeveloper opens up the applications that you had open last time when you worked in your IDE.

Every now and then you may want to do some cleanup in your development environment. The good news is that it's a lot easier than cleaning up your desk.

You can close any tab in JDeveloper, whether it's a system tab, such as the Application Navigator or Structure panel, or a tab displaying one of your application files. If you accidentally close a system tab (or simply want to open a new one), just select it from the View menu; this menu lists all your tabs. For example, the previously mentioned Application Server Navigator and Run Manager panes are not shown by default; you can open them through the View menu (Figure 2-28).

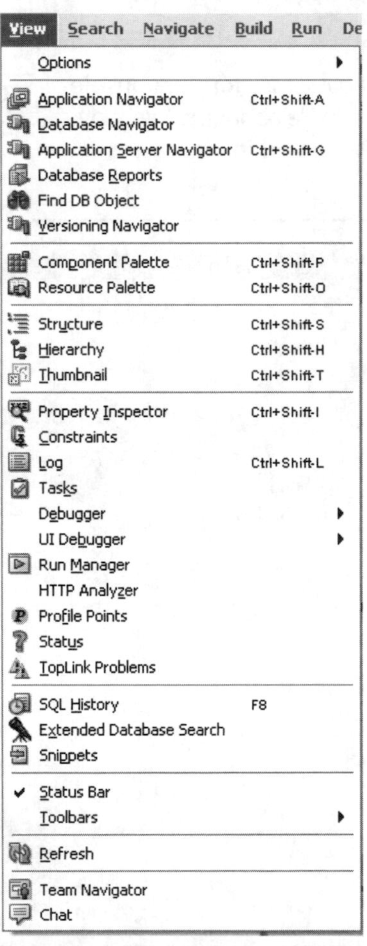

FIGURE 2-28 *The View menu containing the system tabs*

When you close your application in JDeveloper, you are prompted to save the changes you made, and the application tree is collapsed. When closing your applications, you have two options, as shown in Figure 2-29:

- Close application
- Close application and remove it from JDeveloper

The latter option removes the application from the Application Navigator. You can reopen your applications by simply selecting the File | Reopen menu option.

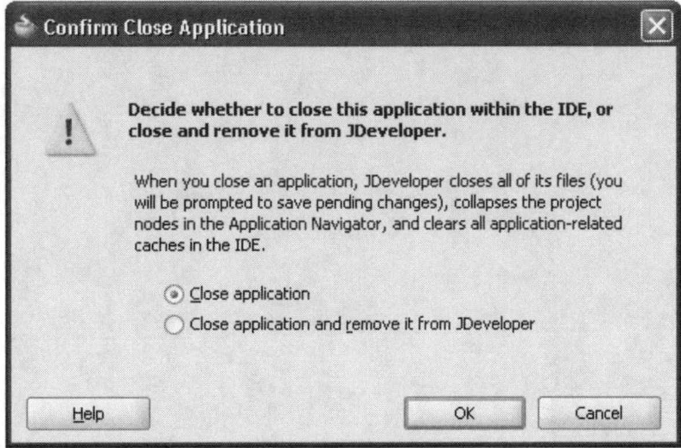

FIGURE 2-29 *Closing your application*

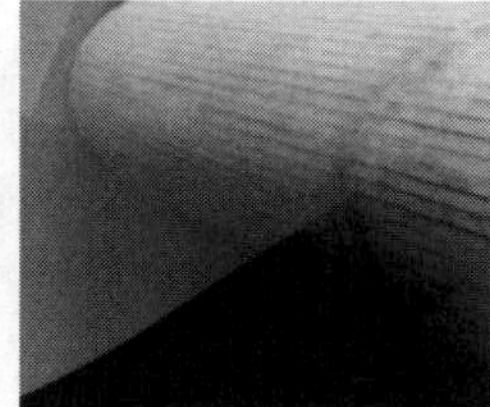

CHAPTER 3

Oracle Application Development Framework

racle WebCenter is, among other things, a building block for your applications. It was not put together from scratch: it uses Oracle's own ADF framework extensively. The WebCenter programming model, offered in WebCenter Framework, is simply an extension of the ADF one; to use the former, you must master the latter. Obviously, we don't pretend to provide a comprehensive overview of ADF here. This is what *Oracle JDeveloper 11g Handbook: A Guide to Fusion Web Development* by Duncan Mills, Peter Koletzke, and Avrom Roy-Faderman is for. Our aim is to give an overview of the features and capabilities of the framework and to illustrate how they enable the realization of rich and customizable applications.

ADF Concepts and Used Standards

Application Development Framework may seem like a utilitarian name, but it perfectly reflects the product's origins. Introduced in 1999 in Oracle's E-Business suite as a data access and business logic layer, ADF has since grown into a comprehensive and integrated framework, covering all aspects of web and client/server applications. ADF 11*g* is the cornerstone of the Fusion Applications project. Obviously, the functional requirements covered by ADF are mainly those of Oracle's own development teams. Although this situation may skew things in a certain way, ADF strongly benefits from the fact it is engineered to build real-world applications and integrates significant feedback from paying customers.

The design of ADF can be summarized in a few basic tenets:

- **Separation of concerns** ADF is a clean implementation of the MVC model, as it facilitates correct isolation of the business logic from the user interface.
- **Declarative development** Validation rules, navigational structure, and other artifacts are defined through declaration instead of code. This enables visual application development, as well as easier application customization through metadata layering.
- **Extensibility** The framework can be extended and adapted as needed. Nearly every part of it can be tailored through code overrides.
- **Standards based** ADF is rooted in the Java Enterprise Edition standards, and some of its constituent parts have been proposed to the Java Community Process.

Overall, those tenets result in a framework that heavily relies on a layered approach. Figure 3-1 illustrates an ADF application's structure as well as the corresponding layers. While these are tightly integrated, it must be noted that Oracle JDeveloper 11*g* offers the possibility to replace some of them. Data access and business logic, for example, can be implemented using Oracle's own TopLink, which is an implementation of the Java Persistence Architecture (JPA) specification, or through Enterprise JavaBeans, both a part of the Java Enterprise Edition standard. The downside of such substitutions would be the loss of some productivity aids available in the IDE. Oracle JDeveloper includes many visual and declarative features to provide the best possible developer experience, many of which are fully realized only when you're using the full ADF stack. And Oracle WebCenter is built with ADF from top to bottom.

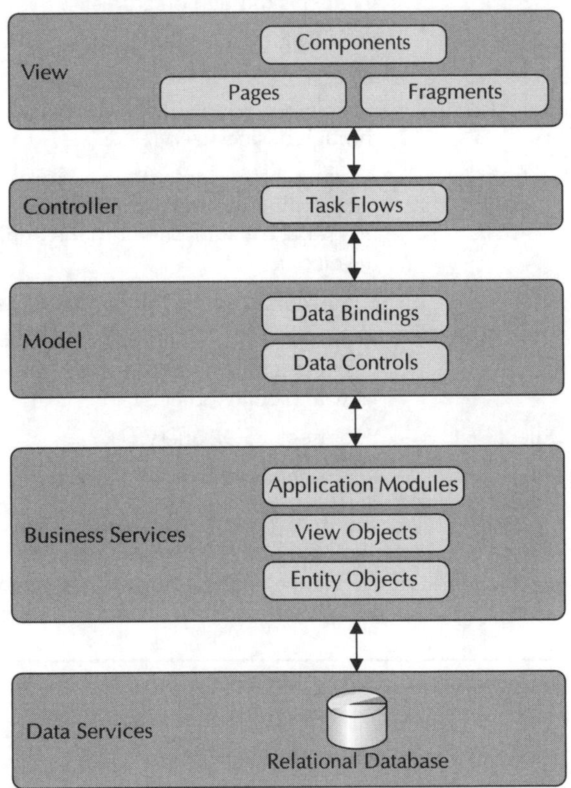

FIGURE 3-1 *Structure of an ADF application*

Layer	Component	Role
View		Supply the application's user interface.
	Components	Provide for layout, input, and output. Can be rendered using a variety of technologies, DHTML being the typical choice.
	Pages	Assemble components to represent a whole applicative panorama.
	Fragments	Assemble components to represent a reusable part of an applicative panorama.
Controller		Manage the user interface flow.
	Task Flows	Embody a business process using pages or fragments through diagrams.
Model		Deal with user-provided values in memory for use by the other layers.
	Data Bindings	Link view components to data manipulated through business services.
	Data Controls	Abstract the business services accessed through data bindings so the technology implementation of a service is transparent to the application developer.
Business Services		Supply business logic and data access.
	Application Module	Represent a service interface, since it concentrates business logic and provides access to underlying view and entity objects.
	View Object	Represent a SQL query.
	Entity Object	Represent a single row in a database table or database view for transactional purposes.
Data Services		Store application data.
	Relational Database	Define the application's data model with relations and provide for data access and storage.

TABLE 3-1 *Structure Components of an ADF Application*

Table 3-1 lists each of the components of the structure.

We will now examine each of the constituent parts of ADF.

View: ADF Faces Rich Client

ADF's view layer is probably the area that has experienced the most changes over the years. The roots of the current ADF Faces Rich Client component library can be traced back to ADF UIX, which was introduced with JDeveloper 9.0.2 in May 2002.[1] At the time, the UIX model was a tremendous innovation; it brought a component-oriented approach to the market when separation of business logic from presentation was usually achieved through JSP tag libraries. The expertise gained on UIX enabled Oracle to play a significant role in the birth of Java Server Faces (JSF), a user interface standard for Java web applications.

Basically, JSF is an implementation of the Model-View-Controller paradigm focused on the separation between the definition of the user interface and its rendition. This separation is achieved through components: reusable bits of code that translate the intended controls in a target markup language, such as DHTML. The existence of components makes it possible to build teams where component and application developers have distinct focus areas. This means application developers do not have to care about the target markup, as they assemble components to produce the application's pages and fragments. Component developers, on the other hand, must build their components and check the correctness of the rendering on all the supported clients or devices. In the case of AJAX-enabled components, such as those offered in the ADF Faces Rich Client 11*g* library, this implies validation of the rendered UIs in supported browsers as well as verification of the behavior of the client-side JavaScript code.

JSF was brought to market through the Java Community Process. As such, it was an open specification. It was selected as the basis of Oracle's next generation of web view technologies, since it is component based, thus enabling the company to start from the UIX code base instead of building from scratch. JSF benefits from strong IDE support, obviously, because of its openness and its focus on components, which lend themselves to visual and declarative development.

UIX's successor was ADF Faces, which was made generally available in January 2006 with the 10.1.3.0.4 version of JDeveloper. ADF Faces is a complete overhaul of UIX in which the various components were redeveloped as JSF components. Thus, one could see ADF Faces as a productivity layer placed on the top of standard JSF. This drive toward standardization of the underlying platform was accompanied by an overture to the open source community. As ADF Faces reached production,

[1] This was stated in an entry of Steve Muench's blog. See http://radio.weblogs.com/0118231/stories/2005/02/25/historyOfJdeveloperReleases.html for more details.

The Java Community Process

Introduced by Sun Microsystems in 1998, the Java Community Process (JCP) is a participative process to develop and revise Java specifications. Members of the JCP can be either corporations or individuals. New specifications are brought through a Java Specifications Request (JSR), which is a document submitted to the JCP's Project Management Office to propose the development of a new specification or significant revision of an existing one. JSRs undergo a stringent approval process and are presented to public review before being submitted to an approval ballot. A JSR becomes an official Java specification if this approval ballot is positive.

All approved JSRs must have their own Reference Implementation and Technology Compatibility Kit. This ensures that all would-be implementers can measure the faithfulness of their implementation to the specification.

Oracle is a major player in the JCP, and several of its employees participate in various JSRs. Some parts of the ADF framework were proposed to the community as JSRs.

Oracle announced the library would be donated to the Apache Software Foundation. It is now known as Apache MyFaces Trinidad. Oracle employees and partners still contribute code to Trinidad, which is an integral part of the 10*g* and 11*g* releases of ADF.

Recent developments in the web application space have seen the rise of the AJAX programming model, which made the advent of Rich Internet Applications (RIA) possible. While very powerful, AJAX adds complexity to an application's architecture. Developers must master not only Java on the server side, but also JavaScript for browser-based interaction. Obviously, while it is possible to implement AJAX functionality from scratch, it is much easier to use existing building blocks. In the last few years, literally dozens of mutually incompatible AJAX client libraries made it to market. Those cannot be combined because there is no standardized way to process client events and server responses.

The main design goal for ADF Faces Rich Client 11*g* was to extend the 10*g*R3 components with built-in AJAX capabilities. This explains why the library's name was changed to ADF Faces Rich Client. Oracle now positions ADF Faces Rich Client

What Is AJAX?

AJAX means asynchronous JavaScript and XML. AJAX-based technologies provide a way for developers to build richer and more interactive applications. Suppose you are developing a web application in which the user must provide his or her account number to complete a transaction. This number must respect a specific format, and, obviously, must exist in the system. Wouldn't it be great to validate the account number before sending the transaction to the server? AJAX makes this possible.

The key here is JavaScript. HTML, by itself, is just a *markup* language. It is optimized for rendering of static content, but does not possess any intrinsic dynamic rendering capability. JavaScript, which runs in the browser, can interact with both the HTML content and the server. Within AJAX, JavaScript code is used to send XML requests to the server, and to process XML responses. The whole process is asynchronous, since it would not be desirable to freeze the user interface while the requests and responses are processed. In any case, since the HTTP protocol is stateless, the web browser does not have a permanent connection to the server. Asynchronous processing enables developers to work around this limitation.

as the ideal foundation for RIA, as the components in the library encapsulate both the server-based HTML rendering and the JavaScript code needed by client-side behaviors. Feature-wise, ADF Faces Rich Client has much to offer: drag-and-drop facilities, page hierarchy management, and support for lightweight dialogs are some standouts. All components support skinning and internationalization; they also provide accessibility support for special needs users.

There are more than 150 ADF Faces Rich Client components available in the library. They are divided in the following categories:

- **Layout components** Used to organize the contents of the page. Some of them are interactive; they enable the user to show or hide content. Certain components can also adjust their size and position according to the size of the browser windows, thus ensuring correct rendering of the user interface. Figure 3-2 illustrates some of the layout components in a real application; the list of items uses one, and separators can be seen left and right.

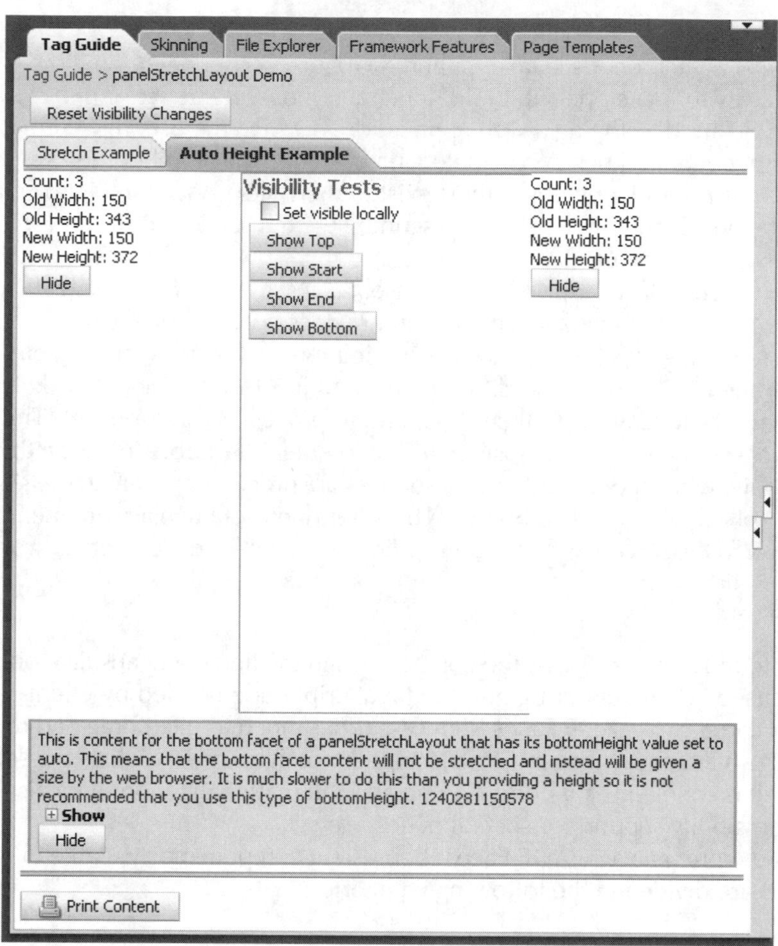

FIGURE 3-2 *Real-world use of ADF RC layout components*

- **Input components** Allow users to enter data and even enable file upload. Figure 3-3 displays typical input components.

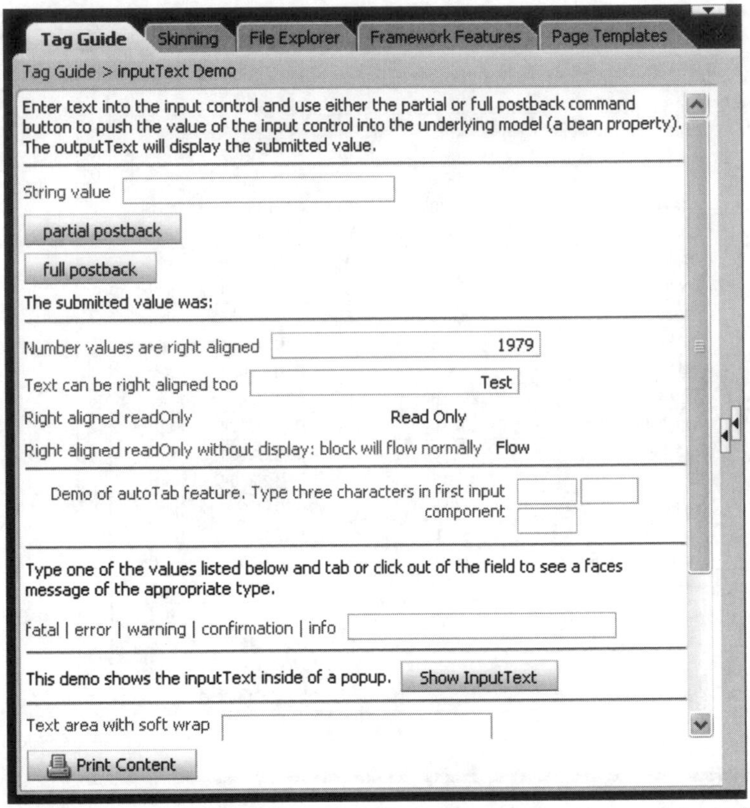

FIGURE 3-3 *Typical input components*

- **Structured data components** Display tabular or hierarchical data in tables or trees, with sorting and filtering functionality. Figure 3-4 shows an ADF rich client table implementing sorting functionality.

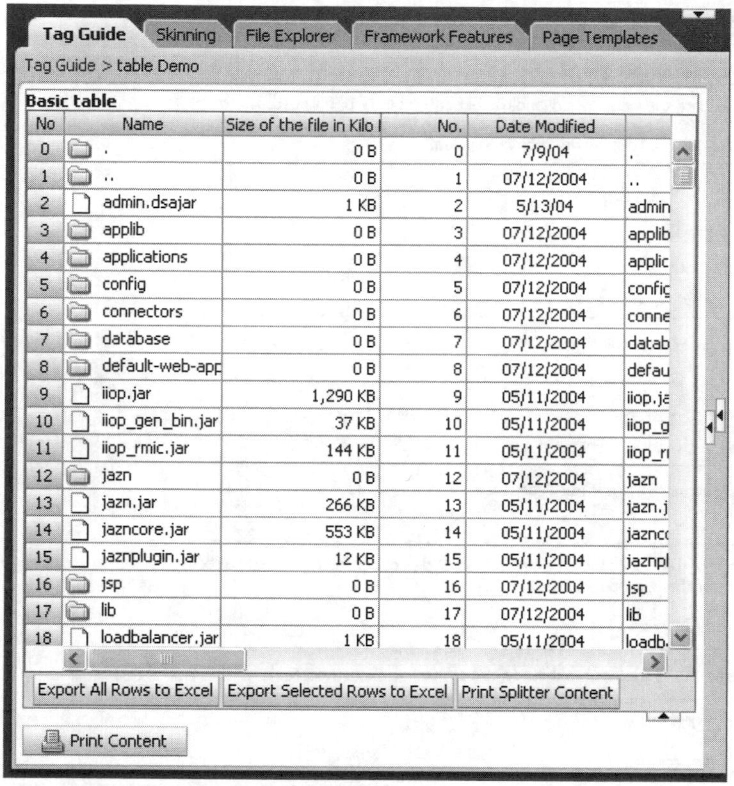

Tag Guide | Skinning | File Explorer | Framework Features | Page Templates

Tag Guide > table Demo

Basic table

No	Name	Size of the file in Kilo I	No.	Date Modified	
0	.	0 B	0	7/9/04	.
1	..	0 B	1	07/12/2004	..
2	admin.dsajar	1 KB	2	5/13/04	admin
3	applib	0 B	3	07/12/2004	applib
4	applications	0 B	4	07/12/2004	applic
5	config	0 B	5	07/12/2004	config
6	connectors	0 B	6	07/12/2004	conne
7	database	0 B	7	07/12/2004	datab
8	default-web-app	0 B	8	07/12/2004	defau
9	iiop.jar	1,290 KB	9	05/11/2004	iiop.ja
10	iiop_gen_bin.jar	37 KB	10	05/11/2004	iiop_g
11	iiop_rmic.jar	144 KB	11	05/11/2004	iiop_r
12	jazn	0 B	12	07/12/2004	jazn
13	jazn.jar	266 KB	13	05/11/2004	jazn.j
14	jazncore.jar	553 KB	14	05/11/2004	jaznco
15	jaznplugin.jar	12 KB	15	05/11/2004	jaznpl
16	jsp	0 B	16	07/12/2004	jsp
17	lib	0 B	17	07/12/2004	lib
18	loadbalancer.jar	1 KB	18	05/11/2004	loadb.

Export All Rows to Excel | Export Selected Rows to Excel | Print Splitter Content

Print Content

FIGURE 3-4 *ADF RC table with sorting*

- **Output components** Present text and graphics. Components for labels, tips, and messages are available and used in conjunction with other components. Figure 3-5 illustrates the run-time appearance of a message.
- **List components** Users can select from model-driven lists. Search functionality is also provided. Figure 3-6 shows a typical list of values.

Choose some values to see messages. In the property editor try setting the 'inline' attribute

Critical Error

Please read this carefully:
Fatal message DETAIL text.

OK

warning
confirmation
info

The content of these global scope messages are formatted, for example the message contains bold text.

Page Level Formatted Message
fatal
error
warning
confirmation

FIGURE 3-5 *A message in action*

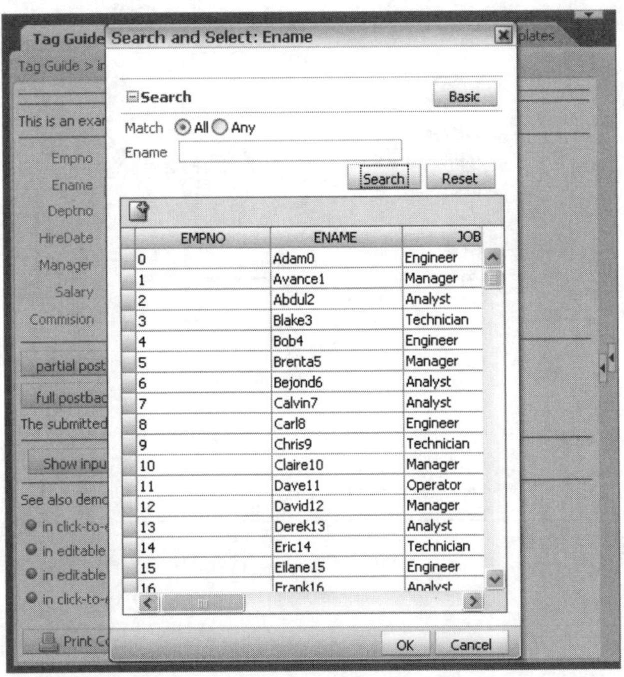

FIGURE 3-6 *A list-of-value component*

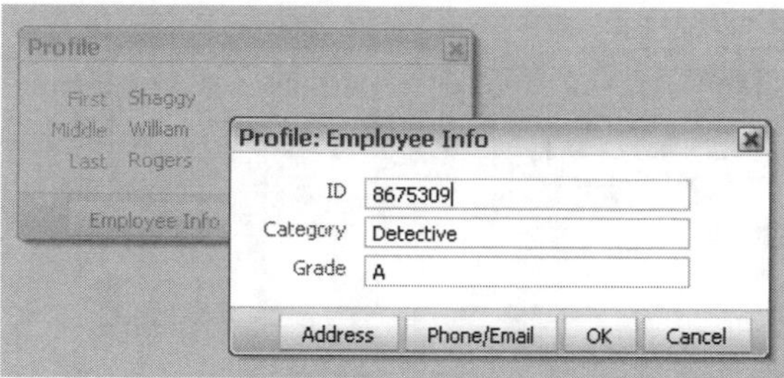

FIGURE 3-7 *Dialog box*

- **Pop-up components** Pages and page fragments can be displayed in their own pop-up browser windows or in modal windows. A comprehensive dialog framework is provided. Figure 3-7 presents a sample dialog box.
- **Menu and toolbars components** Application actions can be launched through menu and toolbar components. Figure 3-8 exemplifies the kind of menus that can be built with those components.

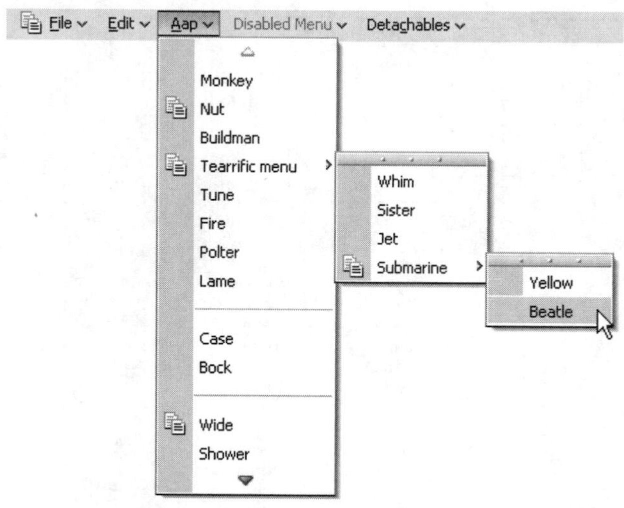

FIGURE 3-8 *Menu and toolbars*

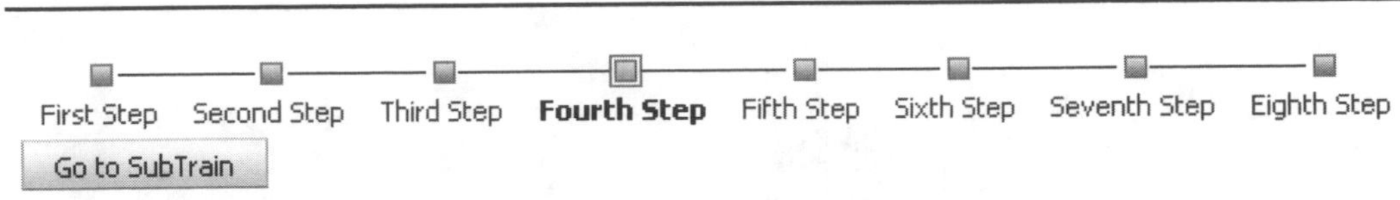

FIGURE 3-9 *The train component*

- **Navigation components** The various navigation components, like buttons, links, and menus, can be configured to provide access to a specific page or can interact with more complex page flows. A fine example is the train component, in which each page or fragment materializes a step in a business process. The component will inform the user if some of the steps contain errors or if mandatory steps were skipped. Figure 3-9 shows the train component's main features.
- **Query components** The two components in this category support single item search and multiple criteria search, respectively. The multiple-criteria search query is displayed in Figure 3-10.
- **Data visualization components** This family of components offers graphs, gauges, pivot tables, Gantt charts, and geographic maps. The data visualization components can be rendered with either Adobe Flash or SVG. Most of them support drill-down operations for data mining purposes. Some examples of ADF data visualization graphs can be found in Figure 3-11.

Employees (header)
This search panel can be used to search for Employees.
Cancel Actions Apply
Search
Basic Saved Search System Search 1
* Required
Match All Any
* Employee Name Joe
* Department Number Equals 529
Hire Date Less Than 6/8/2007
Search Reset Save... Add Fields

FIGURE 3-10 *Multiple-criteria search query*

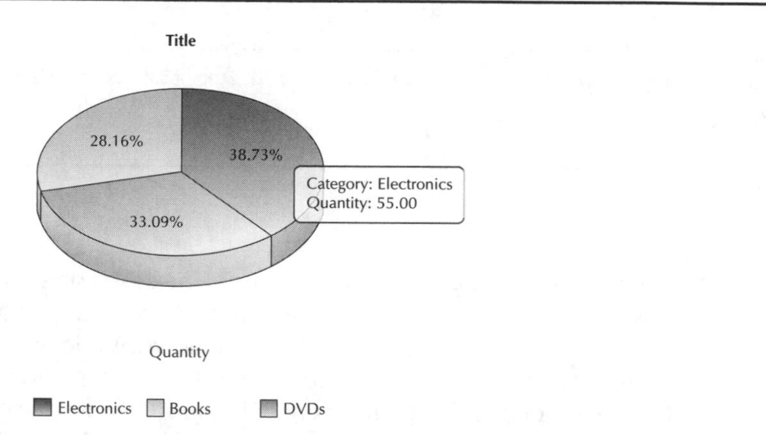

FIGURE 3-11 *Data visualization graph*

There is one key capability of the ADF RC components we still have not discussed: customization. Several of the components enable users to alter their display at run time; a good example of this behavior is the splitter, which can be moved to fit user preferences. Those alterations can be preserved automatically for the duration of the user session through a mechanism called *change persistence*. While efficient, change persistence may not offer the granularity and layering required by some business scenarios. This was to be expected, as change persistence concerns itself with run-time user customizations only. However, the ADF framework also supports *seeded* customizations—by which a generalized baseline is tailored to the needs of a specific group. And the base ADF customization capabilities can be extended through the use of WebCenter Framework, which enables layered run-time customization of applications. Behind the scenes, all these customization scenarios exploit the capabilities of the Oracle Metadata Services framework (MDS). Chapter 14 explains the architecture and capabilities of the MDS framework.

While ADF Faces Rich Client components offer much functionality, they cannot by themselves manage the application's flow as well as user input. This is where ADF Controller comes into play.

Controller: ADFc

Of all the layers that compose the framework, ADF Controller (ADFc) is at the same time the most strategic and the less visible. This can be explained easily. In version 11*g*, ADF Controller is basically a run-time execution engine for ADF Task Flows.

However, Oracle JDeveloper 11*g* offers alternatives to ADFc. Those are the standard JSF controller and Apache Struts, respectively. The former is included since ADF is built on the JSF standard, while the latter ensures the support of legacy applications. Both of them offer less functionality than ADFc, and cannot execute ADF Task Flows.

In ADFc, page requests and submissions invoke the ADF page life cycle, which is an extension of the standard JSF life cycle. The JSF life cycle takes charge of the values submitted on the page, validates those, handles navigation to pages, renders the components on the resulting page, and will save or restore the state. The ADF life cycle, on the other hand, will deal with data model preparation and updates, model layer data validation, and business methods execution. Data is made available to the page through a dedicated object.

Like its JSF counterpart, the ADF life cycle was designed to be easily extended. Developers can create custom phase listeners that invoke custom code, and register them within the life cycle to execute during a specific phase. It is even possible to customize the life cycle of a single page or fragment by adding an entry to the appropriate page definition.

Now that we have described their supporting infrastructure, it is time to delve into ADF Task Flows.

Task Flows

At their core, ADF Task Flows are just configuration files meant for consumption by the ADF Controller. Since they are built at design time, they expose all of the controller's underlying features. One of the design goals behind ADF Task Flows is to promote reuse of pages and fragments. They allow encapsulation and enable navigation while managing the life cycles of managed beans. One innovative feature they have is that they can define transactions that span pages and fragments without requiring changes to the data access layer—something unheard of in web application frameworks before. Task flows are one of the most significant new features in ADF 11*g*.

Task flows are a combination of activities, control flow rules, and memory scopes. Activities are the actual steps of a specific business process. These steps can be anything from the display of a page to the invocation of a Java method. As for control flow rules, they simply describe the possible transitions between the activities. They are similar in concept to JSF navigation rules, but they capture additional information. Finally, managed beans are meant to handle events or data manipulations that are related to the user interface. They can be referenced in expression language (EL) expressions from ADF Rich Faces components or from task flows.

Task flows are defined in Oracle JDeveloper 11*g* using diagrams. Each node in the diagram represents an activity. Table 3-2 lists all available activity nodes and describes their roles.

Icon	Name	Description
view1	View	Displays a page or fragment.
urlView1	URL View	Displays a URL external to the application.
router1	Router	Enables conditional navigation according to an expression language (EL) expression.
methodCall1	Method Call	Invokes a specific method in a Java class, typically a managed bean.
taskFlowCall1	Task Flow Call	Calls another task flow from the current one.
taskFlowReturn1	Task Flow Return	Identifies task-flow completion and returns control to the caller when applicable.
savePointRestore1	Save Point Restore	Restores application state and data from the last save point reached.
parentAction1	Parent Action	Allows a flow to invoke a navigation case in the parent flow as well as a local navigation case.

TABLE 3-2 *Activity Nodes and Their Roles*

Figure 3-12 shows a complete task flow diagram as displayed in the visual editor provided by Oracle JDeveloper 11*g*.

There are two distinct types of task flows: bounded and unbounded. An ADF 11*g* web application always contains a single unbounded task flow, even if it is empty. This unbounded task flow contains the application's entry points. The view activities it contains can be designated as bookmarkable, if needed.

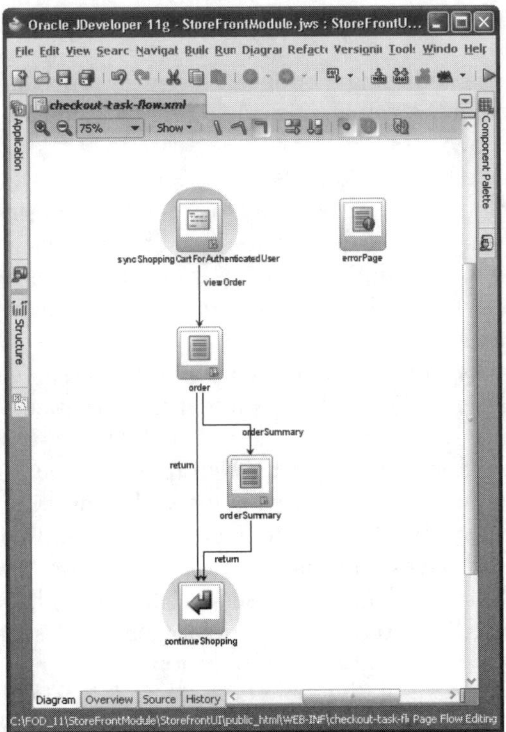

FIGURE 3-12 *Task flow as displayed in Oracle JDeveloper 11*g

Bounded task flows are meant to encapsulate a piece of reusable business logic, and they possess several defining characteristics:

- Single point of entry.
- One or several return values, if needed.
- Declarative input parameters.
- A dedicated page flow scope instance to control managed bean life span.
- Transaction management. Developers can specify in a declarative manner if the task flow must create a new transaction, join an existing one, or be excluded from the current transaction.
- Reentry, if needed. This enables support for the browser back button if the application's logic permits.
- Support nesting and recursion.

The Task Flow Call activity enables developers to chain task flows one to another, thus maximizing reuse possibilities. For example, suppose an online store lets new users create an account only at checkout time. The account creation process could be implemented using a bounded task flow. This task flow could then be called from anywhere in the application, including the checkout task flow, or from a registration task flow.

Chaining is one way to reuse task flows; ADF regions are another. They enable extracting and packaging a bounded task flow to add it to other pages. ADF regions can receive input parameters. These parameters must be passed, either by reference or by value, at the beginning of the task flow. It is also possible to exchange information after the start of the task flow with event passing. This ensures maximum reactivity of the user interface.

From a WebCenter perspective, task flows are a fundamental feature on which to build customizable applications. Since they represent reusable pieces of business logic, they naturally lend themselves to inclusion in a variety of contexts. Their isolated memory and transaction scopes decouple them from the surrounding application. This explains why task flows can be included in the WebCenter Composer resource catalog. When declared correctly, WebCenter Framework enables drag-and-drop of task flows in customizable pages, thus making task flows a first-rate option on the same footing as portlets. In fact, task flows represent a lightweight alternative to JSR 168 and JSR 286 portlets, since they do not require deployment in a separate container at run time to be deployed in a WebCenter application.

Be warned, however, that task flows can be built and consumed by ADF applications only. This limitation is mitigated by the existence of Oracle's JSF Portlet Bridge, which enables exposure of task flows as JSR 168 portlets that can be integrated to any standards-based portal.

While task flows are high-level implementations of business processes, they are not meant to host data access or business logic. They must interact with data controls and declarative bindings for these purposes. But these controls and binding are merely indirection mechanisms, since data access and business services are provided by the ADF Business Components framework (ADF BC).

Business Services: ADF BC

ADF BC is the most mature part of ADF. Born in 1999 under the name Java Business Objects, it was quickly renamed Business Components for Java (BC4J) and was adopted in several Oracle products over the years. In its current form, it is both a solid object to relational mapping tool (ORM) and a business logic layer. ADF BC implements several key patterns[2], such as Business Delegate[3] and Service Locator[4],

[2] See http://www.oracle.com/technology/products/jdev/tips/muench/designpatterns/index.html for more details.

[3] http://java.sun.com/blueprints/corej2eepatterns/Patterns/BusinessDelegate.html

[4] http://java.sun.com/blueprints/corej2eepatterns/Patterns/ServiceLocator.html

thus favoring an interface-based style of programming. Consequently, ADF BC is well suited to support service-oriented architecture (SOA), since it regroups data access, business domain validations, and business logic in a single location.

While the ADF BC framework is made up of hundreds of Java classes, developers typically manipulate only three main components:

- **Entity object** Represents a row in a database table and handles create, update, and delete operations. Validations can be defined at the entity object level to ensure data quality. Those validations can be defined in a declarative way or through code overrides if they are more complex.
- **View object** The view object represents a SQL query, and can be linked to other view objects to create master-detail hierarchies. It handles read operations. View objects cooperate with entity objects to validate user data.
- **Application module** A transactional component that plays the role of a work unit–related container. It contains instances of the view objects related to the use case and defines the service methods related to an end-user task.

Those three components are defined in a declarative manner with the help of XML files. Their default behavior comes from the base classes of the ADF BC framework. This behavior can be customized by associating a Java class to a specific component to override or extend the basic functionality.

Oracle JDeveloper 11*g* offers a visual environment to create and update entity objects, view objects, and application modules. The IDE provides property editors for each of these types of components, and is able to generate them from an existing database. In addition, developers can use ADF BC diagrams to model the object structure of their business logic layer. JDeveloper can create the corresponding database objects from the diagram. It can as well create a diagram from existing objects. Figure 3-13 shows such a diagram. In addition, JDeveloper can create diagrams reflecting the physical data model and supports multiple database-related tasks since it is built on the same code base as Oracle SQL Developer and, as such, inherits most of its features.

One interesting innovation brought by the 11*g* version of ADF is the inclusion of the Groovy scripting language. More specifically, several tasks related to Business Components support the use of Groovy. These include validator definition, error message tokens definition, and conditional execution conditions for validators, as well as default value assignment to view criteria bind variables, view object attributes, and entity attributes. Entity object and view objects may also have values calculated for their transient attributes by Groovy expressions.

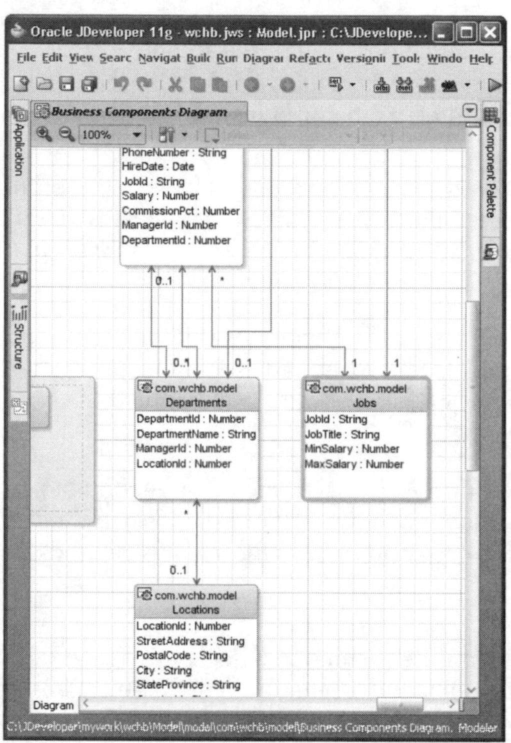

FIGURE 3-13 *ADF Business Components diagram in JDeveloper 11g*

The Groovy Language

Groovy is a dynamically typed scripting language that runs on the Java Virtual Machine (JVM). This can be achieved because the output of the Groovy compiler is straight Java bytecode. Groovy was proposed as a Java specification to the JCP through JSR 241.

One of Groovy's design objectives was to increase developer productivity by reducing scaffolding code and providing streamlined syntax constructs while being friendly to Java developers. Since they are compiled as needed at run time, Groovy scripts can be stored in XML files and alter the application's behavior without having an impact on the base Java/ADF code.

Since it provides a simpler syntax than Java, Groovy is a great productivity aid for developers. However, please note it is not possible at this time to code an entire ADF application using Groovy. Its use is limited to the ADF BC tasks mentioned previously. Figure 3-14 shows a typical Groovy expression edited in Oracle JDeveloper 11*g*.

We have given lots of attention to design-time features. Some of ADF BC's run-time features are also worth mentioning. The BC framework, for example, synchronizes data changes between the various view objects involved as long as they are based on the same entity object. Moreover, ADF BC takes charge of per-row state management by means of dynamic attributes added at run time. Performance and scalability features were also added by Oracle at various levels of the framework. Application modules, for example, are pooled by default. Since application modules are stateful, their state is persisted if the pooling algorithm decides to reuse them to process new requests. Run-time optimizations ensure that the same application module instance will be reassigned, if possible, to the last user session that returned it to the pool. In addition, it is possible to adjust the pool parameters to better fit current usage patterns.

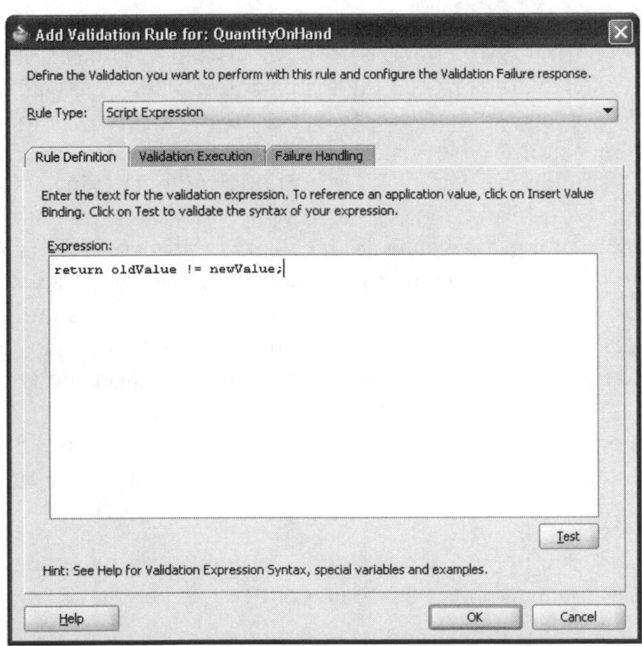

FIGURE 3-14 *Groovy expression in Oracle JDeveloper 11*g

Finally, it is worth mentioning that the ADF BC framework makes it possible to call PL/SQL procedures and functions easily—even if they are not part of a package. This makes ADF one of the premier options for organizations wanting to migrate from Oracle Forms to a Java platform.

You may wonder how ADF BC fits in the overall Oracle WebCenter context. By itself, WebCenter does not mandate its use. Alternative technologies supported by Oracle JDeveloper, such as Oracle TopLink or Enterprise JavaBeans, could be used in its place. It must be noted, however, that parts of WebCenter were built using ADF BC, more specifically Spaces and some of the Web 2.0 Services. The same goes for Oracle Fusion Applications, as the current and previous versions of Oracle E-Business suite. This means ADF BC packs a great deal of real-world expertise and has reached a level of maturity uncommon among its peers. Whatever business logic layer you choose, however, it will have limited impact on developer interaction with the model layer. ADF data controls can be used with all JDeveloper-supported alternatives.

Model: ADFm (JSR 227) Data Bindings and Data Controls

As we wrote earlier, one of the central tenets of ADF is separation of concerns. Oracle ADF Model (ADFm), which is an implementation of JSR 227, was designed to enable decoupling of the user interface from the business service implementation. This decoupling comes from two levels of encapsulation. The first level is the data control, which is a definition of a service's operations and data using standardized metadata. The second level is the data binding, which abstracts the data control's operations and data from the ADF Faces Rich Client components that employ them in the pages and fragments composing the application. This way, developers are insulated from changes in the business service internals as long as the service's interface—its contract to the outside world—is untouched. In a typical ADF application, it must be noted that the data controls have a one-to-one relationship with the ADF Business Components application modules (see previous section).

In ADFm, the connection between the user interface and the business service is two-way and declarative, since data controls and data bindings are defined in an XML file. ADFm defines three different types of binding objects:

- **Action** UI components, such as buttons or links, use this binding to invoke operations on data collections or data controls.
- **Iterator** Handles scrolling and paging through collections.
- **Value** Data consuming UI components possess value bindings. Specialized versions of these bindings exist for lists, trees, and tables.

All bindings supporting a specific page or fragment are defined in an XML file called the *page definition* file. This file is particular to a page or fragment. Oracle JDeveloper offers a graphical editor for these files, as shown in Figure 3-15.

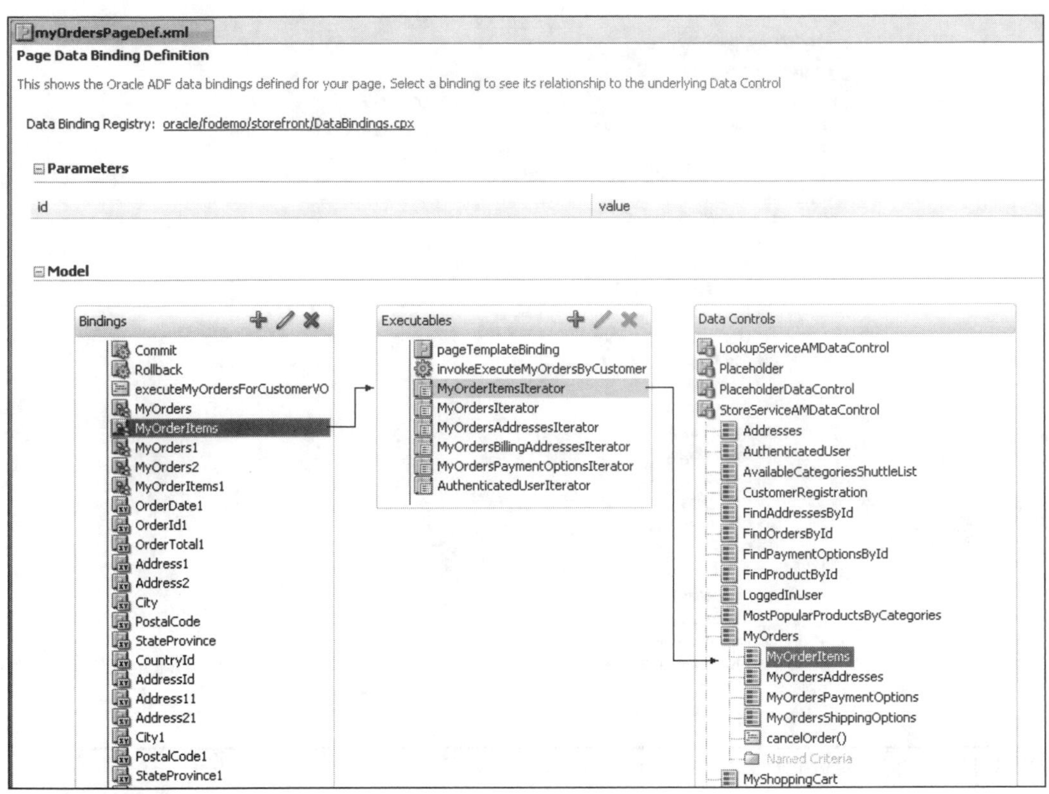

FIGURE 3-15 *The JDeveloper 11*g *page definition editor*

At this point, you are probably asking yourself how to populate the page definition. It is certainly possible to use the page definition editor for that purpose. However, in order to create data-bound user interfaces, developers typically drag-and-drop elements from the Data Controls panel (Figure 3-16).

When an application's business logic is implemented using ADF BC, this panel exposes each application module as a data control and lists the view object instances that the module contains. The view links establish the hierarchy for the objects contained by the data control. Methods defined in the application modules and view objects are listed in the panel, whether they are built-in or custom; these are also called *operations*. Furthermore, it is possible to add to the panel an interesting new feature in JDeveloper 11*g*: the *placeholder data control*. This special data control is incredibly useful for prototyping purposes, since it makes it possible to bind the UI without having actual application modules or view objects linked to it. The placeholder data control defines both the expected data structures and sample data; at run time, the pages will work as if they were bound to a real data source.

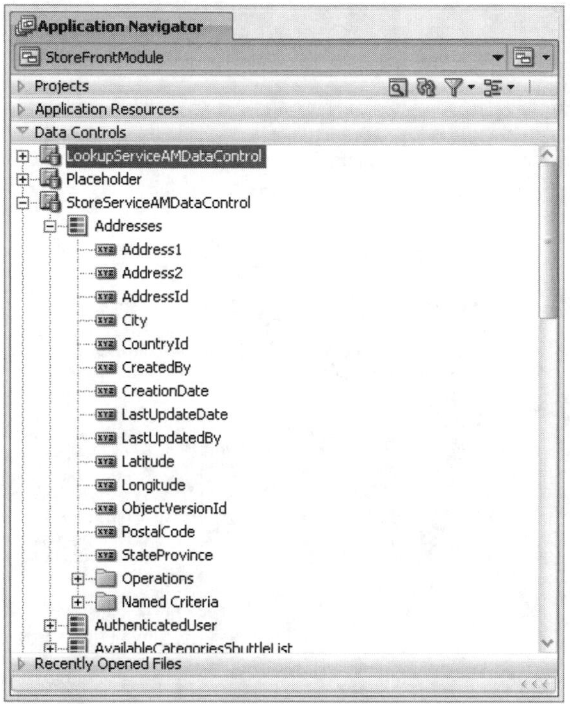

FIGURE 3-16 *The JDeveloper 11*g *Data Controls panel*

Several WebCenter features are exposed as data controls. This is the case of the page service; developers can list and delete the customizable pages available in the application. The content JCR adapter is another example.

How It All Fits Together

We now have reviewed all of Oracle ADF 11*g*'s components. But how do they fit together, and what does the development process of a typical application look like? Data model definition usually comes first. Business analysts or developers could choose to create diagrams using Oracle JDeveloper 11*g* or Oracle SQL Developer data modeling to visually depict the objects and their relationships. Once the data model is available, developers can use the ADF BC wizard to create default business components. Validations can then be added to the entity objects as needed, while queried rows are refined through view objects. Business methods are added to application modules as needed.

User interface definition will begin with the creation of the pages and fragments required by the application's use cases. Layout components will structure the look and feel of the application. ADF bindings will then connect the ADF Faces Rich Client components found in the pages and fragments to the underlying data model. The application's navigation rules, on the other hand, are defined in ADF Task Flows as well as reusable application tasks. Those task flows may then be published and consumed in WebCenter applications as needed.

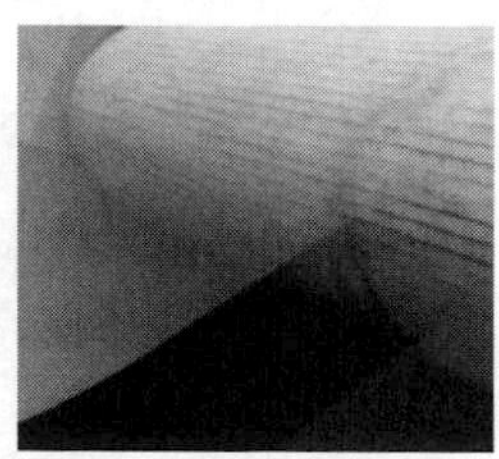

PART II

Building WebCenter Applications

CHAPTER 4

Building Your First WebCenter Page

ebCenter applications are based on open industry standards such as XML, Web services, and JavaServer Faces. In theory, you can use any open source or third-party development environment, even Emacs, vi, or Notepad to build your WebCenter applications.

However, one of the most important differentiators of Oracle WebCenter is that instead of exclusively focusing on your application's run-time behavior (performance, high availability, scalability), it also provides an elaborate design-time experience to ensure that the development process is straightforward, productive, and consistent. If you decided that Oracle WebCenter is for you, our recommendation is to use the free Oracle JDeveloper as your IDE. It will save you a lot of time and effort. And there are certain tasks that are incredibly hard to do if you're using different IDEs. These include consuming portlets or integrating the WebCenter Web 2.0 Services, such as threaded discussions or instant messaging. Another essential capability of WebCenter is that it enables any application with run-time customization and personalization capabilities, which allow the tailoring of an application to a user's exact requirements after the application has been deployed. The advantage of this over traditional application development is an increase in application agility as there are no development round trips needed for those changes. Also the user's acceptance and productivity is increased as the application fits the individual's work flow perfectly.

The data needed to facilitate customization and personalization are stored as layered metadata in the Meta Data Services (MDS). This layered metadata is applied to the base application to create the changed view of the application. Through this mechanism, new application versions can be rolled out while preserving the user's personalization and any customizations done to the application, significantly increasing the productivity of rolling out new application versions.

To start off into WebCenter, we are going to create our first WebCenter application with JDeveloper.

Creating an Application

To create an application in JDeveloper:

1. Invoke the New Gallery (Figure 4-1) through File | New or use the New icon from the toolbar and then select Applications from the Gallery selection and select WebCenter Application from the items.

2. Drop down the Application selector from the Application Navigator and select New Application (Figure 4-2).

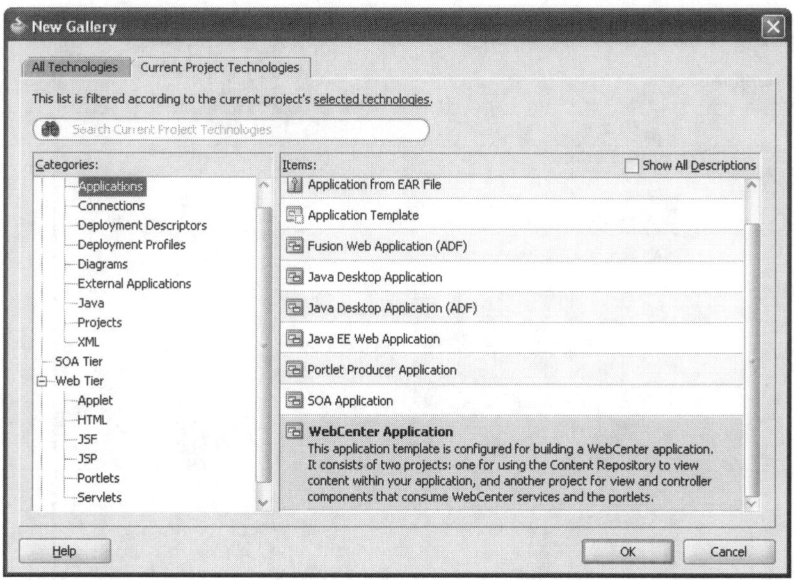

FIGURE 4-1 *New Gallery*

After this, JDeveloper will present the Create Application wizard. Here is where you can select the type of application you are about to create. JDeveloper provides Application Templates, which define the structure and necessary libraries for a certain type of application. This feature helps you hit the ground running instead of having to set up the necessary things over and over again.

Since we are about to create a WebCenter application, we are going to select the WebCenter Application template, shown in Figure 4-3, and continue.

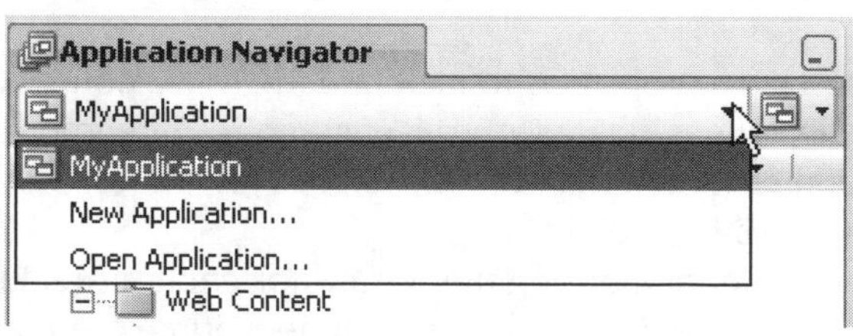

FIGURE 4-2 *The Application Navigator*

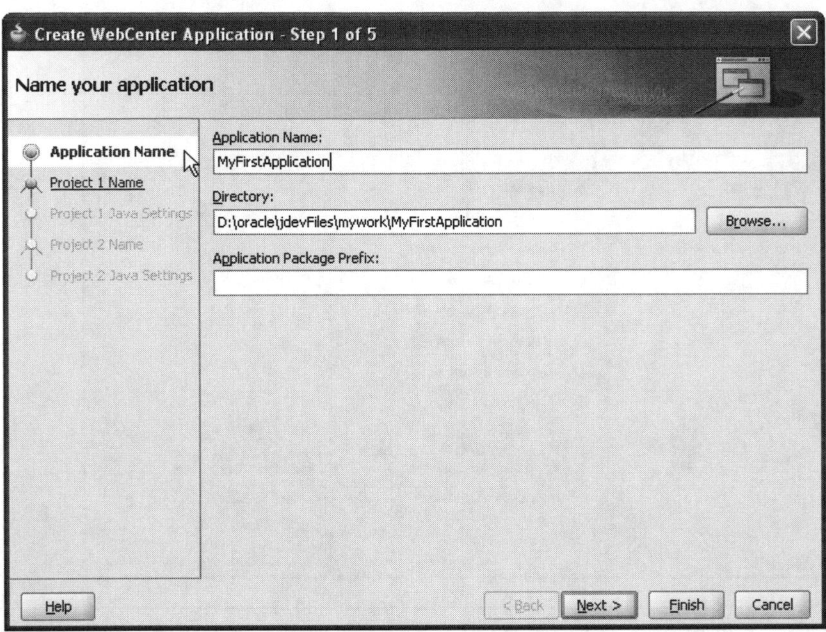

FIGURE 4-3 *The New Application wizard for WebCenter applications*

Now that we have selected the WebCenter template, the wizard will create two application projects, one called Model and one called ViewController (Figure 4-4). Each application project has individual settings for project technology, generated components, and associated libraries.

From the template these settings have preset entries relevant for the application type, but during the wizard (and afterward) you can modify those settings so they fit your requirements.

The purpose of these two projects is to facilitate the MVC concept where all model-related components (e.g., Data Controls) will go into the model project and where all view- and controller-related objects, such as JSF pages, page flows, etc., will go into the ViewController project.

Also, Java settings are defined during the wizard for each project in the application. You can define the default package name, source path, and output directories (Figure 4-5). Again there are default values preseeded, but they can be changed anytime to fit your requirements.

The wizard will guide you through both projects; on finishing you will end up with an application skeleton, shown in Figure 4-6, with two projects and all necessary libraries and technologies ready to start creating a WebCenter application.

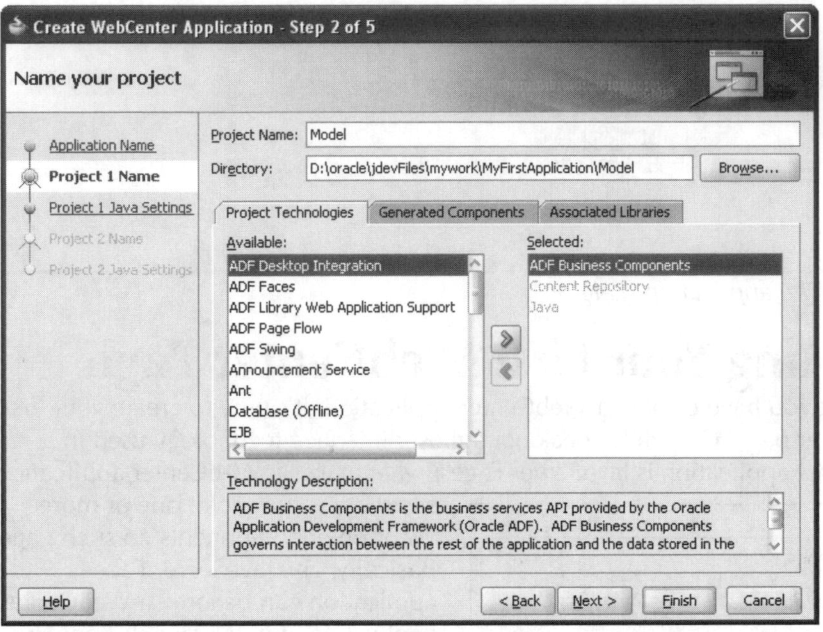

FIGURE 4-4 *Project settings*

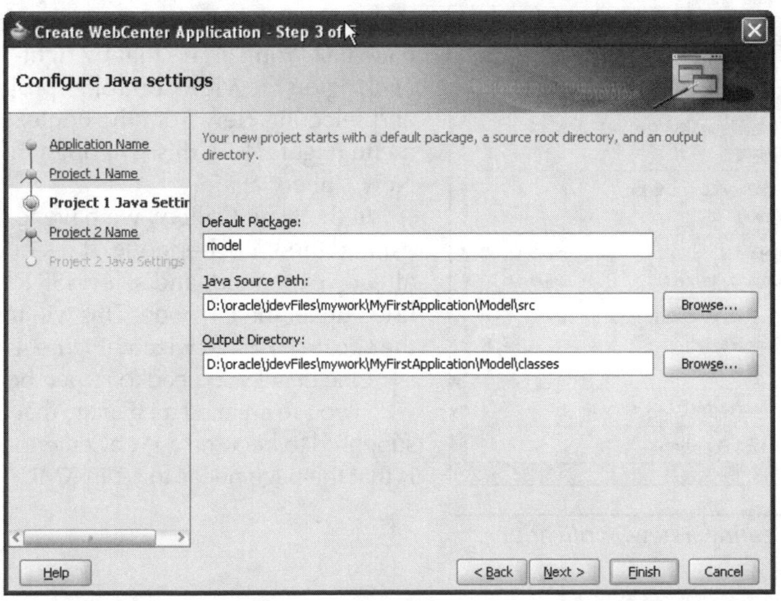

FIGURE 4-5 *Java settings*

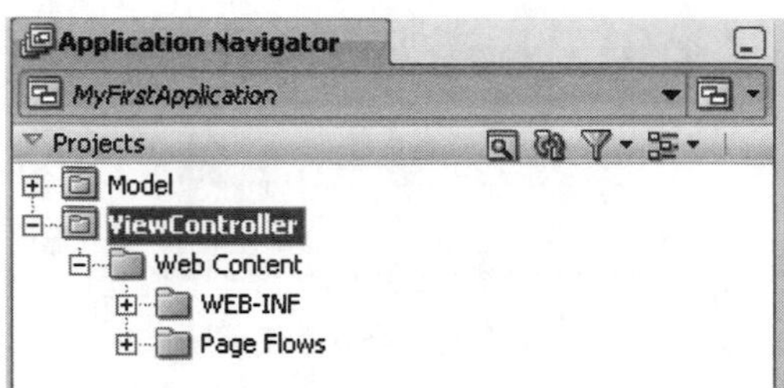

FIGURE 4-6 *The application skeleton*

Creating Your First WebCenter Page

Now that you have created a WebCenter application, it's time to create your first WebCenter page. Generally speaking, the user interface technology used in a WebCenter application is JavaServer Faces; what makes a WebCenter application stand out is the use of one or more WebCenter components on such page. Basically, any JavaServer Faces application can become a WebCenter application and leverage its benefits, either from the get-go or later through enhancement.

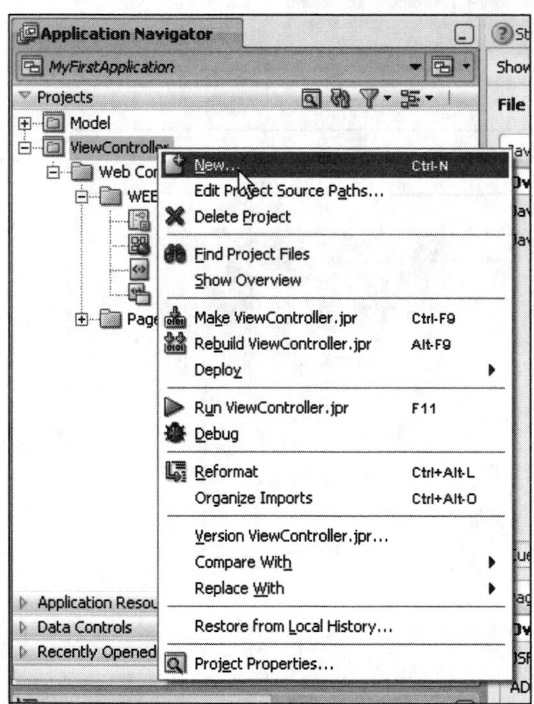

FIGURE 4-7 *Creating a new application component*

To create your first WebCenter page we need to create a JavaServer Faces page first. You can do that by right-clicking on the ViewController project and selecting New from the context menu (Figure 4-7); this will open the New Gallery again.

In the New Gallery, we have to expand the Web Tier node, if it's not already expanded, and select JSF Page listed under the JSF node. This will invoke the Create JSF Page wizard (Figure 4-8).

One detail you need to remember when you're creating a JSF page that is supposed to become a WebCenter page is that the page needs to be in XML

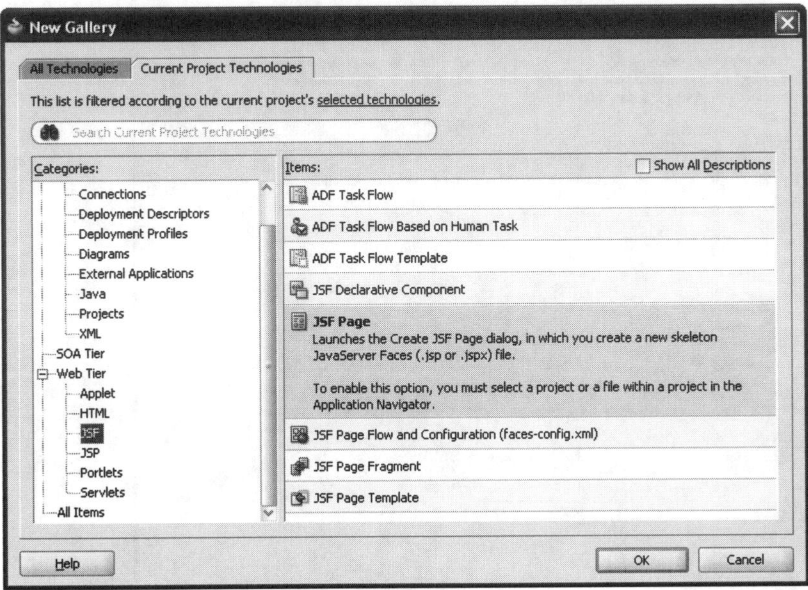

FIGURE 4-8 *The Create JSF Page wizard*

format and hence be a JSPX page. This is necessary to allow the run-time customization and personalization capabilities that come with WebCenter. Those changes are stored in XML form in WebCenter's Meta Data Services and are, at run time, applied to the page. Since only XML has a strict syntax and grammar, we need to use JSPX as the page syntax. To create a JSPX page you simply click the Create as XML Document checkbox on the Create JSF Page dialog (Figure 4-9).

Enter the name and directory and choose OK. When JDeveloper creates the page and opens it in the editor, we are ready to add components to the page. In order to select components to be added, you should use the Component Palette, which is normally located on the right-hand side of your JDeveloper window. In case the Component Palette is not visible you can bring it back using View | Component Palette.

The Component Palette, shown in Figure 4-10, is divided into several sections; components are grouped. You can switch groups by selecting the one you are looking for from the drop-down at the top of the Component Palette.

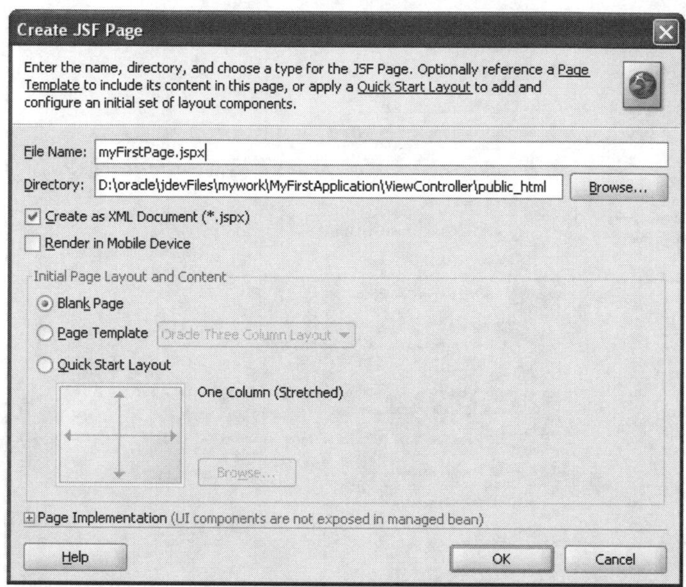

FIGURE 4-9 *The Create JSF Page dialog*

FIGURE 4-10 *Changing component groups*

Adding Your First Component

To create your first WebCenter page you are going to add three WebCenter components to the page. The first one is Panel Customizable, which sets the groundwork for allowing a user personalizations at run time. First you need to change the group in the Component Palette to Oracle Composer where you will find all components related to Oracle Composer. What Composer is and what it can do for us we will see in a later chapter. For now let's just drag-and-drop the component named Panel Customizable onto our new, empty page. The component will show up on the page as a dashed box, as shown in Figure 4-11.

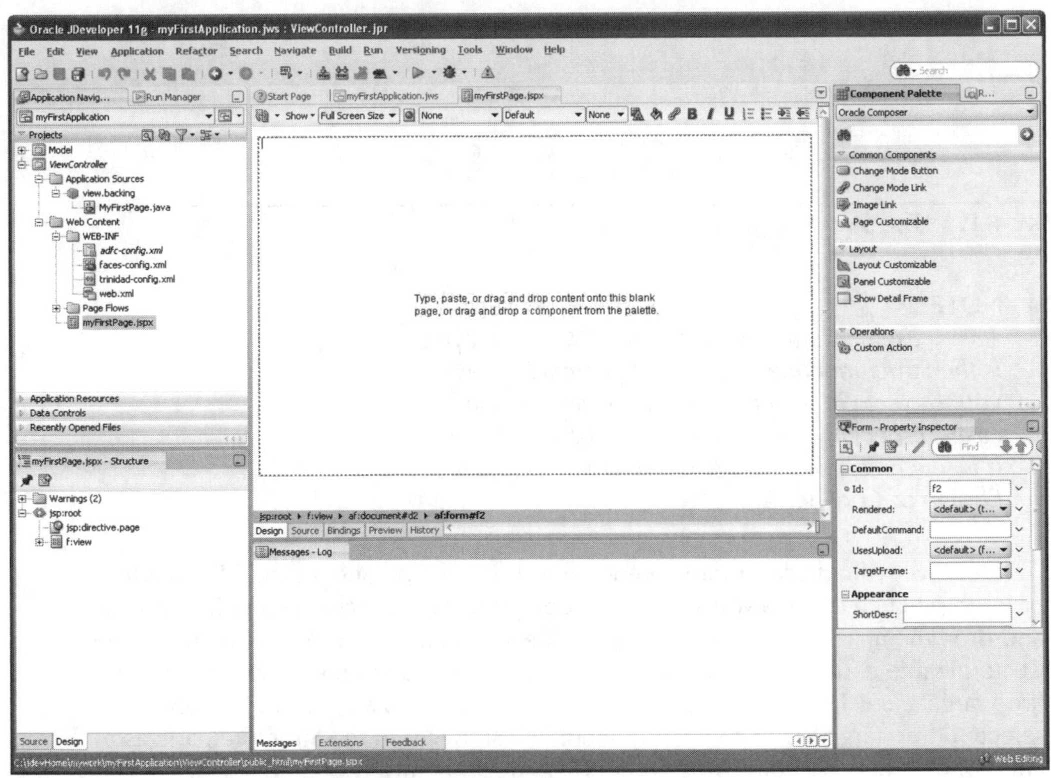

FIGURE 4-11 *JDeveloper with open editor*

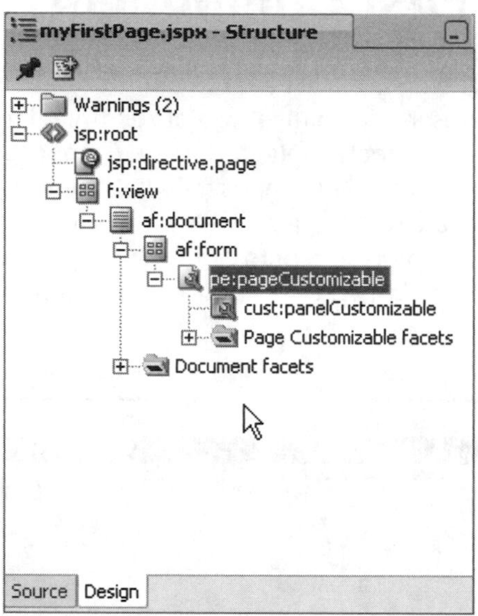

FIGURE 4-12 *The Structure panel*

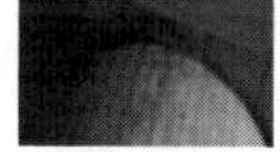

NOTE
A very useful tool for working with WebCenter pages is the Structure panel (Figure 4-12), which shows you the page in a hierarchical tree view. In some cases, especially with complex nested constructs, it is much easier to navigate there than using the Design or Code view.

Now we will add two more components, both of type Show Detail Frame. In order to practice the two ways of adding components to a page, you will now drag-and-drop the first one directly to the page. Be sure that you drop it inside the Panel Customizable component, which is indicated by the blue frame around the active drop target (see Figure 4-13, which shows Panel Customizable as the currently selected drop target). The new component will show up in the Structure pane as a child of the Panel Customizable component in the hierarchy (Figure 4-14).

Now, for the second instance of Show Detail Frame, take it from the Component Palette and drop it onto the Panel Customizable node in the Structure panel.

Let's take a look at the page now. You will see two objects on the page, or rather two boxes with headers and a small icon on the right. These are the two Show Detail Frame components (Figure 4-15). In the Structure panel select one of the two Show Detail Frame components and you will see the associated properties in the Property Inspector.

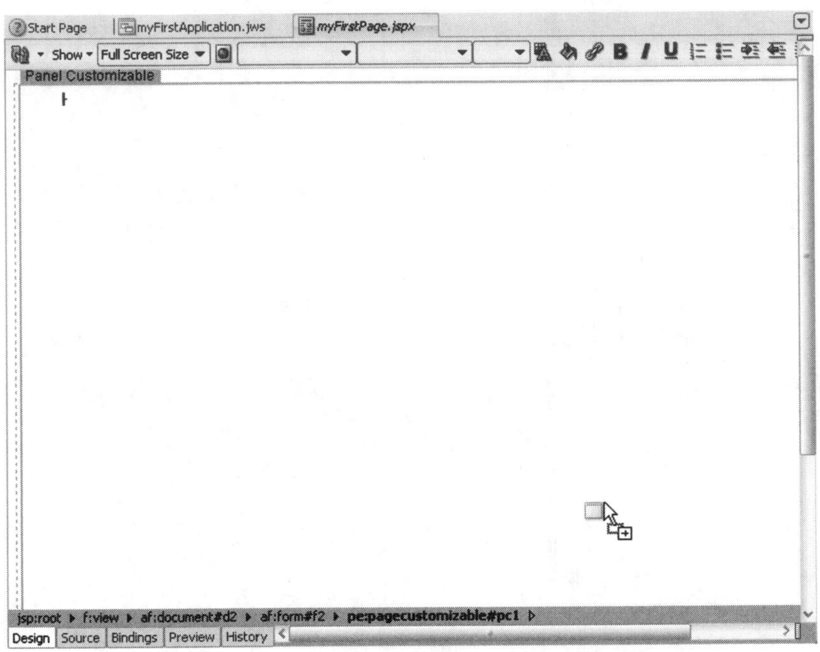

FIGURE 4-13 *Dropping a component onto a visual editor*

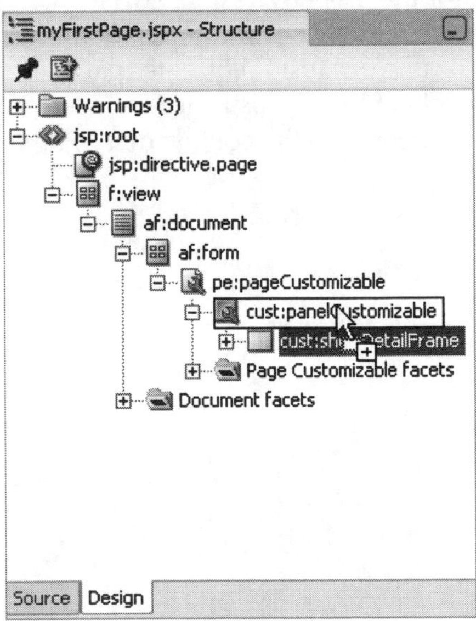

FIGURE 4-14 *Dropping a component onto the Structure panel*

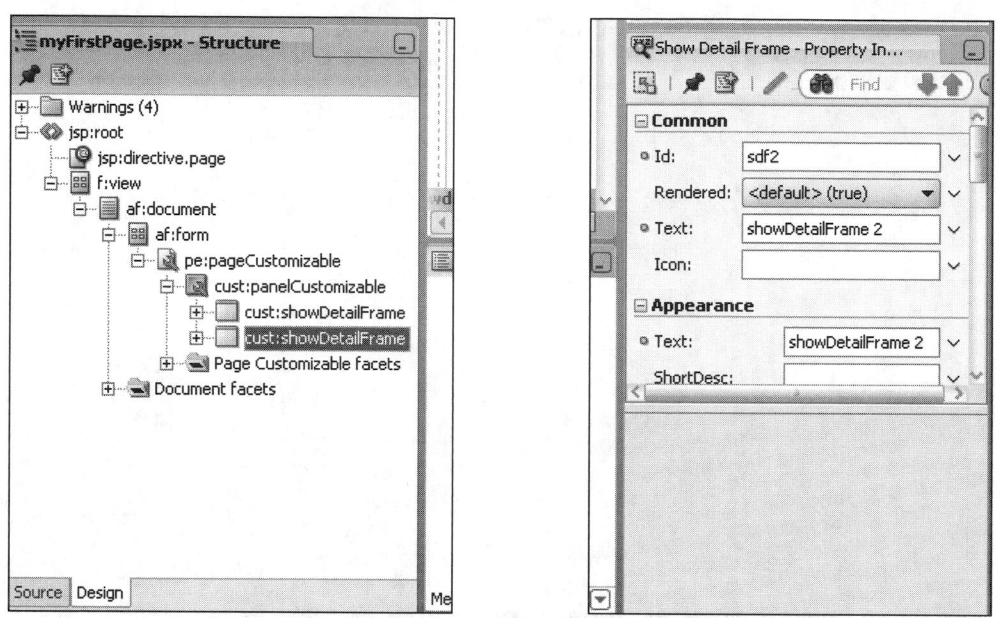

FIGURE 4-15 *Setting properties for a specific component*

Now change the value for the property Text to My First Frame. Do the same for the second Show Detail Frame, but change the value to My Second Frame. And now—drumroll—it's time to run your first WebCenter page.

To do so, simply right-click on the myFirstPage.jspx node in the Application Navigator and select the Run item from the context menu, as shown in Figure 4-16.

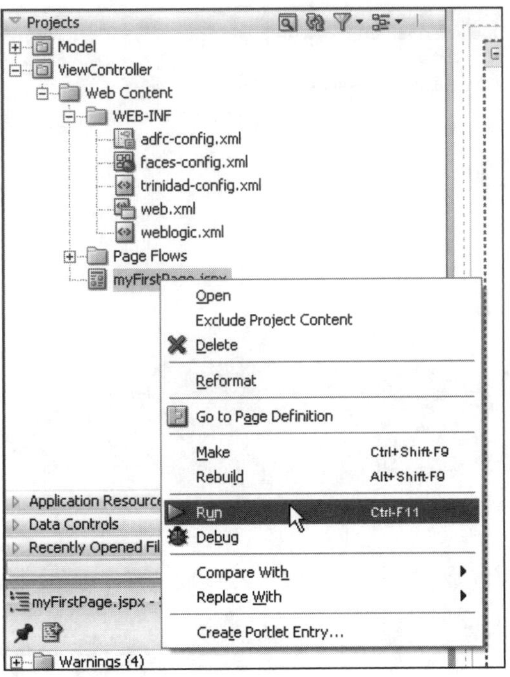

FIGURE 4-16 *Executing a page*

Once the Integrated WebLogic Server is started and the page is ready for execution, your favorite browser will pop up and present the result of your hard work, the first WebCenter page showing two empty frames. Be patient, especially if you run a page for the first time. Starting the Integrated WebLogic Server can take time, depending on the speed of your machine.

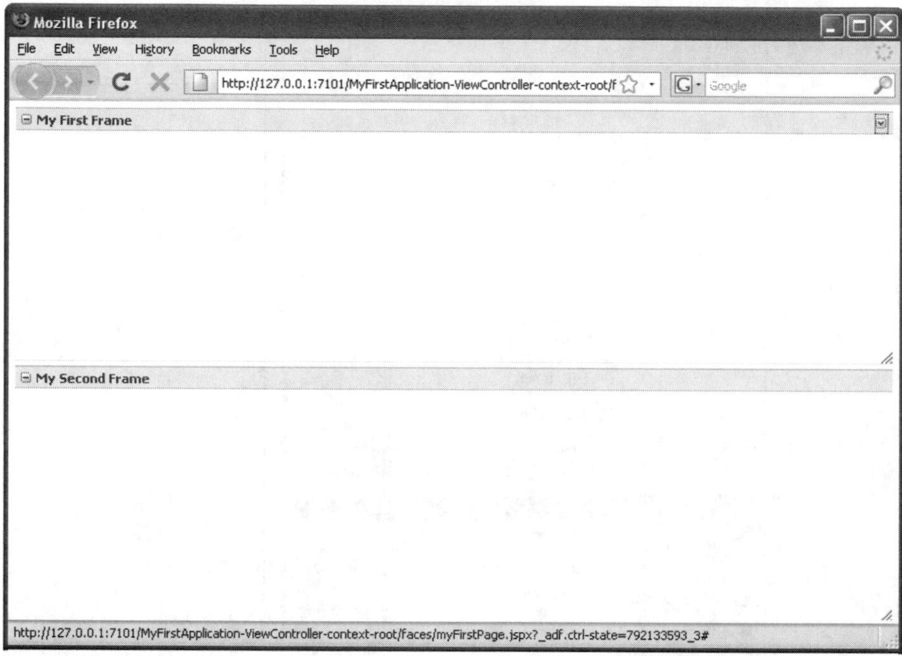

FIGURE 4-17 *The running page*

Let's examine the rendered page a bit closer (Figure 4-17). You will find each frame to have

- A header with expand icon, title, and a menu on the right.
- A resize indicator in the lower-right corner.

Without any further coding you can now

- Expand/contract the region using the icon left of the title text.
- Reorder frames using the menu items of the menu behind the icon on the right.
- Reorder through drag-and-drop by grabbing the frame at the header.

All those changes are being persisted in MDS and will be preserved even if you restart the application. This behavior is the basis for creating more complex scenarios where you can then add new components at run time or dynamically change the page layout without having to touch the underlying application code.

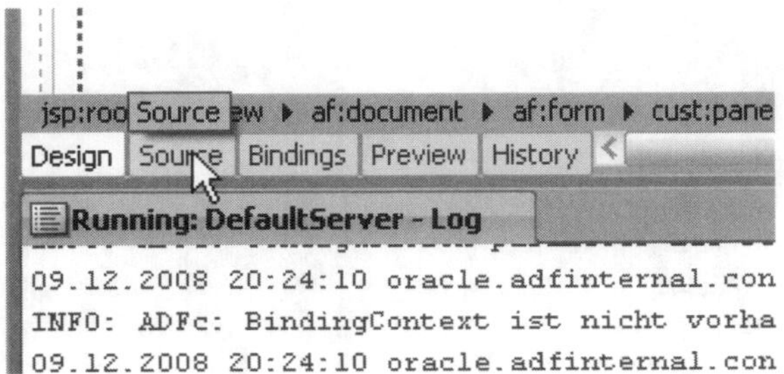

FIGURE 4-18 *Switching to Code view*

The Inner Makings—the JSP Tag Structure

Now that you have succeeded in creating our first WebCenter page, take a look at the page to see what it is made of. To do so, switch from Design to Code view (Figure 4-18) in your editor window in Oracle JDeveloper by selecting the Source tab at the bottom of the page editor.

```
<?xml version='1.0' encoding='windows-1252'?>
      <jsp:root xmlns:jsp="http://java.sun.com/JSP/Page" version="2.1"
               xmlns:f="http://java.sun.com/jsf/core"
               xmlns:h="http://java.sun.com/jsf/html"
               xmlns:af="http://xmlns.oracle.com/adf/faces/rich"
               xmlns:cust="http://xmlns.oracle.com/adf/faces/customizable">
        <jsp:directive.page contentType="text/html;charset=windows-1252"/>
        <f:view>
          <af:document id="d2" binding="#{backingBeanScope.backing_welcome.d2}">
            <af:form id="f2"  binding="#{backingBeanScope.backing_welcome.f2}">
              <cust:panelCustomizable
                          binding="#{backingBeanScope.backing_welcome.pc1}"
                          id="pc1">
                <cust:showDetailFrame text="My First Frame"
                           binding="#{backingBeanScope.backing_welcome.sdf1}"
                           id="sdf1"/>
                <cust:showDetailFrame text="My Second Frame"
                           binding="#{backingBeanScope.backing_welcome.sdf2}"
                           id="sdf2"/>
              </cust:panelCustomizable>
            </af:form>
          </af:document>
        </f:view></jsp:root>
```

All that is WebCenter-specific are the Panel Customizable and the Show Detail Frame tags; everything else is plain JavaServer Faces and JavaServer Page components.

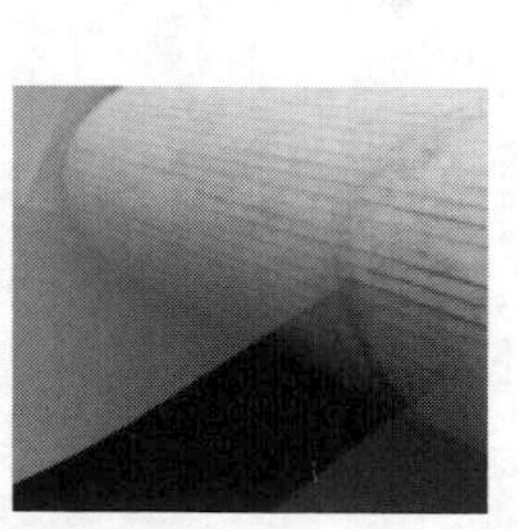

CHAPTER 5

Consuming and Building Portlets

Portlets are the key building blocks of portals; they are reusable web components or page fragments that you can plug in to your pages. Examples of portlets are a report of top sales by region, an order entry form, or a threaded discussion forum. Portlets are frequently used by Enterprise Resource Planning (ERP), Customer Relationship Management (CRM), or systems to publish well-defined, often self-contained business facts. In this chapter you will learn what portlets are, what it takes to build portlets, and how to consume them in your WebCenter applications.

We cannot go into great detail about portlet development, but fortunately there is a lot of information available about portlet development online. First and foremost, you can refer to the Java Portlet Specification (JPS), http://jcp.org/en/jsr/detail?id=168 and http://jcp.org/en/jsr/detail?id=286. Secondly, you can look up the official Oracle documentation, the Oracle WebCenter Developer's Guide that contains plenty of details about portlet development. And last but not least, Stefan Hepper, the specification lead for JSR 168 and 286, co-authored a book, *Portlets and Apache Portals*. The book, containing a wealth of information, has not been published, but the manuscript is freely available from the publisher's web site on http://www.manning.com.

What Are Portlets?

Portlets (Figure 5-1 provides an example) are often compared to web services. While the two are fundamentally different technologies, there are certain similarities between them.

Weather Portlet

Day	Lo	Hi	Sky
Monday	45	55	Rainy
Tuesday	80	85	Sunny
Wednesday	50	61	Partly Cloudy
Thursday	70	80	Cloudy
Friday	50	63	Rainy
Saturday	55	70	Rainy
Sunday	50	68	Partly Sunny

FIGURE 5-1 *Example of a portlet*

Both portlets and web services provide well-defined functionality and are invoked by consumer applications. While the information coming from web services is meant to be processed by the consuming application, portlets themselves are the consumed entities. For example, a weather or stock quote web service returns data based on the ZIP code or stock ticker information. On the other hand, portlets also provide the user interface on top of their data, so the application developer consuming the portlet doesn't have to build a UI. Web services, as their name suggests, are accessible through the Web, typically over HTTP. The user interface for web services is mostly defined on the consumer end. The most common markup types that portlets generate are HTML and XML. Portlets can be accessed both locally (deployed along with the consumer application or portal) and remotely.

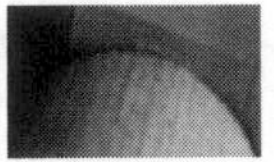

NOTE
*To accommodate the scalability and flexibility requirements of large-scale enterprise deployments, Oracle has a history of supporting remote portlet technologies. In the 11*g *release, Oracle WebCenter supports remote portlets only. WebLogic Portal supports local portlets as well. Oracle WebCenter was architected so that local portlet support can be added easily in future releases.*

Another core functionality of portlets is that they provide customization and personalization capabilities. Administrators, for example, may set the default stock ticker for the stock quote portlet, which end users can override by personalizing the portlet.

Portlet Standards: Java Portlet Specification and WSRP

There are widely used open industry standards for portals and portlets, which ensure that portlets built and deployed on one vendor's platform work well when deployed to or consumed by another company's infrastructure.

The Java Portlet Specification defines the API to build standards-based portlets. The initial 1.0 version of the Java Portlet Specification,[1] often referred to as JSR 168, addresses the basic portlet functionality, such as the portlet life cycle, portlet request and response, portlet context, and portlet display modes. The Java Portlet Specification 2.0 (JSR 286) elevated the portlet standards to the next level by adding key functionalities, such as inter-portlet communication and event support.

[1] While in development, the Java Portlet Specification 1.0 was managed under Java Specification Request (JSR) 168. Java Portlet Specification 2.0 was developed by the JSR 286 Expert Group.

Just as you deploy servlets to a servlet container, portlets live inside a portlet container. The portlet container provides portlets with a run-time environment: it manages their life cycle and provides a persistent storage for portlet preferences (Figure 5-2).

The Oracle Portlet Container, part of Oracle WebCenter, allows you to access portlets remotely. Portlets deployed to the Oracle Portlet Container are automatically exposed for remote access through Web Services for Remote Portlets (WSRP).

WSRP, an Organization for the Advancement of Structured Information Standards (OASIS) web services standard, is the communication protocol that defines what it takes to interact with portlets remotely. WSRP 1.0 is dealing with fundamental portlet functionalities, such as registering a remotely running portlet producer with the portlet consumer application, retrieving the portlet markup from the portlet producer, and mapping roles between the portlet consumer and the portlet producer application. WSRP 2.0 addresses a number of additional capabilities, such as inter-portlet communication through navigation parameters, export and import of portlet customizations, event support, and support for rich AJAX user interactions.

Remote portlets play very well in a service-oriented world. Very much like web services, remote portlets provide an extended level of flexibility and scalability. Most

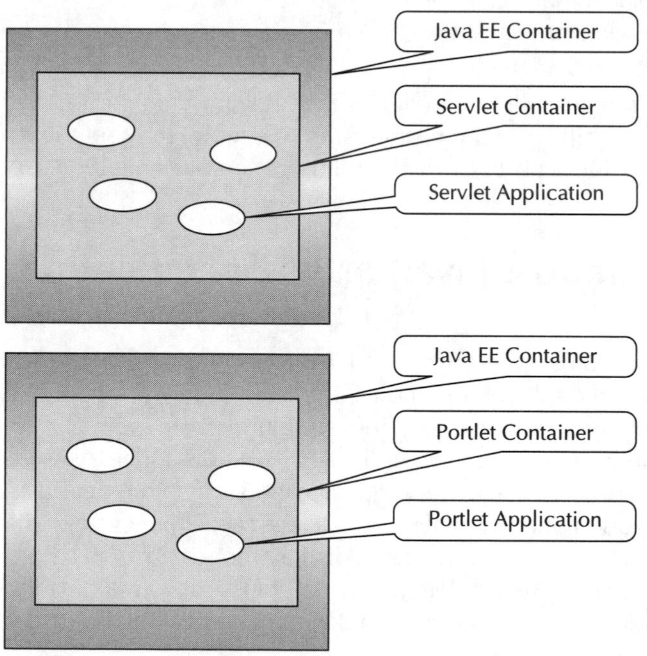

FIGURE 5-2 *Servlet and portlet containers*

important, WSRP supports federated deployments, allowing you to consume remotely running portlets in multiple portlet consumers. WSRP is often used when interoperability is crucial between portals of different vendors. For example, through WSRP, Oracle WebCenter can easily consume the standards-based portlets deployed to Oracle Portal or WebLogic Portal. At the same time, Oracle WebCenter and WebLogic Portal portlets are available to Oracle Portal or any other third-party portlet consumer with WSRP support.

What makes WSRP especially powerful is that it's a communication protocol and therefore is independent of the underlying language used to build the portlet. There are WSRP portlet containers and bridges available for different programming languages, including Java, PHP, and .NET.

Although WSRP is language-independent, WSRP 1.0 was designed to work well with JSR 168 while WSRP 2.0 goes hand in hand with JSR 286.

For a long time, standards-based portlets were inferior to vendor-specific portlets. Fortunately, this has changed with JSR 286 and WSRP 2.0. In this section we primarily focus on standards-based portlets. If you are interested in building and consuming Oracle-specific PDK-Java portlets, the product documentation provides plenty of information about it.

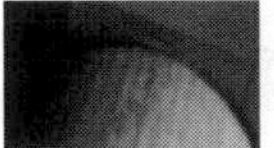

NOTE

Be warned that by using PDK-Java, you are tied to the Oracle Portal offerings: Oracle Portal and Oracle WebCenter. Given that PDK-Java doesn't offer significant advantages over standards-based portlets, our recommendation is to go with standards-based portlets. An even better reason to walk the standards-based path: Oracle invests most of its development effort into standards-based portlets. While WSRP 2.0 portlets are pretty much first-class citizens in the WebCenter world, PDK-Java portlets have various limitations, including lack of support for events and limited partial page refresh support.

WSRP 2.0 provides functionalities that JSR 168 does not support. To be able to build feature-rich WSRP 2.0 portlets with capabilities such as parameters and support for export and import of portlet customizations, Oracle extended the portlet container to provide these features using WSRP 2.0. While JSR 168 portlets can be deployed to any vendor's portlet container, JSR 168 portlets using the Oracle extensions to support WSRP 2.0 must be deployed to the Oracle Portlet Container. If deployed to a third-party JSR 168 container, the Oracle specific extensions will be ignored.

NOTE
Oracle WebCenter 11gR1 supports JSR 168, WSRP 1.0, and WSRP 2.0. JSR 286 support is planned for a future release.

Consuming Portlets in JDeveloper

WebCenter allows you to consume portlets at design time in JDeveloper, or run time in your WebCenter application. There are some differences between the exact steps of consuming portlets at design time versus run time, but the concepts are the same for the two approaches. First, let's focus on how to consume portlets in the design-time environment.

You need to follow four easy steps when consuming portlets in your WebCenter applications:

1. **Register portlet producer** The first step before adding portlets to your applications is the portlet producer registration. You have to point your WebCenter application to the portlet producer endpoint: the WSDL URL in the case of WSRP, or the producer test page URL in the case of PDK-Java portlets.

2. **Drop portlet onto the page** The newly registered portlet producer shows up under your connections, and you can drop the portlet onto the page.

3. **Specify portlet view tag attributes** The portlet view tag allows you to control behavior like rendering or hiding the portlet header, which portlet modes the portlet should expose, or whether the portlet should be rendered in an inline frame (iframe).

4. **Wire portlet parameters and events** If the portlet supports navigational parameters in the case of WSRP 2.0 portlets or public portlet parameters in the case of PDK-Java portlets, you can wire them up with other components on the page. You can also specify partial page refresh behavior.

Now let's take a closer look at these steps.

Before Consuming Portlets

If you created your application using the WebCenter Application template, shown in Figure 5-3, it includes the WebCenter Portlet View technology scope, and you can go ahead and start consuming portlets right away. This technology scope adds the necessary libraries and JSP tag libraries to the project and performs the necessary configuration so that the portlet producer registration wizards show up in JDeveloper's New Gallery.

We recommend that until you get more familiar with the technology, use the WebCenter application template and technology scopes. Later on, you will probably build your applications and projects without applying any of the templates and technology scopes to it, and will most likely manually configure your environment. The Oracle WebCenter documentation lists the libraries and JSP tag libraries pulled into your project when you're using the WebCenter Portlet View technology scope (Table 5-1).

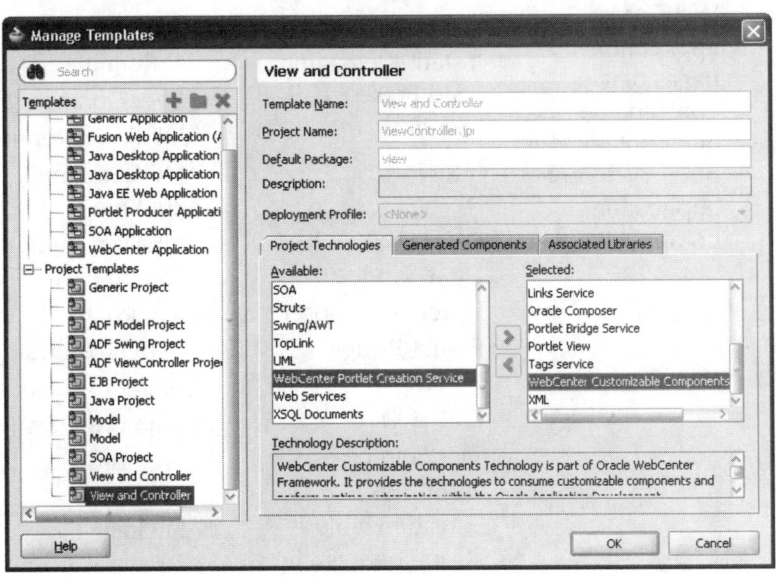

FIGURE 5-3 *WebCenter application template and technology scopes*

Project	Purpose	Technology Scope	Associated Libraries
Model	Use this project to define data controls that pull in content from selected data repositories.	ADF Business Components Content Repository Java	ADF Model Runtime BC4J Oracle Domains BC4J Runtime BC4J Security BC4J Tester MDS Runtime MDS Runtime Dependencies Oracle JDBC
ViewController	Use this project to build WebCenter application pages that consume portlets and contain your other WebCenter application components.	ADF Faces ADF Page Flow HTML Instant Messaging and Presence (IMP) Service Java JSF JSP and Servlets Links Service Oracle Composer Portlet Bridge Service Portlet View Tags Service WebCenter Customizable Components XML	*JSP Tag Libraries:* JSF Core JSF HTML JSP Runtime *Other Libraries:* ADF Faces Runtime ADF Common Runtime ADF Web Runtime MDS Runtime MDS Runtime Dependencies Commons Beanutils Commons Logging Commons Collections ADF Page Flow Runtime ADF Controller Runtime

TABLE 5-1 *WebCenter Application Template Projects, Technology Scopes, and Libraries*

Registering Portlet Producers

In the Oracle world, portlets tend to be remote. WSRP requires portlet consumers to register the portlet producer they intend to use. The producer registration is the time when the portlet producer tells the portlet consumer about the portlets it offers, how many portlets it provides, what they are called, and what portlet modes they support.

When you're using the Oracle Portlet Container, the easiest way to access the portlet producer endpoint URL is to point your browser to the test page (Figure 5-4) of your portlet application: http://host-name:port-number/context-root. For example, when you're using the Integrated WebLogic Server in the JDeveloper development environment, the sample WSRP portlet producer is accessible at http://localhost:7101/portletapp.

By clicking on the WSDL URL links on the bottom of the portlet producer test page, you can access the WSRP WSDL documents (Figure 5-5). The Oracle Portlet Container provides access to your portlets both through WSRP 1.0 and WSRP 2.0. You will need to provide the WSRP WSDL URL to the portlet producer registration wizard.

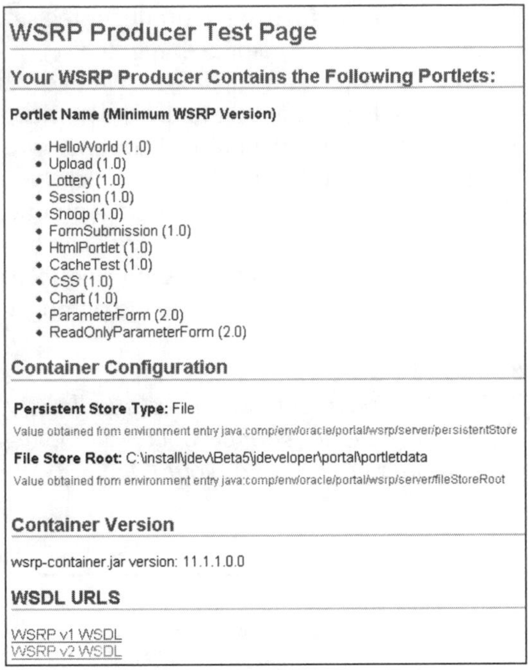

WSRP Producer Test Page

Your WSRP Producer Contains the Following Portlets:

Portlet Name (Minimum WSRP Version)

- HelloWorld (1.0)
- Upload (1.0)
- Lottery (1.0)
- Session (1.0)
- Snoop (1.0)
- FormSubmission (1.0)
- HtmlPortlet (1.0)
- CacheTest (1.0)
- CSS (1.0)
- Chart (1.0)
- ParameterForm (2.0)
- ReadOnlyParameterForm (2.0)

Container Configuration

Persistent Store Type: File

Value obtained from environment entry java:comp/env/oracle/portal/wsrp/server/persistentStore

File Store Root: C:\install\jdev\Beta5\jdeveloper\portal\portletdata

Value obtained from environment entry java:comp/env/oracle/portal/wsrp/server/fileStoreRoot

Container Version

wsrp-container.jar version: 11.1.1.0.0

WSDL URLS

WSRP v1 WSDL
WSRP v2 WSDL

FIGURE 5-4 *The test page of a WSRP portlet producer*

```
- <definitions targetNamespace="urn:oasis:names:tc:wsrp:v2:wsdl">
    <import namespace="urn:oasis:names:tc:wsrp:v2:bind" location="http://localhost:7101/portletapp
    /portlets/wsrp2?WSDL=wsrp_v2_bindings.wsdl"/>
  - <service name="WSRP_v2_Service">
    - <port name="WSRP_v2_ServiceDescription_Service"
      binding="bind:WSRP_v2_ServiceDescription_Binding_SOAP">
        <soap:address location="http://localhost:7101/portletapp/portlets/wsrp2"/>
      </port>
    - <port name="WSRP_v2_PortletManagement_Service"
      binding="bind:WSRP_v2_PortletManagement_Binding_SOAP">
        <soap:address location="http://localhost:7101/portletapp
        /WSRP_v2_PortletManagement_Service"/>
      </port>
    - <port name="WSRP_v2_Markup_Service" binding="bind:WSRP_v2_Markup_Binding_SOAP">
        <soap:address location="http://localhost:7101/portletapp/WSRP_v2_Markup_Service"/>
      </port>
    - <port name="WSRP_v2_Registration_Service"
      binding="bind:WSRP_v2_Registration_Binding_SOAP">
        <soap:address location="http://localhost:7101/portletapp/WSRP_v2_Registration_Service"/>
      </port>
    </service>
  </definitions>
```

FIGURE 5-5 *The WSDL of a WSRP portlet producer*

After having successfully accessed the WSDL document, copy the WSDL URL to the clipboard and invoke the producer registration wizard.

When it comes to producer registration, you can decide if you want to register the producer with your application or with your IDE. You should register the producer with your IDE if you expect to use the portlet producer repeatedly in other consumer applications. If you are new to WebCenter, we recommend that you register the WSRP Sample Portlet Producer with JDeveloper through the Resource Palette (Figure 5-6). This will allow you to reuse the portlet producer across your applications by simply dropping a portlet from the Resource Palette onto your page or by dropping the portlet producer connection onto the Application Resources section in the Application Navigator without going through the producer registration process over again.

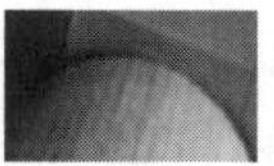

NOTE
The producer registration wizard allows you to specify whether your producer will be registered for your application or your IDE.

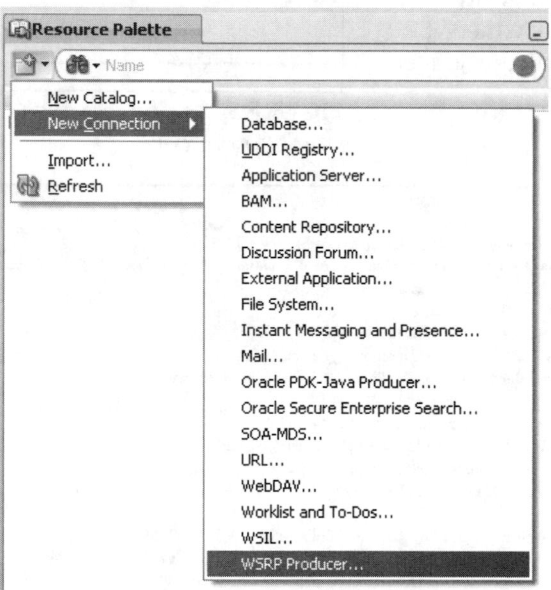

FIGURE 5-6 *Registering a portlet producer against the Resource Palette*

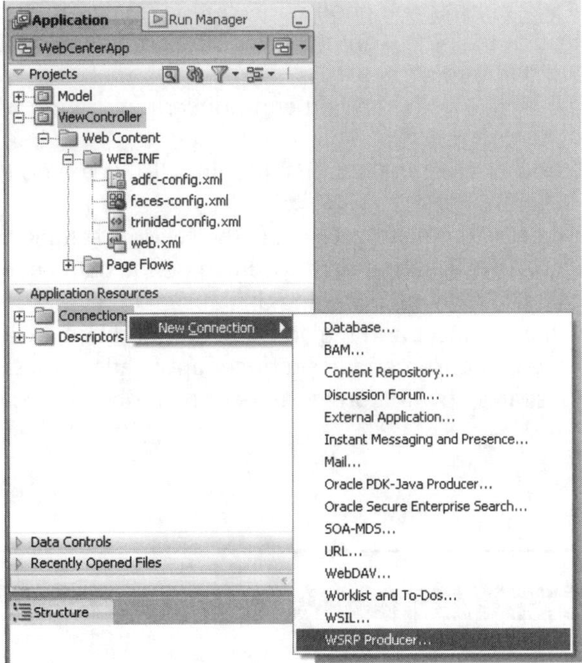

FIGURE 5-7 *Registering the portlet producer against your application*

Take the following steps to register a portlet producer against JDeveloper using the Resource Palette (Figure 5-7):

1. Click on the New icon in the Resource Palette.
2. Select New Connection | WSRP Producer from the pop-up menu.
3. Follow the steps of the producer registration wizard.

Follow these steps to register a portlet producer against the application, using the Application Resources under your project:

1. Invoke the context menu (right mouse click) of your project's Application Resources | Connections.
2. Select New Connection | WSRP Producer from the context menu.
3. Follow the steps of the producer registration wizard.

You can invoke the producer registration wizard from the New Gallery as well: File | New | Web tier | Portlets. If you choose this option, make sure you select the project in your application that you want to register the portlet producer against, typically the ViewController project.

Figure 5-8 shows how to invoke the portlet producer registration wizard in the New Gallery.

Figure 5-9 shows how to enter the WSRP endpoint URL in the portlet producer registration wizard.

The registration process allows you to specify the security settings for your portlet producer as well. At registration time, you can define data encryption, for example, by using SSL, data authenticity using digital signature, and secure identity propagation between the producer and the consumer. In addition, you can perform role mapping between your consumer and producer application roles.

Figure 5-10 demonstrates how to configure security attributes for portlet producers.

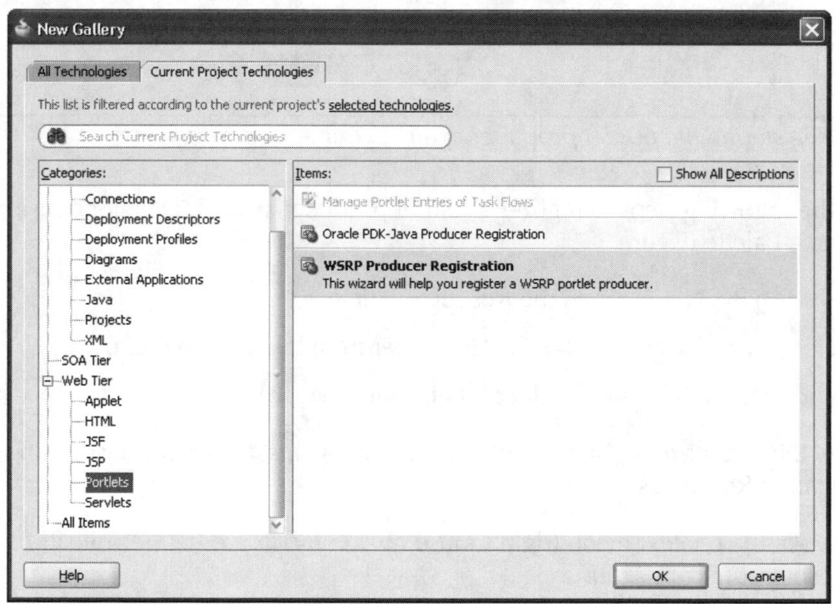

FIGURE 5-8 *Invoking the portlet producer registration wizard through the New Gallery*

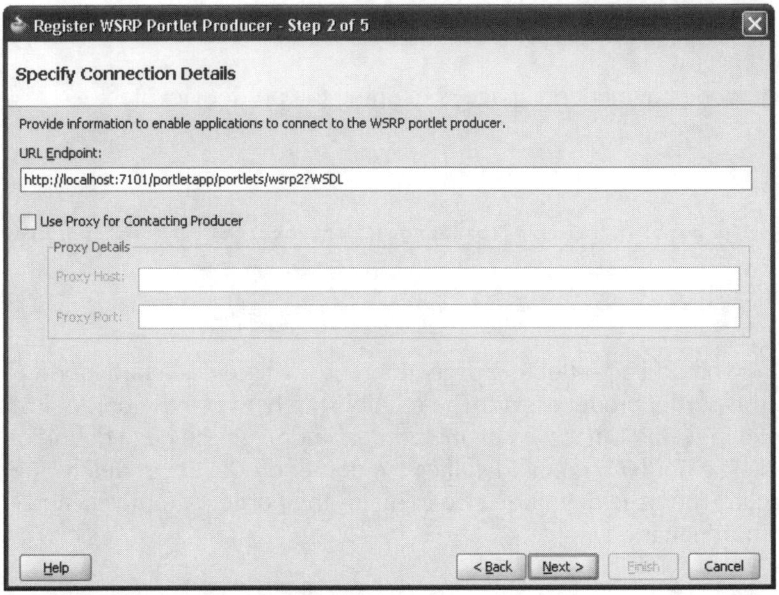

FIGURE 5-9 *Providing the WSRP endpoint URL*

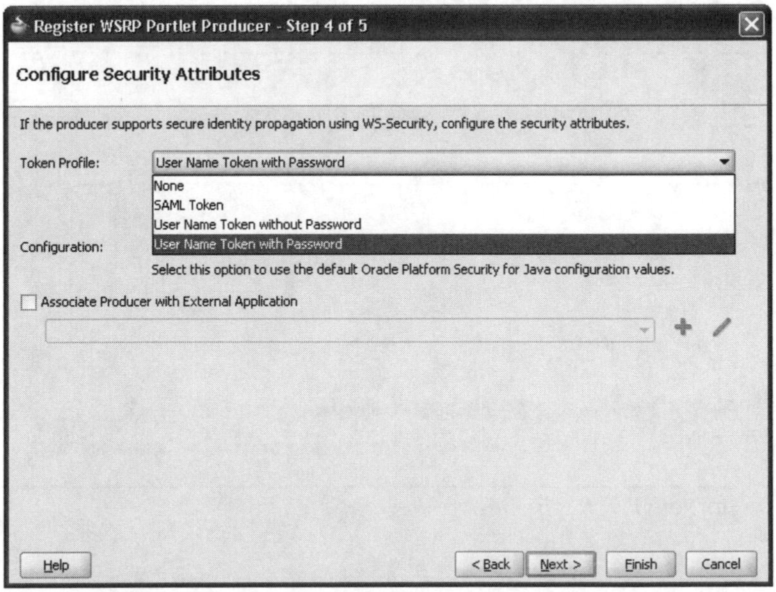

FIGURE 5-10 *Configuring security attributes for the portlet producer*

Dropping Portlets onto the Page

When dropping a portlet onto a page, JDeveloper adds a portlet view tag to your page (Figure 5-11).

This is the code fragment of a page containing the portlet view tag:

```
<f:view>
  <af:document>
    <af:form>
      <adfp:portlet value="#{bindings.ChartPortlet1_1}" id="portlet1"/>
    </af:form>
  </af:document>
</f:view>
```

Every time you add a portlet to a page, the producer creates a new portlet instance on the portlet producer end. The relationship between the portlet instance and the portlet view tag is handled by the portlet binding in the page definition (Figure 5-12). The portlet binding identifies the portlet producer, as well as the portlet instance. The page definition also contains the portlet parameters and events if the portlet has any.

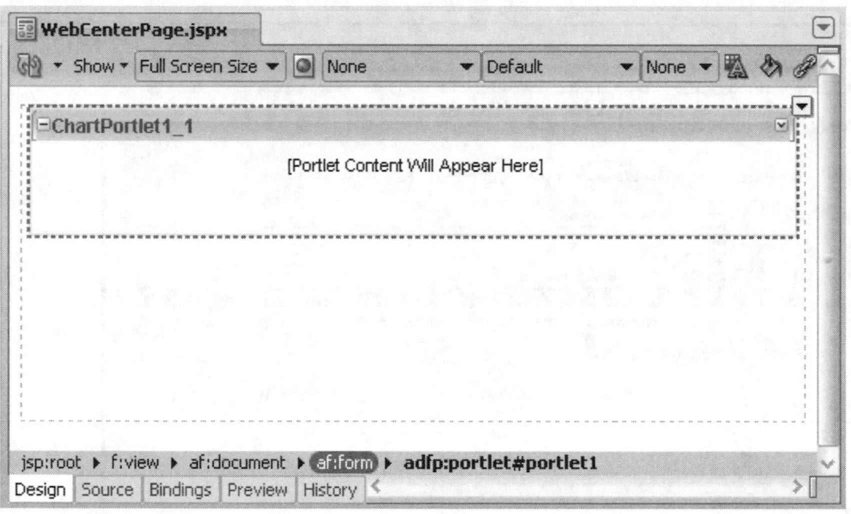

FIGURE 5-11 *The portlet view tag in Design View*

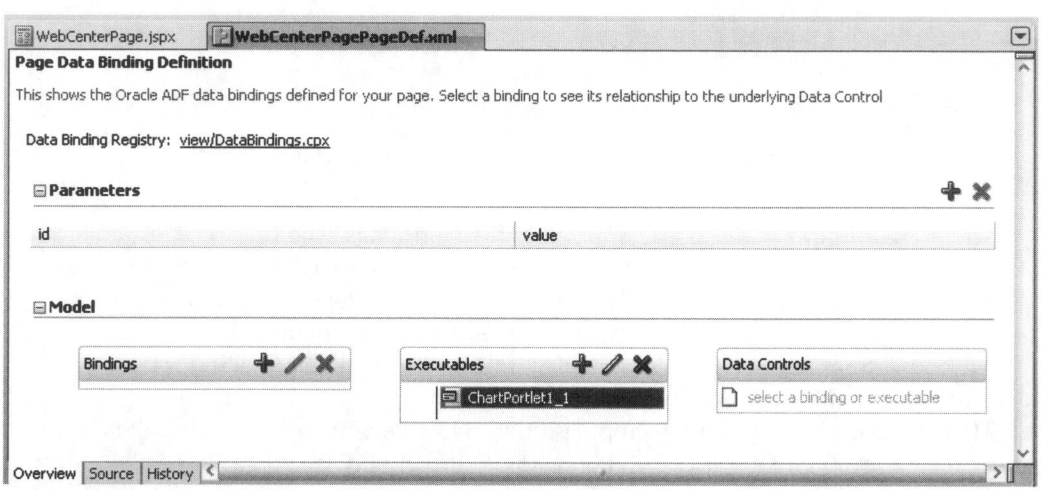

FIGURE 5-12 *Overview of the portlet binding in the page definition*

This is the code fragment of the page definition, containing the portlet binding:

```
<executables>
   <portlet id="ChartPortlet1_1"
portletInstance="/oracle/adf/portlet/WSRPSampleProducer/ap/
Ei14default_ed6a9439_011e_1000_8001_8d90a04566f8"
             class="oracle.adf.model.portlet.binding.PortletBinding"
             retainPortletHeader="false"
             xmlns="http://xmlns.oracle.com/portlet/bindings"/>
</executables>
```

Portlets Rendered in iFrames

WebCenter offers you two options when you're rendering portlets on a page. They can be rendered inline or in an iframe. Sometimes portlets have to be rendered in iframe.

Let's take a look at what the main reason is for requiring portlets to be rendered in iframes. Interactive JSF pages often use HTML forms. According to the portlet specification, portlets are allowed to render any HTML page fragment, including HTML forms. However, HTML doesn't support nested form tags.

```
<!-- JSF Page -->
. . .
<form>
```

```
<!-- Portlet starts here -->
. . .
<form>
. . .
</form>
. . .
<!-- Portlet ends here -->
</form>
```

There are multiple ways to avoid nested HTML form tags. The first and desired approach is having the WebCenter Framework parse the markup that the portlet returns and replacing the form, form field, and form submit tags with meaningful JavaScript code. This allows the browser to render the portlet in the page, without nested HTML form tags. When the portlet's form is submitted, the JavaScript code kicks in and submits the form on behalf of the portlet.

This approach works well for simple portlets. However, there are portlets that use complex JavaScript libraries, which makes it virtually impossible to parse the portlet markup in a reliable and flawless manner. When parsing of the portlet markup fails, the framework falls back to using an iframe.

WebCenter offers a certain level of control for you to specify how the portlet should be rendered on the page. The portlet view tag has a `renderPortletInIFrame` attribute allowing you to specify if the portlet should be rendered inline (`renderPortletInIFrame=false`) or in an iframe (`renderPortletInIFrame=true`). The third option is setting the `renderPortletInIFrame` attribute to `auto`, which causes the WebCenter Framework to render the portlet in an iframe if any of the following conditions are true:

- The portlet is built using the JSF Portlet Bridge. When you add a JSF portlet to your page, `renderPortletInIFrame` is set to `true` by default as JSF pages within portlets are too complex to render inline.
- The portlet contains a file upload element.
- The parser is not able to parse the markup.

If you, as a portlet developer, want to ensure that your portlet is always included in an iframe, you can declare it in the oracle-portlet.xml file by setting the `<prefer-iframe>` element to `true` in the `<portlet>` section.

The code below shows the contents of the oracle-portlet.xml file:

```
<?xml version="1.0" encoding="UTF-8" standalone="yes"?>
<portlet-app-extension xmlns=
        "http://xmlns.oracle.com/portlet/oracle-portlet-app">
    <portlet-extension>
        <portlet-name>CalendarPortlet</portlet-name>
        <portlet-id>1244584713031</portlet-id>
        <allow-export>true</allow-export>
```

```
            <allow-import>true</allow-import>
            <require-iframe>true</require-iframe>
        </portlet-extension>
        <allow-export>true</allow-export>
        <allow-import>true</allow-import>
    </portlet-app-extension>
```

Specifying Portlet View Tag and Binding Attributes

The portlet view tag attributes control the visual appearance and behavior of the portlet on a page. Just like for any other tag attribute, you can either hard code these values or use an expression language to evaluate them at run time. Table 5-2 describes the portlet view tag attributes.

Attribute	Description
Common	
Id	The identifier of the portlet view tag; it has to be unique on the page. `id="p1"`
Text	The portlet title displayed in the portlet header. If the portlet view tag text value is not defined, it is defined by the portlet response. If the portlet response doesn't define the text attribute, it is defined by the portlet definition: portlet.xml. `text="Weather Information"`
Width	The width of the area to allow for portlet display. If the actual portlet width is larger than the width value entered here, a scroll bar appears, provided the `displayScrollBar` attribute is set to `auto` or `true`. If `displayScrollBar` is set to `false`, and the actual portlet width exceeds the value expressed for the `width` attribute, the `width` attribute value is considered and the portlet content is truncated.
Height	The height of the area to allow for portlet display. If the actual portlet height is larger than the height value entered here, a scroll bar appears, provided `displayScrollBar` is set to `auto` or `true`. If `displayScrollBar` is set to `false`, and the actual portlet height exceeds the value expressed for the `height` attribute, the `height` attribute value is considered and the portlet content is truncated.
Icon	A URI specifying the location of an image to use as an icon, displayed to the left of the portlet title in the portlet header. This can be used to indicate the portlet's purpose, to reinforce branding, as a content indicator, or for some other reason.
PartialTriggers	The IDs of the components that trigger a partial update of the portlet. The portlet listens on the specified trigger components. If one of the trigger components receives a trigger event that causes it to update in some way, this portlet also requests to be updated.

TABLE 5-2 *The Portlet View Tag Attributes*

Attribute	Description
Appearance	
ExpansionMode	The default state of the portlet: `maximized`—The portlet's default display mode is expanded to the width of its parent `panelCustomizable` component, displacing all other components in the `panelCustomizable.` This option applies only to portlets placed inside a `Panel Customizable` component. `minimized`—The portlet's default display mode is collapsed (minimized). `normal`—The portlet's default display mode is neither collapsed nor expanded to the width of the page.
AllModesSharedScreen	The choice of whether a change in portlet mode renders the new mode on a new page, rather than the page on which the portlet resides. `false`—All portlet modes, except View (JSR 168) or Show (PDK-Java), are rendered each on their own page. This is useful for portlets such as OmniPortlet and the Web Clipping portlet, which require that modes other than Show mode display on pages other than the page on which the portlet resides. `true`—All portlet modes are displayed inline. One mode is swapped out for another on the same page. In other words, this attribute enables all portlet modes to display without leaving the context of a given page. `auto`—Portlet modes are displayed as specified in the oracle-portlet.xml file.
RenderPortletInIFrame	The choice of whether the portlet is rendered in an iframe: `auto`—The portlet is rendered in an iframe if parsing of the content fails, or if a form in the content contains an input of type `file.` For more information refer to the "Portlets Rendered in iFrames" section in this chapter. `false`—The portlet is rendered inline. HTML markup from a portlet that is not rendered in an iframe may interfere with other components on the Oracle ADF page. `true`—The portlet is rendered in an iframe.
DisplayScrollBar	The choice of whether a scroll bar is displayed: `auto`—Render a scroll bar if the portlet content does not fit the `width` and `height` specified. `false`—Never render a scroll bar. If the portlet content does not fit the `height` and `width` specified, the portlet renders in its actual size. `true`—Always render a scroll bar.
DisplayHeader	The choice of whether the portlet header is displayed: `false`—The portlet header is not displayed. Icons and links normally displayed in the header are hidden. If `isSeededInteractionAvailable` is set to `true`, users can access portlet menus and icons by rolling the mouse over the portlet. A fade-in/fade-out toolbar appears, from which users can select Actions menu options. `true`—The portlet header is displayed. Consequently, header-based icons and links are displayed.
DisplayShadow	The choice of whether to display a shadow decoration around the portlet: `false`—Do not display a shadow decoration. `true`—Display a shadow decoration.

TABLE 5-2 *The Portlet View Tag Attributes* (continued)

Attribute	Description
Rendered	The choice of whether the portlet is rendered. `false`—Do not render the portlet. No output is rendered. `true`—Render the portlet. This is the recommended setting. Setting this attribute to `false` will cause problems when you run the page.
Background	The style selector to apply to the skin used by the portlet: `dark`—Apply the dark style selector to the skin. `light`—Apply the light style selector to the skin. `medium`—Apply the medium style selector to the skin. This provides a way for you to apply a different look and feel to each portlet on a page.
ShortDesc	A short description of the portlet.
DisplayActions	The choice of whether seeded interactions for the portlet are shown: `always`—Always show seeded interactions. `never`—Never show seeded interactions `onHover`—Show seeded interactions when users move the mouse over the portlet.
ShowMoveAction	The choice of whether to display the Move command in the portlet's Action menu: `menu`—Display the Move command on the portlet's Action menu. `none`—Do not display the Move command.
ShowRemoveAction	The choice of whether to display the Remove icon on the portlet chrome: `chrome`—Display the Remove icon on the portlet chrome. `none`—Do not display the Remove icon.
ShowMinimizeAction	The choice of whether to display the Minimize icon on the portlet chrome: `chrome`—Display the Minimize icon on the portlet chrome. `none`—Do not display the Minimize icon.
Behavior	
PartialTriggers	The IDs of the components that trigger a partial update. The portlet listens on the specified trigger components. If one of the trigger components receives a trigger event that causes it to update in some way, this portlet also requests to be updated.
SubmitUrlParameters	The choice of whether parameters in portlet links that point to the page on which the portlet is placed are made available to the page: `false`—Parameters are not made available to the page. Rather, they are available only inside the portlet initiating the request. `true`—Parameters are available on the container page.
ShowResizer	The choice of whether the portlet can be vertically resized. `false`—The portlet cannot be resized. `true`—The portlet is resizable.
Portlet Modes	
IsAboutModeAvailable	The choice of whether to render an About command on the portlet's Actions menu.
IsConfigModeAvailable	The choice of whether to render a Configure command on a JSR 168 portlet's Actions menu.

TABLE 5-2 *The Portlet View Tag Attributes* (continued)

Attribute	Description
IsCustomizeModeAvailable	The choice of whether to render a Customize command on the portlet's Actions menu.
IsDetailModeAvailable	The choice of whether to render a Details command on a PDK-Java portlet's Actions menu.
IsHelpModeAvailable	The choice of whether to render a Help command on the portlet's Actions menu.
IsPrintModeAvailable	The choice of whether to render a Print command on a JSR 168 portlet's Actions menu.
IsNormalModeAvailable	The choice of whether to render a Refresh command on the portlet's Actions menu.
IsPersonalizeModeAvailable	The choice of whether to render a Personalize command on the portlet's Actions menu. Users choose Personalize to alter their personal view of the portlet. This mode is equivalent to the Edit mode selection in the Standards-based Java Portlet (JSR 168) wizard. The Personalize command displays on the Actions menu only to authenticated users (that is, users who are logged in). It does not display to public or unauthenticated users. You must implement some form of application security for users so they can personalize their portlet views.
IsPreviewModeAvailable	The choice of whether to enable previewing of portlet content. This mode has no particular application in WebCenter applications, but it is used in Oracle Portal's Portlet Repository, where it renders as a magnifying glass icon, which users click to preview a portlet.
Style	
ContentStyle	The CSS style to apply to the portlet content. Values entered here take precedence over styles specified in the `inlineStyle` attribute and those included in a CSS or skin on the specific portlet instance.
InlineStyle	The CSS style to apply to the whole portlet. Values entered here take precedence over styles included in a CSS or skin on the specific portlet instance.
Customization	
CustomizationAllowed	The choice of whether customizations are allowed on this portlet.
CustomizationAllowedBy	The roles for which customizations are allowed. This enables you to allow customizations, but restricts who can actually perform them.

TABLE 5-2 *The Portlet View Tag Attributes* (continued)

Attribute	Description
Annotations	
Other	
IframeDTD	The DTD, if any, that is specified in the `doctype` declaration created when the portlet content is rendered inside an `iframe`: `none`—No DTD is specified. This relaxes the restrictions on the HTML content being technically conformant HTML. Browsers will usually handle such HTML acceptably, however, because a CSS style sheet from the ADF Faces page consuming the portlet is also imported into the `iframe` document; for that style sheet to work correctly, it may be necessary to declare the content conformant to the loose or strict DTDs. `loose`—The DTD `http://www.w3.org/TR/html/loose.dtd` is used. `strict`—The DTD `http://www.w3.org/TR/html/strict.dtd` is used.

TABLE 5-2 *The Portlet View Tag Attributes* (continued)

Another essential task of consuming portlets is to contextually wire them to their environment. They may refresh other components on the page, and they may be refreshed as well. The term wiring also includes the notion of components passing parameters to and receiving parameters from each other. This topic is covered in Chapter 6.

Consuming Portlets at Run Time

Using an IDE to build pages is a very natural choice. You create your page, drop components on it, specify certain attributes as well as the relationship between components, and sometimes write code to incorporate custom business logic.

One of the great innovations portals have introduced is to empower business users by allowing them to create pages and assemble them at run time, all from within a simple web browser. Portals provide easy-to-use UI to perform these tasks, without the need to install and master a full-blown IDE. Furthermore, this is all happening in place at run time, and therefore the application or portal doesn't have to be redeployed.

WebCenter provides you the tools to build applications to meet all these requirements. If you are interested in other aspects of the run-time customization process, such as how to create pages, how to make the pages customizable, or how to control what resources are available to the business users, please refer to Chapter 11.

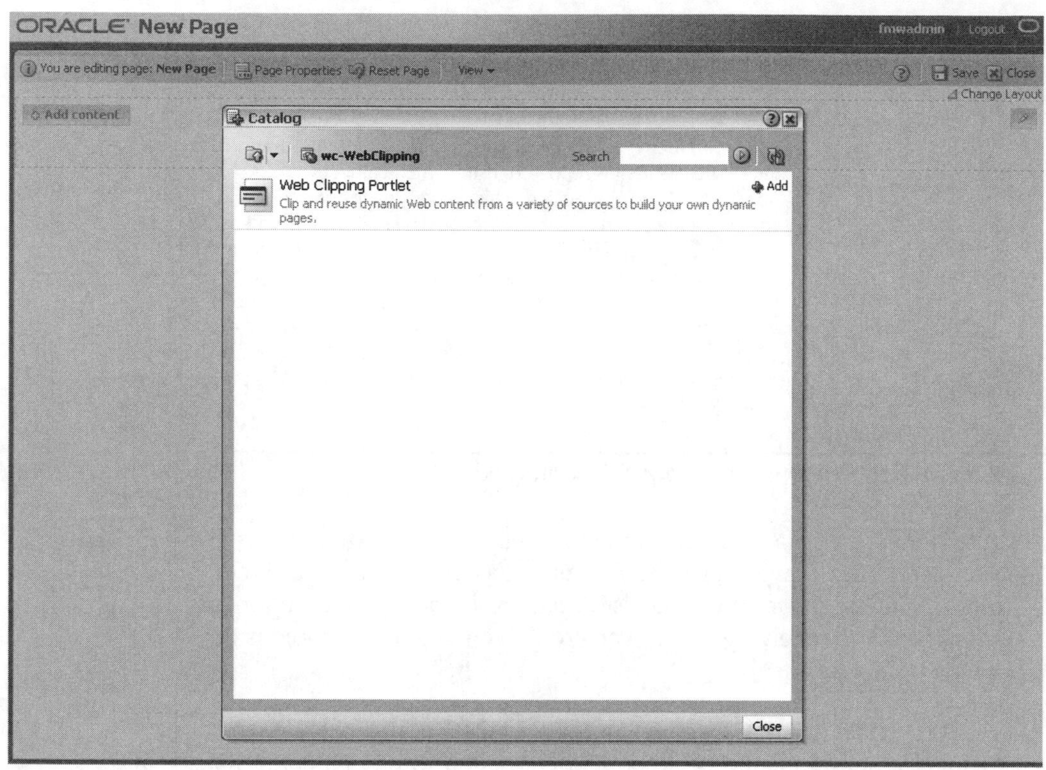

FIGURE 5-13 *The WebCenter resource catalog containing portlets*

Most portals provide a repository or catalog of portlets (Figure 5-13). After locating the portlets you're looking for, you can drop them onto your pages.

Like any other customization, when you're dropping portlets onto a page, the customization is saved to MDS. As portlets are made up of the portlet view tag and the portlet binding, when you're dropping a portlet on a page at run time, both of these entries are created in MDS as well.

NOTE
Since by default MDS uses the file system store in the development environment, you can take a look at the MDS entries created when a portlet is dropped onto the page. You can learn more about this in Part III: Customization.

Building Portlets

The portlet creation wizards offered by the Oracle WebCenter extension in JDeveloper allow you to build two types of portlets: standards-based JSR 168 portlets and Oracle-specific PDK-Java portlets. The portlet creation wizards generate the skeleton of your portlet code that you can extend with your business logic.

To create a portlet, it is recommended that you create a new application based on the Portlet Producer Application template.

Building Standards-Based Portlets

In this section we will walk through the portlet creation wizard, then take a closer look at the code that the wizard generates.

Building a JSR 168 Portlet Using the Portlet Creation Wizard

Portlets are reusable components across your consumer applications, so let's create a dedicated application for your portlets. When you're creating the application, select Portlet Producer Application (Figure 5-14) as the template.

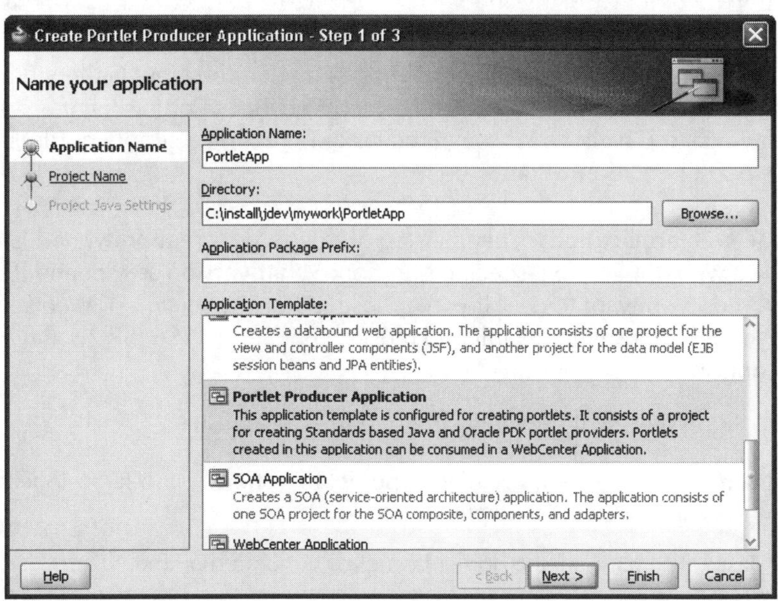

FIGURE 5-14 *Creating an application using the Portlet Producer Application template*

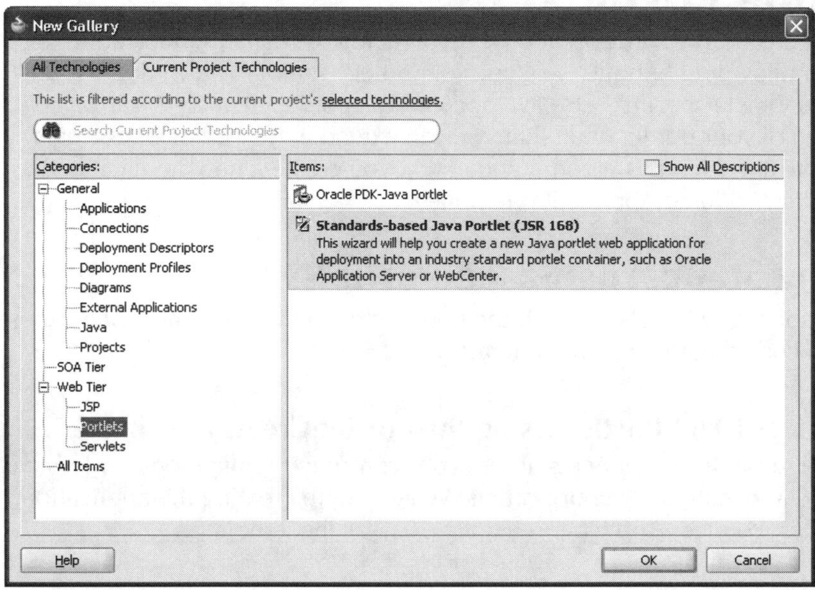

FIGURE 5-15 *Portlet creation wizards in the New Gallery*

Your application contains one project, Portlets. Invoke the New Gallery (Portlets context menu | New… or File | New…) and select Web Tier | Portlets (Figure 5-15).

The following steps walk you through the task of creating a simple portlet using JDeveloper's portlet creation wizard.

1. **Create web application** The first step of the portlet creation wizard is a generic web application–specific question: What version servlet and JSP version do you want to use? If you are using the 11*g* version of WebCenter, you should choose the default and most recent Servlet 2.5/JSP 2.1 (Java EE 1.5) option.

   In this step you specify several generic portlet properties:

   - **Name** The display name of your portlet that shows up in JDeveloper, as well as in Composer at run time.
   - **Class** The name of the portlet Java class generated by the wizard.
   - **Package** The package created for the portlet Java class.

- **Language** The default locale language of the portlet. You can add additional languages to your portlet after the portlet skeleton code has been generated.
- **Enable users to edit portlet content** By selecting this option the wizard assumes that you want your portlet to support the Edit mode, so it generates the necessary portlet.xml entries and supporting files.
- **Enable inter-portlet communication using Oracle WSRP V2 extensions** Select this checkbox to indicate that this portlet will support Oracle WSRP 2.0 capabilities. By selecting this option, shown in Figure 5-16, the wizard creates the oracle-portlet.xml file, which is used for WSRP 2.0 features such as navigation parameters.

2. In this step, you specify additional portlet information (Figure 5-17):

- **Display Name** This attribute may be used by portlet consumers when they present the list of portlets available to be added to pages. Oracle WebCenter does not use this attribute.

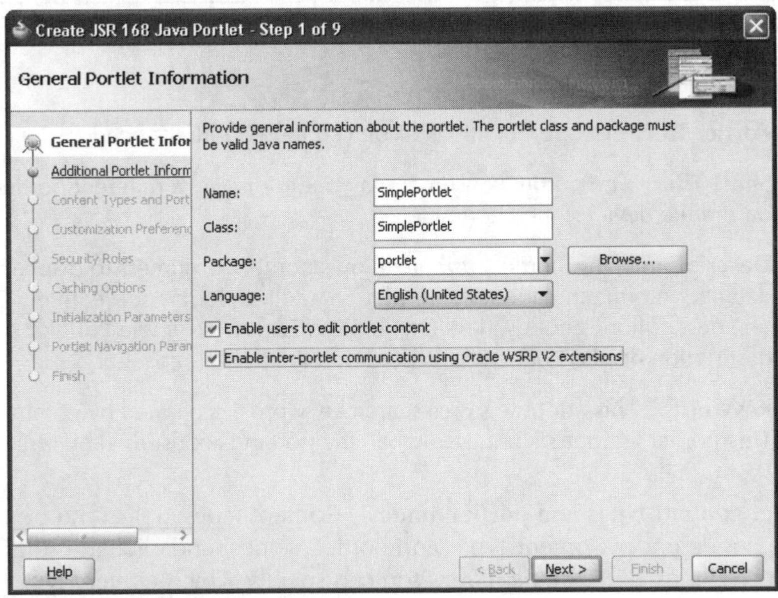

FIGURE 5-16 *Specifying general portlet information*

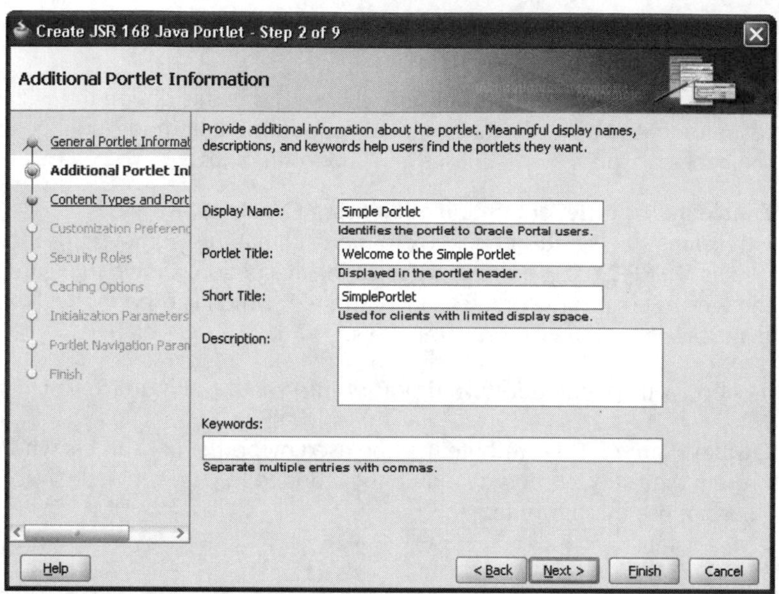

FIGURE 5-17 *Specifying additional portlet information*

- **Portlet Title** The portlet title is displayed in the portlet's header.
- **Short Title** The portlet consumer may opt to display a different portlet title on mobile devices: the Short Title.
- **Description** This portlet attribute allows portlet consumers to display detailed information about the portlet, in addition to the portlet title. The description is not used by Oracle WebCenter. In Oracle Portal the description displays beneath the portlet in the portlet repository.
- **Keywords** This attribute stores search keywords, separated by commas. This portlet attribute is not used when the portlet is consumed by Oracle WebCenter.

3. **Select content types and portlet modes** Content types: Select the `text/html` node under Content Types and Portlet Modes, and click the Add button (Figure 5-18). In the dialog you can specify which content types you want your portlet to support. Also, if you need to specify a content type not available in the list, you can do so by clicking the New button.

- **Portlet modes** Select a portlet mode under Content Types and Portlet Modes, such as `view`, and click the Add or Remove buttons to create new or delete existing portlet modes you want your portlet to support.
- **Implementation method** Select a portlet mode under Content Types and Portlet Modes, such as `view`, and select one of the available implementation methods.
- **Generate JSP** This option generates both a JSP for the selected portlet mode and Java code that dispatched the requests for the given mode to the generated JSP. The Java code resides in the portlet Java class that you provided earlier in the wizard.
- **Generate ADF Faces JSPX** This option generates a JSF page. You can use all the tools and techniques you use to build a JSF page, including the ADF data binding capabilities and the ADF Rich Client functionality—in other words, take advantage of the full power of ADF.

NOTE
This option uses the JSF Portlet Bridge behind the scenes, covered later in this chapter.

- **Map to path** Map the selected mode to an existing (or planned) target. Enter the URL in the provided field. With this selection, you must write the targeted resource or file yourself. The target could be, for example, a JSP, a servlet, or an HTML file. This selection enters code in the generated portlet Java class that routes requests for the given mode to the specified target.
- **Custom code** Implement the selected mode through your existing (or planned) custom Java method. This option creates a skeleton method in the generated portlet Java class to render content. You must update this code to render useful content. The name of the generated method is `privatevoid do`*`ModeName`*`Html`.

4. **Select customization preferences** If your portlet supports the Edit mode, you can specify the preferences you want your portlet to handle (Figure 5-19). The default preference supported by the portlet is the portlet title. As a best practice, all portlets should allow page designers and end users to provide their custom portlet title if they wish to do so. You can also create your own portlet preferences or delete existing ones using the Add and Remove buttons. In addition to choosing a name and a default value for your portlet preferences, the wizard can also generate a resource bundle class to store and manage the translations for your portlet preferences.

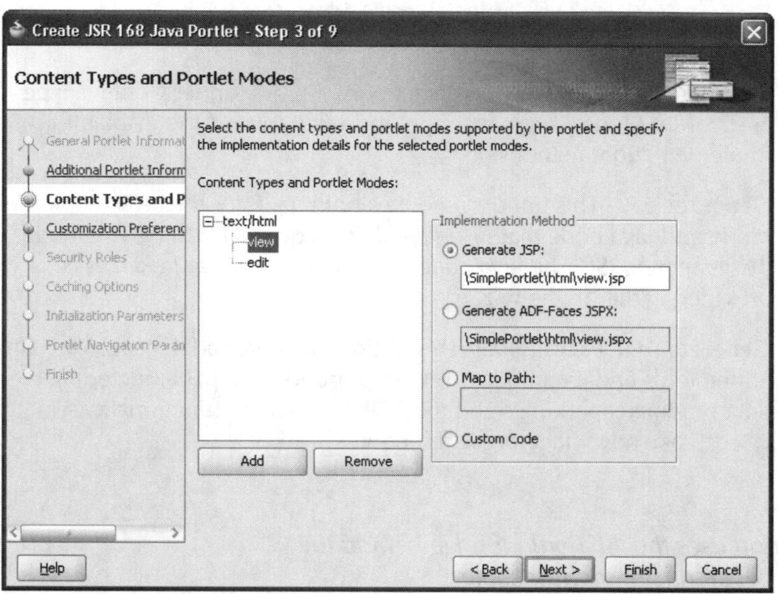

FIGURE 5-18 *Specifying content types and portlet modes for your portlet*

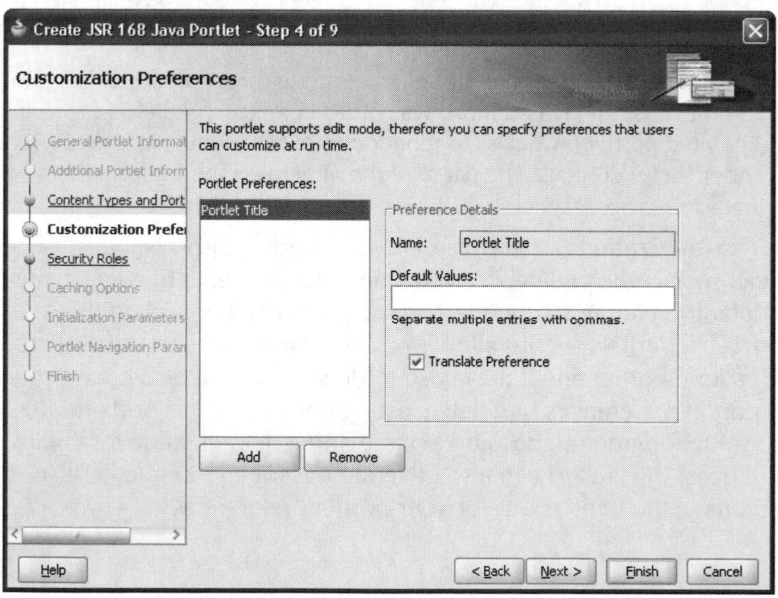

FIGURE 5-19 *Specifying customization preferences for your portlet*

5. **Specify security roles** This step allows you to specify which of your Java EE security roles, defined in the `web.xml`, are exposed to your portlet and surfaced to the portlet consumer (Figure 5-20). Roles surfaced to the portlet consumer can then be mapped to the portlet consumer's enterprise roles at producer registration time.

   For example, you built a large application, which contains two application roles: `administrator` and `participant`. Your portlet exposes a small subset of the functionality of your application. You would like to allow the administrator of your portlet consumer to perform a role mapping at producer registration time. The mapping needs to take place from the portlet application's `participant` role and the portlet consumer's `finance-users` role. At the same time, you don't want to make the `administrator` role available to your portlet.

   Below are the contents of the `web.xml` file:

```
<security-role>
    <description>Participant role</description>
    <role-name>participant</role-name>
</security-role>
<security-role>
    <description>Administrator role</description>
    <role-name>admin</role-name>
</security-role>
```

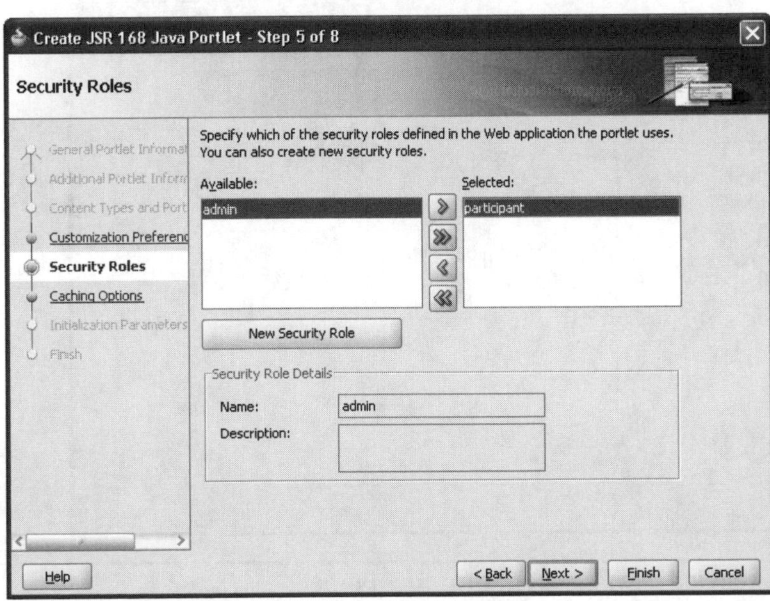

FIGURE 5-20 *Specifying security roles for your portlet*

The contents of the `portlet.xml` file follow:

```
<security-role-ref>
    <role-name>participant</role-name>
</security-role-ref>
```

6. **Specify caching options** To improve the scalability of your portlets, JSR 168 allows your portlet to support expiration-based caching (Figure 5-21). You can define the expiry time in seconds. The caching of the portlet content is managed by the portlet container.

   When your portlet is initially invoked, the cache is empty; it's a cache miss. In subsequent invocations the cache may contain the previously generated markup. In this case, the portlet code doesn't get invoked; the markup is served from the cache.

   When the expiration period is over, the portlet content is to be removed from the cache—subsequent requests will result in invoking and executing the portlet code.

7. **Specify initialization parameters** These are parameters your portlet can use when it initializes (Figure 5-22). Initialization parameters are defined as a name-value pair, along with a description, and they provide an alternative to Java Naming and Directory Interface (JNDI) parameters.

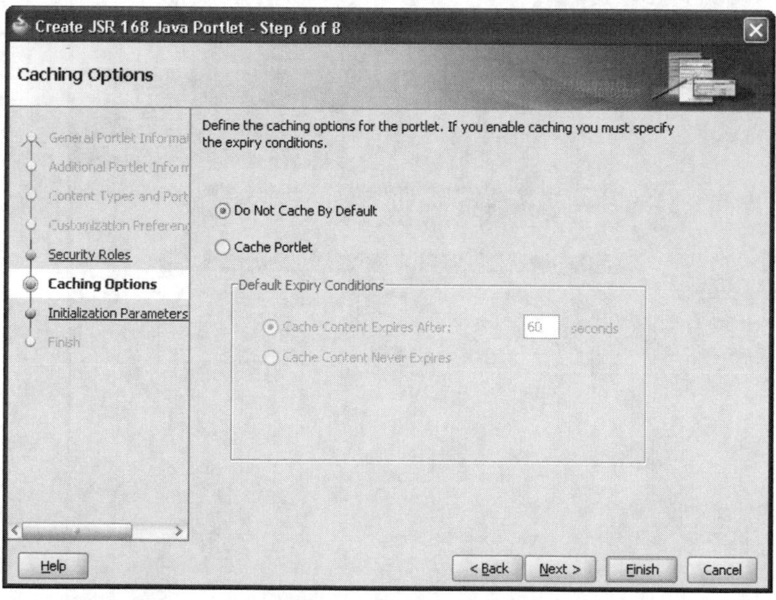

FIGURE 5-21 *Specifying caching options for your portlet*

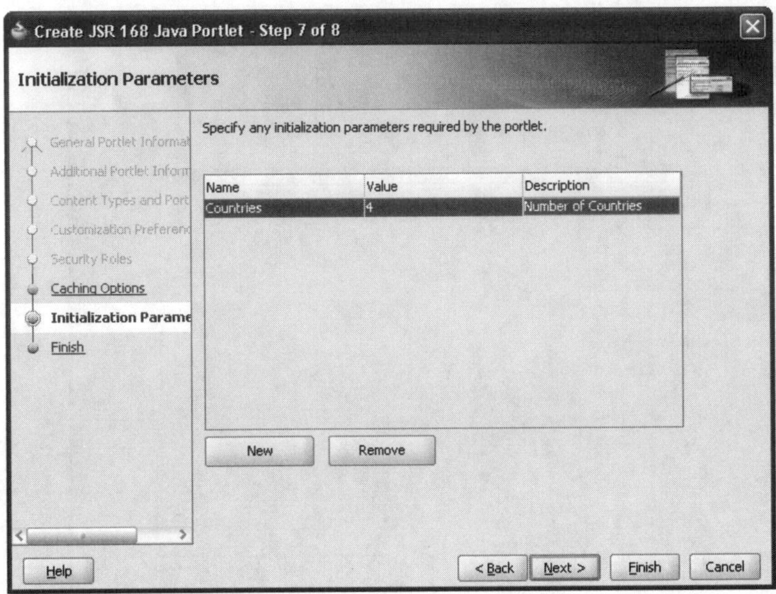

FIGURE 5-22 *Specifying initialization parameters for your portlet*

8. **Specify portlet navigation parameters** WSRP 2.0 portlets use navigation parameters for inter-portlet communication. As shown in Figure 5-23, you can define the navigation parameters for your portlet by providing a parameter name, a label, and a translatable hint text.

NOTE
This option is available only if you have selected the Enable Inter-portlet Communication Using Oracle WSRP V2 Extensions checkbox in the General Portlet Information wizard step, shown in Figure 5-16.

Understanding the Generated Portlet Skeleton Code

Figure 5-24 shows all the files that the portlet creation wizard generated for us. In this section we explain the generated files:

- **portlet.xml** The portlet deployment descriptor file is the most important of all the generated files in a portlet application. It contains information about the portlets and their attributes that the application contains. Attributes

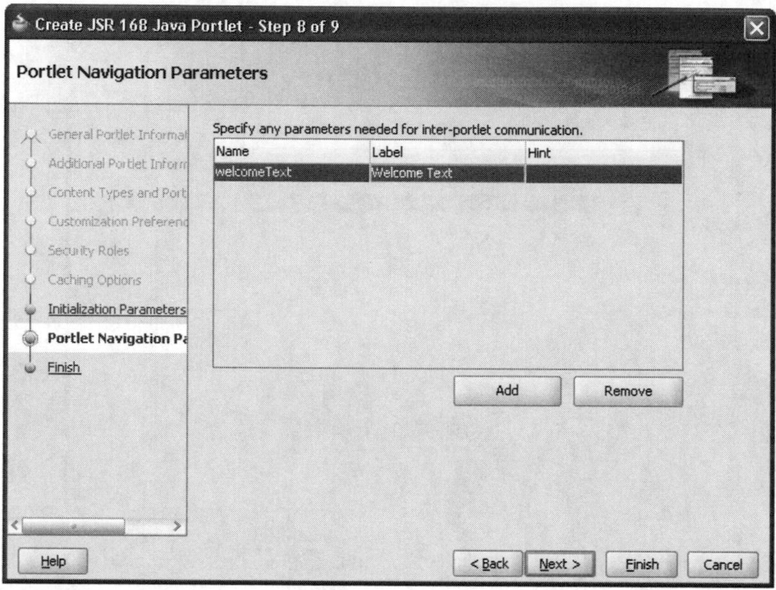

FIGURE 5-23 *Specifying navigation parameters for your portlet*

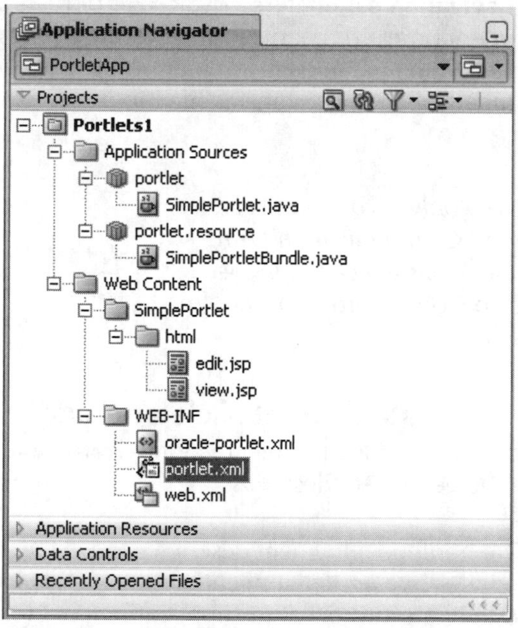

FIGURE 5-24 *Files generated by the portlet creation wizard*

include the portlet's unique ID, the portlet name, and display name, as well as the display modes that the portlet supports.

```
<?xml version="1.0" encoding="UTF-8" standalone="yes"?>
<portlet-app version="1.0"
xsi:schemaLocation="http://java.sun.com/xml/ns/portlet/portlet-app_1_0.xsd
http://java.sun.com/xml/ns/portlet/portlet-app_1_0.xsd"
xmlns="http://java.sun.com/xml/ns/portlet/portlet-app_1_0.xsd"
xmlns:xsi="http://www.w3.org/2001/XMLSchema-instance">
    <portlet id="1232667183625">
        <portlet-name>SimplePortlet</portlet-name>
        <display-name xml:lang="en-US">Simple Portlet</display-name>
        <display-name xml:lang="en">English Display Name</display-name>
        <portlet-class>portlet.SimplePortlet</portlet-class>
        <expiration-cache>0</expiration-cache>
        <supports>
            <mime-type>text/html</mime-type>
            <portlet-mode>edit</portlet-mode>
        </supports>
        <supported-locale>en-US</supported-locale>
        <resource-bundle>portlet.resource.SimplePortletBundle
        </resource-bundle>
        <portlet-info>
            <title>Welcome to the Simple Portlet</title>
            <short-title>SimplePortlet</short-title>
            <keywords/>
        </portlet-info>
        <portlet-preferences>
            <preference>
                <name>portletTitle</name>
            </preference>
        </portlet-preferences>
    </portlet>
    <custom-portlet-mode>
        <portlet-mode>about</portlet-mode>
    </custom-portlet-mode>
    <custom-portlet-mode>
        <portlet-mode>config</portlet-mode>
    </custom-portlet-mode>
    <custom-portlet-mode>
        <portlet-mode>edit_defaults</portlet-mode>
    </custom-portlet-mode>
    <custom-portlet-mode>
        <portlet-mode>preview</portlet-mode>
    </custom-portlet-mode>
    <custom-portlet-mode>
        <portlet-mode>print</portlet-mode>
    </custom-portlet-mode>
</portlet-app>
```

- **oracle-portlet.xml** This file contains Oracle-specific deployment information about the portlet. Since WSRP 2.0 features are implemented as extensions on top of JSR 168, this file is generated when you select the Enable Inter-portlet Communication Using Oracle WSRP V2 Extensions checkbox, as shown in Figure 5-16. In addition to defining navigation parameters, this file also allows you to control whether the portlet should be rendered in an inline frame.

```
<?xml version="1.0" encoding="UTF-8" standalone="yes"?>
<portlet-app-extension
xmlns="http://xmlns.oracle.com/portlet/oracle-portlet-app">
    <portlet-extension>
        <portlet-name>SimplePortlet</portlet-name>
        <navigation-parameters>
            <name>welcomeText</name>
            <type xmlns:xsd=
            "http://www.w3.org/2001/XMLSchema">xsd:string</type>
            <label xml:lang="en-US">Welcome Text</label>
            <hint xml:lang="en-US"/>
        </navigation-parameters>
        <portlet-id>1232667183625</portlet-id>
        <require-iframe>false</require-iframe>
    </portlet-extension>
</portlet-app-extension>
```

- **<portlet-name>.java** This Java class is referenced from portlet.xml, and its methods are invoked by the portlet container. This class extends the `GenericPortlet` class by default and contains among others a `doDispatch(RenderRequest request, RenderResponse response)` and a `processAction(ActionRequest request, ActionResponse response)` method. The former is responsible for dispatching the request to other Java classes or JSPs (view.jsp and edit.jsp). The `processAction()` method plays a key part in the portlet life cycle, and it is invoked when the user is interacting with the portlet and clicks a link or submits a form.

```
package portlet;
import java.io.IOException;
import java.util.StringTokenizer;
import javax.portlet.ActionRequest;
import javax.portlet.ActionResponse;
import javax.portlet.GenericPortlet;
import javax.portlet.PortletContext;
import javax.portlet.PortletException;
import javax.portlet.PortletMode;
import javax.portlet.PortletPreferences;
import javax.portlet.PortletRequestDispatcher;
import javax.portlet.RenderRequest;
import javax.portlet.RenderResponse;
import javax.portlet.WindowState;

import portlet.resource.SimplePortletBundle;

public class SimplePortlet extends GenericPortlet {
  protected String getTitle(RenderRequest request) {
     // Get the customized title. This defaults to the declared title.
```

```
        PortletPreferences prefs = request.getPreferences();
        return prefs.getValue(PORTLETTITLE_KEY, super.getTitle(request));
    }

    protected void doDispatch(RenderRequest request,
                     RenderResponse response) throws PortletException,
                                                     IOException {
        // Do nothing if window state is minimized.
        WindowState state = request.getWindowState();
        if (state.equals(WindowState.MINIMIZED)) {
            super.doDispatch(request, response);
            return;
        }

        // Get the content type for the response.
        String contentType = request.getResponseContentType();

        // Get the requested portlet mode.
        PortletMode mode = request.getPortletMode();

        // Reference a request dispatcher for dispatching to web resources.
        PortletContext context = getPortletContext();
        PortletRequestDispatcher rd = null;

        // Dispatch based on content type and portlet mode.
        if (contentType.equals("text/html")) {
            if (mode.equals(PortletMode.VIEW)) {
                rd =
context.getRequestDispatcher("/SimplePortlet/html/view.jsp");
            } else if (mode.equals(PortletMode.EDIT)) {
                rd =
context.getRequestDispatcher("/SimplePortlet/html/edit.jsp");
            } else {
                super.doDispatch(request,response);
            }
        } else {
            super.doDispatch(request,response);
        }
        if (rd != null) {
            rd.include(request, response);
        } else {
            super.doDispatch(request, response);
        }
    }
    public static final String APPLY_ACTION = "apply_action";
    public static final String OK_ACTION = "ok_action";
    public static final String PORTLETTITLE_KEY = "portletTitle";

    private String[] buildValueArray(String values) {
        if (values.indexOf(',') < 0) {
            return new String[] {values};
        }
        StringTokenizer st = new StringTokenizer(values, ",");
        String[] valueArray = new String[st.countTokens()];
        int i = 0;
        while (st.hasMoreTokens()) {
            valueArray[i] = st.nextToken().trim();
            i++;
        }
```

```
        return valueArray;
    }

    public void processAction(ActionRequest request,
                  ActionResponse response) throws PortletException,
                                                      IOException {
        // Determine which action.
        String okAction = request.getParameter(OK_ACTION);
        String applyAction = request.getParameter(APPLY_ACTION);

        if (okAction != null || applyAction != null) {
            // Save the preferences.
            PortletPreferences prefs = request.getPreferences();
            String param = request.getParameter(PORTLETTITLE_KEY);
            prefs.setValues(PORTLETTITLE_KEY, buildValueArray(param));
            prefs.store();
            if (okAction != null) {
                response.setPortletMode(PortletMode.VIEW);
                response.setWindowState(WindowState.NORMAL);
            }
        }
    }
}
```

- **view.jsp** This JSP file is generated by the portlet creation wizard for your convenience, allowing you to quickly and easily define the portlet's behavior. By default, this file shows a welcome message.

```
<%@ page contentType = "text/html; charset=windows-1252"
        pageEncoding = "windows-1252"
        import = "javax.portlet.*, java.util.*, portlet.SimplePortlet,
portlet.resource.SimplePortletBundle"%>
<%@ taglib uri = "http://java.sun.com/portlet" prefix="portlet"%>

<portlet:defineObjects/>
<p class="portlet-font">Welcome, this is the ${renderRequest.portletMode}
mode.</p>
```

- **edit.jsp** This file contains starter code to add customizations to your portlet.

```
<%@ page contentType = "text/html; charset=windows-1252"
        pageEncoding = "windows-1252"
        import = "javax.portlet.*, java.util.*, portlet.SimplePortlet,
portlet.resource.SimplePortletBundle"%>
<%@ taglib uri = "http://java.sun.com/portlet" prefix="portlet"%>

<portlet:defineObjects/>
<%
    PortletPreferences prefs = renderRequest.getPreferences();
    ResourceBundle res =
        portletConfig.getResourceBundle(renderRequest.getLocale());
%>

<form action="<portlet:actionURL/>" method="POST">
  <table border="0">
    <tr>
```

```
      <td width="20%">
        <p class="portlet-form-field" align="right">
          <%=  res.getString(SimplePortletBundle.PORTLETTITLE) %>
        </p>
      </td>
      <td width="80%">
        <input class="portlet-form-input-field"
               type="TEXT"
               name="<%= SimplePortlet.PORTLETTITLE_KEY %>"
               value="<%= prefs.getValue(SimplePortlet.PORTLETTITLE_KEY,
res.getString("javax.portlet.title")) %>"
               size="20">
      </td>
    </tr>
    <tr>
      <td colspan="2" align="center">
        <input class="portlet-form-button" type="submit"
                                    name="<%=SimplePortlet.OK_ACTION%>"
                                              value="<%=res.getString(SimplePor
tletBundle.OK_LABEL)%>">
        <input class="portlet-form-button" type="submit"
                                              name="<%=SimplePortlet.APPLY_
ACTION%>"
                                              value="<%=res.getString(SimplePor
tletBundle.APPLY_LABEL)%>">
      </td>
    </tr>
  </table>
</form>
```

- **<portlet-name>Bundle.java** This is the resource bundle the view.jsp and edit.jsp files use, by default.

```
package portlet.resource;

import java.util.ListResourceBundle;

public class SimplePortletBundle extends ListResourceBundle {
    public static final String OK_LABEL = "oklabel";
    public static final String APPLY_LABEL = "applylabel";
    public static final String PORTLET_INFO_TITLE = "javax.portlet.title";
    public static final String PORTLET_INFO_SHORT_TITLE =
"javax.portlet.short-title";
    public static final String PORTLETTITLE =
"javax.portlet.preference.name.portletTitle";
    private static final Object[][] sContents =
    {
    {OK_LABEL, "OK"},
    {APPLY_LABEL, "Apply"},
    {PORTLET_INFO_TITLE, "Welcome to the Simple Portlet"},
    {PORTLET_INFO_SHORT_TITLE, "SimplePortlet"},
    {PORTLETTITLE, "Portlet Title"},
  };

    public Object[][] getContents() {
        return sContents;
    }
}
```

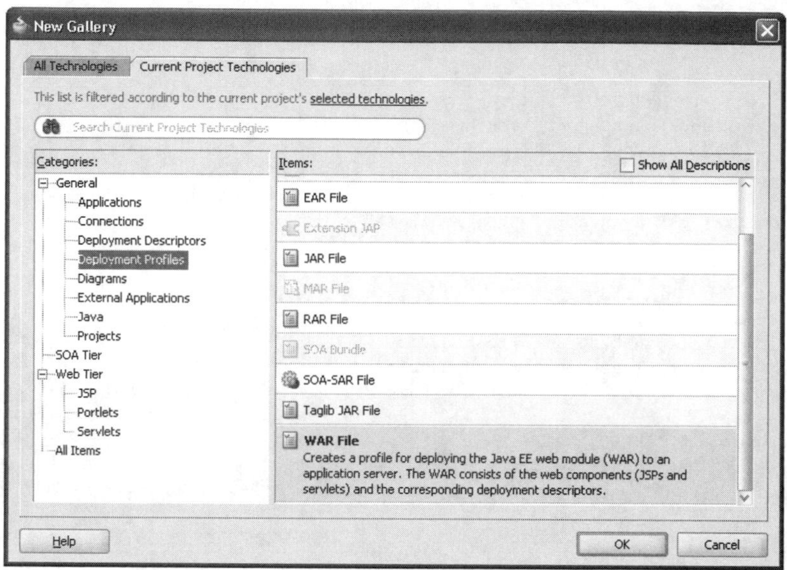

FIGURE 5-25 *Creating a WAR deployment profile using the New Gallery*

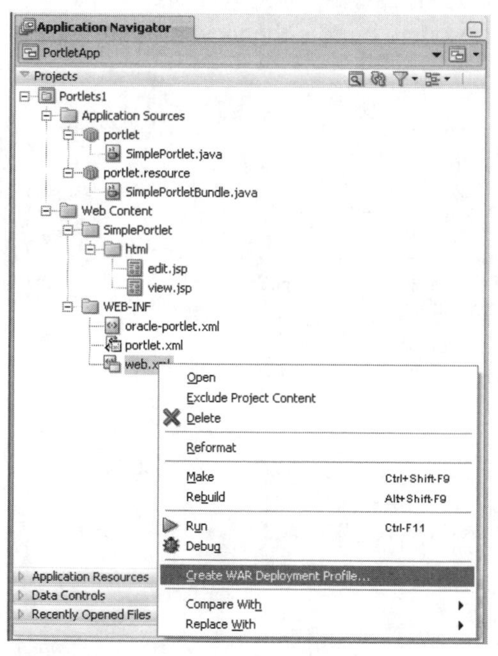

FIGURE 5-26 *Creating a WAR deployment profile using the context menu of web.xml*

Deploying Your Portlet

Your portlet application is essentially a web application; therefore the steps of deploying a portlet application are the same.

First, you have to create a WAR deployment profile. You can do it either through the New Gallery: File | New | Deployment Profiles | War File, as shown in Figure 5-25, or through the context menu of the web.xml file, as demonstrated in Figure 5-26.

In Figure 5-27 you can see that JDeveloper prompts you to enter the name for your WAR deployment profile, and allows you to set certain attributes of your WAR deployment profile, such as the Java EE Web Context Root, as shown in Figure 5-28.

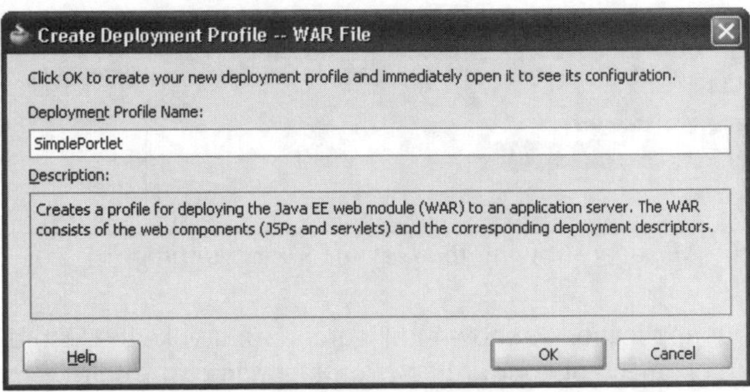

FIGURE 5-27 *Providing the deployment profile name*

Before deploying your portlet application, be sure that your Default Server has been started. One way of doing so is by opening the Run Manager through the View | Run Manager menu item. When your Default Server is running, your Run Manager should be similar to the one shown in Figure 5-29.

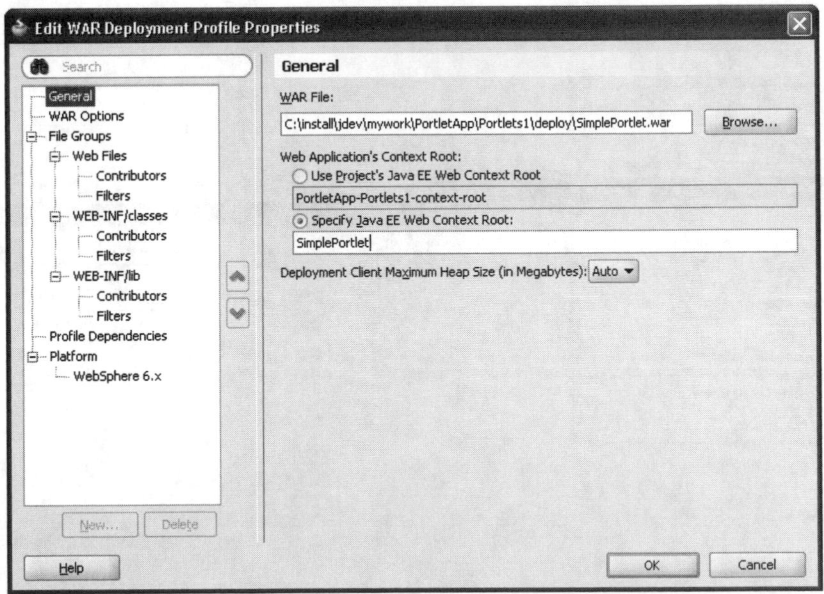

FIGURE 5-28 *Editing the WAR deployment profile properties*

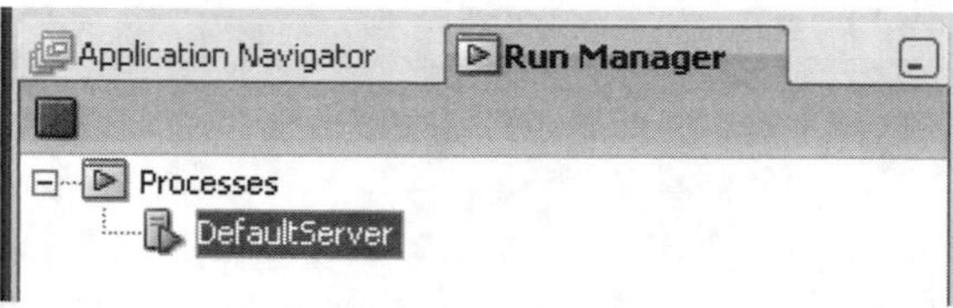

FIGURE 5-29 *The Run Manager showing the Default Server running*

To deploy your application as shown in Figure 5-30, invoke the Deploy menu item from the context menu of your project: <project-name> | Deploy | <portlet-name> | to | IntegratedWLSConnection.

The Select Deployment Type dialog, shown in Figure 5-31, prompts you to select whether you want JDeveloper to inject the WSDLs into your portlet, which is needed to expose the portlet through WSRP. When you're deploying to the Oracle Portlet Container, which is the case when using the Integrated WebLogic Server, select Yes.

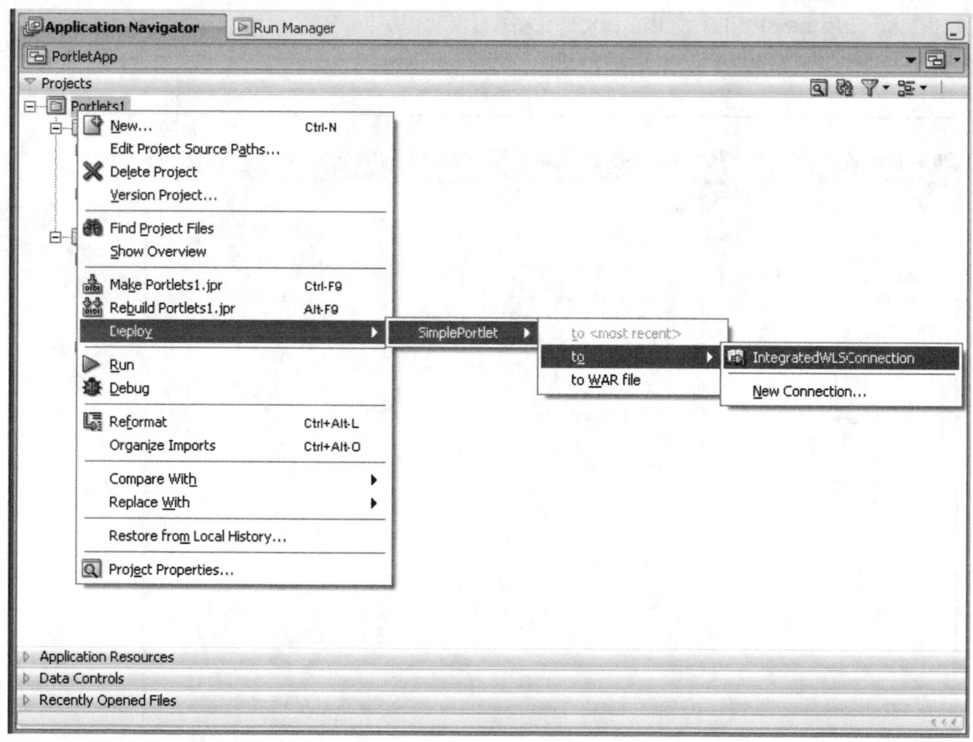

FIGURE 5-30 *Deploying your portlet application to the Integrated WebLogic Server*

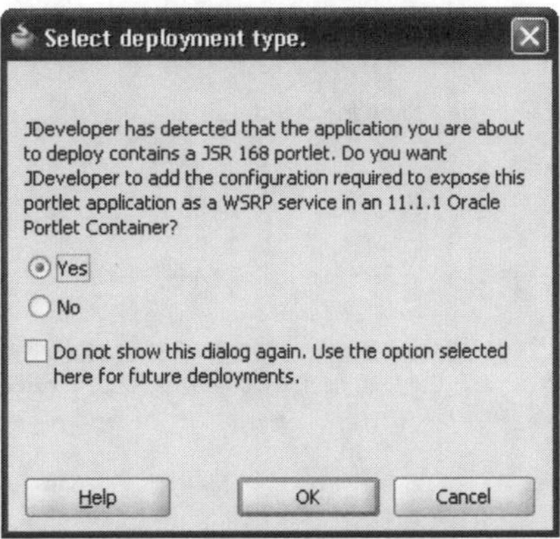

FIGURE 5-31 *Select deployment type dialog*

As Figure 5-32 shows, you can keep track of the various stages of the deployment in JDeveloper's Log window.

You can access the test page of the newly deployed portlet producer through the following URL:

http://localhost:7101/<context-root>

The portlet producer test page is shown in Figure 5-33.

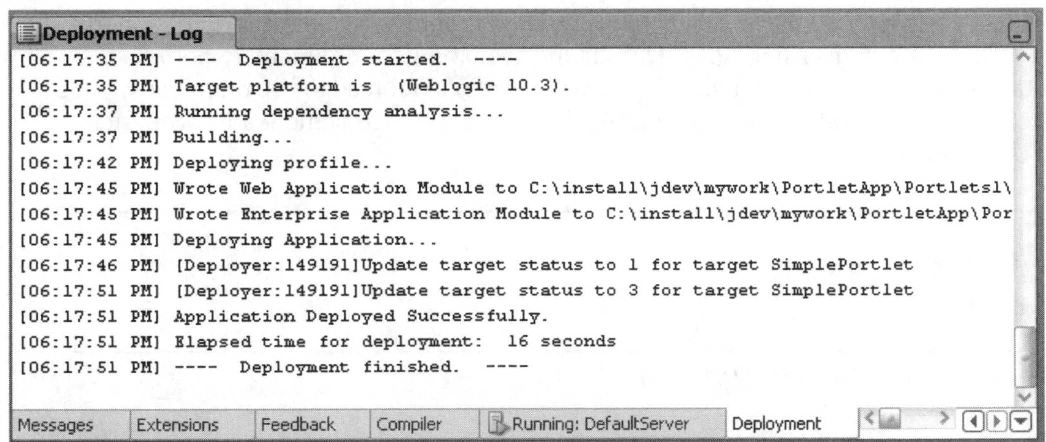

FIGURE 5-32 *Deployment status shown by the JDeveloper Log window*

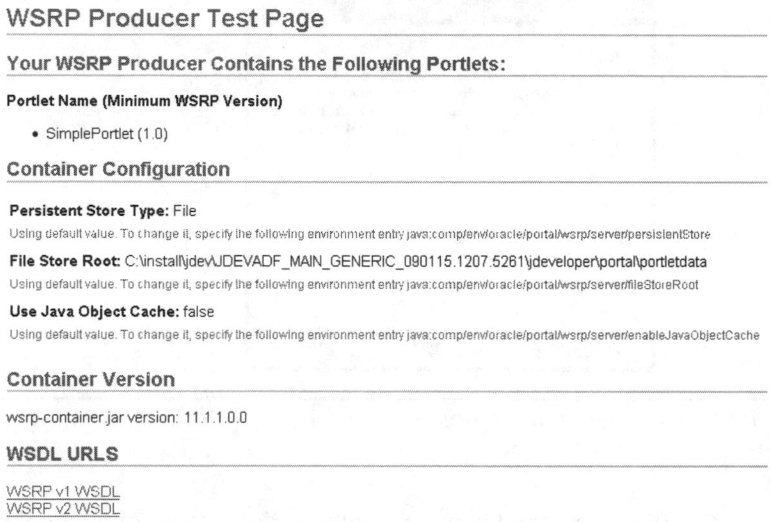

WSRP Producer Test Page

Your WSRP Producer Contains the Following Portlets:

Portlet Name (Minimum WSRP Version)

- SimplePortlet (1.0)

Container Configuration

Persistent Store Type: File

Using default value. To change it, specify the following environment entry java:comp/env/oracle/portal/wsrp/server/persistentStore

File Store Root: C:\install\jdev\JDEVADF_MAIN_GENERIC_090115.1207.5261\jdeveloper\portal\portletdata

Using default value. To change it, specify the following environment entry java:comp/env/oracle/portal/wsrp/server/fileStoreRoot

Use Java Object Cache: false

Using default value. To change it, specify the following environment entry java:comp/env/oracle/portal/wsrp/server/enableJavaObjectCache

Container Version

wsrp-container.jar version: 11.1.1.0.0

WSDL URLS

WSRP v1 WSDL
WSRP v2 WSDL

FIGURE 5-33 *The test page of your newly deployed portlet producer*

If you got to this point, you have successfully deployed your first portlet application. When you're consuming the portlet, it looks as shown in Figure 5-34.

Building PDK-Java Portlets

Using proprietary APIs to build portlets was a necessity for a long time. The first versions of the portlet standards, JSR 168 and WSRP 1.0, defined the foundation of the portlet technologies, but lacked many important capabilities, including inter-portlet communication, the ability to export/import portlet customization, or support for rich interactions using AJAX. Despite the availability of rudimentary portlet standards, portlet and portal developers were very often forced to use proprietary, vendor-specific portlet APIs if they wanted to take advantage of more advanced, rich portlet functionalities.

Welcome to the Simple Portlet

Welcome, this is the view mode.

FIGURE 5-34 *Your newly deployed portlet*

Oracle PDK-Java was born long before the inception of the portlet standards. In fact, the remote nature of PDK-Java portlets served as an inspiration for WSRP.

The second-generation portlet standards, JSR 286 and WSRP 2.0, fill most of the gaps of JSR 168 and WSRP 1.0. Therefore, in almost every case you will be building standards-based portlets. To save space for more important and exciting topics, we cover only the first steps of creating PDK-Java portlets. If for some reason you are required to build portlets using PDK-Java, the Oracle WebCenter documentation contains a lot of useful information and examples.

As in the JSR 168 portlet creation wizard, you can create a new PDK-Java portlet by creating a dedicated application based on the Portlet Producer Application template, as shown in Figure 5-35.

In Figure 5-36 you can see that right next to the JSR 168 portlet creation wizard, the New Gallery contains a dedicated PDK-Java portlet wizard that will generate the skeleton code for your portlet application.

For more information on PDK-Java portlets, please refer to the Oracle WebCenter Developer's Guide.

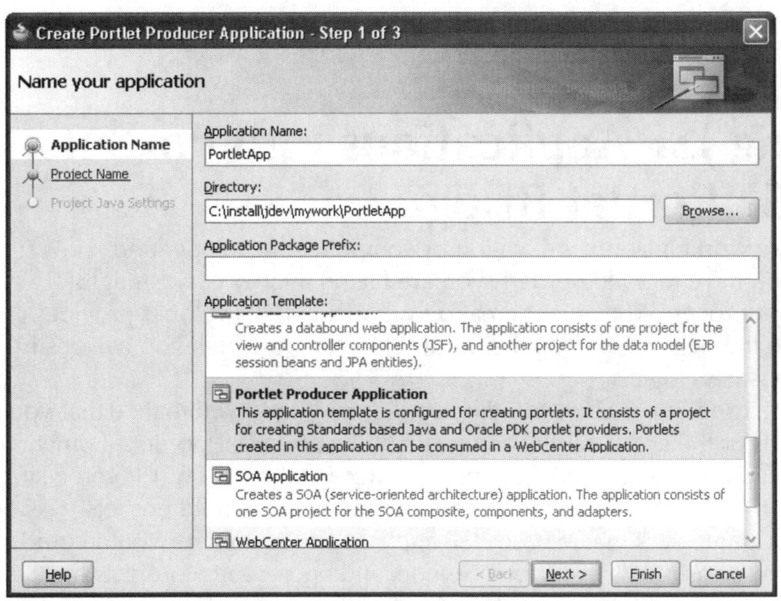

FIGURE 5-35 *Creating an application using the Portlet Producer Application template*

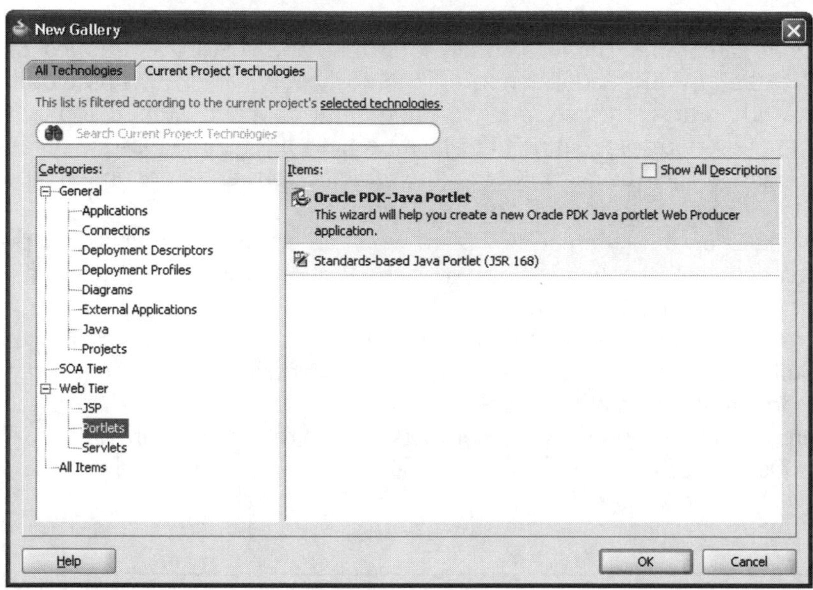

FIGURE 5-36 *Portlet creation wizards in the New Gallery*

Turning JSF Applications into Portlets: The JSF Portlet Bridge

When you're working as an application or component developer and know up front that you have to build portlets, you are facing a fairly easy, straightforward development process. The portlet creation wizards that JDeveloper provides guide you through the steps of creating the portlet skeleton, to which you can easily add your own business logic.

Very often, though, you are building applications, and you realize that you need to make parts or the entire application available to portals as portlets. Sometimes there is a need for your JSF applications to be accessed remotely. Or you'd simply like to use an MVC framework with rich UI capabilities to build portlets.

A tool or framework that exposes JSF applications as portlets would come in handy for these cases. While various vendors and open source projects have been experimenting with such implementations, they didn't provide interoperability; there was no standard that identified the requirements for this. Challenges of such implementations included mapping WSRP to the JSF life cycle and dealing with rich AJAX behavior. With WebCenter, Oracle introduces the JSF Portlet Bridge, a framework that allows exposing JSF applications as portlets.

In 2006 Oracle initiated a Java Specification Request to address this problem. JSR 301 is supported by the major portal vendors, including IBM, Sun, eXo, and SAP.

Terminology

The task of turning applications into portlets is sometimes referred to as "portletizing" the application. While this is not a commonly accepted term, and obviously you don't find it in English dictionaries, it is being used quite widely. An even more unusual and unfortunate terminology you may see in this context is "portalizing" the application. This doesn't even express the task we're performing (we are not turning an application into a portal, but into a portlet). Despite the spread of these terms, we try to stay away from them, but at the same time we find it important to clarify that they tend to mean the same thing.

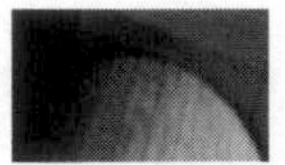

NOTE

The JSR 168 portlet creation wizard offers various technologies to build portlets, one of them being JSF. When you choose JSF as the implementation style, it is the portlet bridge that's used under the covers.

How Do You Do It?

JDeveloper provides very simple and powerful design-time support for exposing JSF applications as portlets. You can simply invoke the Create Portlet Entry action from the context menu of any Faces page in your application. This is often referred to as the JSF Portlet Bridge design-time experience (Figure 5-37).

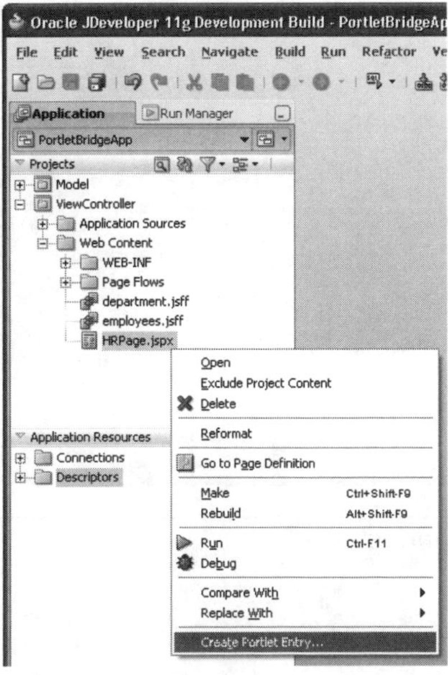

FIGURE 5-37 *JSF Portlet Bridge design-time experience*

NOTE
Earlier in this chapter we covered how to build portlets using the portlet creation wizards. One of the view technology options offered by the JSR 168 portlet creation wizard is ADF Faces. While the portlet creation wizard and the JSF Portlet Bridge design-time experience provide two fundamentally different paths to build portlets, the underlying enabling technology is the same: the JSF Portlet Bridge.

When you're building portlets, you have to define a number of attributes, such as their name, display name, and the portlet title. The dialog that displays after selecting the Create Portlet Entry (Figure 5-38) lets you provide these values, or simply accept the default ones.

Create Portlet Entry

Enter portlet information to generate a portlet entry. The name must adhere to Oracle naming standards. Other values are for display purposes only.

Portlet Name:
PortletBridgeApp_HRPage_jspx

Display Name:
PortletBridgeApp_HRPage_jspx

Portlet Title:
PortletBridgeApp_HRPage_jspx

Short Title:
PortletBridgeApp_HRPage_jspx

Description:
PortletBridgeApp_HRPage_jspx

Help OK Cancel

FIGURE 5-38 *Providing portlet attributes*

As a result of invoking the Create Portlet Entry action from the context menu, several files are created in your project. The two most important ones are:

- **`portlet.xml`** This is the standard portlet deployment descriptor file that has to be present in every JSR 168 portlet application. The `portlet.xml` identifies the portlet class that will be used: `ADFBridgePortlet`, as well as the JSF page that serves as the entry point to the portlet: `/POSubmit.jspx`.

  The following is a relevant code fragment of the generated portlet.xml file:

```
<portlet-class>
    oracle.portlet.bridge.adf.application.ADFBridgePortlet
</portlet-class>
<init-param>
    <name>javax.portlet.faces.defaultViewId.view</name>
    <value>/POSubmit.jspx</value>
</init-param>
```

- **`oracle-portlet.xml`** This is the Oracle-specific descriptor file that contains the extensions required to expose JSR 168 portlets through WSRP 2.0; it allows the portlet to leverage some of the WSRP 2.0 capabilities that JSR 168 doesn't provide.

As a consequence of using the JSF Portlet Bridge, the ADF Portlet Bridge library has been added to your project if it wasn't part of it before.

As applications vary in complexity, the number of portlets you create for them can change too. Remember that when you create a portlet, you specify the JSF page that serves as the entry point to the portlet. Users are free to navigate in the portlet, just like they would do it in the native application. For example, if you have an application consisting of three JSF pages, you may choose to provide only one portlet for the application and have the user navigate between the pages (Figure 5-39). An alternative is to provide a portlet for each JSF page, giving the portlet consumer more options to choose from. Both approaches can be valid depending on the nature of your JSF application.

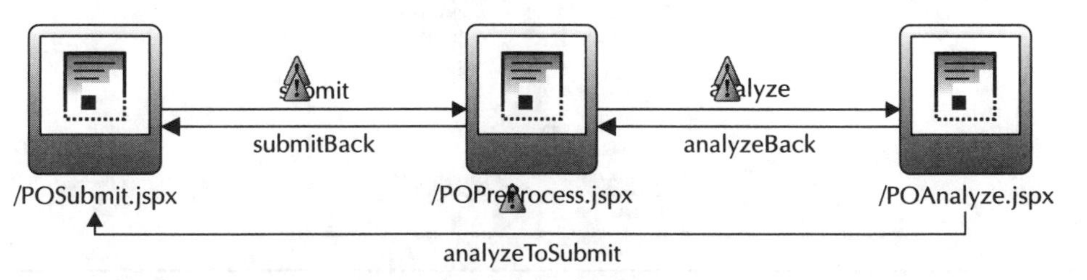

FIGURE 5-39 *JSF application composed of three JSF pages*

Turning Task Flows into Portlets

In addition to applying the JSF Portlet Bridge to JSF pages, you can apply the JSF Portlet Bridge to ADF task flows as well as expose them as portlets (Figure 5-40).

NOTE
You can learn more about task flows in Chapter 3.

When you're turning a task flow into a portlet, a library is added to your project: ADF Portlet Bridge Task Flow. You can easily confirm this by opening the Project Properties dialog and clicking on the Libraries and Classpath entry on the left.

In case you have a large number of task flows, it may easily get overwhelming to manage the task flows exposed as portlets. JDeveloper provides a dialog that simplifies the management of the portlet entries in the portlet.xml file, called the Manage Portlet Entries of Task Flows dialog (Figure 5-41); to invoke it, select Web Tier | Portlets | Manage Portlet Entries of Task Flows from the New Gallery (Figure 5-42). This dialog contains a shuttle UI component with a list of available task flows (task flows that have not been exposed as portlets) and a list of selected task flows

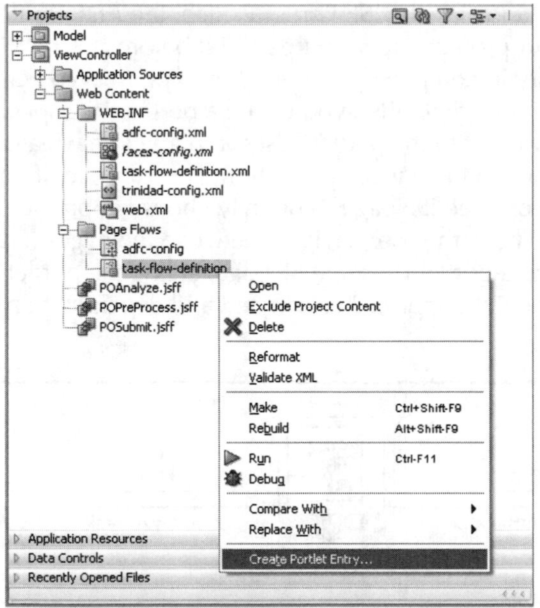

FIGURE 5-40 *Design-time support for turning task flows into portlets*

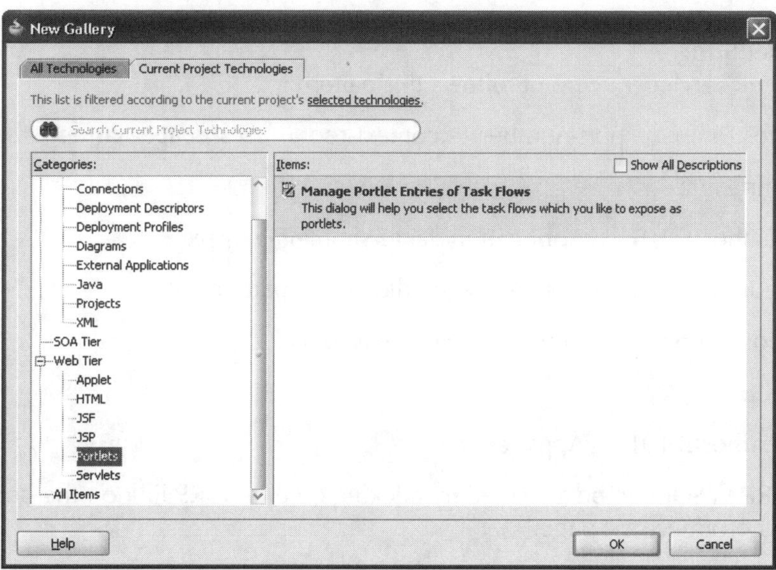

FIGURE 5-41 *Invoking the Manage Portlet Entries of Task Flows dialog*

(task flows that have been made available as portlets). Moving a task flow from left to right is equivalent to selecting the Create Portlet Entry option from the context menu of the task flow. Moving a task flow from right to left has the same effect as removing the task flow's portlet entry from the portlet.xml.

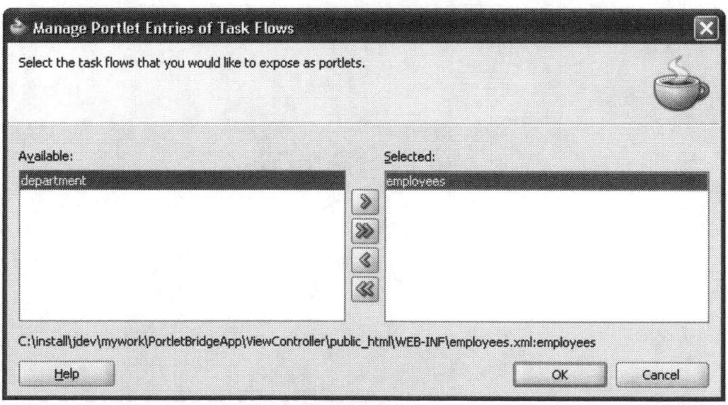

FIGURE 5-42 *The Manage Portlet Entries of Task Flows dialog*

After deploying your "portletized" application, you can access it via the traditional servlet entry point, as well as the portlet entry point, provided by the JSF Portlet Bridge.

The default servlet entry point follows this pattern:

http://<host-name>:<port-number>/<context-root>/faces/<page-name>

For example:

http://localhost:7101/MyApplication /faces/simplePage.jspx

The default portlet producer test page follows this pattern:

http://<host-name>:<port-number>/<context-root>

For example:

http://localhost:7101/MyApplication

The WSRP WSDL can be accessed by clicking on the WSRP link on the bottom of the portlet producer test page.

CHAPTER 6

Inter-component Communication

omposite applications and portals share a common root in many aspects. In this chapter we focus on the aspect that they both promote the building of a site or application on top of existing functions and services; they often do so by leveraging reusable components. When you are implementing such solutions, it is imperative that the building blocks are able to communicate with each other so they can be synchronized in the page.

Let's take a simple example. The user of an enterprise application is interacting with orders: the user can see the order date, the status of the order, as well as the items that make up the order. This functionality may be implemented as one single component, or alternatively as two: a master (orders) and a detail (items). The expected behavior is that orders and items are synchronized.

As the user is stepping through the orders, another component in the page displays detailed information about the customer who placed the order. The orders component drives the customer details component—in other words, orders and customer details components are in sync, they share the context, they are contextually wired.

In general, we can say that two components are contextually wired if the following conditions are satisfied:

- Parameters are passed from one component to another.
- The target component is refreshed as a result of a partial page refresh (PPR) event.

In this chapter we will demonstrate the options available to you and give recommendations for when to use which.

Which Technique Is for Me?

ADF and the WebCenter Framework provide several component types, including JSF view components, task flows, and portlets that can be wired in a number of different ways. As a rule of thumb, you should always use the simplest approach that fits your use case and requirements.

The first and simplest scenario that we will discuss is when your data resides in one data source, for example a database, and the native ADF data controls can handle the actual wiring for you, without performing the wiring task explicitly.

Another straightforward wiring option is when you want to use a JSF view component, for example a drop-down list, to drive another component, such as a table, on the page. This can be achieved in two simple steps: you have to pass the information from one component to the other, and you have to make sure that the driven component is repainted with partial page refresh. In this section you will see an example of how a portlet can be driven by a JSF view component as well.

In the context of portals, most of the time, inter-component communication translates to inter-portlet communication. In this chapter you will also learn how two portlets can communicate with each other using navigational parameters, a feature of WSRP 2.0.

Moving to somewhat more complex cases, you can make task flows communicate with each other, using the ADF model layer (ADFm) contextual events. This is a very powerful way of linking ADF task flows that were built independently. In addition to ADF task flows, portlets can expose contextual events, providing an extra level of flexibility when it comes to wiring them.

Contextual Wiring with ADF Data Controls

In enterprise applications, your data often resides in a database and you use ADF data controls to access it. The relational data model inherently supports the notion of relationships between entities.

When you're choosing ADF Business Components or TopLink to access your database, ADF's data controls provide you with easy ways to ensure that the relationship in the data model is reflected in the UI of the application you are building. While it's beyond the scope of this book to go into great detail on how you can use data controls to build master-detail or more complex relationships, we'll take a quick look at what you can achieve in a simple example.

When you want to display a set of master rows, and for each master row a set of coordinated detail rows, then in your application module you can create view links to define how you want the master and detail view objects to relate. You can do this explicitly, or if the primary key–foreign key relationship is defined in your database schema, JDeveloper can do this automatically for you.

In Figure 6-1 you see how a primary key–foreign key database relationship is visualized in the data control panel as a master-detail hierarchy. The OrdersView (called OrdersView1 in the figure) and OrderItemsView (highlighted and called OrderItemsView2 in the figure) are both exposed as data collections. Notice that

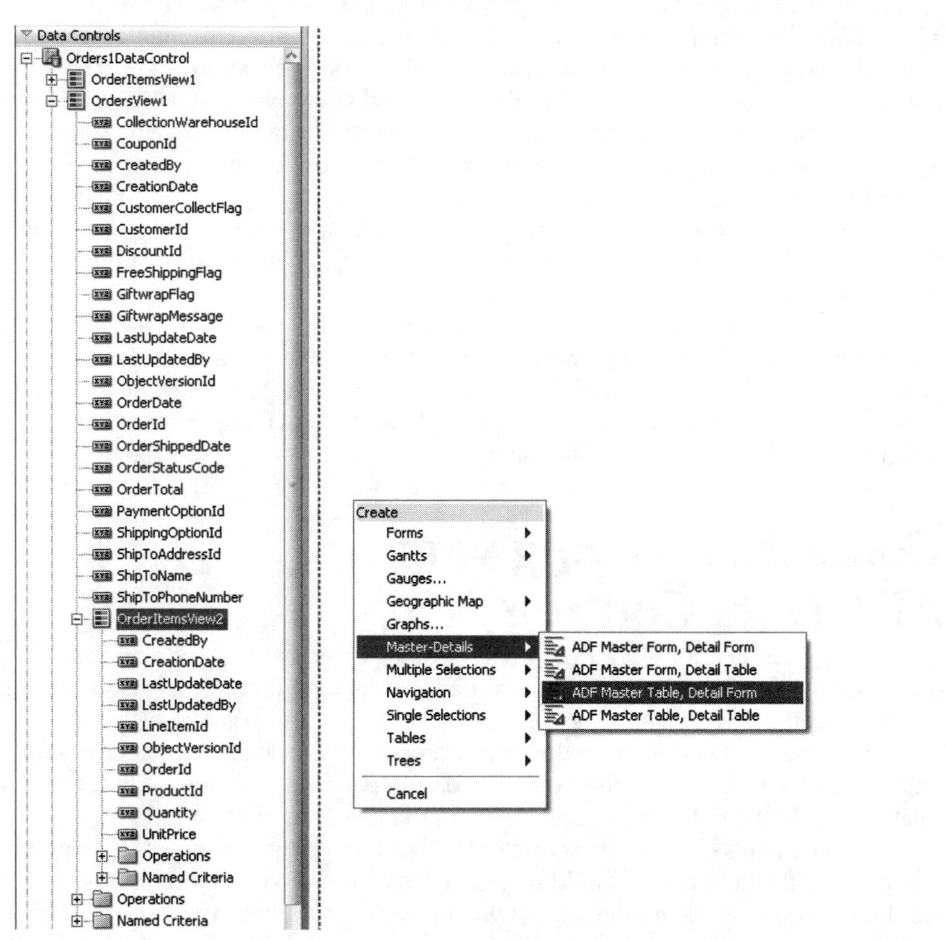

FIGURE 6-1 *Master-detail hierarchy visualized in the Data Controls panel*

the OrderItemsView is nested under the OrdersView. By dropping the OrderItemsView2 on the page, a Master-Details option is offered as well as the usual visualization options.

Figure 6-2 shows the default run-time view that JDeveloper generates for the ADF Master Table, Detail Form visualization option.

OrdersView1

OrderId	OrderDate	OrderShipped
1110	2/26/2009	
1100	2/24/2009	
1001	1/20/2009	1/23/2009
1002	1/30/2009	
1003	1/19/2009	
1004	1/9/2009	
1005	12/15/2008	12/20/2008
1006	1/24/2009	
1007	12/25/2008	12/30/2008
1008	2/2/2009	
1009	1/31/2009	
1010	1/31/2009	
1011	1/28/2009	
1012	2/1/2009	
1013	2/1/2009	
1014	1/14/2009	1/19/2009
1015	2/2/2009	

OrderItemsView2

OrderId 1100
LineItemId 101
ProductId 14
Quantity 1
UnitPrice 49.99
CreatedBy FOD
CreationDate 2/5/2009
LastUpdatedBy FOD
LastUpdateDate 2/24/2009
ObjectVersionId 6

First | Previous | Next | Last

FIGURE 6-2 *Default master-detail visualization*

NOTE
If you want to present the order items to your users without the actual master order records, you can do so by dropping the OrderItemsView1 collection onto the page, displayed as the topmost collection in the Data Controls panel in Figure 6-1.

The technique outlined in this section is a core functionality of ADF. Building data-aware applications with ADF is a big topic. If you are interested in this approach, you can refer to books on ADF as well as the Oracle documentation, including the Fusion Developer's Guide.

Wiring of JSF View Components and Portlets

In this section we discuss another technique provided by ADF to contextually wire two JSF view components. It is essential to understand this method, as certain aspects of portlet wiring are similar.

To demonstrate this technique, we build a simple application, depicted in Figure 6-3. It contains three components: a drop-down list (on the top), a read-only form (on the left), and a portlet (on the right).

The drop-down list drives the two other components on the page, using partial page refresh, shown in Figure 6-4. When selecting EMEA from the list, the form shows EMEA-specific information, and the portlet displays a different image.

As mentioned earlier, at a high level, it takes only two steps to wire two JSF view components together. We have to make sure that the necessary parameter or parameters are passed from one component to the other, and we have to ensure that the driven components refresh using partial page refresh.

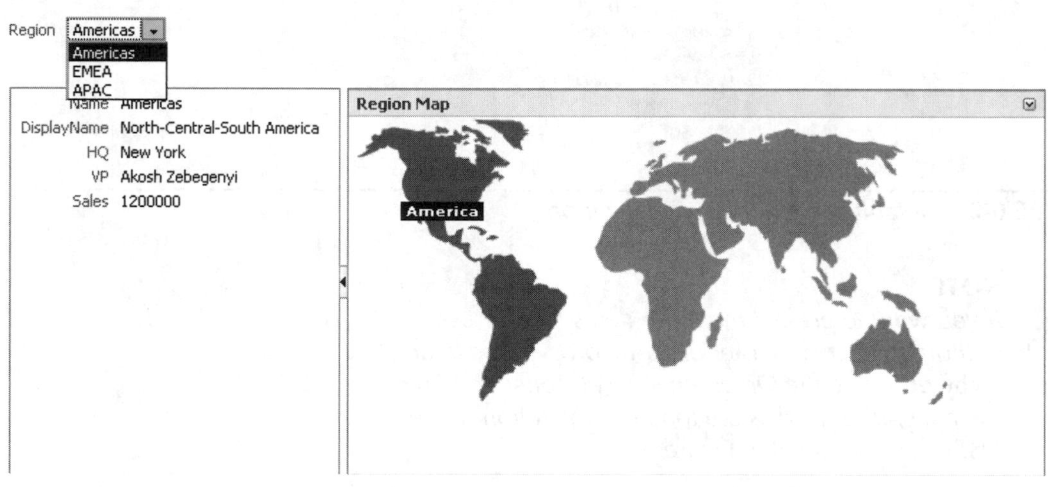

FIGURE 6-3 *Contextually wired components on the page*

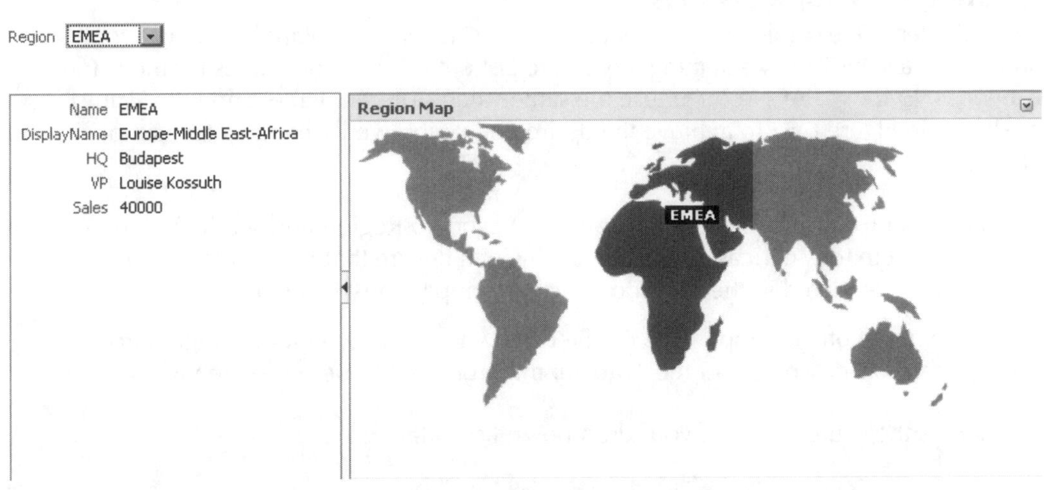

FIGURE 6-4 *Contextually wired components in action*

Building a Simple Contextual Application

Let's see what it takes to build an application containing these three contextually wired components. To build a sample like this, first we need to understand where the data is coming from that the components use.

To keep the scenario simple, the drop-down list is a static list with three values. The form component uses a comma separated value (CSV) data source, and the portlet simply refers to hard coded images depending on the parameter value passed to it.

If you want to follow the steps, get started with a new application based on the WebCenter Application template, and create a new JSF page under the ViewController project, with the Automatically Expose UI Components in a New Managed Bean option selected under Page Implementation in the Create JSF Page dialog. To end up with a similar layout to the one shown in Figure 6-3 and Figure 6-4, drop a Panel Stretch Layout component on the page.

Creating the Drop-down List

Drop a Select One Choice component in the "top" facet of the Panel Stretch Layout, and define a static list by selecting the Create List option. Provide values for the list: Americas, EMEA, APAC. You can use the same values for Item Label and Item Value, as shown in Figure 6-5. To achieve the desired behavior, we'll change a few simple attributes:

1. Under Common Properties, change the Label to Region and set the Value attribute to Americas. This latter setting will ensure that there is always a value rendered in the drop-down list; no empty entry is offered.
2. To notify other components on the page when you select a new region from the drop-down list, set the Auto Submit property to true under Behavior.

Here is the source code of your drop-down list so far:

```
    <af:selectOneChoice label="Region"
binding="#{backingBeanScope.backing_pg1.selectOneChoice1}"
         id="selectOneChoice1" value="Americas"
         autoSubmit="true">
      <af:selectItem label="Americas" value="Americas"
          binding="#{backingBeanScope.backing_pg1.selectItem1}"
          id="selectItem1"/>
      <af:selectItem label="EMEA" value="EMEA"
          binding="#{backingBeanScope.backing_pg1.selectItem2}"
          id="selectItem2"/>
      <af:selectItem label="APAC" value="APAC"
           binding="#{backingBeanScope.backing_pg1.selectItem3}"
           id="selectItem3"/>
    </af:selectOneChoice>
```

Creating and Wiring the Form Component

Before creating the form component, let's drop a Panel Splitter component into the center facet of the Panel Stretch Layout. This layout component allows us to specify at run time how much horizontal space our components require.

To create the form component, we will use a CSV data source that returns its results based on the parameter passed to it. For example, the regionDetails .jsp?region=Americas request returns this CSV:

```
Name, DisplayName, HQ, VP, Sales
Americas, North-Central-South America, New York, Akosh Zebegenyi, 1200000
```

How the parameterized CSV is generated is not really relevant from this chapter's perspective. However, for the sake of completeness, here is the source of the above-mentioned regionDetails.jsp file. If you make it part of your application, it

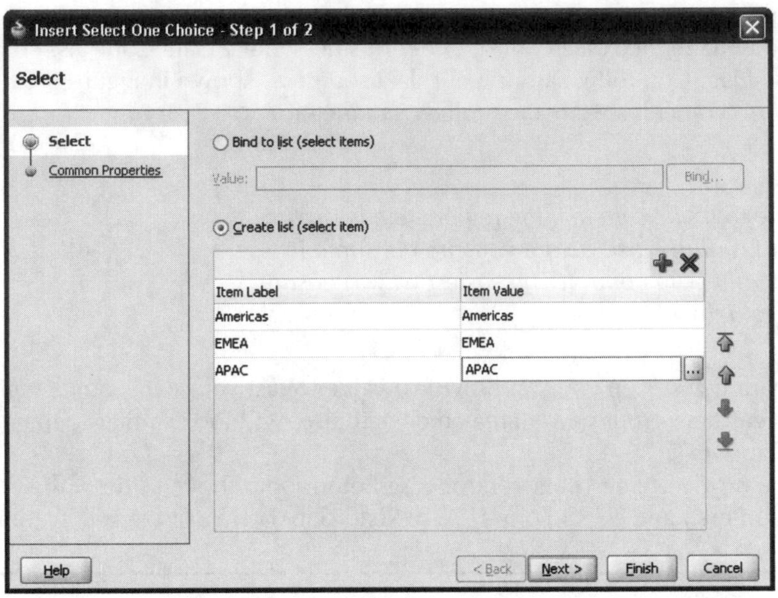

FIGURE 6-5 *Defining a static drop-down list*

gets deployed along with it, and the data source is always available when you run your page.

```
Name, DisplayName, HQ, VP, Sales
<%
if ((request.getParameter("region") != null))
  { if (request.getParameter("region").equals("Americas"))
{%>Americas, North-Central-South America, New York,
Akosh Zebegenyi,1200000
<%}
    else if (request.getParameter("region").equals("EMEA"))
{%>EMEA, Europe-Middle East-Africa, Budapest, Louise Kossuth,40000
<%}
    else if (request.getParameter("region").equals("APAC"))
{%>APAC, Asia Pacific, Beijing, Jin Yi Tsai,1420000
<%}
  }
else
{%>Americas, North-Central-South America, New York,
Akosh Zebegenyi,1200000
<% } %>
```

Now create a new URL Service data control. Invoke the New Gallery through the Model project's context menu. Select All Technologies in the New Gallery, and you find the URL Service data control under Business Tier | Data Controls. Point the URL Service Data Control wizard to your data source as shown in Figure 6-6. In the Source section you can specify the request parameter.

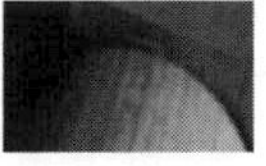

NOTE
You have to make sure that the regionDetails.jsp file is up and running first, before you can consume it through your data control. The easiest way to ensure it is by actually running it.

In the parameters step you can provide a value to test your data source with. Enter **Americas** here. Your newly created data control will look similar to the one shown in Figure 6-7.

From the newly created data control drag Return onto the left side of the Panel Splitter, called first, and select Forms | ADF Read-only Form as the visualization

FIGURE 6-6 *The URL Service Data Control wizard*

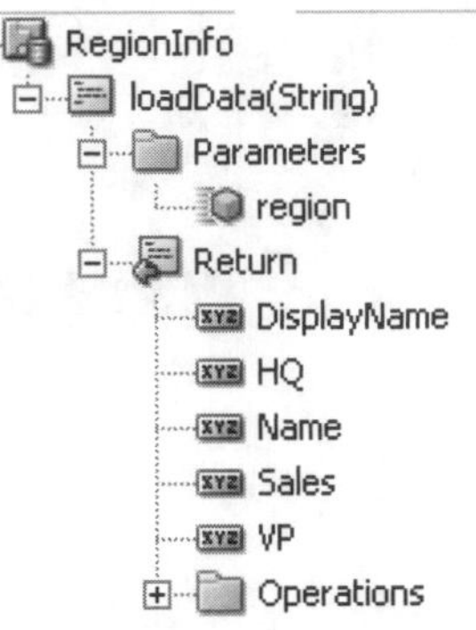

FIGURE 6-7 *Data control with parameter*

option from the pop-up menu. Click OK in the Edit Form Fields dialog. Because the data control takes a parameter, region, the Edit Action Binding dialog pops up, allowing you to pass the value selected in the drop-down list to the data control. The value of the region parameter should be similar to this:

```
${backingBeanScope.backing_pg1.selectOneChoice1.value}
```

If you switch to the page definition, the source of the method action binding section looks similar to this:

```
    <methodAction id="loadData" RequiresUpdateModel="true"
Action="invokeMethod"
            MethodName="loadData" IsViewObjectMethod="false"
            DataControl="RegionInfo" InstanceName="RegionInfo"
                    ReturnName="RegionInfo.methodResults.loadData_
RegionInfo_loadData_result">
      <NamedData NDName="region"
        NDValue="${backingBeanScope.backing_pg1.selectOneChoice1.value}"
        NDType="java.lang.String"/>
    </methodAction>
```

Now that we took care of the parameter that is passed from the drop-down list to the form, the second thing we have to do is ensure that the form refreshes with PPR when a new value is selected in the drop-down list. To do so, switch to your JSPX page and select the Panel Form Layout that surrounds the newly added form. Edit its Partial Trigger attribute and select the selectOneChoice component, residing in "facet (top)" under the Panel Stretch Layout (Figure 6-8).

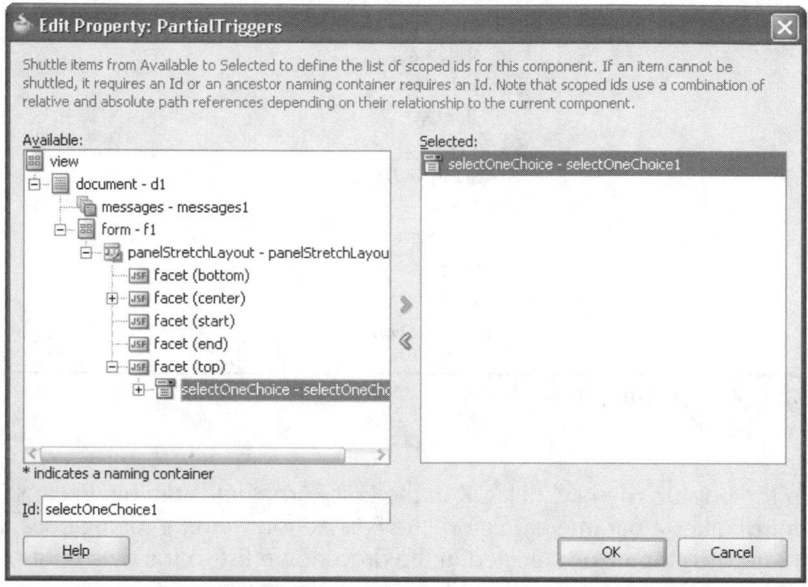

FIGURE 6-8 *Setting the Partial Trigger attribute of the form component*

When you run the page, the drop-down list and the read-only form are displayed in the page and they are contextually wired. When selecting a region, the form updates with partial page refresh.

Creating and Wiring an OmniPortlet

Now that we are done with the drop-down list and it's wired to the form, the third component we have to add to the page is an OmniPortlet.

To be able to consume OmniPortlet in your application, first you have to register the OmniPortlet producer. To do so, you'll have to know what your portlet producer URL is. The one deployed to your Default Server instance can be found under the following URL, by default:

http://localhost:7101/portalTools/omniPortlet/providers

To test this URL, you can access the URL from your browser, and make sure that you see the portlet producer test page, as shown in Figure 6-9.

After successfully testing the URL in your browser, you will use it to register the portlet producer with your application. Under Application Resources | Connections, invoke the context menu and select New Connection | Oracle PDK-Java Producer.

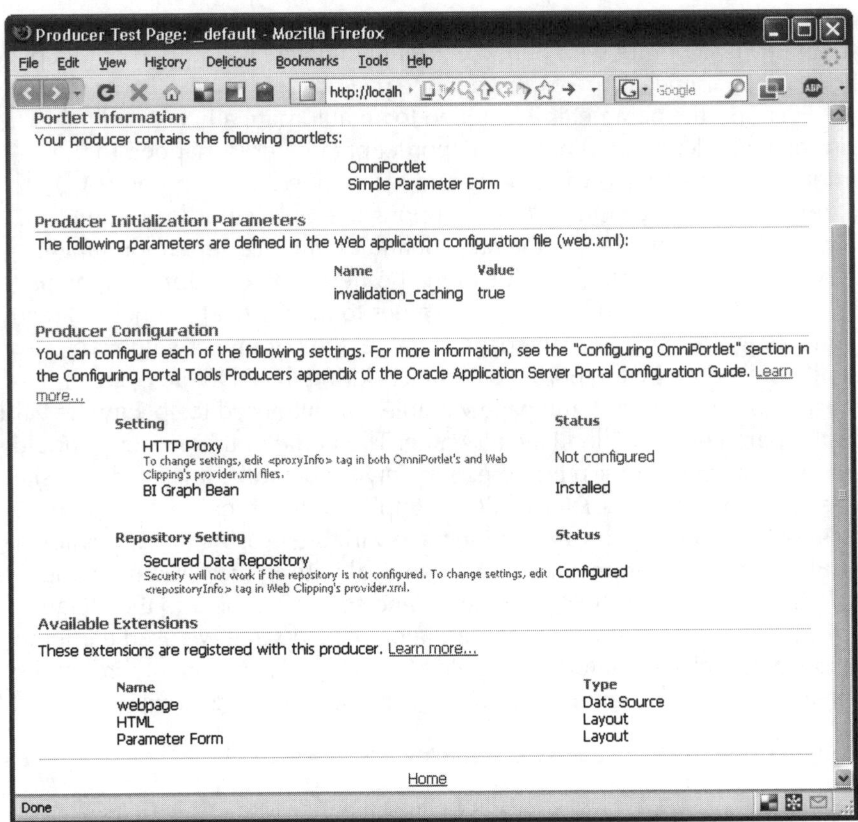

FIGURE 6-9 *The OmniPortlet producer test page*

Provide a producer registration name, such as OmniProducer. For the URL endpoint enter your OmniPortlet endpoint URL, for example http://localhost:7101/portalTools/omniPortlet/providers, and click Finish.

Expand the newly registered portlet producer under Application Resources | Connections and drop OmniPortlet into facet "second" of the Panel Splitter component.

NOTE
Your newly registered OmniPortlet is located under Application Resources | Connections | Oracle PDK-Java Producer | OmniProducer.

To wire OmniPortlet to the drop-down list, switch to the page definition file by invoking the context menu of the JSPX page and selecting Go to Page Definition.

When a PDK-Java portlet with public portlet parameters is dropped onto a page, the public portlet parameters are exposed in the page definition file, under the portlet tag. Every portlet parameter is mapped to an automatically created page variable in the page definition file. Param1 portlet parameter is mapped to the OmniPortlet1_1_Param1 page variable, Param2 is mapped to OmniPortlet1_1_Param2, and so on. Because OmniPortlet supports five public portlet parameters, you see five of these parameters in the page definition file. It's very important to know that you can manipulate the value of the portlet parameter, through the page variable, but you cannot do so by assigning values to the portlet parameter directly. When you're assigning a value to the page variable, the parameter value is automatically picked up by the portlet parameter during the ADF life cycle.

As unusual as it may sound, the page variable attribute used to specify the value for the portlet parameter is called Default Value. The name of the property should not mislead you, as the value isn't used exclusively for defaults; it is used to assign new values to the portlet parameter while the application is running.

The easiest way to assign a value to the page variable is using an expression language (EL). Select the parameter you want to deal with in the Structure pane (in our case, let's select OmniPortlet1_1_Param1) and select Edit next to the Default Value attribute. The same expression editor dialog pops up that we used earlier to select the currently selected value of the selectOneChoice component through its backing bean. We'll do the same thing and specify the following value:

```
#{backingBeanScope.backing_pg1.selectOneChoice1.value}
```

Now that we took care of the parameter wiring, the last thing we have to do is set the Partial Trigger attribute of the portlet to ensure that it gets refreshed when a new value is selected in the selectOneChoice drop-down list component. Switch back to your JSPX file, select OmniPortlet in the page, and set the Partial Trigger attribute to SelectOneChoice1. Again, remember that you find it under the "top" facet of the Panel Splitter (in case you use the partial trigger editor dialog), shown in Figure 6-8.

When you re-run the page, your OmniPortlet is undefined. You can customize the portlet and walk through a five-step wizard to define its contents. In our simple sample, we use JavaScript to render an image conditionally, depending on the parameter that is passed to the portlet.

From the action menu of the portlet select Customize. In the first screen of the wizard, don't change anything and click Next. In the Source screen specify a default value for the first parameter, Param1: Americas. Don't change anything in the Filter screen. In the View screen change the portlet title to Region Map and the Layout Style to HTML. In the Layout screen clear all the fields by selecting Clear Fields from

Quick Start and clicking the Apply button. In the Non-Repeating Heading Section enter your code. Here is some sample code that you can use as a starting point:

```
<script type="text/javascript">
if ("##Param1##" == "Americas") {
 document.write ("<img src=http://127.0.0.1:7101/WCHBChapter15Sample1/images/map_
america.gif>");
}
else if ("##Param1##" == "EMEA") {
 document.write ("<img src=http://127.0.0.1:7101/WCHBChapter15Sample1/images/map_
emea.gif>");
}
else
 document.write ("<img src=http://127.0.0.1:7101/WCHBChapter15Sample1/images/map_
apac.gif>");
</script>
```

As you return to the page, OmniPortlet displays an image, specific to the Americas region. As you select another region from the drop-down list, both the form and portlet components refresh with partial page refresh and render their new content, relevant to the region selected.

Inter-portlet Communication: Wiring Portlets

Because WebCenter applications are built on the foundation of JSF and ADF, most of the time you are required to wire portlets with other JSF view components. However, wiring two portlets on a page remains a key functionality, and the WebCenter Framework gives you full power to leverage it.

We will start off with an application that was created based on the WebCenter Template containing two WSRP 2.0 portlets: the Parameter Form and Parameter Display portlets. These two portlets are very useful when you want to learn and experiment with portlet wiring: the Parameter Form portlet can drive the Parameter Display portlet.

To register the portlet producer containing these two portlets, point your browser to your producer's test page, for example http://localhost:7101/portletapp/info. Confirm that you see the ParameterForm (2.0) and ReadOnlyParameterForm (2.0) portlets in the list. Copy the WSRP 2.0 WSDL URL to your clipboard, and use it to register the WSRP portlet producer with your application. After a successful registration you can drop the Parameter Form and Parameter Display portlets onto the page.

Open the page definition file by invoking the context menu of the JSPX page and selecting Go To Page Definition from the menu. In the Structure panel shown in Figure 6-10, you can see the two portlets: ParameterFormPortlet1_1 and ParameterDisplayPortlet1_1, each featuring three parameters, called ora_wsrp_navigparam_Parameter< >. Navigational parameters serve both as input and output parameters.

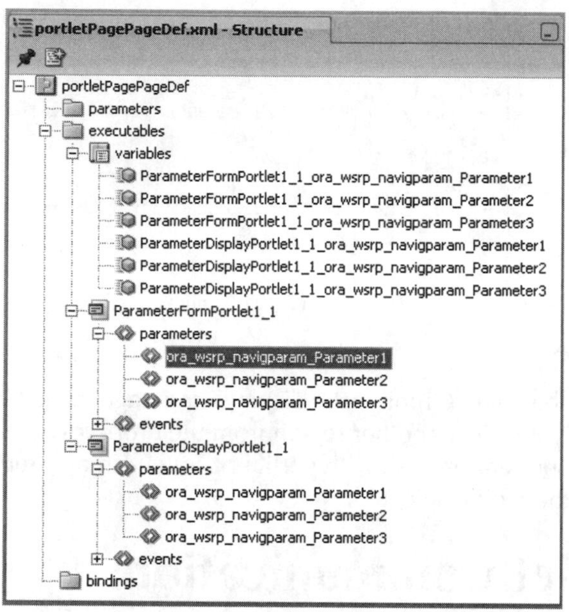

FIGURE 6-10 *WSRP 2.0 navigational parameters in the Page Definition*

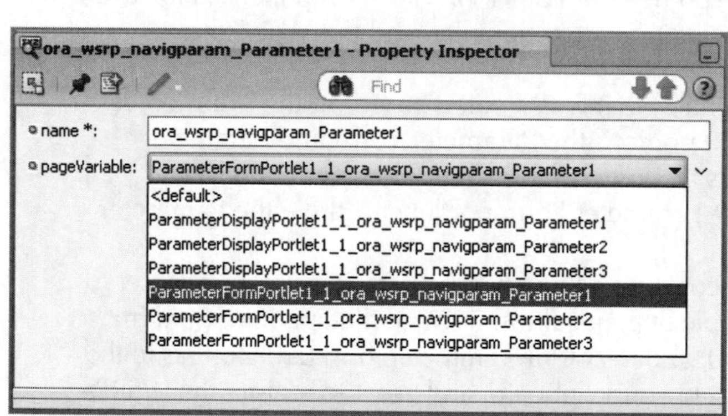

FIGURE 6-11 *Portlet parameters mapped to page variables*

Under executables | variables, you can see that for each portlet parameter a page variable is created automatically. Each portlet parameter is mapped to a corresponding page variable and the link is established through the Page Variable attribute of the portlet parameter, shown in Figure 6-11.

Portlet variables cannot be manipulated directly. If you want to change their value, you have to do so by going through the page variables' Default Value attribute.

For example, if you want to pass a string value to the portlet parameter, simply assign it to the Default Value of the corresponding page variable.

```
<variable Name="ParameterDisplayPortlet1_1_ora_wsrp_navigparam_Parameter1"
          Type="java.lang.Object" DefaultValue="#{'constant'}"/>
```

Alternatively, you can use expression language to define the default value of your page variables. In this example we use EL to retrieve and pass to the portlet the current user's time zone.

```
<variable Name="ParameterDisplayPortlet1_1_ora_wsrp_navigparam_Parameter2"
          Type="java.lang.Object"
          DefaultValue="#{generalSettings.userTimeZone.displayName}"/>
```

Most of the time, however, you want to ensure that portlets exchange data with each other, which means you need to wire portlet parameters together. The easiest way to achieve this is by ensuring that the portlet parameters of the two portlets point to the same page variable. In Figure 6-12 you see three lines highlighted. The first one is the page variable, where the name attribute is ParameterDisplayPortlet1_1_ora_wsrp_navigparam_Parameter3. The second highlighted line belongs to our first portlet and it is pointing to the above-mentioned page variable. The last highlighted line, which belongs to the Parameter Display portlet, mimics what the Parameter Form portlet does: it points to the same page variable.

By pointing to the same page variable, the framework ensures that when one parameter changes, it gets propagated to all other parameters as well.

The second and last step is to be sure that the driven portlet listens to the user interactions that are taking place in the first portlet. You have to set the Partial Trigger attribute of the Parameter Display portlet by providing the ID of the first portlet:

```
<adfp:portlet value="#{bindings.ParameterDisplayPortlet1_1}"
     id="portlet2"
     binding="#{backingBeanScope.backing_portletPage.portlet2}"
       partialTriggers="portlet1"/>
```

```
<?xml version="1.0" encoding="UTF-8" ?>
<pageDefinition xmlns="http://xmlns.oracle.com/adfm/uimodel"
                version="11.1.1.52.88" id="portletPagePageDef"
                Package="view.pageDefs">
  <parameters/>
  <executables>
    <variableIterator id="variables">
      <variable Name="Para ... "java.lang.Object"/>
      <variable Name="Para ... "java.lang.Object"/>
      <variable Name="Para ... "java.lang.Object"/>
      <variable Name="Para ... ltValue="constant"/>
      <variable Name="Para ... Zone.displayName}"/>
      <variable Name="ParameterDisplayPortlet1_1_ora_wsrp_navigparam_Parameter3"
                Type="java.lang.Object"/>
    </variableIterator>
    <portlet id="ParameterFormPortlet1_1"
             portletInstance="/oracle/adf/portlet/WSRPSampleProducer/ap/Ei4default_dd440b20_01
             class="oracle.adf.model.portlet.binding.PortletBinding"
             retainPortletHeader="false"
             xmlns="http://xmlns.oracle.com/portlet/bindings">
      <parameters>
        <parameter name="ora ... gparam_Parameter1"/>
        <parameter name="ora ... gparam_Parameter2"/>
        <parameter name="ora_wsrp_navigparam_Parameter3"
                   pageVariable="ParameterDisplayPortlet1_1_ora_wsrp_navigparam_Parameter3"/>
      </parameters>
      <events> <event name ... sChange"/> </events>
    </portlet>
    <portlet id="ParameterDisplayPortlet1_1"
             portletInstance="/oracle/adf/portlet/WSRPSampleProducer/ap/Ei5default_dd4427a1_01
             class="oracle.adf.model.portlet.binding.PortletBinding"
             retainPortletHeader="false"
             xmlns="http://xmlns.oracle.com/portlet/bindings">
      <parameters>
        <parameter name="ora ... gparam_Parameter1"/>
        <parameter name="ora ... gparam_Parameter2"/>
        <parameter name="ora_wsrp_navigparam_Parameter3"
                   pageVariable="ParameterDisplayPortlet1_1_ora_wsrp_navigparam_Parameter3"/>
      </parameters>
      <events> <event name ... sChange"/> </events>
    </portlet>
  </executables>
  <bindings/>
</pageDefinition>
```

FIGURE 6-12 *Portlet parameters referencing the same page variable*

Figure 6-13 shows you what your page looks like after performing the above-outlined wirings.

Wiring PDK-Java Portlets

The WebCenter Framework treats WSRP and PDK-Java portlets in most aspects the same way. However, there are significant differences between the two portlet types, especially in the contextual wiring realm.

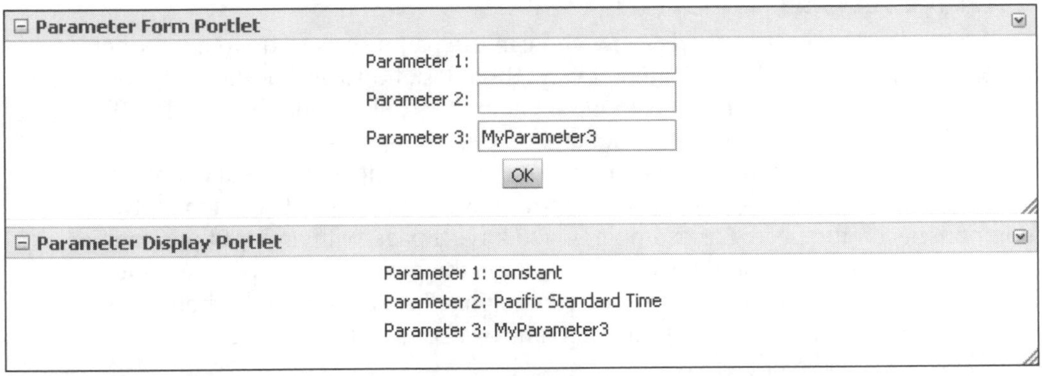

Parameter Form Portlet

Parameter 1:

Parameter 2:

Parameter 3: MyParameter3

OK

Parameter Display Portlet

Parameter 1: constant

Parameter 2: Pacific Standard Time

Parameter 3: MyParameter3

FIGURE 6-13 *Two contextually wired WSRP 2.0 portlets*

When looking at the consumer side of portlet wiring, the same wiring techniques apply to PDK-Java portlets as to WSRP 2.0 portlets. The public portlet parameters of PDK-Java portlets, conceptually similar to the WSRP 2.0 navigational parameters, are automatically wired to page variables. As shown earlier in this chapter, through the automatically linked page variables, PDK-Java portlets can be driven by other components or portlets in the page.

Workaround for PDK-Java Portlets to Drive Other Components on the Page

A significant limitation of PDK-Java portlets is that they cannot drive other portlets or components in the page. If this is a requirement, you should seriously consider using different view technologies to build your components, such as task flows or WSRP 2.0 portlets.

If for some reason you don't have a choice and you have to use PDK-Java portlets, you can use a simple workaround. Since the portlet cannot drive other components on the page, the only way to pass information to other components on the page is by rendering HTML links and/or forms in your portlet that point back to your page. When users click on the link or submit the form, the entire page refreshes, and the link or form parameters are passed to the page. At that point, the request parameters can be wired to any other component on the page.

By default, parameters submitted to the same page are not made available to portlets on the page. To make them available, you have to set the master or driver PDK-Java portlet view tag's Submit URL Parameters attribute to true.

Mind you, the above-outlined technique has to be treated as a workaround and is not a recommended technique to be used in large-scale production deployments. It performs a full page refresh, and therefore you lose your Faces context on your page and it will render as if it was rendering for the first time.

Contextual Events

Earlier in this chapter we covered how you can use parameters to drive components on pages. Although in slightly different ways, both task flows and portlets support parameters: task flow parameters are input parameters only, while the WSRP 2.0 navigational parameters are both input and output parameters.

ADF offers another way for components to keep in sync: contextual events. The main benefit of contextual events is that they allow you to cascade content between components on the page. For example, if you have a page with an input parameter of Order Number, you could have task flow A on the page that accepts that input parameter and displays customer order information. Task flow A could then raise an event with a pay load of Customer Info and a second task flow on the page could display Customer Details.

Very much like task flows, portlets support contextual events as well: they can be both event consumers and event producers. As an event producer, portlets that contain navigational parameters have a predefined event called *parameter changed*. The pay load of this event contains all the portlet parameters. As event consumers, the event pay load elements are mapped to the input parameters of the detail portlet.

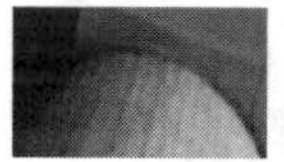

NOTE
While task flows do not require partial trigger settings when they are wired using contextual events, portlets do require you to specify partial triggers to have the listening portlet update when the detail portlet receives an event.

Wiring Portlets Using Contextual Events

In this section we walk you through the steps you have to take to wire two portlets using contextual events. The assumption is that you have a page containing a WSRP 2.0 Parameter Form and a WSRP 2.0 Parameter Display portlet.

First, you need to switch to the page definition of your page, where the parameter wiring is taking place. In the Structure pane invoke the context menu on the root element, and select Edit Event Map, as shown in Figure 6-14.

In the Event Map Editor dialog click the Add a New Event Entry icon, shown in Figure 6-15.

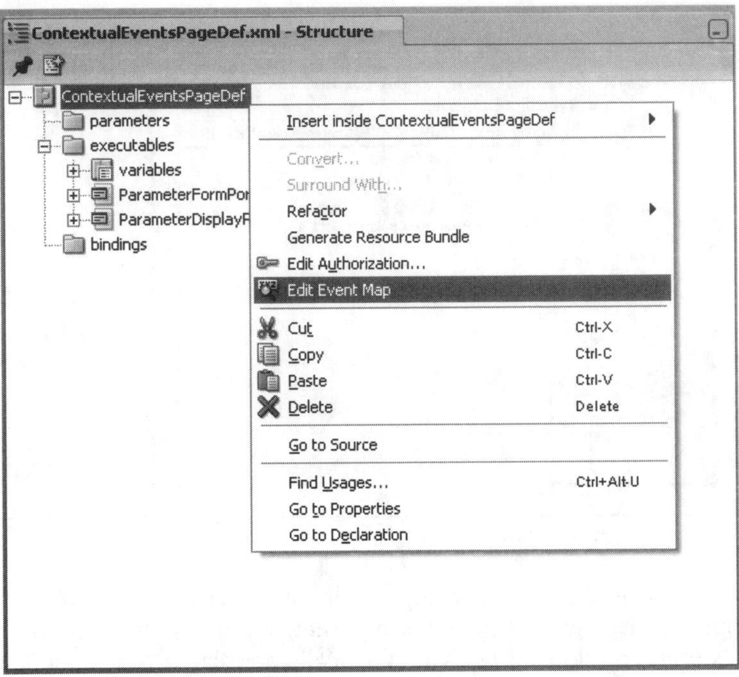

FIGURE 6-14 *Invoking the Event Map Editor*

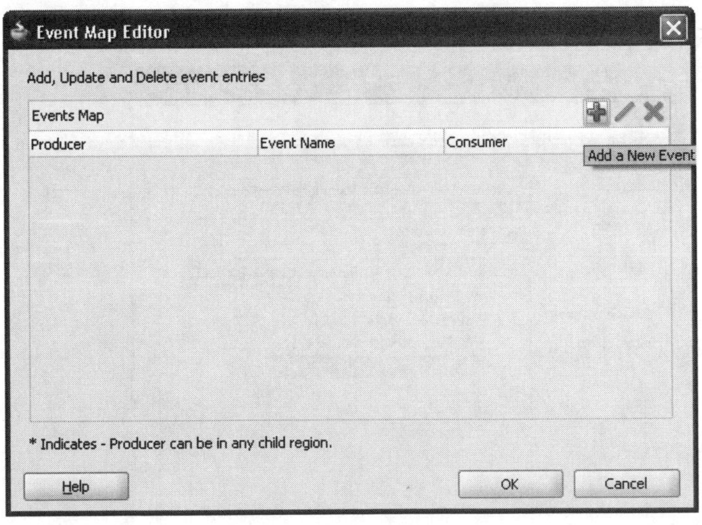

FIGURE 6-15 *Adding a New Event map entry*

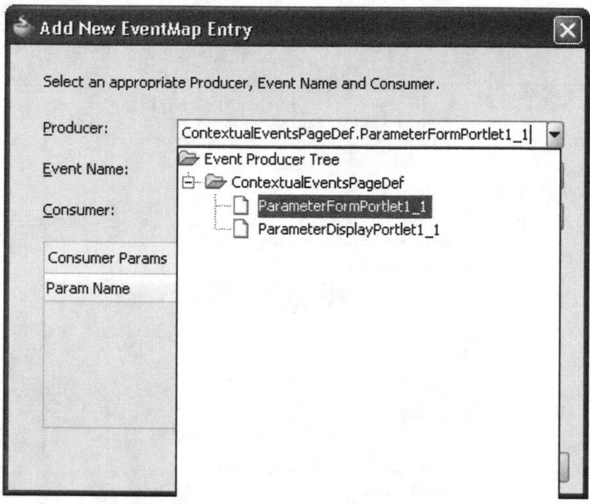

FIGURE 6-16 *Selecting the Event Producer*

In the Add New EventMap Entry dialog you'll have to specify the event producer. In our case it's the Parameter Form portlet, shown in Figure 6-16.

The Event Name drop-down list gets automatically populated. Since our Parameter Form portlet offers only one event, ParameterFormPortlet1_1_Event, the list contains only one element.

Then, you have to select the event consumer: the Parameter Display portlet, as shown in Figure 6-17.

FIGURE 6-17 *Selecting the event consumer*

After selecting the event consumer, you have to specify the consumer parameters by clicking the Add Consumer Parameter icon. You can provide any valid identifier for the parameter name. To define the parameter value, click on the ellipses and select the value using the following EL expression:

```
${payLoad.ora_wsrp_navigparam_Parameter1}
```

Figure 6-18 shows that the EL editor allows you to select the event pay load. It even introspects the pay load and allows you to select a particular parameter.

The last step is adding the partial triggers if they're not already there.

Task Flows Exposed as Portlets

A task flow can have "input" parameters to receive values but no similar mechanism for providing "output." How do you get around this when task flows are exposed as portlets using the Oracle JSF Portlet Bridge? The Portlet Bridge maps the task flow functionality so that a task flow that is exposed as a portlet can both receive and produce context.

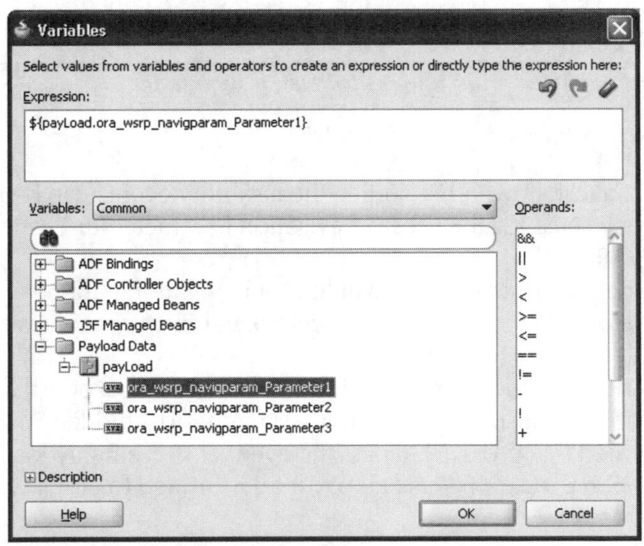

FIGURE 6-18 *Specifying the event pay load*

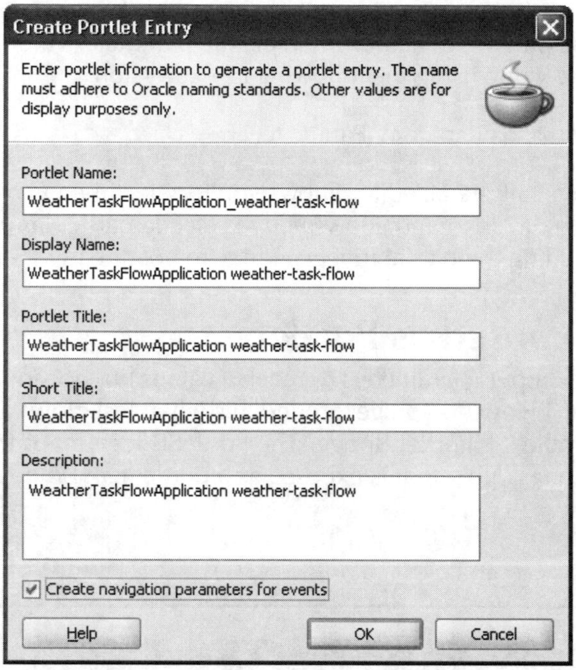

FIGURE 6-19 *Creating navigation parameters for task flow events*

When you turn a task flow into a portlet, the task flow events can be mapped to portlet parameters by selecting the Create Navigation Parameter for Events checkbox, shown in Figure 6-19.

As a result of the above setting, you will have a navigation parameter entry in the oracle-portlet.xml file for each of your contextual events, as shown in Figure 6-20.

For output, ADF contextual events within the task flow are exposed as ADF contextual events in the consumer application. A number of "hidden" portlet parameters are created that are used to pass the event and event pay load.

At present, support for parameters and pay load is limited to String types.

```
<?xml version="1.0" encoding="UTF-8" standalone="yes"?>
<portlet-app-extension xmlns="http://xmlns.oracle.com/portlet/oracle-portlet-app">
    <portlet-extension>
        <portlet-name>WeatherTaskFlowApplication_weather-task-flow</portlet-name>
        <navigation-parameters>
            <name>_adf_event_zipcodeEnteredEvent</name>
            <type>String</type>
            <label xml:lang="en">_adf_event_zipcodeEnteredEvent</label>
            <hint xml:lang="en">_adf_event_zipcodeEnteredEvent</hint>
        </navigation-parameters>
        <portlet-id>adf_taskflow_WEB_INF_weather_task_flow_xml</portlet-id>
        <allow-export>true</allow-export>
        <allow-import>true</allow-import>
        <require-iframe>true</require-iframe>
        <minimum-wsrp-version>2</minimum-wsrp-version>
    </portlet-extension>
</portlet-app-extension>
```

FIGURE 6-20 *Navigation parameters created for task flow events in oracle-portlet.xml*

Contextual Wiring of Portlets at Run Time

Oracle Composer is a very powerful tool allowing you to edit pages, add and remove components to and from your pages, and set component and page attributes. In addition to these capabilities, probably the most sophisticated functionality it provides is allowing business users to contextually wire two or more components in the browser at run time.

While you as the developer will perform most of the component wiring in JDeveloper at design time, there may be a requirement to empower your business users to do this at run time. WebCenter Spaces is a great example for this scenario: WebCenter Spaces is an application that is built by Oracle, and therefore when you install it, it's accessible only from your browser and has a run-time interface only.

In this section we walk through the simple steps of wiring two portlets: the Parameter Form and Parameter Display portlets. First we use navigational parameters, then do the same using ADF contextual events. Our environment is WebCenter Spaces, but the steps are very similar in any customizable WebCenter application that features WebCenter Composer.

Wiring Portlets with WSRP 2.0 Navigational Parameters

Wiring two portlets using navigational parameters at run time is essentially identical to wiring them at design time. It consists of two simple steps:

1. Wire the parameters of the two portlets by ensuring that the navigational parameters refer to the same page variable.
2. By defining the partial trigger attribute, set up the partial page refresh behavior by pointing to the Parameter Form portlet from the driven Parameter Display portlet.

Take the page into edit mode, and select the Edit action (pencil icon) of the Parameter Form portlet. Under Choose a Value select Page Parameter from the first drop-down list, and one of the parameters from the second one, as shown in Figure 6-21. You will have to make sure that the same value is selected in the Parameter Display portlet as well.

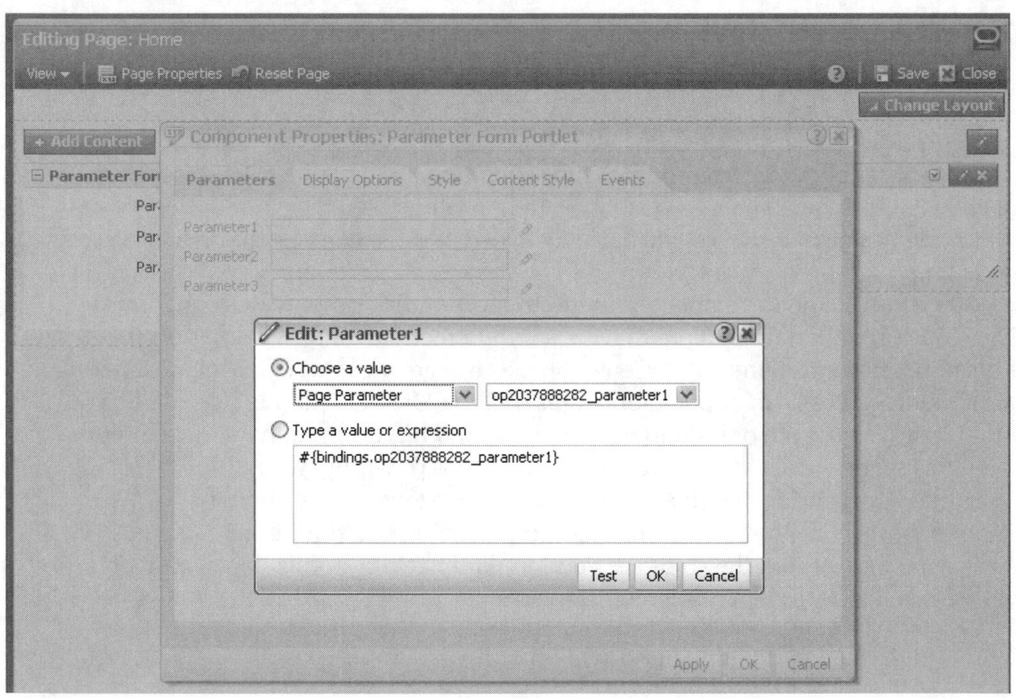

FIGURE 6-21 *Mapping the portlet parameter to the page variable*

We are not quite done with step 1, as we will have to wire the Parameter Display portlet's navigational parameter to the same page variable. But while we are here, let's take this opportunity to copy the system-generated ID of the first portlet to the clipboard. This ID will be needed for step 2: setting up the Partial Trigger attribute for the Parameter Display portlet, shown in Figure 6-22.

Let's close the Component Properties dialog and edit the properties of our Parameter Display portlet. On the Parameters tab point Parameter1 to the same page variable as shown in Figure 6-21.

And finally, switch to the Display Options tab and paste in the Parameter Form portlet's ID in the Partial Triggers field, as shown in Figure 6-23.

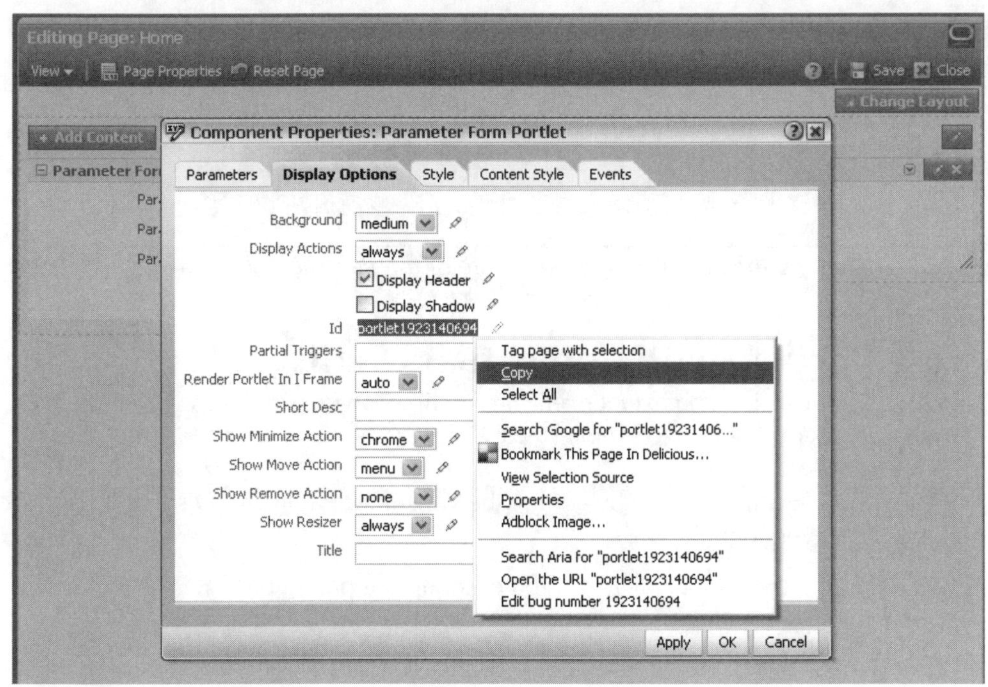

FIGURE 6-22 *Copying the ID of the Parameter Form portlet to the clipboard*

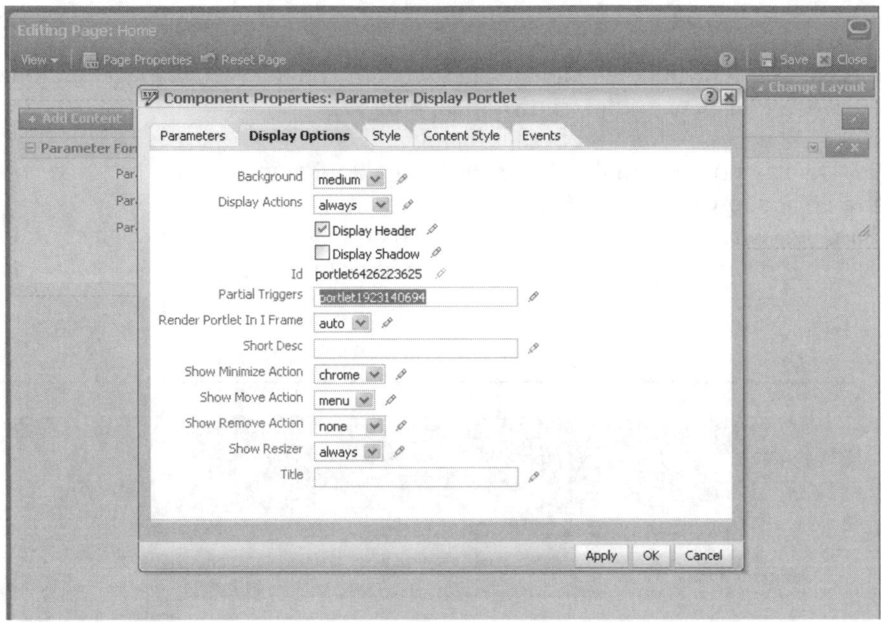

FIGURE 6-23 *Specifying the Partial Triggers attribute of the Parameter Display portlet*

Wiring Portlets with Contextual Events

Wiring two portlets using contextual events at run time is very similar to wiring them at design time. It consists of two simple steps:

1. Define the event mapping by editing the consumer Parameter Display portlet's event definition.
2. By defining the Partial Trigger attribute, set up the partial page refresh behavior by pointing to the Parameter Form portlet from the driven Parameter Display portlet.

Both steps are performed by editing the Parameter Display portlet's properties. However, the second step requires you to have the Parameter Form portlet's ID. Therefore, before actually getting started with the first step, get a hold of this ID.

Take the page into edit mode, and select the Edit action (pencil icon) of the Parameter Form portlet. In the Display Options tab of the Component Properties dialog, select and copy the value of the ID attribute to your clipboard. Close the Component Properties dialog of the Parameter Form portlet.

Select the Edit action (pencil icon) of the Parameter Display portlet. Navigate to the Events tab and select the event name that belongs to the event producer Parameter Form portlet. In our example, you see two events: one belongs to the Parameter Form portlet, the other one to the Parameter Display portlet. Since the automatically generated event names contain the unique portlet ID to which they belong, identifying the one that belongs to the event producer Parameter Form portlet is not too hard. In the Action field select the only action available, and make sure the Enable Action checkbox is selected. When you're selecting Constant, you can specify an EL in the actual parameter value field. Enter the following EL in the field:

```
${payLoad.ora_wsrp_navigparam_Parameter1}
```

Figure 6-24 shows how to define the event mapping for the Parameter Display portlet.

Last, switch to the Display Options tab, where you can the Partial Triggers attribute of the Parameter Display portlet. The value will be the ID of the Parameter Form portlet that you copied to the clipboard earlier in this section.

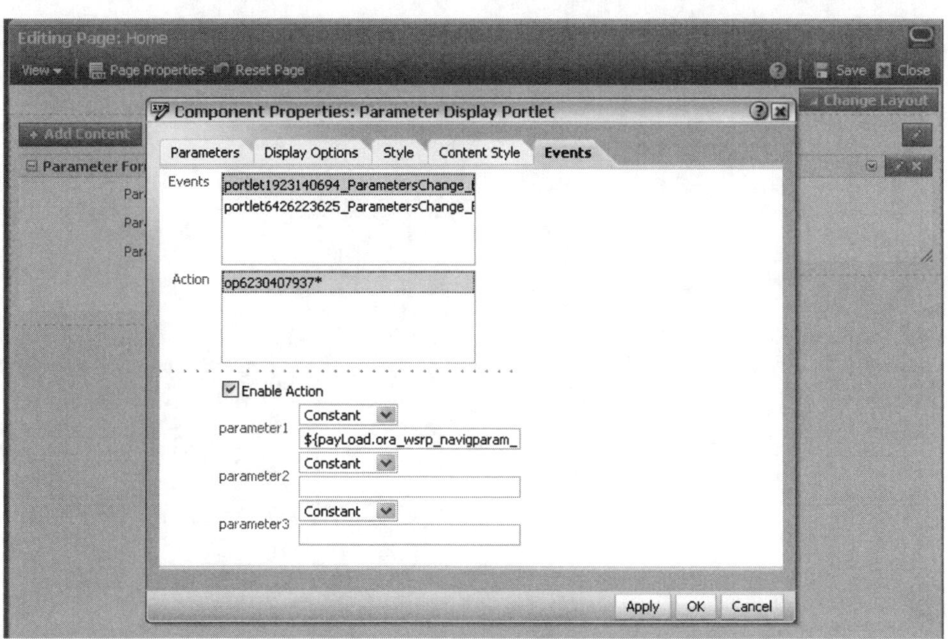

FIGURE 6-24 *Creating the event mapping in Composer at run time*

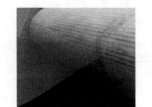

CHAPTER 7

Integrating Content Systems

An essential part of any application is content. Content can be various things, the most obvious one being pictures of some kind (product pictures, personnel pictures, etc.), but it can also be document-style content. If you are using a project management application, you might want to manage structured data about the project, like open tasks, through the application. Projects usually also include unstructured information in the form of documents such as reports and meeting minutes; this information needs managing and, ideally, should be managed and accessible through the same application as the structured information about the project.

Oracle WebCenter provides mechanisms that allow you to manage unstructured content in a professional content management system and expose that content in your WebCenter application. In addition, you can expose content from third-party content management systems through the use of adapters adhering to the Java Content Repository (JCR) standard.

NOTE

The Java Content Repository standard (JCR, aka JSR 170 and JSR 283) describes the access to content stored in a content management system through Java APIs as well as a common object model representing the content itself. The idea behind JCR is similar to the idea behind Java Database Connectivity (JDBC): to provide a common interface to access information from a Java application regardless of the type of repository (or storage mechanism) used. In order to do so, a group of industry experts created an API definition and object model that provided a base set of capabilities in read, query, write, and search. This initial release was JCR 1.0, also known as JSR 170. JCR works by way of adapters, similar to JDBC, that represent the interface between native repository APIs and the standard-defined JCR APIs.

Oracle WebCenter provides a set of JCR adapters (File System, Oracle Portal, and Oracle Universal Content Management) out of the box and ones (e.g., Microsoft SharePoint, EMC Documentum, and Lotus Domino) that can be licensed separately.

Because the JCR standard is quite complex and hard to get used to, Oracle WebCenter includes a Data Control to simplify the interaction with JCR within a WebCenter application. In this chapter we will discuss the mechanisms you can choose from to integrate content into your application.

There are two main mechanisms to choose from:

- **Content Repository Data Control** If all you want to do is provide read-only access to the content repository, but want to completely control the way the results are presented, you can use the Content Repository Data Control to bind regular view components, such as tables, to the data set returned through the JCR adapter.
- **Document Service** The Document Service provides several task flows, complex reusable components, that facilitate various aspects of document management, such as a complete file management component (Document Library) and various document presentation components. These components can be bound to a Content Repository Connection to present the content items.

Connecting to Content

Before you can think about how and what you want to expose from your content repository, you need to create a connection to that repository. To do so, you need to expand the Application Resources panel and right-click on the Connections folder to invoke the context menu. There you simply select the New Connection and then the Content Repository entry (Figure 7-1), which will bring up the Create Content Repository Connection wizard.

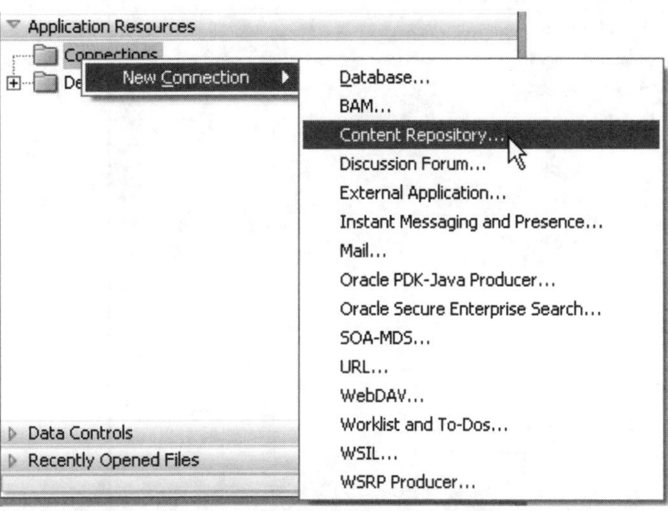

FIGURE 7-1 *Invoking the Create Content Repository Connection wizard*

The wizard lets you create a new connection using one of the installed adapters. For your first connection you are going to connect to the file system as your content repository of sorts.

You will create the connection in Application Resources and name it MyFirstConnection. For the Repository Type select File System (Figure 7-2). The File System adapter is provided so you can easily try content applications without the need of a proper repository. It is, however, not meant for production use. So once you are familiar with the content integration you should develop your applications against the target repository (Oracle Universal Content Management (UCM) is an example). You don't need to worry about the default connection setting yet. A bit later in this chapter you are going to use the Document Service and then decide which connection needs to be set as the default connection.

Next you need to provide the values for the necessary adapter parameters. In the current case, with the File System adapter, the only parameter needed is the path that the adapter should use as its root. You can specify any path you want—let's choose d:\. Now you can use the Test Connection button to see if the adapter works fine.

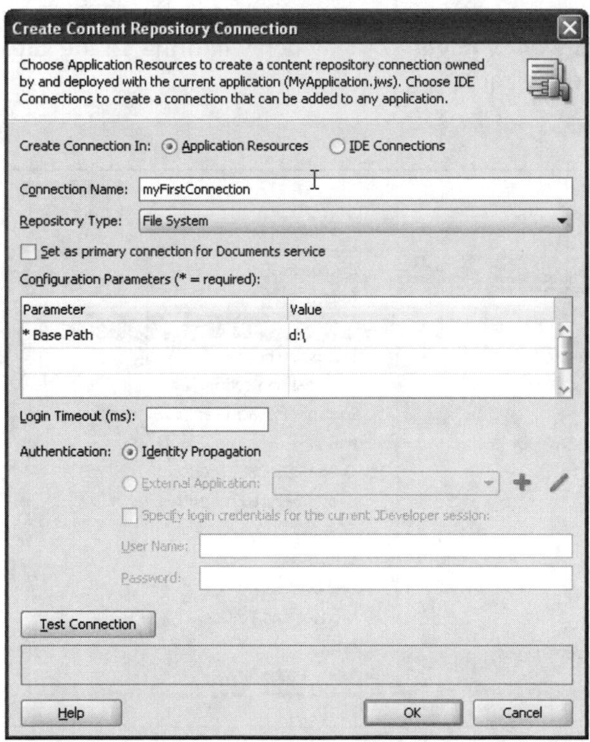

FIGURE 7-2 *Browsing the repository through the JDeveloper Connection dialog*

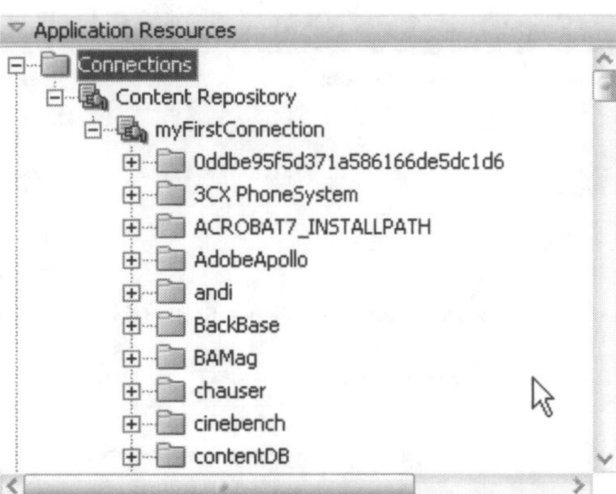

FIGURE 7-3 *Invoking the Create Content Repository Data Control wizard*

To see if the adapter works correctly and retrieves the content items you can expand the Connections node in the Application Resources panel; you should see the content stored at the location provided as the root folder for the connection (Figure 7-3).

Simple Table of Content

You have just created a multipurpose connection that you will first use to create a simple table of files stored at that location. To do so you have to create a data control using this connection. Simply right-click on the model project and invoke the New Gallery by clicking on the New icon in the context menu. From the New Gallery select the Content Repository Data Control, which can be found under the Business Tier | Content Repository section.

Another way to create a data control is to right-click on the respective connection and choose Create Data Control from the context menu.

Now you will be presented with the Create Content Repository Data Control wizard. There you need to specify the necessary information for the data control, starting with the name for it. Then you can select the connection you want to use. In your case, the choice is simple, as you have defined only one connection so far (Figure 7-4).

Finally, there is the list of custom attributes. A custom attribute can be used to expose adapter-specific content metadata. In this simple example you'll leave the custom attributes unchanged. What you have created is a data control that you can

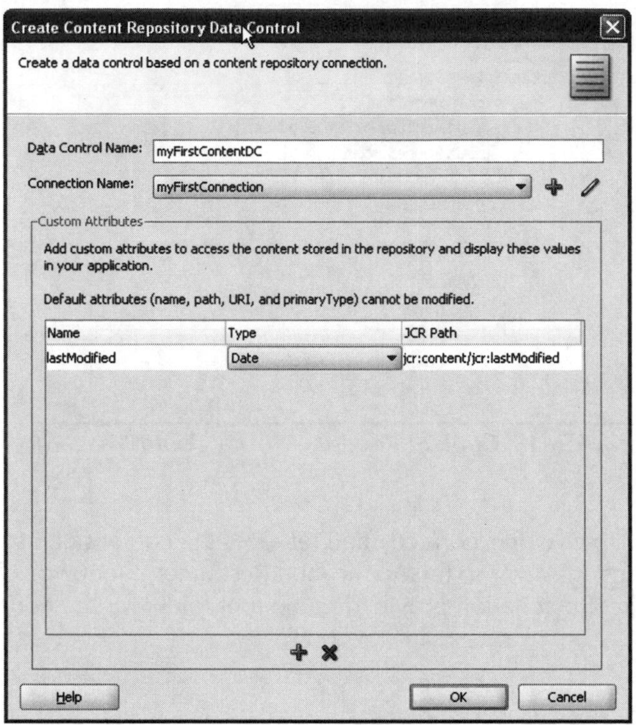

FIGURE 7-4 *Creating a content data control*

examine in the Data Controls panel exposing a set of operations you can perform with the content (Figure 7-5):

- **advancedSearch** Performs a search for attribute values or full-text.
- **getAttributes** Returns a list of attribute and their values for a given folder or a document.
- **getItems** Returns the list of nodes (files and/or folders) at a given location.
- **getURI** Returns the URL that can be used to return the binary content of a given item in the content repository.
- **search** Performs a simple version of search that lets you search using full-text or name pattern search.

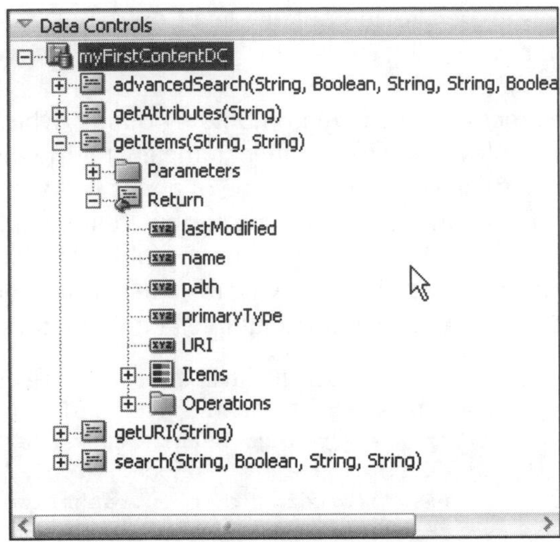

FIGURE 7-5 *The content data control*

In the current example you are going to use the getItems method to present a list of files using a simple ADF Table. You simply drag-and-drop the return node of the getItems method to the page and select ADF Read-Only Table from the Create menu (Figure 7-6).

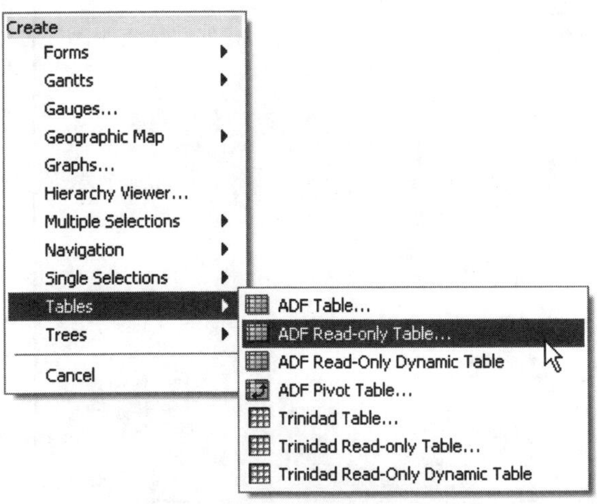

FIGURE 7-6 *Creating an ADF Read-Only Table*

The Edit Table dialog shows all attributes that the return set contains. Had you defined custom attributes in the Create Content Data Control wizard, they would also be shown. You can now modify the column headers and remove unwanted columns, among other things.

Another step in the process, the Edit Action Binding dialog (which is brought up automatically for you) allows you to specify parameters for the method (Figure 7-7)—in your case, the starting folder and the type of nodes you want returned. Let's specify / for the starting folder and leave the Type attribute empty (alternatively you could nt:file or nt:folder to limit the result set to files or folders).

Let's take a look what was created by the wizards. First switch into Code view. There you can see an af:table tag containing multiple af:column tags.

```
<af:table value="#{bindings.Return.collectionModel}" var="row"
          rows="#{bindings.Return.rangeSize}"
          emptyText="#{bindings.Return.viewable ?
          'No data to display.' : 'Access Denied.'}"
          fetchSize="#{bindings.Return.rangeSize}">
  <af:column sortProperty="name" sortable="false"
             headerText="#{bindings.Return.hints.name.label}">
    <af:outputText value="#{row.name}"/>
```

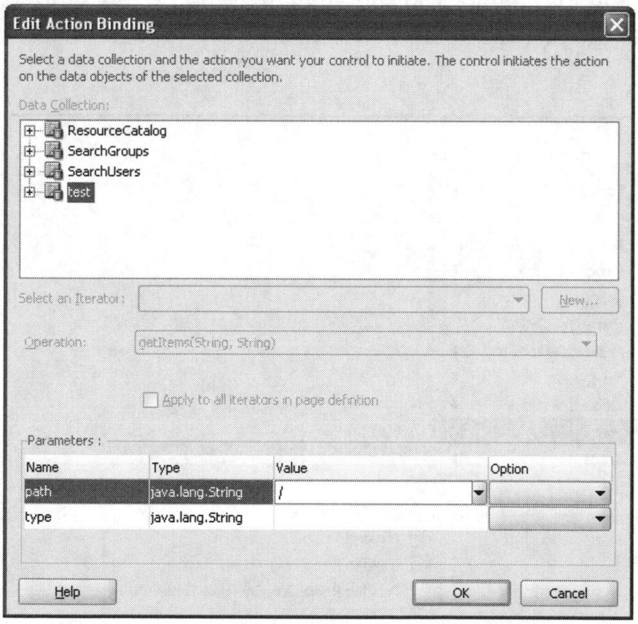

FIGURE 7-7 *The Edit Action Binding dialog*

The af:table contains several references to objects starting with bindings and row. *Bindings* refer to definitions in the Page Definition, which you will take a look at in a second. The *row* references (e.g., ${row.name}) are the references to columns in the result set, which are the attributes you defined during the Data Control creation plus the default ones like name, etc.

To look at the bindings, switch into the Bindings view by clicking the Bindings tab of the editor at the bottom of the window (Figure 7-8).

There you can follow all the bindings that are used on the page, and by clicking on the link at the top of this page you can open the Page Definition. This file will be your friend later on when you dig deeper into WebCenter. Just out of curiosity, click on the link and then switch into Source view for the Page Definition (Figure 7-9).

If you look closely you will find familiar names in that file. This is the XML representation of the bindings you saw earlier in the graphical view on the Bindings view.

You are ready to run your first Content page. Simply go back to the JSPX file in the editor and click Run. After a bit your browser will present you with a table that might look familiar. Comparing it with your file system, you fill find that all files and folders are listed in this table. The column PrimaryType, for example, indicates whether the respective item shown in this row is a file (nt:file) or a folder (nt:folder).

Through some simple maneuvers you can achieve some nice user interaction enhancements. For example, you could convert the filename into a link and then use the URI attribute to point the link to the file binary.

Simply right-click on the outputText element representing row.name and select Convert from the context menu. It can be a bit tricky sometimes to select nested items in the Design view, so you can use the Structure panel to verify that the correct element is selected, or select it there in the first place. Because you want to create a link to the binary file, you need to convert the name into a goLink component.

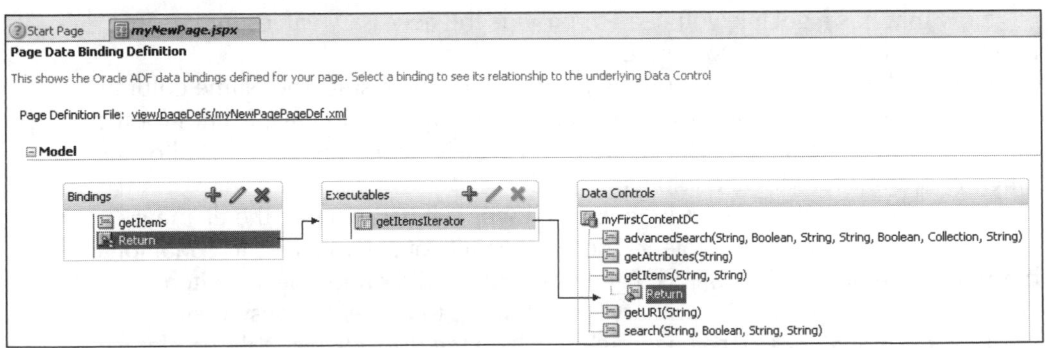

FIGURE 7-8 *The Bindings view*

Start Page | myNewPage.jspx | myNewPagePageDef.xml

Find

```
<?xml version="1.0" encoding="UTF-8" ?>
<pageDefinition xmlns="http://xmlns.oracle.com/adfm/uimodel"
                version="11.1.1.52.3" id="myNewPagePageDef"
                Package="view.pageDefs">
  <parameters/>
  <executables>
    <methodIterator Binds="getItems.result" DataControl="myFirstContentDC"
                    RangeSize="25"
                    BeanClass="model.myFirstContentDC.getItems_return"
                    id="getItemsIterator"/>
  </executables>
  <bindings>
    <methodAction id="getItems" RequiresUpdateModel="true" Action="invokeMethod"
                  MethodName="getItems" IsViewObjectMethod="false"
                  DataControl="myFirstContentDC" InstanceName="myFirstContentDC"
                  ReturnName="myFirstContentDC.methodResults.getItems_myFirstContentDC_getItems_result">
      <NamedData NDName="path" NDValue="\" NDType="java.lang.String"/>
      <NamedData NDName="type" NDType="java.lang.String"/>
    </methodAction>
    <tree IterBinding="getItemsIterator" id="Return">
      <nodeDefinition DefName="model.myFirstContentDC.getItems_return">
        <AttrNames>
          <Item Value="name"/>
          <Item Value="path"/>
          <Item Value="URI"/>
          <Item Value="primaryType"/>
          <Item Value="lastModified"/>
        </AttrNames>
      </nodeDefinition>
    </tree>
  </bindings>
</pageDefinition>
```

FIGURE 7-9 *The Page Definition XML*

Now that it is a goLink, you need to provide the necessary values for the Text and the Destination property (Figure 7-10).

Having done that, you can run the page and see the result. The Name column now has links in every line. However, what you really want to have is links for files only. This can be achieved by introducing an af:switcher component that allows different options for files and folders.

As described earlier, the attribute primaryType defines whether the element returned represents a file or a folder. The functionality of af:switcher is to conditionally branch to one of its child objects. Facets are valid children for the af:switcher component. You will use the primaryType attribute to trigger the af:switcher.

To add the switcher to the page, right-click on the respective af:column element and select Insert Inside af:column | ADF Faces from the context menu (Figure 7-11).

FIGURE 7-10 *Property Inspector*

To switch between the facets, you need to use the Property Inspector to set the value of the switcher's FacetName attribute. Since your condition depends on the value of PrimaryType, you are going to set the value of FacetName to #{row.primaryType}. You could also set the defaultFacet attribute value to a valid one, such as nt:file.

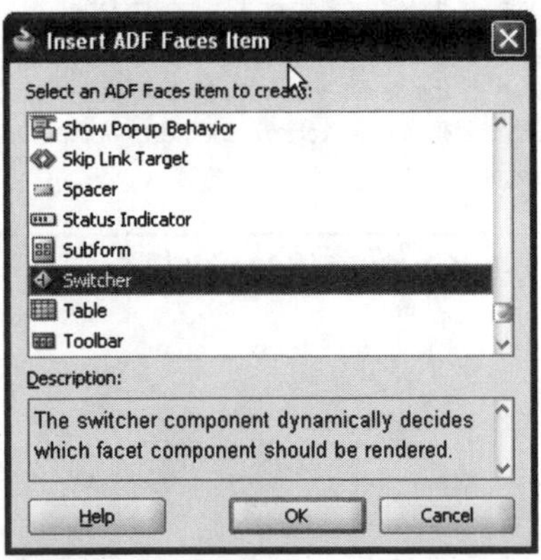

FIGURE 7-11 *The Insert ADF Faces Item dialog*

Next you need to add the options for the af:switcher component (Figure 7-12). You need a facet for each possible value of primaryType. Luckily there can only be two: nt:file and nt:folder. Following the example from earlier, you want the name column of the table to be a link for files and just text for folders. To get that you need to add two facets as children to the af:switcher.

Simply right-click on the af:switcher, select Insert Inside af:switcher, and select the Facet from the context menu. You will be presented with a dialog where you can specify the name for the facet; specify the string nt:file there and click OK. Repeat, but this time specify nt:folder for the name of the facet.

Now you can start fleshing out what you want to see for each of these facets. For nt:files, where you want a link to the file's binary, you can simply drag-and-drop the af:goLink you already have into the facet.

For the nt:folder simply right-click on the nt:folder facet and select Insert Inside f:facet | ADF Faces from the context menu. You will be presented with a dialog to select the Faces component. Select OutputText from there. You will see the outputText component in the nt:folder facet. Select it and in the Property Inspector provide #{row.name} as the value for the Value property.

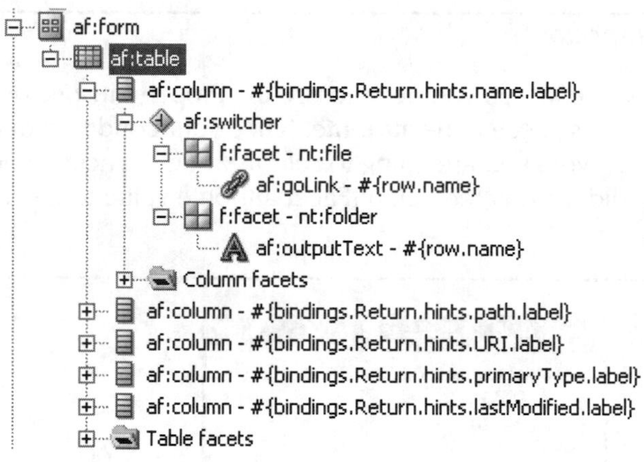

FIGURE 7-12 *The page structure after adding the switcher*

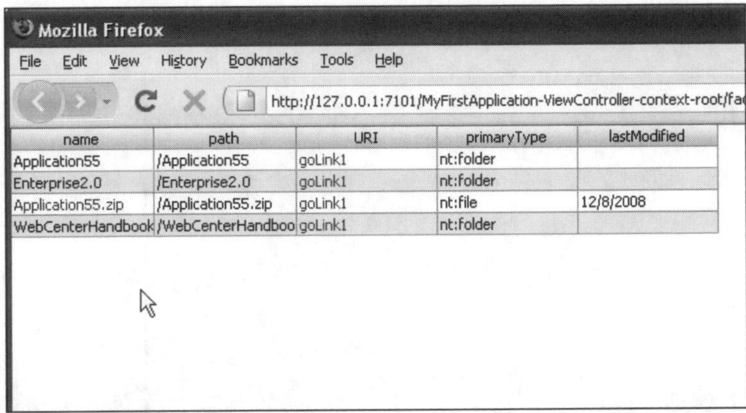

FIGURE 7-13 *Rendered table with af:switcher*

Now if you run the page you will see the table with the entries listed (Figure 7-13). The files are displayed as links; the folders are displayed as simple text.

Performing a Search with the Data Control

Our next challenge will be to allow passing in parameters to the Data Control to perform operations such as search. The basic method is the same. All you need to do is drag-and-drop three relevant things.

First you take the Search node and drop it as a Command Button. You can find this under the Methods menu. Like earlier, the Edit Action Binding dialog will show up. This time a couple of other attributes are shown. Specify / for the path and true for the attribute isRecursive (Figure 7-14).

Next you need to create an input field so a user can enter the search term. For simplicity let's do a name search. Expand the Parameters node and drag the namePattern node onto the page. From the menu select ADF Input Field /w label. Last, but not least, you need to create a table for the search results. For this, like

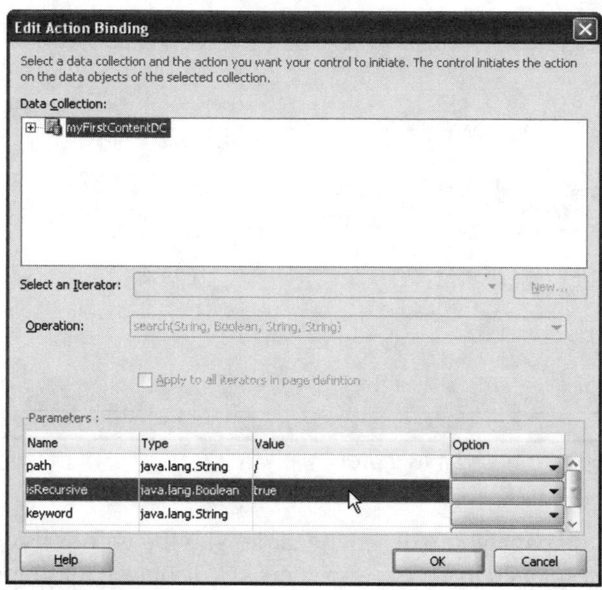

FIGURE 7-14 *The Edit Action Binding dialog*

earlier, take the Returns node (this time from the search method though) and drop it as an ADF Read-Only Table on the page (Figure 7-15).

All the necessary wiring is done by the wizard. Imagine how long it would have taken you to do all that in plain Java.

FIGURE 7-15 *The resulting page*

One small detail to mention here: for namePattern searches, the JCR standard used under the covers requires % to be used as the wildcard character. So either you train your users accordingly or you provide some Java code that scans for the commonly used * and replaces it with %, to be on the safe side.

Using Images from the Content Repository in Your Application

Another common requirement for applications is using images to enhance the visual appearance of your application. Usually such images are part of your application resources. In certain cases, for example in the context of a product information application, the requirement could be that the images should come from the content repository. The easiest way to achieve this is to browse the content repository in the Connections panel and simply drag the required image onto the page. JDeveloper will give you the option to (1) move the asset into the project and, by doing that convert it into an application resource, or (2) leave it in the repository and access it via the connection.

Using the Document Service Components

Another, and much more convenient, way to create a content integration is the Document Service. It comprises various components that you can use to present content in your application. The components can be found under the Document Library group in the Component Palette.

- **Document Library—List View** Here you can display a list of content items (Figure 7-16). This component is highly customizable and lets you specify the location and other query criteria to select content from and whether users should be allowed to browse through the resulting content. When used within the context of a composer/page editor page this component can be further customized in page edit mode.

- **Document Library—Recent Documents** The Recent Documents task flow (Figure 7-17) allows you to present the user with a list of documents that were recently accessed. This can come in handy when you want to provide a view of recent activities across your document repository.

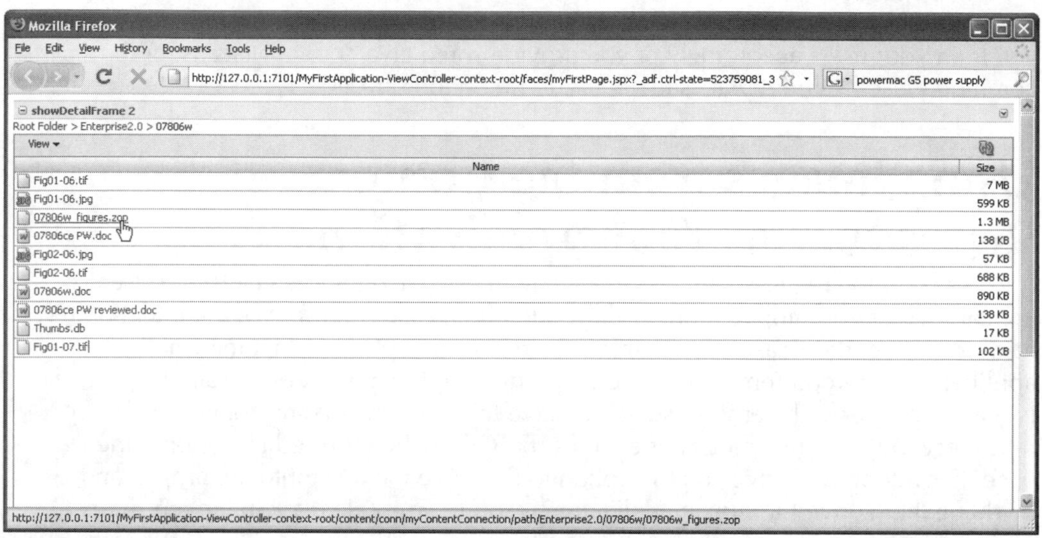

FIGURE 7-16 *The List View task flow*

- **Document Library—Document Library** This is a complex component that allows you to perform complex document management functions, such as uploading documents, inspecting and changing file properties, and much more (Figure 7-18). You will go more into the functionality of the Document Library region later in this chapter. Depending on the capability of the connection, the features allow read-only or read/write access.

FIGURE 7-17 *The Recent Documents task flow*

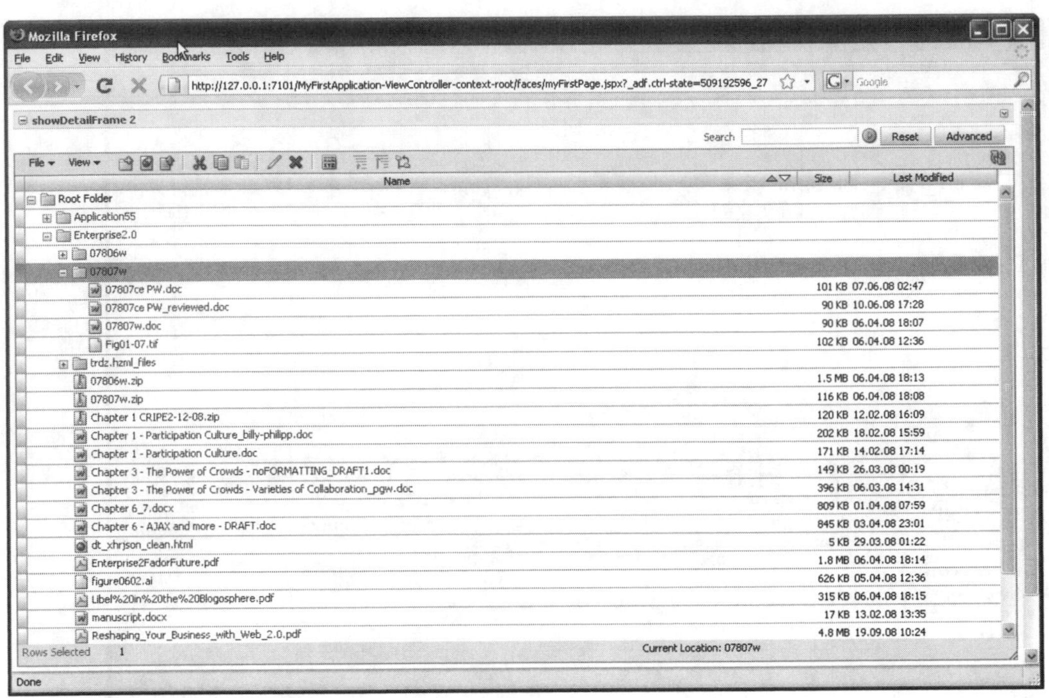

FIGURE 7-18 *The Document Library task flow*

Content-Enabling Your First Application

In Chapter 5 you created your first WebCenter application. Granted it was not very glamorous, but you will change that here and now. The idea is to content enable the application you created earlier.

Let's create a Document Library and a List Viewer instance on the page, each in a separate ShowDetailFrame on the page (Figure 7-19). You already have the ShowDetailFrames from earlier. The easiest way to add a UI element for a given content repository connection is to simply drag-and-drop the connection from the

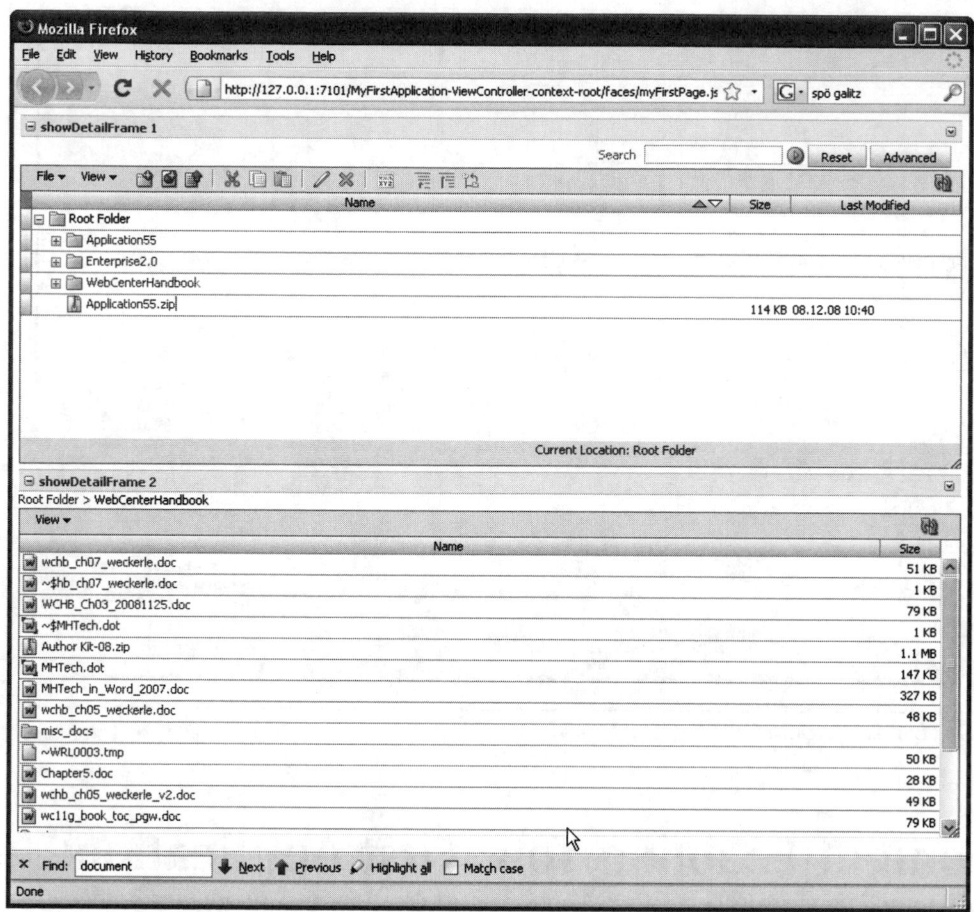

FIGURE 7-19 *Comparison Document Library with List View task flow*

Connections panel into the respective ShowDetailFrame on the page (Figure 7-20). You will be presented with a drop menu where you can select what UI element you want to create. For the top ShowDetailFrame we will choose Documents, which represents the Document Library task flow.

The Edit Task Flow Binding dialog will come up. Here you can specify the necessary values for the task flow. Because you have invoked the Binding editor by dropping a connection onto a page, the dialog is already prefilled with certain values,

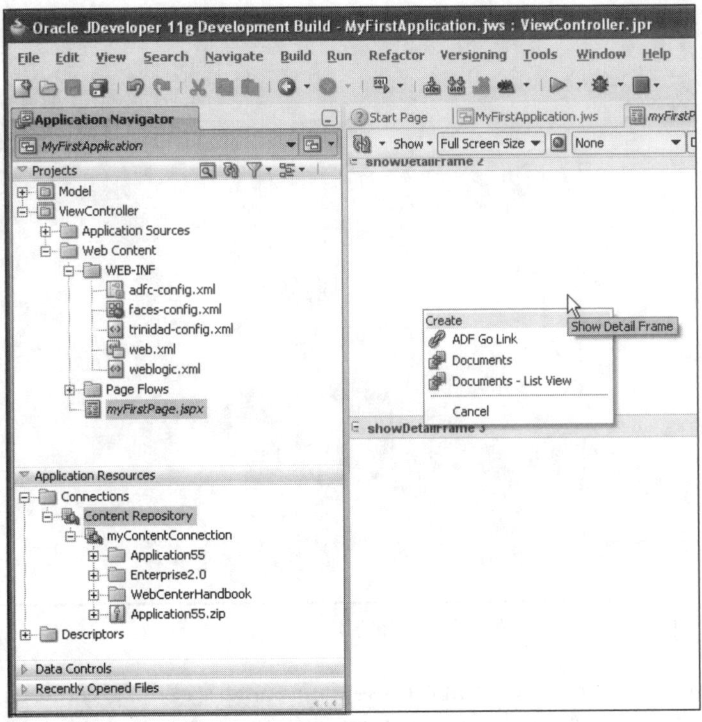

FIGURE 7-20 *Dropping the connection on a page*

like the name of the connection to use and the starting folder (Figure 7-21).

As we discussed earlier, you can actually drill down into your connection within the Connections panel, and instead of dropping the whole connection, you could drop a folder or subfolder onto the page. This would set the startFolderPath parameter respectively.

Done! Well, not quite. But before you continue on to adding the List View task flow, take a closer look at the Document Library task flow.

FIGURE 7-21 *The Edit Task Flow Binding dialog*

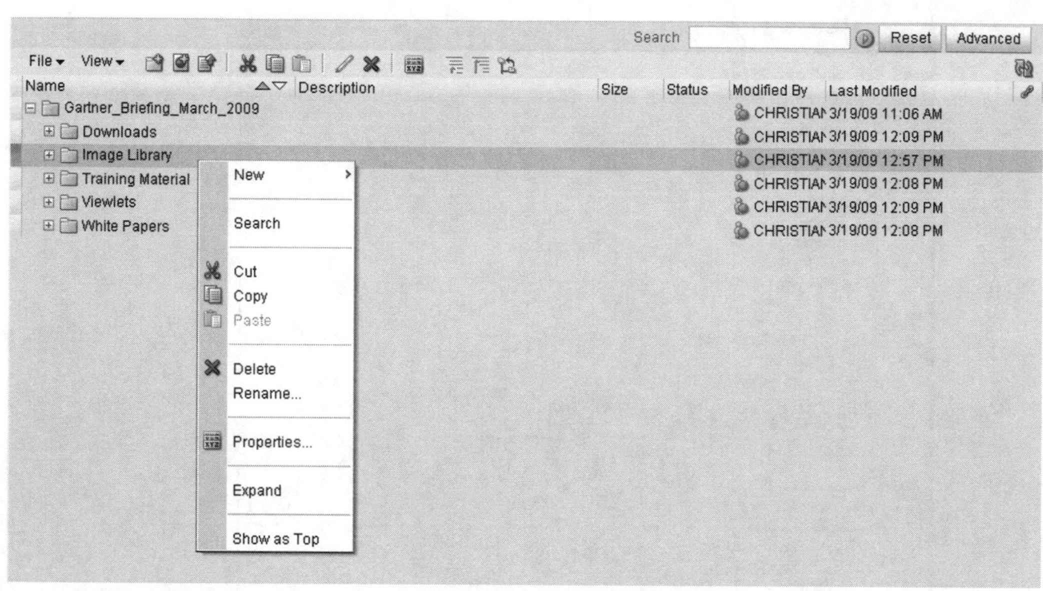

FIGURE 7-22 *Document Library base functionality*

Using Document Library you can browse your content at the given location. By clicking on the right mouse button you can invoke the context menu for the selected item (Figure 7-22). The context menu gives you access to relevant operations for the selected file or folder:

- **Edit in Rich Text Editor** Document Library allows you to edit HTML documents in-place in your application. For this it provides a built-in rich text editor (Figure 7-23) where users can edit in a WYSIWYG style, with no HTML knowledge needed. For files with .htm or .html extension, this option will be active.

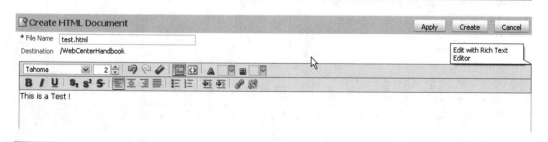

FIGURE 7-23 *The Rich Text Editor*

- **Email URL** This will open your standard Compose e-mail dialog (e.g., Thunderbird, Outlook, etc.) with the URL to the selected document in the mail body. This is helpful if you want to perform a Send to Friend operation for a particular document.
- **Cut/Copy/Paste** Document Library also supports regular clipboard actions to move elements around in the content system; however, this Cut/Copy/Paste is limited to the Document Library's internal clipboard and will not link up with the operating-level clipboard. This also requires a connection with read/write support. The same operations can be performed directly with simple drag-and-drop. Cut/Copy/Paste is internally handled like regular document operations, so for Paste, for example, the underlying repository will handle the action as a regular document creation or check-in, so if this operation requires workflow approvals, the result might not be immediately visible to the users performing the operation.
- **Delete** Deleting requires a read/write-enabled content connection. This will, however, honor any workflows or delete protection defined by the back-end system. This could result in unexpected behaviors if delete is specially handled in the back-end repository.
- **Rename** This operation will rename the file. (It requires connection with read/write support.)
- **Properties** Here you can see the files properties.
- **Show As Top** Usually you would provide a starting folder for a Document Library task flow. This folder is used as the root in your view. With Show As Top you can promote a subfolder to become the root of this particular view. This is useful if your application should always start at a certain level but the users should then have the ability to change the starting folder easily.

In addition to Show As Top (second from the right) there are two more icons on the toolbar, immediately left of Show As Top, that allow navigation relative to the set starting folder. Go Up and Go To Top allow navigation to the set starting folder or to the one defined by the developer, once you browse deeper down in the hierarchy.

While the toolbar (Figure 7-24) and the context menu will be the two most popular access mechanisms for operations, some of the features from the context menu are exposed through the toolbar menu—the File menu (Figure 7-25).

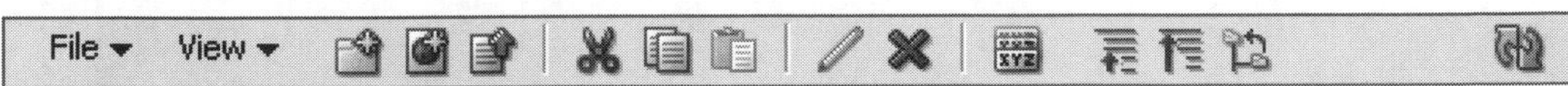

FIGURE 7-24 *Document Library toolbar*

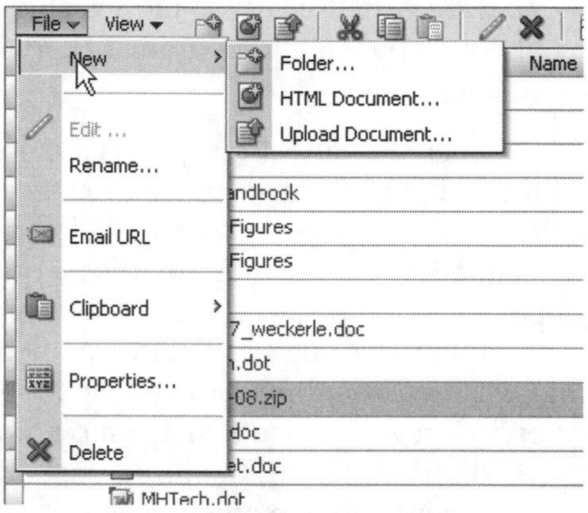

FIGURE 7-25 *The File menu*

Here you can, for example, create a new folder or document, or upload a document. The invoked operation is still the same.

Leveraging the List View

In certain cases, all an application needs is a read-only view on a particular folder to limit the possible operations to browse and open, and prevent the user from uploading new documents. For this purpose, Oracle WebCenter provides the List View task flow (Figure 7-26).

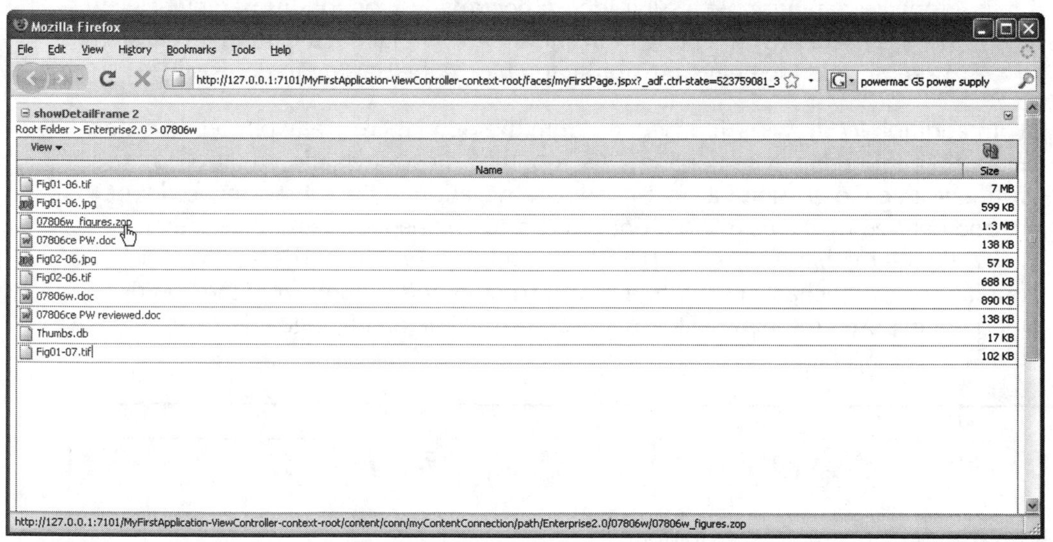

FIGURE 7-26 *The List View task flow*

The purpose of the List View task flow is to provide more control over the way files are presented. You can limit the list through various parameters:

- **Show Folders** The parameter defines whether the List View should allow drilling down into subfolders or just display the files in the given location.
- **Connection Name** Here you provide the name of the connection to use (e.g., ${'myCSConnection'}).
- **Start Folder Path** Here you can specify the starting location, like you can with the Document Library task flow.
- **Last Modifier** Only documents are listed that were last modified by the specified user (e.g., ${'Philipp'}).
- **Last Modified After, Last Modified Before** Only documents modified after or before the given date will be listed. The date needs to follow ISO8601 (e.g., `${'2008-08-07T18:24:36.000Z'})`. Actually the JCR specifications demand the format `sYYYY-MM-DDThh:mm:ss.sssTZD`, which is one of the valid ISO8601 formats.
- **Max Documents** This parameter specifies how many entries should be shown by the task flow.
- **Most Recent First** This Boolean parameter specifies whether the most recently modified document should be listed first or last, defining the sort order within the list.

Content Server—WebCenter's Built-in Enterprise Content Management

So far you have seen the WebCenter content integration components and their functionality using the simple File System adapter. In a professional environment, however, storing an application's content in the file system will not suffice for various reasons, and a content management system will take its place.

Oracle WebCenter Suite includes Content Server, the foundation behind Oracle's Enterprise Content Management solution called Oracle Universal Content Management (Oracle UCM). Content Server provides all the necessary functionality that is required to perform document management at an enterprise scale from within your WebCenter application.

Because it is the foundation for Oracle Universal Content Management, the choice is yours whether you want to expand the scope for content management beyond pure document management into more sophisticated areas, such as Records Management, Digital Asset Management, or Web Content Management, all of which are covered by Oracle's Enterprise Content Management platform (Figure 7-27).

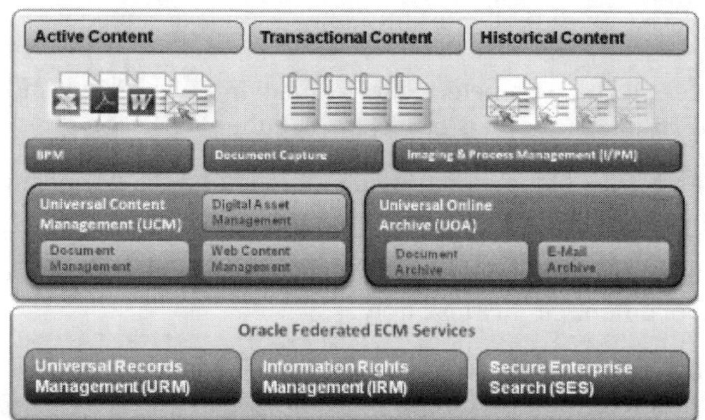

FIGURE 7-27 *The Oracle Enterprise Content Management platform*

To understand the integration between Oracle Content Server and Oracle WebCenter you first have to understand the basic concepts behind Oracle Content Server.

Content Server facilitates the basic aspects of document management. It allows the administrator to set up different kinds of constructs that allow the efficient storage and retrieval of documents as well as their attribution and full-text indexing for search.

Concepts

A main element in Content Server is an item. An item is the atomic entity that represents a document stored in the system by combining the binary document and its associated attributes into one object.

Within an item, the content can be versioned, which allows us to keep track of document changes and, if necessary, roll back to a previous version if the edits were proven wrong.

More advanced features, such as Records or Digital Asset Management, are available only in Oracle Universal Content Management, the product that is built on Content Server as a foundation.

Oracle Content Server comes with a comfortable web user interface that can be used to manage stored content. In addition the so-called Desktop Integration Suite allows accessing Oracle Content Server from your Windows Explorer, the Microsoft Office Suite, or through the Lotus Notes Client. It ensures an even smoother integration into existing client environments. Users can interact with content directly in Windows Explorer or the MS Office dialogs to locate, open, or save documents.

Oracle Content Server also provides a number of additional mechanisms through which you can extend the content management experience or integrate it with other applications:

- **Web services** Pretty much every operation in Content Server can be exposed as a web service following both SOAP and REST. Through this, content management can be integrated into pretty much any application that supports either of those standards.
- **Content Integration Suite** This Java™ API is geared toward more complex integration scenarios. It requires a separate Java™ application, the CIS Server, to run alongside Content Server. It handles the communication between the third-party application and the Content Server back end.

One big advantage of CIS is the fact that an application can be considered "trusted," which means it can simply hand over a user's identity, as determined by a login process, to Content Server and therefore achieve Single Sign-On. The SOAP web services, while simple and easy to use, would require a login with each request to ensure the user's identity.

In order to leverage CIS, there are several setup steps that need to be performed on the application server side, to enable and configure CIS for use with Content Server.

These steps are documented in the Content Integration Services Installation Guide on Oracle's Technology Network and exceed the scope of this book.

Content Server Web UI

As we mentioned, Content Server has a comfortable web user interface (Figure 7-28) that users can use right out of the box to manage documents.

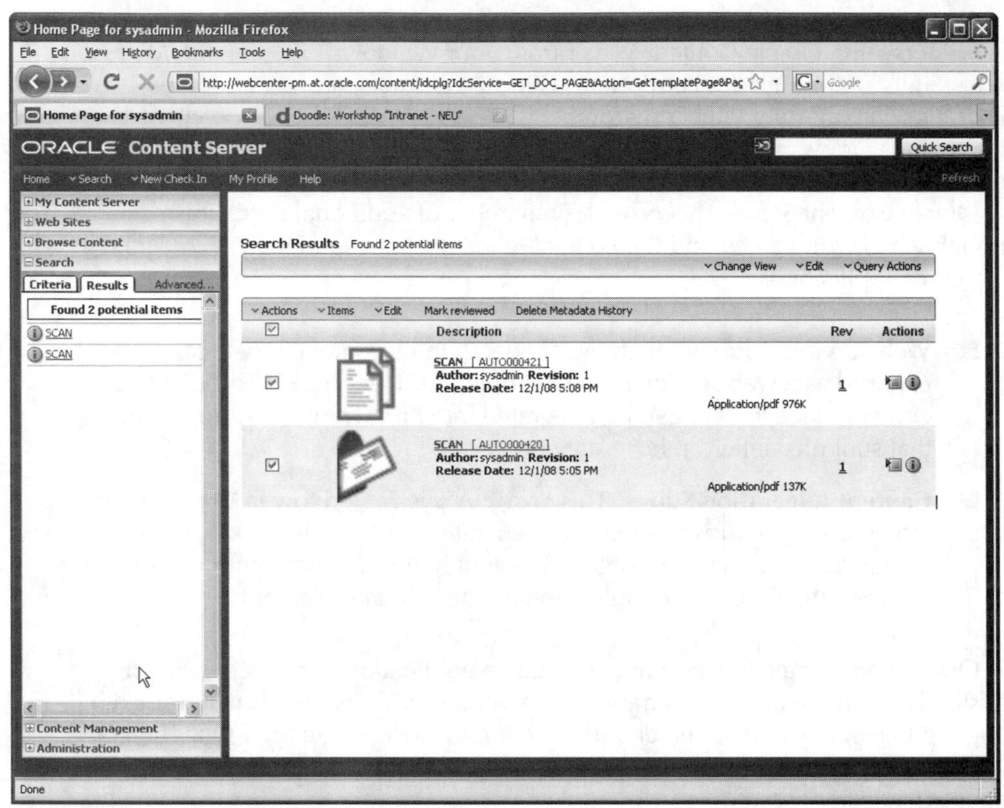

FIGURE 7-28 *The Content Server web UI*

All major operations, such as uploading, attribution, modifying, and searching, are exposed there. This user interface can be used to communicate with Content Server and manage content. Another possible way is to use Content Server's Desktop Integration Suite (Figure 7-29), which will install an extension on your Windows system allowing you to access content server functionality from Windows Explorer.

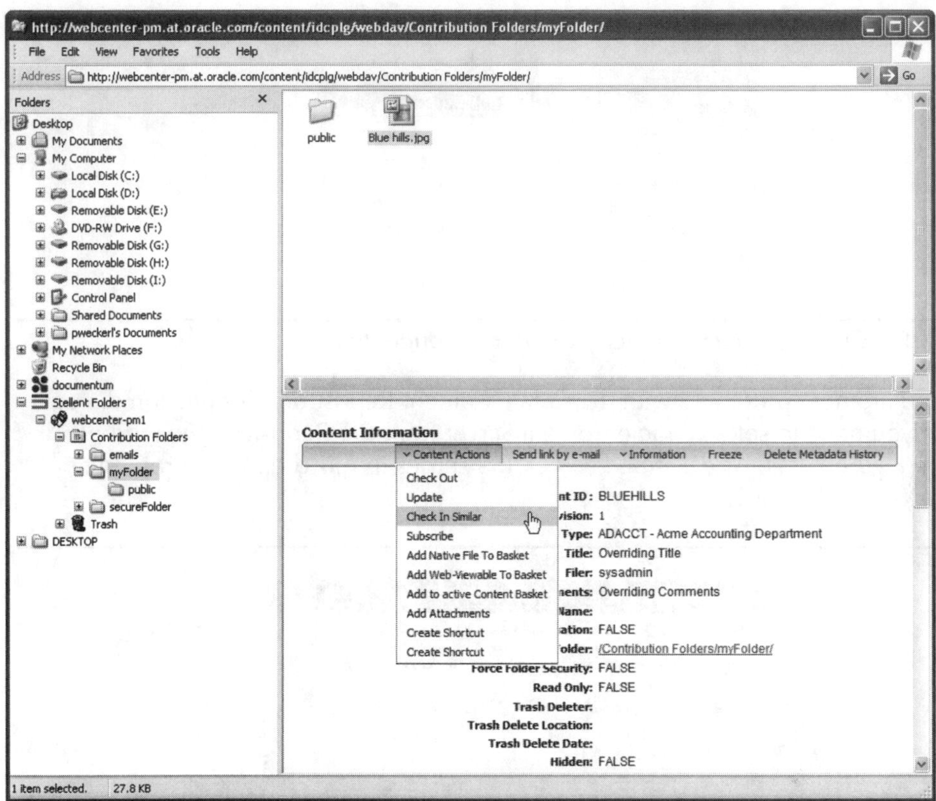

FIGURE 7-29 *Desktop integration*

Setting Up the Data Control with Content Server

In order to use Content Server as your content source, you need to configure a Content Server connection and create a Data Control for it. To do so, simply right-click on the Content Repository node under Connections in the Application Resources panel. Alternatively you can always go via File | New or the New button in the toolbar (Figure 7-30).

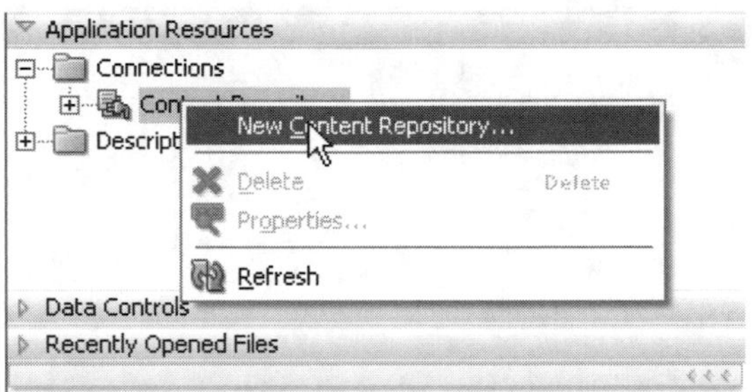

FIGURE 7-30 *Creating a New Content Repository connection*

You are now presented with the Create Content Repository Connection dialog. There you need to select Oracle Content Server from the Repository Type drop-down (Figure 7-31). As described earlier, the entries in this drop-down represent the registered JCR adapters.

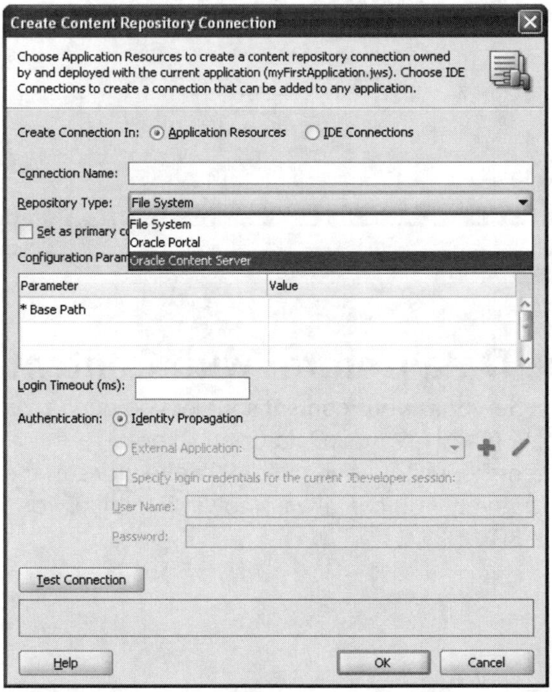

FIGURE 7-31 *Selecting the Content Server Repository Type*

Once you select Oracle Content Server you will see the list of necessary attributes change to those necessary for Oracle Content Server:

- **CIS Socket Type** This attribute determines whether CIS connects on the content server listener port or the web server filter. It accepts `socket`, `socketssl`, or `web`.
  - **socket** Uses an `intradoc` socket connection to connect to the Oracle Content Server. The client IP address must be added to the list of authorized addresses in the Oracle Content Server.
  - **socketssl** Uses an `intradoc` socket connection to connect to the Oracle Content Server that is secured using the SSL protocol. The client's certificates must be imported in the server's trust store for the connection to be allowed.
  - **web** Uses an HTTP(S) connection to connect to the Oracle Content Server.
- **Server Host Name** Name of the Oracle Content Server instance; for example, `content-server.mycompany.com`.
- **Content Server Listener Port** Port of the server specified in the Server Hostname field; for example, `4444`.
- **URL of the Web Server Plugin** If the CIS socket type is `web`, then the URL must be in this format: `http://hostname/webroot/idcplg`.
- **CIS Temporary Directory** This is blank, by default.
- **KeyStore File Location** The keystore location can be a relative path.
- **KeyStore Password** The password required to access the keystore.
- **Private Key Alias** The client private key alias in the keystore. The key is used to sign messages to the server. The public key corresponding to this private key must be imported in the server keystore.
- **Private Key Password** The client private key password required to retrieve the key from the keystore.

The Recent Documents Task Flow

The main reason we discuss the Recent Documents task flow after the introduction into Content Server (Figure 7-32) is that this task flow is supported only in conjunction with Content Server due to limitations in the other supported JCR adapters. After adding the task flow to a page, you can set parameters to limit the list of files displayed (Figure 7-33).

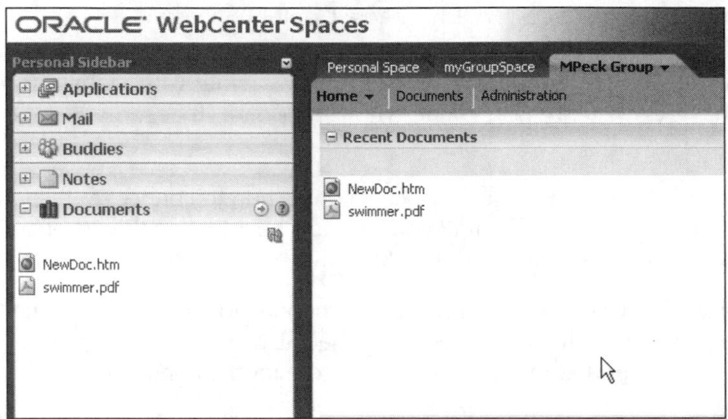

FIGURE 7-32 *Recent Documents task flow used in WebCenter Spaces*

All parameter values need to be specified in EL syntax, being ${'…'}. Below are the parameters and tips on their use:

- **Connection Name** You provide the name of the connection to use (e.g., ${'myCSConnection'}).
- **Last Modifier** Only documents are listed that were last modified by the specified user (e.g., ${'Philipp'}). If left blank, it will default to the currently logged-in application user. You can use a wildcard (e.g., %) if you want to list all documents, regardless of their modifier.
- **Last Modified After, Last Modified Before** Only documents modified after or before the given date will be listed. The date needs to follow ISO8601 (e.g., `${'2008-08-07T18:24:36.000Z'})`. As mentioned earlier, the JCR specifications actually demand the format `sYYYY-MM-DDThh:mm:ss.sssTZD`, which is one of the valid ISO8601 formats.
- **Max Documents** This parameter specifies how many entries should be shown by the task flow.
- **Most Recent First** This Boolean parameter specifies whether the most recently modified document should be listed first or last, defining the sort order within the list.

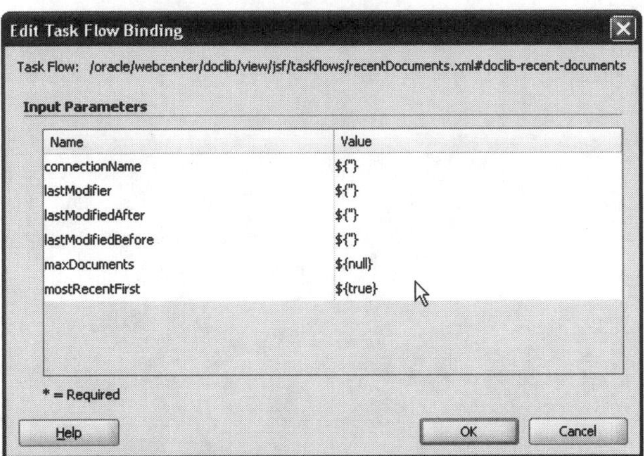

FIGURE 7-33 *The Recent Documents task flow parameters*

Deployment

When you're deploying an application that uses content integration, keep in mind that you need to take care of the necessary content connections. What exactly you need to do will be described in Chapter 19.

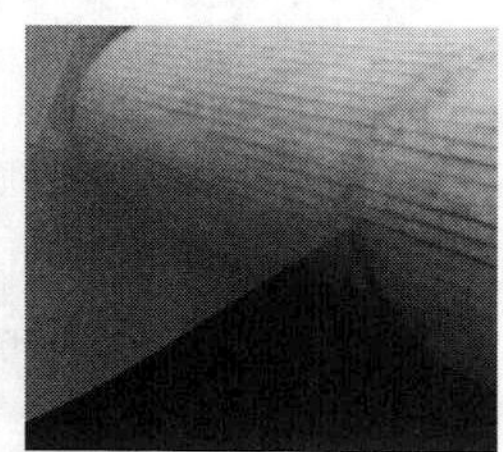

CHAPTER 8

Overview of WebCenter Web 2.0 Services

he birth of personal computers (PCs) in the 1970s was a major milestone in the evolution of networked computers. PCs featuring graphical displays provided a wide spectrum of personal productivity, data processing, and gaming applications.

One of the biggest contributions of the '80s was the wide adoption of networking techniques. Local area networks (LANs) were initially used to share resources, such as hard disks and printers. Networks also encouraged the installation of several, and sometimes dozens or hundreds, of computers on the same site. By the end of the '80s the advancement of networking software and operating systems, such as Novell NetWare, blurred the physical implementation differences between networking solutions; computers and networks could be easily connected and integrated.

The spread of computers connected into LANs played a key role in making client-server computing a success. The role of the server is very often played by an e-mail or database server, while the client software the end user is interacting with is an e-mail program or a database-driven enterprise application. Oracle pioneered the client-server database application market and for a long time client-server applications were built using Oracle Forms and Reports, which in turn connected to an Oracle database as the server.

Later, the appearance of web technologies introduced new color to the client-server world. The Web implements a special type of client-server computing using HTTP as the communications protocol. The client is a web browser that initiates HTTP requests and interprets responses received from the Web or an application server in the form of HTML, XML, and JavaScript.

The evolution of browsers, JavaScript, and HTML made it possible for web applications to become richer and more interactive. The World Wide Web turned from an interconnected information sharing and publishing media into an environment promoting teamwork and collaboration. The richness of the browser-based applications' user interfaces allowed end users to easily build and maintain social connections. Online retail stores like Amazon.com transformed their customers into an active, self-organizing community, influencing purchasing decisions of millions of people. Sites like Wikipedia fundamentally changed the way information is shared and accessed.

The richness of these applications is achieved by using AJAX technologies. AJAX allows browsers to submit asynchronous requests to the server, process the response that is returned, and update certain parts of the page displayed to the end user without refreshing the entire page. All of this is happening without interfering with the behavior of the web page rendered by the browser.

Without major technical inventions or revolution, the way the Web is being used has changed. This new way of leveraging web technologies for social and community-focused applications is very often referred to as Web 2.0. AJAX is an integral part of Web 2.0, since it makes it possible to build interactive web applications needed for true online collaboration.

The term Web 2.0 was coined at an O'Reilly Media Web 2.0 conference in 2004, where Tim O'Reilly argued that by taking advantage of native features and services of the Internet, users turn the Web into a platform—a platform fostering contribution and participation, and thus creating network effects. According to Tim O'Reilly: Web 2.0 is the business revolution in the computer industry caused by the move to the Internet as a platform, and an attempt to understand the rules for success on that new platform.

One of WebCenter's key missions is to integrate many of the Web 2.0 concepts that have been introduced and vetted by the consumer web space into enterprise applications. WebCenter was architected to provide a pluggable framework allowing existing and future Web 2.0 services to be plugged in seamlessly.

While the Oracle WebCenter license includes a number of back-end servers (such as Universal Content Management for enterprise content management and Jive for threaded discussions), the main objective that Oracle has set with WebCenter is to easily integrate the services of your choice. For example, you can connect to any e-mail server using IMAP. In addition, Microsoft Exchange is a supported e-mail server out of the box.

What Are the WebCenter Web 2.0 Services?

The WebCenter Web 2.0 Services expose personal productivity and social networking capabilities. Some services provide features for both personal productivity and social networking, some of them connect two or more services; the latter are called shared services.

- **Personal productivity service** An example of a personal productivity service is RSS. The RSS reader, as shown in Figure 8-1, allows you to subscribe to and display RSS feeds on your pages.

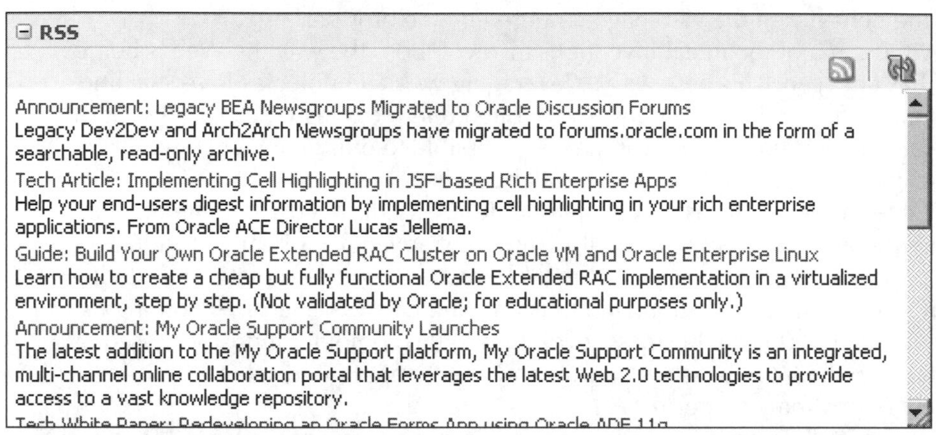

FIGURE 8-1 *RSS reader*

- **Social networking service** A typical social networking service is threaded discussions, displayed in Figure 8-2, which allow the users of your site to exchange information by posing and responding to questions.
- **Shared services** When you're thinking of shared services, linking may come to mind. Links, depicted in Figure 8-3, create a relationship between two objects or services in your application. For example, you can link a document to a discussion forum thread, providing easy access from the thread to the document.

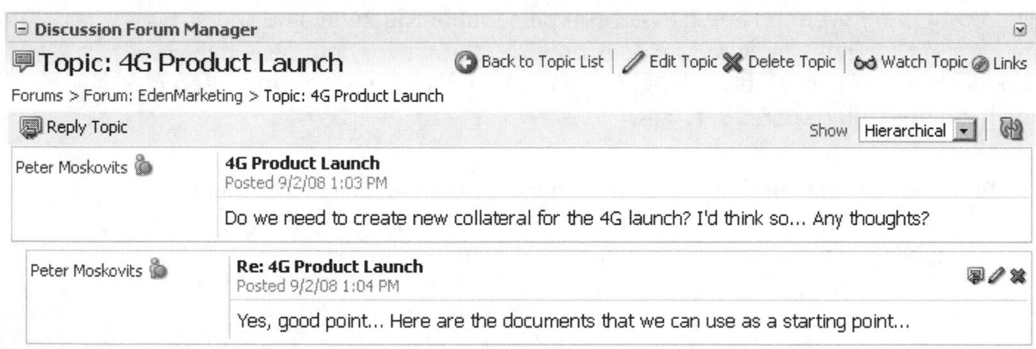

FIGURE 8-2 *Threaded discussion forum*

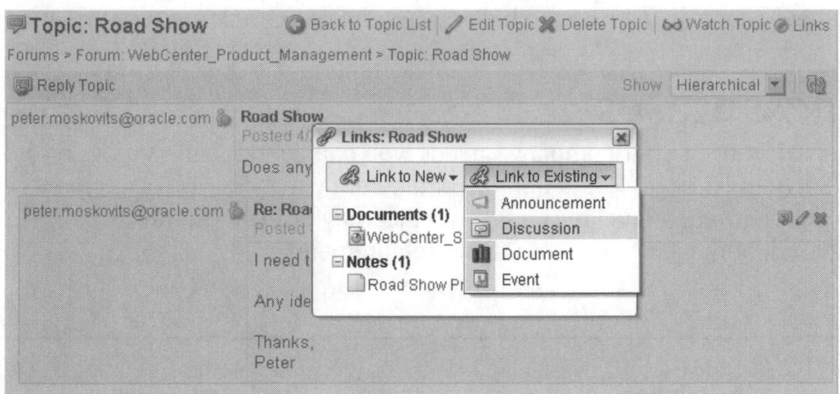

FIGURE 8-3 *Links*

Figure 8-4 provides a summary of the personal productivity and social networking services.

In a typical deployment, WebCenter services talk to a back-end server, where service-specific data is stored. For example, the Discussions service data is managed by the Jive Discussion data store.

Instead of talking to the back-end servers directly, WebCenter accesses them through a thin adapter layer, thus allowing the WebCenter Framework to abstract the communication interface.

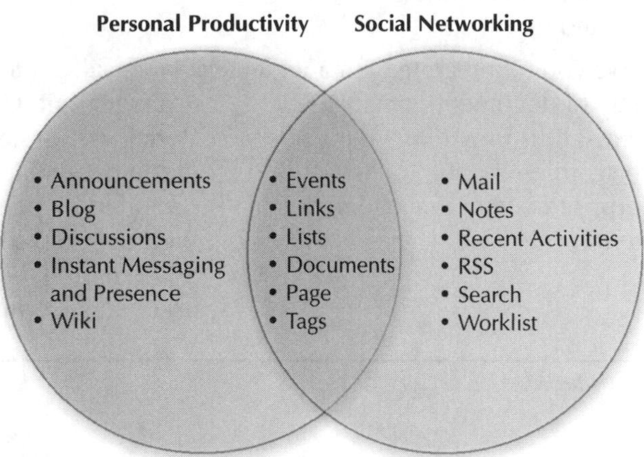

FIGURE 8-4 *Personal productivity and social networking services*

If the need arises to connect to another back end, the only thing you need to build is a new adapter. Adapters are built by Oracle and Oracle partners.

Business Cases

Depending on your or your company's needs, you can leverage the WebCenter Web 2.0 Services (Table 8-1) in a number of different ways. In this section we discuss a couple of high-level business cases that may come in handy as you are trying to identify which services fit your requirements.

WebCenter Web 2.0 Service	Description	Back-end Server
Announcements	Allows you as an administrator to broadcast important messages to the community of your users.	WebCenter Discussions (Jive Discussion Server)
Blog	Allows your users to create and maintain a blog in the context of your application.	WebCenter Wiki and Blog Server (JZonic wiki and blog server)
Discussions	Allows your users to pose questions, submit answers, and search for answers in a threaded discussion forum environment. Also, they can watch threads that they are interested in.	WebCenter Discussions (Jive Discussion Server)
Documents	Allows you to integrate with a wide variety of document management systems, thus providing your users with seamless access to these enterprise content management systems.	Universal Content Management, Oracle Portal, File System (additional adapters provided by partners include Microsoft Sharepoint, Documentum, and Lotus Domino)

TABLE 8-1 *Oracle WebCenter Web 2.0 Services*

WebCenter Web 2.0 Service	Description	Back-end Server
Instant Messaging and Presence (IMP)	Allows your users to see the presence status of other authenticated users and initiate instant communication with them through a number of different channels, including chat, e-mail, and voice over IP.	Microsoft Office Communication Server
Links	Allows your users to establish and discover relationships between two objects or services in your application.	WebCenter database schema
Lists*	Allows your users to create, publish, and manage data as a list, in a similar fashion to spreadsheets.	WebCenter database schema
Mail	Allows your users to access their e-mail. Supported operations include reading, composing, responding, forwarding, creating, and deleting e-mail messages.	Any IMAP/SMTP standards-based e-mail server, including Microsoft Exchange
Notes*	Allows your users to take a quick personal note and save it for future reference.	WebCenter database schema
Page	Allows your users to create, delete, and manage pages at run time.	Metadata Services
Recent Activities	Allows your users to monitor the recent changes in other services in the application, such as discussions, announcements, documents, and the page service.	All the services configured with your application (no additional back-end server required)
RSS	Allows your users to subscribe to and display RSS feeds on their pages.	No back-end server required

TABLE 8-1 *Oracle WebCenter Web 2.0 Services* (continued)

WebCenter Web 2.0 Service	Description	Back-end Server
Search	Allows your users to search WebCenter applications. Search returns results from all the WebCenter services that manage data, including discussions, documents, announcements, and tags. The Search service integrates with Oracle Secure Enterprise Search, too.	All the services configured with your application, Oracle Secure Enterprise Search (optional)
Tags	Allows your users to assign keywords to any uniquely identifiable object in your applications. Tags used in the application show up in search results and are presented in the tag cloud.	WebCenter database schema
Wiki	Allows your users to collaborate on HTML documents.	WebCenter Wiki and Blog Server (JZonic wiki and blog server)
Worklists	Allows your users to view the tasks that are assigned to them and that are generated through business processes, such as an approval or review request.	BPEL

*These services are not available in custom applications, only in WebCenter Spaces.

TABLE 8-1 *Oracle WebCenter Web 2.0 Services* (continued)

Customer Relationship Management Application

The traditional objective of CRM applications is to help companies store, maintain, and manage data and business processes related to their customers, prospects, and partners. CRM applications often set goals to improve interactions initiated with and services provided to customers.

CRM applications tend to be highly transactional by nature. Sales and marketing teams enter data about customers and prospects and often record interactions with them.

Injecting simple Web 2.0 services, such as instant messaging and presence (IMP) into CRM applications, can very quickly and easily improve the usability of the application, and provide a new level of service to customers, as well as other employees within your company.

By presence-enabling your application, your company's employees will see the presence status of other employees, allowing them to initiate an instant chat, web conferencing, VoIP call with video, or even click-to-call. By using click-to-call, you don't have to look up a person's phone number: first the presence server will ring your phone, then the other phone, and connect the two.

As your company most likely would not be sharing your presence server with your customers and partners, with them you can take advantage of the click-to-call and web conferencing capabilities.

Enterprise or Departmental Portal

WebCenter is often positioned and considered to be Oracle's next-generation user interaction and portal product. While enterprise portal capabilities vary from deployment to deployment, most of them share certain functionalities, including the following:

- **Run-time customization** The ability to make changes to your pages at run time without taking back the application to the design-time deployment and redeploying it. These tasks include changing the layout of pages (e.g., from two-column layout to three-column), adding and removing resources to and from the pages, as well as rearranging the components on the page.
- **Run-time page creation** A capability that you take for granted when talking about a portal, but is not a common use case for traditional J2EE or Java EE applications. This capability includes page permission management and navigation controls between pages.
- **Content integration** The ability to surface documents from document managements systems is again a classic use case for portals, and is rarely seen in Java EE applications.
- **Portlet support** Portals introduced the notion of reusable web components: portlets. Portlet standards define APIs that portlet developers can use to build interoperable portlets: JSR 168 and JSR 286. Portlets can be deployed along with the consumer application or portal, or they can be remote. If they are remote from the consumer, the communication standard between the portlet consumer and the portlet producer is Web Services for Remote Portlets (WSRP). WSRP has two versions: 1.0 and 2.0. WebCenter supports all these portlets standards, thus allowing it to consume portlets from third parties, as well as producing portlets to third-party portlet consumers.

If you are looking for a solution that has characteristics of an enterprise portal, WebCenter has a wealth of supporting capabilities for you.

Community-centric Group Site with Rich Collaboration

Many enterprises have geographically spread-out teams. Such teams find group sites very useful, allowing them to share and collaborate on documents and to manage their work in a well-organized fashion.

In other companies there's a need to form virtual teams in an ad hoc manner to achieve a certain objective. For example, if a company is bidding for a sales opportunity, a virtual team of domain experts, sales representatives, and marketing analysts is formed. The team can use threaded discussions to converse about the bidding process, leverage wiki pages for shared content authoring, and utilize project management tools to define tasks, set deadlines, and assign them to owners. Bid-related documents, such as company profile, bidding template, and bid document drafts, are stored in the company's enterprise content management system and can be linked to discussion forum threads related to the documents. Users can assign keywords (or tags) to discussion forum threads as well as documents, allowing them to easily find the information later on. Tags can be represented by a tag cloud, providing an easy-to-navigate visualization of the wisdom of the crowd.

The Landscape Is Changing

Today's IT application ecosystem is changing. While in the past applications were designed to purely replicate business tasks, they did not take organizational or even informal social aspects and resulting differences between individuals and the way they work into account.

With the rise of corporate portals, the goal was to provide individuals with the ability to surface and combine the business applications in a way that would best fit the individual's focus areas or manner of working.

However, the original goal of portals—to provide users with a personalizable environment to work in—had shortcomings. Because the only building blocks for those portals were portlets, the possibilities of creating specialized working environments were limited by the real estate available as well as interactivity due to the standards involved. Nevertheless, portals gained wide popularity.

Information Sharing Is Becoming Collaborative

As the IT ecosystem changed, so did the overall working environment. Corporations became global, and organizations started to span geographies; what were formerly known as virtual teams, groups of people who worked across organizational structures on projects, became common; and organizations were now spread out rather than concentrated in a single location. At the same time a new generation of workers is starting to enter today's working environments. These workers grew up with the emerging social components of a World Wide Web that is changing from a pure community of consumers of content provided by a small group of publishers to a collaborative environment, one where everyone can be a contributor and at the same time consume and collaborate on the contributions of others. Web 2.0 is the idea of collaboratively defining and creating content for a wider audience.

It all started with things like discussion forums where people could exchange information, discuss asynchronously, and build online communities. The next steps were weblogs, so-called blogs, shown in Figure 8-5, where people could easily share their thoughts on various topics. While used as public diaries to share more or less private information, blogs soon became a new kind of web site. Earlier sharing information on web pages mainly focused on creating HTML pages that contained information and structured it in a hierarchical way. With blogs as hosted services, publishing information became more of a linear or chronological exercise that could also be performed by nontechnical individuals. Soon a lot of blogs changed from being simply a diary to a diary-style source of high-quality information—allowing subject matter experts to share information in an informal way.

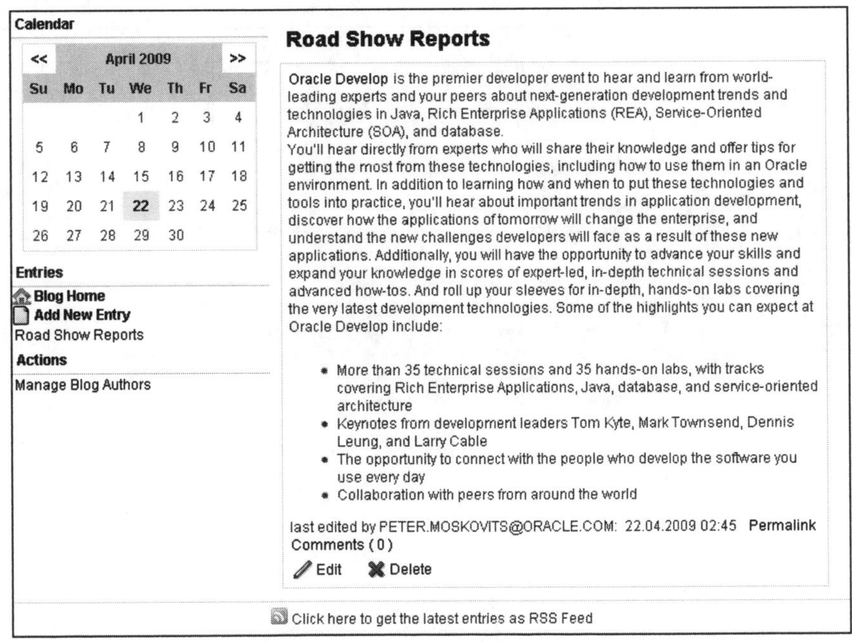

FIGURE 8-5 *Weblogs becoming a way for informal information sharing*

One could argue that this was also possible with normal web sites. True, but a main aspect of blogs is that readers can leave comments on those expert postings to either augment the information or simply support the content with their experience. Additionally some blog systems allow readers to rate the postings, leveraging the power of the crowd to enrich the information available with relevance.

The next logical evolution of these concepts was a way for a group of people to easily work on information, to share and update it to—again—leverage the power of the crowd to raise the quality of the information available and decrease the time it takes to create that information.

By providing a simple syntax to allow formatting the information, those systems became popular among distributed teams to share information in a self-service manner. Those systems are called wikis. The most well-known implementation of a wiki is Wikipedia, shown in Figure 8-6, where an open source wiki system has evolved into the largest online encyclopedia in the world.

The characteristics of Wikipedia, like any wiki, is that anybody can become an author. Originally information was available immediately as soon as it was created by an author. These days, because of numerous false and joke entries, Wikipedia has implemented a review mechanism to ensure the quality of the information stored.

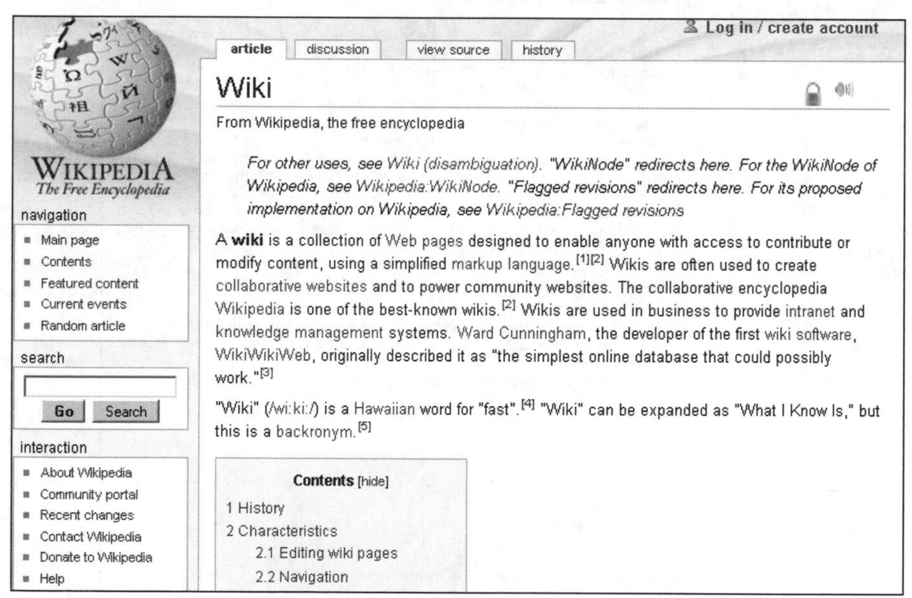

FIGURE 8-6 *Wikipedia as an example of a public wiki used by millions of people*

CHAPTER 9

Social Web 2.0 Services—New Concepts in the Application Landscape

raditional services in the Web 2.0 space such as discussion forums, wikis, and blogs can be integrated as individual information sources into your application. The main concept of Enterprise 2.0, however, is the ability to not only present information from different sources but to present information in context and provide the ability to model interconnection between information artifacts. Another fundamental idea behind Enterprise 2.0 is collaboration, more precisely to combine Web 2.0 collaborative and communal services for the information users to process. Oracle WebCenter provides the necessary components and services to cater toward both fundamental principles. Services such as the Link Service provide the ability to link artifacts of disparate services to each other, despite the fact that the services and their artifacts do not know about each other.

Services such as tagging and presence facilitate modern concepts of collaborative attribution and support communication between participants by directly exposing modern communication mechanisms such as instant messaging, e-mail, and even Voice over IP (VoIP) or web conferencing in context, within other services, in relevant places.

The idea behind those overarching services is to be auto-detective, so that a developer would not have to worry which service was enabled with another service, but rather auto-detect exposed services on a page and act accordingly.

So let's take a closer look at those overarching services and their role in creating modern, Enterprise 2.0 applications.

Configuring Your Application for the WebCenter Web 2.0 Services

WebCenter Web 2.0 Services have different configuration requirements. Some of them, such as e-mail, simply connect to a back-end server. Other services, for example the Tagging Service or the discussion forums, have a dependency on a database schema where they store their metadata, which can include information about the tags assigned to pages, or about the relationship created between discussion forum threads and documents residing in your enterprise content management server.

Often there is a requirement to implement identity propagation between your application and a back-end server. For example, user john.doe in your application should be mapped to jdoe in the back-end document management system. The task of credential mapping in WebCenter is performed by external applications.

In this section we will cover these dependencies and the steps you need to follow to successfully use the services in your applications.

To install the database schema and schema objects, you can either use the Repository Configuration Utility, or simply run a script in JDeveloper. To do so, first you have to create a connection pointing to the database that you will use as your linking and tagging metadata repository. You can create the database connection either in the Application Navigator under Application Resources or in the Resource Palette. Invoke the database connection dialog through the New Gallery: File | New | Database Tier | Database Connection. If the schema already exists that will hold your WebCenter metadata, simply connect to that database schema. If your WebCenter schema doesn't exist yet, create your database connection as sys, and the script will create the new schema for you.

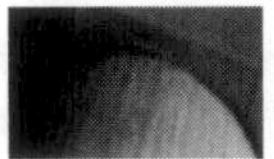

NOTE
If you are connecting to the database as sys, remember to change the connection properties of your WebCenter connection from sys to <your_schema_name>, for example WebCenter, so that you connect to the WebCenter schema of your database, rather than to sys.

As Figure 9-1 shows, you have to provide the connection name, username, password, host name, SID, and port number. Be sure to name your connection **WebCenter**, as this is how your application will find the right database connection to use. If for some reason you want or need to give a different name to your connection, you can follow the instructions in the Additional Prerequisites section in the WebCenter Developer's Guide.

FIGURE 9-1 *Creating a database connection*

The script creates a database schema, grants privileges, and creates the necessary database objects. You can invoke the script from SQL*Plus if you have it installed, or from the integrated SQL Worksheet that comes as part of JDeveloper. Be aware, however, that most likely your DBA will have to run the script since it requires the SYSDBA role.

To start SQL Worksheet, select Tools | SQL Worksheet from the menu. Invoke the script as shown in Figure 9-2. Here is an example of the path to the setup script:

```
<JDEV_HOME>\jdev\extensions\oracle.webcenter.install\sql\wc_schema.sql
```

To invoke it, simply use the @-operator, for example:

```
@c:\jdeveloper\jdev\extensions\oracle.webcenter.install\sql\wc_schema.sql
```

The script prompts you for the schema name, schema password, default tablespace name, and temporary tablespace name. If you want to use easy-to-remember, simple names, you can consider the following values:

- Schema name: *webcenter*
- Schema password: *<a password>*
- Default tablespace: *users*
- Temporary tablespace: *temp*

Steps in Case the WebCenter Schema Already Exists

If the schema that will hold your services metadata already exists, there are two steps you must take:

1. Grant the following to your schema, where `&&1` is the schema name:

```
grant execute on dbms_lock to &&1;
grant resource to &&1;
grant connect to &&1;
grant create sequence to &&1;
Execute the following script to populate your schema with
the WebCenter database objects:

@<JDEV_HOME>\jdev\extensions\oracle.webcenter.install\sql\
wc_objects.sql &&1
```

where `&&1` is the schema name. For example:

```
@c:\jdeveloper\jdev\extensions\oracle.webcenter.install\
sql\wc_objects.sql &&1
```

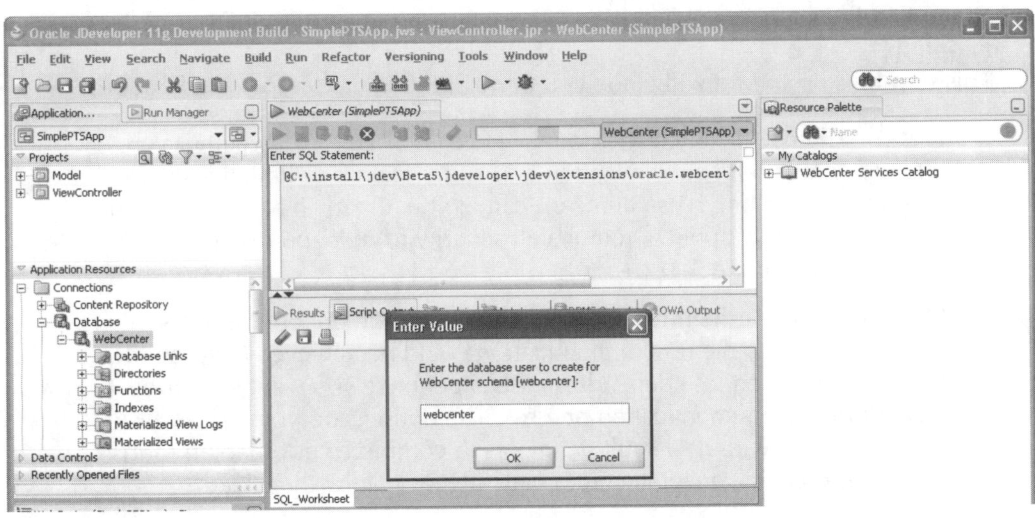

FIGURE 9-2 *Executing the WebCenter database script in the SQL worksheet*

If you are using SQL*Plus, you can use the following command to invoke the schema creation script similar to the way described above:

```
SQL> @@wc_schema.sql schema_name schema_password dflt_tblsp tmp_tblsp
```

If you want the script to prompt for the above arguments, you can invoke the script without the parameters as well:

```
SQL> @@wc_schema.sql
```

In addition to those dependencies, some services require security to be enabled on the application to provide a user scope. Details on securing an application are covered in Chapter 19. For the purpose of this chapter you are going to apply basic security to show the services in action.

Setting Up Basic ADF Security

Security for applications is becoming more and more important. JavaEE and ADF, through Java Platform Security (JPS), provide a sophisticated and open security framework for your application. While getting security up and running is quite simple, understanding all the possibilities the security framework provides is quite complex, and describing it exceeds the scope of this chapter. That's why you can find a complete chapter about security, what it is, what it does, and what it can do for you (or rather your application) later on in this book.

The easiest way to enable security for your application is to use the ADF Security wizard. You can invoke it using the Application | Security | ADF Security menu option.

This step-by-step wizard will guide you through the initial setup of ADF security.

- **Step 1—Choose the Security Model** Here you can select whether you want to enable both authentication and authorization or limit the security to authorization only. Also here you can, if you already have an application with ADF security applied, remove all security from it and restore it to its original state (Figure 9-3).
- **Step 2—Select Authentication Type** The available options here describe the possible ways the user authentication could be achieved (Figure 9-4). Which one you choose depends on the experience you want your users to have during the authentication process. The options are from HTTP Basic Authentication with its default behaviors to complete custom login forms (which also can be generated automatically for you by the wizard).

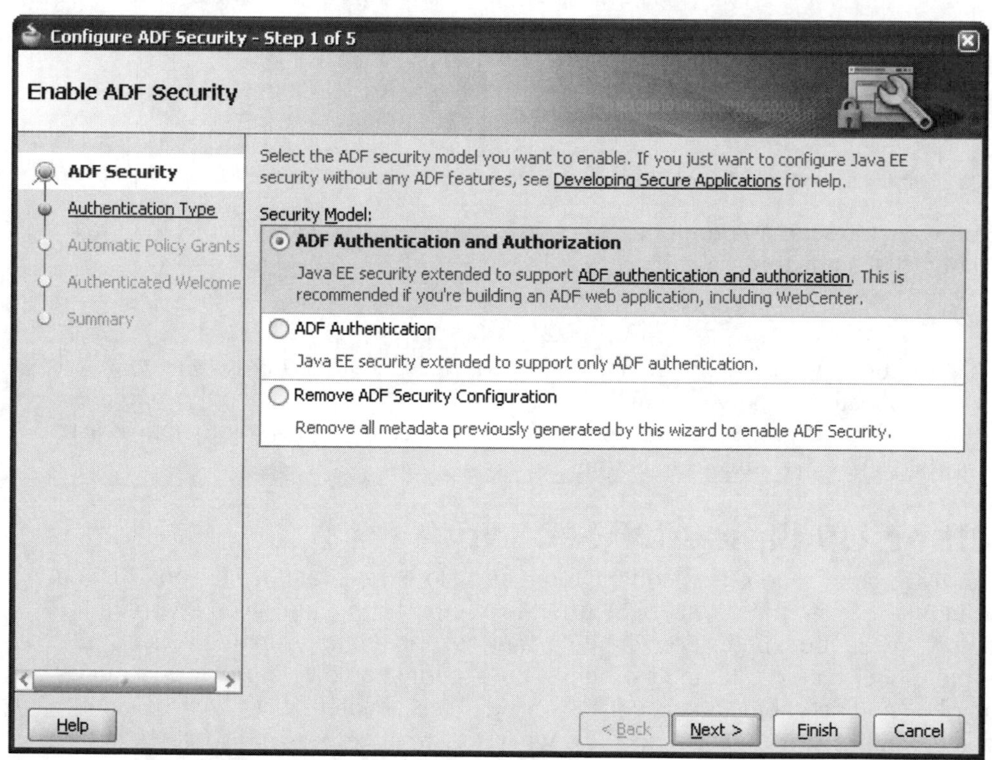

FIGURE 9-3 *Choosing the security model*

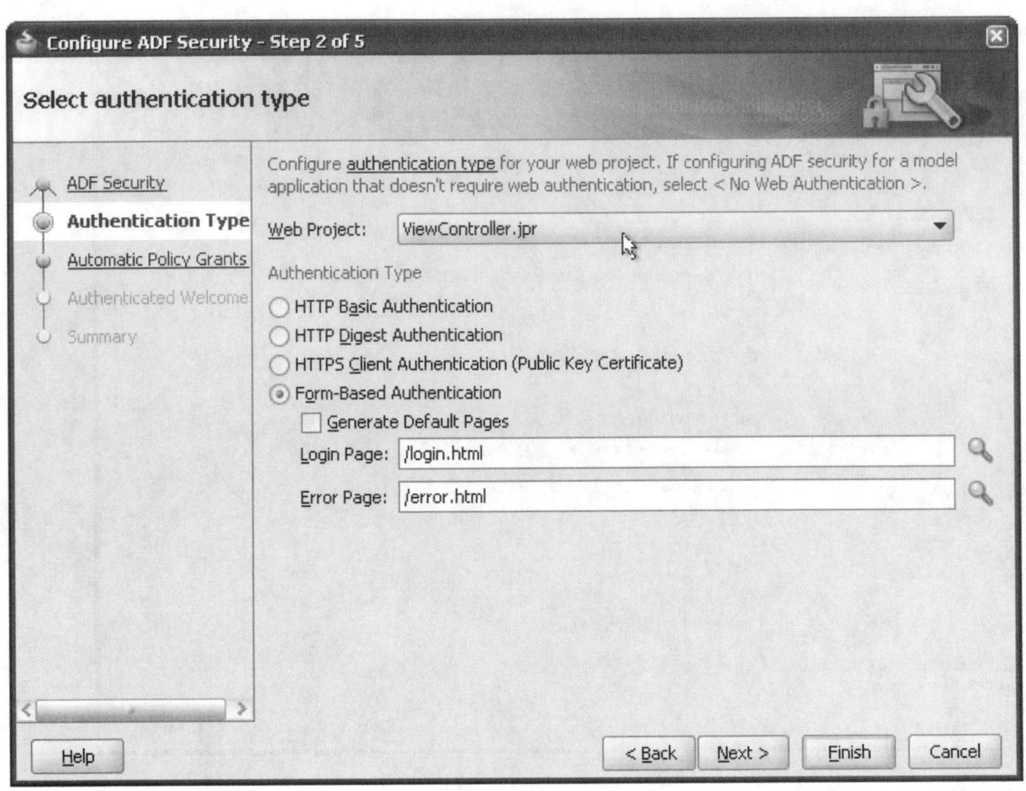

FIGURE 9-4 *Choosing the authentication type*

- **Step 3—Automatic Policy Grants** By default, as soon as security is applied to an application, the access to any object within this application, such as pages and task flows, would be restricted, and hence the application would not work properly until you created the appropriate policies for each object. To avoid this initial hassle you can choose from one of three options here (Figure 9-5): (1) not automatically grant any privileges, which would require your manual intervention as described, (2) automatically grant only existing objects that might already be in the application when you run the wizard, or (3) do so only for new objects, even if they are created after the wizard was run for the first time. Regardless of which option you choose, what is being granted is the view privilege for the test-all role. The idea behind this is to allow easy testing of the application right away without having to explicitly create policies for the whole application. Proper object-level privileges need to be granted later on, once you have defined which role will be allowed access to what objects.

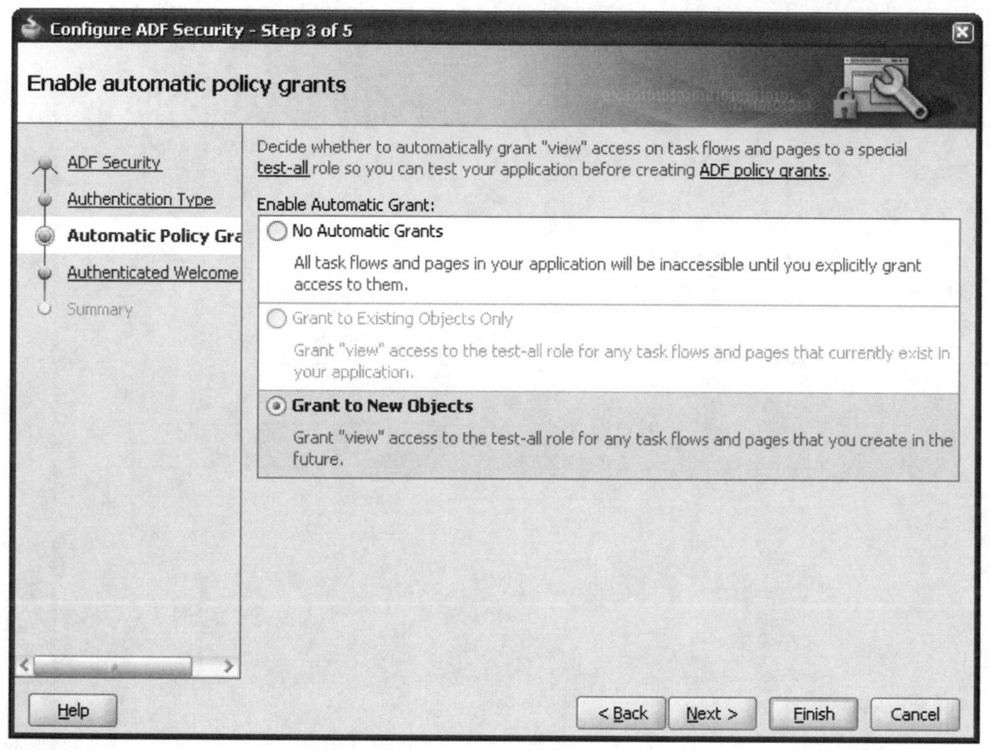

FIGURE 9-5 *Choosing the policy grants process*

NOTE

The test-all role ensures that all pages are accessible when they're run from the IDE without having to authenticate. If you want to test with proper authentication, you need to revoke the view privileges from the test-all role. With WebCenter, however, the running application relies on the presence of a security context which is created only if the login process is being performed. So for WebCenter applications you should create your own roles and assign them accordingly. Simply select the No Automatic Grants option.

- **Step 4—Redirect** Optionally you can redirect to a special welcome page upon successful login (Figure 9-6). This option is useful if your application uses a dedicated login page rather than a login component on a partially public main page.

Once you are finished with the wizard, your application is secure. To run a secure application you need to add some users and roles, or at least create a test user (we will discuss how to do that in a bit) and make him or her a member of the test-all role.

To investigate what was created by the wizard, you can inspect the applications security information by invoking the ADF Security Policies option from the applications menu, which is the icon next to the Application Selector in the Application Navigator (Figure 9-7).

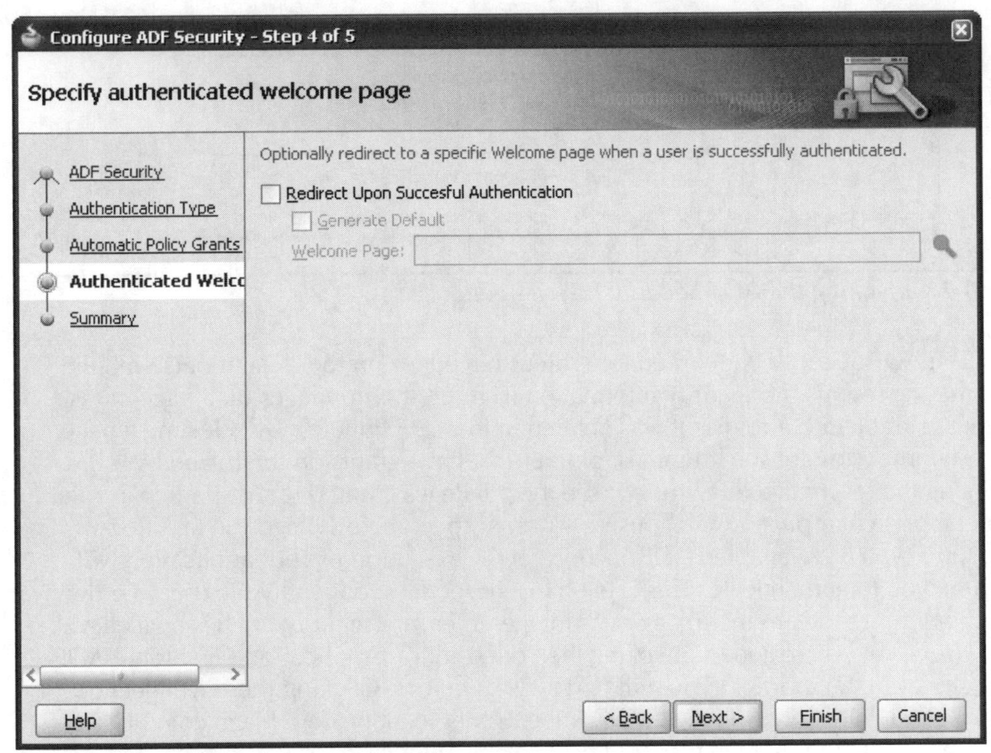

FIGURE 9-6 *Defining the redirect rule*

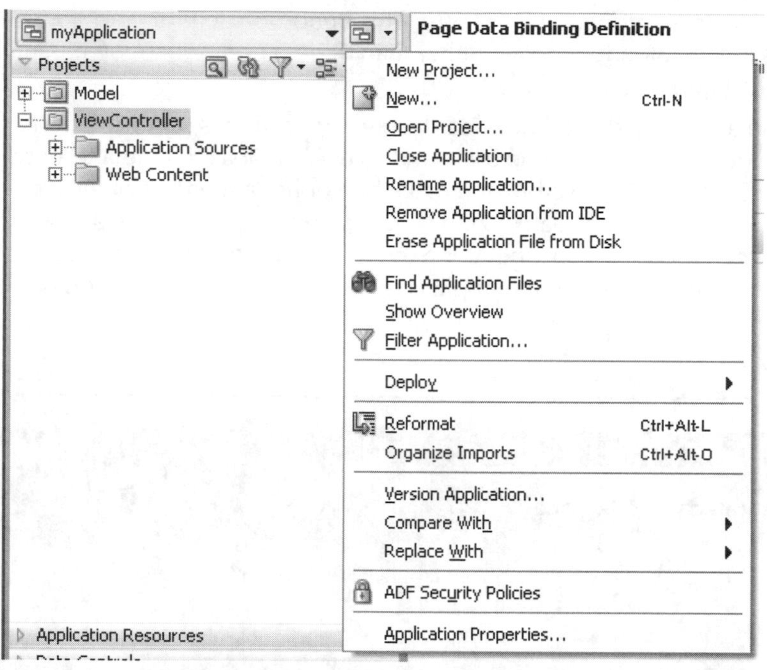

FIGURE 9-7 *Invoking the ADF Security Policies editor*

The ADF Security Policies editor is a custom editor on top of jazn-data.xml, the file that represents the security information (Figure 9-8). Privileges on a page or task flow are granted to a role as it was defined in the ADF Policies. By selecting a page, for example, you are shown the list of roles that have grants on them, and by clicking the respective role you can see the privileges granted to that particular role on that particular page. Analogously you can inspect the privileges on task flows.

Once you have enabled ADF Security, every execution of your application will require you to authenticate. This is the basis for services to identify the user in order to authenticate toward their back-end storages to ensure security on the service level.

Users can be created by invoking the Policy Editor (Application | Security | ADF Policies). On the top-right you will find a Users button. Clicking there will get you to the Edit JPS Identity & Policy Store dialog. Under Identity Store | jazn.com | Users you can create the users that should be available. Under Roles you can create container-level roles. Roles for the application, in case you need those, can be created under Application Policy Store | "your application's name" | Application Roles. There you can also assign membership in roles.

The security concept used in WebCenter applications is role-based: the application defines a set of roles and privileges are associated with these roles. A user is assigned

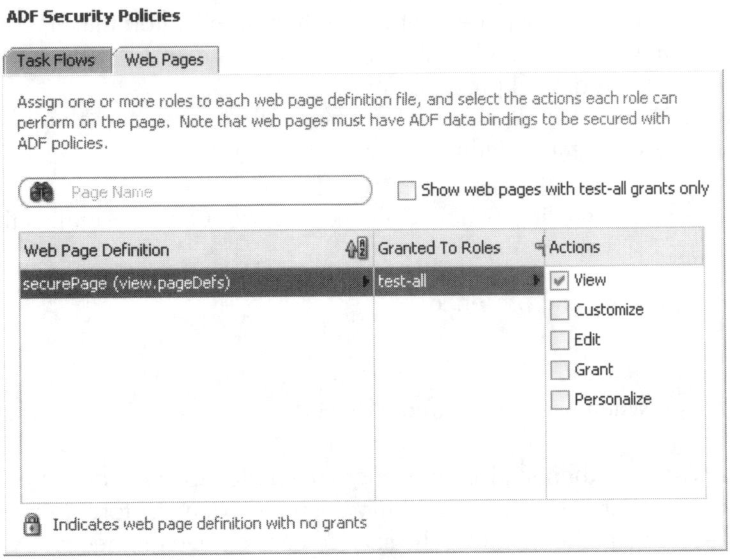

ADF Security Policies

Task Flows | Web Pages

Assign one or more roles to each web page definition file, and select the actions each role can perform on the page. Note that web pages must have ADF data bindings to be secured with ADF policies.

Page Name | Show web pages with test-all grants only

Web Page Definition	Granted To Roles	Actions
securePage (view.pageDefs)	test-all	[x] View [ ] Customize [ ] Edit [ ] Grant [ ] Personalize

Indicates web page definition with no grants

FIGURE 9-8 *ADF security policies in jazn-data.xml*

one or more roles and receives privileges on applications objects. This assignment happens at the container level; the application knows only about roles, not the users directly.

There are two levels of roles because you might want to encapsulate roles within your application during development time—for example, moderator, participant, and viewer, which will later be mapped to roles on the container to which the application is deployed.

That way you can keep a clean container-level role hierarchy, regardless of the applications installed. You do not have to pollute your container's role model with the sum of all applications, and your application does not have to be tied to the role model of a particular container setup, giving you the most flexibility when you're creating secure applications.

For services that leverage the same user-store as your application, for example, your corporate directory following the Lightweight Directory Access Protocol (LDAP), the users' identity can simply be propagated to the back-end service in a secure and trusted manner governed by web service security or, if you choose, simple and unsecured. The task flow will propagate the user context to the service to specify the users' identity.

In other cases, when the service does not use the same identity store and it is not possible to make it use the same identity store, for technical, organizational, or security reasons, the External Application Connection can be used.

External Application Connections

When a WebCenter Web 2.0 Service interacts with an application that handles its own authentication, you can associate that application with an external application definition to allow for credential provisioning.

The following WebCenter Web 2.0 Services let you use an external application to connect with the service and define authentication for it:

- Documents (when using Oracle Content Server or Oracle Portal as the content repository)
- Instant messaging and presence
- Mail
- RSS viewer (when using a secured RSS feed)

For the purpose of authentication, the External Application service stores credentials on a per-user, per-service level in a secure credential store. During service invocation and authentication, the service can retrieve the necessary user credentials from this store for the accessing user to authenticate on his or her behalf to the back-end storage.

The good thing in most cases is that you as the developer do not have to worry about any implementation details because the respective task flows will have the necessary functionalities already integrated so the end user can provide the credentials on initial use or when login attempts using the stored credentials fail. More details on External Application Security can be found in the Securing Your WebCenter Application of the Oracle Fusion Middleware's Developers Guide for Oracle WebCenter.

Services Inside and Out

Now you are ready to take a closer look at the services available. In the following section you will group the services in somewhat thematically related groups which, by the way, has nothing to do with any physical grouping in the product.

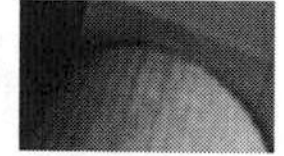

NOTE

Most services perform tasks asynchronously, using AJAX communication. In order to give the user an indication of whether there is still processing going on, you should always add the Status Indicator component to your application and educate your end users to watch it while they're working with the application.

Collaborative Services

In this category you can put all services that support collaboration among the users of an application. They can collaborate about topics and create a collective knowledge pool of sorts.

Discussion Forums

The most traditional one is, no doubt, the discussion forum. Used widely for many years, the discussion forum's functionality and purpose is widely known and accepted. However, forums today usually are stand-alone entities, represented by some kind of web user interface where users can create threaded discussions and, depending on the capabilities of the used software, apply more sophisticated tasks, such as attaching documents, ratings, etc.

One problem, however, remains in most implementations today—context. As discussion forums are stand-alone collections of discussion threads, the connections to their potential counterparts in other information repositories are usually difficult to make out. Let's take two simple examples:

- **Presentation of discussions in context** Here you could take Oracle's own discussion forum on Oracle's Technology Network (OTN), otn.oracle.com. It is a silo, parallel to the information pages on OTN. While page authors try to present things in context by providing a link to relevant forums from their product pages, the user leaves the product page to go to the forums. Also, information such as new threads in a particular product topic would be interesting on the product page, rather than somewhere outside that scope.
- **Discussing a document that is stored in the document repository** Here is a pretty common use case: The author of a document wants to discuss details about the document's content with a group of subject matter experts. Both the document and the discussion thread are stored in two separate repositories. So how could the author create a connection between these? One option could be to paste a link to the document (if the document repository provides web access) in the initial discussion thread entry. This would work if the entry point was the discussion forum, but if somebody browsed the document repository, there would be no indication that a particular document was the subject of a discussion. If the document repository does not provide web access, a descriptive entry with the document's location would be the only option. The least desirable option is to attach a version of the document to the thread since it causes information duplication and could cause confusion and circulation of different document versions.

These two examples show that the value of discussion forums can be significantly raised if there is an ability to present its functionality in context. Oracle WebCenter Discussions can provide such in-context discussion capabilities with your application.

COLLABORATIVE SERVICE CHARACTERISTICS

REQUIRES WEBCENTER SCHEMA: no
REQUIRES BACK-END SERVICE: yes—Oracle WebCenter Discussions
REQUIRES APPLICATION TO BE SECURE: yes
OTHER DEPENDENCIES: none

AVAILABLE TASK FLOWS

- **Discussion Forums** This task flow displays the Oracle Discussions Manager View, which allows the user to see all the discussions and their respective replies. It also allows users to perform various operations based on their privileges. A moderator can perform create, read, update, and delete operations on all objects. A participant can create a topic, edit a topic that has been created by him or her, and reply to a topic. A viewer can only view objects.
- **Popular Topics** This task flow provides a view that allows users to see all the popular topics under a given category ID or forum ID.
- **Recent Topics** This task flow displays a view that allows users to see all the recent topics given a category ID or forum ID.
- **Watched Forums** This task flow displays a view that allows users to see all their watched forums under a given category ID.
- **Watched Topics** This task flow displays a view that allows users to see all their watched topics under a given category ID or forum ID.
- **Sidebar View** This task flow displays a combined view of the Popular Topics, Recent Topics, Watched Topics, and Watched Forums task flows. This task flow was designed to work in limited horizontal space, such as an Microsoft Outlook–style sidebar.

Creating a Discussion Connection

Before you can integrate the discussion forum in your application, you need to create a connection to the Discussion Service. To do so, right-click on Connections in the Application Resources panel and select Discussions from the list of available connection types. You will be presented with a connection creation wizard, specific to discussion connections (Figure 9-9).

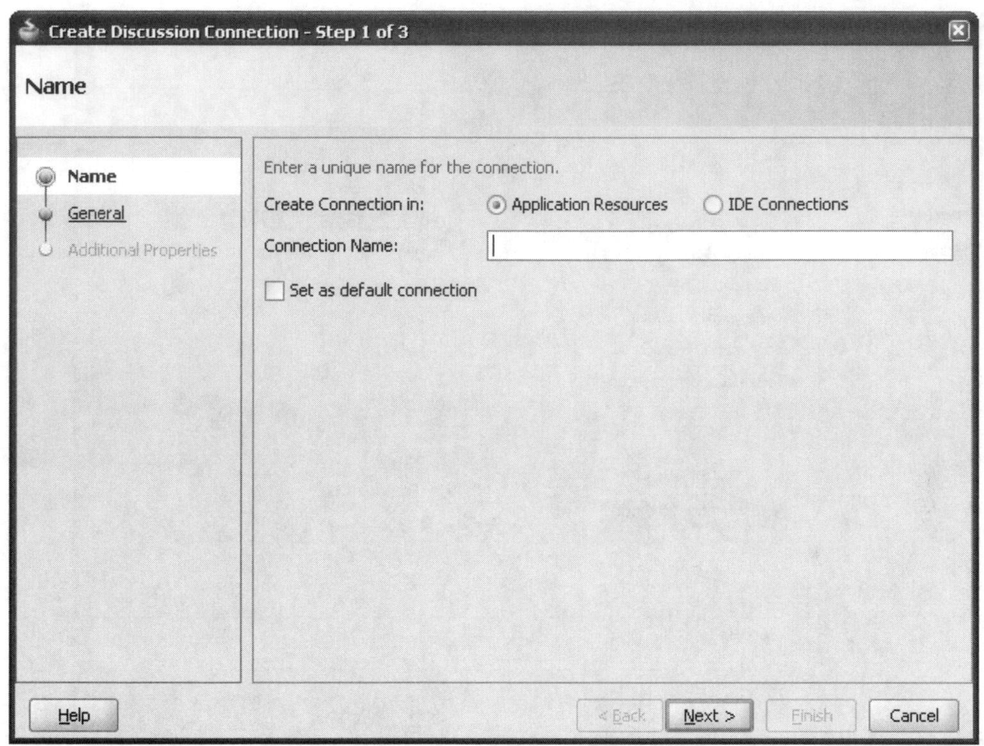

FIGURE 9-9 *Discussion Connection wizard*

Creating a connection to Application Resources will restrict its scope to the application it was created in, while an IDE connection can be used by all applications. The default connection topic was already discussed earlier in Chapter 7. Similarly here with discussion connections, a connection can be named as the default connection. The default connection will be picked up by the task flow if no connection name is explicitly specified in its attributes.

You might need to use more than one connection if there is more than one discussion forum system in use (e.g., multiple regions, departments, etc.).

To establish the connection, information such as the URL to the back-end system needs to be provided (Figure 9-10). Here you also see the ability to choose between Identity propagation and the External Application connection. While Oracle WebCenter Discussions can be used with Identity propagation, the Discussion Service's architecture can support the extension to other discussion systems in the future, which might require External Application.

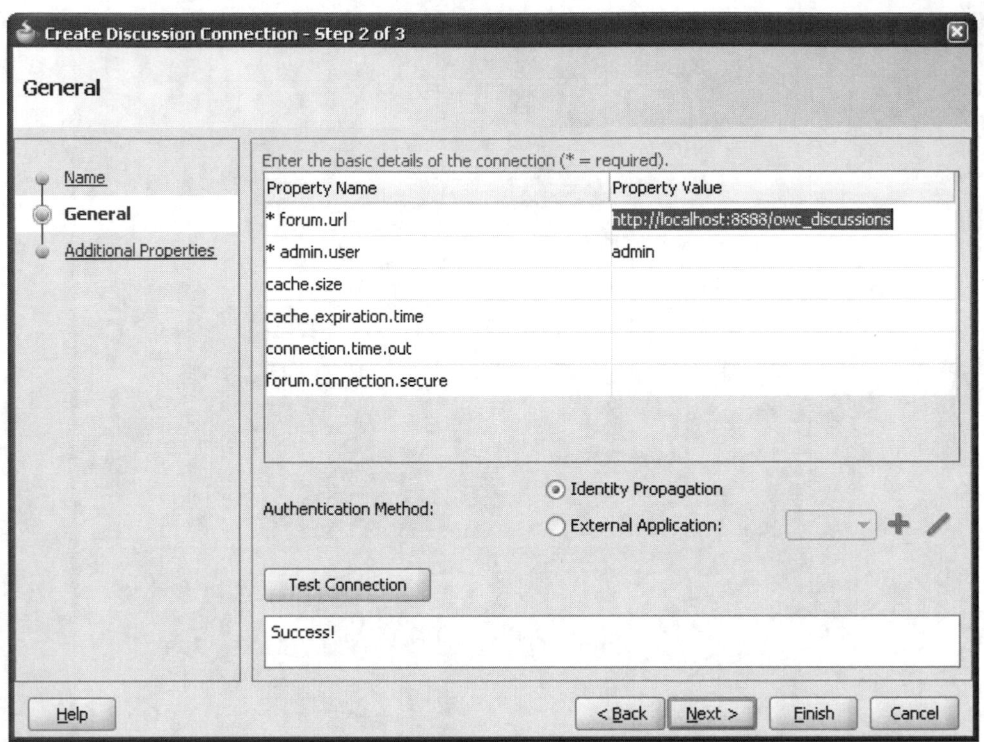

FIGURE 9-10 *Specifying connection parameters*

Oracle WebCenter Discussions provides web services for external access. The base URL under which the system is available acts as a base for the web service URL and needs to be provided here.

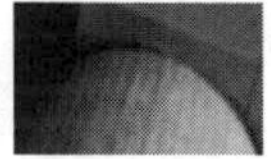

NOTE
For some services, such as Links, that are integrated with the Discussion Service, it is necessary to define the root category from where the hierarchy should be exposed. To do so, open the adf-config.xml (found in the Application Resources panel under Descriptors | ADF META-INF*) and look for a service definition with the service id oracle.webcenter .collab.forum.*

There you need to add an <adapter></adapter> element as follows:

```
<adapter name="Jive">
  <adapter-class>
  oracle.webcenter.collab.forum.internal.jive.JiveForumSession
  </adapter-class>
  <property name="application.root.category.id" value="XX"/>
  <property name="recent.topics.days" value="2"/>
  <property name="group.mapping" value="forum"/>
</adapter>
```

XX in application.root.category.id stands for the number of the category that should be used as the root (e.g., 2).

Adding Discussion Capabilities to Your Application

Adding discussion capabilities to an application is as simple as adding a component to a page. Simply select one of the Discussions task flows from the Resources panel and drag it onto your page (Figure 9-11).

You will be presented with the bindings dialog where you can specify further details for publishing discussions (Figure 9-12).

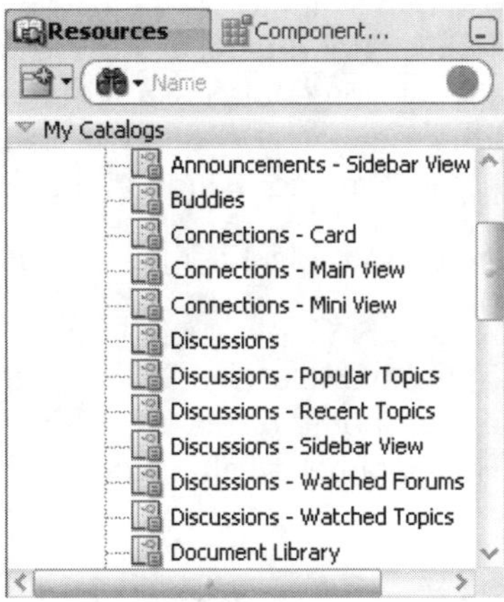

FIGURE 9-11 *Discussions task flows in the Resources panel*

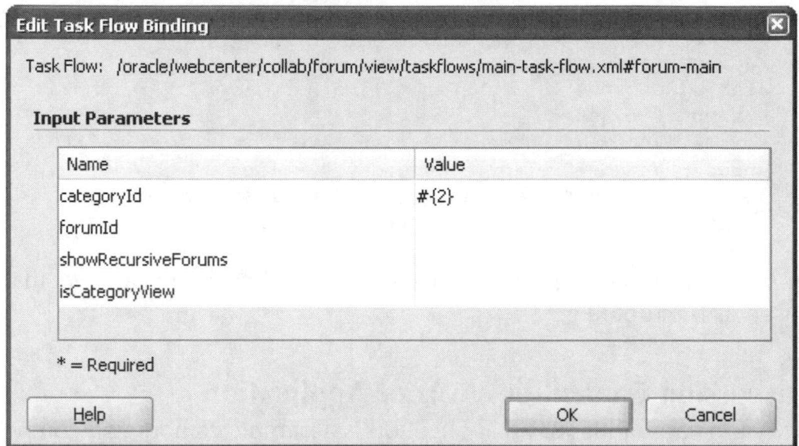

FIGURE 9-12 *The bindings dialog for discussions*

The Discussions task flow can be parameterized using a set of attributes:

- `categoryId` This parameter is an identifier for an existing category in your Oracle Discussions instance to which the view should be scoped. For testing purposes, you may want to create a new category through the Oracle Discussions administrator interface and then reference that category identifier here. Alternatively, you could enter a numeric value of `${1}`, but this value refers to the root category and will cause the application to retrieve and display all of the information in the discussion.
- `forumId` This parameter is an identifier for an existing forum that resides inside the given category.
- `isCategoryView` This parameter defines how the view should be presented; for example, if it should display recursively all forums inside the given `categoryId`. This parameter value works in combination with other parameters.
- `showRecursiveForums` This parameter determines if you show forums either in one category or in subcategories.

About Security

You might notice that after adding the Discussions task flow to your page and executing it, you will see the discussion threads, but you will miss icons to create a new thread, for example. This is because you have not yet assigned one of the three roles to the user and hence, as far as the discussion forum service is concerned, the user currently running the application is not a member of any discussion forum role. By default, the discussion forum has three roles: administrator, writer, and viewer. Through the WebCenter discussion administration, you have to assign the appropriate role to the user. In the current release, this is a manual or semi-manual process. WebCenter Discussions provide APIs to programmatically set and revoke roles from users.

WebCenter Application and Discussions services are joined by similar usernames. So users on the WebCenter side need to match the users on the Discussions service side. If you decide to use LDAP as your user store, you can bind both WebCenter and Discussions services to this user store, and by doing so obtain matching names.

Wiki and Blog Service

Sharing information has become a vital part of everyday business. When you look at sharing information you can identify two major models, the create-review-publish model and the ad hoc publishing model; both have their advantages and disadvantages. While the traditional create-review-publish model's goal is to provide high-quality information to a large number of people, the turnaround time is quite long and, interestingly enough, the create/review phase will require collaborative concepts if there is more than one person involved in the creation. Still, this model is valid in certain cases where the life span of the published information is relatively long and the information itself stays solid once it has been reviewed. This model is also characterized by a formal process of create-review-publish.

The ad hoc publishing model, on the other hand, is more of a collaborative working environment where a group, somewhat in parallel, is responsible for creating and/or reviewing on a more informal level. This model is usually used by larger project teams to document ongoing findings to build up a proper information source that, once completed, can be published. This is also a more iterative model, where the creation and review of information is more ongoing than precisely timed.

The latter model has gained in popularity over the last years, not only because ongoing project documentation has always been a hassle due to technical limitations of the infrastructure available, but also because project teams are starting to spread geographically and sharing information informally in the hallway has become increasingly difficult. In the past, technologies like word processors were used to create such ad hoc documentations or, if online capabilities were required, web pages were used for this purpose. However, neither was quite capable of facilitating the simultaneous nature of ad hoc publishing, so another technology, the wiki, gained in popularity.

Wiki, Hawaiian for "fast," soon became a synonym for a simple, web-based tool where users could share information online. Every person could become an author quickly, and the simple wiki syntax allowed even novice users to publish nicely formatted information on the Web, without HTML knowledge. There are several large-scale wiki sites today; possibly the largest and most well-known is Wikipedia (Figure 9-13), the online encyclopedia project. Wikipedia is also a very good

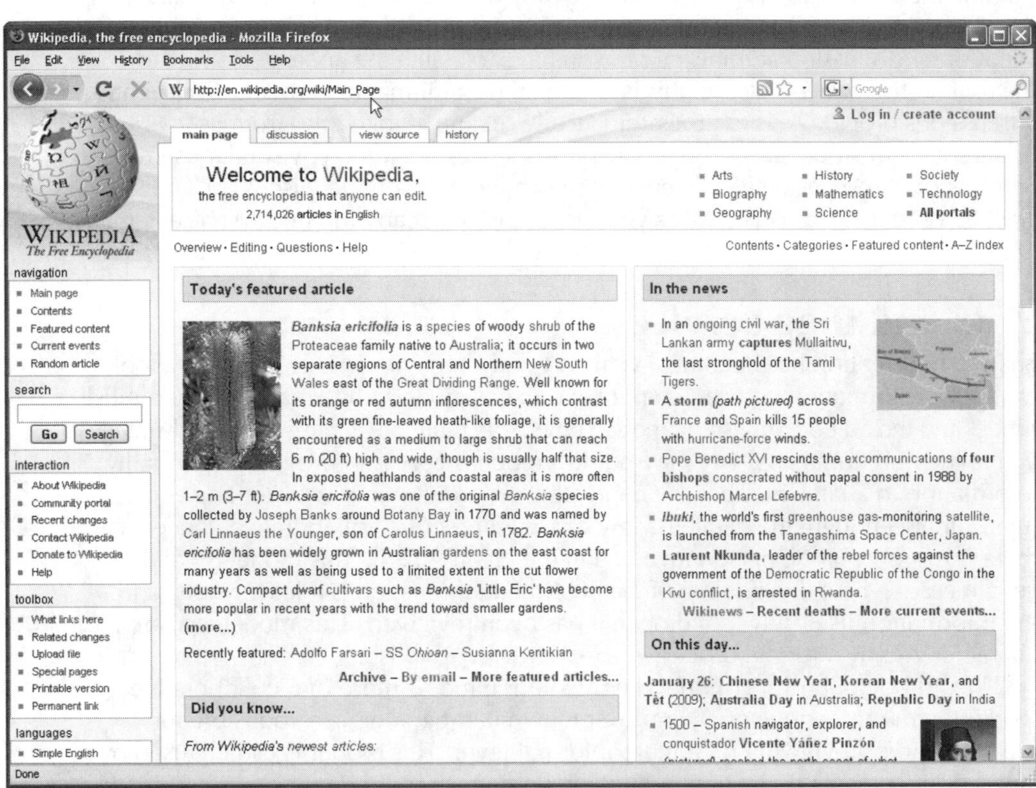

FIGURE 9-13 *Wikipedia—one of the most popular public wikis*

example of the idea behind wikis, to create and share information in a large group of people and therefore leverage the knowledge of the crowd to enhance the quality of information.

Soon those simple wiki environments evolved into publishing environments combining the ease of use and simplicity of the original idea with more enterprise-grade features such as versioning, approval capabilities, etc.

Weblogs (Figure 9-14), or blogs for short, are online diaries where individuals share information with others and usually allow the readers to comment on their postings. Originally blogs were diaries in the proper sense, where people shared experiences from travels or other adventures, but soon they became more of general purpose information publishing environments. Mainly because of their ease of use, blogs became popular for sites dealing with news-style sites, where the author publishes information on a more or less regular basis, while still retaining a personal perspective since blogs are usually run by individuals or a small group of people.

They have also become quite popular in the technology area where subject matter experts can quickly and easily publish personal experiences, observations, and findings for the good of a wider audience. The audience, on the other hand, can usually comment on those posts and, depending on the blogging environment used, even rate the postings, their usefulness, or their accuracy.

Oracle WebCenter's Wiki and Blog Service allows you to integrate wiki or blog capabilities into your WebCenter application. The service can be easily integrated using a URL-consuming portlet or an iframe component.

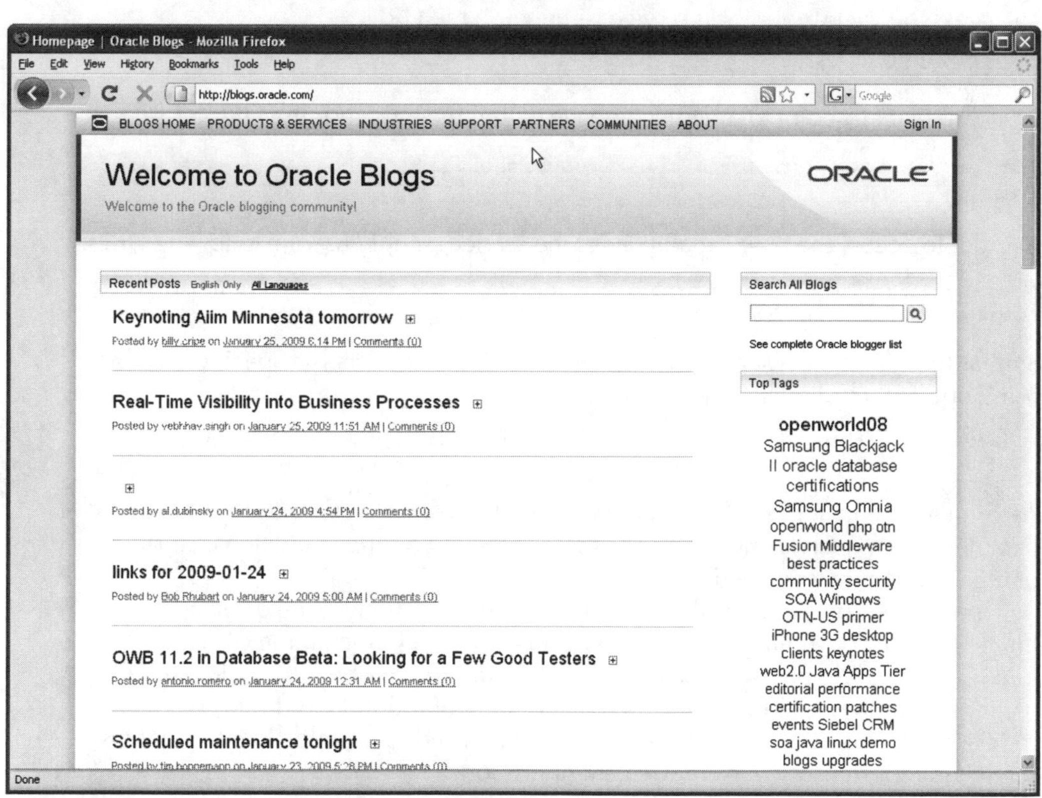

FIGURE 9-14 *Blogging site about Oracle products*

WIKI AND BLOG SERVICE CHARACTERISTICS

REQUIRES WEBCENTER SCHEMA: no
REQUIRES BACK-END SERVICE: yes—Oracle WebCenter wiki
REQUIRES APPLICATION TO BE SECURE: yes
OTHER DEPENDENCIES: none

AVAILABLE TASK FLOWS
none

Adding Wiki or Blogs to Your Application

To access the WebCenter wiki service, simply use the URL

```
http://<server>:<port>/owc_wiki/page/show.jz?inline=1&scope=<domain>
```

or, if you want to point to a particular page within the wiki, use the URL

```
http://<server>:<port>/owc_wiki/page/show.jz?inline=1&page=<domain>:
<wikiPageName>
```

In order to access the blog capabilities of the service, simply use the following URLs:

```
General Blog: http://<server>:<port>/owc_wiki/blog/list.jz?inline=1&name=<domain>
Personal Blog: http://<server>:<port>/owc_wiki/blog/list.jz?inline=1&name=<user>
```

Similar to addressing a specific wiki page, you can also address a specific blog by using one of the following URLs:

```
General Blog: http://<server>:<port>/owc_wiki/blog/list.jz?inline=1&name=<domain>
Personal Blog: http://<server>:<port>/owc_wiki/blog/list.jz?inline=1&name=<user>
```

As you can see in Table 9-1, the addressing of the service is done using regular URL parameters in a query string. By adding those to the query string, additional capabilities of the wiki can be leveraged.

The integration for the Wiki and Blog Service is currently done using a regular iframe or URL consuming portlet. For example, add an Inline Frame component to your application page and point the Source attribute to one of the URLs shown earlier in this chapter to access the respective area of the Wiki and Blog Service.

There will also be a set of portlets that can be used to seamlessly integrate this service into portals or your WebCenter application.

What about Security?

For the Wiki and Blog Service, the security is relatively simple. All you need to do is ensure that the users created in the Wiki and Blog Service follow the same model as the one in your application. So, for example, john.doe in your application should also be named john.doe on the service side. In the current release, the wiki service

Session Variable	Description
`inline`	Value of 0 sets the view to normal, displaying the Oracle Wiki Server default user interface and features. This is the recommended mode for wiki administrators. Value of `1` strips away nonessential wiki and blog chrome. It also renders left-side navigation that lists all wiki or blog pages within the current domain. This is the recommended mode when integrating with a custom application. Value of 2 is similar to `inline=1`, except it turns off left-side navigation.
`name`	Facilitates navigation to a specific blog, attributed to a particular domain or user.
`page`	Facilitates navigation to a specific page in a specified domain. This variable follows the syntax: `page=<domain>:<wikiPageName>`.
`scope`	Creates a new domain with the name specified for the `scope` variable. If such a named domain already exists, `scope` navigates to it. If the `scope` variable creates the domain on the fly, it also creates the home page (WelcomePage) and redirects the user to that page. Domain creators can specify another name besides WelcomePage for the start (default) page.
`theme`	Dynamically applies the specified wiki theme to the requested page (the theme must already exist on both Oracle Wiki Server and the application server). ■ `none` turns off CSS. ■ `default` applies the default theme specified on the server. ■ `<theme_name>` applies the specified wiki theme/CSS to the wiki page and all its children. Oracle Wiki Server provides seeded wiki themes, which you can include in your wiki and blog URLs. Use any one of the following (use the value in parentheses in the session variable): ■ Wiki Default (`default`) ■ Blue (`blue`) ■ Red (`red`) ■ WebCenter (`webcenter`) ■ Flatirons (`flatirons`) ■ Sand (`sand`) ■ Tech Gray (`tech_gray`) To ensure that your application chrome renders consistently, you'll want to additionally place a copy of all seeded CSS files on your application server. The list of themes is growing and will most likely be extended over time.

TABLE 9-1 *List of URL Parameters (Source: Oracle WebCenter Developers Guide)*

cannot share the same user store with your application. The service pages will automatically determine the logged-in user based on the JAAS context and assume its identity.

Announcement Service

When you look at the traditional use cases for community-style portals, one capability can be found across various portals, regardless of their type or topic: the ability to make announcements to the community, by publishing information to a main page or some other central place within the hierarchy.

Adding Announcements to Your Application

Oracle WebCenter uses its Discussion Service and a specialized task flow to allow the publishing of announcements. If you decide to add announcements to your application, make sure you have a forum set up to store the announcements, or you can decide to mix the announcements in with regular forum posts. An announcement is a special type of post and requires certain privileges to create it in the back-end repository. When you're adding the task flow to the page, the bindings dialog will let you specify which forum you want to use by providing a value, the ID of the forum, for the parameter ParentID.

ANNOUNCEMENT SERVICE CHARACTERISTICS

REQUIRES WEBCENTER SCHEMA: no
REQUIRES BACK-END SERVICE: yes—Oracle WebCenter Discussions
REQUIRES APPLICATION TO BE SECURE: yes
OTHER DEPENDENCIES: Discussion Service Connection

AVAILABLE TASK FLOWS

- **Announcements** This task flow displays a view that allows the user to see all current announcements and perform operations based on their privileges. For a moderator, all command buttons are shown, but for a reader, only the refresh and personalization options are shown. The personalization option lets users select the number of days to display announcements. The `parentId` parameter is the forum ID in the discussions server under which announcement objects are maintained.
- **Announcements—Sidebar View** This task flow displays a view that shows various categories of quick links to announcements. The look and feel of this view changes with the optional parameter values given for rendering the task flow region.

There are additional attributes for the Announcement Sidebar task flow:

- **`freeFlowView`** If this is set to true, then WebCenter removes the title/subject of all announcements in the task flow and shows only the announcement body with the HTML formatting. When `freeFlowView` equals `true`, the values for `truncateAt` and `expandedAnnouncements` are ignored. When `freeFlowView` equals false or is not set, announcements are controlled by the `expandedAnnouncements` and `truncateAt` parameters.
- **`expandedAnnouncements`** This parameter enables users to specify how many announcements show announcement details (that is, the body of the announcement). All other announcements display only their titles, which users can click to display the full announcement. The value you enter for `expandedAnnouncements` is ignored if `freeFlowView` is set to `true`.
- **`truncateAt`** For announcements that display announcement body details, this value specifies how many characters to display for each announcement. Enter an expression language (EL) expression. For example, when the value is set to the EL expression `${50}`, following their titles, announcements display no more than 50 characters. Users can click announcement titles to display the full announcement. If no value is specified, then WebCenter displays 50 characters. This parameter takes effect in conjunction with `expandedAnnouncements`. The value you enter for `truncateAt` is ignored if `freeFlowView` is set to `true`.

The capabilities of the task flow are driven by the security settings in the Discussions' back end. If the currently authenticated user has moderator or admin privileges in the back end, then the Create Announcement button is visible; otherwise, it is not.

Information Discovery Services

The next group of services we characterize as those that help locate or discover information. The classic term locate information refers to the process of looking up information by some kind of hierarchy, whether it's storage, attribute, or some other predefined hierarchy that documents adhere to. Another way of information discovery is by searching for terms or attributes that identify the information. The third, not so traditional way is by alternative characteristics, such as tags or the pure relationship between different pieces of information.

To support those different approaches, Oracle WebCenter provides a set of services that cater toward those requirements.

Links Service

Oftentimes, information stored in a different repository is semantically related; however, this relationship is not formally defined or known to users outside the immediate area where this information comes from. Technology barriers, more often than not, prevent tight integration between those systems. Oracle WebCenter provides the Links Service, which allows the linking between different information sources within your application.

Imagine an application where you provide the ability to store documents in the document repository and discussion threads in the discussion forum. Each service is encapsulating the functionalities and artifacts of its purpose but is oblivious to other services around it. A possible use case could be that authors want to open a discussion about a particular document. Obviously those could be created independent of each other, but then you would face the problem of communicating the fact that there is a discussion thread about a particular document somewhere in the discussion forum. Also, from the discussion forum point of view, how would a user there find the relevant document?

Ideally one would have a link between the document in the repository and the forum in the discussion system. The Links Service allows exactly that, without forcing information duplication or hard linking via URL.

There are certain interdependencies shown in Table 9-2. There are limitations to the list of services from where links can be initiated as well as to the list to which services links can be established. Some services allow linking to existing (E) artifacts, some support linking only to newly created artifacts (N). The Links Service automatically detects all configured services in your application and will show the corresponding entries in the Links dialog.

Link From	**Link To**							
	Announcements	Discussions	Documents	URLs	Mail	Worklist	Search	Custom
Announcements	E	N/E	N/E	N	✓	✓	✓	✓
Discussions	E	N/E	N/E	N	✓	✓	✓	✓
Documents	E	N/E	N/E	N	✓	✓	✓	✓
URLs	✓	✓	✓	✓	✓	✓	✓	✓
Mail	✓	✓	✓	✓	✓	✓	✓	✓
Worklist	✓	✓	✓	✓	✓	✓	✓	✓
Search		✓	✓	✓	✓	✓	✓	✓
Custom	E	N/E	N/E	N	✓	✓	✓	✓

TABLE 9-2 *Service Interaction*

LINKS SERVICE CHARACTERISTICS

REQUIRES WEBCENTER SCHEMA: yes
REQUIRES BACK-END SERVICE: none
REQUIRES APPLICATION TO BE SECURE: yes
OTHER DEPENDENCIES: auto-detects existing other services

AVAILABLE COMPONENTS

- **Links Detail Button** This displays an icon and (optionally) a hyperlink that when clicked opens the Links panel.
- **Links Detail Menu Item** This adds a menu item that opens the Links panel. You can embed this item in an ADF menu.
- **Links Status Icon** This displays an icon if links exist on a particular resource; otherwise, it displays nothing.

How to Prepare for Using the Links Service

The Links Service uses the WebCenter database schema to store its necessary metadata. Therefore you need to create a connection to the database schema (Figure 9-15).

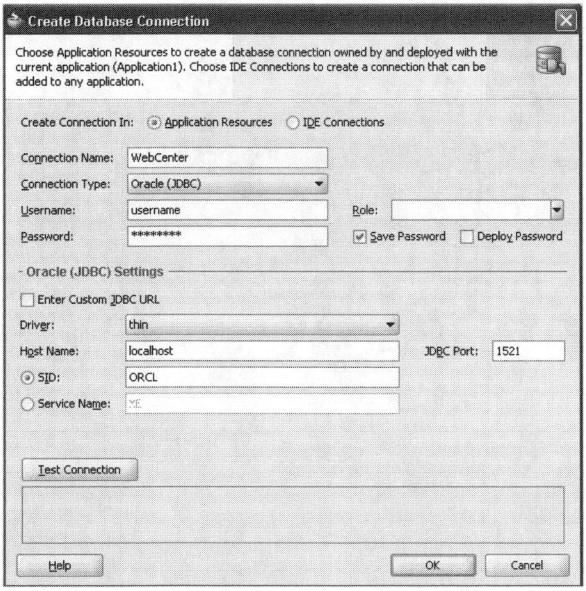

FIGURE 9-15 *Database connection wizard*

NOTE
In order to identify the connection, the Links Service assumes the connection name to be `WebCenter`*. If you decide to use a different database connection name, then you must add the following* `<data-source>` *tag as a child of the* `<wpsC:adf-service-config>` *element in the* `adf-config.xml` *file. (*`<data-source>` *should be a sibling of* `<extension-registry-config>`*.) Example:* `<data-source jndi-name="jdbc/<database_connection_name>DS"/>`*, (*`database_connection_name` *stands for the name of your database connection).*

How to Add Linking to Your Application

Different from other services, the Links Service is exposed in an application not only through a task flow, but through one of three components. In fact, the associated task flow represents the Links dialog, while the user interaction element is one of the three components. You can find the components in the Component Palette in the WebCenter Links Service group (Figure 9-16).

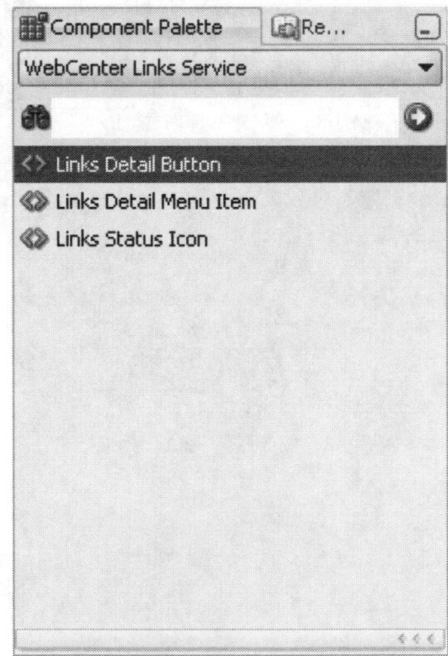

FIGURE 9-16 *Links Service components*

Once you drop one of them on your page, you will find the Insert … Details dialog asking for certain values to uniquely identify the object this particular component (or instance) should be bound to. It could be there to link the whole page, or it could be in a table to identify the records. For this, rather than providing fixed values, you would have to provide EL expressions with, for example, the primary key of the row for the project ID to facilitate identification at the row level.

- **objectDescription** The description of the object to which you are binding the Links Detail Button.
- **objectId** A unique ID that identifies the object to which you are binding the Links Detail Button.
- **objectName** The name of the object to which you are binding the Links Detail Button.
- **serviceId** The service identifier that you will eventually add to `service-definition.xml` when adding the resource viewer.

Adding this component will allow your users to see the status, whether there is a link available or not, and invoke the Link Details dialog. However, this dialog is a separate task flow and needs to be added to the application as well. Simply drag-and-drop the Links Dialog task flow from the Resource Palette to the page (Figure 9-17). It will not create any visible object on the page, but it provides the dialog that will be invoked if a user invokes the Links Service via one of the components. The Links Services will auto-detect the services available in your application and adjust the available link targets accordingly.

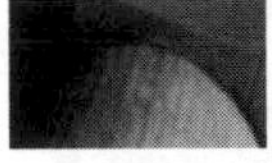

NOTE
If you experience problems when you're trying to link to a discussion, such as the message "No Forums were found," make sure you followed the steps described earlier for defining the root category by modifying adf-config.xml.

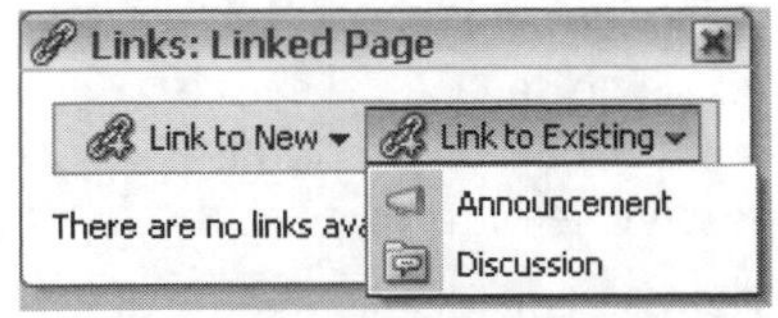

FIGURE 9-17 *The Links Service dialog at run time*

You will notice that the Links icon has two states, white and golden. Whenever the icon is golden, there are links defined for this particular resource.

For certain services, the Links Service is automatically activated by simply adding the corresponding service task flow to your application page. So, for example, the Document Library task flow would automatically offer the Links capabilities.

Tag Service

Very similar to the Links Service, the Tag Service is targeted toward simplifying information location and classification. Tags are user-chosen words attached to some artifact. Those keywords are tracked and analyzed across users and build up the tag cloud where the occurrence and combination of terms creates a web of interconnection between artifacts across different sources. That way, a user searching for a particular tag will be able not only to locate artifacts with the same tag from different sources, but he or she may be guided by the tag cloud to other, related tags or artifacts.

TAG SERVICE CHARACTERISTICS

REQUIRES WEBCENTER SCHEMA: yes
REQUIRES BACK-END SERVICE: no
REQUIRES APPLICATION TO BE SECURE: yes (for personal tags)
OTHER DEPENDENCIES: none

AVAILABLE TASK FLOWS

- **Tagging—Dialog** Similar to the Links Service, there is also a required task flow to display the operational dialog for this service. You need to add this task flow so the Tag Link component can invoke it to allow the user to enter tags.
- **Tagging—Personal View** This task flow shows the tags created by the current user and objects tagged by those tags. (It requires authentication.)
- **Tagging—Related Links** This task flow shows all related objects relative to the object whose ID was passed into the task flow. You can control the accuracy by a threshold value.
- **Tagging—Tag Cloud** The Tag Cloud shows a visual representation of the popularity of tags by their usage numbers. You can invoke a search for a tag by clicking on one of the tags in the tag cloud.
- **Tagging—Tagged Items** This displays a list of tagged items. The list can be refined by passing in a tag. Tagged items can be combined with the Tag Cloud task flow. The Tag Cloud can raise events that can be consumed by, for example, the tagged items to drive its contents.

Adding Tagging to Your Application

Along the lines of the Links Service, the Tag Service also consists of several task flows and two UI components (Figure 9-18). These components represent the elements that you can use to invoke the tagging capability.

FIGURE 9-18 *The Tag Link component with tag rollover at run time*

Among the various task flows there is one that is required on all pages that leverage the tagging feature. This task flow, the Tagging Dialog, represents the user dialog to create and modify tags of a given item (Figure 9-19). It has no UI rendering at design time and gets rendered only once a user clicks on the Tag link or menu item at run time. You will find a checkbox on that dialog that determines whether the tag you provide would be available to you personally or would be shared with other users.

Once you drop in the Tag Button or Tag Menu Item component, a similar dialog like the one with the Links Service appears. You are required to enter certain mandatory values in order to identify the artifact you want to tag.

- **ResourceId** The unique identifier for your custom component or object. In this case, enter `customComponent123`. Note that the value in this field need not be static. You can use EL, too. For example, you might use EL to insert a unique value for each row in a table.
- **ResourceName** The name of the custom component. In this case, enter `Custom Component 1`. Note that the value in this field need not be static. You can use EL, too. For example, you might use EL to insert a unique value for each row in a table.
- **ServiceId** The service identifier that you will eventually add to `service-definition.xml` when you're adding the resource viewer.

FIGURE 9-19 *The Tagging Dialog task flow at run time*

Search Service

Being able to search is one of the most common requirements across applications. Users want to be able to search the artifacts of the application they are working with. Given that you are moving into the Enterprise 2.0 era and considering the fact that now applications leverage multiple services and information repositories, search becomes quite a complex topic. But it's an even more important requirement for users. The more information sources are combined in a single application, the more crucial it becomes to allow a search across those sources, presenting the result back in a single view. It is all about presenting information in context.

Oracle WebCenter Search works as a search federator where search criteria are distributed to all services registered in your application. The search result is presented and grouped by source in a single list, allowing the user to get a unified view of the search result from all relevant sources.

Additional sources, such as Oracle Secure Enterprise Search, can be registered to provide an even wider view for the user.

SEARCH SERVICE CHARACTERISTICS

REQUIRES WEBCENTER SCHEMA: no
REQUIRES BACK-END SERVICE: no—auto-detects services used
REQUIRES APPLICATION TO BE SECURE: no—unless searching secure content
OTHER DEPENDENCIES: no

AVAILABLE TASK FLOWS

- **Search** This task flow provides a rich search experience with several options for searching and the ability to refine and save the search results.
- **Search—Saved Searches** This task flow lets you access previously saved searches.
- **Search Preferences** This task flow lets you select which WebCenter Web 2.0 services to search. It also allows users to select and order the columns available in the search results.
- **Search Toolbar** This task flow lets users quickly enter simple search criteria and run the search from any page of the application.

Adding Search to Your Application

In general, Oracle WebCenter Search does not require any setup steps. If, however, you want to use additional sources, like Oracle Secure Enterprise Search (SES), those need to be configured, and in case of Oracle SES, a connection needs to be created, so Oracle WebCenter Search can access the SES search engine (Figure 9-20).

The simplest way to add search capabilities to your application is to simply drop the Search Toolbar task flow onto your page (Figure 9-21). It allows the user to perform simple searches across the registered sources. To add richer search experience, complete with search refinement capabilities, simply drag the Search task flow to your page.

How Do You Add Search Sources?

As described, Oracle WebCenter Search will auto-detect the WebCenter Services used in your application and automatically search them. You can, however, register additional sources to expand the view your users get.

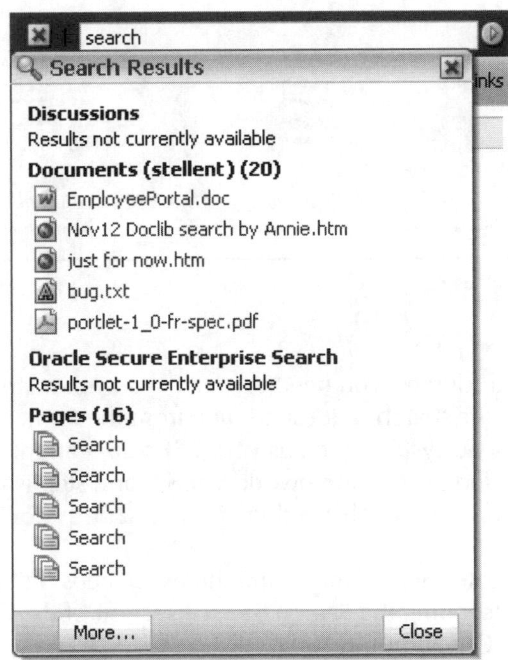

FIGURE 9-20 *Search Toolbar task flow*

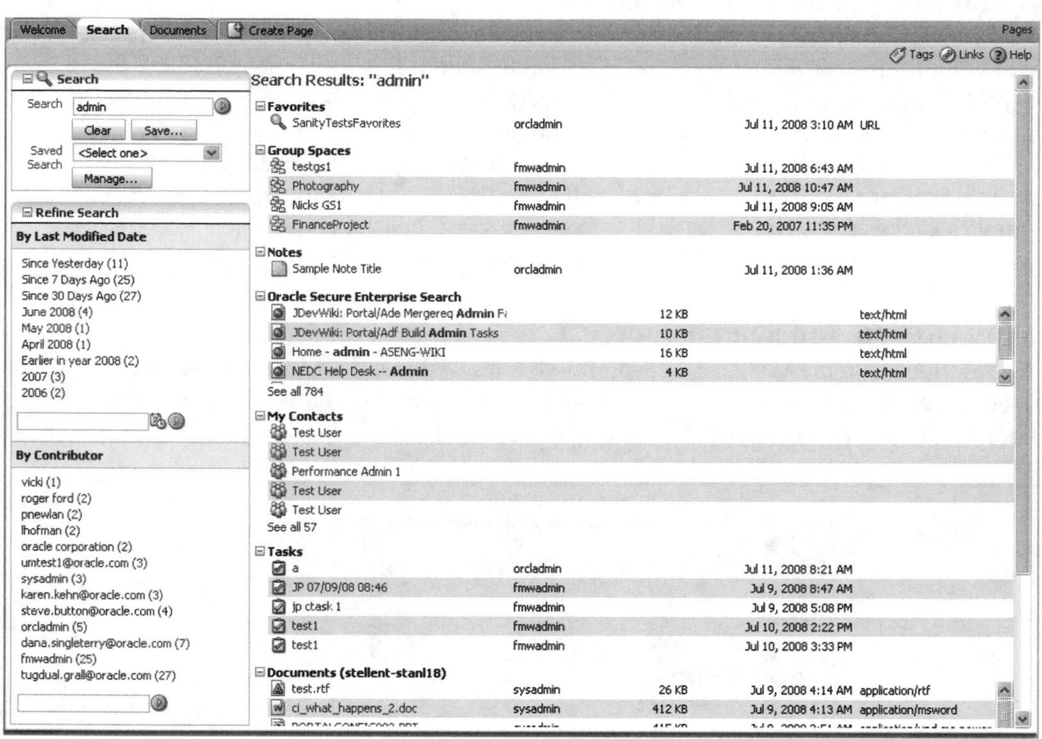

FIGURE 9-21 *Search task flow*

To add those external sources, you need to create a search adapter which is responsible for handling the search request coming from the framework, dispatching it to the respective back-end system (such as your ERP application), then delivering the search result back to the Search framework. The second step is to register this source with the Search framework. This is done in `services-config.xml` within your application.

Details on how to create such adapters and the exact steps on how to register them can be found in Integrating the Search Service section of the Oracle Fusion Middleware Developers Guide for Oracle WebCenter.

Communication Services

For Web 2.0 and Enterprise 2.0, communication between individuals is more important than ever before. The services in this category will allow us to add communication capabilities to any application.

Mail Service

One of today's most widely used electronic communication services is, no doubt, e-mail. Most of us use it multiple times a day for business and personal communication. Life without e-mail, for a lot of us, would be an unthinkable scenario; it has even become business critical in many areas.

A lot of companies use e-mail systems today for business communication, and employees use it on a day-to-day basis, so integrating their e-mail system into those business applications, alongside other services, is becoming more and more important.

Oracle WebCenter provides a service that allows you to consume your corporate e-mail service and expose your users' e-mail in your application. This service does not try to replace traditional desktop or web e-mail clients such as Microsoft Outlook, Mozilla Thunderbird, Zimbra, or Microsoft Outlook Web Access, but can be used to provide a simple yet productive way to keep track of your e-mail communication. It also allows simple e-mail operations, such as read, reply, forward, and create e-mails.

Adding E-mail Capabilities to Your Application

Before you can add e-mail capabilities to any application, you need to create a connection to the e-mail system of choice.

Simply right-click on the Connections node in the Application Resources panel and select Mail from the list of available connection types. You will be presented with the connection wizard.

MAIL SERVICE CHARACTERISTICS

REQUIRES WEBCENTER SCHEMA: no
REQUIRES BACK-END SERVICE: yes—e-mail Server (IMAP, incl. Microsoft Exchange)
REQUIRES APPLICATION TO BE SECURE: no (If Application is not secured, the mail connection needs to be configured to use External Application Authentication and has to have Public Credentials defined. Those credentials will be used to authenticate toward the e-mail server if no specific user is authenticated.)
OTHER DEPENDENCIES: no

AVAILABLE TASK FLOWS

- **Mail** This task flow can present your e-mail inbox in two ways, one being a traditional, tabular view, the other a more compact view that can be used in a sidebar, for example.

NOTE
Remember to set the Default Connection flag. This is how the mail service will identify which connection should be used.

On the second screen of the wizard you need to provide the necessary parameters for the connection to your mail server (Figure 9-22).

- `mail.imap.host` Location of your IMAP server.
- `mail.imap.port` Your IMAP server port number. The default is -1.
- `mail.smtp.host` Location of your SMTP server.
- `mail.smtp.port` Your SMTP server port number. The default is -1.
- `(optional) mail.imap.secured` Takes a value or true/false to indicate if you should use secure SSL connection.
- `(optional) mail.smtp.secured` Takes a value or true/false to indicate if you should use secure SSL connection.
- `(optional) ldap.host` and `ldap.port` Are needed only if MS-Exchange 2003 is the mail server and you intend to leverage create distribution lists.

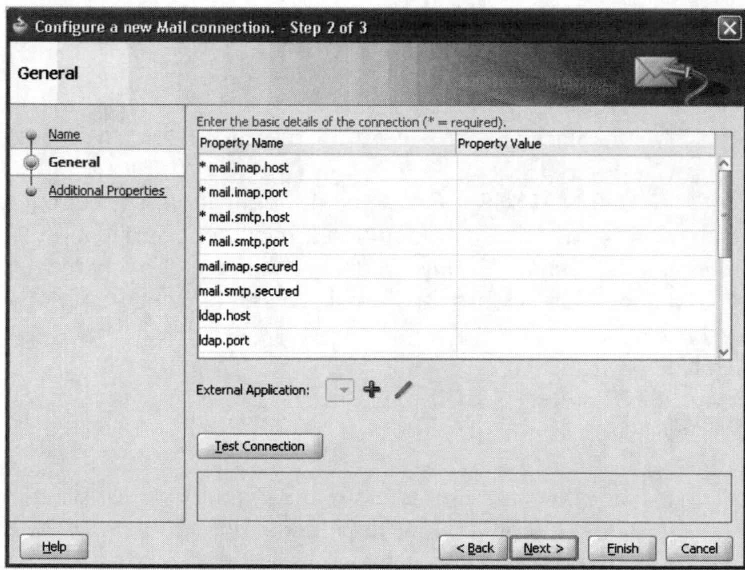

FIGURE 9-22 *Connection parameters for the mail server connection*

Also, you need to create an application ID for the External Application framework right from within the wizard. To do so, simply click on the plus sign next to the ApplicationID drop-down or select an existing ID from that drop-down.

Once you created the connection you can add the e-mail task flow from the Resources Palette to your page (Figure 9-23). The Mail task flow has two rendering modes which can be toggled by setting the `tabularView` task flow attribute. If set to `true`, the task flow will render the e-mails in an inbox-like table, while it will render it in the sidebar view if the attribute is left empty or is set to `false`.

If there have been no credentials pre-populated into the credential store, the first time users visit the mail service, the Mail task flow will present only a Login to Mail link. If users click on it, a dialog allows them to provide their e-mail server credentials which are securely stored in the credential store for them (if they check the Remember My Login Information checkbox). To let the user change those credentials, you can create a page to change the password stored for the mail service. This can easily be done by leveraging the External Application—Change Password task flow. You create a page in your application that would hold this task flow. From this page the user would be able to modify the stored credentials for each registered service.

Instant Messaging & Presence Service

A more direct way of communication and a highly productive way of determining a person's availability is instant messaging, a channel with instant response but still asynchronous and hence less intrusive than a regular phone call, though more instant than e-mail communication.

Most instant messaging systems, besides the chatting capabilities, provide some kind of presence service. Users can set their status as available or unavailable and, depending on the service, a more fine-grained status can be set.

In a collaborative system, communication is key, and if the system is able to convey the status of a person and the communication channels available to a

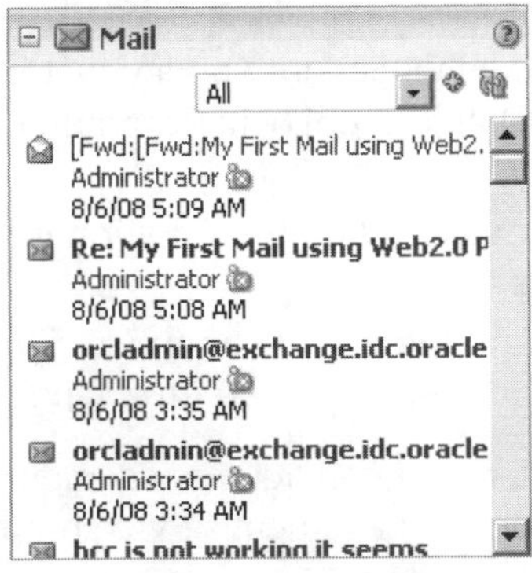

FIGURE 9-23 *The Mail task flow's sidebar view mode*

particular person, then users of this system don't have to embark on a hunt for their counterparts, but can simply choose one of the currently available communications channels.

Oracle WebCenter's Instant Messaging & Presence service (IM&P) tries to provide exactly this service. Tied to a back-end IM system, it up levels this information to any application. The IM&P service connects to a back-end system through an adapter framework. Oracle WebCenter bundles Oracle WebLogic Communications Services, but other SIP-based IM services, such as Microsoft's Live Communication Server, can be used with IM&P. Which third-party systems are supported should be verified with Oracle Support Services, as this list will most likely expand over time.

Adding Presence Capabilities to Your Application

Like other services, you need to create a connection to the Presence server before you can use the service in your application. Simply right-click on the Connections node in the Application Resources panel and select Presence & IM from the list of available connection types.

You will be asked to provide the necessary connection information for the connection to either Microsoft's Live Communication Server or to WebLogic Communication Server. Be sure to provide a full URL for the server info, not just the server name.

- `base.connection.url` and `domain` Enter the location of your OWLCS instance. The following properties are optional.
- `cache.expiration.time` The time (in minutes) the cache should live in memory. After this time, the cache will be removed.
- `connection.time.out` The time (in seconds) the service should wait for the server to respond while making the connection. If the discussions server does not respond in the given time then it will abort the connection and report an error.
- `policyURI` URI to the WS-Security policy that is required for authentication on the Oracle WebLogic Communication Server.

The following parameters can be added on the Additional Parameters tab:

- `presence.url` URL to the presence service. This needs to be supplied if the presence service has been deployed on a separate server.
- `contacts.url` URL to the contact management service. This needs to be supplied if the contact management service has been deployed on a separate server.

INSTANT MESSAGING & PRESENCE SERVICE CHARACTERISTICS

REQUIRES WEBCENTER SCHEMA: no
REQUIRES BACK-END SERVICE: yes—Instant Messaging (such as Oracle WebLogic Communications Services)
REQUIRES APPLICATION TO BE SECURE: yes
OTHER DEPENDENCIES: External Application Security, IM client install

AVAILABLE TASK FLOWS

- **Buddies** Represents the buddy list as it is stored in the underlying IM system.
- **Presence** (component) Represents the icon indicating the presence status of a given user. It also allows the initiation of an IM conversation, an e-mail, a phone conference, or an online meeting. It requires Presence Data (component) to be present on the page.

- `call.url` URL for the third-party call server. If no value is supplied, then this uses the same value as `base.connection.url`.
- `call.method` Supports values `sip` and `pstn`. When set to `sip`, the IMP service will forward the user's SIP address to the third-party call service. The third-party call service must decide on the routing of the call. If it is set to `pstn`, then the user's phone number is based on the user's profile attribute (`BUSINESS_PHONE`). This default profile attribute (`BUSINESS_PHONE`) can be changed to any other attribute with the connection property `call.number.attribute`.
- `call.domain` The domain name of the `pstn` gateway. If no domain name is supplied, then this uses the same value as the `domain`. This should be supplied only when `call.method` is set to `pstn`.
- `contact.number.attribute` The attribute used to read users' phone numbers from the user profile. The default is `BUSINESS_PHONE`. This should be supplied only when `call.method` is set to `pstn`.
- `primary.domain` If the WebCenter user identity is qualified with a domain (for example, `john.deo@oracle.com`), and if the presence server domain is different (for example, `john.deo@example.com`), then the primary domain `oracle.com` should be specified here. If the user identity is qualified with a domain and the presence server uses the same `oracle.com` domain, then you do not need to specify the `primary.domain`.

FIGURE 9-24 *Presence tag*

The presence service itself is visually represented by the Presence component and the Buddies task flow. The Presence component renders the Presence tag (Figure 9-24), which indicates a user's status as well as provides access to the communications menu where you can select the channel of communication you want to use.

The Presence component requires the Presence Data component to be on the page with it; however, there needs to be only one Presence Data component on any given page. Its purpose is to establish the connection to the IM service and provide the status for all the Presence components on the page. Because this component initiates communication with the service in the background, you should have it as one of the last elements on a page to avoid render delays. The presence service presents itself through the Presence context menu (see Figure 9-25).

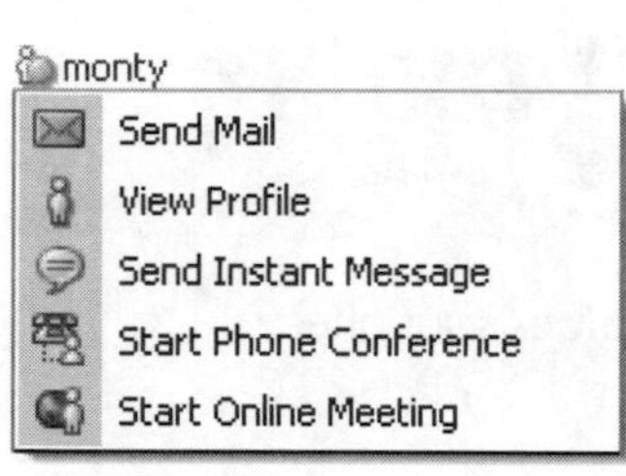

FIGURE 9-25 *Presence context menu*

The Buddies task flow represents the user's buddy list as it is retrieved from the back-end IM system. This task flow is very helpful if you want to provide generic IM and presence capabilities without adding individual Presence components onto the page.

When you're adding the Presence tag onto a page, you will be asked for the user name of the user that this particular tag should represent. Keep in mind that the name you enter there has to be the username in the back-end IM system. Ideally your usernames would be identical across the services, but sometimes this is not possible, so you need to find a way to translate between the different username nomenclatures you might have.

Like with Tagging and Linking, some services task flows (such as Document Library) implicitly use and surface the presence service.

Miscellaneous Services

There are a couple of services that are hard to categorize or that fall into multiple categories due to their nature.

Documents Service

We have discussed integrating content at length in the previous chapter, so in this section we will cover only a few.

DOCUMENTS SERVICE CHARACTERISTICS

REQUIRES WEBCENTER SCHEMA: no
REQUIRES BACK-END SERVICE: yes—Content Repository (e.g., Content Server)
REQUIRES APPLICATION TO BE SECURE: no
OTHER DEPENDENCIES: none

AVAILABLE TASK FLOWS

- **Document Library—List View** Here you can display a list of content items at a given location. This component is useful if all you want to do is to show content items and allow your application user to browse through this content.
- **Document Library—Recent Documents** The Recent Documents task flow allows you to present the user with a list of documents that were recently accessed. This can come in handy when you want to provide a kind of recent activities view across your document repository.
- **Document Library—Document Library** A complex component that allows you to perform complex document management functions, such as uploading documents, inspecting and changing file properties, and much more. We will go more into the functionality of the Document Library region later in this chapter. Depending on the capability of the connection, the features allow read-only or read/write access.

Recent Activity Service

In collaborative environments it can become hard to keep track of what is happening in the different information repositories. Modern social networking sites introduced activity streams, a steady list of all events that had taken place over time. That way, people can keep track of what happens around them. A similar concept is behind the Recent Activity Service. It tracks events in various WebCenter services and exposes them as a kind of activity stream. Just consider the way you normally locate elements: you search or locate them. With Recent Activities you can get a bird's-eye view of what has happened and avoid a long search. Another interesting fact is that, like most of the WebCenter services, Recent Activities can be consumed via RSS. So if your users already have RSS Readers in use, they could subscribe to the Recent Activity feed and won't even have to actively visit the web application to see what's new there.

The Recent Activity Service can track:

- Documents
- Announcements
- Discussion forums
- Pages created or modified by the page service
- Oracle Secure Enterprise Search repositories

How to Add Recent Activities to Your Application

Before you can add Recent Activities to your application, you need to make sure that at least one of the tracked services already exists on the page (Figure 9-26). While you can still add the task flow, if there is no other service, your application will display an error at run time.

Once you add the Recent Activities task flow to your page (Figure 9-27), you will be asked for a set of parameters to define the task flow.

- `groupSpace` Leave the value of this parameter as null. This value is used only if the task flow is used as part of WebCenter Spaces.
- `timePeriodShort` Default value: `Today`. Possible values: `Today`, `Yesterday`, or a `Time in Minutes`.

RECENT ACTIVITY SERVICE CHARACTERISTICS

REQUIRES WEBCENTER SCHEMA: no
REQUIRES BACK-END SERVICE: no
REQUIRES APPLICATION TO BE SECURE: no
OTHER DEPENDENCIES: Tracks other services. At least one has to exist in the application, otherwise an error is displayed.

AVAILABLE TASK FLOWS

- **Recent Activities** Shows the list of recent events with the different services.

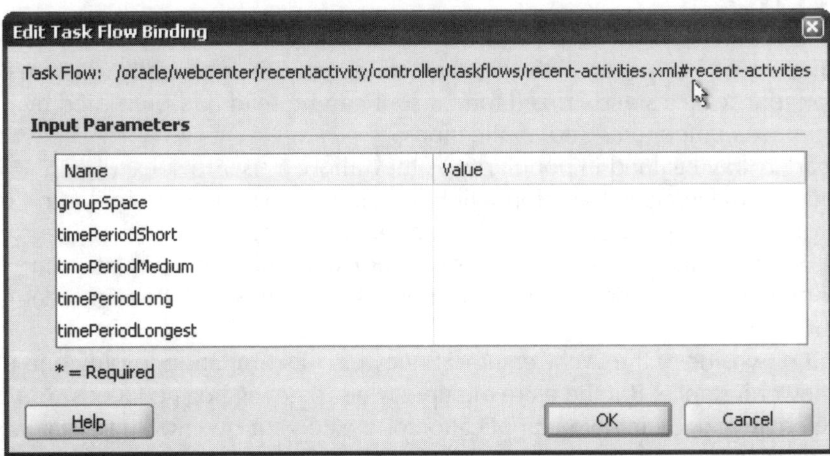

FIGURE 9-26 *The Binding dialog for the Recent Activities task flow*

- `timePeriodMedium` Default value: `Since Yesterday`. Possible values: `Today`, `Yesterday`, or a `Time in Minutes`.
- `timePeriodLong` Default value: `10080`. (10,080 minutes is equivalent to 7 days.) Possible values: `Today`, `Yesterday`, or a `Time in Minutes`.
- `timePeriodLongest` Default value: `43200`. (43,200 minutes is equivalent to 30 days.) Possible values: `Today`, `Yesterday`, or a `Time in Minutes`.

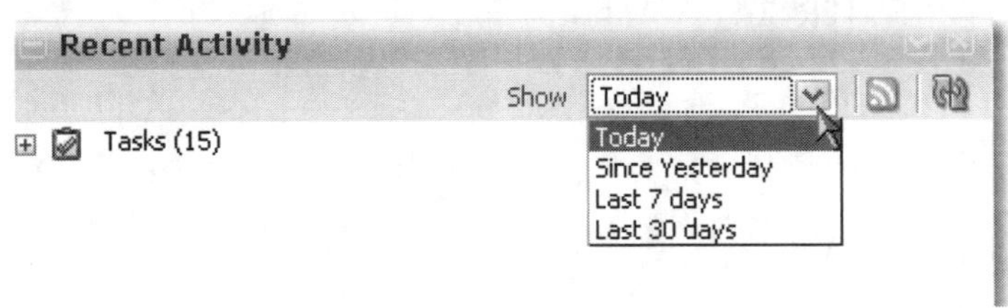

FIGURE 9-27 *The Recent Activities task flow*

RSS Service

Real Simple Syndication, or RSS, is a widely used XML grammar for providing feeds of news items, news being used in the most general sense. RSS is basically a stream of information following a standardized format so it can be read and presented by general-purpose components and applications.

RSS readers have gained in popularity as they allow a user to subscribe to various feeds and aggregate the information in a unified experience, similar to the goal Enterprise 2.0 applications and Mash-Ups are pursuing.

The RSS Service in Oracle WebCenter is responsible for surfacing data from the other services as RSS and it provides a simple RSS Viewer task flow in order to consume RSS feeds.

A small downside of the WebCenter RSS Viewer is its limitation to only one RSS feed per viewer instance. But there are multiple ways to get aggregated feeds. You can integrate Google gadgets into your application or create your own RSS aggregator.

Adding an RSS Feed to Your Application

The RSS Viewer task flow does not have any external dependencies and can be used simply by placing it on the page (Figure 9-28). All you need to provide is the location of the desired RSS feed in URL format for the `rssFeedLocation` parameter (e.g., ${'http://www.oracle.com/rss/rss_ocom_pr.xml'}). In some cases, RSS feeds require authentication, especially if the content has to be paid for. In this case, you need to provide an External Application ID for the parameter `extAppId` (e.g. ${'myRssCredentials'}) so the component can leverage the External Application framework and the Credential Store to store and retrieve the credentials to authenticate to the RSS feed.

RSS SERVICE CHARACTERISTICS

REQUIRES WEBCENTER SCHEMA: no
REQUIRES BACK-END SERVICE: no
REQUIRES APPLICATION TO BE SECURE: no
OTHER DEPENDENCIES: no

AVAILABLE TASK FLOWS

- **RSS Viewer** Publishes the items from a given RSS feed in your application page.

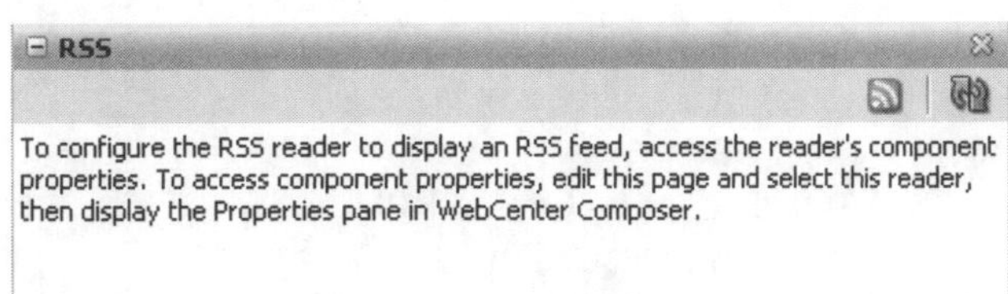

FIGURE 9-28 *RSS Viewer at run time*

NOTE
In most cases, those RSS feeds will come from some external source, and in order to access the feed, a proxy server needs to be defined. When you're executing the application from JDeveloper, the proxy settings will be set for you. You will find out how to define the proxy in your deployment environment in Chapter 19.

Worklist Service

The Worklist Service can be used to visualize open tasks, or process, from Oracle BPEL assigned to the currently authenticated user. It provides an at-a-glance view of all open business processes that require the user's attention (Figure 9-29).

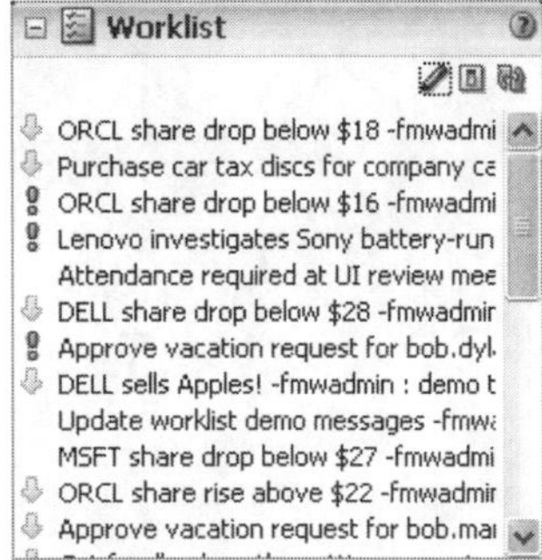

FIGURE 9-29 *Oracle WebCenter Worklist task flow*

WORKLIST SERVICE CHARACTERISTICS

REQUIRES WEBCENTER SCHEMA: no
REQUIRES BACK-END SERVICE: yes—Oracle BPEL
REQUIRES APPLICATION TO BE SECURE: yes
OTHER DEPENDENCIES: none

AVAILABLE TASK FLOWS

- **Worklist** Displays all open BPEL tasks.

How to Add the Worklist to Your Application

The Worklist task flow requires a configured connection to your BPEL server. Simply right-click on the Connections node in the Application Resources panel and select Worklist from the list of available connection types.

In the Create Connection dialog you need to provide the necessary values to establish the connection to your BPEL server (Figure 9-30):

- URL: Enter the location of your BPEL/SOA server, such as `http://bpel.example.com`. This is the URL for the managed server running the SOA processes.

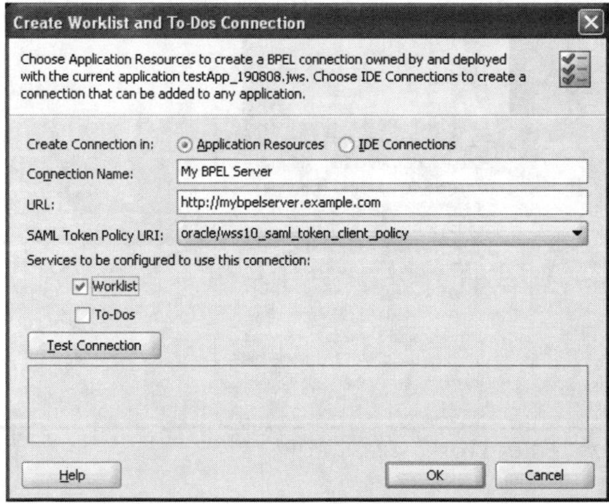

FIGURE 9-30 *Creating a BPEL connection*

- Select the SAML Token Policy URI to use for this server. SAML (Security Assertion Markup Language) is an XML-based standard for passing security tokens defining authentication and authorization rights. An attesting entity (which already has a trust relationship with the receiver) vouches for the verification of the subject by a method called sender-vouches. Options available are
  - **SAML Token Client Policy (oracle/wss10_saml_token_client_policy)** Select to verify your basic configuration without any additional security. This is the default setting.
  - **SAML Token with Message Client Policy (oracle/wss10_saml_token_with_message_protection_client_policy)** Select to increase the security using SAML-based BPEL Web Services. If selected, you must configure keys stores both in your custom WebCenter application and in the BPEL application. To learn more about this configuration, refer to Chapter 9, "Configuring Policies," in Oracle Fusion Middleware Security and Administrator's Guide for Web Services.

Once the connection has been created, you can drop the Worklist task flow onto the page, by dragging-and-dropping from the Resources Palette.

Extending the Services Concept in Your Application

While WebCenter's Web 2.0 services provide a wide spectrum of functionality, they are most certainly not an exhaustive set of every possible service of interest to every user out there. Also, some services might provide too much or don't have enough functionality.

In these cases, you might decide to create your own custom components and integrate those into the overall WebCenter experience. You especially might want to enable them for horizontal services such as Links, Tags, Search, and Recent Activities.

The Resource Action Handler framework is one of these hooks that a custom component can provide to existing WebCenter Services to integrate. It allows a service to look up the method of how to render an artifact of a given service. For example, the Resource Action Handler invokes the compose e-mail dialog if a user clicks on an e-mail that was returned during a search for a certain keyword in the search result screen.

Services that invoke resource views using the Resource Action Handler framework are

- Search
- Tags

- Links
- Recent Activities

Services that own task flows that can be invoked by the Resource Action Handler framework are

- Announcements
- Discussions
- Documents (Resource URL rewriter to point to GET handler)
- Mail
- Page (Resource URL rewriter to point to page URL)
- Search—Main View
- Tags—Tag Center

More details about this can be found in the Oracle Fusion Middleware Developers Guide for Oracle WebCenter.

Tying It All Together

Now that we have discussed Oracle WebCenter Web 2.0 Services individually, it is time to explain the benefit and, more importantly, show how easy it is to build an application that leverages those services.

So let's say you want to build an application that shows a list of files stored in the content repository at a given location. For each file you want the ability to attach a tag to the file and link the file to some other service's elements. Also, you want to let users contact the author of the document. Last but not least, you want to provide an overall search capability.

While this task sounds daunting, in fact we have discussed all necessary services already.

- **Document Service** To display the table of files, you will use the Content Repository Data Control to access the content item list.
- **Links & Tags Service** You will use the components of these services to attach the linking and tagging functionality to your table of files.
- **IM & Presence Service** In order to provide the communication capabilities you will use the IM&P component to enhance the author column of the files table.
- **Search Service** With no significant effort you will add global search capabilities to the application.

First of all, you need to create a new JSPX page. Invoke the New option from the menu or the toolbar and select JSF Page from the list of available objects to create. Now you can specify the details for this page in the New dialog.

Creating the Documents Table

Next you need to create a content repository connection. This can easily be done by right-clicking on the connection node of the Application Resources panel and selecting Content Repository from the list of available connections. You select a connection type, for example Content Server, and fill out all the necessary connection values (for details, please see Chapter 7). Once the connection is created, right-click on the connection name and select the Create Data Control option from the context menu. The Create Data Control wizard will allow us to create the data control for this content connection.

Now all you need to do is to create an ADF Table for this content repository. Expand the Data Control panel and then expand the Data Control node and farther down the GetItems node.

Drag the Returns node onto the blank page and select ADF Table | ADF Read-Only Table from the context menu (Figure 9-31).

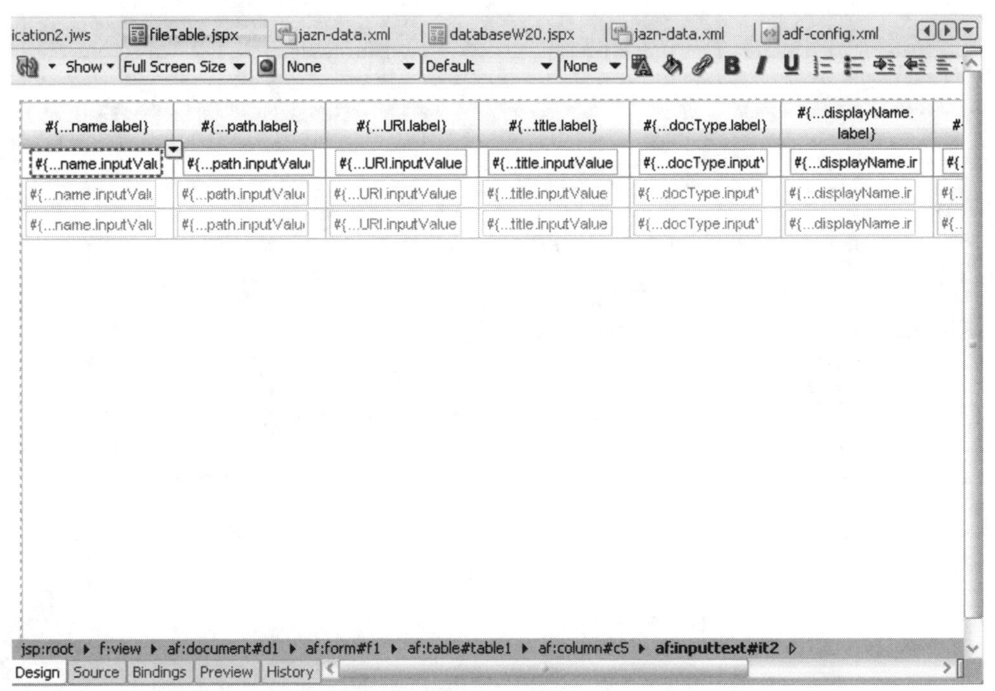

FIGURE 9-31 *The ADF Table listing the files coming from Oracle Content Server*

Securing Your Application

Before you go any further, secure this application. You need to do this, because some of the services you are going to use require the user to be authenticated. To secure an application, invoke the ADF Security wizard through Application | Security | Configure ADF Security.

Then step through the wizard as we described earlier in this chapter. If you want to get details on the role of ADF Security in a WebCenter application, see Chapter 19.

Once ADF Security is configured, you need to set the correct policies for your page. To do so, invoke the policies editor via Application | Security | ADF Policies (Figure 9-32).

In this example, the name of the page is fileTable. So on the Web Pages tab simply select this page. Now you see the assigned roles and privileges. Right now, the only role that has privileges assigned is the test-all role with the view privilege. Uncheck View to disable this.

Next you add a new role to the list by clicking on the green + sign in the Granted to Roles column. For simplicity, select the authenticated role, which is a blanket role for all users authenticated to the system. After adding it, select it in the Granted to Role column and select the View privilege for this role.

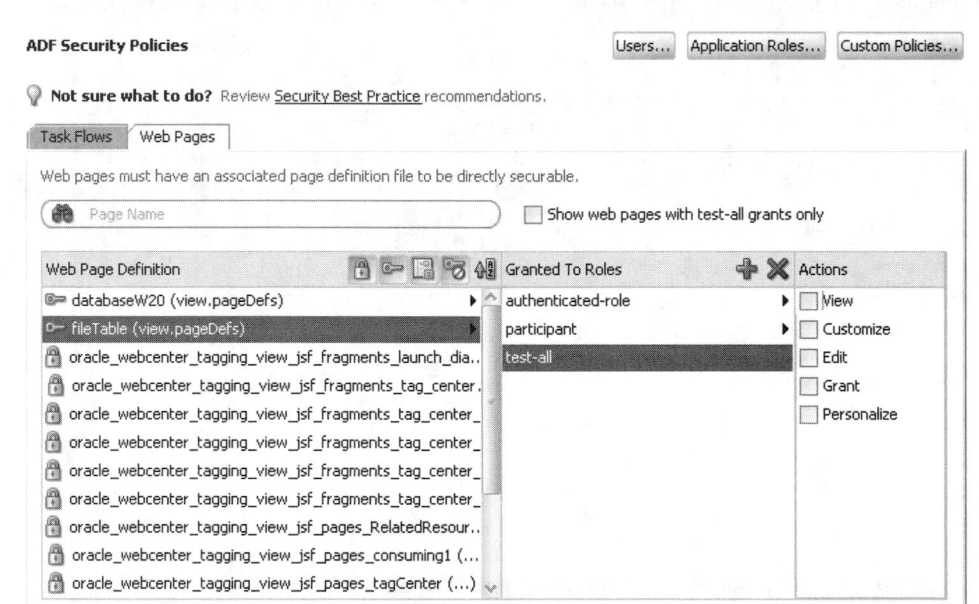

FIGURE 9-32 *The ADF Security Policies*

Adding Linking and Tagging

Next, you'll add linking and tagging to the application. As we discussed earlier, linking and tagging both require a connection to the WebCenter database schema, as well as a secured application. The latter requirement we just satisfied by configuring ADF Security. The database connection, however, you still need to create (unless you are working in a project with the connection already created).

Simply right-click on the Connections node in the Application Resources panel and select Database from the list of available connection types, provide the connection details to the WebCenter schema, and you are good to go. Just keep in mind that the name of the connection should be **WebCenter**; otherwise you need to modify the adf-config.xml.

Now that the two prerequisites, the database connection and security, are satisfied, add the service components and task flows.

First add the two dialogs required for the services. Select the Resource Palette and expand the WebCenter Services Catalog | Task Flows node. Drag-and-drop the Links Dialog and the Tags Dialog task flow onto the page. As described earlier, those two will not render in the design time and will be used by the Links Detail button and Tagging button to render the necessary dialogs during link creation or tagging.

Now switch to the Component Palette and bring up the WebCenter Links Service components. Drag-and-drop the Links Detail button into the first-row column underneath the heading #{...name.label}. You will be presented with the Insert Links Detail button dialog, asking for the necessary attributes. This is where it gets a bit tricky for a second. The Links Service needs some unique identification for the artifact that is going to be linked. Besides a unique objectID it also needs some name and description, as well as a serviceID; the latter is used to identify where this link is coming from to potentially link back to its source. This is where the Resource Action Handler and the resource viewer comes into play, but for now, you don't really care about it, though you'll still provide a value, such as application.employee.list. For the other values you need to set some relevant values. How do you do that?

Well, what is going to happen at run time? When the application is executed, the ADF table will be fed with records from the database and create rows for each record, according to the template row defined at design time. All elements in there will be dealt with at the instance level. So, therefore, your Links Detail button also will be dealt with (Figure 9-33), and whatever values you provide for ObjectID; ObjectDescription and ObjectName need to be dynamic rather than static.

If you take a closer look at the table that was generated earlier, you can see that the row template also has, for obvious reasons, dynamic references in EL for the field values.

In this particular case you can identify the name (filename) as the fitting value for ObjectName and ObjectDescription, and the URI (link to the physical file and hence unique) fits the requirements of ObjectId. So you'll reference these values in the dialog.

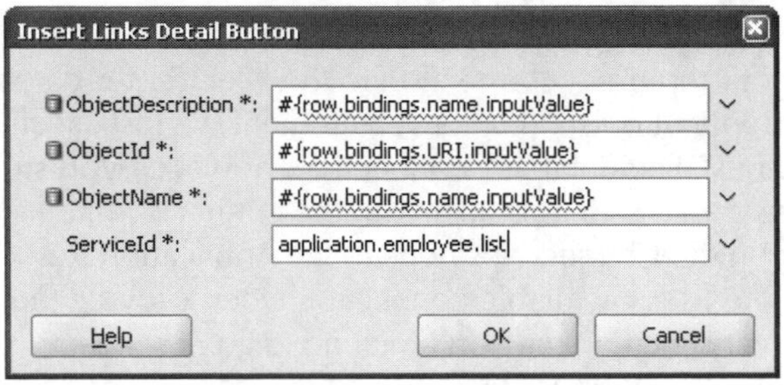

FIGURE 9-33 *Referencing dynamic values*

Using EL, for example `#{row.bindings.name.inputValue}`, you can reference those dynamic values and ensure that the rendered table will have the corresponding values for the attributes of each instance of Links Detail button (Figure 9-34).

OK. So, being as brave as you are, you want to take a look at what you have created so far. Save your work, right-click on the page, and select Run. After a few seconds you will be prompted for your credentials. Specify the user credentials you created earlier when you were securing the application and the page should render your first Enterprise 2.0 application.

To prove that the links will be created for each individual element, click on one of the Links buttons and the Links dialog will show you the name of the associated item in the dialog title (Figure 9-35).

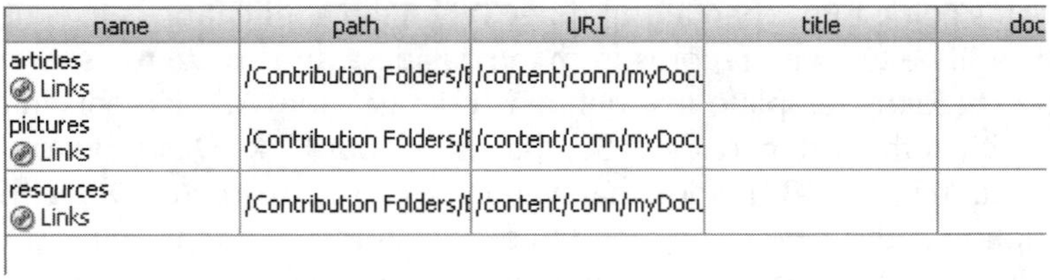

name	path	URI	title	doc
articles Links	/Contribution Folders/E	/content/conn/myDocu		
pictures Links	/Contribution Folders/E	/content/conn/myDocu		
resources Links	/Contribution Folders/E	/content/conn/myDocu		

FIGURE 9-34 *The link files table with a link tag for each element*

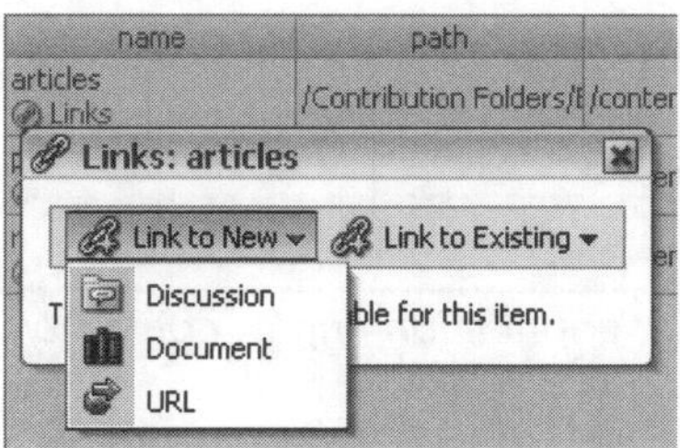

FIGURE 9-35 *Links dialog for the "articles" element on the list*

By closing this dialog and opening another one you will see that the dialog heading and therefore all corresponding other attribute values are indeed different for each instance. This is exactly what you wanted.

NOTE
The list of available services to link to will depend on the services that were added to your application. If you have not yet added any service, the Links dialog might look slightly different.

Similar to adding Links, when you add the Tag button to the page, right next to the Links Detail button, you can use the same technique to reference the necessary values (Figure 9-36). The only difference would be the ServiceId which would have to be different from the one used in the Links dialog. Use something like application.employee.list.tag.

FIGURE 9-36 *Insert Tagging Button dialog*

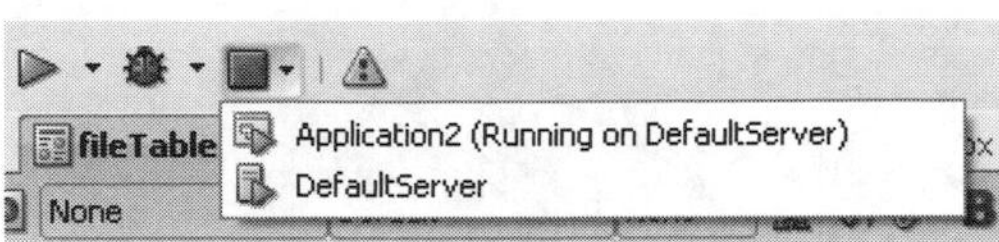

FIGURE 9-37 *Stopping the running application and/or container*

Again, it is time to review your work. Before you do, restart the container. You actually only need to stop it, because JDeveloper starts it automatically once you run your application (Figure 9-37).

Just select the big, red stop button in the toolbar to stop either the running application or the whole container. It is wise to stop the application after every major change and stop the container after a couple of executions, just to free up some memory resources.

When you're stopping the application or container be sure to watch the messages in the message window until they clearly state that it was successfully stopped.

Once it's stopped, you are ready to run the application. Right-click on the page in the Application Navigator and select Run. After a couple of seconds you should, as before, be asked to authenticate; once authenticated, the application will show a similar table as before with the Links Detail button, but you will also see the Tag button. Click on one of them and the Tag dialog (Figure 9-38) will open for that particular one (check out the dialog title).

Type in a tag or two and click Save. After a couple of seconds you will be back at the table view. Now, if you hover your mouse pointer over the Tag button you just clicked, you will see that your tag has been added and is now listed in the Tag summary (Figure 9-39).

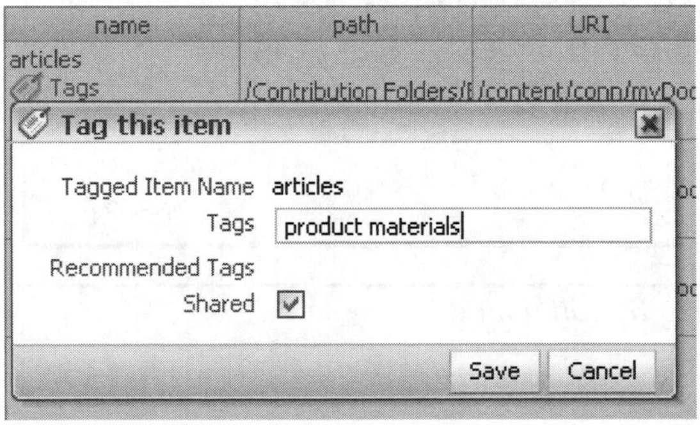

FIGURE 9-38 *The Tag dialog in action*

name	path	URI
articles Tags My Tags materials product Popular Tags None	/Contribution Folders/E	/content/conn/myDocu
	/Contribution Folders/E	/content/conn/myDocu
resources Tags Links	/Contribution Folders/E	/content/conn/myDocu

FIGURE 9-39 *The Tag summary*

If you click on one of the tags in the summary it will bring you to the Tag Center. You will notice that your tag is highlighted in the tag cloud, but the search does not return any results. This is because the service this tag came from (remember we defined it as application.employee.list.tag) has not yet been registered and has no associated resource viewer and hence there is no way Tag Center could know how to access those artifacts. Registration is a bit complex and would exceed the scope of this example.

Adding Search

Adding Search is possibly the easiest thing to do here. All you need to do is to drag-and-drop the Search toolbar to the page. We discussed earlier that search will auto-detect the services used in your application and determine what sources should be searched. After dropping the Search Toolbar task flow on the page, simply run the application. Easy enough, right?

You will be asked to authenticate and see the same table with link and tag buttons, but now there will be a search box also (most likely on the top, but it really depends where you dropped it).

To show the power of WebCenter's integrated services, submit a search for one of the tags you entered earlier. After a couple of seconds, you will see the search result showing you the tag (Figure 9-40).

Clicking on the tag will, as described before, invoke Tag Center.

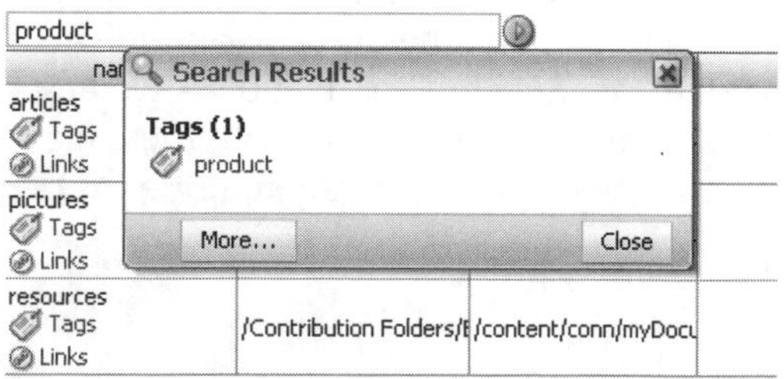

FIGURE 9-40 *Search with invoked result*

Adding Instant Messaging & Presence Capabilities

Last but not least, you want to add Presence to your file table. From the perspective of a user browsing the files in the table, it would be ideal to be able to contact a document's author directly from the table. With Oracle WebCenter Instant Message & Presence you can provide exactly that.

First you need to create a connection to the back-end IM system by right-clicking on the Connections node in the Application Resources panel. Select Instant Messaging & Presence from the list of available connection types. Then you need to provide the necessary data for the connection. Be sure you check the Use as Default Connection checkbox. Once the connection is created, add the Presence Data component at the bottom of the page.

Now you are ready to Presence-enable your table. What you want is for the Owner column to become the Presence tag. To do that, you can use the Convert operation in JDeveloper. Simply right-click on the InputField for the Owner and select Convert from the context menu.

You will be presented with the Convert dialog. Here you need to choose the WebCenter Instant Messaging & Presence Service group of components and click on the Presence component.

Once you click OK, the Presence Properties dialog is shown (Figure 9-41). There you can provide all the necessary attributes for the component and, in certain cases, check the mapping between the attributes of the previous component and the newly chosen one.

On the Other tab you will see the mandatory property Username. Here you need to provide, similar to tagging and presence, an EL expression to fill it with dynamic data, as there will be one instance of the Presence component per row. In your example you want to reference the value of the column owner for each row, so the EL expression would look something like `#{row.bindings.owner.inputValue}`.

Now, when you execute the page, you will see that a Presence tag is being rendered for every cell in the Owner column (Figure 9-42).

The Status Indicator

You might notice that sometimes there are delays in the application, although the browser does not indicate any data transfer. This is caused by AJAX communication happening behind the scenes. To add an indication when the AJAX communication is done, meaning the application is waiting for user input, you can add the Status Indicator component anywhere onto the page. You can find the Status Indicator component in the Component Palette under ADF Faces | Common Components.

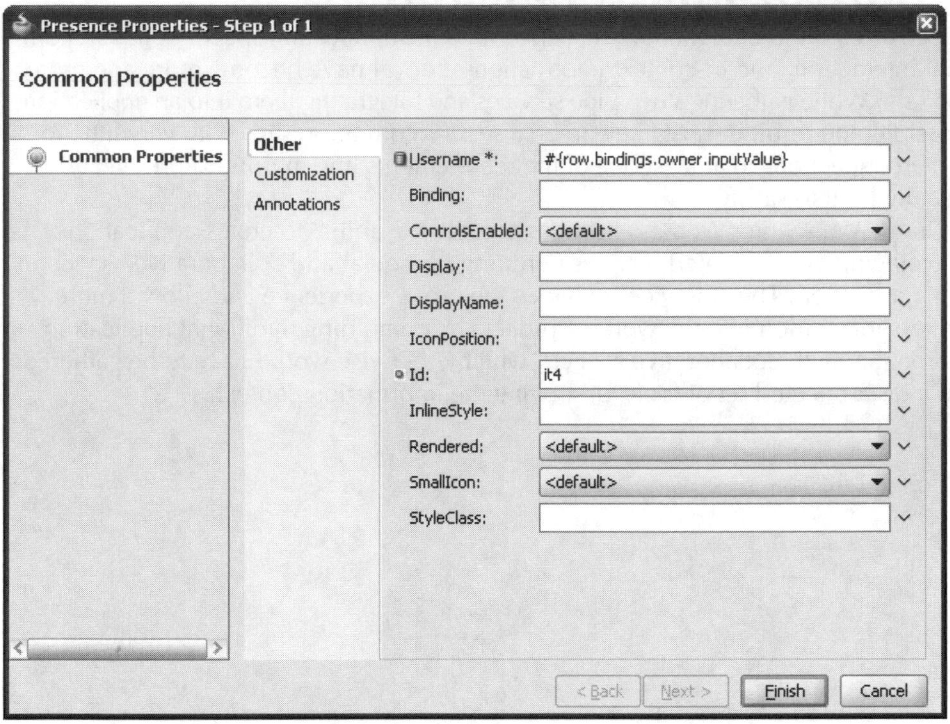

FIGURE 9-41 *The Presence Properties dialog during the conversion*

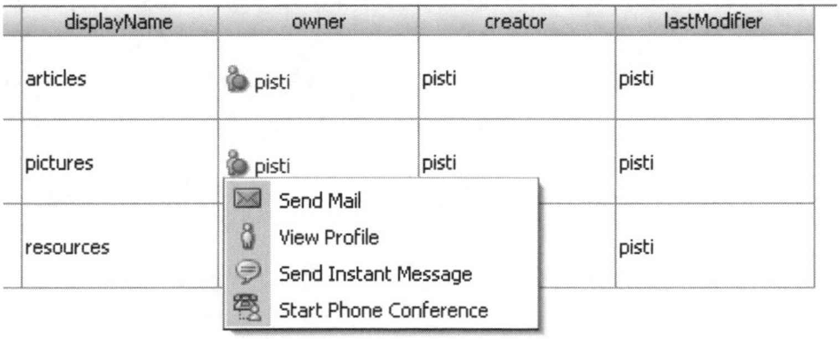

FIGURE 9-42 *The Presence-enabled owner column values*

A More Seamless Integration

The age of Web 2.0 brought new challenges into the application space. Collaboration, social interaction, and in-context information retrieval have become more and more important. While gathering stove-pipe services and integrating them into an application is possible, the result is most likely to be a set of information silos with very little to no interconnection, so at least one of the requirements, the in-context presentation, is usually hard to satisfy.

Oracle WebCenter Web 2.0 Services provide the ability to create applications by leveraging pre-integrated services nurturing the social and collaborative aspect of an application. These services enhance the user's experience and allow a more seamless integration into the working process by combining traditional application functionality with collaborative aspects, which otherwise would have to be gathered from a disconnected set of tools, destroying the information context.

CHAPTER 10

Setting Up Your Development Environment for Success

As you have seen in the previous chapters, the toolbox offered to developers by Oracle WebCenter 11*g* is quite extensive. This was to be expected. Oracle WebCenter's ultimate goal is to enable the creation of rich composite web applications; customization and service orientation were two of its key design principles. The various services offered by the product come either as Java Enterprise Edition (JEE) web applications or, in Oracle Content Server's case, as a Java executable wrapped in an operating system–specific service. To work effectively on such composite applications, project teams will need to share code and customizations. They will also require access to private service instances for test and development purposes.

Even though current high-end workstations can hold enough random access memory to accommodate all of the required software components on a developer's machine, such a concentration would not lend to development process efficiency. The cost of such a machine would also be prohibitive. Quality assurance of a composite application can be cumbersome and time consuming, especially as even unit tests could involve several back-end services. A single task flow deployed in a dynamic page created by Oracle WebCenter Page Service, for example, could call the Oracle WebCenter Spaces API, consume data fetched from an ADF BC Application Module instance, and call an external web service. Consequently, composite application testing supposes that comprehensive and synchronized sample data sets covering all the involved services are available. Deploying and maintaining such data sets on individual team members' computers would be counterproductive.

To tackle these challenges we just highlighted, it is essential to put into place a flexible development environment where service instances will be shared between developers. Strong configuration management processes and tools must also be deployed in the project team. Finally, automation is essential, as it will reduce the potential for human error and promote process reuse inside the team and between projects.

No One Is an Island: Topology Matters

Infrastructure sizing for production purposes is a whole book in itself. We won't even pretend to cover such matters exhaustively here. Our aim is simply to illustrate the basic principles that should guide the deployment of a robust development environment. This does not mean the matter at hand is not important; quite the contrary. In fact, topology is one of the most important factors determining a development environment's fitness to the task.

Principle 1: Service Isolation

Service decoupling is an integral part of service-oriented architectures. Service implementations must be encapsulated in order to facilitate their maintenance and, eventually, their replacement. All of Oracle WebCenter 11*g* services except for content management, provided by Oracle Content Server, are either ADF or Java Enterprise Edition applications deployed on an Oracle WebLogic Server container. You could deploy all of these applications on a single Oracle WebLogic instance. This, however, means that maintenance operations and some administrative processes will impact all of the services available in the development environment at the same time. On the other hand, completely isolated service instances will require more time to set up and manage, because of the added complexity. Thus, it is essential to strike the right balance between concentration and isolation.

We strongly recommend you isolate the most strategic services and give them their own Oracle WebLogic Server instance. You may consolidate the others as needed. Obviously, the list of strategic services will vary from one project to another and between organizations. It must be noted that service isolation, in our view, does not extend to hardware. Virtualization solutions, such as Oracle VM, can be put to good use in service isolation scenarios. In other words, service isolation must not lead to server proliferation.

Principle 2: Use Corporate Resources for Ancillary Services

Service isolation, while useful, must be applied to the appropriate scope. To the project team, the development environment is a tool; the services it contains must bring value to developers. Ancillary services, such as e-mail, enterprise directories, and content management, could be sourced from outside the development environment depending on the resources available inside the organization. Corporate policies will probably influence decisions in such matters.

As a rule of thumb, it is better to keep a specific service in the development environment scope if it is expected to be upgraded frequently and if several custom-built use cases (task flows or portlets) need to consume it.

Principle 3: Consolidate Your Database Schemas

Several of the Oracle WebCenter services require their own database schema. One could design a development environment where each service instance is linked to its own database; however, this will not enhance service isolation and will result in a marked increase in infrastructure maintenance efforts. Consequently, while we advocate service isolation, we suggest you consolidate these schemas on a single Oracle Database instance.

To achieve schema consolidation, we recommend you avoid using Oracle Database Express Edition (XE) 10*g* in your development environment. The storage and memory limitations of this particular product do not fit well with the load you should expect from your project teams. This was to be expected, as Oracle Database XE was designed to be an excellent choice for very specific use cases, such as demos, learning, and individual development projects. Our scope is much more ambitious here.

Principle 4: Implement Actual Security from the Start

Security is an integral but often overlooked part of software design. Customizable composite applications, such as the ones you can build with Oracle WebCenter, rely on roles implemented through standard ADF Security mechanisms. One could be tempted to code the use cases using a simplified security model, then retrofit the target security mechanisms in the finished application. This is a very dangerous approach. Security impacts each and every layer of the application; it can be found in the JSF fragments making the user interface, as well as in the ADF Business Components implementing the business services layer. It may even require adjustments at the data services level; data filtering according to the user's role, for example, could be implemented though the Virtual Private Database (VPD) option of Oracle Database Enterprise edition. In more complex cases, an application security could even require changes to be made to the enterprise directory; LDAP schema extensions are a common occurrence.

We advise you to take security into account right from the start of your requirements management process. It is also essential for the development environment to have access to actual instances of the products that are part of the security infrastructure planned for production.

Sample Development Environment

To better illustrate the principles mentioned before, we have built a diagram illustrating a sample development environment, seen in Figure 10-1.

A few remarks are in order:

- Each of the service instances is fully isolated. These are labeled instance 1 to instance 4.
- The Oracle WebLogic Server instances dedicated to services are administered from a central location, called instance 5 in this case.
- All of the database schemas needed are deployed on a single Oracle Database instance residing on a physical machine.
- The e-mail ancillary service is provided as an enterprise-level resource. This includes SMTP traffic as well as mailboxes devoted to unit tests and such.
- Portlets are deployed both on developer workstations and in the development environment. Those found on shared servers should be production-quality, feature-complete components specific to the project or belonging to the corporate repository. Conversely, portlets deployed on a developer

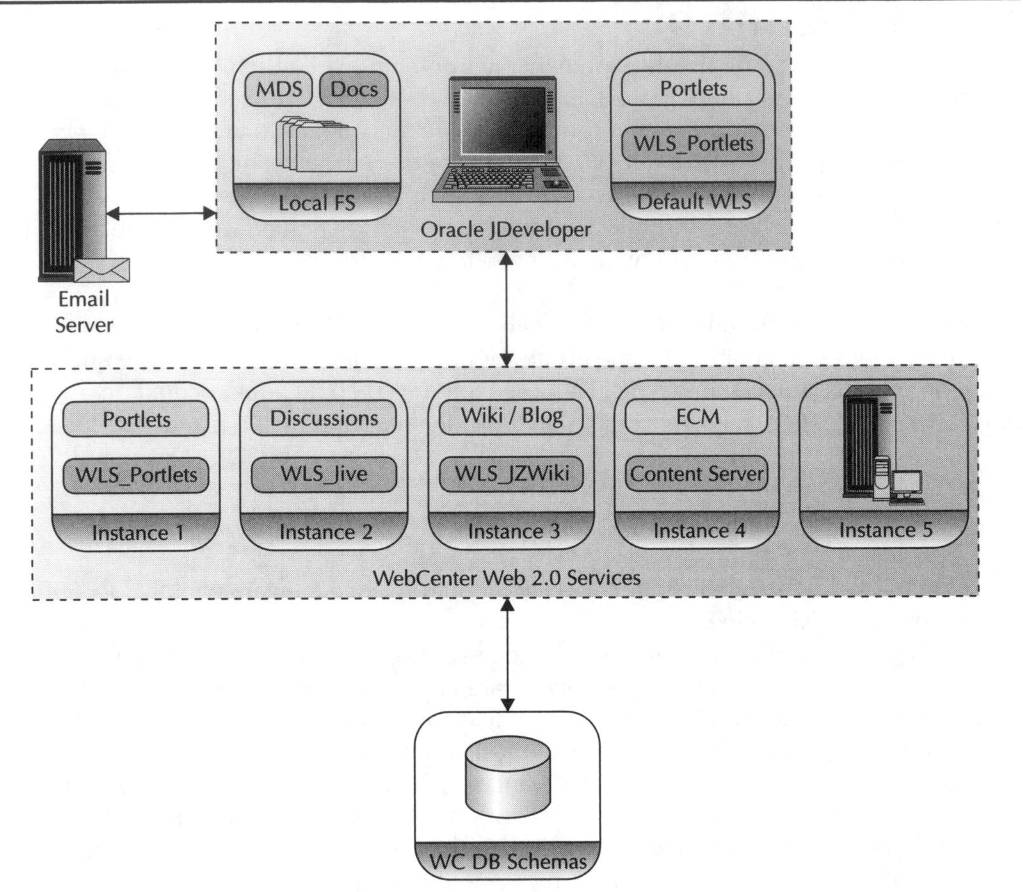

FIGURE 10-1 *Sample development environment*

workstation should be at an earlier phase in their life cycle. These must be transferred to the development environment as soon as they are completed.

- MDS customizations are stored on the local file system of the developer workstation. This is the default mode when you're running and deploying the application on the Oracle WebLogic Server instance embedded in Oracle JDeveloper.

We want to stress that the sample topology we propose may not necessarily fit the specific needs of your team or project. Carefully plan your environment by assessing your needs and analyze your requirements in a structured fashion.

Version Control

Pooling shared services in the development environment, while useful, will not ensure project success alone. Project team efficiency is strongly linked to the quality of your configuration management processes. While this applies to any current web development project, it is especially vital in the case of WebCenter applications. In order to develop and test correctly, you will need to manage, share, and version not only JSF pages and Java classes, but also sample data and document sets. If your application is customizable, you will also need to take customizations into account in your test scenarios.

Predefined MDS customizations, also called seeded customizations, will need to be put under version control; this means developers will have to put extra care and attention into the process. In a typical MDS-enabled web application located on a developer workstation, customizations can typically be found in two places:

- [Application root]\ViewController\public_html\mdssys
- [Application root]\ViewController\public_html\WEB-INF\mdssys

It is essential to put both folders under version control, since they are equally needed by the MDS engine.

The keystone of any configuration management process is the version control system (VCS). It lets project team members share application code efficiently, while enabling them to trace developer actions. Oracle JDeveloper, fortunately, offers rich version control features. Since Oracle is not itself a player in the application life cycle management space, the VCS implementation is completely encapsulated from the development environment. This means most features will work the same independently of the VCS you elected to use. At the time of writing, the following VCS products were officially supported in Oracle JDeveloper 11*g*:

- CVS
- IBM Rational ClearCase
- Microsoft Team System
- Perforce
- Serena Dimensions
- Subversion (SVN)

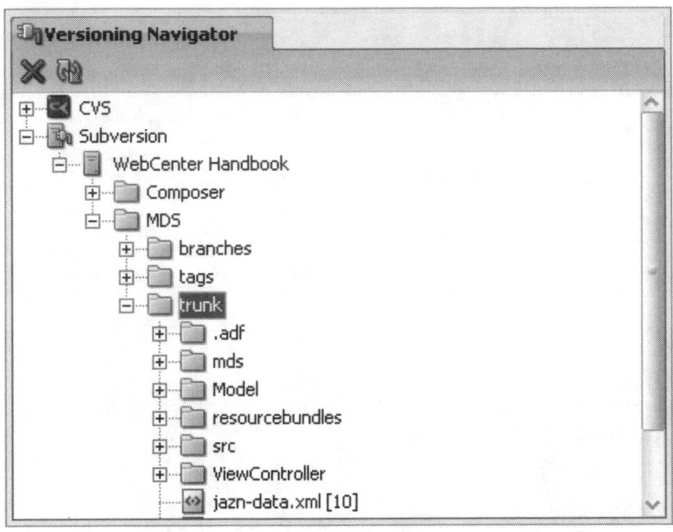

FIGURE 10-2 *Versioning Navigator in Oracle JDeveloper 11*g

Figure 10-2 displays Oracle JDeveloper 11*g*'s Versioning Navigator, which you can use to navigate any repository you have defined a connection on.

One thing to remember is that Oracle JDeveloper 11*g* VCS support is done through software extensions. This means you will have to install a client native to your operating system in order for some of these extensions to work, since not all VCSs offer a Java API. CVS and SVN, however, do not need such clients since Oracle JDeveloper ships with the required Java libraries. In addition, while comprehensive, the VCS support offered by Oracle JDeveloper may lack some of the features found in native clients. In particular, we strongly encourage you to install TortoiseSVN if you connect to a Subversion server on a Windows operating system. TortoiseSVN nicely integrates to Windows Explorer contextual menus, and handles complex operations well. Figure 10-3 shows a screen capture of TortoiseSVN's repository browser.

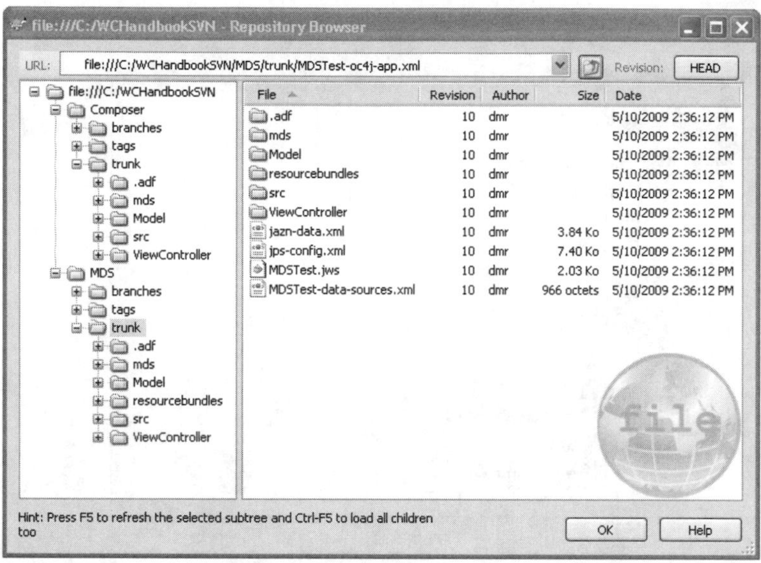

FIGURE 10-3 *TortoiseSVN repository browser*

Automation through Apache ANT

Separation of concerns is integral to well-designed applications. The same can be said about project teams. A successful development environment will be one that will enable developers to concentrate on their core competencies, which are technical design, coding, and unit testing. This is why it is so important to automate deployment tasks. While Oracle JDeveloper 11*g* offers strong wizard-driven deployment features, we feel deployment tasks are better handled through scripting. In release 1 of Oracle JDeveloper 11*g*, such scripting is done through Apache ANT (http://ant.apache.org).

ANT is a Java-build system originally created by the author of the Tomcat web container, and is now maintained by the Apache Software Foundation. The scripts it can run are defined in XML files calling out a target tree where various tasks get executed. Each task is run by a Java object implementing a particular Task interface. Introduced in 2000, ANT has seen several releases since. It is very mature and widely deployed; several components of Oracle Fusion Middleware rely on it. Oracle WebLogic Server ships with several ANT tasks you can use to create JMS queues or deploy entire applications, for example. Oracle SOA suite also uses ANT to deploy Business Process Execution Language (BPEL) processes to server instances.

The following listing illustrates how to define an ANT target that will deploy to Oracle WebLogic Server:

```
<target name="deploy" depends="clean,compile,copy,buildJar,buildEar">
    <property file="${project}.properties"/>
    <property file="project.properties"/>

    <echo message="Undeploying application..."/>
    <wldeploy action="undeploy" verbose="true" debug="true"
        name="${project}"  adminurl="t3://${host}:${port}"
        user="${username}" password="${password}"
        targets="${target.server}" failonerror="false"/>

    <echo message="Deploying application..."/>
    <wldeploy action="deploy" verbose="true" debug="true" name="${project}"
        adminurl="t3://${host}:${port}"
        user="${username}" password="${password}" targets="${target.server}"
        failonerror="false"
        source="${project.home}/${global.deploy.dir}/${deploy.file}"
        remote="true" upload="true"/>

</target>
```

It is not our intent to illustrate the inner workings of ANT scripts. There is one thing we want to highlight in the sample above, though: ANT support for user-defined variables is pervasive. You can define such variables in scripts themselves or in property files, and even pass them to the script as command-line arguments. References to variables always begin with the dollar sign and are enclosed inside curly brackets. Variables can make your scripts more dynamic, and promote their reuse since they can be more generic in nature.

There are several commercial and open source alternatives to ANT available. The most widely used is without a doubt Apache Maven (http://maven.apache.org). Maven's philosophy in quite different from ANT's, since it imposes a mandatory folder structure for project artifacts. On the other hand, Maven integrates several tools geared toward code quality and collaboration; it can, for example, create a full-blown web site aggregating the project's JavaDoc documentation, code quality reports, and activity logs. For the time being, Maven is not integrated in Oracle JDeveloper, and ANT is the only officially supported option. It is possible to use Maven anyway, but this will require manual tinkering and will make migration to newer Oracle JDeveloper releases harder. Oracle is reportedly considering adding native Maven support to JDeveloper in the post 11*g* Release 1 time frame.

There is an intrinsic connection between build automation, software deployment, and quality assurance, especially in composite applications. Technical architects increasingly need to monitor the quality of the code base on an ongoing basis. Continuous integration, which is a software development practice in which members of a team integrate their work frequently[1], enables that. Each time a developer integrates his or her work by checking in the work in the VCS, an automated

1. Martin Fowler, *Continuous Integration.* http://www.martinfowler.com/articles/continuousIntegration.html

build is launched and tests are run. The key here is that ANT scripts can automate not only deployment, but also unit tests through the JUnit framework. JUnit tests can even be run on ADF BC components, if needed. In order to implement continuous integration, you will need to deploy a dedicated piece of software. There are several alternatives available on the market, most of them being JEE web applications, and some are even open source. Apache Continuum and Cruise Control are two of the most popular. Figure 10-4 shows the main screen of Apache Continuum.

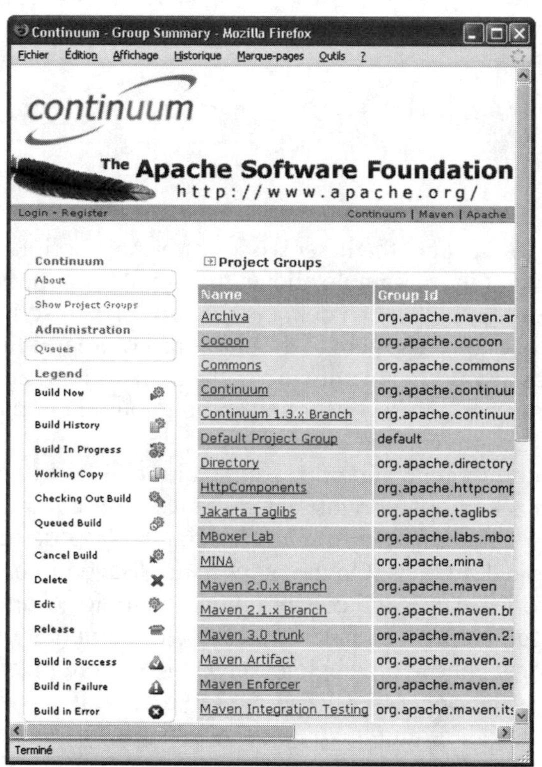

FIGURE 10-4 *Apache Continuum*

PART III

Tailoring Your Applications

CHAPTER 11

Run-Time Customization

If you have ever been part of building and deploying enterprise applications, you may have faced the following challenge: business users who come forward with requirements when it's too late in the game, when the application has either been rolled out or entered a state from which there is no return. Very often all they want is a tiny little functionality change: a slightly different page layout here, a simple announcement there, maybe content showing up on the page in a different order. To accommodate these types of business requirements most of the time you have to implement the changes in the development environment, and after going through thorough testing and staging, you have to deploy your application over again. Not only can this be a very time-consuming and complex process, you also have to bring down your systems, often compromising your company's or customer's core business.

Wouldn't it be nice if, instead, you could perform certain changes to your applications without going through the testing and re-deployment process and you could make these changes from within the deployed application? Or even better: if you as a developer had the means to design your applications in a way that empowers your business users to perform some or all of these tasks themselves simply by interacting with the running application?

If you have used portals before, it's no news to you that what we've just described is a core functionality in the portal space and that it has been maturing for over a decade now. While the implementation may differ slightly, the following tasks can be performed in most of the enterprise portal products available in the market today:

- Edit content in the pages.
- Add new and delete unneeded components from pages.
- Rearrange the order of components on the pages.
- Rearrange the layout of pages.
- Contextually wire components on pages.
- Edit component and page properties.
- Create and delete pages at run time.
- Control page permissions at run time.

The promise of Oracle WebCenter is that you as an application developer can provide the above capabilities to your application administrators or business users at run time.

In the not too distant past you had to weigh what was more important to you: building a transactional Java EE or JSF application, or providing the above-listed portal capabilities. If you chose the former, you had limited or no portal capabilities. The latter implied you couldn't take advantage of many features that development frameworks provide.

With the WebCenter Framework being an integral part of Oracle's Fusion Middleware development platform, you don't have to make this choice anymore. You can build your transactional composite SOA applications and pull in portal capabilities on an as-needed basis. This chapter explains how you can add all these functionalities to your ADF applications.

Run-Time Customization Concepts

Before diving into the details of building customizable applications, let's discuss some of the most important concepts and building blocks that you'll use.

Run-time customization is an idea that portals have introduced to the Internet world. The way it's implemented may well be very different, but what the portal subculture means by run-time customization is very much the same: you can use a simple web browser to perform fundamental changes to an already deployed application; you can create new pages, define and change the page layout, and add new content and components to the pages by selecting them from a repository. Let's take a quick look at the key players in run-time customization in Oracle WebCenter:

- **Oracle Composer** The user interface that the WebCenter Framework provides administrators and business users to perform the different types of run-time customizations. Oracle Composer provides means to actions, such as taking a page into Edit mode, changing the layout of your pages, or moving components around on the page using drag-and-drop. The changes you make to your pages are persisted by the Metadata Services (MDS).
- **Metadata Services (MDS)** The infrastructure responsible for storing and managing customization data. MDS provides a unified architecture for defining and using metadata in an extensible manner. MDS stores metadata in XML format. When you customize a page, your changes, often referred to as the delta, are stored by MDS in an XML representation. When a request is received by MDS, it takes the base XML document, applies all the changes (or deltas) on top of that, and returns the result to the requester. MDS supports layered customization. For example, the administrator can add an announcement component on the front page of the application, group managers can add components to pages relevant to their team, and end users can personalize their pages and components, visible only to themselves.

- **Resource Catalog** A read-only repository of objects that can be dropped onto pages. Examples for resources: portlets, task flows, JSF view components, and documents. It's important to note that the same resource catalog infrastructure is used by business users for run-time customization as is is by JSF developers for building applications using JDeveloper.

The three key players of run-time customization, Oracle Composer, the resource catalog, and MDS, are very tightly integrated. In this chapter you learn how to build customizable applications by leveraging these three building blocks. If you are interested in the details of how MDS works and how ADF applications can take advantage of the capabilities MDS provides, refer to Chapter 13 and Chapter 17.

The Oracle Composer Toolbox

To familiarize yourself with the tool set provided by Composer, build a simple application that contains the Composer components. By the end of this section you will know how to build an application that features the following capabilities:

- End users can add components to the page as they wish and change the height of the portlets and task flows by dragging the bottom-right corner of these components. These changes are persisted to MDS as end-user personalization.
- Users with edit privileges can take the page into edit mode and do the following:
    - Change the page layout, for example from two-columns to three-columns.
    - Browse the resource catalog and drop new resources onto the page.
    - Remove resources from the page.
    - Edit resource and page properties.
    - Wire components contextually to enable inter-component communication.

The Oracle Composer capabilities are surfaced in JDeveloper as JSF view components. As shown in Figure 11-1, the WebCenter Framework provides eight JSF view components to allow you to build customizable pages.

- **Page Customizable** This component defines the area of the page that is editable at run time. When you add the Page Customizable component to the page, a Page Editor panel is added as well as a facet. The Page Editor panel provides the user interface to perform run-time customization operations, such as page and component property editing, contextual wiring, and showing the resource catalog.

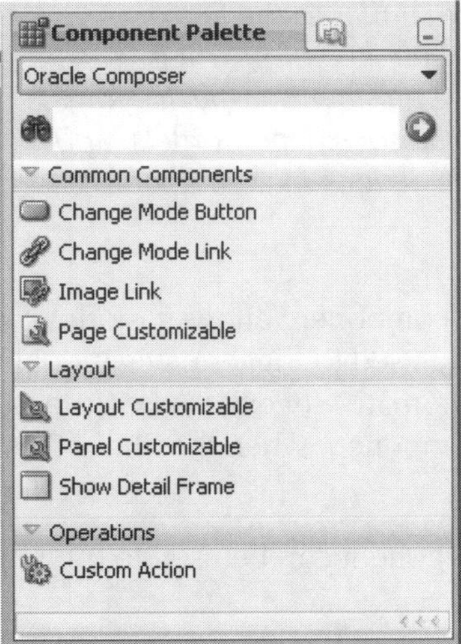

FIGURE 11-1 *Oracle Composer on the Component Palette*

- **Change Mode Button and Change Mode Link** These components allow users with page customization permission to switch the page from View mode to Edit mode.
- **Layout Customizable** This component allows privileged business users to select from a set of predefined layouts, such as two-column or three-column, and apply the layout to the page.
- **Panel Customizable** This component is a valid drop-target; portlets, Show Detail Frames, task flows, and JSF view components can be dropped into the Panel Customizable component from the resource catalog, and existing components on the page can be moved into them. In addition, all components within the Panel Customizable can be selected and edited at run time.
- **Show Detail Frame** This component renders a header or chrome along with an optional border around its children components. The Show Detail Frame and its children can be dragged-and-dropped on the page from and to Panel Customizable parent components. The Show Detail Frame chrome provides the UI for dragging the component. In addition, the Show Detail Frame provides collapse/expand capabilities. It can also surface the custom actions of its child task flow. The Show Detail Frame can contain only one child component; that is, it renders only the first of its children. If you would like to surround multiple components with a Show Detail Frame, first lay them out in a grouping component, like Panel Group Layout, which can then be dropped inside a Show Detail Frame.

NOTE
The portlet view tag is very similar to the Show Detail Frame (in fact, it's a subclass of it). Their behavior is very similar in a number of aspects: you can drag-and-drop and collapse/expand portlets, and portlets can present custom actions in their action menus as well.

- **Custom Action** This component allows task flows to define task flow–specific actions that are used to trigger navigational flow in the task flow. Custom actions are automatically exposed on the UI in the action menu of a Show Detail Frame component when the Show Detail Frame is the parent of the task flow.
- **Image Link** This component can be used to include an HTML link as an image in the page.

Building a Customizable Application

Let's create a new application based on the WebCenter application template. For simplicity's sake don't secure this application. When you're running the application from JDeveloper, you can perform all the tasks an administrator can. You can test most of the functionality using a nonsecure application. If you secure your application you can restrict the various tasks to users and roles with the right privileges.

If you don't have any application open in your Application Navigator, you can click the New Application placeholder. Alternatively, you can invoke the New Gallery by selecting the File | New menu option. In the New Application dialog as well as in the New Gallery be sure to select WebCenter Application as your application template.

Call your application Customizable Application; you can leave all other application properties unchanged.

Create a new page, called customizablePage.jspx. Since MDS mandates us to use the XML representation of the page, select the Create as XML Document (*.jspx) option.

NOTE
The Create as XML Document (.jspx) option and the extension of the name of the page you are about to create are synchronized to make the developer's life easier. When you check the option, the file extension changes to *.jspx, and vice versa: when you specify your file extension as *.jspx, the checkbox is checked automatically.*

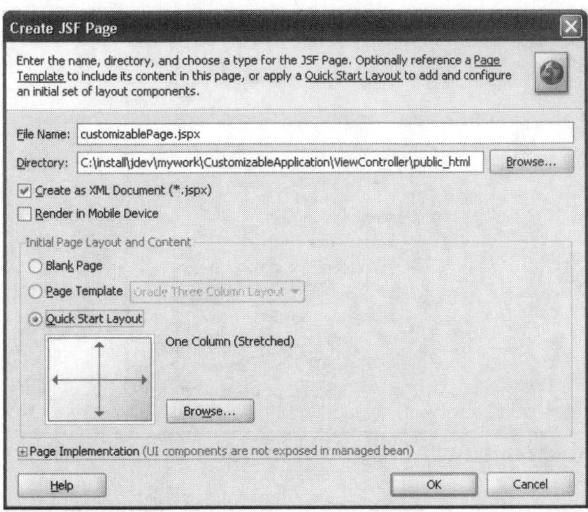

FIGURE 11-2 *Create a new JSF page*

Also, to make sure that the contents of our page fills the entire browser page, select the Quick Start Layout option under Initial Page Layout and Content, as shown in Figure 11-2. If you plan to build a slightly more complex page, click on the Browse button to choose from a variety of one-, two-, or three-column page layouts. To keep this sample simple, we use the One Column (Stretched) layout option.

On the Component Palette select Oracle Composer from the page selector drop-down list; to make the page customizable, drop a Page Customizable component onto the page. Figure 11-3 demonstrates that the Page Customizable component pulls in a Panel Customizable component, as well as the Page Editor panel in the edit facet. These additional components ensure that the desired customization capabilities can be achieved quickly and easily.

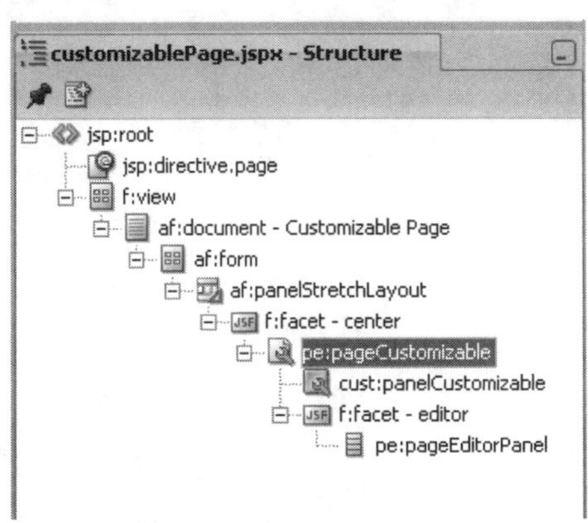

FIGURE 11-3 *Page Customizable component dropped onto a page*

In addition to the Page Customizable, you will need a button or link that will take the page into Edit mode. Add a Change Mode Button right above the Page Customizable component. When you're doing so, notice (Figure 11-4) that a Panel Group Layout is automatically added too.

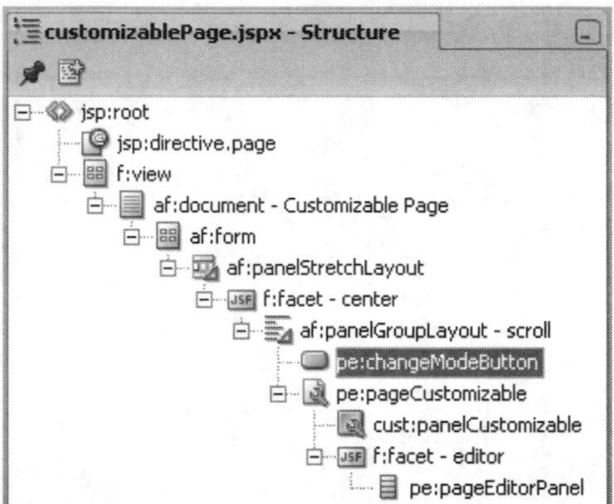

FIGURE 11-4 *Customizable page with Change Mode Button*

After adding just these two components to the page, your application has a lot of customization capabilities. You can test at this point if you like. What you see after clicking the Edit button is presented in Figure 11-5.

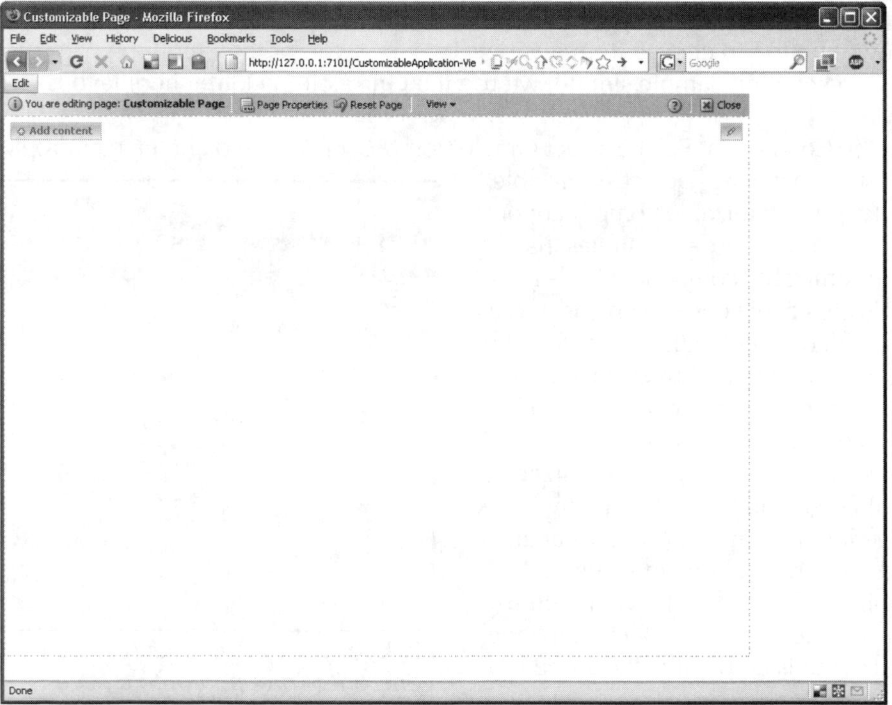

FIGURE 11-5 *Running the simplest customizable page*

You may notice that the Page Customizable component doesn't stretch in the browser window. This is due to the behavior of the automatically added Panel Group Layout, which is a component that doesn't stretch its children.

There are several ways to make your Panel Group Layout stretch; here is one:

1. Enable the Top facet of the Panel Stretch Layout, as shown in Figure 11-6.
2. Move the Change Mode Button to the Top facet of the Panel Stretch Layout.
3. In the Source editor delete the Panel Group Layout.
4. Set the TopHeight attribute of the Panel Stretch Layout to 20px.

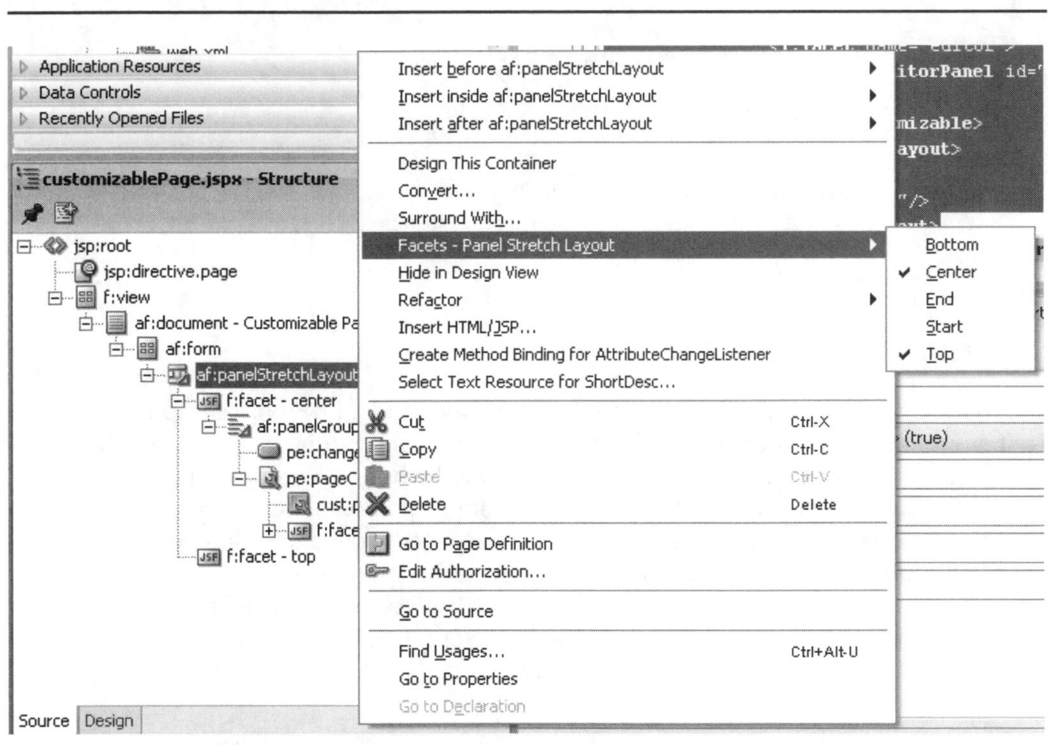

FIGURE 11-6 *Enabling the Top facet of the Panel Stretch Layout component*

Here is the source of the page after the above-suggested modifications:

```
<?xml version='1.0' encoding='windows-1252'?>
<jsp:root xmlns:jsp="http://java.sun.com/JSP/Page" version="2.1"
          xmlns:f="http://java.sun.com/jsf/core"
          xmlns:af="http://xmlns.oracle.com/adf/faces/rich"
          xmlns:pe="http://xmlns.oracle.com/adf/pageeditor"
          xmlns:cust="http://xmlns.oracle.com/adf/faces/customizable">
  <jsp:directive.page contentType="text/html;charset=windows-1252"/>
  <f:view>
    <af:document title="Customizable Page" id="d1">
      <af:form id="f1">
        <af:panelStretchLayout id="psl1" topHeight="20px">
          <f:facet name="center">
              <pe:pageCustomizable id="pageCustomizable1">
                <cust:panelCustomizable id="panelCustomizable1"
                                        layout="scroll"/>
                <f:facet name="editor">
                  <pe:pageEditorPanel id="pep1"/>
                </f:facet>
              </pe:pageCustomizable>
          </f:facet>
          <f:facet name="top">
            <pe:changeModeButton id="cmb1"/>
          </f:facet>
        </af:panelStretchLayout>
      </af:form>
    </af:document>
  </f:view>
</jsp:root>
```

To make our example a little more interesting, let's add a few more components. First, you want to allow the page layout to be changed at run time. Let's replace the Panel Customizable (which was automatically added when you dropped the Page Customizable onto the page) with a Layout Customizable component. The Layout Customizable component allows us to change the page layout at run time as well as at design time. By default, the Layout Customizable component is visualized as a farily small icon on the page. If you would like to display a text or label next to the icon, you can use the Text attribute to do so; for example: Select Layout.

Figure 11-7 shows how you can specify the seeded or default value for the desired page layout.

The Layout Customizable component manages three Panel Customizables and lays them out in the page as specified by its Type attribute. The Layout Customizable offers eight content arrangement layout types. Their names are pretty descriptive:

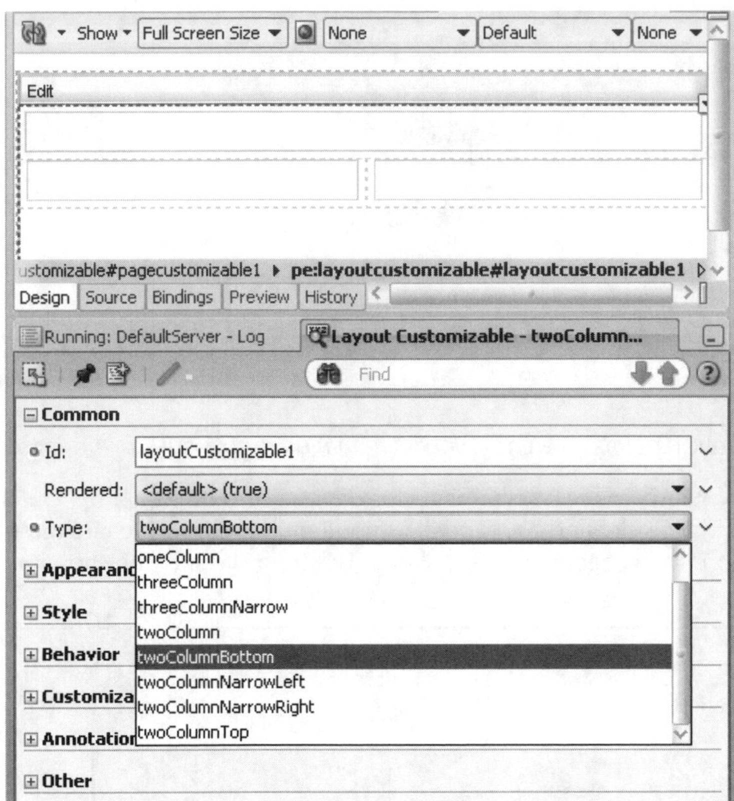

FIGURE 11-7 *Specifying the page layout type in JDeveloper*

oneColumn, twoColumn, twoColumnNarrowLeft, twoColumnNarrowRight, twoColumnTop, twoColumnBottom, threeColumn, and threeColumnNarrow. You will see the layout types later in Figure 11-11. To restrict the offered layouts, you can provide a space-separated list in the showTypes attribute of the Layout Customizable tag:

```
<pe:layoutCustomizable type="oneColumn" id="l1'
  showTypes="oneColumn twoColumn twoColumnNarrowLeft twoColumnNarrowRight">
```

As shown in Figure 11-8, one of the Panel Customizables is the child, and two others reside in the contentA and contentB facets.

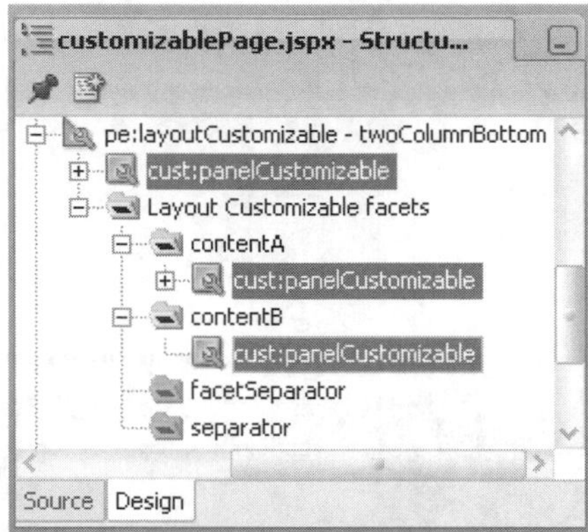

FIGURE 11-8 *Panel Customizable components managed by Layout Customizable*

Now that you are done with the page customization settings, let's populate the page. You'll add a portlet and a calendar component in a Show Detail Frame.

When you run the page, your view should be similar to the one shown in Figure 11-9.

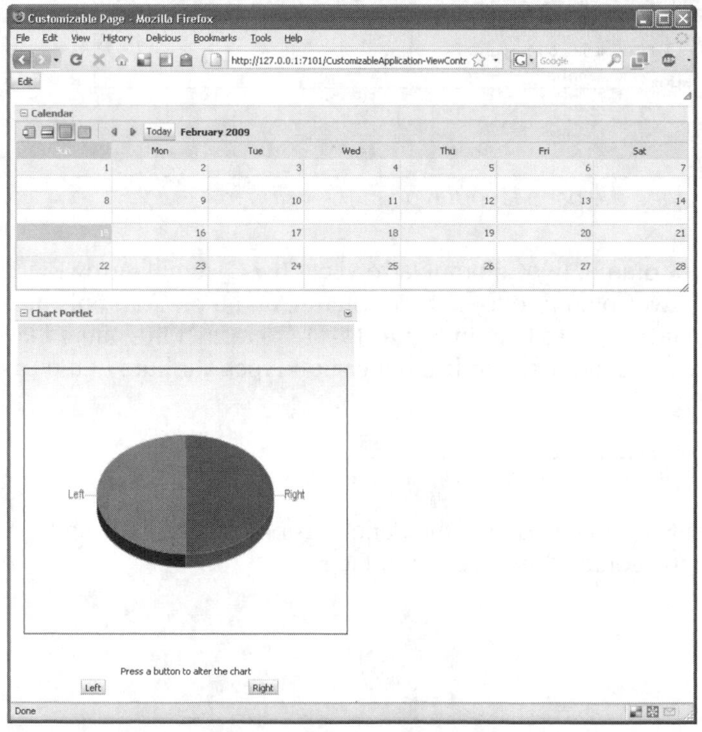

FIGURE 11-9 *A Customizable Page with components on it*

Interacting with Oracle Composer

Now that you've built a customizable application, discover what you can do with Composer at run time.

The first thing you may notice is that both the portlet and the Show Detail Frame components provide a handle in their lower-right corner that allows you to vertically resize them. Both of them support drag-and-drop as well, demonstrated in Figure 11-10.

In the top-right corner of the page click the little triangle icon. A layout selector panel will pop up, shown in Figure 11-11, allowing you to select the layout for your page.

To take the page into Edit mode, click the Edit button. The information bar on the top of the editable section, shown in Figure 11-12, displays the name of the page that you are currently editing. By clicking the Page Properties button, you can change the name of the page as well as add parameters to the page that can then drive and synchronize other components on the page. The Reset Page control removes all the run-time customization from MDS that was earlier applied to the

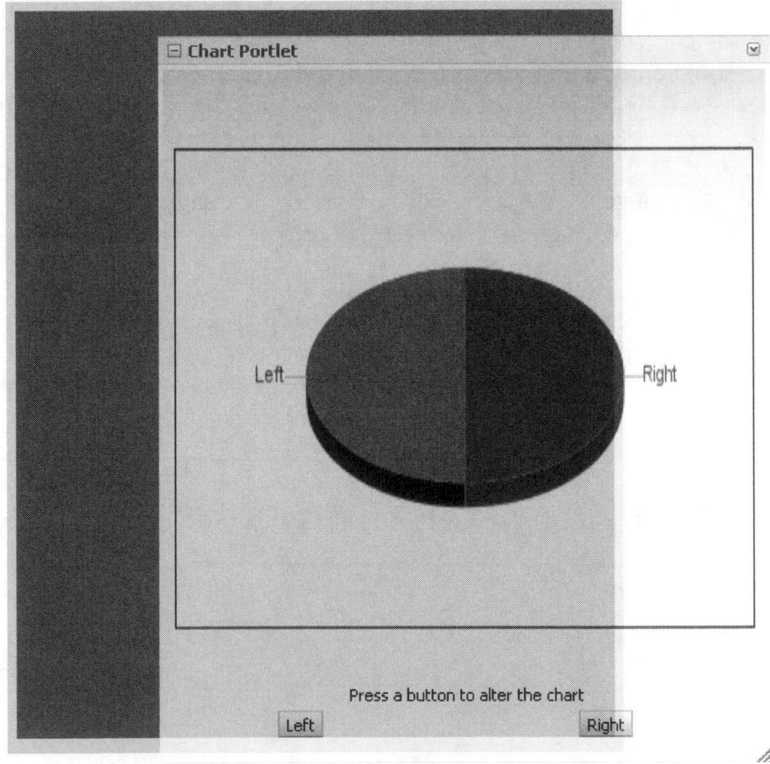

FIGURE 11-10 *Dragging-and-dropping components on the page*

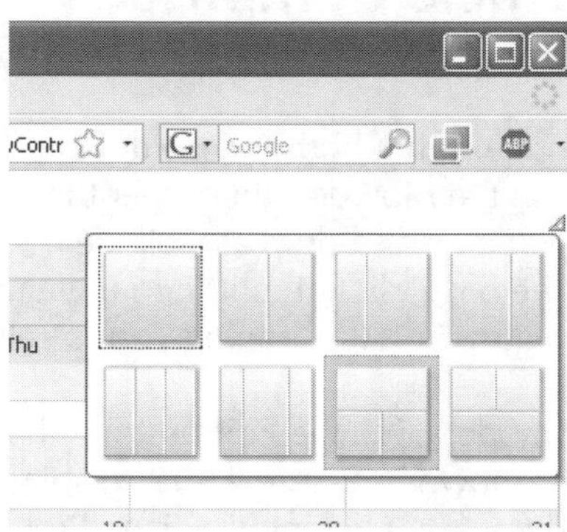

FIGURE 11-11 *The layout selector panel*

page. By selecting the View Design or View Source options, you specify whether you want to exclusively see a WYSIWYG representation of the page, or you want to display a simplified tree view of the page as well. The latter may come in handy when you have many nested components on the page and you want to select a specific one to set its properties.

To edit component properties, click on the Edit link, represented by a pencil, in the top-right corner. The properties are shown in a floating pop-up panel and are organized in tabs. Most of the properties offer editor panels as well. Figure 11-13 gives you an idea of what the Component Properties editing panel looks like. This panel allows you to change the component title or to contextually wire the component with other components on the page. Components can provide custom property editing panels as well.

To add a new component to the page, select the Add content button in the Panel Customizable where you want to add the content to. This brings up the resource catalog pop-up panel.

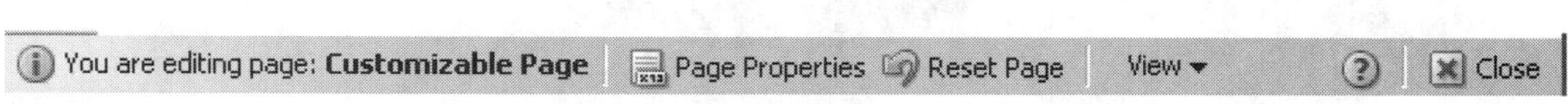

FIGURE 11-12 *The information bar in Composer*

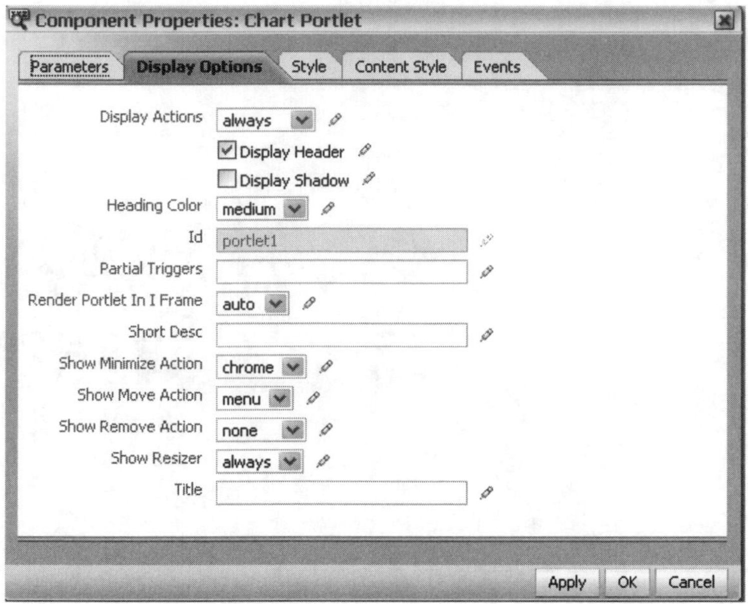

FIGURE 11-13 *The Component Properties editing panel*

If you have registered portlet producers with your application before, the Portlet Producers folder shows up automatically in the resource catalog as shown in Figure 11-14. When you're drilling down in the Portlet Producers folder, all the registered portlet producers are listed. Selecting a specific portlet producer returns the list of portlets the producer offers. In your example you registered the Sample WSRP portlet producer with the application; therefore, now you can add the Lottery Portlet, offered by this producer.

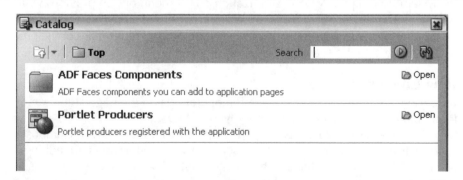

FIGURE 11-14 *The run-time resource catalog viewer*

FIGURE 11-15 *Page modified at run time*

When you're done, delete the Chart Portlet from the page by clicking on the Remove icon in the top-right corner of the portlet.

Your view of the page should look similar to the one shown in Figure 11-15. To save some real estate, we collapsed the calendar component on the page.

Cleaning Up Run-Time Customizations

You saw earlier that Composer's Reset Page control on the information bar, demonstrated in Figure 11-12, removes all run-time customization applied to the page. The Build | Clean Run-time MDS Customizations menu option in JDeveloper does the same but for the entire application. It simply deletes the directory from your file system holding the MDS customizations. This menu option provides you an easy way to find the location of the file system repository MDS uses for your application at design time. By the way, this information is stored in adf-config.xml and can be changed for your application if need be.

Handling Concurrency

If multiple users are performing customization operations on the page at the same time, then all the independent changes get saved to MDS/.

If two users are customizing a page at the same customization layer, Composer's information bar displays a message letting users know that other users are editing the page as well. In this case changes that are committed last overwrite previous customizations.

Advanced Composer Configuration

In this section we take a closer look at some of the more sophisticated capabilities of Oracle Composer.

Controlling Customization Options

The Show Detail Frame and Layout Customizable components provide you a lot of flexibility to control what you do and don't want to expose to your users. Both components can hide the edit action. In addition, the Show Detail Frame can hide all or some of the actions, including minimize, move, resize, and remove. These options are controlled by the ShowMoveAction, ShowRemoveAction, ShowResizer, ShowMinimizeAction, and ShowEditAction properties.

Concurrent Page Editing Using Composer Sandbox

When two users are editing the page at the same time, the information bar, presented by the Page Customizable component, gives you a warning message about it. If you would like to turn off this the warning, you can do so by setting the Page Customizable component's ShowMessage attribute to false.

One of the reasons web applications are so successful is that they support the simultaneous access of the same application by a large number of users. When such applications offer features beyond read-only capabilities, dealing with concurrent access becomes essential.

When Composer is configured to use the file system repository, which is the default in a development environment, managing concurrent access is limited to displaying warnings to users. This can be elevated to the next level by configuring Composer to work against a database MDS repository. In this case you can enable Composer's so-called sandbox functionality. Sandbox in the Composer world is a temporary storage area to save run-time page customizations before they are either committed to the back end or canceled. If you don't use sandbox, your users' changes are automatically and immediately committed. If you are familiar with SQL, sandbox gives you the Composer version of savepoint-rollback-commit functionality.

Since the exact steps are documented in the Oracle WebCenter Guide, here we review only the high-level steps to configure sandbox for Composer:

1. To enable sandbox, you have to make sure that your MDS uses a database repository. If it doesn't, you have to reconfigure and/or migrate your file system–based MDS repository to a database repository.
2. The next step is editing your adf-config.xml, declaring for which metadata you want to enable sandboxing. Most likely you want to enable sandboxing for your *.jspx and page definition files.

3. In the adf-config.xml file turn sandboxing on.
4. Define a Composer-specific filter in your application's web.xml, before the ADF bindings filter. This will ensure that all requests are routed through the Composer-specific filter first.

At run time, when you switch to Edit mode, the presence of a Save button on the header of the Composer panel is the most obvious indication that sandbox creation is enabled for the application.

After you make the required changes in Edit mode and are satisfied with the changes you have made, you can commit the changes by clicking Save on the Composer panel. Alternatively, you can click Close to close the Composer panel, and then you'll be prompted to save or cancel your changes.

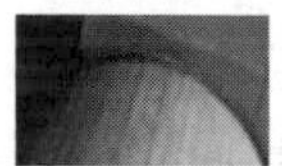

NOTE
Oracle WebCenter Spaces takes advantage of the sandboxing feature, shown in Figure 11-16.

Custom Actions

In addition to the common capabilities of the Show Detail Frame component, such as drag-and-drop or collapse and expand support, a less frequently used but quite powerful functionality it provides is the action menu in its top-right corner. The flexible custom action framework allows you to plug in and surface task flow actions in this menu.

Let's take a look at the following example. Your calendaring task flow has a main view and a view showing print preview. The two views, demonstrated in Figure 11-17, are implemented as ADF task flow view activities. Now, in addition to (or instead of) providing navigation controls between the two view activities

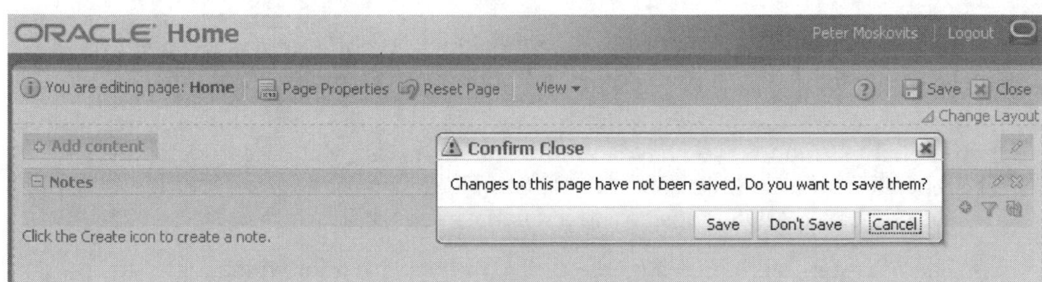

FIGURE 11-16 *Composer sandbox used by WebCenter Spaces*

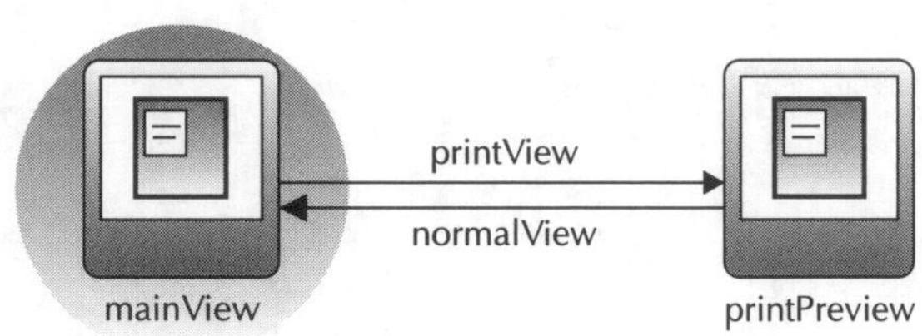

FIGURE 11-17 *A task flow with two view activities*

inside your task flow, you can also surface action menus in the Show Detail Frames surrounding the task flow, to provide the navigation between the two views.

The first view activity provides two ways to navigate to the print preview: a traditional button on the bottom of the task flow, labeled as Print Preview, and a custom action link, demonstrated in the top-right corner of Figure 11-18: Print Preview, with a printer icon next to the label.

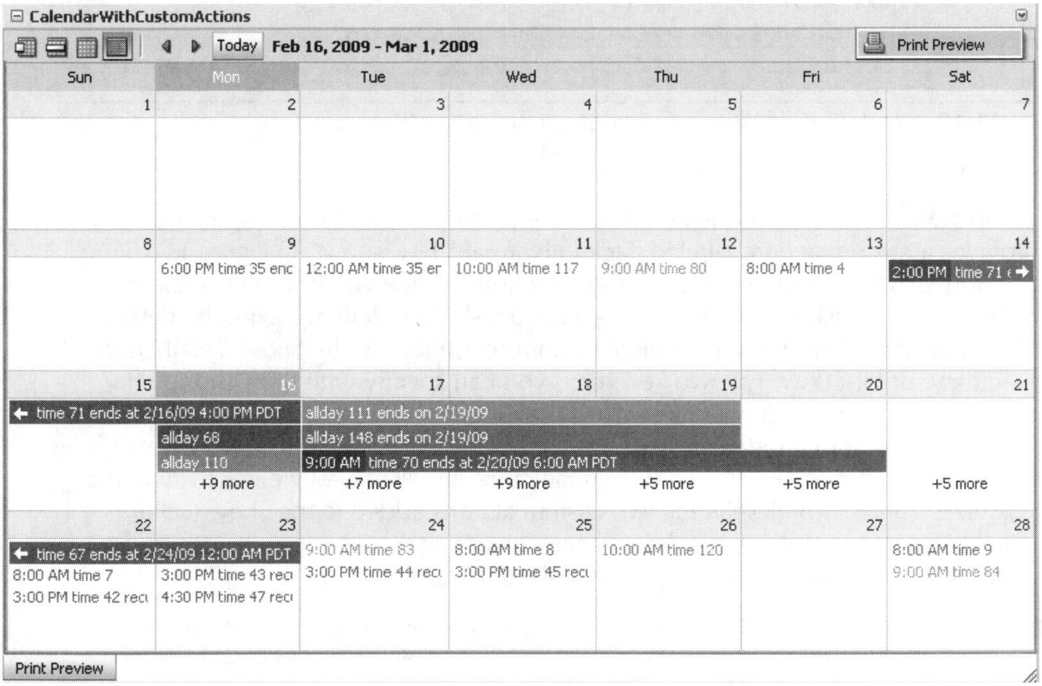

FIGURE 11-18 *Task flow view with two navigation options to Print Preview*

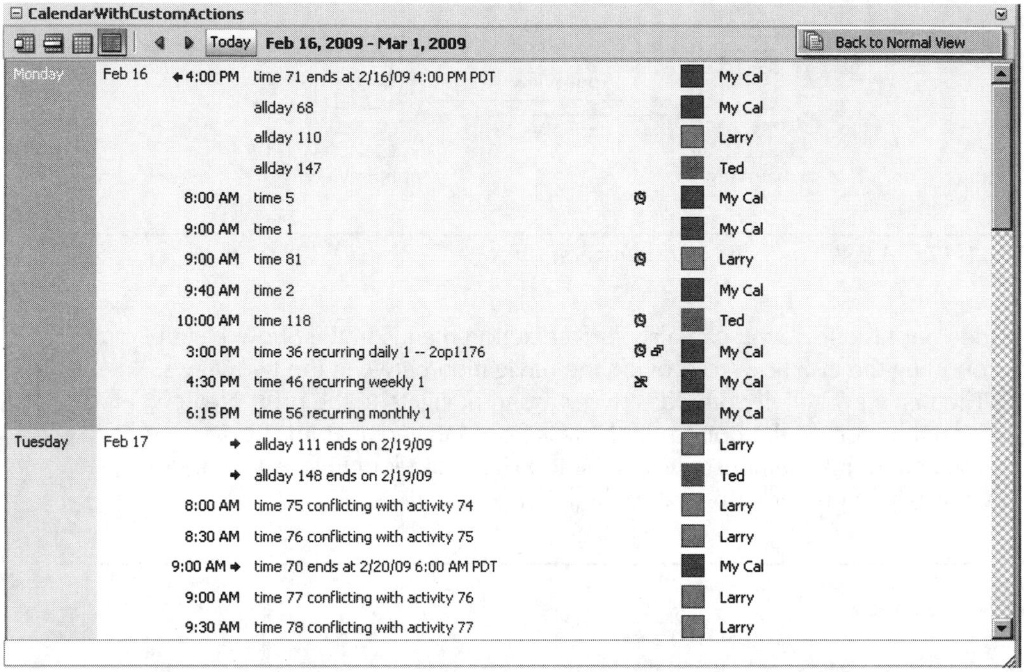

FIGURE 11-19 *Task flow featuring a custom action navigation option*

To navigate back from the printPreview view activity to mainView, the task flow provides a custom action, labeled Back to Normal View, shown in Figure 11-19.

How can you create your own custom actions? Once you have the actions defined in your task flow definition file (called task-flow-definition.xml, by default), all you need to do is add one or more customAction tags to the Show Detail Frame holding your task flow. The two key things you can specify with the customAction tag: the label and the icon shown in the Show Detail Frame menu.

It's important to remember that the only actions displayed in the Show Detail Frame are valid navigation actions from the currently displayed view activity in the task flow. This is why despite the two custom actions added to the Show Detail Frame, in our case only one is shown at any given time.

Here is the source code for your Show Detail Frame:

```
<cust:showDetailFrame text="CalendarWithCustomActions" id="sdf1">
  <af:region value="#{bindings.taskflowdefinition1.regionModel}"
          id="r1"/>
  <cust:customAction action="printView" text="Print Preview"
id="ca1" icon="iconpath/print_ena.png"/>
```

```
        <cust:customAction action="normalView" text="Back to Normal
View" id="ca2" icon="iconpath/pages_qualifier.png"/>
       </cust:showDetailFrame>
```

On top of defining custom actions for individual Show Detail Frame components, you can also provide global custom actions, applied to all Show Detail Frames in the application.

A logical question at this point is, Which of the globally defined actions show up in the menu of the Show Detail Frame? The behavior is the same as you saw before: only those actions that have a corresponding control flow in the currently displayed view activity of the task flow are present in the menu. If you are in Normal mode, the print preview action is displayed, and vice versa; if you are in Print Preview mode, the normal view item is shown.

You can declare your global custom actions in the adf-config.xml:

```
<cust:adf-config-child>
    <enableSecurity value="true" />
    <customActions>
      <cust:customAction action="printView" displayName="Print Preview"
                         id="gca1" icon="iconpath/print_ena.png"/>
      <cust:customAction action="normalView" tooltip="Back to Normal View"
                         id="gca2" icon="iconpath/pages_qualifier.png"/>
    </customActions>
</cust:adf-config-child>
```

Creating Pages at Run Time Using the Page Service

Very much like making changes to page content and layout, creating pages at run time is a typical functionality that every portal product provides. While the way business users and developers interact with it is very different, the Page Service is most of the time discussed on the same page with Oracle Composer. They both provide powerful run-time application customization capabilities and both use MDS as their repository.

The page service lets the authorized business users of your application create new pages, delete pages, copy pages, and change page properties.

The Page—Create New Task Flow

The button responsible for creating a new page has been implemented as an ADF task flow called Page—Create New. In addition to the Create Page button the task flow also provides a modal dialog window displaying the page styles that the user can choose from.

The Page—Create New task flow, just like any other WebCenter task flow, resides in the WebCenter Services Catalog, in the Resource Palette in JDeveloper.

It accepts seven parameters. The easiest way to define values for the parameters is by navigating to the page definition file of the page containing the task flow, and opening the Parameters section in the Property Inspector. This is the list of the task flow parameters and what they control:

- **Scope name** By assigning pages to scopes using the scope name parameter, you can group your pages.
- **Outcome** The outcome parameter defines the Java method that gets invoked after the page is created. For example, this allows you to provide visual feedback to the user after the page is created, or to navigate to the newly created page and take it into Edit mode.
- **Page style file** This parameter allows you to point to an xml file (called template.xml, by default) that describes the page styles that the user can pick from when creating a new page. Page styles are basically jspx pages, optionally accompanied by a page definition file, that is copied as the newly created page.
- **ADF template** Here you can define the ADF page template that you'd like your page to use. If your page style is based on an ADF template, you can configure the page-creation task flow such that a different ADF template is used based on different criteria such as user or scopes.
- **User interface type** This parameter allows you to specify whether you want your Page—Create New task flow to render as a link or a button. By default it renders as a button. To render as a link, the parameter value has to be ${'link'}.
- **Icon** The icon parameter allows you to specify a custom icon that will appear on your button or next to your link.
- **Label** This parameter provides you with control over the label that is rendered.

Figure 11-20 shows two visualizations of the Page—Create New task flow. The first one is the default, the second one with different icon and label.

FIGURE 11-20 *Page—Create New task flow: two visualizations*

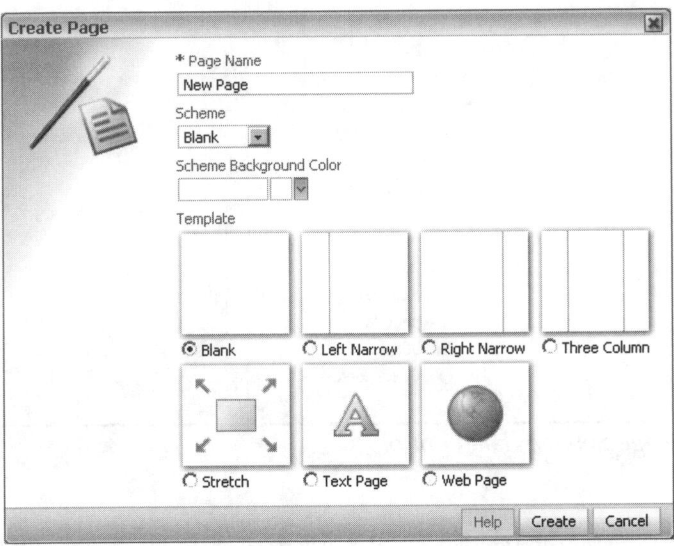

FIGURE 11-21 *The Create Page dialog*

When users click the button, a dialog is displayed allowing them to specify the name, color scheme, background color, and style for the new page, shown in Figure 11-21.

The Page Service Data Control

The Page Service data control, PageServiceDC, gives you access to information about your pages at run time. It also lets you delete any of your pages at run time.

In the following simple example you will see how to use the Create Page task flow to create pages at run time, and what it takes to display the pages using the Page Service data control.

Create a new application using the WebCenter Application template. Create a page using a two-column Quick Start Layout. In the WebCenter catalog locate the Page—Page Service task flow, and drop it onto the narrow column in your page (labeled as first).

Locate the PageServiceDC under Data Controls in your applications. Expand it, expand the getPageTree(String) node, and drop the PageTreeNode onto the wide column of your page (labeled as second), shown in Figure 11-22.

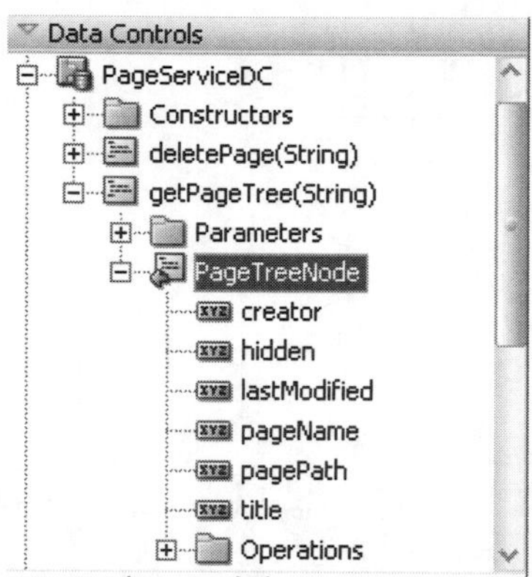

FIGURE 11-22 *The Page Service data control*

Visualize the data on the page as an ADF Read-Only Table. Select the defaults, and click OK. When prompted for the scopeName parameter, you can leave it empty, and click OK again.

This table will display metadata about the pages in MDS. You will make one minor change to it: add a Go Link that will allow you to navigate to the page displayed in the table.

Drop a Go Link into the first (title) column of the table, and delete the original Output Text rendering the title. Select the newly added Go Link, and change the following three properties:

Text: #{row.link}

Destination: /faces#{row.pagePath}

Target Frame: _blank

Let's run the page. Click the Create Page button, and specify a name, scheme, and page style you want to base your new page on.

Since our application is very simple, you'll have to perform a manual page refresh in the browser for the newly created page to show up in the table, as shown in Figure 11-23.

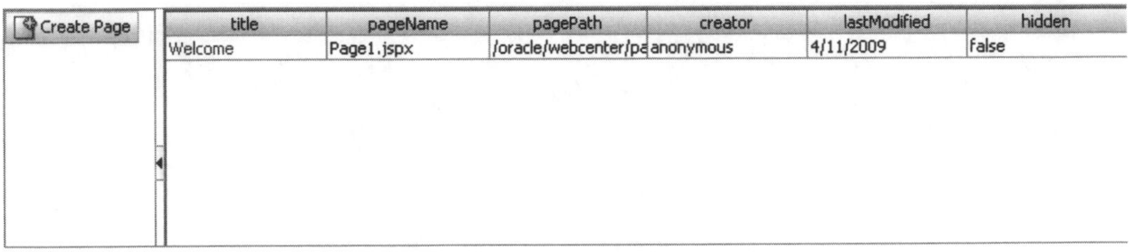

Create Page

title	pageName	pagePath	creator	lastModified	hidden
Welcome	Page1.jspx	/oracle/webcenter/pa	anonymous	4/11/2009	false

FIGURE 11-23 *Creating pages at run time*

Clicking on the link takes you to the newly created page, called Welcome. In our example we used the Text Page as the page style (or template), shown in Figure 11-24.

The official Oracle documentation, the WebCenter Developer's Guide, available online on OTN, discusses the Page Service capabilities in a lot more detail. If run-time page creation and management is your bread and butter, the Developer's Guide, presenting nice examples, is a great resource to read.

Edit

Text

FIGURE 11-24 *Page with Rich Text Editor, created by the Page Service*

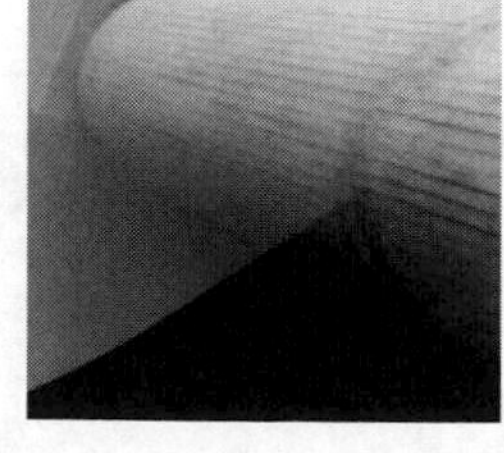

CHAPTER 12

Resource Catalog

ow that we have discussed run-time customization, one question seems painfully obvious: What do I need to do to enable my own components in run-time customization? The answer lies in the mechanism called the *resource catalog.*

The resource catalog, both at design time and at run time, represents the list of components that can be added to a WebCenter page. Elements that can be added to a page at run time are:

- **Box** A container component represented by a dotted line, inside which you can add any other components from the run-time resource catalog viewer. Child components can be moved around inside this container. Any new components can be added only inside such a container component. The box is analogous to the Panel Customizable component that is available in Oracle JDeveloper.
- **Hyperlink** Analogous to the ADF Faces Link component in Oracle JDeveloper; it creates a link to a page or web site.
- **Image** A default image with a link that navigates to another location. You can change the properties to add any image from your File System repository and provide a destination for the link.
- **Movable Box** Similar to a box component, but enables you to group components as one movable unit. This component provides a place to drop documents, page links, web page links, and web pages such that they can be moved on the page. Movable Box is analogous to the Show Detail Frame component that is available in Oracle JDeveloper.
- **Text** Analogous to the Rich Text Editor component in Oracle JDeveloper; provides a text editor that enables you to add richly formatted text to the page.
- **Web Page** Analogous to the Inline Frame component in Oracle JDeveloper; creates an inline frame tag.
- **Portlets** From any producer that was registered at design time and is therefore displayed in the Portlet Producers list.
- **Task flows** Available under WebCenter Libraries in the Catalog. While the design-time resource catalog, also called Resource Palette in Oracle JDeveloper, contains registered task flows and visualizes IDE Connections created to various services (e.g., portlets, content repository, etc.) , the Runtime Resource Catalog is the collection of all components that can be added to a page at run time.

Contents of the Resource Palette are available for developers to use in any application, while run-time catalogs are integral components of an application, just like the application pages. Each run-time catalog contains an application-specific set of components that are organized according to the requirements of the application users.

The resource catalog will combine components from different sources in a single view.

How the Resource Catalog Gets into Your Application

You might wonder how the resource catalog magically gets into the application. When you add the Composer (aka PageCustomizable) tag to your application, two things happen behind the scenes:

1. A default resource catalog definition file (`default-catalog.xml`) is copied to `<ApplicationRoot>\<Application_Name>\mds\oracle\adf\rc\metadata`.
2. A default resource catalog viewer (Figure 12-1) is configured to use the default resource catalog definition.

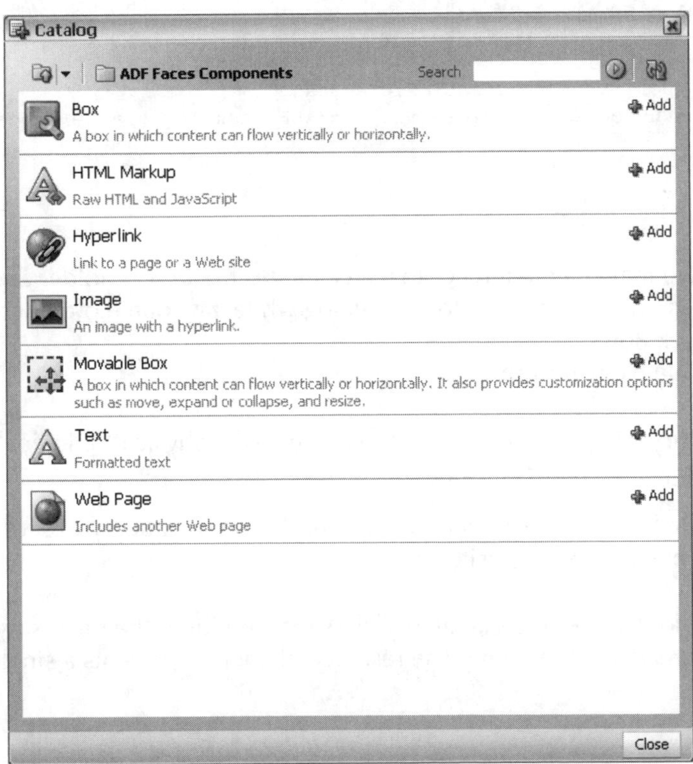

FIGURE 12-1 *A resource catalog viewer in Oracle Composer*

If you want to change the contents of the default catalog you can either modify the default-catalog.xml or create a new catalog definition and configure your application to use it as the default run-time catalog.

Default_catalog.xml defines the content of the default run-time catalog. The XML below shows a default-catalog.xml that has been slightly modified.

```
<?xml version = '1.0' encoding = 'UTF-8'?>
<catalogDefinition xmlns="http://xmlns.oracle.com/adf/rcs/catalog"
    id="catalogDefinition"
    name="Default Resource Catalog"

    description="Default resource catalog ">
  <contents>

    <!-- *************************************************************
    * Custom folder exposing ADF Faces components                  *
    * Comment out this element if you want to remove it from the catalog.*
    *************************************************************** -->
    <customFolder id="facesComponents" name="ADF Faces Components"
      description="ADF Faces components you can add to application pages"

factoryClass="oracle.adfinternal.view.page.editor.componentcatalog [...]
  <resource id="doclibMainView"
          name="Documents Task Flow"
          description="Main view of the Documents service"
          repository="application.classpath"
          path="doclib-service-view.jar/ADF_TaskFlow/oracle+webcenter+
[...]
...
</contents>
</catalogDefinition>
```

There are two main element types that a catalog is made of: a folder and a resource. Folders provide structure to the catalog while a resource provides content in the form of task flows.

Other possible elements are:

- **Repository** Repository exposes the content of a physical or logical repository (e.g., Portlet Producer).
- **Dynamic folder** This folder has contents based on a query executed against one or more repositories.

The custom folder references a factory class that produces the necessary information to create the hierarchy. The resource element represents a single resource in the catalog. It would point, for example, to a task flow that should show up in the catalog. There are several other valid elements that can be used in the catalog definition. We will discuss those later in this chapter.

Enabling an Existing Task Flow

If you open the default-catalog.xml of your application, you will find a sample reference to the Document Library task flow in there, but surrounded by comment tags:

```
<resource id="doclibMainView"
      name="Documents Task Flow"
      description="Main view of the Documents service"
      repository="application.classpath"
      path="doclib-service-view.jar/ADF_TaskFlow/oracle+webcenter+ [...]
```

If you take a closer look at the tag, you can see a set of attributes:

- **id** A unique ID for the specific component.
- **name** The name that will show up in the resource catalog viewer.
- **description** The longer text you will see in the resource catalog viewer below the name.
- **repository** The attribute that defines where the resource can be found. If you are adding a task flow that is packaged with your application, you would put in application.classpath.
- **path** The path to the task flow definition.

NOTE
You might wonder how to get the cryptic value that you need to provide for path. The easiest way is to right-click on the respective task flow in the Resource Palette (see Figure 12-2) in Oracle JDeveloper. By invoking the Show Catalog Reference option, JDeveloper will hint at the necessary values, as seen in Figure 12-3.

This is quite helpful in determining what you need to provide to get the respective task flow into the resource catalog.

To add the Document Library task flow, remove the comment tags around the tag. Simple enough, right?

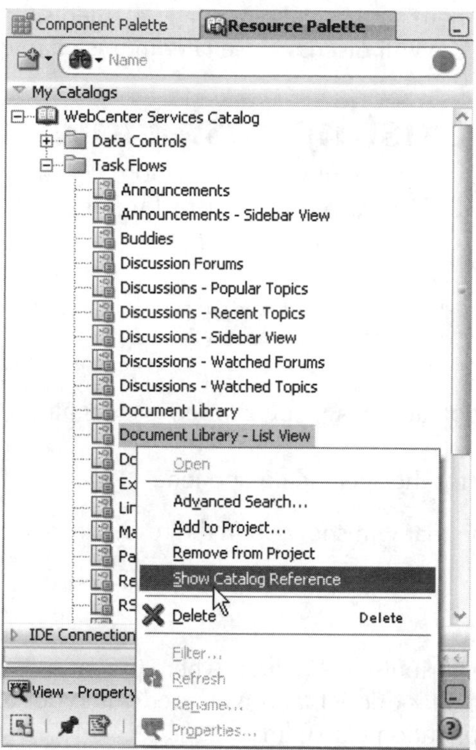

FIGURE 12-2 *Figuring out the values for the resource catalog definition*

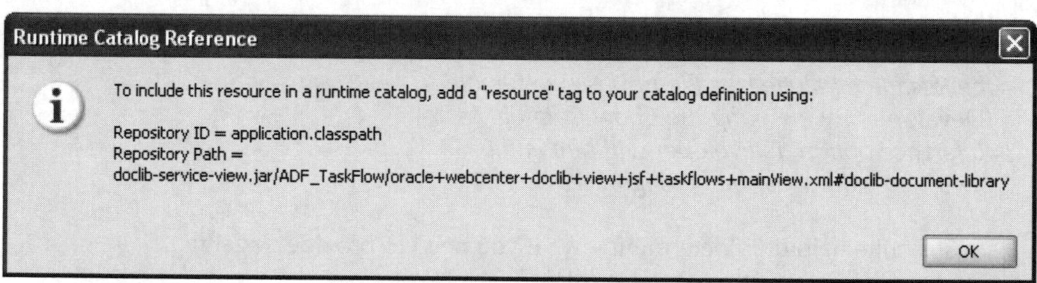

FIGURE 12-3 *Runtime Catalog Reference dialog*

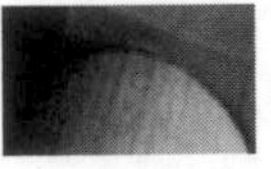

NOTE
To actively use the Document Library, your application needs to have one (or more) content connections created. See Chapter 7 for further details.

Now to add another task flow to the catalog, say the Discussions task flow, expand the WebCenter Services Catalog in the Resource Palette and expand the task flows. There you can find the Discussions task flow.

NOTE
Just as for any service, your application needs to have the Discussion Service enabled. This is done automatically when you add the Discussions task flow onto a page in JDeveloper, or if you explicitly select Add to Project from the task flow context menu in the Resource Palette in JDeveloper. Also, to use the task flow properly, your application needs to have one (or more) connections of the respective type (in this case Discussions) available.

First you need to add the associated Java Archive (JAR) file to the project. To do so, you need to right-click on the task flow in the Resource Palette and choose Add to Project. This will add the associated JAR file to the project classpath.

Now you need to modify the default-catalog.xml. Simply browse to the file in your Windows Explorer and open it in your favorite text editor. The file is located in <application root>/mds/oracle/adf/rc/metadata/default-catalog.xml. Of course you can also add it to your JDeveloper project.

Once it's open in an editor, add the resource tag to it.

```
<resource id="discussionsMainView"
          name="Discussionforum"
          description="Main view of the Discussions service"
          repository="application.classpath"
          path="forum-view.jar/ADF_TaskFlow/
oracle+webcenter+collab+ […]
```

Remember, you can get the value for the path attribute by right-clicking on the task flow in the Resource Palette to invoke the Show Catalog reference option from the context menu.

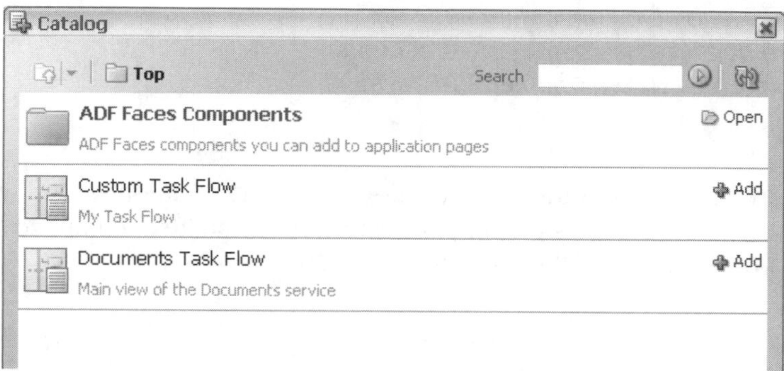

FIGURE 12-4 *The modified resource catalog viewer*

Please keep in mind that in order for the task flows to work, you also need to create the necessary connection (as we have stated in the notes above). If you do not do that, you can still run the application, but the task flows that you add to the page will not work until connections are configured in your application.

Now save the changes and run the application. When you now invoke the resource catalog from Composer you will see two new task flows, the Custom Library task flow and the Documents task flow (see Figure 12-4).

Getting Custom Task Flows into the Resource Palette

So now that we have discussed how to add existing task flows to the resource catalog, the next step is to register your own task flows with the resource catalog, first in JDeveloper and then in Composer.

In JDeveloper this task is simple enough. First you need to create a new File System IDE connection. To do so, expand the IDE Connections section of the Resource Palette and right-click on the File System node (Figure 12-5).

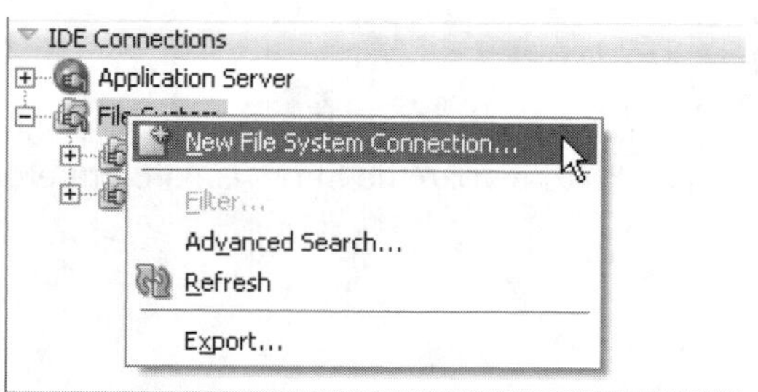

FIGURE 12-5 *Adding a new File System connection*

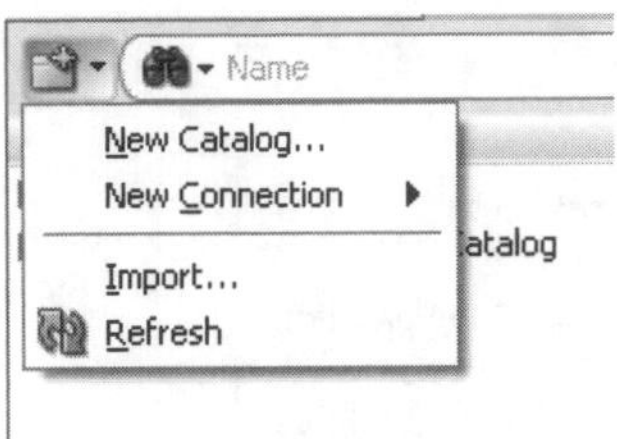

FIGURE 12-6 *Adding a new File System connection via the New icon*

It could be that your IDE Connections section does not have such a node, because a connection of that type has not been defined yet. In that case, simply click on the New icon at the top-left of the Resource Palette and select New Connection and the File System type (Figure 12-6).

You are presented with the dialog for a new File System connection. Simply provide a name and the path to the directory where you have ADF Library files (Figure 12-7). Then click OK.

Task flows are packaged in ADF Libraries. These are JAR files that contain additional information identifying the task flows, data controls, app modules, etc., that are included in the library.

To create an ADF Library, create your task flows/data controls in a JDeveloper project, then create a deployment profile of type ADF Library and deploy to that profile.

Once it's created, this connection allows you to browse the content of the provided location (see Figure 12-8). If there are any ADF Libraries present, you can drill down to reveal the task flows available. You can either leave it at that or add the task flow to the My Catalogs section of the Resource Palette.

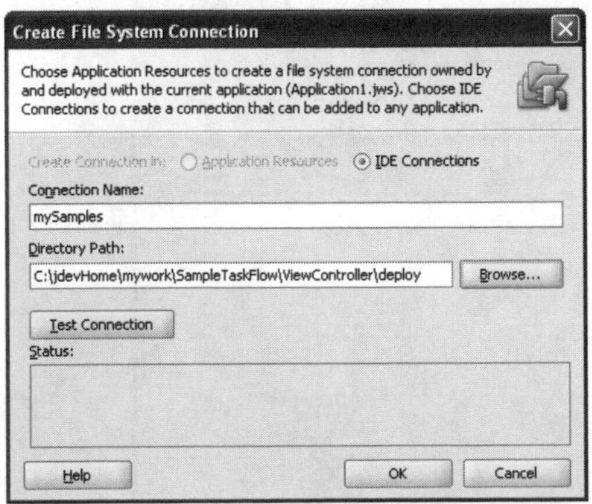

FIGURE 12-7 *The new File System Connection dialog*

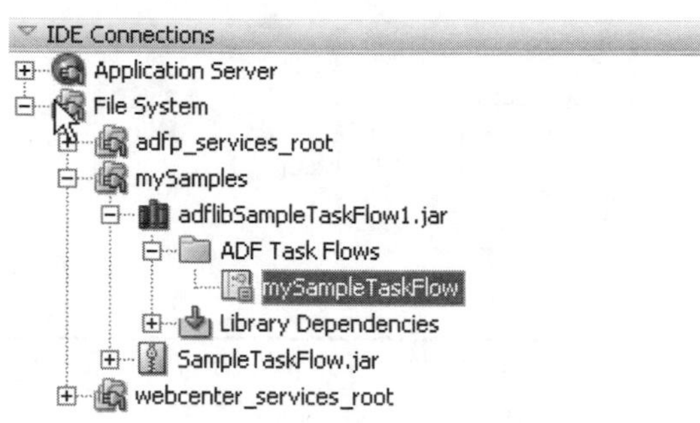

FIGURE 12-8 *Browsing the connection*

To do so, simply drag-and-drop the task flow from the connection to the desired position in the My Catalogs panel. Another way is to right-click on the task flow and select Add to Catalog, which will bring up the corresponding dialog (Figure 12-9). There you can decide where to add your component in the hierarchy.

To keep the section tidy, you can create catalogs and folders. These catalogs can be organized to your liking and can be exported and imported if needed.

In the Add to Catalog dialog you can select the position where you would like your task flow to be added or decide to create a new catalog altogether (or new folders).

Don't worry if you realize that either the necessary hierarchy is not available or you placed it at a wrong position; elements in the Resource Palette can be rearranged easily using drag-and-drop.

Well, guess what? You're done. Now you can select your custom task flow and drop it onto a page in your application, just like you can do with the built-in task flows from WebCenter.

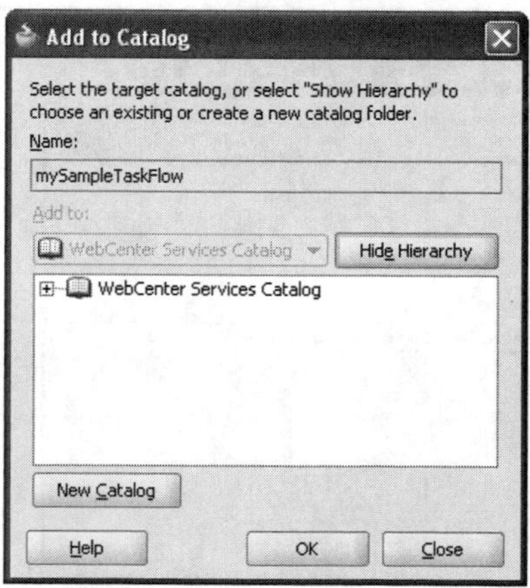

FIGURE 12-9 *Adding a component to the My Catalogs section of the Resource Palette*

Adding Your Own Task Flow to the Catalog

Granted, so far we have revealed only half the greatness of the resource catalog. Now that you have successfully added your own task flow to the Resource Palette in JDeveloper, the next logical step is to add it to Runtime Resource Catalog in Composer.

The steps to do that should be known to you already; they are in no way different from the ones you used to add one of the built-in task flows to the catalog.

1. Open the default-catalog.xml file.
2. Create a new resource element.
3. Fill in the necessary values for the path attribute. To get to them, simply right-click on the task flow in question and invoke the Show Catalog Reference to get the Cheat dialog.
4. Don't forget to add the task flow to your project by selecting the Add to Project option from the same context menu you used to bring up the Cheat dialog.

   Now your entry should look something like this:

   ```
   <resource id="mySampleTaskFlow"
       name="A Sample Task Flow"
       description="This is a very simple Hello World Task Flow to [...]
       repository="application.classpath"
       path="adflibSampleTaskFlow1.jar/ADF_TaskFlow/WEB-INF+ [...]
   ```

Granted, the path will most likely look different since your task flow, your JAR, or both will be named differently, but overall it should compare.

Now when you run a page and invoke the resource catalog through Composer, you will find your custom task flow there.

Using Your Custom Task Flow

Once your task flow is available in the resource catalog, you can go ahead and add it to your page at run time. When you're in Edit mode, you will find a small pencil icon for every component added to your page. This will bring up the settings dialog for this component. The first tab of this dialog holds the parameters. If a task flow has input parameter definitions, they will automatically show up there; there's nothing more for you to do.

Input parameters are useful if you want to connect elements on a page (task flows, portlets) by passing parameter values to them. For example, you could have multiple elements on the page take in a customer ID and pass a common value for those parameters to the components so the data they provide is synchronized.

NOTE
To reference your input parameters inside your task flow, simply use EL to reference it; for example, #{pageFlowScope.myFirstParameter}.

Another thing you might notice is that all custom task flows in the catalog viewer have the same icon, while pre-defined task flows or components have their own, nice-looking icons. You can control this by overriding the IconURI of the respective resource.

To do so, add an <attributes>...</attributes> section as a child of the resource tag into the catalog definition.

```
<resource ...>
   <attributes>
     <attribute value="/adf/webcenter/announcements_qualifier.png"
      attributeId="IconURI"/>
   </attributes>
</resource>
```

The referenced icon needs to be available in the META-INF directory on the application classpath. Ideally you would add it to the archive that contains the task flow.

You need to provide two sizes of icons named <name>_qualifier and <name>_lg_qualifier. A complete list of parameters can be found in the Oracle Fusion Middleware Developers Guide for Oracle WebCenter.

Organizing the Run-Time Resource Catalog

Eureka! Now you can happily create your run-time resource catalog. But hold on one second. If you now create a massive amount of components, the catalog will soon become bloated and very confusing. You need to create some kind of hierarchy.

To do so, you can use the <folder> element in the catalog definition.

```
<folder id="sampleFolder" name="Sample Folder"
    description="This Folder helps to keep things tidy.">
 <contents>
    <resource id="mySampleTaskFlow"
          name="A Sample Task Flow"
          description="This is a very simple Hello World Task [...]
              repository="application.classpath"

              path="adflibSampleTaskFlow1.jar/ADF_TaskFlow/ [...]
 </contents>
</folder>
```

It will create a folder in your catalog and can contain resources, dynamic folders, and resources. Using this you can now easily create a hierarchy and thereby keep your catalog neatly organized.

Creating a Custom Catalog Definition

So far you have modified the default catalog definition. This is the easiest way to get a customized catalog. However, in certain instances you might want to create your own catalog definition or even a set of catalog definitions (if, for example, you want to have different catalogs on certain pages or for certain user roles).

In this instance you need to manually create the catalog definition. You might want to start off by copying the default-catalog.xml to some other name and start to edit this copy. Then you need to configure your application to actually pick up this new catalog definition instead of the default catalog. These changes need to be made in adf-config.xml. Adding, for example, the `<rcv-config>` tag will allow you to point to a different catalog XML file.

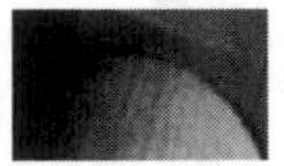

NOTE
adf-config.xml is located in .adf/META-INF of your application root. Do not confuse *adf-config.xml* with *adfc-config.xml. The latter file is visible by default in your Application Navigator, but has nothing to do with resource catalog.*

Add this section accordingly to point to your new catalog definition file. Notice that you do not need to provide the file extension (in this example the new name of the catalog definition would be my-custom-catalog.xml and it would be located in the same location as default-catalog.xml).

```
<rcv-config xmlns="http://xmlns.oracle.com/adf/rcs/viewer/adf-config">
  <default-catalog catalog-name="my-custom-catalog"/>
</rcv-config>
```

Multiple Catalog Definitions

As we described, not only can you provide your own catalog definition file, but you can also provide multiple definitions paired with a selector class that decides, based on some rule that you can define, which catalog to show. That way you could, for example, provide different catalogs for different user roles, or application sections.

Simply create a class implementing the oracle.adf.rc.model.config. ResourceCatalogSelector interface which implements the logic to select the correct template. It could, for example, use the page_id (via context.get(RCVContext.PAGE_ID)) to determine which page is invoking the viewer and by that determine which catalog to choose.

All you need to do then is to register this class with the resource catalog viewer by modifying adf-config.xml.

```
<rcv:rcv-config xmlns="http://xmlns.oracle.com/adf/rcs/viewer/adf-config">
  <catalog-selector class-name="your_catalog_selector_class"/>
  <default-catalog catalog-name="default-catalog"/>
</rcv:rcv-config>
```

This will invoke the class, and in the case of the class not returning any catalog name, it will use the name specified in the default-catalog element which, of course, could also point to a custom catalog definition file as described in the previous section.

Advanced Resource Catalog Definition Changes

Besides the already described elements in the catalog definition there are a couple more that need mention.

<attributes>...</attributes>

Each element can contain any number of attribute elements (surrounded by an <attributes> element). You would use <attributes> to override existing task flow properties. So, for example, if you wanted to change the task flow title, simply create an attribute with the name Title and provide the desired title.

```
<attribute value="My Sample Title" attributeId="Title" isKey="false"/>
```

Another use of attributes is to provide resource IDs in case you wanted to use resource bundles instead of hard-coded values. This will also allow you to translate those bundles and create multilanguage applications.

```
<attribute value="CUSTOMTASKFLOW.TITLE" attributeId="Title" isKey="true"/>
```

If you decide to define attributes, you also need to provide a <schema> element with further descriptions for the resource catalog service on how to treat those attributes in relation to the user.

```
<descriptor searchable="true" labelKey="TITLE.PROMPT_KEY"
endUserVisible="true"shortLabelKey="TITLE.SHORT_PROMPT_KEY"
attributeId="Title" multivalue="false"/>
```

Adding Portlets to the Catalog

The last remaining element you might want to add to the catalog is a portlet, or rather a portlet producer serving a number of portlets. The way you would add portlets to your catalog is to create a connection to a producer (either PDK Java or WSRP). The default catalog contains the definition for a customFolder that will dynamically show all registered producers and their portlets.

However, you might want to show individual portlets in your catalog, just like you do with task flows. In that case, you would simply create a <resource> tag, just like you did for getting a task flow into the catalog, and point it to the respective portlet. The only twist here is what values to provide for the resource entry:

- Repository would take the provider connection name.
- Path would take the portlet ID on the provider side.

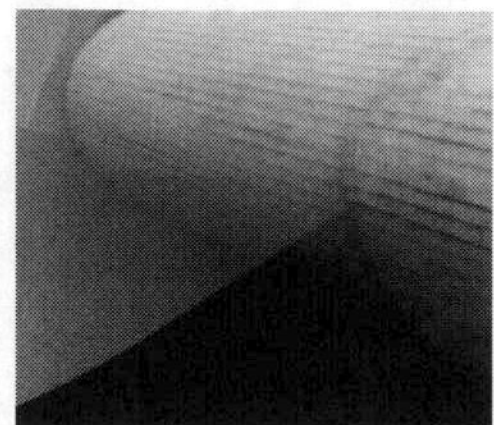

CHAPTER 13

Skinning Your WebCenter Applications

eauty lies in the eye of the beholder" is a common phrase to explain the difference in aesthetic understanding and the subjective nature of visual appeal. As this is true for everything from art to personal appearance, it is also true for the visual design of software, known as *usability*, which combines the visual and functional design of an application.

While functional design is driven by the process the application represents and commonly used principals, the visual appeal, more often than not, is often considered less important.

But the market trend has proven that the level of visual appeal has as much impact on the user as the functional design does. All around us we see an emphasis on designing the appearance as well as the functional experience. Companies like Apple have pioneered this field; their success—and the fact that more and more vendors follow this trend—has shown that users not only support it but demand it.

In application development, designing the look of an application is commonly known as *skinning*. Skinning encompasses the overall application appearance, such as color schema, icon style, and graphical identity. Especially with the move into the Web, designing the look of an application has become very similar to designing web pages, although the requirements for web pages are somewhat different from the ones for applications.

In the recent past, several examples have shown how much effort is being put into the visual appeal of software. Apple's OS X, Microsoft's Windows Vista or Office 2007, IBM's Lotus suite, and various online services have undergone significant visual redesign compared with their predecessors. The more focus that is put on visual appeal, the higher the bar is raised for new applications.

Another driving factor for skinning is an application's identity and its role in an enterprise environment. Within an enterprise, a user's expectation is that applications look and feel as similar as possible. Also, corporate identity calls for skinning an application.

It would go far beyond the scope of this book to discuss the theories about good user interface design, and there are plenty of books on this topic. In this chapter we want to explain the techniques you can use to skin your application—to apply the styles that were the result of the user interface design to your ADF environment so the applications you are creating follow the required design specifications.

Skin vs. Style: What Is the Difference?

Among web site developers, the expectation usually is that the generated HTML will contain lean, well-structured HTML with style names for the respective objects. The designer will then create the corresponding style sheet definitions to implement the look and feel of the site.

With web applications, this process is not quite practical; on the other hand, skins—server-side definitions for look and feel—are a widely used concept. The main reason behind skinning is that only at run time is the actual HTML being created and, although in the case of ADF Faces the skin definition itself follows the CSS 3.0 specifications, the generated HTML and style information might be created for an earlier browser version. To achieve the best possible result in the application, ADF Faces does not limit itself to generating basic HTML but renders the component in a way that it will produce the expected behaviors. This will result in somewhat complex HTML code being generated. The good news is that the developers really do not have to worry about it, as this code is being generated for them by the ADF Faces component. On the downside, however, this makes it tricky to simply create a Cascading Style Sheets (CSS) style sheet and attach it to the generated HTML page. To solve this, ADF Faces provides the developer with the ability to create a skin and with it to control the visual properties of the components. This is the most efficient and productive way to adjust the look and feel of your application. The model used is geared toward the ADF component model and not toward the generated HTML. This ensures that the skin will work, even if the component-generated HTML changes down the road for performance or feature improvements.

About Skins

The idea behind a skin is to provide all of the information in one place, rather than having it spread out across components. To get you started, ADF provides three predefined skins for you to use:

- `simple` Contains only minimal formatting.
- `blafplus-medium` Provides a modest amount of styling. This style extends the `simple` skin.
- `blafplus-rich` Defines the default styles for ADF Faces components. This skin extends the `blafplus-medium` skin.

But skins are more than just CSS and styles for objects. The skin definition is processed by the skin framework and can facilitate additional capabilities, such as:

- defining platform- and/or browser-specific skins that are chosen by the framework automatically or explicitly by the application depending on the client that accesses the application
- creating an accessible profile for fonts and colors
- defining special styles for right-to-left presentation

Before we dig deeper into the skins topic, let's take a closer look at some fundamentals.

A CSS Primer

In order to understand ADF Faces skinning, you need to understand the way cascading style sheets are built and how you need to address particular elements to specifically set styles for elements on the page.

One of the main concepts heavily used by CSS is a selector. Using a selector, you can specifically address visual aspects of an element on the page. Not only can you address individual elements, but also individual aspects or states. So you can change the color of your link elements on the page, and you can specifically define the color for new, visited, and active links.

CSS by itself is worth a book or two, so it would most certainly exceed the scope of this book to go deeply into the details, but we wanted at least to scratch the surface to help you better understand the techniques used with ADF Faces skinning.

Type Selector

A type selector refers to the reference of a particular element type on the page. For example, if you wanted to modify the properties of all <H1> elements on the page, you would add something like this to the CSS:

```
H1 { font-size:100pt; }
```

Now all <H1> elements on the page would take on the new font size.

Class Selector

Elements on the page can also provide a class attribute which allows the developer to explicitly define the style definitions by name. The CSS would then include the definitions for that particular name.

```
.myStyle {font-size:100pt;}
```

Now if you assign this style name to a particular element using the class attribute of the element, it will take on the defined changes.

If, however, you want to distinguish between different elements and have different styles depending on the type, you can combine type and class selectors.

```
H1.myStyle {font-size:100pt;}
H2.myStyle {font-size:50pt;}
```

Now if you assign myStyle to an H1 element, it would take on the 100-point size; if you assign it to an H2 element it would take on the 50-point size. Any H1 or H2 element without any class assigned will still take on the default settings.

Pseudo Class Selector

Lastly, there are special definitions, called pseudo classes, which allow the definition of styles for particular states of an element. For example, `:hover` would be the pseudo class that can be used to define the color of a link once the mouse moves over it.

```
A:hover {color:red;}
```

In this case, a link on a page would become red once the mouse moves over it, and fall back to the default color once the mouse moves away.

Skin Style Selectors

Skin style selectors are defined in the CSS file corresponding to the skin and are used to define style elements for components at different levels using two categories of selectors.

Global selectors define style information at a global level, affecting all components that consume that given selector.

```
.AFDefaultFontFamily:alias {
        font-family: Tahoma, Verdana, Helvetica, sans-serif;
}
```

If the default selector name ends with `:alias` (a pseudo-class), it will most likely affect more than one component. For example, pretty much all components use `.AFDefaultFontFamily:alias` to specify their default font. If you decide to redefine this selector in your skin, it is highly likely that this will affect all components in your application. In most cases this is exactly why you would use skins, but in some cases it might have unwanted side effects.

Component selectors manipulate style settings for a single component only.

```
af|inputText::content {
          background-color: red;
}
```

In the above example, the selector would control the content's background color in an af:inputText component.

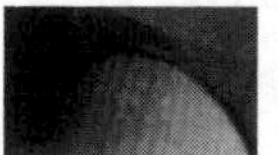

NOTE

You will notice that the style selector name and the component name go in line, except that the component name has a colon (:) where the component selector has a pipe (|) symbol.

Each category can include one or more of the following ADF skin selectors:

- **Standard selectors** Represent directly an element that can be affected by the skin. So `af|body`, for example, stands for the af:body element and you can set CSS style properties, icons, etc.
- **Selectors with pseudo-elements** Used to specify style information of particular parts of a component. You would use a double-colon (::) for this. For example, `af|chooseDate::days-row` provides the styles and properties for the appearance of the dates within the calendar grid.
- **Icon selectors** For all those components that use icons as part of their rendering. Those icons can, although they are not rendered in the normal CSS way, have skin applied to them. To specify this, you would use –icon for component selectors and Icon:alias for global selectors. So to set the changed icon for all components use `.AFChangedIcon:alias`, and to set it only for af:inputDate use `af|inputDate:changed-icon`.
- **Resource strings** Not actual styles, these are represented as references to resource bundles in the trinidad-skins.xml file (we will discuss details about trinidad-skins.xml later on in this chapter). There the <bundle-name> parameter would be used. You could also use the <translation-source> together with EL to point to a map or ResourceBundle. Resource strings are basically text rendered by ADF Faces components. Rather than hard-coding these strings, you create it as a resource string for the purpose of easy translation. For example, `af_dialog.LABEL_OK` is a resource for the label of the OK button of the af:dialog (if configured). All ADF components have default strings (including corresponding translations for the officially supported languages). So if those translations are okay for your application, there is nothing more for you to do.
- **Selectors with style properties** Used to globally control behavior of components. For example, `af|breadCrumbs{-tr-show-last-item: false}` would trigger hiding the last item in the `af:breadCrumbs` navigation path. Those properties, which are not actually styles but nonetheless impact the visual appearance of the application, are stored in the skin object.

There are several other pseudo-classes and small-scale details that you can look up in Chapter 20 of the Oracle Fusion Middleware Web User Interface Developer's Guide for Oracle Application Development Framework.

In some cases it might be necessary to create specific style settings depending on the browser and/or platform of the client accessing the application. To do so you can put your selectors inside a skinning framework rule or use the :rtl pseudo class.

Rules are chosen by the framework depending on the HTTP request header information. The applicable selectors are then merged with the ones outside the rules, and hence are always applicable ones.

Examples for these conditional situations might be extra padding in one browser over the other due to differences in rendering, or different font names on different platforms. In any case, you can adjust the skin so the user experience is identical, regardless of the browser or platform used.

```
/** For IE and Gecko on Windows, Linux and Solaris, make the color pink. **/
@platform windows, linux, solaris
        {
          @agent ie, gecko
          {
            af|inputText::content {background-color:pink}
          }
        }
}
/* The following selectors are for all platforms and all browsers. */
/* rounded corners on the top-start and top-end */
/* shows how to use :rtl mode pseudo-class. */
/* The start image in ltr mode is the */
/* same as the end image in the right-to-left mode. */
af|panelBox::medium af|panelBox::top-start,
af|panelBox::medium af|panelBox::top-end:rtl {
          background-image: url(/skins/purple/images/panelBoxStart.gif);
          width:8px;
          height:8px
        }
```

To control the look and feel of individual component instances within an application (e.g., one particular af:inputText on your page) without impacting the remaining ones on the page, you would use `styleClass` to reference a particular class from a style sheet. Another option to control the look of a component is to explicitly define the visual properties at design time. While skin changes can be performed seamlessly without having to touch the application base, inline-provided style information might have a negative impact if, down the line, the skin of an application is changed.

Applying a Custom Skin to Your Application

Now that you know a little about skins, you are ready to skin your first application. With three easy steps you can get from an application with default skin to your first custom-skinned application:

1. Add a custom skin to your application.
2. Register the custom skin.
3. Configure the application to use the custom skin.

Preparing a Sample Application

Before you can create a skin, you'll need to create a very simple sample application. Using Application | New invoke the New Gallery. Select WebCenter Application from the Application Template list and continue to step through the wizard. (Although this is not necessary, this *is* a WebCenter Handbook, so it's not surprising we are including this example. Instead you could have selected a vanilla application and later added all the necessary libraries to it, but selecting the WebCenter Application template saves you quite a bit of work and time.)

Once the application is created, create a new JSF page in the ViewController project of your newly created application. To do so, invoke the New Gallery by right-clicking the ViewController node in the Application Navigator and selecting New from the context menu.

In the New Gallery, expand the Web Tier node and select JSF Page from the JSF Category (Figure 13-1).

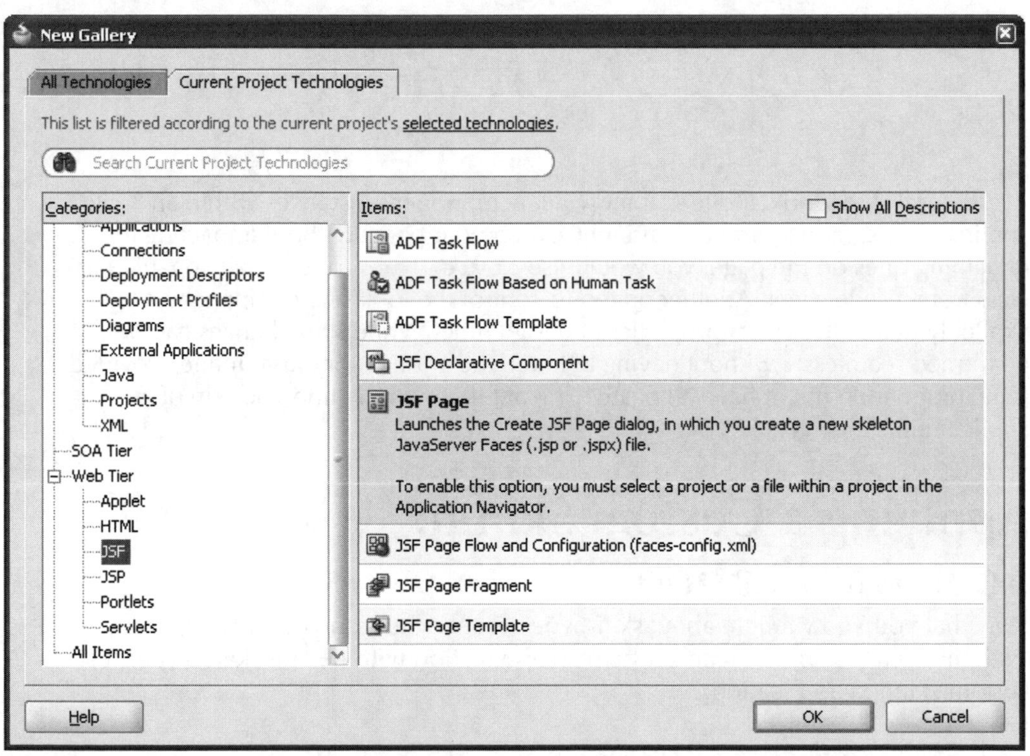

FIGURE 13-1 *Creating a new JSF page from the New Gallery*

Next add some simple ADF components to the page, which you are going to skin further and further through the course of this chapter. Simply drag a goButton component from the Component Palette onto the blank page.

Adding a Custom Skin to Your Application

Now you are ready to create your first custom skin. There are a couple of small steps you need to do before you can create the skin.

Ensure that the built-in CSS editor is set to support CSS 3.0. To do so, invoke the preferences via Tools | Preferences and check under CSS Editor (Figure 13-2). Also check ADF Faces Extension under Supported Components on the same screen.

Next you need to create a CSS file. To do so, invoke the New Gallery, expand the Web Tier node, and select CSS File from the HTML category (Figure 13-3).

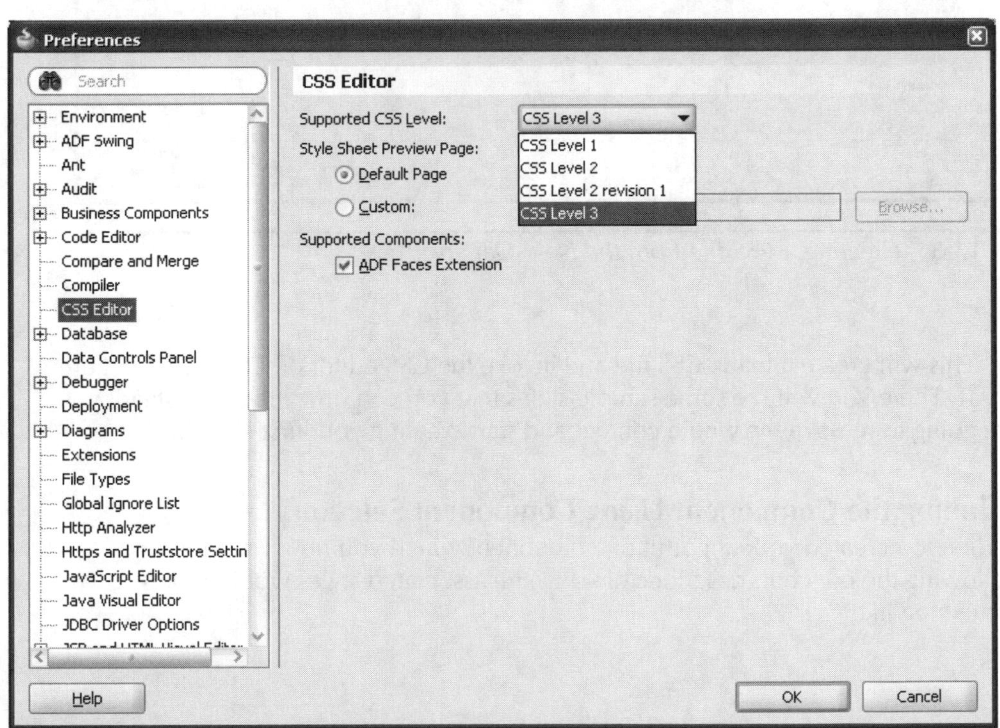

FIGURE 13-2 *Preferences for the built-in CSS editor*

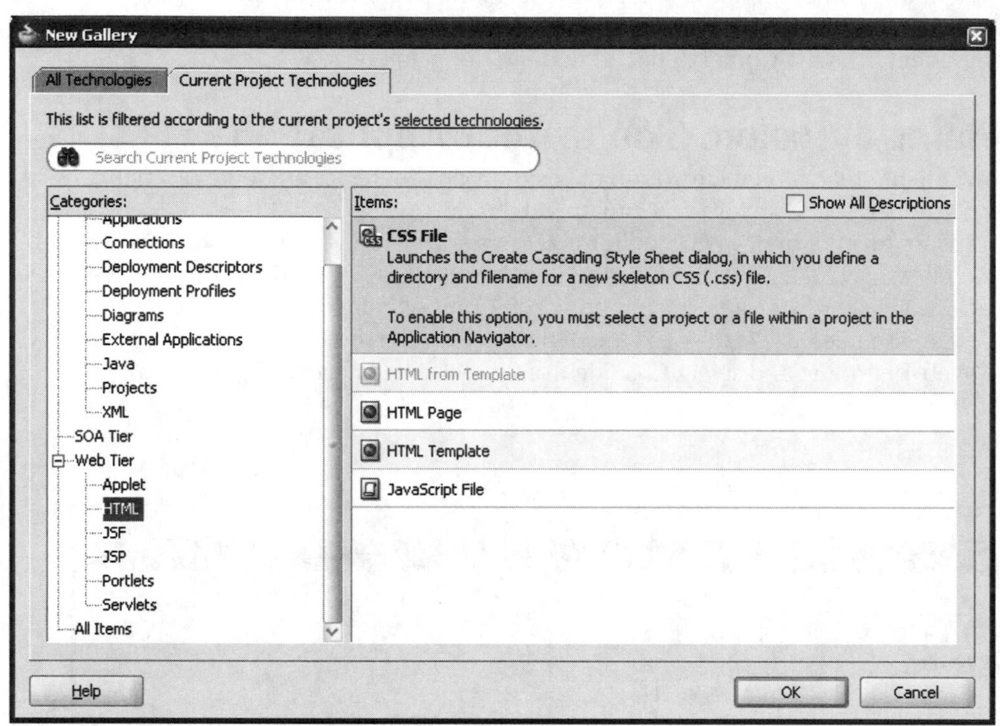

FIGURE 13-3 *Creating a CSS file from the New Gallery*

This will create a blank CSS file and invoke the CSS editor of JDeveloper (Figure 13-4). There you will see some sample styles that you can now modify. Instead, you are going to remove the whole content and start creating your first skin file.

Skinning the Component Using Component Selectors

Earlier you created your af:goButton component which you now want to skin. Following the concepts described already, the associated styles would look something like

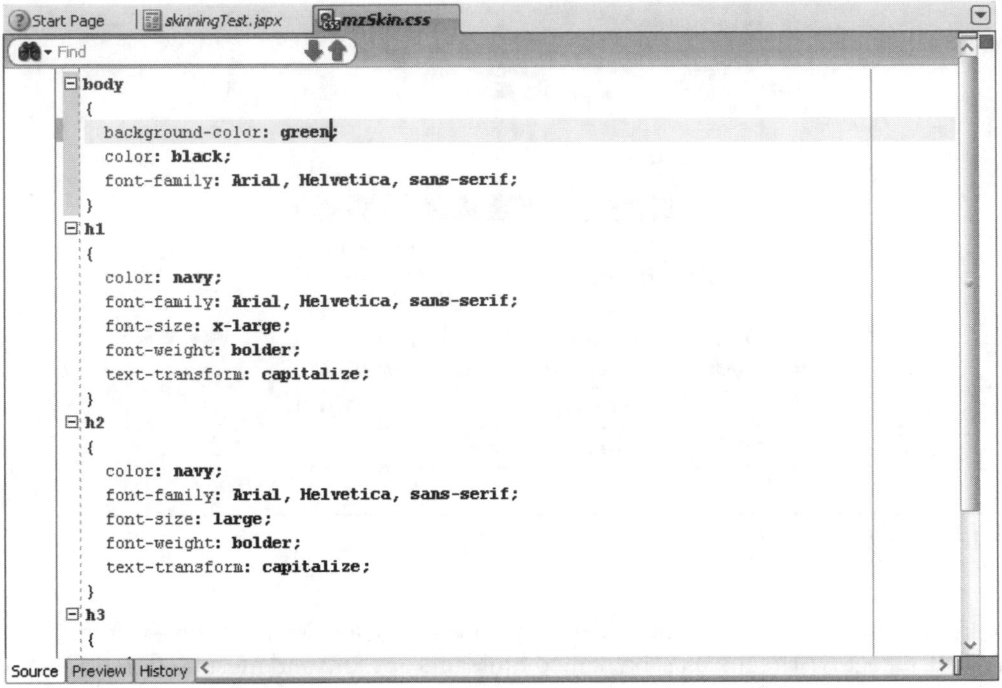

Start Page
skinningTest.jspx
mzSkin.css
Find
body
{
background-color: green;
color: black;
font-family: Arial, Helvetica, sans-serif;
}
h1
{
color: navy;
font-family: Arial, Helvetica, sans-serif;
font-size: x-large;
font-weight: bolder;
text-transform: capitalize;
}
h2
{
color: navy;
font-family: Arial, Helvetica, sans-serif;
font-size: large;
font-weight: bolder;
text-transform: capitalize;
}
h3
{
Source
Preview
History

FIGURE 13-4 *The JDeveloper CSS editor*

```
af|goButton ... { ... }
To start easy, change the color of the button label. The associated class would be
af|goButton {
  color: blue;
}
```

Your first task is done—easy enough, wasn't it?

Register the Custom Skin

Now you need to register this custom skin with the ADF framework. This is done by creating a file called trinidad-skins.xml in the applications WEB-INF directory (Figure 13-5). Simply right-click on WEB-INF in the Application Navigator and invoke the New Gallery.

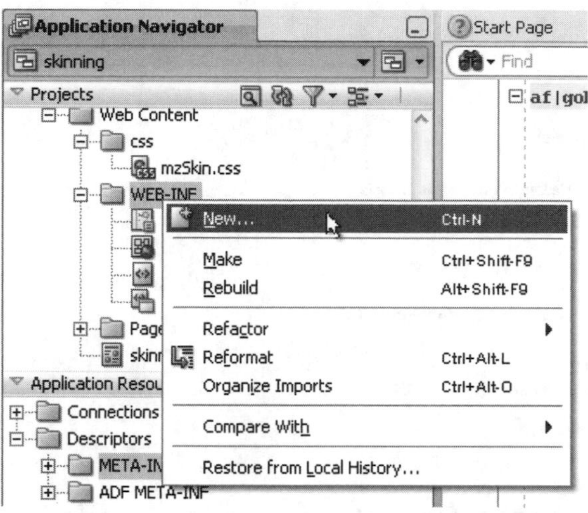

FIGURE 13-5 *Creating a new file in WEB-INF*

In the New Gallery, expand the General Node and select XML Document from the XML category. The file *must* be named trinidad-skins.xml and must be stored in the applications WEB-INF directory.

Now you need to add the skin definition elements to this document.

```
<?xml version="1.0" encoding="ISO-8859-1"?>
<skins xmlns="http://myfaces.apache.org/trinidad/skin">
    <skin>
        <id>
            mySkin.desktop
        </id>
        <family>
            mySkin
        </family>
        <extends>blafplus-rich.desktop</extends>
        <render-kit-id>
            org.apache.myfaces.trinidad.desktop
        </render-kit-id>
        <style-sheet-name>
            css/mySkin.css
        </style-sheet-name>
        <bundle-name>
            myPackage.myBundle
        </bundle-name>
        <translation-source>
```

```
        </translation-source>
    </skin>
</skins>
```

- **id** The unique identification of the skin definition. Per definition it should end with .desktop, .pda, or .portlet.
- **family** Allows you to group skin definitions together for an application to use. The application would reference a family of skins and choose the correct one based on the render-kit-id.
- **extends** Allows you to reference an existing skin that your definition would extend. Usually you would extend one of the existing skins, such as blafplus-rich.desktop, and provide only the changes necessary in your skin definition. This ensures that all components not in your skin definition will still render correctly. You could also use this mechanism to create a hierarchy of skins within your application ecosystem.
- **render-kit-id** Determines which render kit to use for the skin. You can enter one of the following:
  - **org.apache.myfaces.trinidad.desktop** The skin will automatically be used when the application is rendered on a desktop.
  - **org.apache.myfaces.trinidad.pda** The skin will be used when the application is rendered on a PDA.
- **style-sheet-name** Contains the reference to the CSS file to use.
- **bundle-name** The reference to the resource bundle defined with this skin. If you did not create one, you can omit this element and have ADF Faces pick up the default resource bundles and translations.
- **translation-source** Similar to bundle name, this element allows you to define the resource bundle name, but using an EL expression, rather than a static reference.

Make sure you provide the correct filename in the <style-sheet-name> element.

Configuring the Application to Use the Custom Skin

Now that you have created all necessary files for your first skin, you need to tell the skinning framework where to find it and, even more important, to actually use the custom skin (Figure 13-6).

The active skin is defined in trinidad-config.xml, located in the WEB-INF directory of your application.

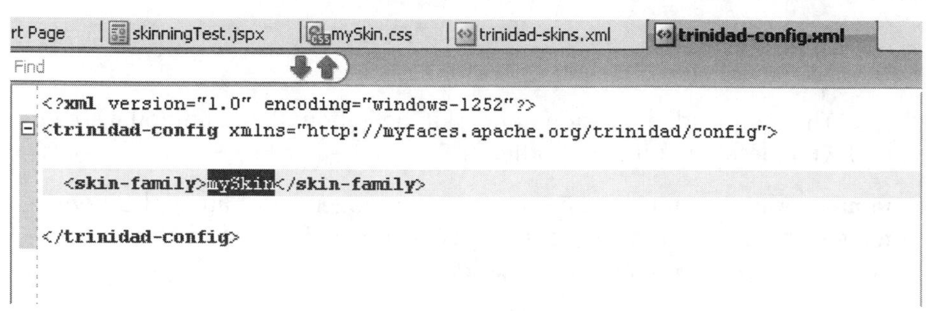

FIGURE 13-6 *Modifying the skin reference in trinidad-config.xml*

NOTE
If you do not see the skin applied to your page, check to see whether the `af:document` *tag has been added to the page. The* `af:document` *tag initializes the skin framework to create the CSS and link it to the page.*

You need to provide the value of `<family>...</family>` from the trinidad-skins.xml as referenced in the trinidad-config.xml.

Now that you have configured the application to use the new skin, see if it works. Execute the page by right-clicking on it in the Application Navigator and select Run from the context menu. Your application should look something like Figure 13-7.

FIGURE 13-7 *Running application with new skin for af:goButton*

Advanced Skinning Techniques

In the above example you have seen that the steps of creating the new skin are actually pretty simple. The tricky part is defining the skin and its properties.

Creating Conditional Skins

As we discussed earlier, the skinning framework allows the creation of conditional skins where certain parts apply to only a specific platform, browser, or both. This is done by embedding the conditional styles in rules. Most often these rules are used to create browser-specific style definitions for certain components or attributes, but even more commonly for creating version-specific skins.

To show the rules working, add a rule to the mySkin.css. You want to have the button label rendered green in IE and red in Firefox (Figure 13-8).

NOTE

The agent rule, like all the other rules, works off the HTTP request information. The tricky part here is that the agent info in the HTTP header does not necessarily correspond with the commonly known product names. So for Firefox, like all Mozilla-based browsers, gecko is the agent you have to specify.

```
@agent ie
{
   af|goButton {
     border-color: rgb(180,0,0);
     color: green;
   }
}
@agent gecko
{
   af|goButton {
     border-color: rgb(180,0,0);
     color: red;
   }
}
```

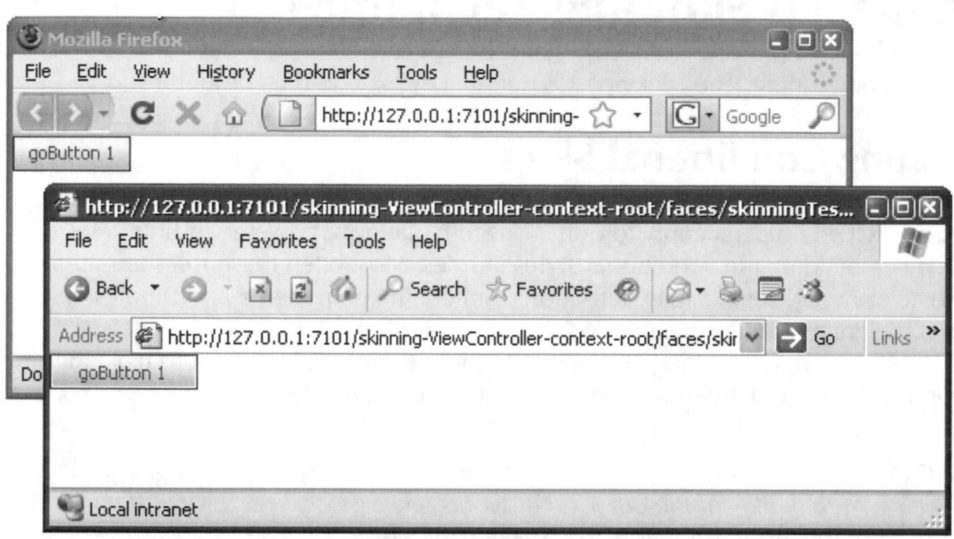

FIGURE 13-8 *Browser-specific skinning*

Skins vs. Themes

Themes are a way to provide a different look for components within a given skin. This might sound confusing, as we said that the idea of a skin was to have a consistent look across your application, and now we have themes introducing different looks within a skin. But it's not contradictory.

Imagine a scenario where the overall look of a button is defined by the designer, but the button has a couple of different tonal or color differences, depending on its position within the application. For example, a button in the menu area, which could have a red background, should be red, but still follow the overall look of a button, while one in the main application area should be a gray color to stand out from the white background. This can be achieved using themes.

Themes cannot be set on just any component; they need to be set on a distinct list. These components setting a theme expose that theme to their child components, and therefore the theme is inherited. Themes can be set (started or changed) by the following components:

- `af:document`
- `af:decorativeBox`
- `af:panelStretchLayout`
- `af:panelGroupLayout`

To create theme-specific entries, simply add a `[theme="..."]` clause to the style definition or to the component that should have theme-level styles.

NOTE
By default, components are not enabled to use themes. In order to enable a component's support for themes, you need to add the `-tr-enable-themes: true;` *value to the skin selector of the particular component.*

The BLAF Plus skins, `blafplus-rich` and `blafplus-medium`, support the following themes:

- Dark
- Medium
- Light
- None (default)

```
@agent ie
{
   af|goButton{
     -tr-enable-themes: true;
     border-color: rgb(180,180,0);
     color: blue;
   }
   af|goButton[theme="Dark"]{
     border-color: rgb(180,0,0);
     color: red;
   }

}
@agent gecko
{
   af|goButton{
     -tr-enable-themes: true;
     border-color: rgb(0,180,180);
     color: yellow;
   }
   af|goButton[theme="Dark"]{
     border-color: rgb(180,0,180);
     color: green;
   }
}
```

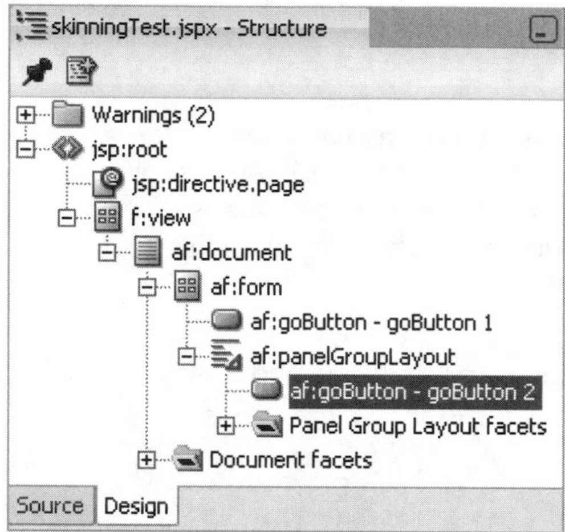

FIGURE 13-9 *Additional components added to the sample page*

Now you have to slightly modify your sample application. You need to add two new objects: an af:panelGroupLayout and another af:goButton. Drag those two components onto your page and make sure the second af:goButton becomes a child of the af:panelGroupLayout (Figure 13-9).

Now, when you execute the page, you will see that the two buttons look different (Figure 13-10). This is where the theme setting of af:panelGroupLayout around goButton2 takes effect.

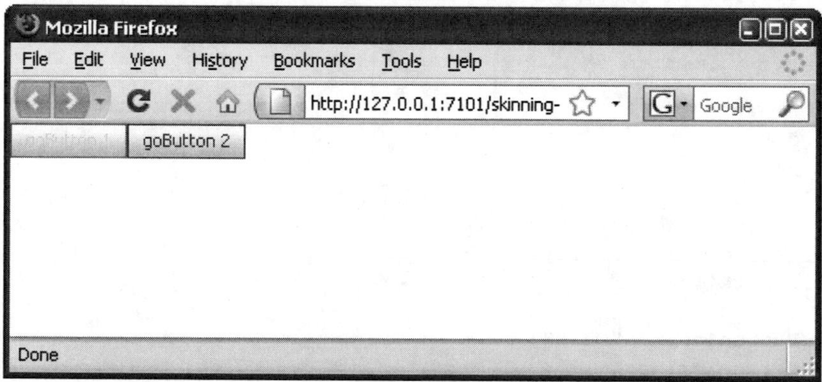

FIGURE 13-10 *Executed page with skins showing effect*

Skinning the Complete Component

In your examples so far, you did not touch the overall graphical appearance of the component, but only changed properties of its look. Now you want to go one step further and actually change the overall look of a component.

Unfortunately, your test subject, the button, is a particularly bad specimen, because the possibilities to change the appearance are quite limited—mainly to changing the background image.

```
.AFButtonBackground:alias{
    background-image:url(/images/aqua/Background.gif);
}
```

So to demonstrate the power of skinning a bit further, you are going to add a new component to your page, the panel box component. It basically is an area on the page that can house other components.

Simply add the panel box to your page and drag the existing goButton1 and panelGroupLayout into the panel box. The easiest way to do this is to drag the elements around in the Structure panel (Figure 13-11).

Each component, obviously, has a default look that can be used or a skin that can be applied. Like you do with skinning the button, you need to know the available selectors for a given component and set the styles there accordingly.

For the panelBox is the name of the component. It should appear like this because this is how it shows up in the product. There are several selectors that can be used. The panelBox also has some specialty in supporting two attributes to define its look, which correspond to two pseudo classes that can be used when defining

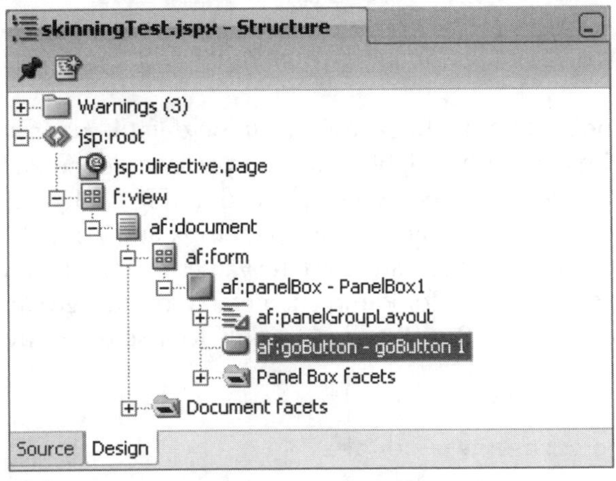

FIGURE 13-11 *Structure after adding and rearranging components*

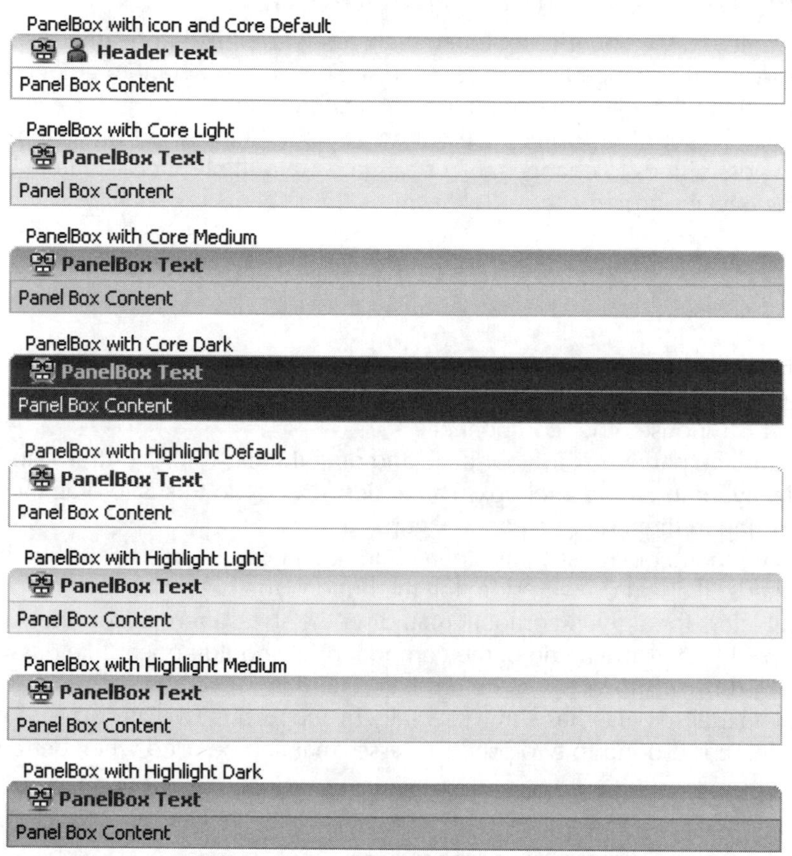

FIGURE 13-12 *The eight default combinations from Ramp and Background*

the styles, Background and Ramp. Background can be default, dark, medium, or light and Ramp can be core or highlight. That way you can define eight looks for panelBox that you can then choose in your application (Figure 13-12).

To change those properties, simply select the panelBox and expand the Appearance section in the Property Inspector. You can select the values there, but for your example, leave the defaults untouched (core for Ramp and default for Background).

To control the look of panelBox, there are mainly four selectors available:

- `af|panelBox::header-start`
- `af|panelBox::header-center`
- `af|panelBox::header-end`
- `af|panelBox::content`

Each can be extended with the corresponding pseudo-classes, corresponding with the values for Ramp and Background (in this order). So to set the image for the start of the header in the core Ramp and for the default Background the selector would be:

```
af|panelBox::header-start:core:default
```

In your example you are going to modify the `core:default` combination as follows:

```
af|panelBox::header-start:core:default {background-image: url(/images/
aqua/Start.gif);}
```

```
af|panelBox::header-center:core:default {background-image: url(/images/
aqua/Background.gif);}
```

```
af|panelBox::header-end:core:default {background-image: url(/images/
aqua/End.gif);}
```

```
af|panelBox::content:core:default {background-color:pink;}
```

Once you add this to the mySkin.css and run the page, you get a modified version of the panelBox with your new graphical look.

Configure a Component for Changing Skins Dynamically

Now that we have discussed how custom skins can be created, one more advanced technique is to allow the application to dynamically apply different skins. This can be useful if your application should be branded depending on the user who is logging in, or similar use cases. In this particular example you are going to allow a user to switch skin at run time, but the techniques can also be applied to other scenarios.

To conditionally configure a component to set the skin family:

1. Open the main JSF page (such as the index.jspx or a similar file) that contains the component that will be used to set the skin family.

2. Configure the page to display the skin family by using the `sessionScope` and binding it to a `selectOneChoice` component.

```
<af:selectOneChoice label="Choose Skin:"
value="#{sessionScope.skinFamily}" autoSubmit="true">
    <af:selectItem value="blafplus-rich" label="blafplus-rich"/>
    <af:selectItem value="blafplus-medium" label="blafplus-medium"/>
    <af:selectItem value="simple" label="simple"/>
    <af:selectItem value="richDemo" label="richDemo"/>
    <af:selectItem value="mySkin" label="mySkin"/>
</af:selectOneChoice>
```

To conditionally configure a component for changing skins at run time, in the trinidad-config.xml file, use an EL expression to dynamically evaluate the skin family:

```
<skin-family>#{sessionScope.skinFamily}</skin-family>
```

Through the `autoSubmit="true"` the page is being redirected once the user changes the `selectOneChoice`, and after this redirect, the page is rendered using the new skin.

Applying Skins to Icons

You can apply skins to the default icons associated with ADF Faces components by specifying the URL path to the icon image in the icon style selector. Note that CSS syntax like pseudo-classes (:hover, etc.) does not work with icon selectors.

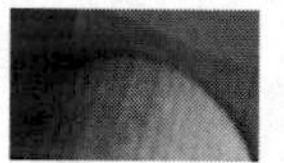

NOTE
If you are overriding a selector for an icon, use a context-relative path for the URL to the icon image (that is, start with a leading slash [/]), and do not use quotation marks. You can also use a relative path by omitting the leading slash (/), or you can provide a server-relative path by providing a leading double-slash (//).

Also, you should include the width and the height for the icon to avoid unwanted rendering results.

```
.AFErrorIcon:alias {
            content:url(/adf/images/error.png);
            width:7px; height:18px
     }
```

Icons and buttons can both use the `rtl` pseudo-class. This defines an icon or button for use when the application displays in right-to-left mode.

```
.AFErrorIcon:alias:rtl {
            content:url(/adf/images/error.png);
            width:16px; height:16px
      }
```

Skinning for HTML Developers

Now that we have discussed basic and more advanced topics of application skinning, we want to spend the last section of this chapter on some guidance for HTML designers to explain the difference between traditional HTML development and application skinning.

In traditional HTML design, you create a set of page templates that later on will be used to create instances of them and fill them with content. Application skinning goes one level deeper by designing the components that make up the application.

HTML developers don't necessarily build a page up from components—a page is the atomic entity and its content is described via HTML, JavaScript, and CSS. In application skinning, on the other hand, the component is the object of interest that needs to be skinned.

Before going about creating a skin, think about the goal for the skin. Is it just to skin a particular application, or should it be an all-purpose skin used across applications? Normally, the latter would be the case, since companies use the same look across their applications. To minimize initial work, you could decide to "skin as you go" and initially skin only the components of a particular application you start off with. Over time, after adding new components used by additional applications, you'll end up with a complete skin.

The next thing to figure out is how the components are built up and what style selectors need to be modified to achieve the desired look. Keep in mind that there are a number of global selectors that can be leveraged to modify certain style attributes across multiple components, while some changes will require overriding the style selectors on the component level. You might not be forced to touch all of them, just the ones you want to modify.

Last but not least is the most difficult work of all: creating the assets (images) needed to create the new look. There are some online tools as well as template resources that can get you started. One tool, for example, is http://kuler.adobe.com/, which helps in choosing color schemas that are pleasing to the eye.

The bottom line is that it usually is significantly more work to create an application skin than styling a web site, but if you are in a situation where you need to fit your application into an existing web site look, then the ADF skinning framework allows you to reuse quite a lot of information or even reference styles from an existing style sheet.

As with creating web sites, the style information should generally be managed in a central place, the style sheet, and all entities should reference those definitions rather than defining their own.

Which tools to use for skinning will be an organizational decision. Skinning is less of a design task and more of a development-oriented one. Our recommendation is that you either have a developer and a designer work together to create the necessary assets (images, color definitions, etc.) or you should explain to your designers what they need to create in terms of style sheets.

Most likely, skinning will also result in some page design templates that then need to be adopted. For example, if a page has tabs for navigation, those tabs could be created in the HTML template, but it would be better done as a tab component. If the decision is for the latter, then the designer needs to take this into account and possibly redesign the layout so the desired look can be achieved.

In the particular example, if the tabs are on top of some background, the designer needs to create the background graphics separate from the tab design elements, so the tab component can be skinned and put in a table cell, for example, that has the respective background image applied. The result is visually the same: a set of tabs in front of a background; however, from a web designer perspective, it requires some rethinking of the approaches. Overall, web developers need to switch from controlling the HTML rendered in the browser to controlling (and skinning) the framework components which, in turn, generate the HTML.

CHAPTER 14

Metadata Services Framework

One of the reasons behind the transition from procedural to object-oriented languages was to further code reuse, since objects were designed as reusable entities that can be incorporated in multiple programs.[1] This made sense from a technical perspective, as well as from a business one. For developers, to reuse exiting classes is a productivity booster; exploiting thoroughly debugged code reduces the probability of anomalies. This results in lowered development and maintenance costs, as well as higher predictability of the system's adherence to its level of service agreement when in production. Code reuse by itself, however, will not reach higher levels of returns on the investment (ROI) for software development or software package implementation projects. To do this, organizations need to make entire systems reusable in a variety of situations. In other words, management needs a way to adapt a single code base to the varied and sometimes conflicting needs of organizational units and lines of business. Superior ROI will be achieved both by keeping development efforts to a minimum and by offering room for local adaptations inside the uniform business processes rooted in the software's code. The ability to customize applications thus appears as an essential component of ROI.

In an ideal world, software systems would simply change their behavior according to their configuration. Current versions of Oracle Applications, such as E-Business Suite or Siebel CRM, implement this pattern. Time after time, organizations found that such packages, while functionally sound and configurable, did not possess the inherent flexibility needed to meet their expectations regarding customization. The underlying business challenge could be expressed this way: how can you tailor a single code base in a standardized way without compromising the link between the original and the customized version? While branch merges or patches can certainly contribute to maintain this link, they generate a significant overhead and require clearly defined processes to be successful. This in turn increases the pressure on the quality assurance team, since it must validate the correctness of the initial implementation as well as the validity of the parts that were customized. Clearly, one of the advantages of a comprehensive customization platform is upgrade safety.

As you probably know, Oracle has a significant investment in software packages. As of 2009, thousands of Oracle developers were working to build Oracle Fusion Applications using Oracle ADF 11*g* as their toolkit. Consequently, it is not surprising to see that one of the design objectives of ADF 11*g* was to provide a standardized way to customize applications without having to change a single line in the original code base. Metadata was selected as the mean to reach this objective.

---

[1] John Lewis and William Loftus, *Java Software Solutions: Foundations of Program Design*, © 1998, Addison-Wesley, p. 55.

What Is Metadata?

The National Information Standards Organization (NISO) explains that "Metadata is structured information that describes, explains, locates, or otherwise makes it easier to retrieve, use, or manage an information resource."[2] This means metadata is essentially data about other data. The real world contains numerous examples of metadata usage. A library, for example, contains thousands of data sources in the form of books. Librarians have defined a standard set of metadata attributes, such as the book's author, title, and International Standard Book Number (ISBN), that describe each book available at the library.

Modern software systems make extensive use of metadata-based mechanisms. Most operating systems, for example, enable users to apply metadata attributes values on the files available to them. Figure 14-1 shows a typical window used for this purpose in Microsoft Windows XP.

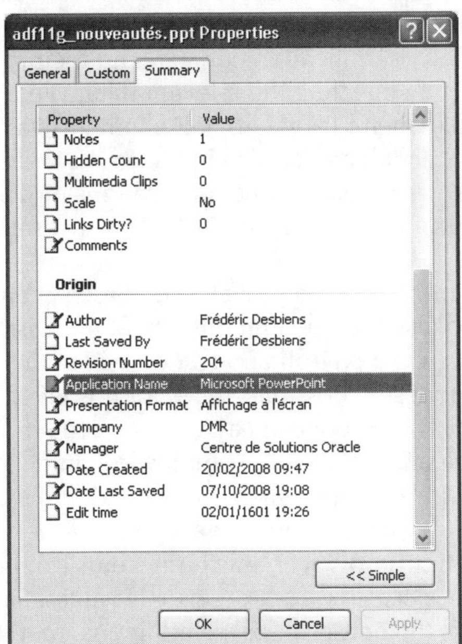

FIGURE 14-1 *File metadata in Microsoft Windows XP*

---

[2] National Information Standards Organization, *Understanding Metadata*, © 2004, Bethesda, NISO Press, p. 1.

Oracle ADF 11*g*'s basic architecture greatly facilitated the implementation of metadata-based customization, since it relied heavily on declaration instead of coding for several critical tasks. This meant that system behavior could be modified by altering the declarations. Metadata Services Framework (MDS) provides a cleanly defined interface to accomplish this very task. In return, MDS enables Oracle to streamline customization data management for both software applications, such as Oracle's own Fusion Applications, and portals built on the Oracle WebCenter stack. This streamlining was made possible by the fact there is a significant overlap in the customization needs between the two. The only difference is the scope of the customizations. Applications will typically be tailored for an industry, market segment, or business unit, while portals will put the emphasis on the personalization needs of individual users.

Architecture

The basic principle of MDS is that the application's data structures and business logic are left untouched; the application could also ship with some predefined metadata that customer customizations will not alter. MDS simply recognizes the metadata to apply according to application context, and then will add, remove, or change declarative artifacts by injecting the relevant data. What exactly are these artifacts? There are several of them: JSF pages, JSF fragments, task flows, data controls, and data bindings are all declarative in nature, as well as ADF business components entity objects, view objects, and applications modules. Since all ADF declarative features store data in XML constructs, the changes managed by MDS are defined the same way.

The aim of MDS customizations is to adapt a software system to a specific business situation. In this context, correct granularity of the customization scope is essential. For example, imagine a payroll application where the top customization layer is the organization's industry. Possible values for this layer could be *financial, healthcare,* and *technology*. Now suppose payroll rules are not the same from one industry to another, and are impacted by the employees' union status. Intuitively, we see the presence of a second layer, for which the value domain could be *union* and *non-union*. Consequently, in this specific scenario, there is a maximum of six possible sets of customizations; however, this limit stems from the fact that the various layers each define a specific number of possible values. Since customizations are hierarchical, each set is the net result of the additions, modifications, and removals accrued from navigating the layers in a top-to-bottom fashion. If a specific element is manipulated through several layers, its ultimate value will be the one resulting from the layer nearest the bottom of the hierarchy. In a way, MDS customizations benefit from inheritance since each layer specifies only the changes required by its core business context. This explains why, in MDS, metadata is layered and hierarchical. Specific customization values are applied to the software system according to the current values given to layers of increasing precision.

By themselves, layers are just functional notions. The values they are assigned simply identify a set of customizations. But how will the system determine the current values for each layer at run time? This is where an MDS concept, *customization classes*, comes into play. Customization classes are simple Java classes that play the role of a layer value selector for a layer name, given a specific run-time context. In fact, they are the layer's embodiment in the application. They do not, however, contain the actual customization values. These are stored in the MDS repository and are applied to the application. The customization value to be applied at run time is returned by the customization class, and is not stored by MDS. On the other hand, the customization document corresponding to a customization value is stored in the MDS repository.

We will study customization classes in greater detail later in this chapter; we even provide concrete code examples. For the time being, please take note that the use of Java classes for layer definition purposes is a requirement set by the MDS engine.

At this point, you probably suspect how Oracle WebCenter 11*g* exploits the possibilities offered by MDS. At its core, the product is built on the idea of customizable pages—pages that are editable by some or all users, thus tailoring the application experience and features to the user's needs. Those customizations can be defined at design or run time, and they simply use the standard MDS apparatus. It must be noted that design-time customizations are sometimes called *seeded* customizations, since they are defined using Oracle JDeveloper but will immediately alter the run-time behavior of the system. For the time being, we will stay in the realm of ADF and will now have a closer look at layers, customization classes, and MDS repositories.

Layers

Ideally, customization layers should be an integral part of the application's specification. However, customization implementation should be done once the initial code base has been completed. To come up with meaningful customization layers for your application is a completely distinct task from building the core features; in fact, layer identification stands as a separate phase of the development process. While the level of parallelism between initial development and customization is open to debate, the main issue rests elsewhere. The key of a good customizable application is not when the customizations are specified, but rather the correct identification of the various layers. Since MDS takes charge of the technical details, this is strictly a business matter.

There are several possible sources for an application's customization layers; organizational structure and business strategy are the most likely to be used. The former is useful for an organization trying to accommodate the needs of its business units while preserving a single code base for its systems. The latter enables an organization to adapt its systems more easily to its customer's needs or to release software packages with predefined customizations directed toward the needs of specific verticals, for example. Whether they reflect internal or external factors, the layers can either possess a finite value domain or be assigned an arbitrary value. The second case applies to layers meant for run-time customization only.

A customized ADF application will store the customizations according to the MDS repository settings found in the adf-config.xml file. By default, on a developer workstation, this repository resides on the local file system. Consequently, applications often sport special folders created by Oracle JDeveloper, named *mdssys*, holding MDS metadata XML files. Figure 14-2 shows the structure of a customized ADF application; the first rectangle highlights pages and fragments customizations while the second one shows task flow customizations.

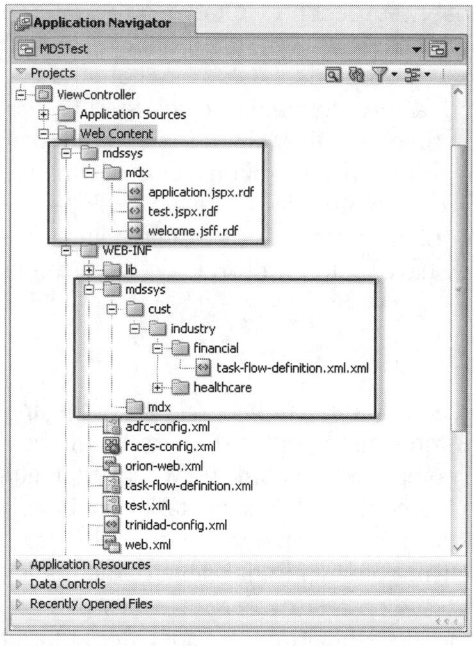

FIGURE 14-2 *Structure of a customized ADF application*

Those customizations are defined by selecting the Customization Developer role when you start Oracle JDeveloper 11*g*. It is also possible for the MDS framework to define the customizations at run time. In other words, an ADF application can be coded in order to customize itself in real time as the result of user interactions. From an MDS perspective, such customizations are stored in the repository and managed all the same.

On a more technical level, all the MDS layers you intend to use at design time must be declared in a specific XML file located in Oracle JDeveloper 11*g*'s folder structure. This declaration is not tied to a specific application, but applies to the IDE as a whole. It fulfills a design-time requirement. The actual path for the XML file is [jdeveloper root folder]\jdev\CustomizationLayerValues.xml. Here is a typical example of the contents of this file:

```
<cust-layers  xmlns="http://xmlns.oracle.com/mds/dt">
   <cust-layer name="industry">
      <cust-layer-value value="financial" display-name="Financial"/>
      <cust-layer-value value="healthcare" display-name="Healthcare"/>
   </cust-layer>
   <!-- Customization layers that are only meant for runtime usage can
   be excluded in design time by defining size as "no_values"-->
   <cust-layer name="userrole" value-set-size="no_values"/>
</cust-layers>
```

As you can see, there are two layers defined in this sample. The first one is called *industry* and has two possible values: financial or healthcare. The name of the second one is *userrole*, and is defined without values since it is meant for run-time usage. It must be noted that declaration is especially important for predefined values belonging to a finite set, as the design-time customization support of Oracle JDeveloper 11*g* relies on the contents of the file to work correctly.

Customization Classes

Once declared in CustomizationLayerValues.xml, each layer needs a Java implementation in order to be used in Oracle JDeveloper. This class essentially contains business logic to determine the actual value for the layer according to a specific context. In order to be recognized as an ADF customization class, Java classes must extend oracle.mds.cust.CustomizationClass, which is provided by Oracle. This class is an abstract one, and defines three methods for its descendants to implement: getCacheHint(), getName(), and getValue(RestrictedSession, MetadataObject). The role of these three methods is explained in Table 14-1.

The possible caching behaviors are listed in Table 14-2.

Method	Role
getCacheHint	Configures the MDS engine's caching behavior for the layer. Possible values are defined in the CacheHint class of the oracle.mds.cust package, and are explained below.
getName	Returns the name of the customization layer represented by the class.
getValue	Returns the current value for the layer. The current MDS session and the metadata object involved in the value check are passed as parameters. The return value is an array. When this array contains more than a single element, customizations are applied to the application in the order in which they appear in the array.

TABLE 14-1 *Customization Class API Methods*

Name	Description
All Users	The layer value will be used indistinctly for all users (evaluated once). The value is applied globally.
Multi User	The same layer value will be used for multiple users, but not for all.
User	The layer value will always be the same for a specific user (evaluated once for each user), as long as his session is valid.
Request	The layer value will be evaluated for each request. This enables real-time changes for the value at the price of higher resource usage.

TABLE 14-2 *MDS Caching Behaviors*

A good example of a real-world customization is ADF's own UserCC class, which defines a user-specific layer. Here is the nearly complete source code for it; import statements were removed for the sake of brevity.

```
package oracle.adf.share.config;
import …
public class UserCC extends CustomizationClass
{
    /** Layer name is an attribute; can change
        according to  context. */
    private String mLayerName;

    public UserCC()
    {
        mLayerName = "user";
    }

    /** This constructor enables class users
      * to specify a custom name for the layer. */
    public UserCC(String layerName)
    {
        $init$();
        mLayerName = layerName;
    }

    public CacheHint getCacheHint()
    {
        return CacheHint.USER;
    }
    public String getName()
    {
        return mLayerName;
    }
    public String[] getValue(RestrictedSession sess, MetadataObject mo)
    {
        // Gets a hold of the principal for the currently logged
        // user.
        Principal p = ADFContext.getCurrent().getSecurityContext().
                      getUserPrincipal();
        if(p != null)
            return (new String[] {
                p.getName()
            });
        else
            return null;
    }
}
```

As you can see, the getValue() method will return the name of the ADF security principal as the value for the layer. In other words, the name of the user account will influence the set of customizations that will be applied at run time. Clearly, the UserCC class was designed to support run-time customization, as it would not be practical to declare all possible user accounts in advance in the CustomizationLayerValues.xml file.

There are some deployment details you should be aware of in order to use customization classes:

- Customization classes must be made available to Oracle JDeveloper through a JDeveloper extension. For the convenience of internal testing, it is also possible to use the JAR file located in the [oracle jdeveloper root]\jdev\lib\patches folder. The best way to achieve this is to create a deployment profile that will take care of the JAR file creation and will place it at the appropriate location. Additionally, you should not forget to integrate this to your automation scripts, if applicable.
- An ADF application must declare all the customization classes it will use in its own adf-config.xml file. Oracle JDeveloper 11*g* helpfully provides an editor to facilitate the process, as displayed in Figure 14-3. To open it, simply double-click on the file. The order in which the classes appear in the editor is essential, since layers will be applied in the order specified in the adf-config.xml file from top to bottom.

Repository Types

Up to now, we have discussed layers and customization classes. As we have seen, layers define the customization structure of an application, while customization classes implement logic to select the correct customization set at run time. It is for customization storage that repositories come into play .

In Oracle ADF 11*g*, there are two types of metadata repositories available to MDS: file based and database. File based is the default, and in fact the only available option inside Oracle JDeveloper 11*g*, since it enables developers to build their application without having to ask for a database schema to collect their customizations. It is not, however, meant for production use. Database repositories, on the other hand, enhance performance and scalability; those will be used by actual applications deployed on Oracle WebLogic Server, for example. Since repository-type selection is made at configuration time, it is possible to migrate seamlessly from one type to another using the Oracle-provided migration tools that ship with Oracle JDeveloper 11*g*. These tools open interesting possibilities for deployment operations; given that they enable exportation and importation of customizations, it is possible to make run-time customizations on a staging environment before migrating them to production, for example.

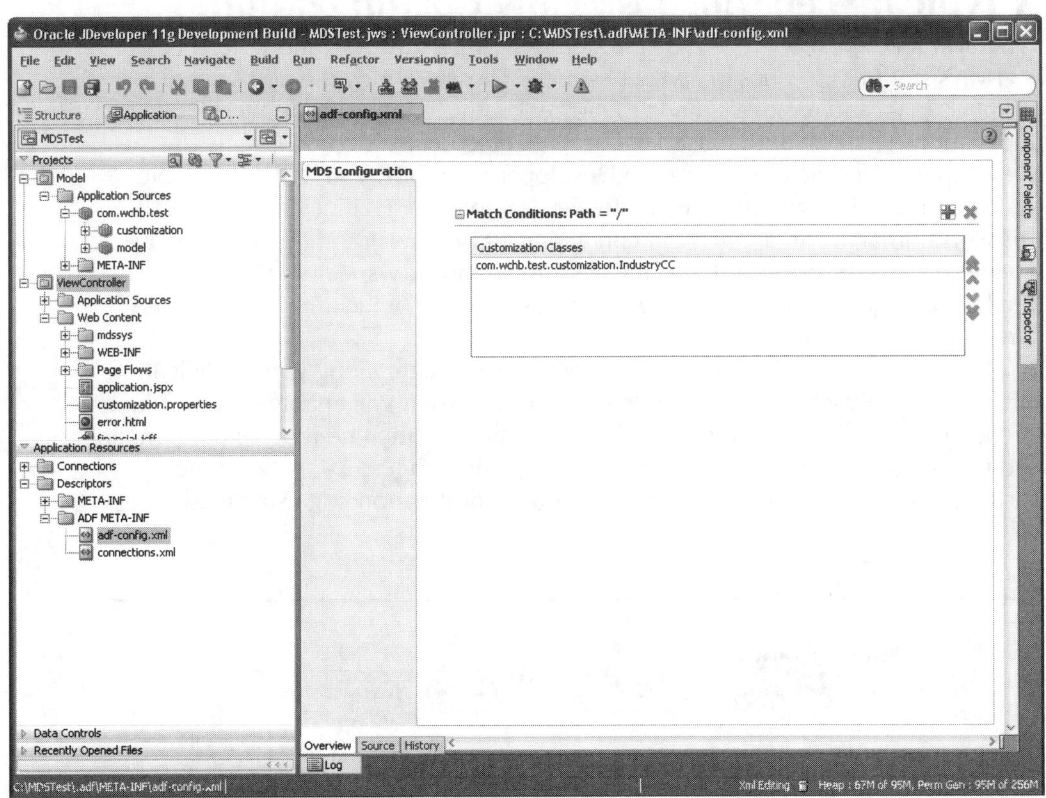

FIGURE 14-3 *The adf-config.xml file in Oracle JDeveloper 11g*

Working on Customizations in Oracle JDeveloper

Up to now, we have described the architecture of MDS and explained the role of its basic constituents: layers, customization classes, and metadata repositories. But how will you use Oracle JDeveloper 11*g* to build a customizable application? The answer to this question will vary according to the type of customizations needed. We will first describe the process for seeded customization. We will also describe a very interesting Oracle ADF 11*g* feature called change persistence, which enables automatic restoration of user preferences throughout application sessions. The topic of run-time-only customizations will be left out of the discussion, since these require a deeper understanding of MDS internals.

A Typical Scenario: Task Flow Customization

Whatever the repository type they are stored in, MDS customization metadata is always stored as a series of XML constructs. These embody the additions, modifications, and removals made to the declarative entities inside the ADF application. Those entities must have been created before starting Oracle JDeveloper under the Customization Developer role; thus, you will not be able to create new JSF pages under this role, for example. Let us illustrate how all of this works. Imagine an application containing a task flow. Our aim is to display a generic welcome page and to bring users to an industry-specific page at the click of a button. The task flow available in the base version of the application is very simple, as seen in Figure 14-4.

It contains only a view activity for the welcome page, along with a navigation rule to itself. This self-referencing rule is essential, since it will enable customizations to change its destination. To change it, simply click on the line representing the link and reroute one of the ends to the actual destination. Figure 14-5 shows the customized task flow, with a healthcare industry destination page specified.

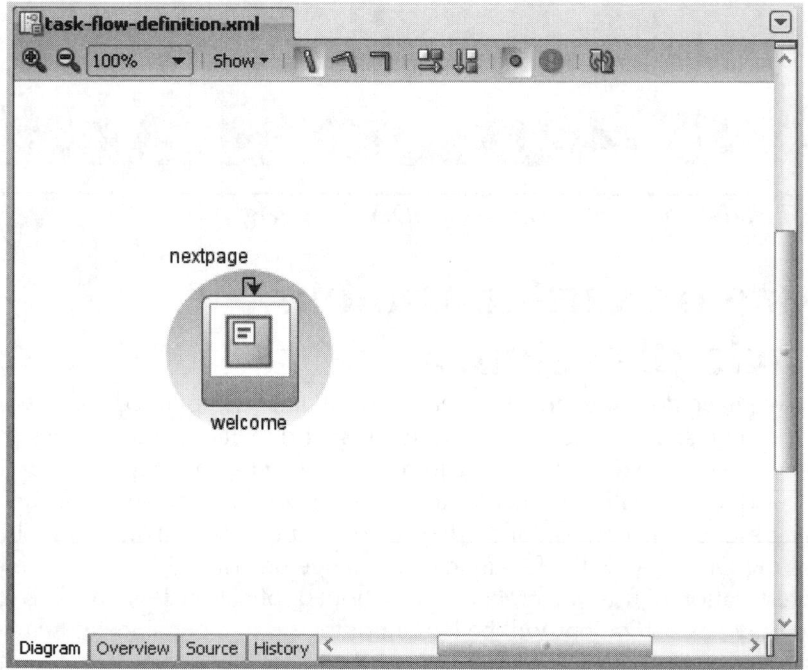

FIGURE 14-4 *A simple example task flow*

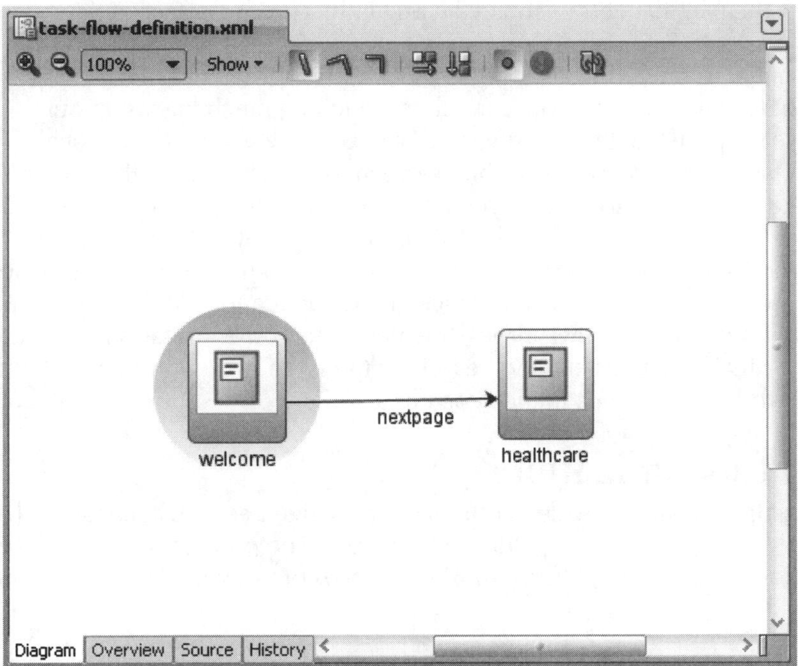

FIGURE 14-5 *The customized task flow, with an industry-specific view activity added*

The XML file expressing these customizations is shown below:

```
<mds:customization version="11.1.1.50.66"
                   xmlns:mds="http://xmlns.oracle.com/mds">
  <mds:insert after="welcome">
    <view id="healthcare" xmlns="http://xmlns.oracle.com/adf/controller">
      <page>
        /healthcare.jsff
      </page>
    </view>
  </mds:insert>
  <mds:replace node="welcome-cf(xmlns(mds_ns1=http://xmlns.oracle.com/
adf/controller))/mds_ns1:to-activity-id/text()">
    healthcare
  </mds:replace>
</mds:customization>
```

Its contents are fairly easy to understand. The `<mds:insert>` tag describes the addition of the view activity. The children of this tag are identical to those of a standard task flow definition; this was expected, since the whole concept behind the MDS engine is to substitute the application's original XML definitions with the ones supplied by way of customization. The `<mds:replace>` tag, on the other hand, materializes the fact that you swapped the original `nextpage` control flow with your own.

It is essential to mention that MDS customizations should not be used as a replacement to standard ADF flow control or branching mechanisms. In our example, we suppose that the industry-specific pages vary wildly in functionality—so much in fact that no reuse is possible between them. The rule of thumb in the case of customizations is to ask yourself if the modifications you envision to the base application are cases of a standard algorithm or if they are extensions of a business process to a specific context. In other words, do the modifications belong to various user types using a single instance of the application? In this case, you will probably provide task flows, pages, fragments, and other artifacts in the base application. MDS will be useful in cases where the various user types must be segregated while preserving a unified code base.

Seeded Customizations

As we have already said, a seeded customization designates a customization that was created at design time using Oracle JDeveloper. The process of creating seeded customizations is fairly straightforward. We will now broadly explain each of the required steps.

1. Create the base ADF application.
2. Identify the various layers and define their values in the CustomizationLayerValues.xml file.
3. Create customization classes matching the layers you defined, and deploy them in the appropriate Oracle JDeveloper 11*g* folder. You could also package the class in a JDeveloper extension and deploy it.
4. Launch Oracle JDeveloper and select the Customization Developer role. This role selection can be done using the appropriate dialog at startup (Figure 14-6) or in the JDeveloper Preferences panel (Tools | Preference menu).
5. Using the Customizations panel, select the current values for the layers. In Figure 14-7, the *healthcare* value was chosen for the industry layer.
6. If customizations to JSF pages or JSFF fragments are needed, ensure that the Enable Seeded Customizations checkbox was checked in the project properties for the web application (see later in Figure 14-9). It is essential that all component IDs in the page are non-null, since those will not be specified automatically by ADF Controller (ADFc).

FIGURE 14-6 *The role selection dialog*

Customizations
View without Customizations
Specify the customization layer values for application : MDSTest

Tip layer	Name	Value
⦿	industry	Healthcare (healthcare).

Customization Context : **industry/healthcare**

FIGURE 14-7 *Customizations panel in JDeveloper*

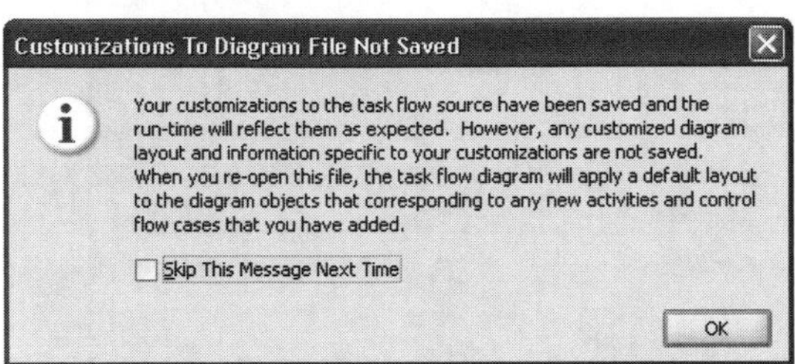

FIGURE 14-8 *Layout changes warning in Oracle JDeveloper 11g*

7. Customize the application. All changes will be stored according to the layer values selected in step 5. When the customizations are applied through diagram changes, such as in the case of task flows, you may receive a warning such as the one in Figure 14-8. Customizations do not extend to design-time layouts and will not be preserved.

Once the application is customized, you can execute it. The actual customizations applied will be determined according to the logic present in the customization classes.

A Dynamic Customization Class: Real-World Problems

We feel the standard Oracle documentation does a great job of explaining the basic MDS mechanisms. Section 33.2.1 of the Oracle Fusion Middleware Fusion Developer's Guide for Oracle Application Development Framework, for example, contains an interesting customization class sample. This sample class reads the current layer value from a property file available on the file system. In such a scenario, the layer value is then tied to a pre-deployment decision; it will not be possible to change it at run time. But what if you want to use a more dynamic approach and store this value in the database? Let's expand the Developer's Guide sample with our own custom logic.

In an ADF application, the obvious choice would be to create an ADF business components entity and view objects, in addition to an application module. The customization class could then instantiate the application module through the Configuration#createRootApplicationModule method in order to access the data. MDS customizations, however, are pervasive throughout the ADF framework. Customization classes will always be instantiated by the container's class loader when a customizable entity is created; consequently, trying to obtain an application module instance from a customization class will trigger a recursive endless loop of instantiations for the customization class.

Since ADF BC is not an option in this scenario, the obvious choice is to use bare JDBC. While this alternative is functional, it is not necessarily convenient and productive. However, if the target database structure is simple enough, there are open source libraries that can ease the pain. A typical example is Apache Commons Configuration,[3] which is an abstraction layer used to manipulate configuration values inside Java applications. In this library, configuration values can be stored in a variety of media, including property files and database tables, as long as they adhere to a simple key/value format. Imagine a table containing three columns: id (integer), name (varchar2[80]), and industry (varchar2[80]). The id column is fed through a database sequence, while the name column matches the user ids exploited by the application. The code listing below shows how you could use Commons Configuration to retrieve the layer value matching a specific user.

```
package com.wchb.test.customization;

import ...

public class IndustryCC extends CustomizationClass {
    private static final String mLayerName = "industry";
    private ADFContext mADFContext;
    private String mUser;
    private boolean mInited;

    public IndustryCC() {
        mUser = null;
        mInited = false;
    }

    public CacheHint getCacheHint() {
        return CacheHint.USER;
    }

    public String getName() {
        return mLayerName;
    }

    public String[] getValue(RestrictedSession sess, MetadataObject mo) {
        String value = null;
        init();

        try {
            // JNDI Context to retrieve DataSource,
            Context ctx = new InitialContext();

            // JDBC DataSource.
            DataSource ds =
                (DataSource)ctx.lookup("jdbc/Connection1CoreDS");
```

[3] See http://commons.apache.org/configuration for details.

```
                // Parameters here are: JDBC DataSource, name of the
                // table holding the config data, column name for the
                // key, column name for the value.
                Configuration conf =
                    new DatabaseConfiguration(ds, "USERS", "NAME",
                                                          "INDUSTRY");
                value = conf.getString(mUser);

            } catch (NamingException ex) {
                System.out.println(ex.getMessage());
            }
            return new String[] { value };
        }

        private void init() {
            if (mInited) {
                return;
            }

            /* This piece of code returns the user name. It compares the
             * login name with the user name referenced by MDS and will
             * ensure a valid name is returned.
            mADFContext = ADFContext.getCurrent();
            String userName = mADFContext.getSecurityContext().getUserName();
            String loginStr = mADFContext.getMDSLogin();
            if (userName != null &&
                (loginStr == null || userName.equals(loginStr))) {
                mUser = userName;
            }
            mInited = true;
        }
    }
```

As you can see, the only JDBC-related complexity in the code above is Datasource retrieval through Java Naming and Directory Interface (JNDI). The user name is fetched once and the first time `init()` is called, since caching will use user scope.

There are several alternatives to the database-driven approach shown in our example. You could use some kind of preference store, or even manage the user-industry association in a lightweight directory access protocol (LDAP) compliant directory, such as Oracle Internet Directory (OID). Reliability, manageability, and solution complexity must all be taken into account.

Change Persistence

While application customization involves a fair share of work, personalization is a nearly automated process in Oracle ADF 11*g*. But what is the distinction between customization and personalization? Essentially, personalization is a specific case of customization where the scope is limited to a single individual; the changes you make impact your own view only; others will not see them. ADF applications where personalization is permitted usually offer their users the possibility to adapt the user interface to suit their taste. This is why the term *change persistence* is also used to describe Oracle ADF 11*g* personalization. User changes to the interface may be persisted through MDS if the application is configured accordingly. A good example of this is column reordering in the ADF table component; alterations made by users could be brought back through change persistence as needed.

In order to enable change persistence, developers must access the properties for the web application project in Oracle JDeveloper, then select the ADF View category. Simply activate the checkbox Enable User Customizations and select the appropriate radio button reflecting the duration of the change persistence. Possible values are For Duration of Session and Across Sessions Using MDS, as shown in Figure 14-9.

It is essential to remember that change persistence, when configured to exploit the MDS repository, will apply to a set of ADF Faces Rich Client component attributes that is explicitly defined in adf-config.xml. Please see the Fusion Developer's Guide for Oracle Application Development Framework for more details on how to accomplish this.

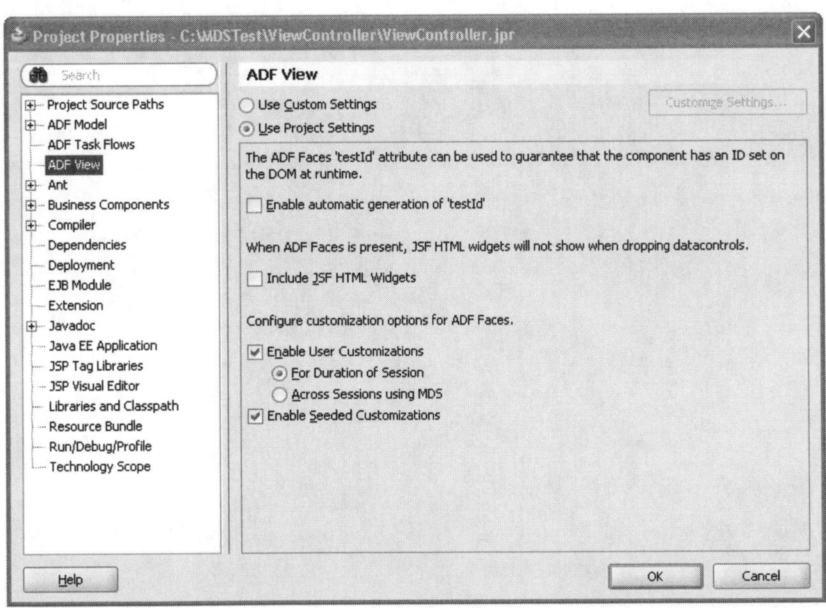

FIGURE 14-9 *Enabling user customizations in Oracle JDeveloper project properties*

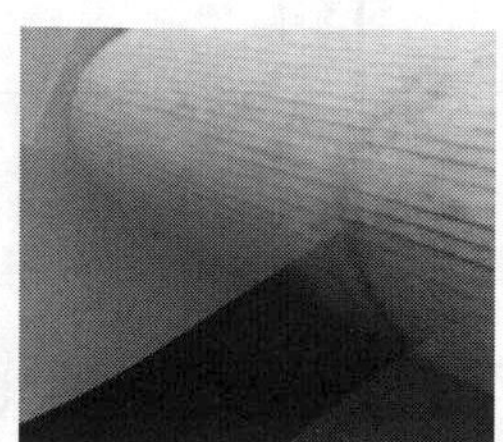

CHAPTER 15

Extending Oracle Composer

racle WebCenter applications are inherently customizable. Oracle Composer, as we wrote in Chapter 11, is the user interface that the WebCenter Framework provides to administrators and business users to perform run-time customizations. Since it is built with ADF Faces Rich Client 11*g* components, Oracle Composer inherits the skinning capabilities available in that component library. The Oracle Fusion Middleware Developer's Guide for Oracle WebCenter contains all the information required to skin Oracle Composer. But what if you want or need to change more than the appearance of the view layer? Fortunately, Oracle Composer's architecture is extendable, which means it is possible for you to augment the run-time capabilities offered to end users.

Skinning notwithstanding, there are three possible ways to alter Oracle Composer's user interface and behavior: add-on panels, property filters, and custom property panels. All three are managed through a single configuration file named pe_ext.xml. This file must be in the META-INF folder, located at the root of the web application. This folder is a sibling of the WEB-INF folder; since Oracle JDeveloper does not provision it automatically, you will have to create it by hand. In addition, do not confuse this META-INF folder with the one typically found in .jar and .war files.

It must be noted that pe_ext.xml is read once at application startup. The web container, usually Oracle WebLogic Server, will not detect that the file has changed if you alter it while running the application. Therefore, changing the file will force you either to redeploy the application or to restart it; an alternative would be to restart the WebLogic instance.

While this chapter covers ways to extend Oracle Composer underlying mechanisms, you must keep in mind that custom task flows and portlets are alternate ways to shape the user experience. The key differentiator here is scope. Custom task flows and portlets exist in the context of a customizable Oracle WebCenter page. On the other hand, you will want to create custom panels and filters to ensure the best user experience for your custom task flow or portlet in the context of Oracle Composer's UI.

Add-on Panels

Simply told, add-on panels are ADF Task Flows displayed in modal dialogs. They are used to manipulate the properties of a page or its constituent parts, such as ADF Faces Rich Client components and task flows. Add-on panels are accessed through buttons placed in the Oracle Composer toolbar when the page is switched to Edit mode.

Oracle Composer ships with four built-in add-on panels:

- **Component catalog** Used to customize a page with user-selected ADF Faces Rich Client components and task flows.

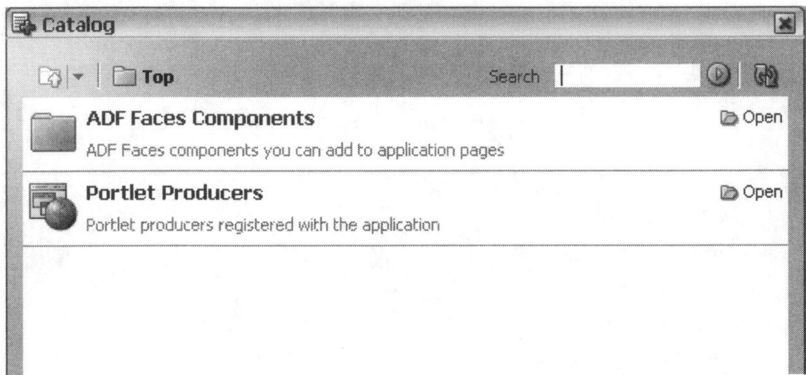

- **Page Properties editor** Controls the page's security settings and parameters. It is also possible to alter the page title through this panel.

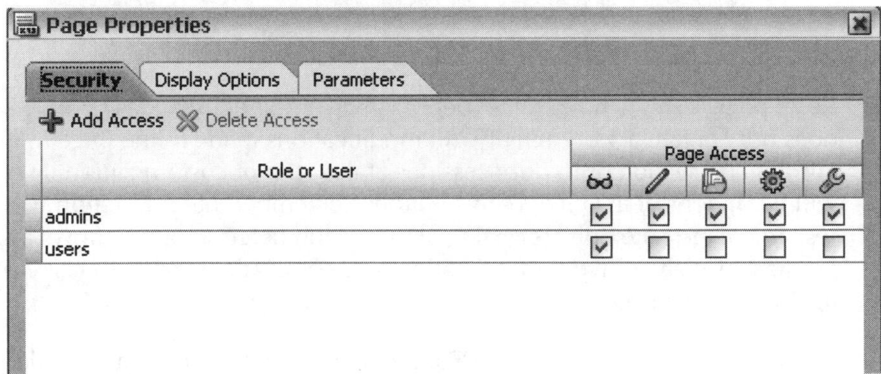

- **Component Properties editor** This panel will display all the properties of a component or task flow except the ones that were excluded through a property filter. Users can change property values as they see fit. This panel applies only to components and task flows that are not linked to a custom property panel.

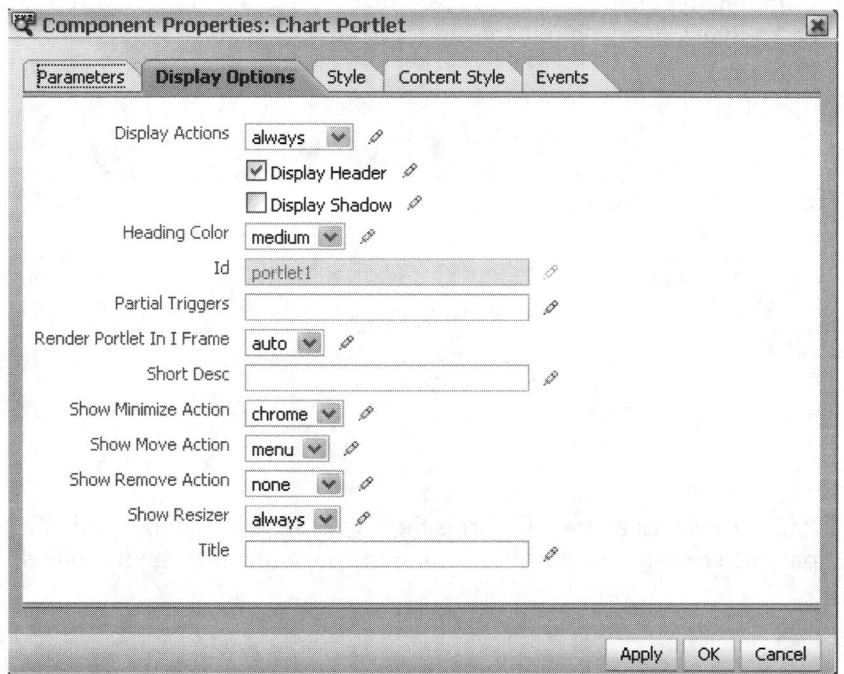

- **Reset page** This is not a panel per se, since the underlying task flow does not contain a *view* activity. All modifications made to the page in the current edit session or in prior sessions at the current customization layer will be undone at the click of this button. Remember that this action will reset the page state only, reversing addition and deletion of task flows and portlets, as well as layout modifications. Customizations made to task flows included in the page will be preserved.

By default, only the Catalog and the Component Properties editor are available. The Page Properties editor and Reset Page button will be rendered only if you declare them in the adf-config.xml descriptor. In order to do this, you must first add the Oracle Composer namespace to the descriptor's header.

```
<adf-config xmlns="http://xmlns.oracle.com/adf/config"
            xmlns:sec="http://xmlns.oracle.com/adf/security/config"
            xmlns:mdsC="http://xmlns.oracle.com/adf/mds/config"
            xmlns:pe="http://xmlns.oracle.com/adf/pageeditor/config"
>
```

Then, add references to the Oracle-provided panels, as below.

```
<pe:page-editor-config
    xmlns="http://xmlns.oracle.com/adf/pageeditor/config">
  <addon-panels>
    <!-- Page Properties add-on panel -->
    <addon-panel name="oracle.adf.pageeditor.addonpanels.page-settings" />
    <!-- Page Reset add-on panel -->
    <addon-panel name="oracle.adf.pageeditor.addonpanels.page-reset" />
  </addon-panels>
</pe:page-editor-config>
```

The appropriate buttons will now appear in the Oracle Composer toolbar.

Custom Panels

Since add-on panels are task flows, it is fairly easy to add your own panel to any Oracle WebCenter application. In order to do this, you must first build a bounded ADF Task Flow that contains JSF fragments. Then, simply add the panel's declaration to pe_ext.xml, as shown in the following XML snippet.

```
<pe-extension xmlns="http://xmlns.oracle.com/adf/pageeditor/extension">
  <addon-config>
    <panels>
      <panel name="com.wchb.preferences" title="Preferences"
             icon="adf/webcenter/images/about.gif"
             taskflow-id="/WEB-INF/preferences.xml#preferences"
      />
    </panels>
  </addon-config>
</pe-extension>
```

It is then necessary to define the panel in adf-config.xml.

```
...
<pe:page-editor-config
    xmlns="http://xmlns.oracle.com/adf/pageeditor/config">
  <addon-panels>
    <addon-panel name="com.wchb.preferences" />
  </addon-panels>
</pe:page-editor-config>
...
```

If you need to grant access to the panel conditionally, simply add a condition to the declaration.

```
<addon-panel name="com.wchb.preferences"
             rendered="#{securityBean.isUserManager}" />
```

FIGURE 15-1 *Oracle Composer header with add-on panels*

The button giving access to the panel will not appear if the condition evaluates to *false*.

Figure 15-1 shows the appearance of the Composer header with buttons to access the Oracle-provided panels added. A custom panel was also declared.

Add-on panels always appear as dialog boxes. You can see a sample custom add-on panel in Figure 15-2.

The typical use case for add-on panels is manipulation of settings specific to the Oracle Composer environment. You may also use them to control properties applying to Oracle Composer pages, task flows, or ADF Faces Rich Client components. For example, you could give users the capacity to change on the fly the ADF skin used in customizable pages through a custom add-on panel.

Property Filters

Among the built-in Oracle WebCenter add-on panels, the Component Properties editor add-on panel possesses a unique feature: filtering. By default, it will display all the available properties for a specific ADF Faces Rich Client component. Via property filters, you can alter the panel's behavior so it will hide specific properties.

FIGURE 15-2 *Custom add-on panel*

Property filters can apply indistinctly to all components, or be scoped to a specific component. They are defined in the pe_ext.xml file. Below is a sample filter definition.

```
<pe-extension xmlns="http://xmlns.oracle.com/adf/pageeditor/extension">
  <addon-config>
    ...
  </addon-config>
  <filter-config>
    <global-attribute-filter>
      <attribute name="autoSubmit"/>
      <attribute name="binding"/>
    </global-attribute-filter>
    <taglib-filter namespace="http://xmlns.oracle.com/adf/faces/rich">
      <tag name="richTextEditor">
        <attribute name="shortDesc"/>
      </tag>
      <tag name="calendar">
        <attribute name="listCount"/>
        <attribute name="startHour"/>
      </tag>
    </taglib-filter>
  </filter-config>
</pe-extension>
```

Figure 15-3 shows the unfiltered property view for the af:calendar ADF Faces Rich Client component; Figure 15-4 shows the filtered view resulting from the sample filters above.

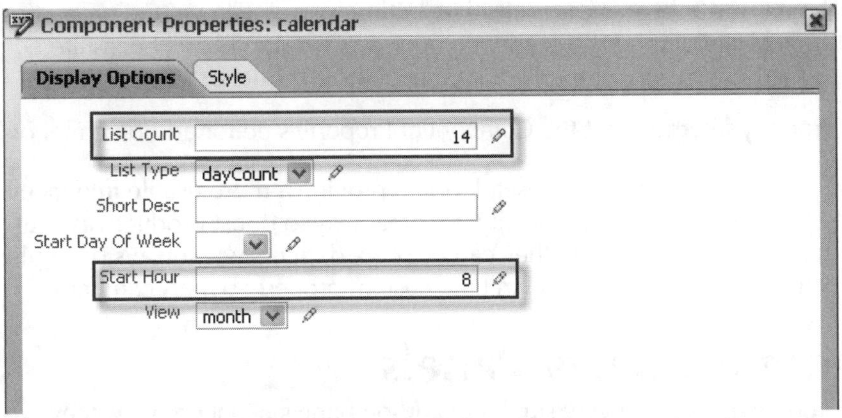

FIGURE 15-3 *calendar properties (unfiltered)*

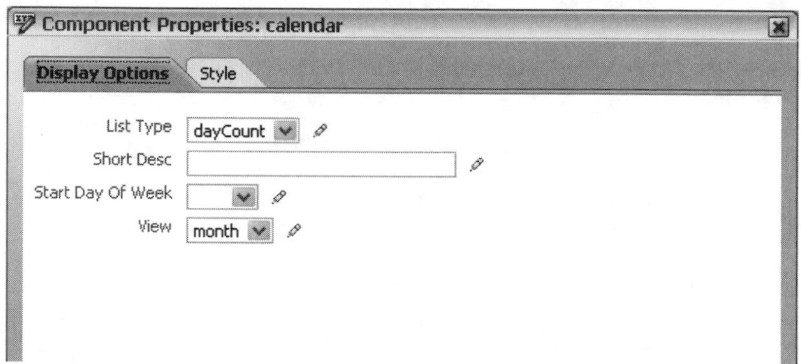

FIGURE 15-4 *calendar properties (filtered)*

Please note the following about property filters:

- Oracle WebCenter possesses built-in filters for several properties.
- It is possible to force display of a property, even if WebCenter filters it by default. In order to do this, simply add `filtered="false"` to any existing filter or create a new one. The filtered attributes takes precedence on any filter defined in other Oracle Composer extension files (pe_ext.xml).
- Filters apply to ADF Faces Rich Client components only. They will not affect task flows.
- The name attribute is case sensitive. In the example above, the properties for the richTextEditor and calendar components wouldn't have been filtered if you did not specify properly the name of the attribute or tag.
- Property filters impact the Component Properties editor add-on panel only.

All in all, property filters are a useful tool to provide a more usable interface to end users. Hiding unneeded complexity is a great way to boost productivity. But property filters have limits; while they can be scoped, filters will always be applied without conditions. If you find this limiting, custom property panels can help.

Custom Property Panels

Custom property panels are very similar to add-on panels. Conceptually, they are property editor overrides. Since they are defined using fragment-based bounded task flows, they give you full control over the user interface and business logic.

This means you can select the properties to be displayed, and implement rendering conditions as needed. It must be noted that property panels can apply either to ADF Faces Rich Client components or to task flows.

A typical use for a custom property panel would be parameter handling for task flows deployed in the Oracle Composer catalog. Values for such parameters are linked to specific task flow instances dropped in customizable pages. These values must be persisted in an appropriate manner and presented to users in the simplest way possible. A task flow presenting sales data using ADF Data Visualization components could offer the choice between bar and pie charts, for example. In this instance, individual user choices would be made through the panel and persisted in the MDS repository. Custom panels may also elect to invoke the Oracle ADF DTRT APIs to alter other properties. A typical example would be to manipulate specific values in the page definition associated with a task flow fragment. Such changes will be persisted through the same MDS session as the one used by the panel itself.

Custom property panels must be declared in pe_ext.xml the same way add-on panels are. The following XML snippet shows how to change the adf-config.xml descriptor accordingly in the case of a component.

```
<pe-extension xmlns="http://xmlns.oracle.com/adf/pageeditor/extension">
...
  <property-panels>
    <property-panel name="cmdbtn">
      <component>
        oracle.adf.view.rich.component.rich.input.RichTextEditor
      </component>
      <panel name="com.wchb.propertypanels.richTextEditor" />
    </property-panel>
  </property-panels>
</pe-extension>
```

In the case of a task flow, the taskflow-id tag is used instead of the component one.

```
<pe-extension xmlns="http://xmlns.oracle.com/adf/pageeditor/extension">
...
<property-panels>
  <property-panel name="salesSummary">
    <taskflow-id>/WEB-INF/salesSummary#summary</taskflow-id>
    <panel name="com.wchb.propertypanels.salesSummaryPanel" />
  </property-panel>
</property-panels>
</pe-extension>
```

Usually, you will need to build custom property panels if you want full control of the property UI for a specific component or task flow. In the case of a component, it is much simpler to use a property filter when applicable. You can also decide to inhibit display of the standard property panels provided by Oracle WebCenter. This is achieved through the rendered attribute of the panel tag in the adf-config.xml descriptor.

```
...
<property-panels>
  <property-panel name="cmdbtn">
    <component>oracle.rich.CommandButton</component>
    <panel name="com.wchb.propertypanels.commandButton" />
    <panel name="oracle.pageeditor.prop-inspector" rendered="false" />
  </property-panel>
</property-panels>
...
```

You may also elect to make the rendering of a specific panel conditional. To do this, simply assign an appropriate EL expression to the rendered attribute, as shown below.

```
<property-panel name="com.wchb.propertypanels.commandButton"
                rendered="#{securityBean.IsUserManager}">
```

UI Event Handlers

Up to now, the Oracle Composer extensions we have discussed concern mainly the view layer. UI event handlers bring to WebCenter developers a way to insert their own business logic when task flows or components are

- Added to a page
- Selected
- Deleted from a page

In addition, it is possible to define UI event handlers of a global scope. Those will be invoked when Oracle Composer saves the current state of the page and switches back to View mode from Edit mode, respectively.

UI event handlers are extremely useful for setup and cleanup purposes. If you choose to implement custom add-on or property panels, we strongly recommend you invoke the save logic for these values through appropriate UI event handlers. Ideally, you should implement the actual business logic in classes distinct from the event handler in order to reuse this logic, when applicable, in various contexts.

To be invoked by Oracle Composer, your handlers must be registered in the pe_ext.xml configuration file. Each registration specifies the UI event the handler will react to and the fully qualified name of the Java class implementing the handler. Your handlers will chain to each other if they process the same event. Thus, the order in which you register them is very important. Moreover, you will need to design your handlers carefully to avoid ripple effects, because Oracle-provided handlers will always run last in each case.

Next is a sample registration.

```
<pe-extension xmlns="http://xmlns.oracle.com/adf/pageeditor/extension">
...
  <event-handlers>
    <event-handler event="save">com.wchb.events.SaveHandler</event-handler>
    <event-handler event="save">com.wchb.custom.CSaveHandler</event-handler>
    <event-handler event="delete">com.wchb.events.DelHandler</event-handler>
  </event-handlers>
</pe-extension>
```

In this specific case, SaveHandler would be invoked before CSaveHandler in the case of a save event. Be careful, however. Oracle Composer uses UI event handlers internally, and those cannot be disabled. There are some things to remember about exception handling in the context of handlers. If an event handler throws AbortProcessingException, then the event is canceled and no further event handlers will be invoked, including Oracle Composer's own handlers. However, if an exception is thrown while instantiating an event handler, then Oracle Composer will simply log a warning and will continue with the next handler in the chain.

In order to create a class implementing a handler, you must implement Oracle-provided Java interfaces. We will now explain the specifics of such implementations.

Save and Close Handlers

Save and Close handlers do not deal with specific task flows, portlets, or components. Instead, they process specific UI actions related to Oracle Composer as a whole. Save handlers are called when a user clicks the Save button on the Oracle Composer toolbar; clicking on the Apply or OK button in the Component Properties add-on panel or Page Properties dialog will also invoke the handlers. Close handlers, on the other hand, will run only when the user clicks on the Close button of the Oracle Composer toolbar.

Table 15-1 provides you all the details you need to implement handler classes. The Event Type column provides you the value you need to fill the event attribute of the event-handler tag in pe_ext.xml.

It must be noted that the processClose and processSave methods each receive an input parameter describing the UI event that occurred.

Event Type	Java Interface	Method
close	oracle.adf.view.page.editor.event.CloseListener	processClose
save	oracle.adf.view.page.editor.event.SaveListener	processSave

TABLE 15-1 *Details for Implementing Handler Classes*

Addition, Selection, and Deletion Handlers

As you may guess, addition and deletion handlers are called when a task flow, component, or portlet is added to the page or deleted from it. On the other hand, selection handlers are invoked when a user selects the Edit icon on a Panel Customizable or Show Detail Frame component in Design mode, a component on the page in Source view, or a component in the hierarchy in Source view.

Table 15-2 provides all the details you need to implement addition, selection, and deletion handler classes. The Event Type column provides you the value you need to fill the event attribute of the event-handler tag in pe_ext.xml.

The processAddition, processDeletion, and processSelection methods are all built on the same model; they all receive a single parameter which is an event descriptor. The AdditionEvent class will enable you to obtain the instance of the UIComponent the portlet or task flow was dropped on, as well as the index it will occupy among the component's children. The getTransferable method can be used to fetch data about the catalog item that was dropped in order to branch correctly. You can use the getComponent method of the DeletionEvent class in order to retrieve the object inheriting from UIComponent that is to be deleted. Finally, SelectionEvent can be used in the same fashion as DeletionEvent in order to get a hold on the instance of the selected UIComponent.

Event Type	Java Interface	Method
Add	oracle.adf.view.page.editor.event.AdditionListener	processAddition
Delete	oracle.adf.view.page.editor.event.DeletionListener	processDeletion
Select	oracle.adf.view.page.editor.event.SelectionListener	processSelection

TABLE 15-2 *Details for Implementing Addition, Selection, and Deletion Handler Classes*

CHAPTER 16

MDS Under the Hood of WebCenter

Oracle Metadata Services Framework (MDS) is an integral component of Oracle ADF 11*g*. As we saw in Chapter 14, all the declarative artifacts that exist in ADF can be customized through MDS. Since Oracle WebCenter is built on the top of ADF, it will not surprise you to learn that WebCenter relies heavily on the capabilities of MDS to support application customization and user personalization. In fact, MDS is central to the Oracle Fusion strategy as a whole, since Fusion applications use it to offer vertical, industry, and customer-specific customizations. WebCenter, on the other hand, concerns itself with design-time and run-time customizations applied to portal-centric use cases. In this chapter, our aim is to describe exactly how various parts of Oracle WebCenter use MDS, with Oracle Composer and Page Service as our focus areas. Special emphasis will also be placed on how to use the programmatic hooks provided by Oracle in order to make Composer rely on your own customization classes to complement or supplant the standard ones.

Oracle Composer

At its heart, Oracle Composer is a management system for run-time customizations. Its scope is rigorously limited to the realm of the user interface. On its own, Composer will not provide business services or manage documents. Instead, it concerns itself with JSF pages and their contents, and more precisely the layout of the services as well as the specific property values that were assigned to them in order to configure them properly. The layout possibilities offered may vary according to the security privileges granted to the user, as well as the basic design of the JSF page. All the layout choices made by users, as well as the values of the properties, are persisted through MDS.

There is a very strong relationship between Page Service and Oracle Composer. This is because Page Service creates dynamically instances of customizable JSF pages that will be edited through Composer. Thus, there are no differences between a customizable page created in Oracle JDeveloper 11*g* and a page created dynamically at run time through Page Service. The same MDS mechanisms ensure persistence of the layout and property values. Consequently, Oracle Composer relies on the mechanisms described in this chapter behind the scenes.

Default Behavior

When you're creating a new application using the WebCenter template in Oracle JDeveloper 11*g*, the IDE will add an MDS-specific section to the adf-config.xml file. The reason for this is twofold. First, it is necessary to configure a basic MDS repository for the application; this repository will reside on the local file system, since this ensures an easy setup on developer workstations. Second, Composer and Page Service, among others, will rely on customization classes. Obviously, you are not forced to use these features if they're not required at the functional level; Oracle JDeveloper simply makes the necessary configuration changes for them to work correctly. By default, a single customization class is used: it is the now familiar UserCC class we have used as an example back in Chapter 14. The extract below shows the section of the XML file we are referring to.

```
<mdsC:adf-mds-config version="11.1.1.000">
  <mds-config xmlns="http://xmlns.oracle.com/mds/config">
    <persistence-config>
      <metadata-namespaces>
        <namespace path="/oracle/adf/rc/metadata"
                   metadata-store-usage="WebCenterFileMetadataStore"/>
        <namespace path="/persdef/"
                   metadata-store-usage="WebCenterFileMetadataStore"/>
      </metadata-namespaces>
      <metadata-store-usages>
        <metadata-store-usage id="WebCenterFileMetadataStore"
                              default-cust-store="true">
          <metadata-store
      class-name="oracle.mds.persistence.stores.file.FileMetadataStore">
            <property name="metadata-path" value="../../mds"/>
          </metadata-store>
        </metadata-store-usage>
      </metadata-store-usages>
    </persistence-config>
    <cust-config>
      <match>
        <customization-class name="oracle.adf.share.config.UserCC"/>
      </match>
    </cust-config>
  </mds-config>
</mdsC:adf-mds-config>
```

At this point, it appears clear that the default type of MDS persistence used by Composer is strictly user related. This means applications will typically allow users to tweak the user interface to their taste, but will not provide for administrators or managers a way to set layout or page contents for other users to see and use. However, the adfshare library contains an alternate customization class, SiteCC. This class can be used to define a group of customizations that will apply to the web application as a whole, since the layer value it returns is a constant. But what will you do if you need to build an application that will combine site-wide customization with personalization? Fortunately, there is a way to achieve this.

Customization Classes and Oracle Composer

The key to understanding Oracle Composer's use of MDS is to remember that Composer manages run-time customizations. In its default configuration, it will use UserCC as described above. In order to make Composer use your own customization classes, you need a way to parameterize the MDS session of the user dynamically. In this case, customizations will be stored according to configuration options specified by you; the whole process will also rely on code you will provide. Specifically, this is achieved by means of a WebCenter-specific HTTP filter, which can be configured to invoke a factory class in order to create an object representing the MDS session's options. The whole run-time dynamics of the process is documented in Figure 16-1.

It must be mentioned that the only pieces that need to be coded are those with light background; shapes with a darker background are of Oracle origin. Let us now study each of the steps listed in Table 16-1 in greater detail.

While there are several participants in Composer's MDS dynamics, the only additional code you need to provide compared with a standard ADF application is the session options factory class.

Design-wise, the role of the session options factory class is simply to parameterize the MDS session in a manner appropriate to the applicative context. All such classes

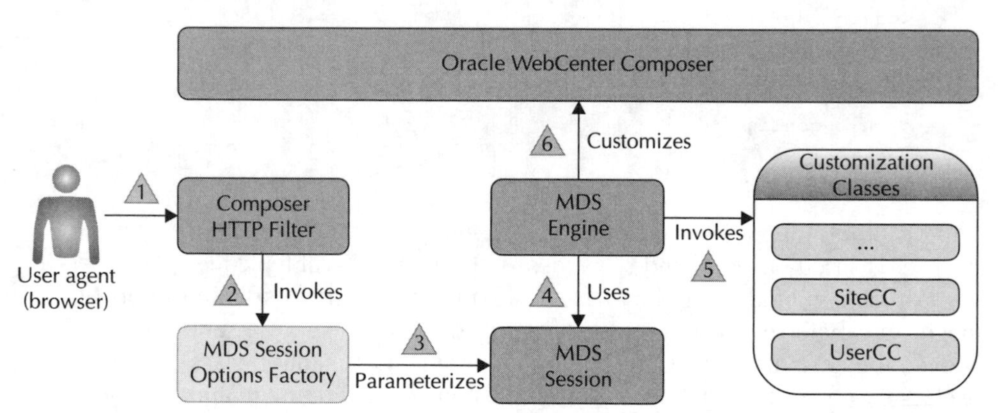

FIGURE 16-1 *Dynamics of custom MDS behavior in Oracle Composer*

Step	Custom Code	Description
1	No	A user agent, typically a web browser, sends a request for a customized Composer page.
2	No	Oracle-provided HTTP filter. Each incoming request goes through it, thus guaranteeing correct parameterization of the MDS session.
3	Yes	This custom class will ensure the appropriate parameters are passed to the session, and is called for each request.
4	No	MDS uses the session pattern in order to manage its connection to the repository. This is conceptually similar to an HTTP session.
5	Yes	The engine invokes the various MDS customization classes needed by the application. Some or all of them can be your own.
6	No	The standard MDS engine pushes the customized pages to Composer, which will then display them to the user.

TABLE 16-1 *Run-time Steps of Custom MDS Behavior in Oracle Composer*

must implement the ComposerSessionOptionsFactory interface defined by Oracle. This interface mandates its implementations to define a single method, for which the signature is

```
public SessionOptions createSessionOptions(SessionOptions, String)
```

The first parameter passed to the method represents the default session options defined at system level, while the second specifies the mode. The default options are defined in the application's adf-config.xml descriptor.

It is worth mentioning that session options factory classes can also alter the list of active customization layers. This is especially useful if you want View and Edit mode customizations to apply to a different set of layers. For example, you might need Edit mode changes to affect the site layer (SiteCC class) while View mode changes affect the combination of site and user layers (UserCC class). The following code sample embodies this approach.

```
package com.wchb

import …
public class ComposerSessionFactoryImpl
                implements ComposerSessionOptionsFactory {

    //Edit mode SiteCC
    private static final CustomizationClass[] EDIT_LAYER =
        new CustomizationClass[] { new SiteCC() };

    //View mode SiteCC + USerCC
    private static final CustomizationClass[] VIEW_LAYER =
        new CustomizationClass[] { new SiteCC(), new UserCC() };

    public SessionOptions createSessionOptions(SessionOptions
defaultSessionOptions,
                                                String mode) {
        CustomizationClass[] custLayer;
        CustConfig custConfig = null;
        if (ModeContext.EDIT_MODE.equals(mode)) {
            //Mode is Edit, change to SiteCC
            custLayer = EDIT_LAYER;
        } else {
            //Mode is View, change to UserCC + SiteCC
            custLayer = VIEW_LAYER;
        }
        try {
            CustClassList custClassList = new CustClassList(custLayer);
            CustClassListMapping custClassListMapping =
                new CustClassListMapping("/", null, null, custClassList);
            custConfig =
                    new CustConfig(new CustClassListMapping[] { cust-
ClassListMapping });
        } catch (Exception e) {
            e.printStackTrace();
        }
        return new SessionOptions(defaultSessionOptions.getIsolationLevel(),
                        defaultSessionOptions.getLocale(),
                        custConfig,
                        defaultSessionOptions.getVersionContext(),
                        defaultSessionOptions.getVersionCreatorName(),
                        defaultSessionOptions.getCustomizationPolicy());
    }
}
```

There are a few remarks to be made about the contents of this sample.

- The code representation of the active customization layers is always an array of type CustomizationClass. Ordering is essential; the classes must be instantiated in a top-to-bottom fashion, meaning index 0 is the topmost class.
- The catch block's content should be replaced with meaningful logging statements before the class is put into production.

To illustrate the simplicity of the whole process, we will now review the tasks required to implement custom MDS behavior in your application.

1. Build your customization classes. These classes are mainly designed to support run-time customization. If design-time customization support is not needed, you do not need to declare them in the CustomizationLayerValues .xml file.
2. Code your MDS session options factory class.
3. Declare the session factory in the adf-config.xml file. This XML fragment demonstrates how.

```
<page-editor-config xmlns="http://xmlns.oracle.com/adf/pageeditor/config">
  <session-options-factory>
      com.wchb.ComposerSessionFactoryImpl
  </session-options-factory>
</page-editor-config>
```

4. Add the Composer HTTP filter to your application's web.xml deployment descriptor. It must be positioned after ServletADFFilter and before ADFBindingFilter. Here is a sample declaration.

```
...
<filter>
  <filter-name>composerFilter</filter-name>
  <filter-class>
     oracle.adf.view.page.editor.webapp.WebCenterComposerFilter
  </filter-class>
</filter>
...
<filter-mapping>
  <filter-name>composerFilter</filter-name>
  <servlet-name>Faces Servlet</servlet-name>
  <dispatcher>FORWARD</dispatcher>
  <dispatcher>REQUEST</dispatcher>
</filter-mapping>
...
```

Implementation of a session options factory, as you can see, is a fairly involved process. Fortunately, it is needed only for a narrow range of use cases, as it is required only when multiple customization layers come into play. If the only thing you want to change is the default layer of the application, a change in adf-config.xml is all you need. Suppose that SiteCC, UserCC, and IndustryCC are configured in your application. The session options factory will need to determine the active layer for applicable actions at run time. For example, in Oracle Fusion Applications, users must select in a dialog the customization layer that will receive the changes before entering the Oracle Composer interface. Behind the scenes, a session option factory ensures the MDS engine will take the user's choice into account.

WebCenter Page Service

As you might expect, Page Service makes extensive use of MDS. The JSF pages it produces are built through Oracle Composer. Consequently, they are subjected to MDS customizations in the same way that the static Composer-enabled pages are built through Oracle JDeveloper. But there is more. In fact, each page instance created through Page Service is a piece of MDS metadata and is saved in the MDS repository. We will now explain why and how.

In custom-built WebCenter applications, there is a strong distinction between static and dynamic content. Static content is built at design time, by the development team, using Oracle JDeveloper and other specialized tools. The pages are not static in behavior, since they are data-driven JSF pages, but their existence is preordained by the application's design. On the other hand, dynamic pages are created by users, using Page Service or a custom UI, and populated with the help of Oracle Composer. While their content and appearance can be oriented through developer-provided templates, they owe their existence to an arbitrary decision made by a user. The application design acknowledges the existence of the dynamic pages by including templates tuned to answer specific expectations, but cannot anticipate user decisions.

Since they do not appear in the design, dynamic pages can be considered customizations of the application. And in Oracle WebCenter, customizations are handled by MDS; Page Service is no exception. But how does all of this work? Figure 16-2 provides an answer.

The key to the whole process is the MDS JSP provider, which is invoked by an Oracle-provided servlet. This provider will redirect all page requests, whether they concern dynamic pages created through Page Service or predefined JSF pages found at the WAR file level, to MDS instead of querying the file system. Dynamic pages are fetched as streams from the MDS repository and passed to the provider, which in turns sends them to the servlet for rendering. Once the stream has been obtained, dynamic page processing is undistinguishable from static page processing. Page definitions, when available, will be loaded over the execution of the JSF life cycle by the MDS engine. The engine will load each of the page definitions either from the WAR file or the MDS repository.

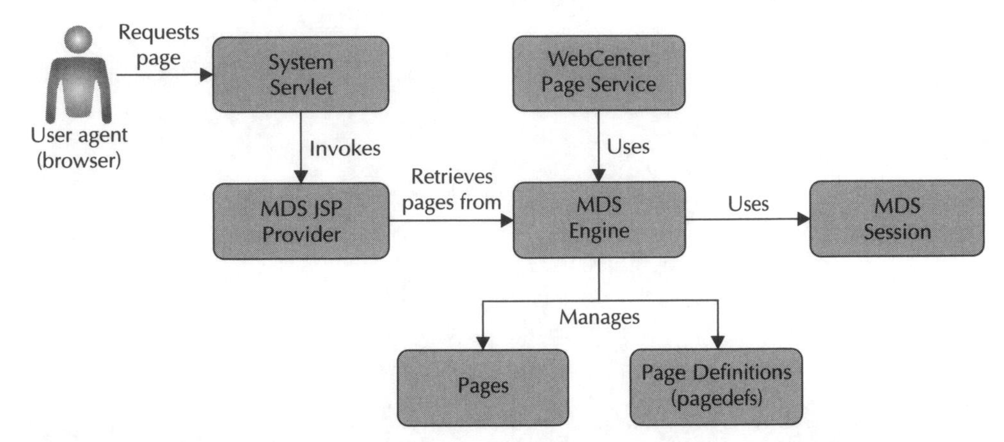

FIGURE 16-2 *Page Service interactions with MDS*

To conclude this section, we must warn you about a potential pitfall. Fundamentally, customizations defined on JSF pages persisted in MDS are identified by the path of the page and the current layer values. When a page contains regions or is based on a template, customizations made on components located in those regions and templates will be propagated to all the pages containing the region or consuming the template. The only exception to this behavior will happen if the layer values for the target page are distinct from those of the page where the customizations were made. Suppose your application contains two pages: one for bills and the other for purchase orders. Both pages are built on the top of the same template, called ERP. Your project plan calls for the implementation of customizations for a single layer, representing the industry. Possible values for this layer are healthcare and financial. If a customization developer alters the bills page by manipulating components belonging to the ERP template, with healthcare selected as the layer value for industry, both the bills and purchase orders pages will reflect the alterations at run time if healthcare is the active layer value. However, changes made to the ERP template will not show if the layer value is financial. Consequently, you need to design your applications and customize them carefully to avoid unintended changes at run time.

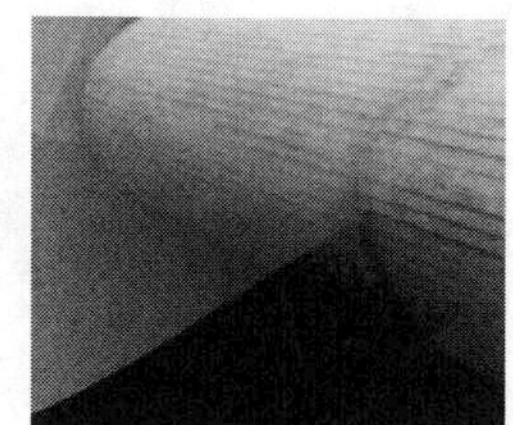

PART IV

Administering Your Applications

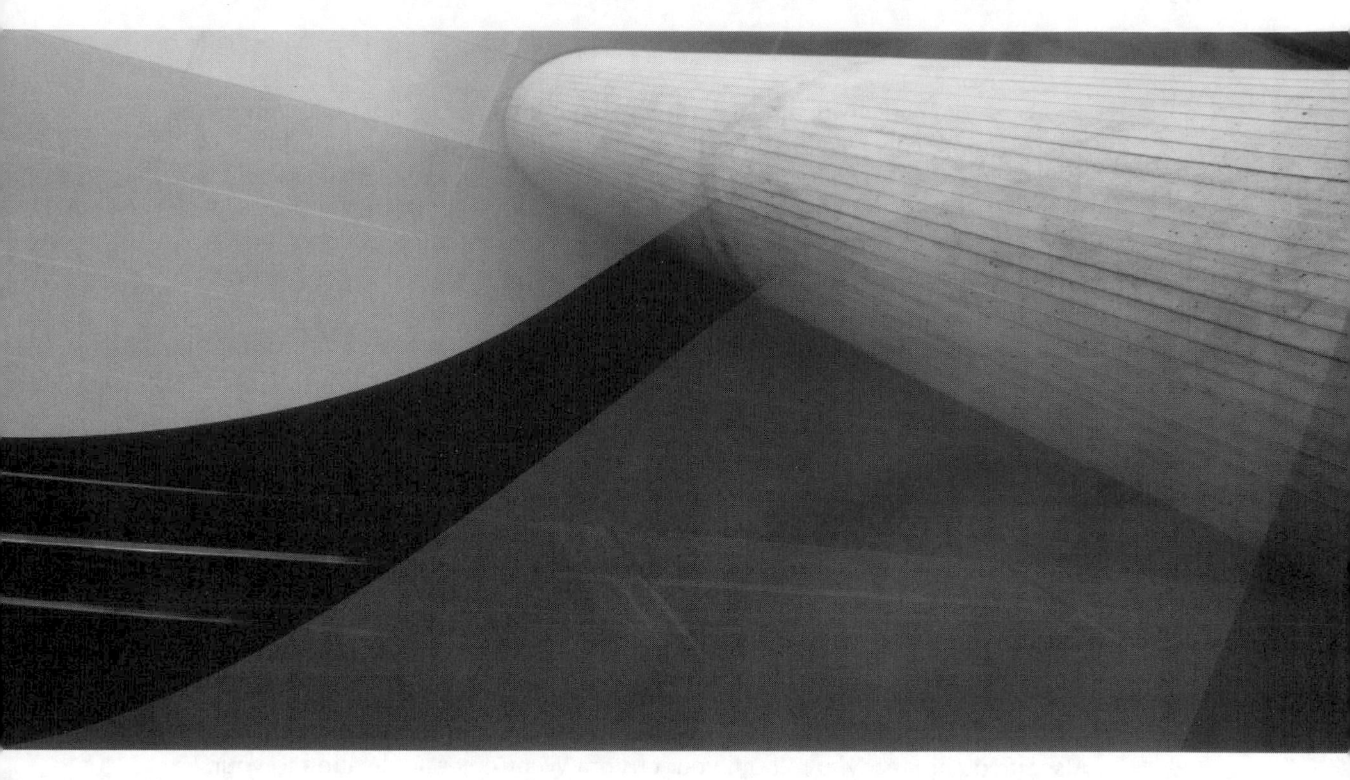

CHAPTER 17

Installing and Managing WebCenter

ost chapters in this book discuss what it takes to build rich, compelling applications with the tool set WebCenter and the Fusion Middleware generally provide. The chapters in Part IV focus on concepts and tasks that are of interest to the Fusion Middleware administrators; we will discuss the installation, management, configuration, security, and deployment aspects of WebCenter applications.

Installing Oracle WebCenter

Luckily, for most of the development tasks of WebCenter, you don't need to perform a full installation of the Oracle Fusion Middleware. By simply installing Oracle JDeveloper, which comes with an Integrated WebLogic Server, adding the WebCenter Extension for JDeveloper and perhaps a database on top of it, you can perform the majority of the development activities. These include building, testing, and deploying WebCenter applications with run-time customization capabilities, portlets, content integration, tagging, linking, security, and much more.

This may not suffice, however, if you want to leverage additional WebCenter Web 2.0 Services, including discussions, wikis, and blogs; or if you want to integrate BPEL or Secure Enterprise Search into your applications. You need to install the back-end servers for these features.

Also, if you are ready to roll out your custom WebCenter application to your user community, install the entire Fusion Middleware along with the required WebCenter components before deploying your application.

In this section we don't explicitly state hardware and operating system requirements, and software version numbers. Rather, we are focusing on concepts. For detailed hardware, OS, and software version requirements refer to the official Oracle documentation.

WebCenter Installation Concepts

Before familiarizing yourself with the actual installation steps, first review a few characteristics about the installation process in general.

The first surprise to those familiar with the Fusion Middleware 10*g* installation is that after completing the Fusion Middleware and WebCenter install steps, you don't end up with a running environment. The install process lays down the binaries only. As a post-installation step, you'll have to step through a configuration process that will result in the running environment, including WebCenter Spaces and out-of-the-box portlets. While some of the WebCenter services require additional, separate installation, the blog, wiki, and discussion services get installed and are ready to be used by users.

Before getting started with the installation, be sure to think through your requirements, including the following:

- **Single-node or clustered environment** While both single-node and clustered options are supported by the installation process, you cannot convert a single-node topology to a clustered environment. If you are thinking about a production setting, chances are you will need to set up a clustered environment. Another advantage of choosing the clustered option is that later on you can scale it out—and you can reduce it to meet your needs.
- **WebCenter Web 2.0 Services needed** It helps during the installation and configuration process if you have a clear understanding of the WebCenter Web 2.0 Services being used. The good news is that the choices you make during the installation and configuration can be adjusted or changed later on.
- **Available and required hardware** Since the Fusion Middleware and the WebCenter components are all loosely coupled, it helps if you have a clear deployment topology planned out before starting the installation.

Installation Steps

Installing WebCenter can be summarized as a 3+1 formula. First, you have to walk through three product installations, then you have to configure the installed products.

The first installation step is getting the database schemas installed. It is performed using the Repository Creation Utility (RCU). This step is responsible for creating the schemas for WebCenter Spaces as well as for some of the WebCenter Web 2.0 Services. RCU provides the flexibility to choose some or all of the services. The prefix you specify will be used to distinguish the schema belonging to multiple instances. It is important to remember the details of the schema along with the prefix and the password. You will require it during the configuration process.

The second step is installing the binaries for the WebLogic Server, the core of the Oracle Fusion Middleware. Again, after completing this step, don't expect the WebLogic Server to be up and running; you have to wait till the configuration process completes.

The third step is installing the binaries for Oracle WebCenter.

The last step is running the configuration wizard to create the domain and servers that contain the out-of-the box applications deployed.

After the configuration wizard has successfully completed, you can invoke the scripts to start up the Administration Server and the managed servers in the domain.

Before reviewing what you end up with after a complete installation, a little terminology:

- **Managed Server** Servers that host applications, portlets, and web services.
- **Cluster** A group of managed servers working together to improve scalability and reliability.

- **Domain** A group of managed servers and clusters.
- **Administration Server** Central control entity to configure the entire domain. The Administration Server manages configuration and distributes changes to servers and clusters.

Figure 17-1 shows a single-node environment that you end up with after completing the installation. The database contains all the necessary schemas and data pre-seeded, including MDS, discussions, wiki, and blog. The database is optionally leveraged by Secure Enterprise Search (SES) or the Oracle Content Server. Note that SES needs to be installed separately (a process not covered by this book).

The WebCenter domain contains several managed servers, such as WLS_Portlets hosting the out-of-the-box portlets, WLS_Spaces hosting WebCenter Spaces, and WLS_Services hosting any additional WebCenter Web 2.0 Services. The Administration Server is responsible for managing and configuring the WebCenter domain.

Figure 17-2 shows the physical representation of a single-node install.

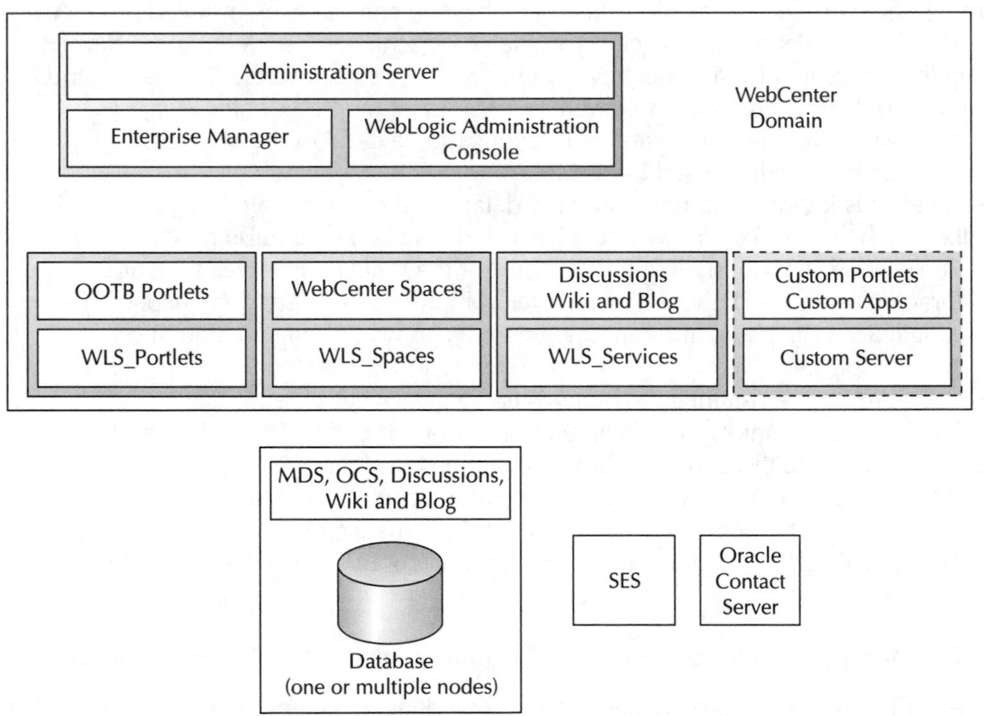

FIGURE 17-1 *Logical view of a single-node topology*

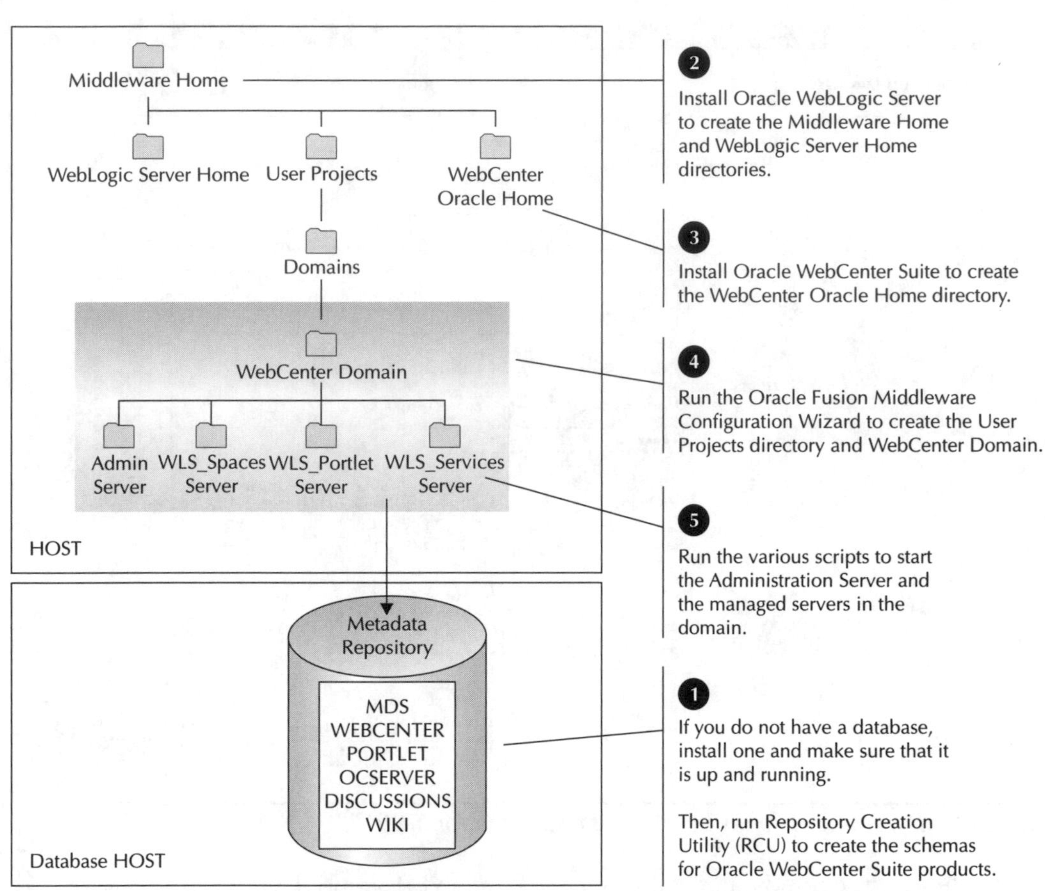

FIGURE 17-2 *Physical view and installation steps of a single-node topology*

Running the Repository Creation Utility

RCU populates the database schemas with the necessary data for WebCenter. You can start RCU from the <RCU_HOME>/bin directory by simply executing

```
$> ./rcu
```

This starts a graphical wizard. After the Welcome screen, select the "Create and load component schemas into a database" option.

Figure 17-3 shows the next step in which you have to provide connection information to your database.

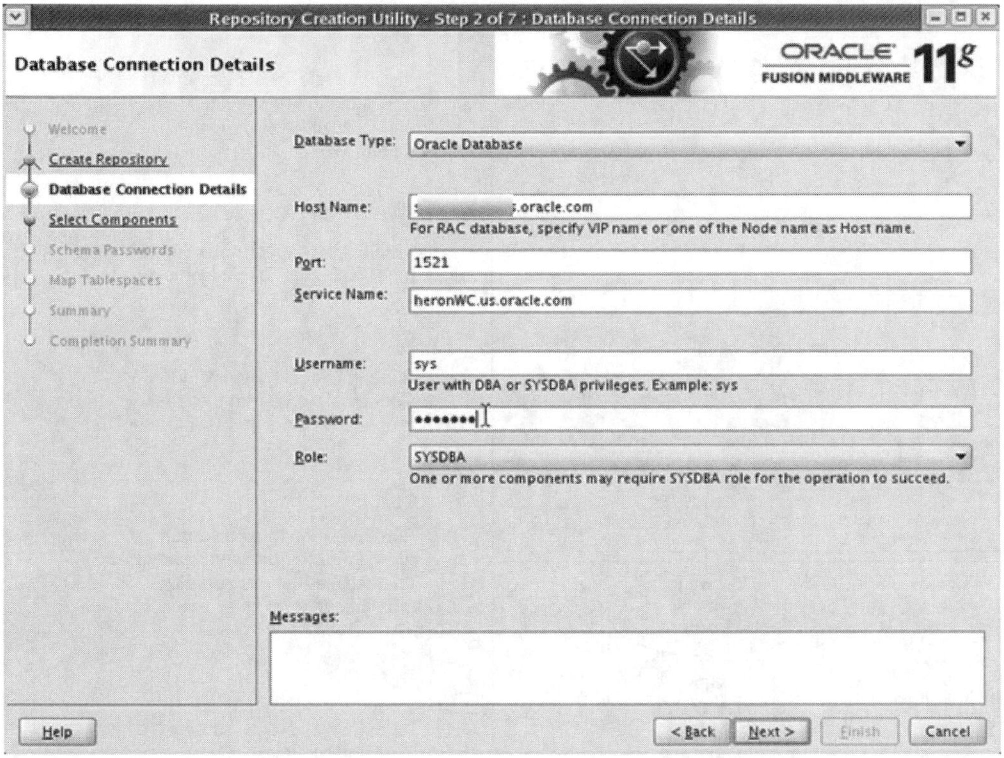

FIGURE 17-3 *Providing database connection information to RCU*

In Figure 17-4 you see the dialog allowing you to select the database schemas you will need. As a minimum, you have to select Metadata Services and WebCenter Spaces. Optionally, you can select Portlet Producers, Oracle Content Server 10*g*, Discussions, and Wiki and Blogs.

After providing passwords for the new schemas and specifying the table space information for them, the wizard allows you to review the information you provided, before populating the schemas. The prefix you provide is used to name the schemas.

Installing the WebLogic Server

In this step you will install the common Fusion Middleware functionalities, including the WebLogic Server.

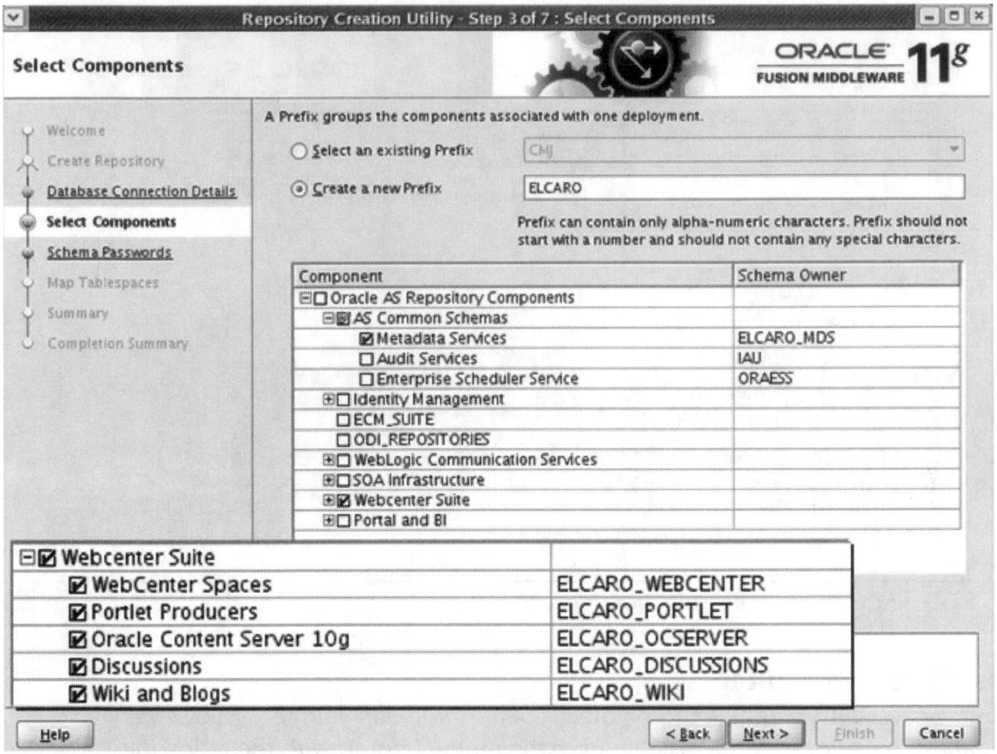

FIGURE 17-4 *Selecting components for installation*

Type the following in the product directory:

```
$> ./server103_linux32.bin
```

The wizard will prompt you to create a new Middleware home. This is a directory in the file system that holds all the common files required by the Fusion Middleware products. Take note of this directory, as you'll need it later on when you're installing WebCenter. Next, you're prompted to select the JDK. For production deployments Oracle recommends the default JRockit JDK. In the last step, you are required to enter the WebLogic Server Home directory, under the Middleware Home. After reviewing your selections, shown in Figure 17-5, you can run the installer.

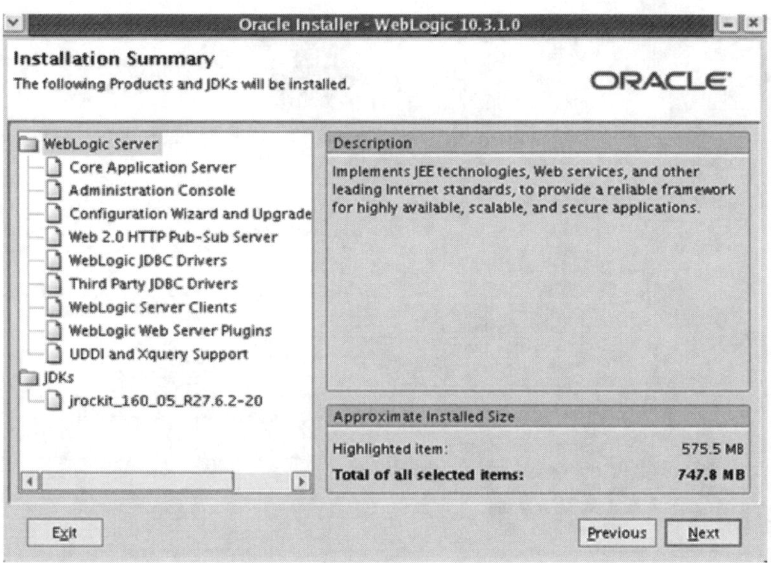

FIGURE 17-5 *Reviewing your selections*

Installing WebCenter

After successfully installing the WebLogic Server, you can start the WebCenter installer. To do so, start the installer from the product home with the following command:

```
$> ./runInstaller
```

The installer asks you to provide a JRE or JDK. Oracle recommends using the bundled JRockit JDK for the installation. Then, you need to provide the location of the Middleware Home, specified during the WebLogic Server installation, and the WEBCENTER_HOME directory (referred to as Oracle Home in the user interface). One thing to pay attention to is that the WEBCENTER_HOME directory has to be under the Middleware Home. Then, you are prompted to specify if you want to install UCM. If you install UCM, you have to have the Oracle HTTP Server installed and up and running to be able to access the web UI of UCM for operations like WebDAV and managing content from your web browser. The Oracle HTTP Server can be installed using the Oracle Web Tier installer. Last, you can review your selections, shown in Figure 17-6.

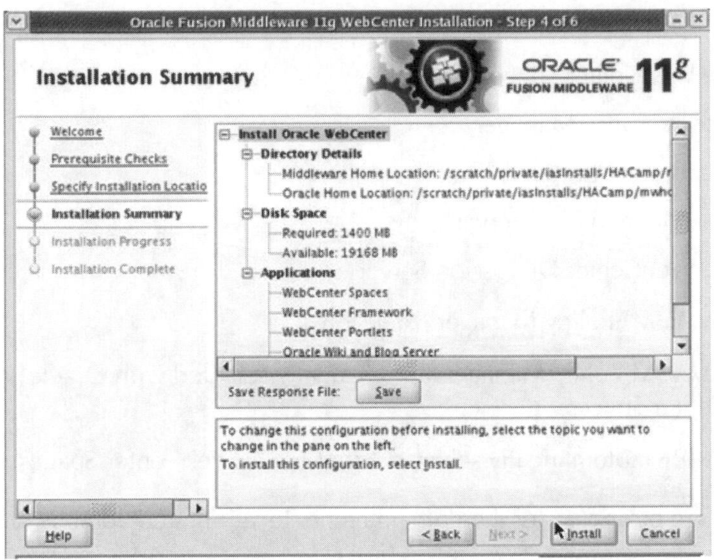

FIGURE 17-6 *Reviewing your selections*

Configuring the WebCenter Installation

After having successfully laid down the binaries, you have to walk through the configuration steps, performing the following tasks:

1. Create the domain and managed servers.
2. Deploy the WebCenter applications and services.
3. Create the data sources for the selected applications and services.

Start the configuration wizard from the `WEBC ENTER_HOME/common/bin` directory with the following command:

```
$> ./config.sh
```

The first dialog prompts you to choose between the following two options: Create a New WebLogic Domain and Extend an Existing WebLogic Domain. Select the first one: Create a New WebLogic Domain.

In the next step, you can specify which products you want to be available in your domain. The options you can choose from:

- Oracle WebCenter Spaces
- Oracle Enterprise Manager
- Oracle Portlet Producers
- Oracle Wiki and Blog Server
- Oracle WebCenter Discussion Server
- Oracle WSM[1] Policy Manager Extension
- Oracle WSM Policy Manager (automatically selected with Oracle WebCenter Spaces)
- Oracle JRF (automatically selected with Oracle WebCenter Spaces)

Then, you are prompted for the domain name, location, and administrator credentials.

In the next step, shown in Figure 17-7, you can specify the JDK; again, JRockit is the recommended JDK. You can also configure your domain either for production mode or development mode. The development mode is lighter weight, it consumes less resources: SSL configuration is simplified using demo SSL certificates, applications are automatically deployed when they reside in the domain_name/autodeploy directory, and the default capacity of the JDBC pool size is 15 connections.

Then, you have to specify the connection information for the database schemas for each component you are installing. This list, shown in Figure 17-8, depends on prior selection of the products. Here, you specify the various schemas you created using the RCU. If the back-end database you are using is Real Application Cluster (RAC), you need to check the checkbox next to "Configure selected component schemas as RAC multi data source schemas in the next panel."

After the schemas are tested and configured, you can select the next configuration activities. Your options are

- Administration Server
- Managed Servers, Clusters and Machines
- Deployments and Services
- RDBMS Security Store

---

[1] Oracle WSM stands for Oracle Web Services Manager, and it provides a stand-alone platform for securing and managing access to web services. It "externalizes" web services security, allowing developers to focus on business logic and security architects and administrators to concentrate on security and management.

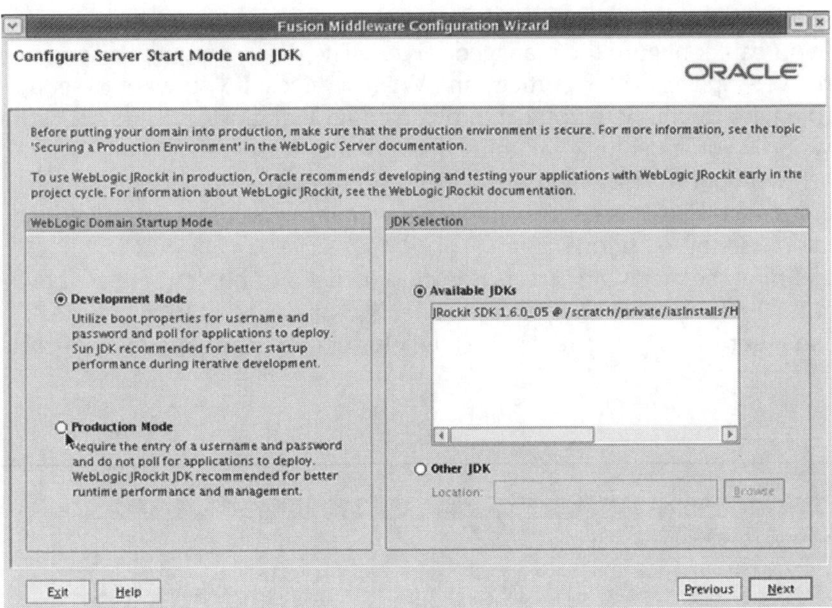

FIGURE 17-7 *Configuration Wizard: selecting the JDK and WebLogic Domain startup mode*

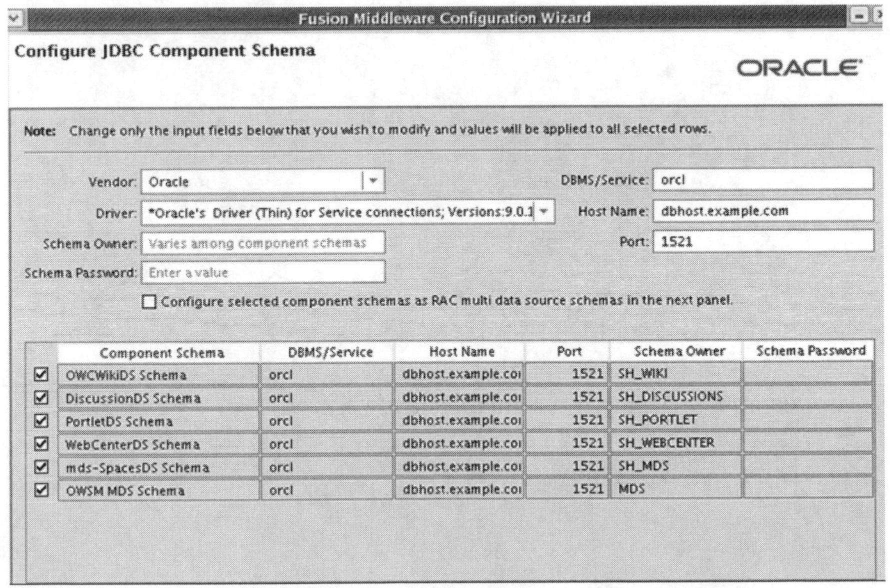

Component Schema	DBMS/Service	Host Name	Port	Schema Owner	Schema Password
OWCWikiDS Schema	orcl	dbhost.example.coi	1521	SH_WIKI	
DiscussionDS Schema	orcl	dbhost.example.coi	1521	SH_DISCUSSIONS	
PortletDS Schema	orcl	dbhost.example.coi	1521	SH_PORTLET	
WebCenterDS Schema	orcl	dbhost.example.coi	1521	SH_WEBCENTER	
mds-SpacesDS Schema	orcl	dbhost.example.coi	1521	SH_MDS	
OWSM MDS Schema	orcl	dbhost.example.coi	1521	MDS	

FIGURE 17-8 *Configuration Wizard: selecting the connection information for the components*

First you are prompted to enter connection information for the Administration Server, including name, listen address, and listen port.

Then, you can configure the managed servers. The default managed servers offered are WLS_Spaces, WLS_Portlets, and WLS_Services. If you want to set up a clustered environment, here you can provide additional clusters to do so. Figure 17-9 shows how you can cluster all three of the managed servers.

The last two options allow you to fine-tune your environment by installing shared libraries on the servers, for example. We recommend that only advanced administrators use these options.

After defining the managed servers, the clusters need to be defined, as shown in Figure 17-10. Then, the managed servers need to be assigned to the clusters, displayed in Figure 17-11. The recommended cluster messaging mode is unicast.

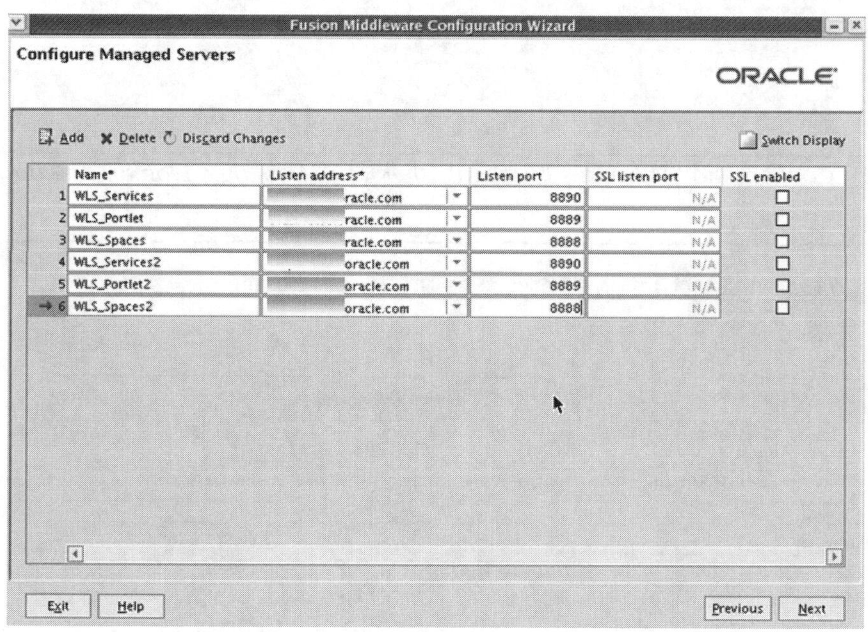

FIGURE 17-9 *Configuration Wizard: creating managed servers*

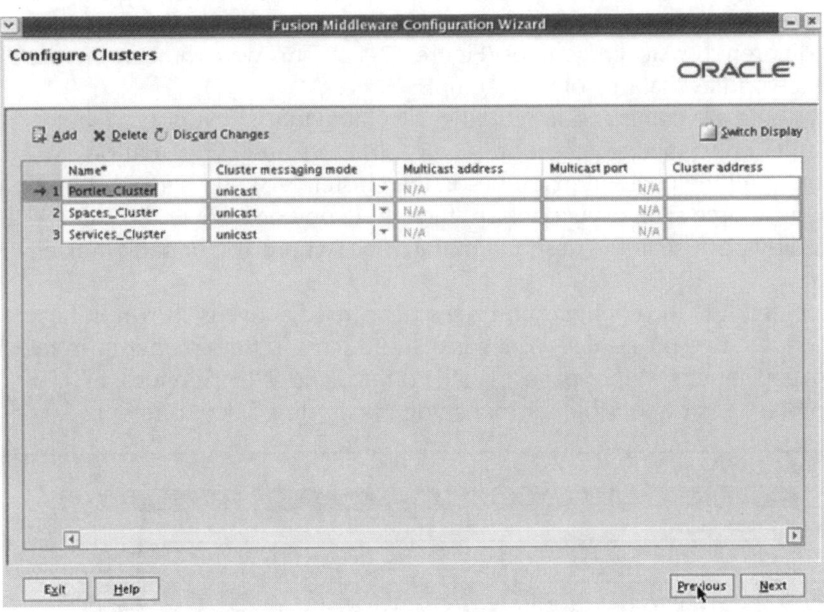

FIGURE 17-10 *Configuration Wizard: creating clusters*

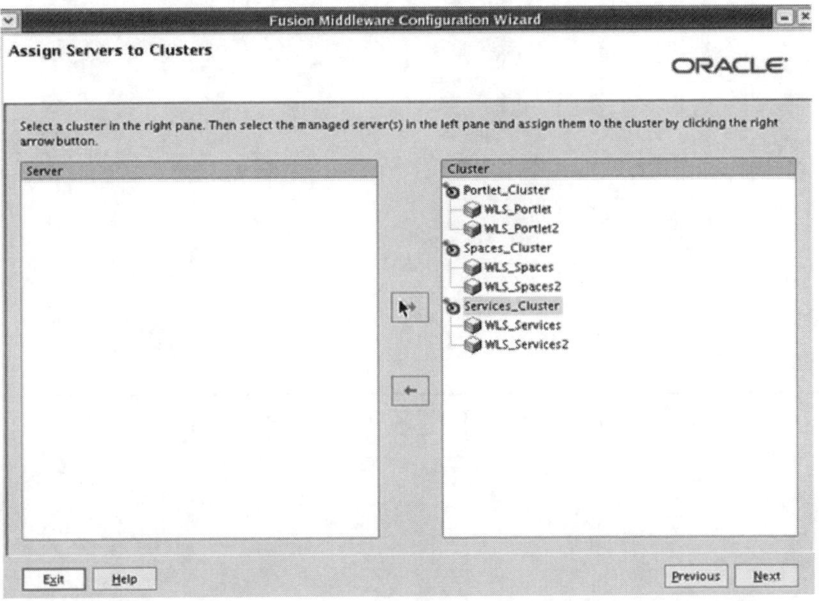

FIGURE 17-11 *Configuration Wizard: assigning managed servers to clusters*

You can assign your managed servers to clusters. If you have set up a clustered topology, you want to spread out your managed servers belonging to the same cluster to different physical machines (Figure 17-12). This way you can increase the resilience and availability of your setup.

Finally, there are command-line utilities available to assist you in packing, copying, and unpacking the domain directory structure and configuration information to all the physical machines in the cluster. First you perform the pack action on the source side, using pack.sh, then you copy or ftp over the JAR file that was created by pack.sh to the destination machine, where you unpack it using unpack.sh.

The end result of the configuration steps performed above is shown in Figure 17-13. There are two physical servers, Host 1 and Host 2. Both of them run the three managed servers, WLS_Spaces, WLS_Portlets, and WLS_Services, as well as a Node Manager, responsible for managing the clustered environment.

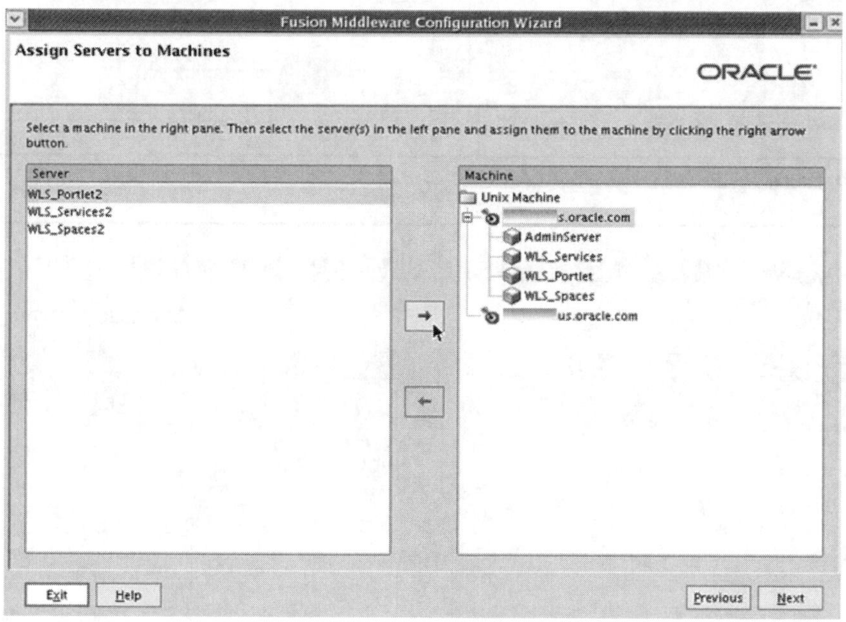

FIGURE 17-12 *Assigning managed servers to physical servers*

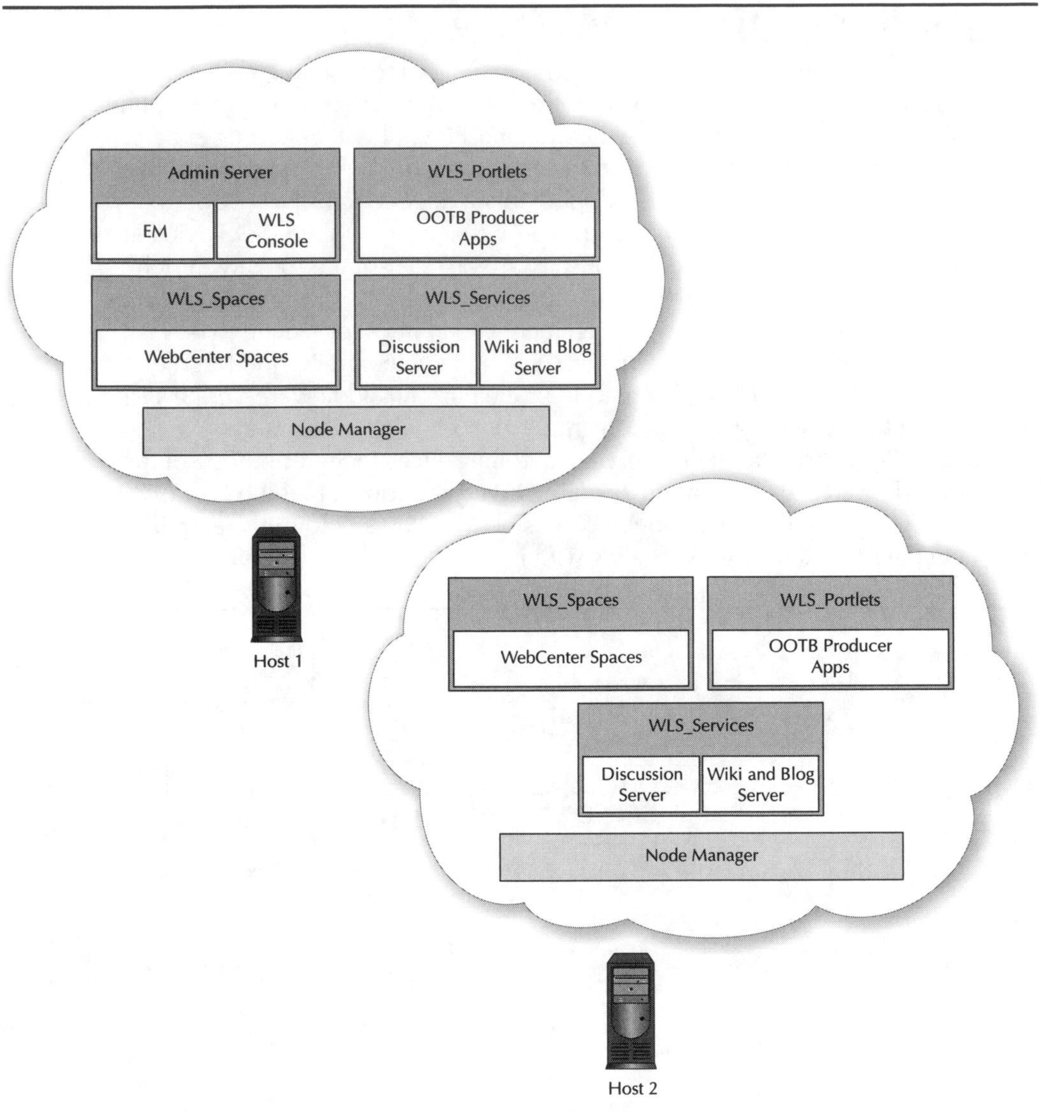

FIGURE 17-13 *A clustered WebCenter topology*

Managing Oracle WebCenter

The Fusion Middleware provides a very comprehensive tool set that assists you in managing and configuring your middleware installation. The WebLogic Scripting Tool (WLST), as its name suggests, is a command-line utility that comes in handy when you want to automate administrative processes such as startup, shutdown, and backup. The Fusion Middleware Control (often referred to as FMW Control, or called by its "umbrella name": Oracle Enterprise Manager) and the WebLogic Server Administration Console (WebLogic Console) are browser-based tools with rich graphical user interface, designed for interactive operations. While the WebLogic Console offers very sophisticated management capabilities, especially when it comes to managing the WebLogic Server, Oracle identified the Fusion Middleware Control as the strategic management tool for the Fusion Middleware. In the 11*g* release the FMW Control is tightly integrated with Oracle WebCenter.

Figure 17-14 shows a quick overview and introduces the terminology of the Fusion Middleware Control. For the first-time user it may appear a little convoluted, but it is a very powerful tool. If you are a Fusion Middleware administrator, it definitely pays to become good friends with it.

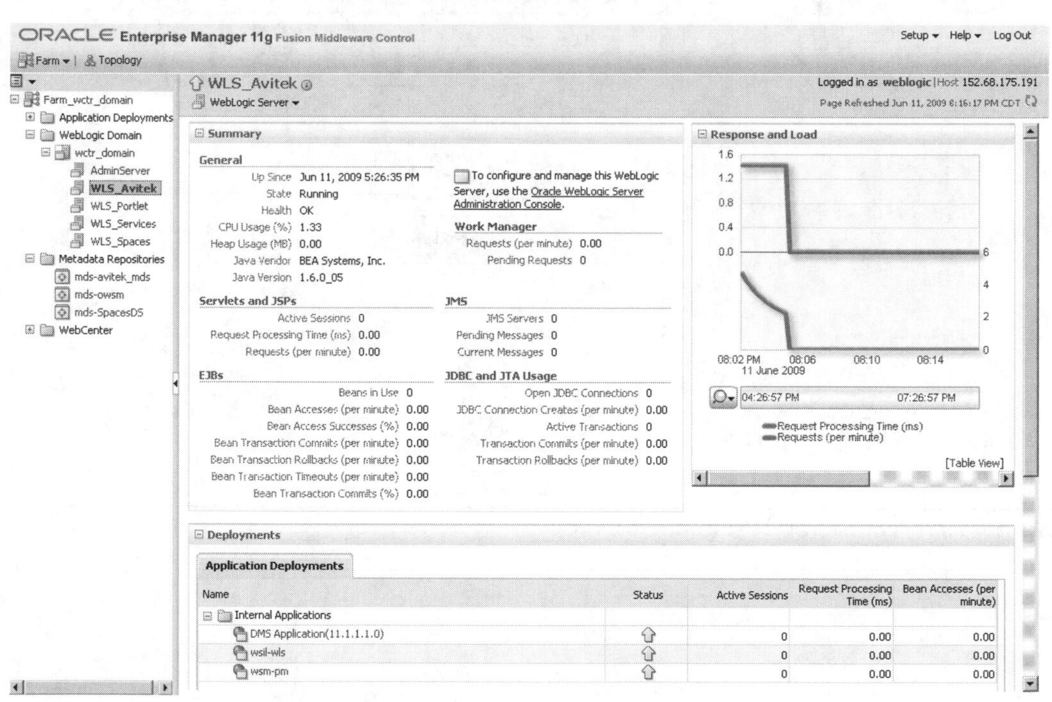

FIGURE 17-14 *Overview of the Fusion Middleware Control*

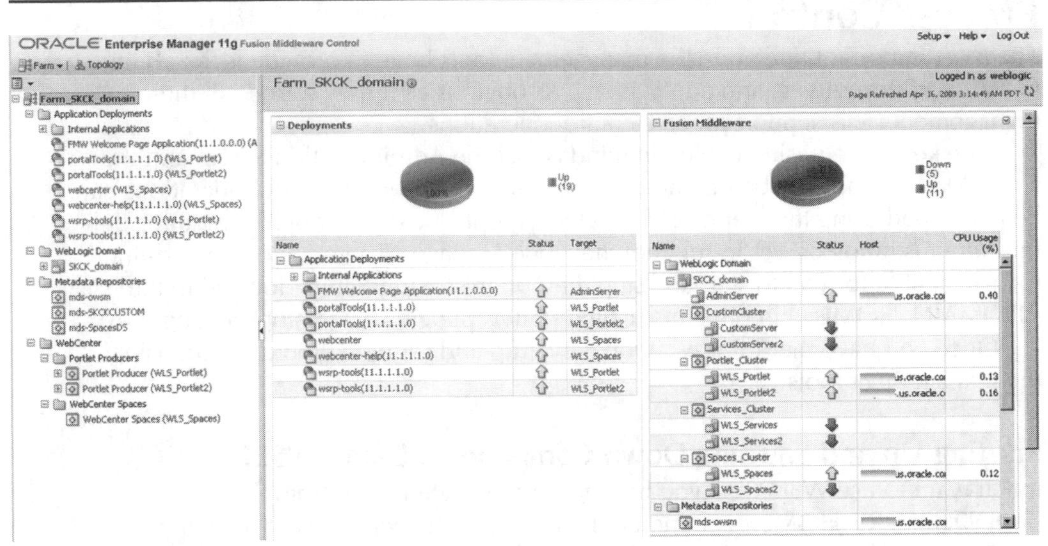

FIGURE 17-15 *Domain, clusters, servers, and deployed applications presented by the Fusion Middleware Control*

Figure 17-15 demonstrates how you can get an overall view of your domain, how the clusters and the servers are laid out, and what their status is.

In Figure 17-16 you get an idea of the other GUI-based management tool, the WebLogic Console.

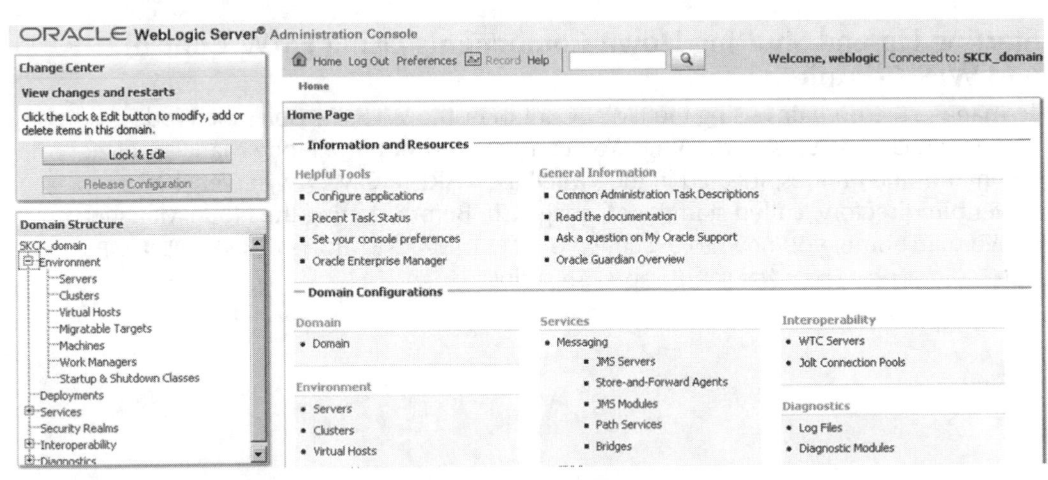

FIGURE 17-16 *The WebLogic Console*

Process Control

The most important operation the management tools have to provide is the ability to start and stop servers and applications. As obvious as it may sound, all three management tools support process control operations.

One key prerequisite to keep in mind is that the Administration Server and the Node Manager have to be up and running before the process control operations can be performed using the graphical UI. WLST is sophisticated enough; it requires only the Administration Server to run, not the Node Manager. There are command-line tools available for you to start and stop the Administration Server, located in the <DOMAIN_HOME>/bin directory, called startWebLogic.sh and stopWebLogic.sh.

Once you have the Administration Server up and running, you can start using the management tools.

Starting Up and Shutting Down Components Using WSLT

If you want to use WSLT, first you have to start the WSLT shell from the <MIDDLEWARE_HOME>/common/bin directory, by executing wslt.sh.

Then, you have to connect to your server by issuing the following command:

```
wls:offline> connect()
```

You will be prompted to enter the server URL, the administrative username, and password.

When you're connected, you can issue the WSLT command to start your server. For example:

```
wls:/WCHB_domain/serverConfig> start('WLS_Portlet', 'Server', block='false')
```

Starting Up and Shutting Down Components Using FMW Control and WLS Console

To manage the domains using the FMW Control or the WLS Console, the Node Manager has to be up and running. You can start and stop the Node Manager using command-line utilities, located in the <MIDDLEWARE_HOME>/wlserver_10.3/server/bin directory, called startNodeManager.sh. Before starting the Node Manager the very first time, you need to execute the `<MIDDLEWARE_HOME>/<WEBCENTER-HOME>/common/bin/setNMProps.sh` script.

You can use the following URLs to access the web user interface of the two management tools:

- FMW Control: http://<ADMIN_HOST>:<ADMIN_PORT>/em
- WLS Console: http://<ADMIN_MOST>:<ADMIN_PORT>/console

The default administration port is 7001, unless changed during installation.

In the FMW Control, you can click any target, including applications, servers, clusters, and portlet producers, shown in Figure 17-15, which take you to specific target pages, containing the Start and Stop options.

For example, when you click on WLS_WebCenter target, the page in Figure 17-17 comes up. It shows the target selected in the navigation pane, on the left: WLS_WebCenter. From the Target menu, you can select WebLogic Server | Control | Start Up.

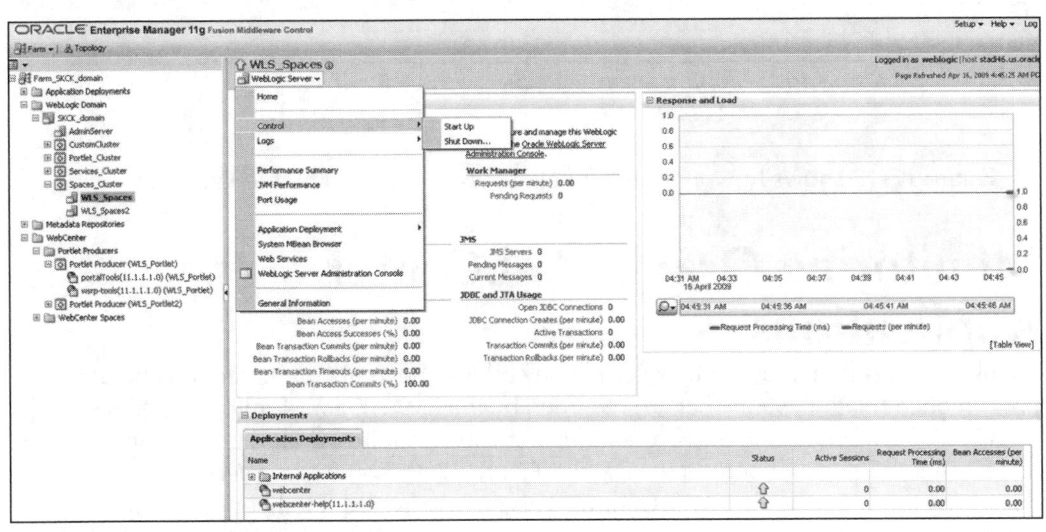

FIGURE 17-17 *Starting and stopping a server using FMW Control*

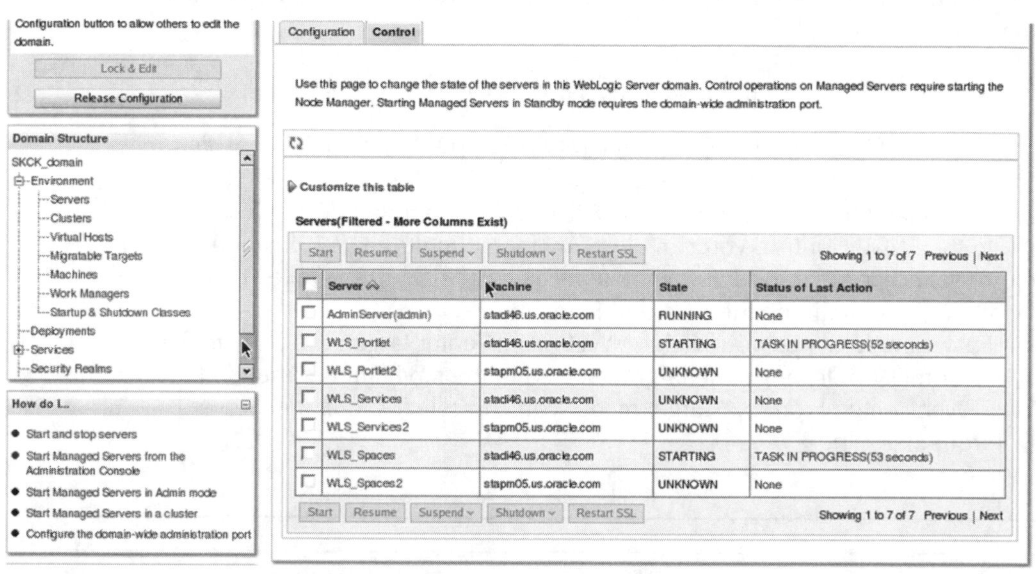

FIGURE 17-18 *Starting and stopping a server using the WLS Console*

Figure 17-18 shows how the same functionality is surfaced by the WLS Console.

Monitoring Oracle WebCenter Applications

Thanks to the fact that the WebCenter Framework has been instrumented to generate performance-related events that are recorded by the FMW Data Monitoring Service (DMS), all WebCenter applications are automatically monitored, and performance intelligence is collected behind the scenes. Figure 17-19 shows the WebCenter Spaces metrics page in the FMW Control. This page provides intelligence about commonly used links, average page response time, slowest group spaces, top accessed group spaces, as well as average page response times.

When you're clicking the More Info link in the Most Active Group Spaces component, located on the right in Figure 17-19, you are taken to a page shown in Figure 17-20. This page shows a table of the most active group spaces on the top, sorted by the number of invocations. All charts on the page show different metrics for the same set of group spaces.

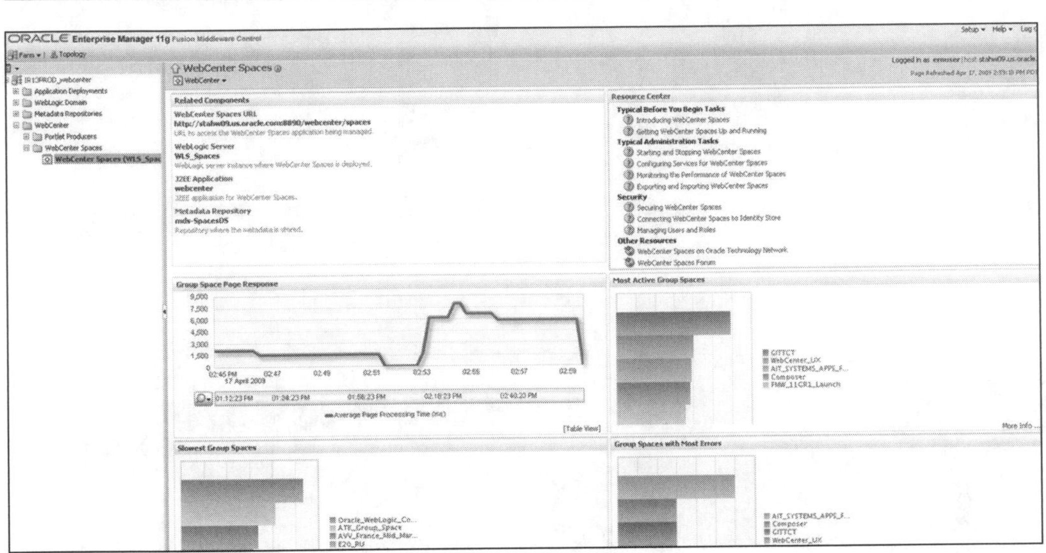

FIGURE 17-19 *The WebCenter Spaces metrics page in the FMW Control*

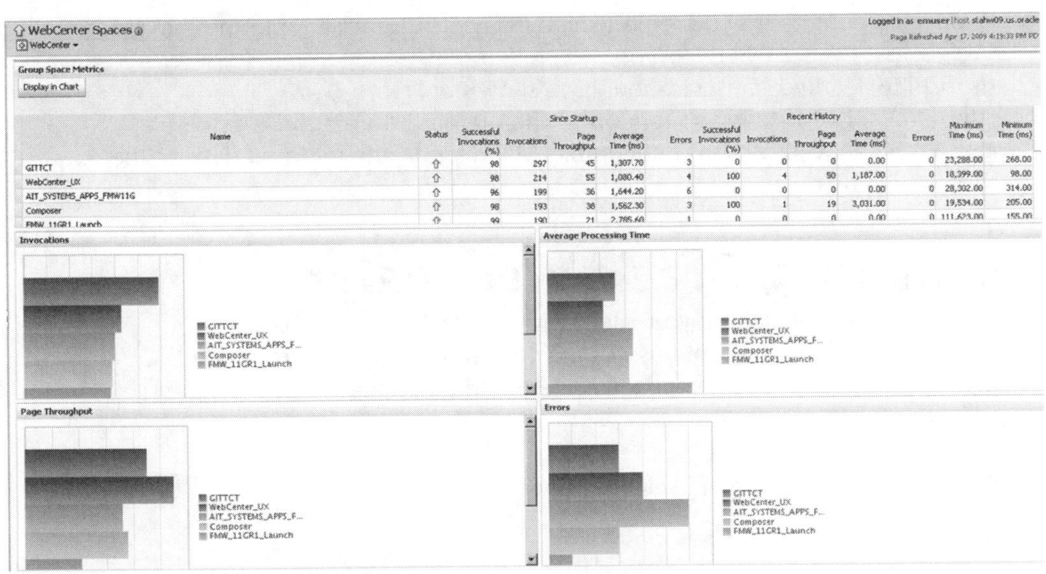

FIGURE 17-20 *The WebCenter Group Space metrics page in the FMW Control*

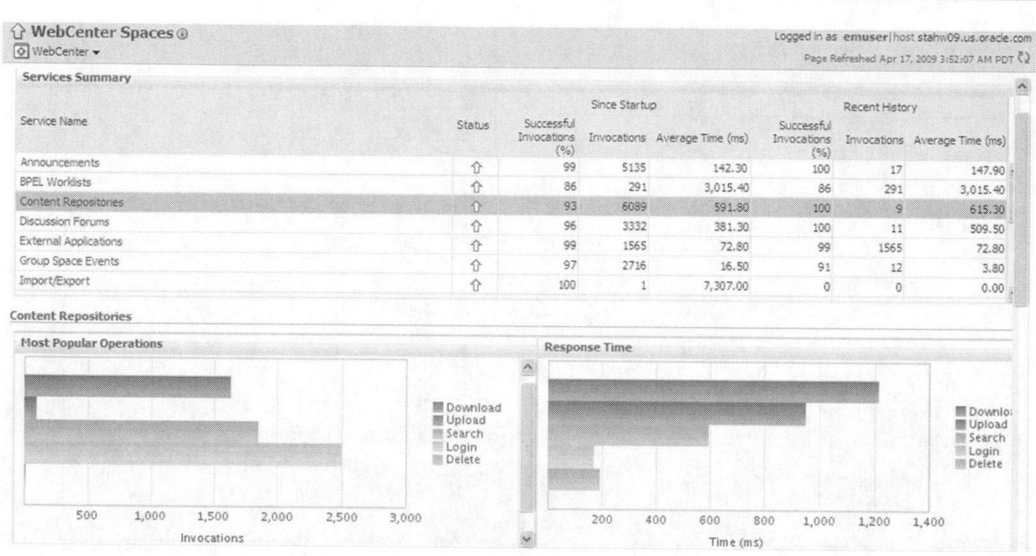

Service Name	Status	Since Startup: Successful Invocations (%)	Since Startup: Invocations	Since Startup: Average Time (ms)	Recent History: Successful Invocations (%)	Recent History: Invocations	Recent History: Average Time (ms)
Announcements		99	5135	142.30	100	17	147.90
BPEL Worklists		86	291	3,015.40	86	291	3,015.40
Content Repositories		93	6089	591.80	100	9	615.30
Discussion Forums		96	3332	381.30	100	11	509.50
External Applications		99	1565	72.80	99	1565	72.80
Group Space Events		97	2716	16.50	91	12	3.80
Import/Export		100	1	7,307.00	0	0	0.00

FIGURE 17-21 *Service-specific metrics presented by the FMW Control*

The FMW Control provides high-level overview or summary information about the WebCenter Web 2.0 Services too. When you're selecting a specific service, the charts display detailed statistics about it, as shown in Figure 17-21.

All of the above-discussed monitoring and metrics information is available through WLST as well. While configurable, WLST prints the returned data on the WLST console, by default.

Configuring Oracle WebCenter

After a successful installation, you often want to tweak your environment by changing the configuration options. All the configuration data is stored and managed by MDS. The most frequently performed configuration options are the following:

- Managing WebCenter Web 2.0 Services
- Managing MDS Repositories
- Remote Portlet Producer Registration

It's important to note that most of the configurations described in this section require you to restart the affected nodes. Exceptions are portlet producer registration and de-registration, as well as external application configuration.

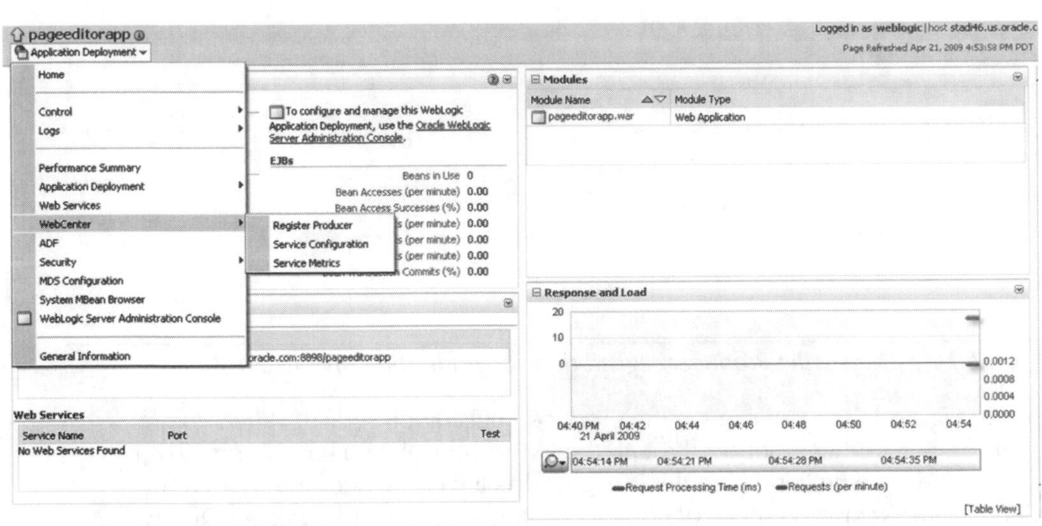

FIGURE 17-22 *Accessing the WebCenter custom application configuration options in the FMW Control*

To configure a custom WebCenter application, navigate to the application home page in FMW Control as shown in Figure 17-22. From the Target menu select WebCenter, and choose either of the two configuration options: Producer Registration or Service Configuration.

Figure 17-23 shows how the individual services can be configured one by one. The service in our example is Oracle Content Server.

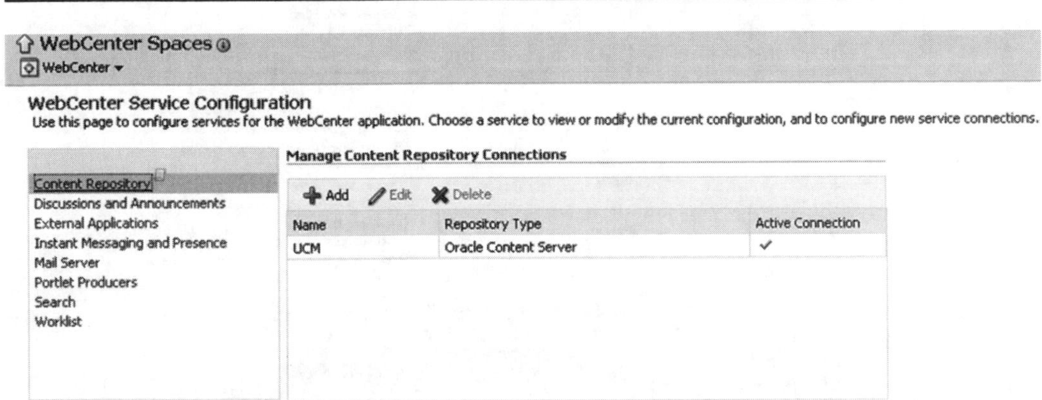

FIGURE 17-23 *Configuring WebCenter Web 2.0 Services using the FMW Control*

FIGURE 17-24 *The Portlet Producer registration screen in the FMW Control*

In Figure 17-24 you can see the producer registration screen. When you're registering a portlet producer through the FMW Control, you have to provide a name, specify whether the portlet is exposed as a web services through Web Services for Remote Portlets (WSRP) or the Oracle proprietary remote PDK-Java protocol, and last but most importantly, provide the producer registration endpoint URL.

Accessing Diagnostics Information

A less frequently used but just as important feature of the FMW Control is that it makes log information easily available to administrators. To access the logging data, choose Logs | View Log Messages from the Target menu, as shown in Figure 17-25.

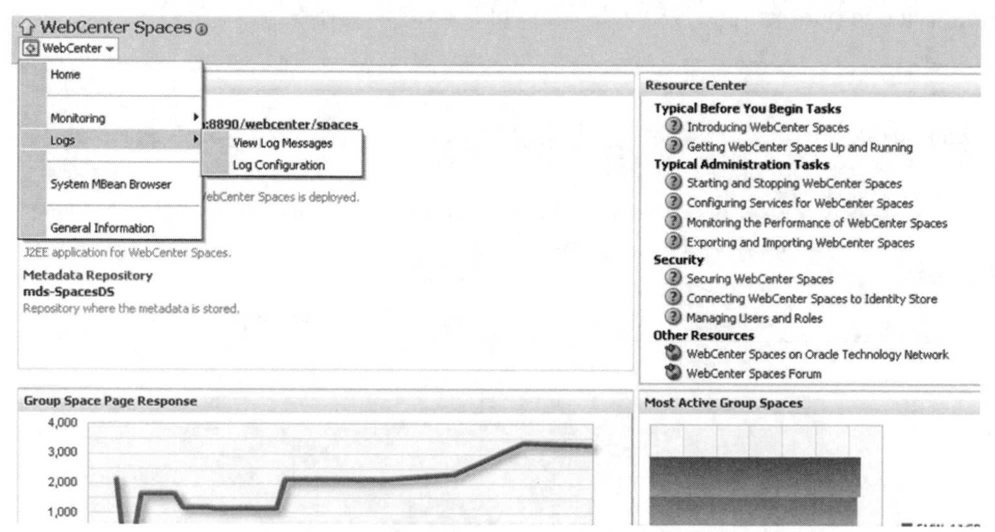

FIGURE 17-25 *Accessing the Log Messages screen in the FMW Control*

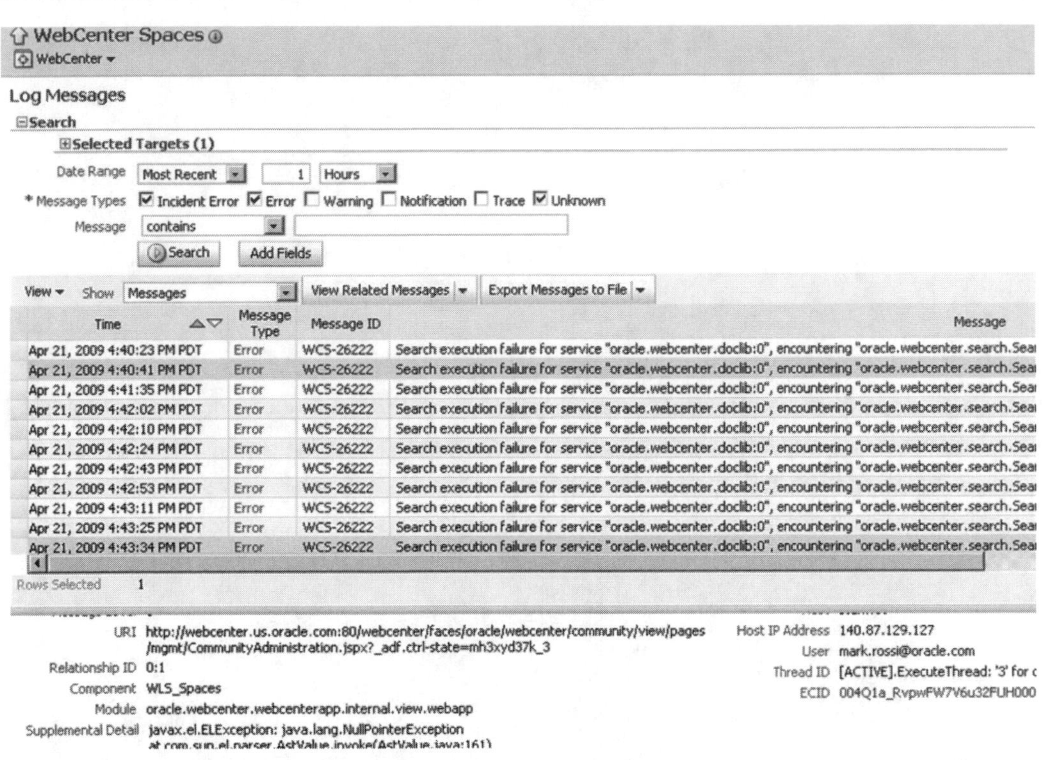

FIGURE 17-26 *The Log Messages screen in the FMW Control*

The Log Messages screen is made up of three parts, shown in Figure 17-26. The top part allows you to specify a search criterion. The middle part displays the search results in a tabular format. The bottom part displays detailed information about the log message or messages selected in the middle part.

To stop and start UCM, execute the `<UCM_HOME>/etc/idcserver_stop` and `<UCM_HOME>/etc/idcserver_stop` commands.

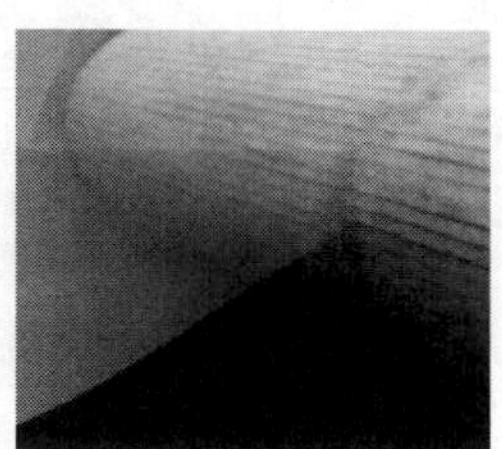

CHAPTER 18

Security

nside organizations, application security is often overlooked because of heterogeneous technology environments, organizational complexity, and limited resources.[1] The depth and complexity of security issues is often underestimated, since security can take many forms—it spans applications, information, and networks. This chapter deals mainly with application and information security from a developer's perspective.

Application security is a subset of information security, since all sorts of information exist outside software systems. At the same time, the ultimate goal of all software is to create, manage, and edit information. Thus, the basic principles of information security—confidentiality, integrity, and availability—apply to software systems. Confidentiality means that information can be accessed by authorized individuals only. Integrity signifies that information was not tampered with while being stored, transferred, or edited. It is essential to ensure the authenticity of information, thus enabling the implementation of business processes based on the legal concept of nonrepudiation. Finally, availability means that authorized users must be able to access information in conformity with the applicable service level agreements. Each of these three basic principles defines a set of possible vulnerabilities and external threats that must be identified, then eliminated or at least mitigated.

The Oracle Application Development Framework (ADF), as well as the Java Enterprise Edition standard it is built on, implements several features intended to facilitate the creation of applications that ensure information confidentiality, integrity, and availability. Table 18-1 lists the most important of those features.

Name	Description
Auditing and logging	Auditing is the record of a user's activity throughout her use of the system, while logging concerns itself with system-level events and errors.
Authentication	The aim of authentication is to validate user identity: is user X the person he pretends to be?

TABLE 18-1 *ADF 11g security features*

[1] Ed Moyle, "Why Application Security Is Often Overlooked," *Ecommerce Times,* September 18, 2007, http://www.ecommercetimes.com/story/59368.html. Accessed January 24, 2009.

Name	Description
Authorization	Authorization verifies the user is granted authority to do a specific action on a system resource: is user X allowed to make operation Y on resource Z?
Cryptography	Cryptography is commonly defined as the enciphering and deciphering of messages in secret code.
Exception management	Exceptions, in object-oriented languages such as Java, are messages sent to the language run time that signal a planned or unplanned anomaly. Those can be handled in a variety of ways.
Input and parameter validation	Validation ensures that the syntax, type, and value of specific bits of information are appropriate according to the system's business rules. Input validation guarantees integrity while parameter validation is geared toward availability, since invalid parameters could compromise system operations or even trigger an application-wide crash.

TABLE 18-1 *ADF 11g security features* (continued)

Oracle WebCenter builds on the strengths of ADF Security to preserve the integrity, availability, and confidentiality of user information and customizations. We will now try to understand ADF Security before describing how its features are put to work in Oracle WebCenter.

ADF Security Overview

At its core, ADF Security encapsulates several other APIs and provides integration features with the rest of the ADF framework. ADF Security resides on the top of a security-related technology stack called Oracle Platform Security Services (OPSS), which was introduced in 2008 as a component of Oracle Fusion Middleware 11*g*. The various features of OPSS, in turn, make extensive use of facilities found in Java Standard Edition such as the specification implemented by all Java virtual machines. Figure 18-1 illustrates the relationship between the different technology layers.

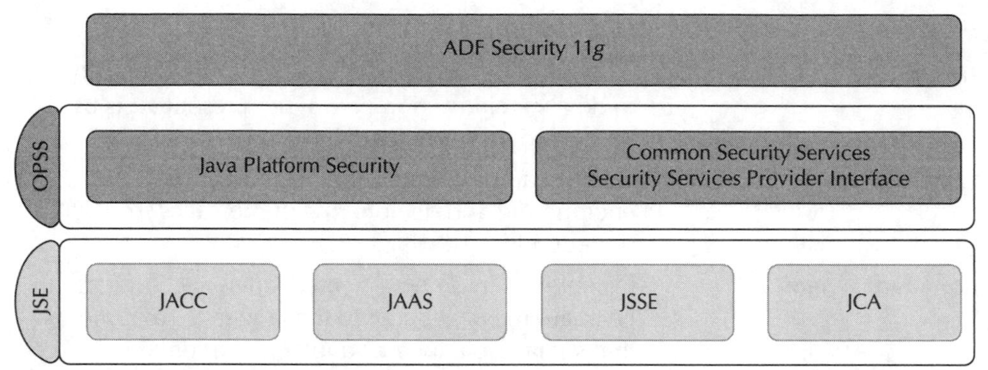

FIGURE 18-1 *Technology dependencies for ADF Security*

Table 18-2 describes each of the components featured in Figure 18-1.

Layer	Name	Description
JSE	Java Cryptography Architecture (JCA)	Built on a provider-based architecture, it offers a set of APIs for digital signatures, message digests (hashes), certificates and certificate validation, encryption, key generation and management, and secure random number generation, among others.[1]
	Java Secure Socket Extensions (JSSE)	Java version of the SSL and TLS protocols. Includes functionality for data encryption, server authentication, message integrity, and client authentication.[2]
	Java Authentication and Authorization Services (JAAS)	Provides authentication and authorization features to the Java Standard Edition platform. Implements the Pluggable Authentication Module (PAM) framework familiar to Linux administrators.[3]
	Java Authorization Contract for Containers (JACC)	Specification that defines classes implementing JEE's authorization requirements.[4]
OPSS	Java Platform Security (JPS)	JPS builds on the JEE permission model (JAAS) and provides granular application-centric authorization.

TABLE 18-2 *Dependencies for ADF Security*

Layer	Name	Description
	Common Security Services (CSS) Security Services Provider Interface (SSPI)	CSS is the set of security services provided for Oracle WebLogic Server, while SSPI enables implementation of pluggable security providers designed to plug into CSS.
ADF	ADF Security	Provides an integrated set of security features to other parts of the ADF. Exploits CSS for authentication and JPS for authorization.

[1] See http://java.sun.com/javase/6/docs/technotes/guides/security/crypto/CryptoSpec.html for details.

[2] See http://java.sun.com/javase/6/docs/technotes/guides/security/jsse/JSSERefGuide.html for details.

[3] See http://java.sun.com/javase/6/docs/technotes/guides/security/jaas/JAASRefGuide.html for details.

[4] See http://java.sun.com/j2ee/javaacc/ for details.

TABLE 18-2 *Dependencies for ADF Security* (continued)

A thorough exploration of all the APIs and technologies mentioned above would warrant a book on its own. We will now focus on the security-related tasks commonly accomplished by ADF developers.

Securing an ADF Application

At its core, ADF Security is an implementation of the Role Based Access Control (RBAC) model. Proposed in 1992[2] by David F. Ferraiolo and D. Richard Kuhn of the National Institute of Standards and Technology, a nonregulatory agency of the U.S. Department of Commerce, it is now a widely used approach. RBAC can be boiled down to three fundamental rules:

1. A subject can execute a transaction only if he or she selected or was assigned to an application role. Thus, all active users must belong to an active role except for login (authentication) purposes.
2. The subject must be authorized to take his or her active role.
3. Roles must be authorized to execute specific transactions; users can execute only the transactions their role is authorized to.

[2] David F. Ferraiolo and D. Richard Kuhn, "Role-Based Access Controls," *15th National Computer Security Conference*, Baltimore, 1992, pp. 554–563.

But how are these implemented in ADF Security? In order to answer this question, we must map the ADF concepts to their RBAC equivalents.

- **Subjects** In ADF, this can be either a user or a group. In Oracle's nomenclature, groups are called *enterprise roles,* since they are often managed through the organization's directory (typically Oracle's own OID, Microsoft Active Directory, or another LDAP-compliant server). Do not confuse these subjects with JAAS subjects.
- **Roles** These correspond to the ADF application roles. Application roles can be organized in a hierarchy, since one role can be listed as another role's subject. By default, ADF defines two standard application roles: anonymous-role and authenticated-role. Using those, you can easily make pages available to all users, or you can restrict access to logged-in users.
- **Authorization** ADF uses the concept of permission to materialize subject authorization. It separates the declaration of the possible permissions from the actual permission grants. The declaration is made through a Java permission class, which we will study in greater detail later on. This class contains a list of operations (transactions) subjects can have the permission to execute. Grants, on the other hand, possess their own name and contain both the fully qualified name of the permission class and the list of authorized operations.

ADF applications define a number of stores where all security-related information is kept. The *identity* store is dedicated to users and enterprise roles. The *policy* store is where all permission grants are kept. The *credential* store encrypts the passwords or other credentials needed at run time. There is also a *key* store available; it is used for digital certificates and encryption keys. All the stores can be either file- or LDAP-based; the latter option requires the use of Oracle Internet Directory (OID) or Oracle Virtual Directory (OVD). LDAP-based stores are useful in clustered deployments and do not necessarily require you to buy additional software, since Oracle WebLogic Server's built-in LDAP server is a simplified version of OID.

The process of securing an ADF application includes four distinct tasks. First, it is necessary to run the ADF Security wizard in order to have Oracle JDeveloper 11*g* configure the application's XML descriptors to enable security. Second, developers have to specify at least users and application roles by editing the jazn-data.xml file. Third, access rights must be granted explicitly on JSF pages and task flows. Finally, ADF BC Entity Objects can be secured as well, if needed. We will now give step-by-step instructions for each of the tasks.

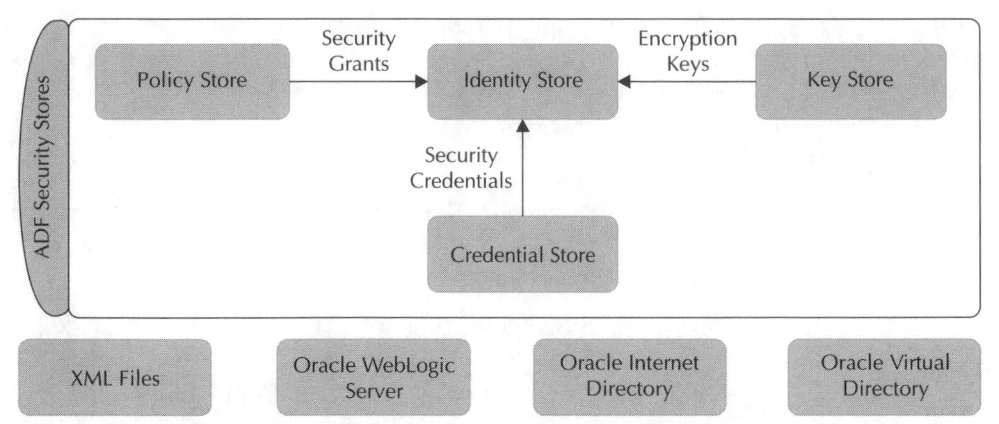

FIGURE 18-2 *ADF Security stores*

ADF Security Wizard

The aim of the ADF Security wizard is to enforce authentication and authorization in the application. In order to achieve this, it will modify several XML files. Table 18-3 below lists the descriptors involved as well as the nature of the modifications made.

File	Modification
adf-config.xml	Declaration of the JAAS security context. Authentication and permission checking enforcement.
jazn-data.xml	Default realm for the file-based identity store.
jps-config.xml	OPSS context for the credential and policy stores.
web.xml	Login configuration. Definition of an ADF authorization HTTP filter (*JpsFilter*). Declaration and configuration of the ADF authentication servlet (*adfAuthentication*).

TABLE 18-3 *Security Descriptors Altered by the ADF Security Wizard*

To launch the wizard, open the Application menu in Oracle JDeveloper 11*g* and select the Configure ADF Security option in the Security submenu. Users of Oracle JDeveloper versions prior to 11*g* R1 (11.1.1.1.0) will notice Application is a new menu option, as the security wizard was found in the Tools menu before. Figure 18-3 shows the wizard's initial screen.

The three possible options are

- **ADF Authentication and Authorization** This enables the most comprehensive set of security features and is the default option. We assume this option was selected for the remainder of this chapter.
- **ADF Authentication** Enables authentication only. You will have to provide your own authorization mechanisms. JAAS could be a great starting point. However, you would forgo several productivity aids found in the IDE.
- **Remove ADF Security Configuration** Will disable security features. Alterations you make to the identity and policy stores will be preserved.

Once your choice was made, click the Next button. The Select Authentication Type screen shown in Figure 18-4 will be displayed.

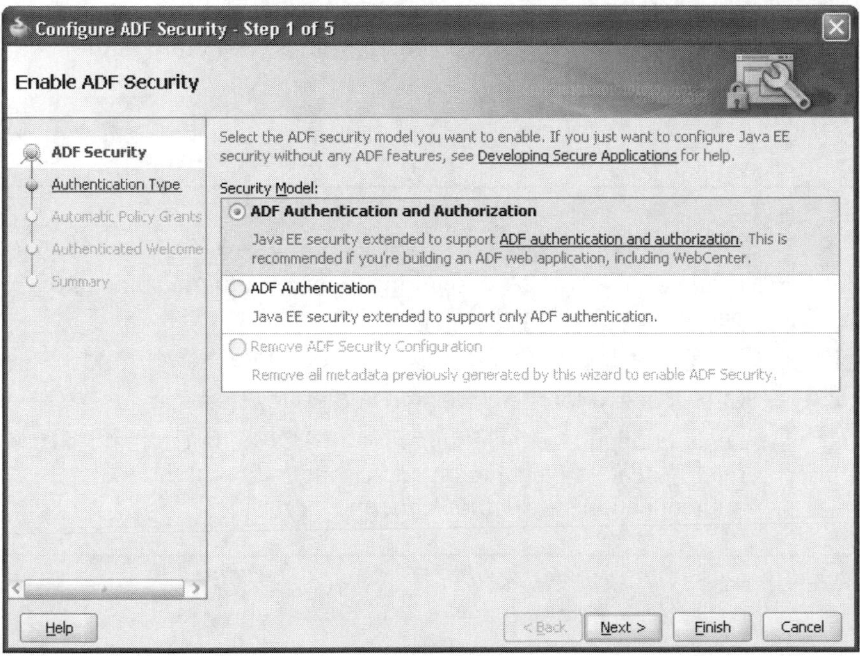

FIGURE 18-3 *ADF Security wizard initial screen*

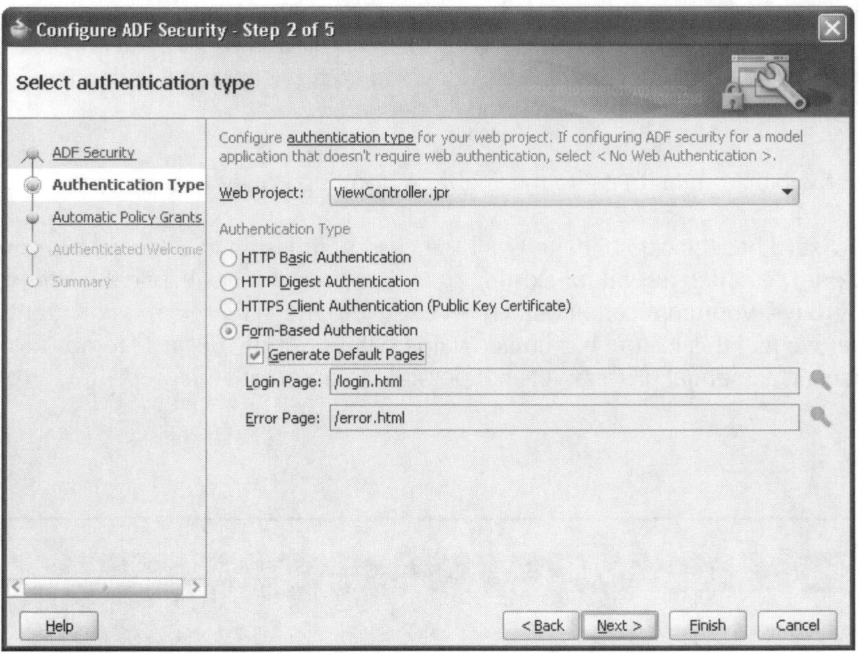

FIGURE 18-4 *ADF Security wizard: authentication type screen*

There are four possibilities here, all of them being mandated by the Java Enterprise Edition specification:

- **HTTP Basic** The browser will display a dialog box asking for an ID and password if the user is not authenticated. This is simple to deploy, but not very secure as the password is sent in clear text.
- **HTTP Digest** Requests an MD5 digest of the password to the user browser for authentication purposes. Support will be dependent on the browser and Java Web Container used, since implementation is optional in the specification. This option is supported by Oracle WebLogic Server, but not commonly used.
- **HTTP Client Authentication** The user browser must present a valid public key client certificate to the server. This is very secure but cumbersome, since the certificate must be deployed on user workstations.
- **Form-Based** The user ID and password will be sent to the server by a web page. This method is as weak as HTTP Basic by itself. Use of the

Secure Sockets Layer (SSL) or Transport Layer Security (TLS) protocols make form-based authentication a compelling option, since all communications between the browser and the server are encrypted, thus guaranteeing password confidentiality. Oracle JDeveloper can generate default pages for login and authentication errors, if needed.

Click the Next button to get to the Enable Automatic Policy Grants screen (Figure 18-5).

The wizard has the capability to grant the view permission to a special-purpose application role called test-all for existing or even future objects. While this could be useful to test your application quickly, even before the actual permission grants are made, we feel this feature has limited value. Why? Mainly because removal of those grants is a manual process; it is not possible to automate the procedure. We

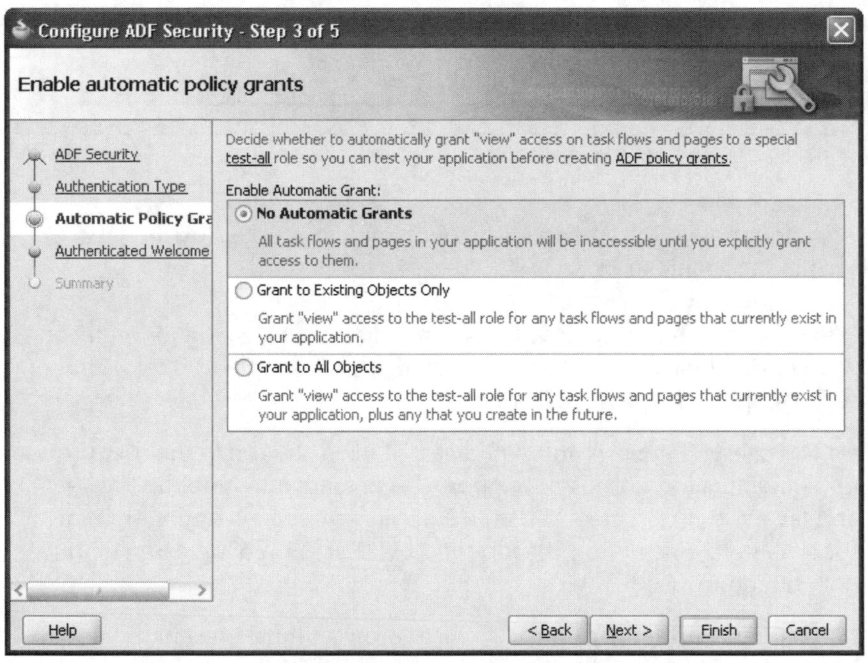

FIGURE 18-5 *ADF Security wizard: Enable policy grants screen*

also think that security is an integral part of a use case's design and that application code will be more robust if all permissions are defined explicitly. For these reasons, we recommend you select the No Automatic Grants option. Click on the Next button to advance to the next step.

The Specify Authenticated Welcome Page screen, pictured in Figure 18-6, is optional.

If you check the Redirect Upon Successful Authentication checkbox, you will need to select an existing page that will serve as the application's welcome page. This means users will be redirected to that page after they log in even if the URL they requested is a different one. You can elect to have the wizard create a default welcome page.

Another click on the Next button will bring you to the last step of the wizard: the Summary page. As you can see in Figure 18-7, it recapitulates the selections you made and lists every XML descriptor impacted by them.

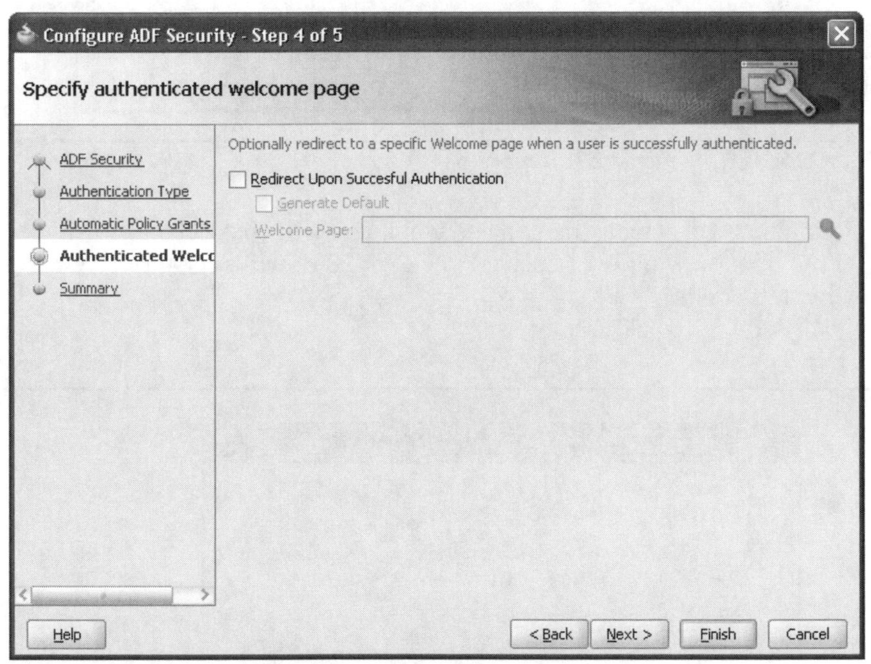

FIGURE 18-6 *ADF Security wizard: specify authenticated welcome page*

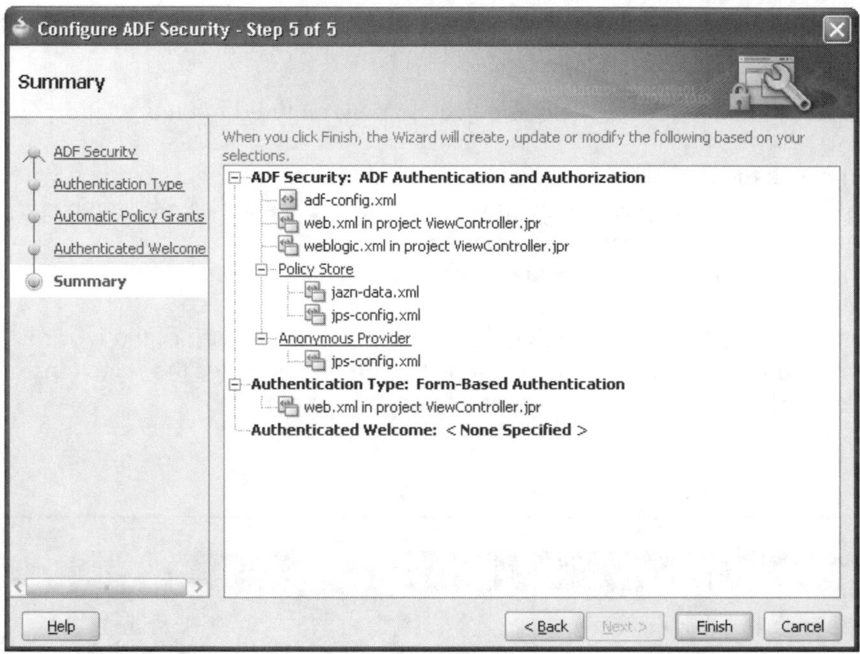

FIGURE 18-7 *ADF Security wizard: summary page*

The descriptors will actually be updated when you will click on the Finish button. A confirmation window, displayed in Figure 18-8, will appear once Oracle JDeveloper will be done.

Simply click on OK to close it.

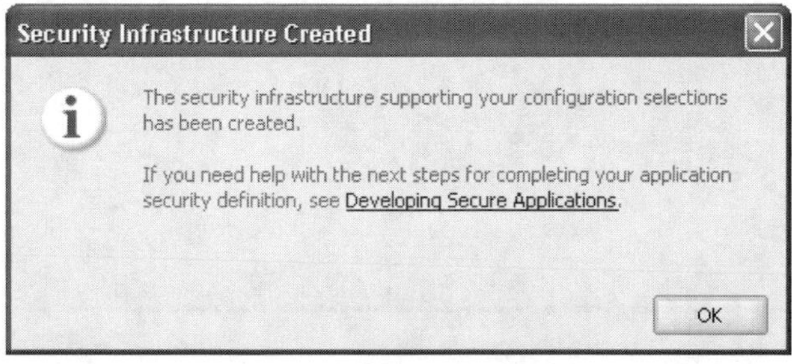

FIGURE 18-8 *ADF Security wizard: confirmation dialog*

jazn-data.xml

If you run the application at this point, you will not be able to log in. This is because the identity and credential stores are empty. In order to populate them, you must edit the jazn-data.xml file. There are a few ways to access it, but the most common is to right-click on the file in the Application Resources panel of Oracle JDeveloper's Application Navigator and select the Properties option in the contextual menu. The file is managed through a specific dialog window, shown in Figure 18-9.

The dialog's Structure panel, located on the left, makes it easy to work on the various sections of the file. To manage users and groups (enterprise roles), simply highlight the appropriate option under the Identity Store label. The user list is pictured above. To create or remove a user, simply use the buttons located on the right of the list.

The JPS Identity & Policy Store dialog makes the difference between enterprise and application roles very clear, since the latter are located under the Application Policy Store label. The user interface employed to manage the application roles is straightforward, as illustrated in Figure 18-10.

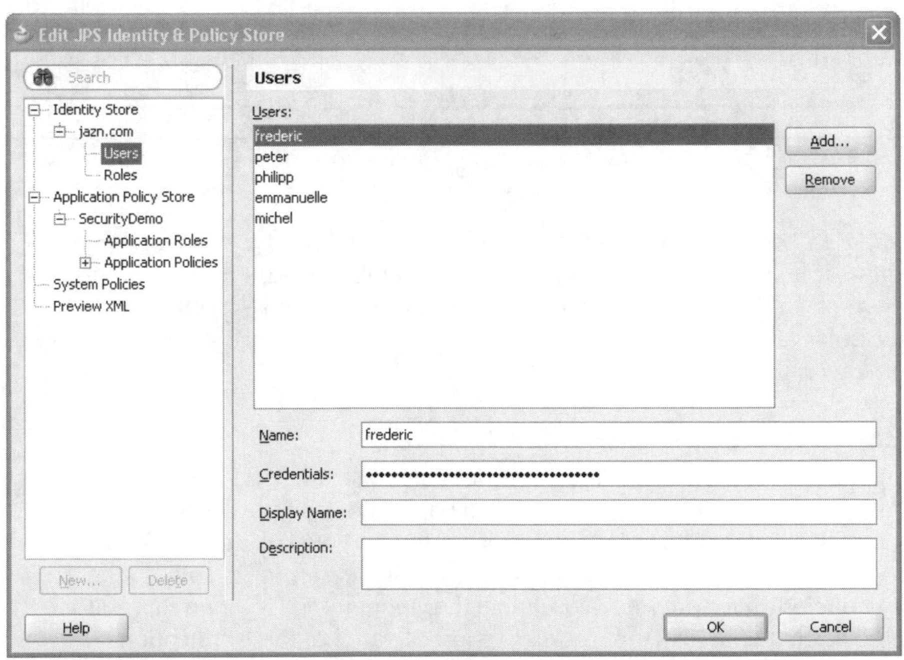

FIGURE 18-9 *JPS Identity & Policy Store dialog: users*

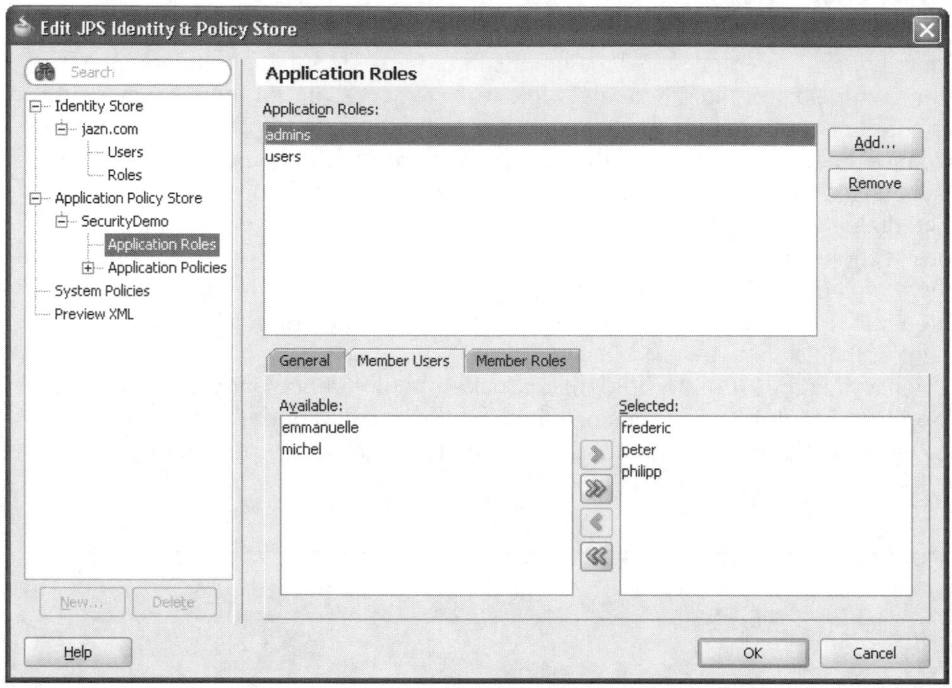

FIGURE 18-10 *JPS Identity & Policy Store dialog: application roles*

In order to add subjects to an application role, highlight it in the list, then use the shuttles available in the Member Users and Member Roles tabs in order to specify which subjects belong to the application role. Please keep in mind the Member Roles tab will list enterprise roles only. Once you're done, simply close the dialog with the OK button.

Pages and Task Flow Permissions

Once application roles are available, it is possible to secure ADF artifacts by creating permission grants. In the case of JSF pages and task flows, this is done by editing the jazn-data.xml file. While it is possible to create such grants manually with the JPS Identity & Policy Store dialog, it is much easier to do so with the ADF Security Policies editor provided by Oracle JDeveloper 11*g*. To open this editor, double-click the file in the Application Resources panel of the Application Navigator. You will obtain a screen similar to the one illustrated in Figure 18-11.

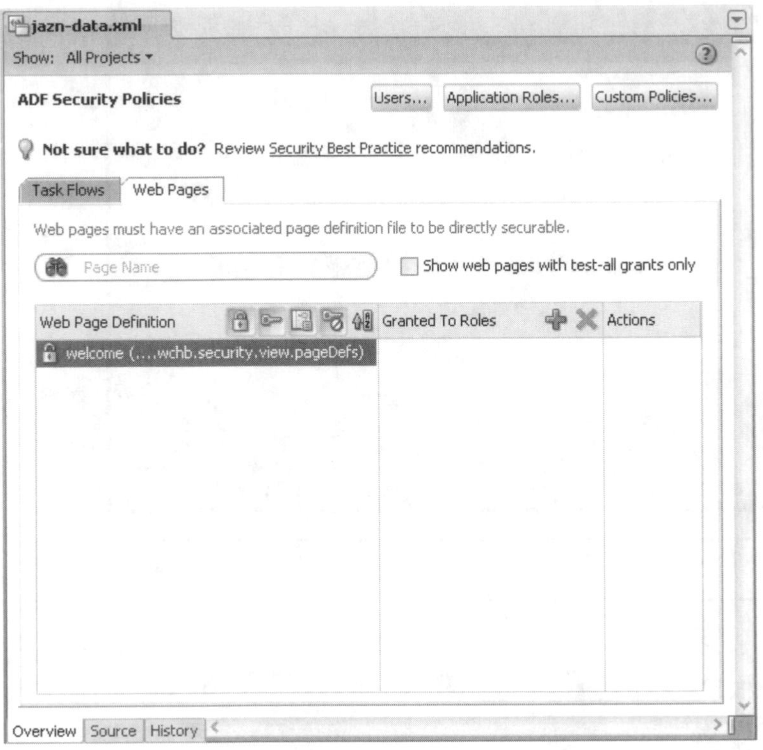

FIGURE 18-11 *ADF Security Policies editor: web pages view*

To secure a JSF page or task flow, select the appropriate tab, then click on the page or task flow in the leftmost column. In Figure 18-11, it is called Web Page Definition. Afterward, simply click on the plus sign found in the Granted To Roles column header. Oracle JDeveloper will present you a dialog, shown in Figure 18-12. It is worth mentioning that only pages associated to a page definition (pageDef) can be secured.

Check a single or several roles, and then click the OK button. You will be returned to the ADF Security Policies editor. The application roles selected will appear in the Granted To Roles column. To specify the authorized actions for a role, highlight the role and, after that, click the appropriate checkboxes in the Actions column. Figure 18-13 illustrates the editor at the end of this process.

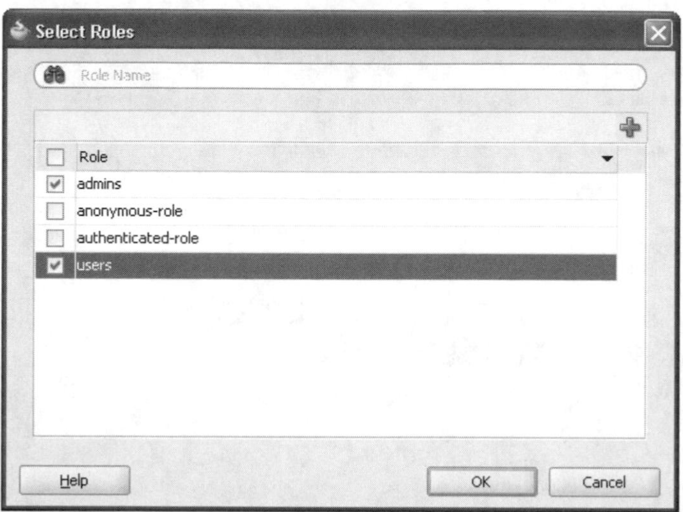

FIGURE 18-12 *Select Roles dialog*

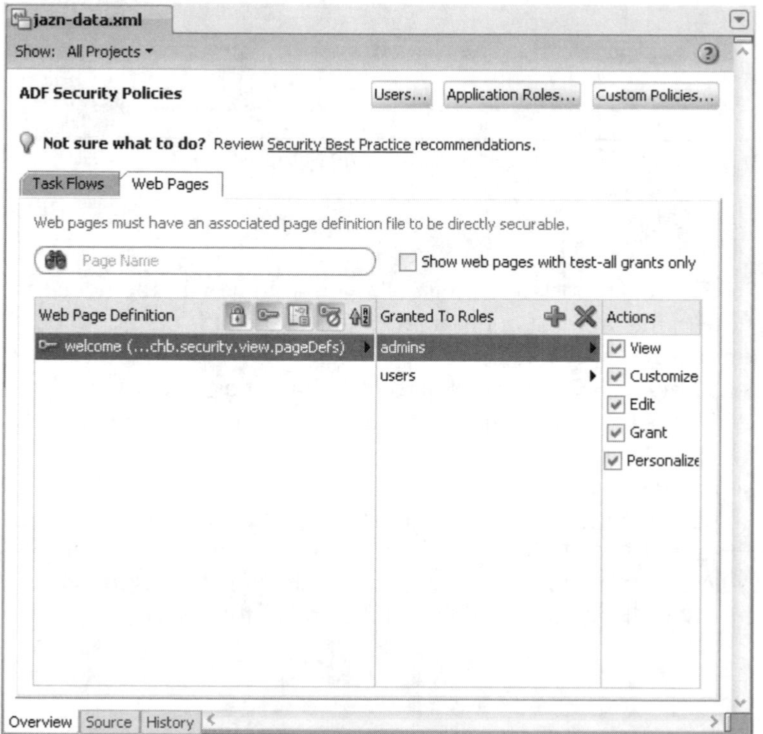

FIGURE 18-13 *ADF Security Policies editor: authorized actions*

Action	Description
Customize	User can apply customizations to the page or task flow.
Edit	In Oracle Composer, user can switch to Edit mode in order to modify the page. This value applies only to pages.
Grant	User has the right to grant the rights he possesses to other users. This is a form of delegation.
Personalize	User can personalize the page or task flow (user scope customization).
View	User can view the page or execute the task flow.

TABLE 18-4 *Actions Defined by the RegionPermission and TaskFlowPermission Classes*

You could ask where the available actions come from. The answer is straightforward: they are defined by the permission classes. In this case, the relevant classes' names are RegionPermission and TaskFlowPermission, respectively used for JSF pages and task flows. Together, those two classes define the actions described in Table 18-4. It must be noted that standard ADF applications support only the view action; all other values are specific to Oracle WebCenter Framework.

The security grants made through the ADF Security Policies editor can also be seen in the JPS Identity & Policy Store dialog, as seen in Figure 18-14.

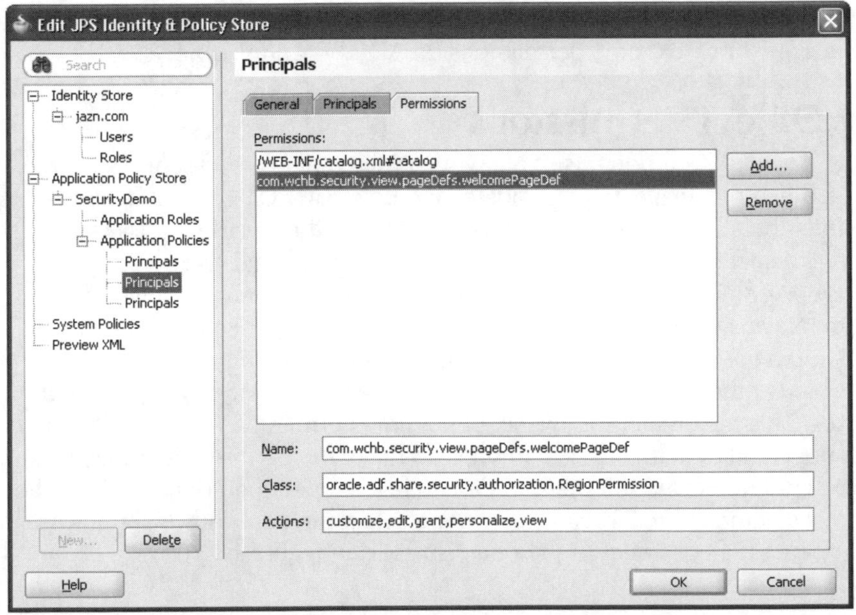

FIGURE 18-14 *JPS Identity & Policy Store dialog: security grants*

As we noted before, the permission is identified by a name and is the combination of the permission class' fully qualified name with the list of authorized actions. This can be seen clearly in jazn-data.xml, since both the ADF Security Policies editor and the JPS Identity & Policy Store dialog are views on this descriptor. The listing below is an extract from that file that matches the contents of Figure 18-14.

```
<grant>
  <grantee>
   <principals>
    <principal>
     <class>oracle.security.jps.service.policystore.ApplicationRole</class>
     <name>admins</name>
    </principal>
   </principals>
  </grantee>
  <permissions>
   ...
   <permission>
    <class>oracle.adf.share.security.authorization.RegionPermission</class>
    <name>com.wchb.security.view.pageDefs.welcomePageDef</name>
    <actions>customize,edit,grant,personalize,view</actions>
   </permission>

   ...
  </permissions>
</grant>
```

Once again, this XML fragment highlights the importance of the permission class in the whole process. But before having a look at the internals of permission classes, we will describe how to define permissions on ADF BC Entity Objects.

Entity Object Permissions

In the ADF Business Components Framework, entity objects represent a specific database table and manage create, update, and delete (CRUD) operations. It is possible to enforce authorization on those operations, thus restricting transaction execution to a specific set of application roles. To achieve this, the first step is to open the selected entity object by double-clicking on it in Oracle JDeveloper's Application Navigator. Afterward, expand the Security group located in the General tab. You should get a screen similar to the one illustrated in Figure 18-15.

Simply select the operations you want to secure by checking the appropriate checkboxes. This merely defines the set of possible permissions on the entity object, and does not result in actual grants. In order to make the permission grants, ensure the desired entity object is still open in Oracle JDeveloper, then right-click on the entity object's name in the Structure panel and select the Edit Authorizations option. This will open a dialog similar to the one displayed in Figure 18-16.

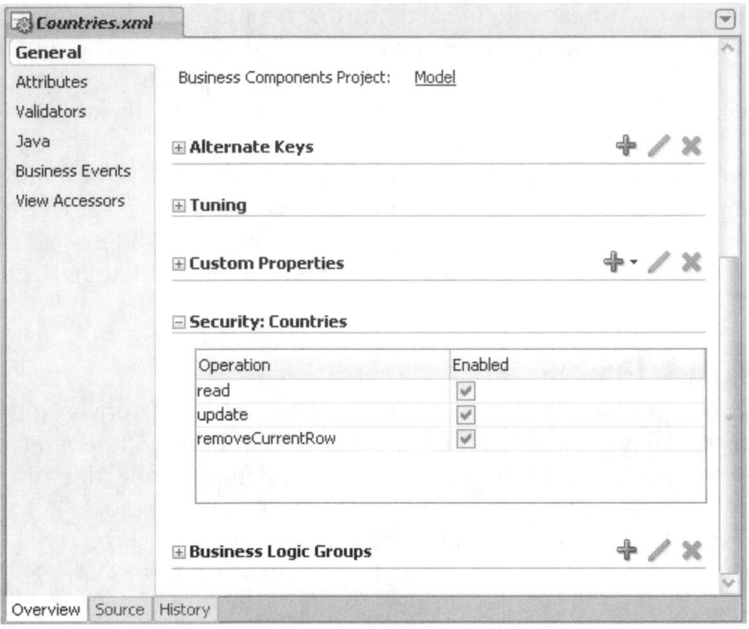

FIGURE 18-15 *Entity Object Security properties*

The dialog is filled with a grid where the columns are the available permissions and the lines present the application roles. To grant permissions, just click the appropriate checkboxes, then close the dialog using the OK button.

Edit Authorization...

Grant privileges to one or more roles.

To Role:

Role	Read	Update	Delete
admins	☑	☑	☑
anonymous-role	☐	☐	☐
authenticated-role	☐	☐	☐
users	☑	☐	☐

Help | OK | Cancel

FIGURE 18-16 *Edit Authorization dialog*

Please note it is also possible to implement authorization on entity object attributes. The process is nearly identical to the one we just described. Attribute authorization covers a single update operation, but is declared and configured in the same way as CRUD row level operations. Please note that entity object permissions are defined in the entity's XML file, and not directly in the jazn-data.xml security descriptor.

At this point, you have secured your pages, task flows, and ADF BC entity objects. There is still a lot of work to do, however. Your application's use cases must handle security exceptions gracefully and ensure users get enough feedback when the transactions they want to execute are denied because of failed authorization controls.

Permission Classes

Permission classes play a central role in ADF Security. Pages, task flows, and entity objects authorization is enforced through them, and ADF ships with several Oracle-provided permission classes. Their responsibility is to define a collection of operations and a scope. Consequently, their structure is quite simple.

The code sample below is a typical custom-built permission class.

```
package com.wchb.security.model.permissions;
...
public class BankChecksPermission extends ADFPermission {
    // This list the possible permissions.
    private static final PermissionActionDescriptor[] actions =
    { new PermissionActionDescriptor("print", "Print Check"),
      new PermissionActionDescriptor("amount", "Change Amount") };

    // This lists the possible targets, e.g. the kind of artefact
    // the permission can be applied to.
    private static final PermissionTargetDescriptor[] targets =
    { new PermissionTargetDescriptor("action", "Method") };

    public BankChecksPermission(String name, String actions) {
        super(name, actions);
    }

    public static PermissionActionDescriptor[]
        getPermissionActionDescriptors() {
            return actions;
    }

    public static PermissionTargetDescriptor[]
        getPermissionTargetDescriptors() {
            return targets;
    }
}
```

The most interesting thing about it is that the permission itself can be applied to a specific set of ADF items: attributes, methods, page definitions, or portlets. The first two obviously concern ADF BC entity objects or custom classes, while the page definition enables use with JSF pages. As for portlets, they represent a type of item that can be added to Oracle Composer's catalog and may be dropped on Oracle WebCenter customizable pages.

Custom permission classes can be useful in several scenarios. But how do you create such a class? Oracle JDeveloper offers a dialog made specifically to handle this task. To invoke it, you must first select the New option in the File menu, then highlight the Security item, located under the Business Tier header, in the Categories panel. You may then select the JAAS Permission in the Items panel and click the OK button. This is displayed in Figure 18-17.

Oracle JDeveloper will display the Create JAAS Permission dialog. The top part is very similar to the standard dialog used to create regular Java classes. The bottom part is specific to permission classes, and enables you to specify the actions and targets for the class. Figure 18-18 shows the dialog.

It must be mentioned that targets are ADF specific, and not part of JAAS. However, the classes produced can be used to enforce any type of authorization check. The class will be created in your project when you click on the OK button. Our sample permission class was built this exact way.

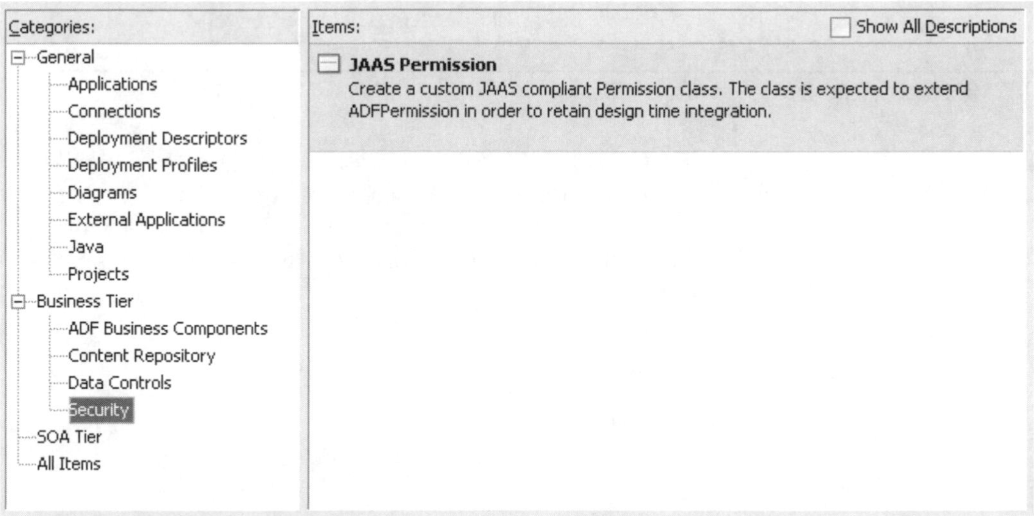

FIGURE 18-17 *Permission class item in the New Gallery dialog*

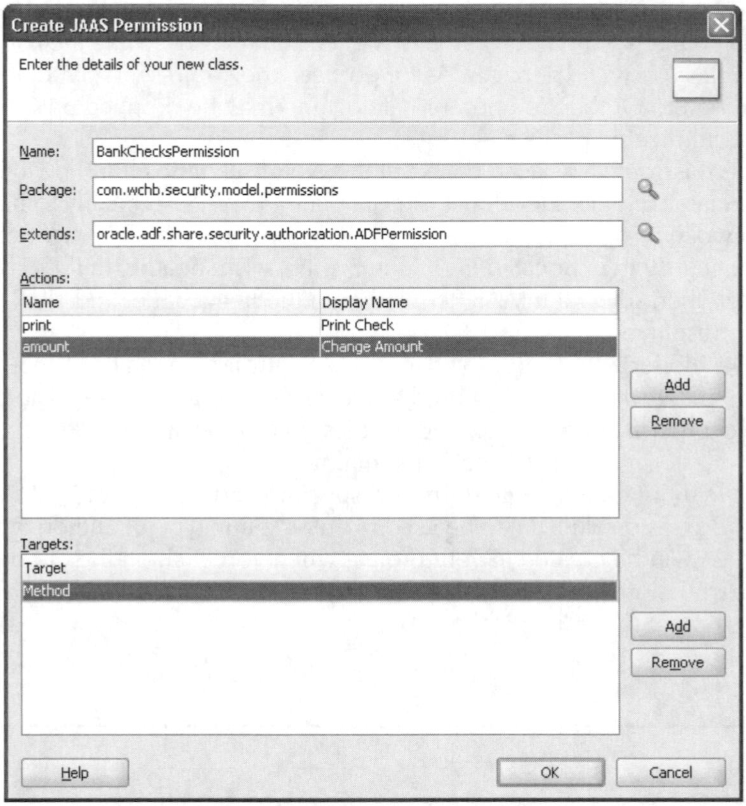

FIGURE 18-18 *Create JAAS Permission dialog*

While ADF makes extensive use of permission classes, it is fairly easy to verify security grants for custom permission classes directly in the code. Typically, this will take place in a managed bean or in the application's business logic. The snippet below shows how to accomplish this.

```
BankChecksPermission p =
    new BankChecksPermission ("com.wchb.chapter19", "amount");
  if (p != null){
    return ADFContext.getCurrent().getSecurityContext().hasPermission(p);
  }
  else{
    return true;
  }
```

There are two key points in this Java code. First, in order to do a permission check, it is necessary to instantiate an object representing the permission. Second, the name of the permission plays a very important role in the process, since the hasPermission method verifies if the user detains a specific instance of permission; the name is the key for permission instance retrieval. An interesting feature of permission names is that it is possible to use wild cards to make the grants. Using hierarchical names similar to Java packages names, such as com.wchb.chapter18, enables you to authorize users on whole branches of the permission tree. A grant referencing com.wchb.*, for example, would authorize a specific role on all permissions whose name begin with com.wchb.

WebCenter and ADF Security

Oracle WebCenter is built on the top of the ADF. Consequently, the standard security behavior for all WebCenter features follows the usual ADF Security patterns. However, Oracle WebCenter Framework brings finer granularity to the authorization process, since it allows applying authorization restrictions on show detail component actions. By default, Show Detail Frame components inherit their authorization behavior from page-level settings. Users who benefit from the Personalize and Customize permissions will be able to manipulate show detail components even while in View mode. It is possible, however, to limit the actions by defining additional restrictions in adf-config.xml. Such restrictions can be defined on either action categories or individual show detail actions.

You may ask, what are action categories exactly? They are simply logical groupings of show detail actions, matching the page-level Personalize and Customize permissions. Table 18-5 shows which categories are defined by Oracle WebCenter.

Category	Member Actions
personalizeActionsCategory	showMoveAction
	showRemoveAction
	showMinimizeAction
	showResizer
	allowAction
customizeActionsCategory	showEditAction
	showAddContentAction

TABLE 18-5 *Categories Defined by Oracle WebCenter*

In order to define Show Detail Frame authorization restrictions, it is required to add specific settings to the adf-config.xml file, as shown below.

```
<cust:customizableComponentsSecurity
xmlns:cust="http://xmlns.oracle.com/adf/faces/customizable">
    <cust:enableSecurity value="true"/>
    <cust:actionsCategory>
      <cust:actionCategory name="customizeActionsCategory"
          value="false"/>
    </cust:actionsCategory>
    <cust:actions>
        <cust:action name="showMinimizeAction" value="true"/>
        <cust:action name="showMoveAction"
            value="#{securityBean.isAdmin}"/>
    </cust:actions>
...
</cust:customizableComponentsSecurity>
```

Use of expression language (EL) constructs is possible in order to assign or remove an action authorization dynamically, as displayed in our example.

Oracle Composer

When a customizable page is built in Oracle JDeveloper 11*g*, it is secured in exactly the same way as a regular JSF page—even if the actual authorization granularity may be set at the component level as we mentioned above. Developers may seed security grants in advance of the actual deployment by editing jazn-data.xml in the IDE. Users with sufficient rights can also alter authorizations on a page at run time. This is done through the Page Properties dialog of Oracle Composer, which is invoked by clicking on the button of the same name in Composer's toolbar, shown in Figure 18-19.

The Security tab of the dialog shows all the permissions currently granted on the page to application roles or user accounts, as is the case in Figure 18-20.

To add a new grant, click the Add Access button. This will pop up another dialog, illustrated in Figure 18-21.

FIGURE 18-19 *Oracle Composer Page Properties button*

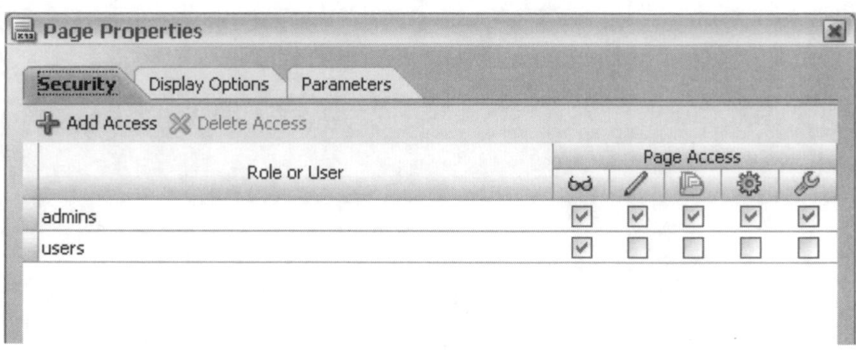

FIGURE 18-20 *Page Properties dialog*

By default, the table used to select users and roles is empty. You must first type a search criterion in the Search text box, then click the arrow button located on the right. After that, highlight the desired user or application role and click the Select button. The dialog will close and the user or role will appear in the Security tab of the Page Properties dialog. Simply check the appropriate checkboxes in order to confer new security rights on the page.

FIGURE 18-21 *Add Access dialog*

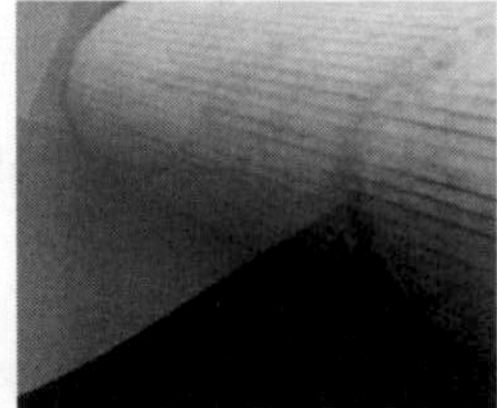

CHAPTER 19

Deployment

Now that we have extensively tested our applications, created skins to influence the look and feel, added various services, and used advanced capabilities such as Composer, it is time to think about finally graduating from JDeveloper. At this point you can tackle deployment to actual application server environments in test, stage, and/or production scenarios, depending on your software development life cycle.

But Where Have All Those Tests I Did So Far Been Run?

To make development, and especially testing, as painless as possible, Oracle JDeveloper comes with an Integrated WebLogic Server (aka default server). This server is started automatically when you run your application. The Integrated WebLogic Server uses the "exploded archive directory" method where all necessary files are hosted on the file system instead of being bundled up into a Java archives (JAR), web application archives (WAR), or enterprise application archives (EAR). Those exploded versions of your application are stored in sysdir/o.j2ee/drs.

This method ensures that you can easily modify static files without having to re-create the archives you would need for an actual deployment; however, experience has shown that in case of unexplainable errors in your application, it is always a good idea to shut down the default server and let it restart with the next run. Some files and definitions are read only once into memory, and just changing out file content will not always result in a reload of the information.

Also, you should never assume that just because an application worked fine with the Integrated WebLogic Server it will work fine on the production system and you can spare yourself the pain of test deployments. As we will see in the coming sections of this chapter, real deployment requires some prerequisite work on the deployment server side, such as re-creating connections, and some conceptual decisions, such as re-wiring producer connections, which are not necessary with the Integrated WebLogic Server.

Understanding the Deployment Concepts

Before we deploy our first application it is important to understand the individual concepts involved in deploying an application.

All application assets need to be packaged for deployment. Available containers for deployment are JARs which would usually be used to package reusable elements that can be used across multiple applications (e.g., task flows), WAR, and EAR.

Creating a WAR file, or rather the deployment profile which, once executed, will result in a WAR file, is done at the project level. You can create deployment profiles either in the Project Properties dialog or directly in the Application Navigator using New from the toolbar, menu, or context menu. EAR files, on the other hand, are created at the application level, so in order to create the deployment profile for EAR files, you need to invoke the Application properties through the Application menu or use the New option from the Application menu.

Another element of pretty much every application is connections. Connections allow access to data of any type, coming from the database, the Document Service, the Discussions Service, or others.

When deploying an application, those connections need to be taken care of after deployment so the application works properly. For security reasons, no credentials are being transported in the WAR or EAR deployment, so the last task you need to do is configure the connections after deployment to provide credentials your application requires. What to do exactly is described in a later section of this chapter.

Preparing for Your First "Real" Deployment

Before you can deploy your application to a remote WebLogic server, you need a WebLogic Managed Server instance that has the necessary shared libraries for WebCenter deployed and targeted. Also you need to create and register an MDS schema for your environment. Provisioning can be done through the administrator server user interface or via WebLogic Scripting Tool (WLST) script. Schema creation is done through the Repository Configuration Utility (RCU) provided with Oracle Fusion Middleware, but these topics have been discussed at length in Chapter 18. Let's focus on the deployment process.

Creating Your First Deployment Profile

The first step in preparing for deployment is to create a deployment profile. It contains all the information needed to get the application off the ground on the application server side. It defines what dependencies are required and at what location the web application can be accessed.

There are different types of deployment profiles. You can create one by selecting File | New to invoke the New Gallery (Figure 19-1). The deployment profiles can be found in the group with the corresponding name.

For your purposes here you are going to create a WAR, so you are going to select that profile type.

The wizard first asks you for the name of the profile. A project in JDeveloper can have multiple deployment profiles, each describing a different deployment scenario.

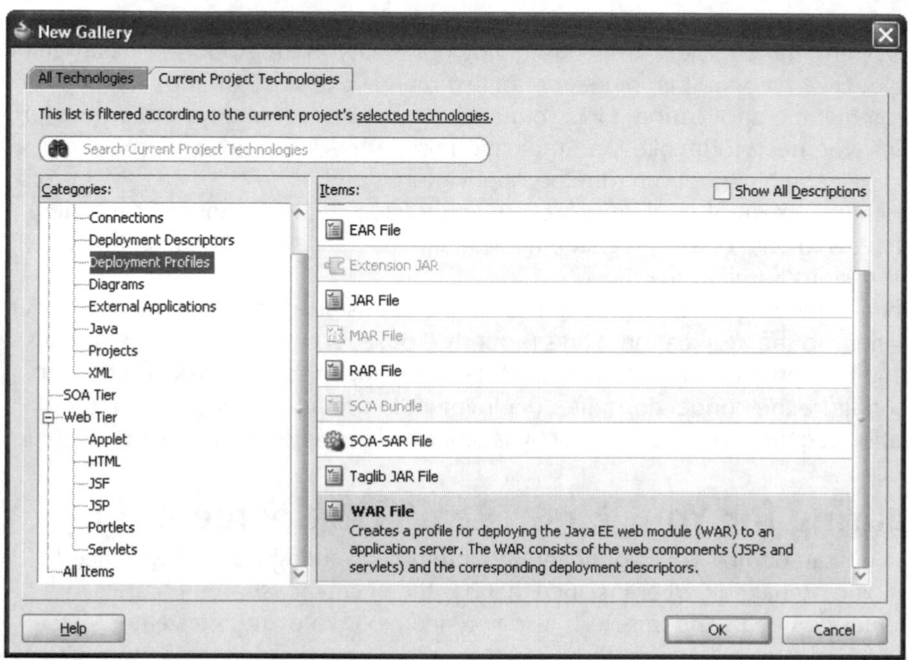

FIGURE 19-1 *Selecting the deployment profile type from the New Gallery*

Next you can provide all the different deployment settings (Figure 19-2). For your purposes there are three major groups of settings you want to explore further.

Under General, we find settings for the location of the generated WAR file. This is important if you want to somehow distribute the created archive, rather than deploying it right from within JDeveloper. Also the Specify J2EE Web Context Root option lets you define at what path on the server your application will be accessible. Usually you would leave the WAR file location unchanged, but the Web Context Root would be something meaningful, for example myApp.

On the Profile Dependencies tab we can specify what other elements this particular web archive depends on (Figure 19-3). This can be JARs or other elements that will then be bundled into the web archive.

Our simple application does not have any dependencies and hence this page will remain unchanged. Last in this first deployment profile we will inspect the Platform page (Figure 19-4). Here we can define the default settings for the deployment target. Platform and connection define how the WAR file should be assembled to work with the respective platform. The Target Connection setting would define a default target that can be overridden when we actually start the deployment process. For Default Platform we select WebLogic 10.3. Initially you will see that the Target connection drop-down is empty, unless you have already created connections of type Application Server.

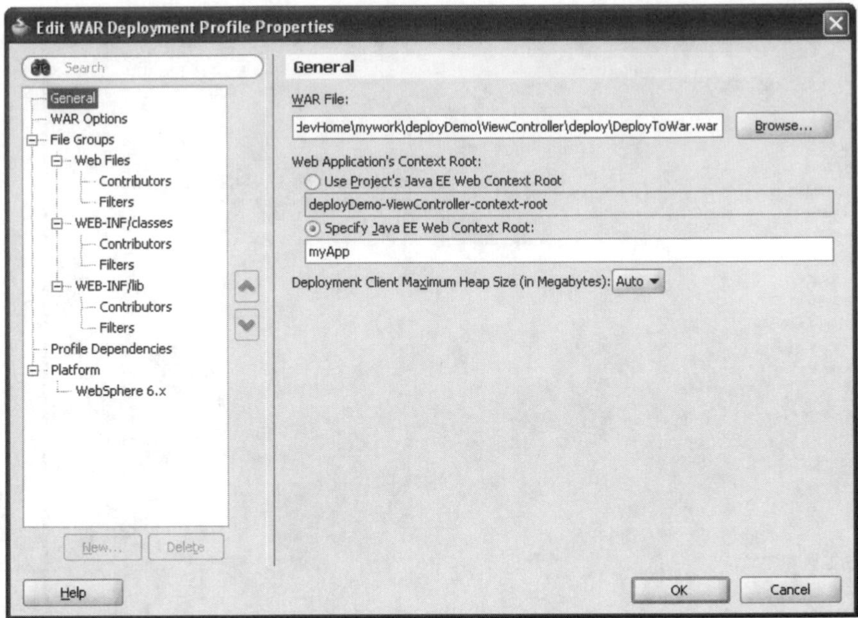

FIGURE 19-2 *The General settings*

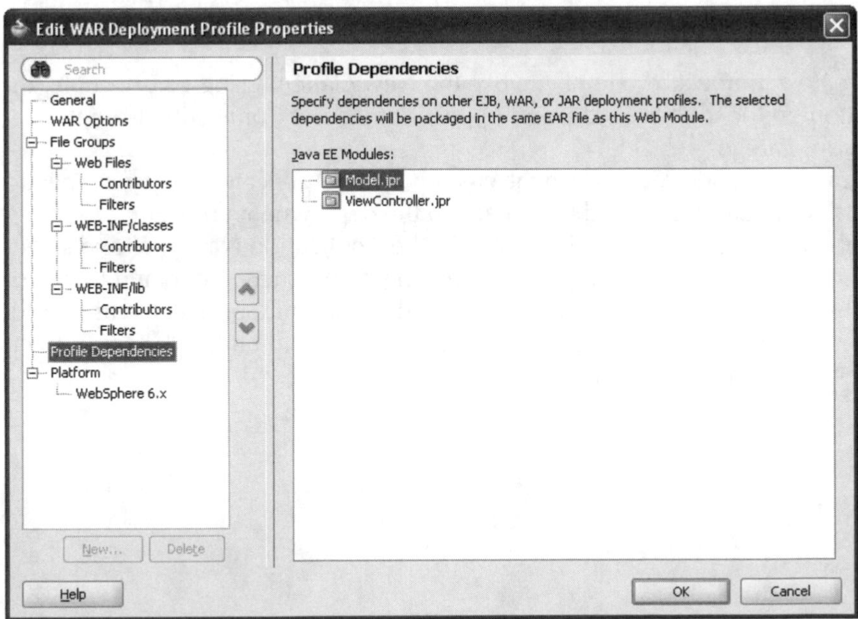

FIGURE 19-3 *The Dependencies settings*

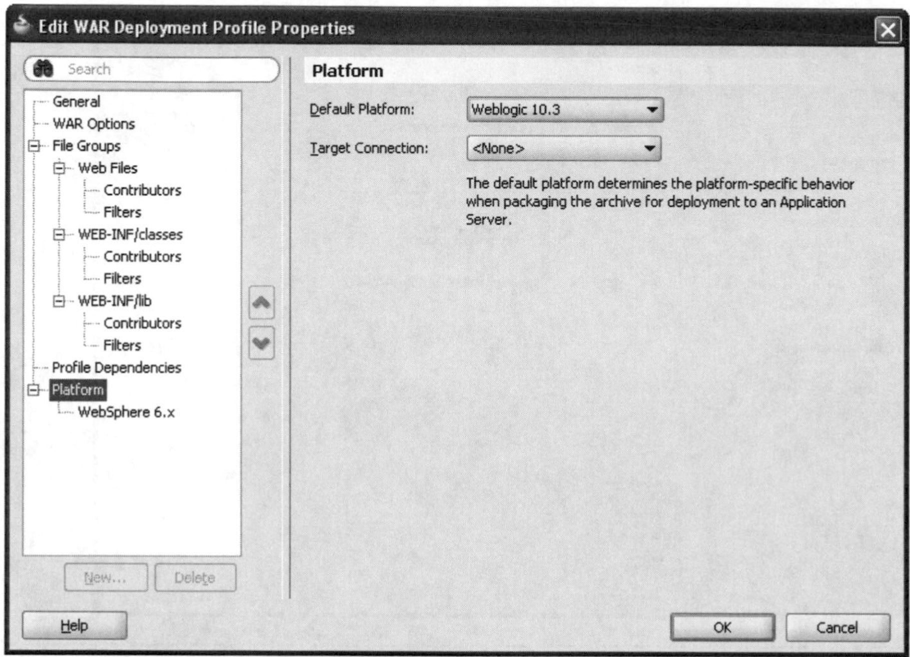

FIGURE 19-4 *The Platform page*

To create a connection, simply invoke the New Gallery using, for example, the New button on the toolbar, and select Application Server Connection from the Connections category.

A wizard will guide you through the creation of the Application Server connection. To set this connection, we need to go back to the deployment profile.

Simply right-click on the Project name in the Application Navigator and select Project Properties. In Project Properties select the deployment group and there you find the list of deployment profiles assigned to this particular project (Figure 19-5).

After selecting the respective project, just click Edit and under Platform you can now select the connection that was just created.

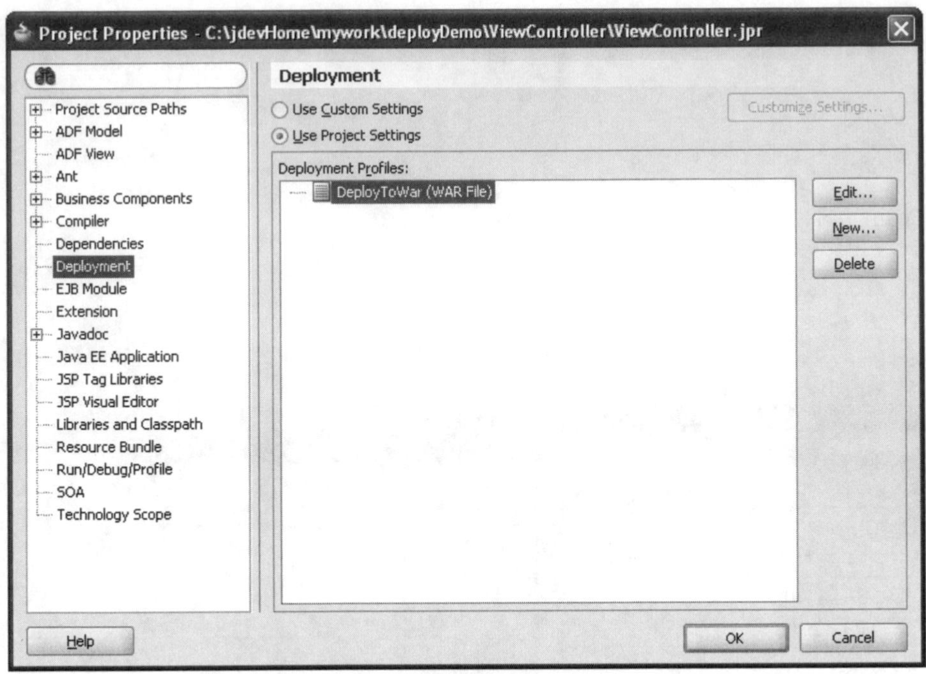

FIGURE 19-5 *Selecting the deployment profile*

Now, in order to successfully deploy the application we need to create a second deployment profile for an EAR file. Invoke the New Gallery again, but this time select the EAR, the type of deployment profile. Provide the necessary information and select the previously created WAR profile on the Profile Dependencies tab. Like before, select WebLogic 10.3 for the default platform and the connection you created for the default connection.

Having set all the necessary values you can go ahead and create your first EAR file. Simply right-click on the project in the Application Navigator and choose Deploy from the context menu (Figure 19-6).

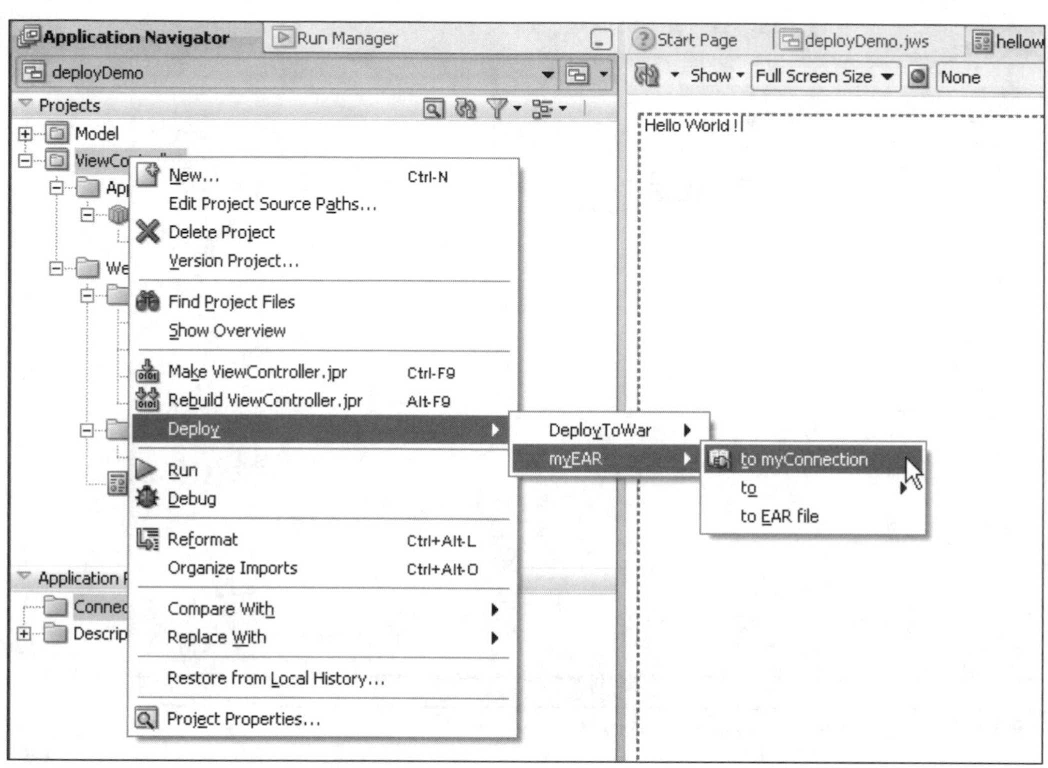

FIGURE 19-6 *Invoking deployment*

Once you have created the EAR file, you can go ahead and deploy the application to your WebLogic server. This can be done via WLS Console, the WLST, or Fusion Middleware Control. The latter has several advantages as it "understands" concepts connected to WebCenter. For example, it allows choosing the correct MDS schema and reassignment of connection endpoints.

The easiest way, however, is to directly deploy your application from inside JDeveloper. Simply choose Application | Deploy | <*yourApplication*> | To | <*yourServerConnection*> and JDeveloper will take care of the deployment.

With WebCenter applications, a central concept is MDS. During testing, MDS data is written to a file in your development environment. When you're deploying to a production environment you need to define a database connection where you want your metadata stored. During deployment, Oracle JDeveloper will present you with the necessary dialog to do that, as seen in Figure 19-7.

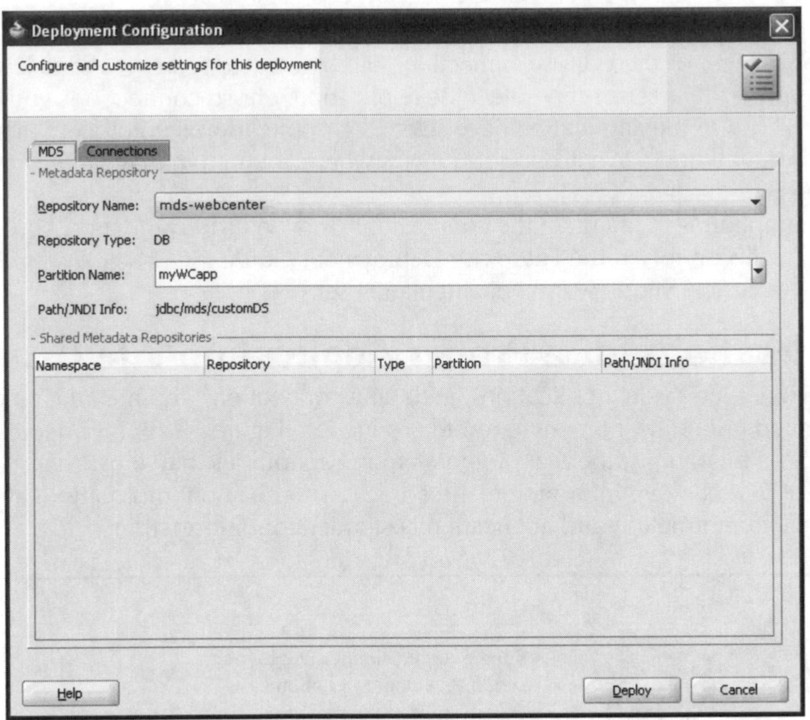

FIGURE 19-7 *Reconfiguration of MDS connection*

Behind the scenes JDeveloper will export the customizations currently active into a metadata archive (MAR) file, package this MAR file with the application, and import it into your new metadata store after deployment.

Congratulations, you have successfully deployed your first WebCenter application. One thing to note: the deployment might take longer than you would expect. Be patient!

What about Creating an EAR File?

If your application requires creating an application archive, you can create the necessary deployment profile from the Application Properties dialog. To get there, simply select Application Properties from the Application menu. In this dialog, under Deployment you can set up the necessary deployment profile. To later deploy the application, simply select Deploy from the Application menu.

Another way to invoke the dialog is by selecting the Application menu right next to the application selector at the top of the Application Navigator.

What to Do about the Connections?

Once the application is deployed, you can manage its connection through Enterprise Manager or the WLST. Connections can be created, edited, and deleted.

In Enterprise Manager simply select the application whose connections you want to modify. On the application page select the Application Deployment menu and there you will find a WebCenter sub-menu where you can manage the connections.

Another option is to maintain the connections using WLST commands. You will find more details on this in the Enterprise Deployment Guide for Oracle WebCenter in the Oracle Fusion Middleware Documentation set.

Considerations for a Proper Application Life Cycle

During a proper life cycle, applications, including connections and metadata, need to be migrated from development to test to production (Figure 19-8). In order to facilitate these migrations, there are import/export capabilities that allow the migration of portlet client information and portlet customization information, as well as service information and application customization information.

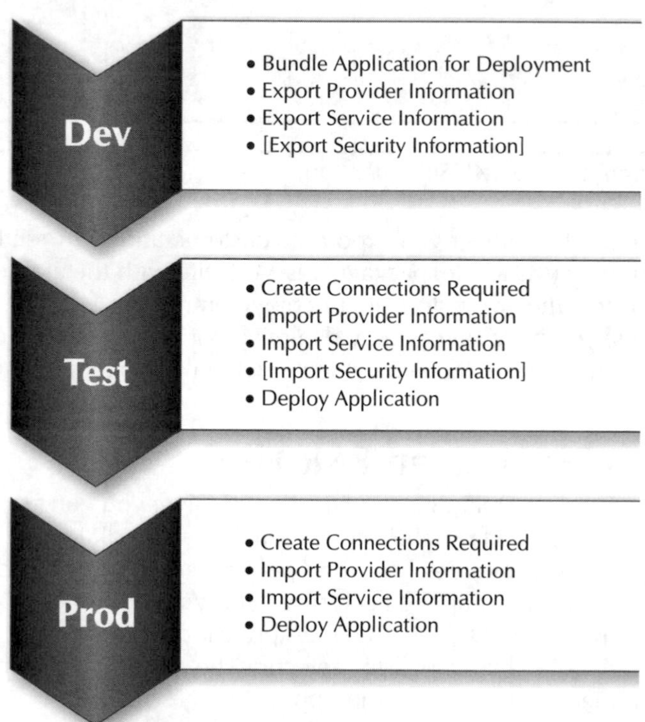
Dev
• Bundle Application for Deployment
• Export Provider Information
• Export Service Information
• [Export Security Information]
Test
• Create Connections Required
• Import Provider Information
• Import Service Information
• [Import Security Information]
• Deploy Application
Prod
• Create Connections Required
• Import Provider Information
• Import Service Information
• Deploy Application

FIGURE 19-8 *From development to production*

Migrating Portlet Information

In order to export portlet client information as well as producer customization information, run the WLST command `exportProducerMetadata`. This command is run for a whole application and therefore exports the data for all used producers; you cannot selectively choose individual producers to export. Analogous to this, for importing the data on the target system, use the WLST command `importProducerMetadata`.

Detailed information on the syntax of these two commands can be found in the Oracle Fusion Middleware WebLogic Scripting Tool Command Reference.

Migrating Service Information

The power of WebCenter applications comes from using Web 2.0 services. Those services, however, also use metadata that potentially needs migration through the life cycle. The WLST provides generic commands, `exportMetadata` and `importMetadata`, to move metadata from one instance of MDS to another.

```
exportMetadata(application='sampleApp', server='myhost',
toLocation='/tmp/myrepos', docs='/**')
importMetadata(application='sampleApplication', server='myhost',
fromLocation='/tmp/myrepos', docs='/**')
```

To use these commands properly, you need to understand the MDS structure a bit in detail, which you should by now, having read the MDS section of this book. In short, for the docs parameter you can provide the branch of MDS you want to migrate. "/**" indicates that all metadata should be migrated. If you want to migrate only a branch of MDS—for example everything related to the Discussions Service—you would use the respective path in MDS (in this example it would be `docs= /oracle/webcenter/collab/forum/**`). A complete list can be found in the Managing Export, Import, Backup, and Recovery of WebCenter section of the Oracle Fusion Middleware Administrator's Guide.

Migrating Back-End Service Information

One more area you need to keep in mind, when you're migrating your application through the life cycle, is the possibility that you might also have to migrate the data of one or more of the back-end services. In short, there are two approaches to this, and each service basically allows one or the other. Either the service provides a specialized export/import mechanism for its data, for example the WebLogic Communication Suite, or you would use database mechanisms like exp/imp, the database export/import utilities, or expdp/impdp, the database data pump mechanism.

Regardless, the steps are different for each service, and the most reliable source for those steps is the section of the administrator's guide we mentioned above. And who knows, maybe over time those steps might be packaged in a handy migration utility.

What If My Application Is Secured?

When you're deploying a secured application, the deployment process provides some capabilities that allow you to deploy security-related information together with your application (Figure 19-9).

Especially in a development-to-test deployment it might be interesting to create the associated users and groups of the development environment to the test environment. If you check the Users and Groups box, those users and groups that are defined in jazn-data.xml of your development environment will be created in the identity store of the new target environment. When you're deploying to a production environment, this option will most likely be unchecked, since users and groups in a production environment should already be created and those should be used by your application. Moving your test users to those systems will most likely be considered a security risk. It also requires the authenticator in your domain to be configured to allow creation of users and groups.

The credentials options take care of deploying any secured attributes and public credentials your application might be using to the production platforms credential store. The assumption, however, is that in most cases those credentials will be different between test, stage, and production environment and hence need to be changed using either WLST or Oracle Fusion Middleware Control.

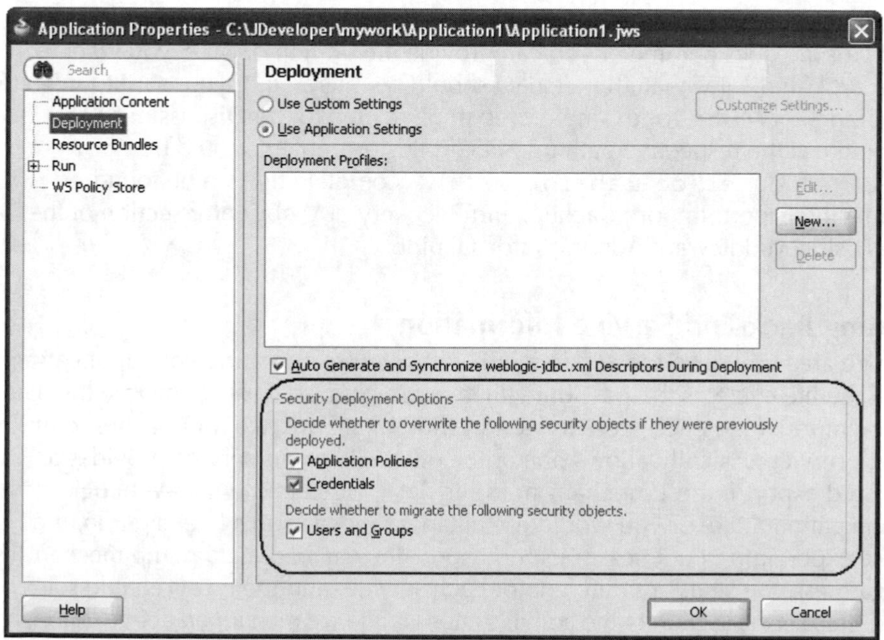

FIGURE 19-9 *The deployment section of the Application Properties dialog*

Migrating Security Information

The last consideration, when looking into a migration scenario, could be the requirement of moving security information across the different environments. While we mentioned that WebCenter security is mainly role-based to simplify production deployment and management, there are certainly cases where you might have to bring production security information back into your development or stage environments.

This can be done by extracting the lightweight directory access protocol (LDAP) information from your production environment via the `ldapsearch` command and then importing that into another system using the `ldapaddmt` command.

```
LDAP_OH/bin/ldapsearch -h ldap_hostname -p ldap_port -D  "cn=ldap_user" -w
password -b "cn=users,dc=example,dc=com" -s subtree "objectclass=*" "*"
orclguid -L > my_users.ldif
LDAP_OH/bin/ldapaddmt -h ldap_hostname -p ldap_port -D "cn=ldap_user" -w
password -c -r -f my_users.ldif
```

A Word of Caution

While it might seem straightforward, security is a very complex topic. You should be sure to develop a good understanding of the way security works: it's WebCenter specific but is dictated by the container, Java, and Oracle ADF.

The more complex your application, and hence your use of security, becomes, the more complex working with security itself gets. Make sure you do a couple of test runs with simple scenarios so you know the inner makings before you attempt setup and deployment of complex applications.

From Manual to Automatic

As you can see, proper deployment can involve quite a number of manual steps that need to be followed. Automation can help a great deal, not only to make deployment more efficient but also to avoid errors during the deployment process. You might want to revisit Chapter 16 of this book, where we discussed automation processes.

When developing a custom WebCenter application, a developer can take advantage of a wide variety of capabilities and services that come with Oracle WebCenter. Not only can the application user significantly benefit from those advanced capabilities, there are also a couple of items the developer and the administrator need to keep in mind when deploying those applications. The most important point is how to move the metadata of all the different services between the stages in the application life cycle, but more to the heart of the matter, WebCenter applications are plain JavaEE applications, and the overall deployment mechanism follows those concepts. No additional proprietary procedures are needed to deploy an application, while at the same time you can take advantage of advanced JavaEE concepts like clustering, etc.

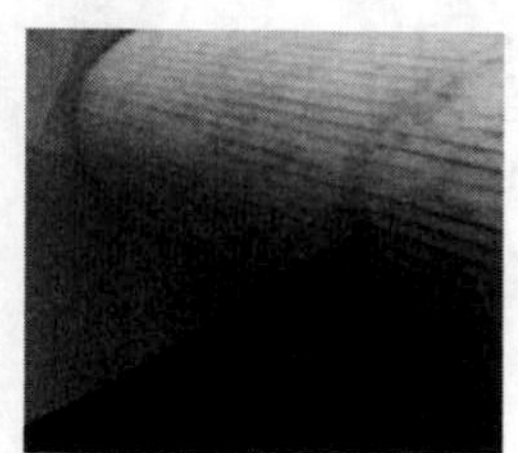

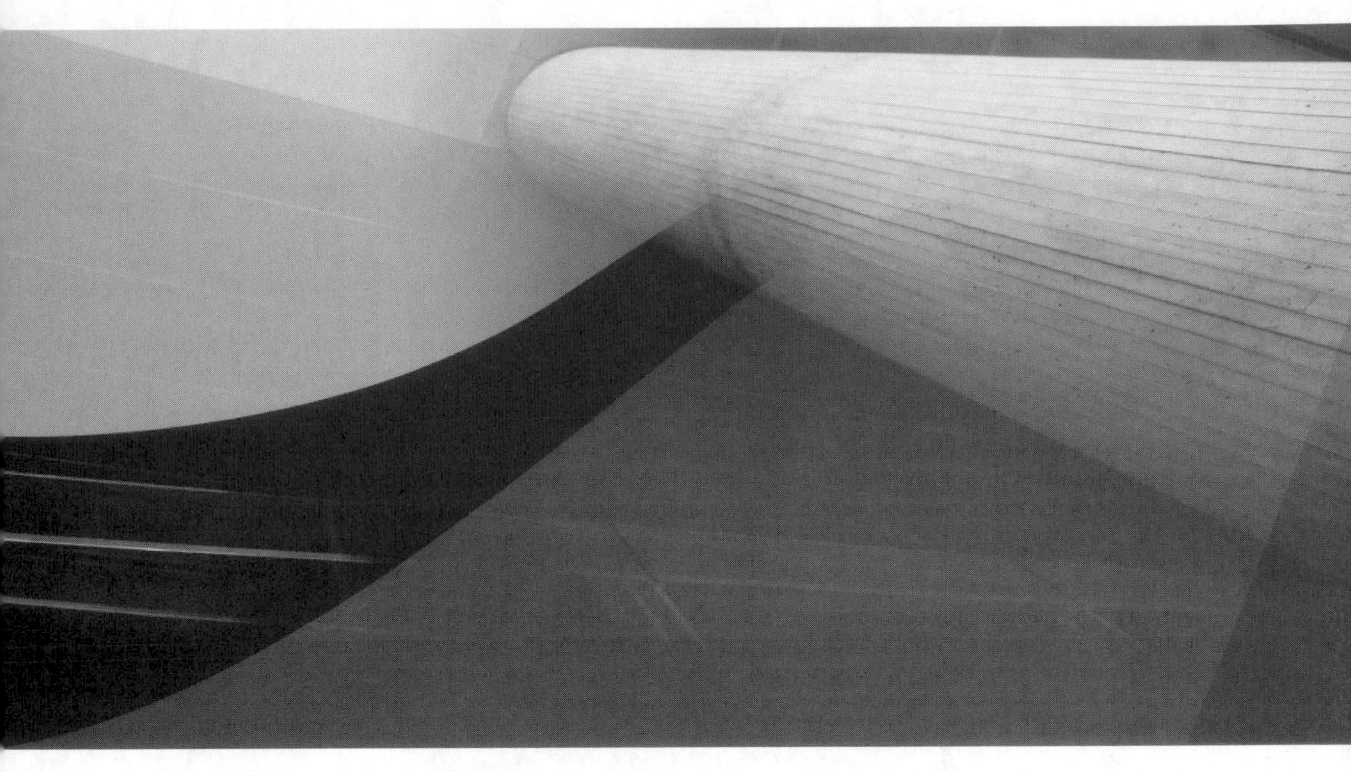

PART V

Oracle Applications Integration

CHAPTER 20

Extending Oracle Applications with WebCenter

ver the course of this book we have introduced you to all aspects of WebCenter development and the concepts of enterprise mashups. One remaining question, however, is where you would get the necessary data for those enterprise mashups, especially if you are using existing enterprise applications, such as Oracle E-Business Suite, Siebel, PeopleSoft, or JDEdwards.

There are two major mechanisms to integrate those into your new WebCenter application:

- Portlet-based integration
- Building Custom UI
    - Using the application's web services
    - Data Binding—JSR 227

While the web service approach might, at first sight, appeal more to the developer crowd from a pure cost perspective, the portlet-based approach should always be favored. This is because any change to the user experience in the application will be propagated to the portlet and would have to be adopted in the custom UI when using the web services, and also because componentizing an application's functionality allows for an easy recombination of those building blocks later on in portal frameworks.

In some cases, creating a composite application is a much more viable solution for getting a specific application than customizing the packaged application. Any customization to a packaged application has risks associated with it and will eventually cost more when you're upgrading the application.

Last, but not least, are portlets, which are providing ready-to-use identity propagation, message integrity, and encryption and hence less work and fewer headaches for the developer.

Portlet-Based Integration with Oracle E-Business Suite

Oracle WebCenter can provide a single customized portal that allows access to one of a variety of enterprise applications, such as Oracle E-Business Suite. This is facilitated through support for Oracle Applications Framework Web Providers and

Oracle Java Portlet Development Kit (JPDK); E-Business Suite links and data are delivered via portlets that can be displayed on customized Oracle WebCenter pages.

Oracle E-Business Suite leverages Oracle Portal to build dashboards within the application and therefore provides an extensive set of portlets. Because they are standards-based, those portlets can also be used by other compatible frameworks. As we discussed earlier, Oracle WebCenter is able to consume both WSRP-based and JPDK-based portlets, which are both the standards and are used by Oracle E-Business Suite.

Portlets installed on an E-Business Suite (Figure 20-1) instance communicate with Oracle WebCenter via web providers that are registered with the respective application.

For Oracle E-Business Suite, the list of available portlets is quite extensive:

- **Navigator portlet** The Navigator portlet allows E-Business Suite users to navigate their responsibilities and menus and launch any functions to which they have access.
- **Favorites portlet** The Favorites portlet allows users to add any E-Business Suite function they have access to as well as any internal or external URLs to a list of favorite links.
- **Daily Business Intelligence (DBI) List of Pages portlet** The DBI List of Pages portlet lists all the DBI overview pages a given user has access to. Leveraging single sign-on, users can easily navigate directly to any of their DBI overview pages.

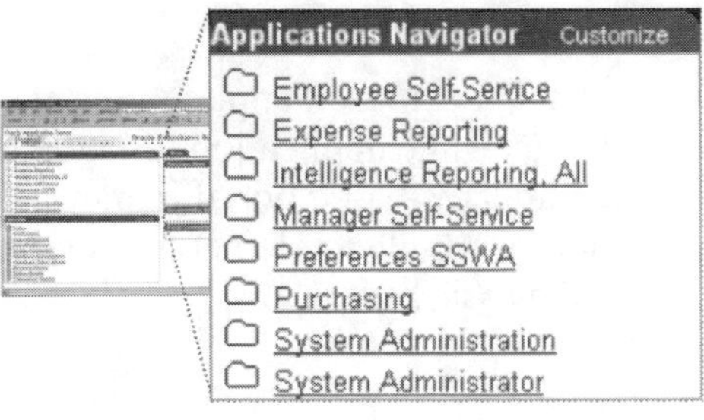

FIGURE 20-1 *E-Business Suite portlets*

- **Worklist portlet** The Worklist portlet provides a single point of interface for accessing any work flow notifications generated by any of the application modules in the E-Business Suite. Examples include expense report approvals and business intelligence performance exception notifications.
- **Balanced Scorecard Key Performance Indicator (KPI) Graph and List portlets** The KPI Graph portlet enables users to select a specific key performance indicator to display in a graphical format. The KPI List portlet enables users to select specific KPIs from a scorecard.
- **Balanced Scorecard Custom View portlet** The Custom View portlet enables customers to design highly graphical scorecard portlets by importing gif or jpg images as the background and adding key performance indicator dynamic color alarm icons. Users can drill from the Scorecard Custom View portlet to KPI drill-down reports to perform additional analysis.

Combining content from all of your business applications, E-Business Suite or other Oracle applications, SAP R3 and mySAP applications, or any application that exposes WSRP or JSR 168–compliant portlets with other transactional content into a single application provides significant business value.

To further enhance the experience, Oracle E-Business Suite is planning to introduce a portlet generator as well as a business service generator, which will allow you to easily and declaratively generate portlets or web services out of the Oracle Applications (OA) framework—the definitions that make up Oracle E-Business Suite.

Integrating Oracle PeopleSoft Applications via Portlets

Like Oracle E-Business Suite, Oracle PeopleSoft applications provide an extensive set of portlets that can be used to integrate application functionality into an Oracle WebCenter application, or any standards-based portal framework for that matter.

Oracle PeopleSoft applications are built on elements called *pagelets* which can be exposed as WSRP portlets quite easily.

You would use the PeopleTools link in your application to navigate to, for example, the Self Service components. On the configuration screen for the component you will find a checkbox for WSRP producible. Once you check this box, you can navigate to WSRP Production in the left-hand menu which will bring you to the producer configuration page. There you will find a section that gives you the web service endpoint URL (Figure 20-2).

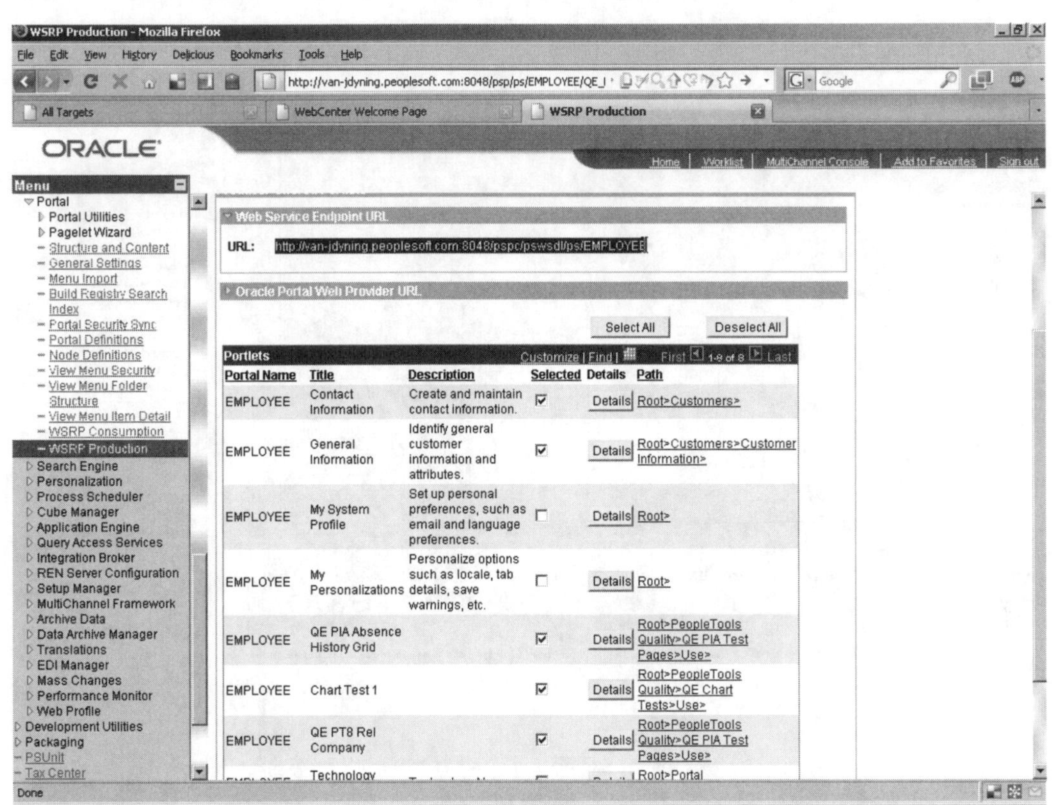

FIGURE 20-2 *Determining the web service endpoint URL for the portlet provider*

Once you register the endpoint URL, representing the Portlet Producer, the portlets will show up in the resource catalog (Figure 20-3), both at run time and at design time, for you to use in your application (Figure 20-4).

The portlet capability is available for all PeopleSoft versions based on PeopleTools 8.4.8 and later.

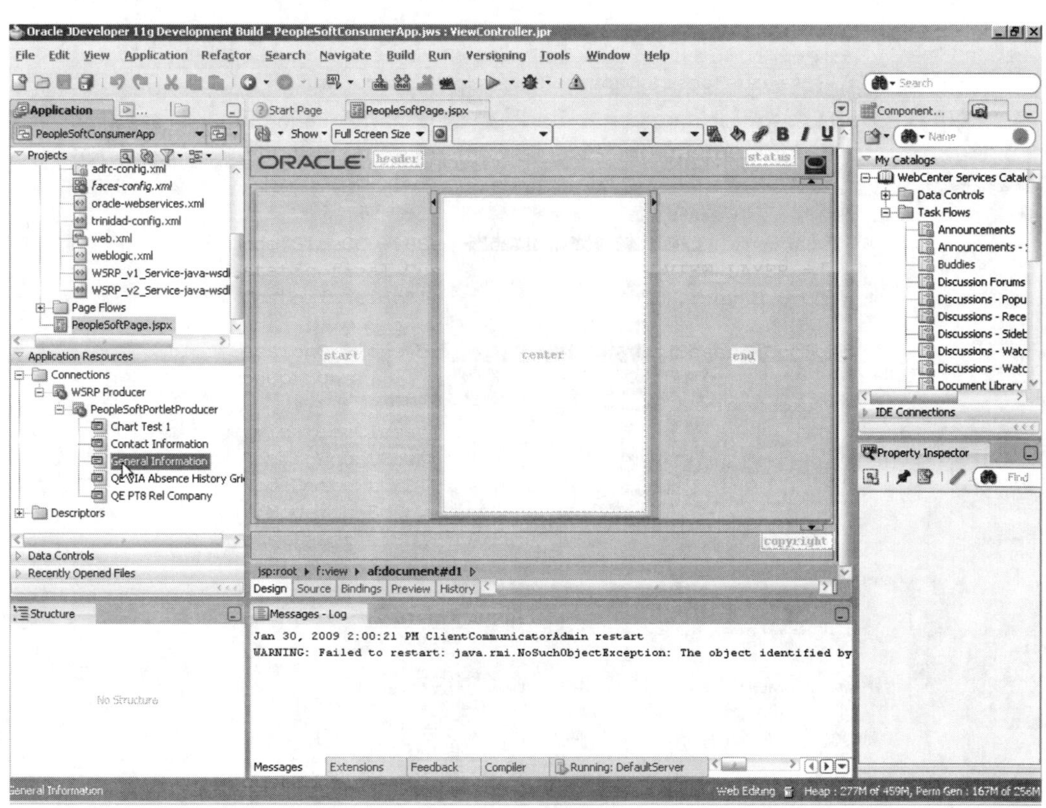

FIGURE 20-3 *Adding a PeopleSoft portlet to an Oracle WebCenter application*

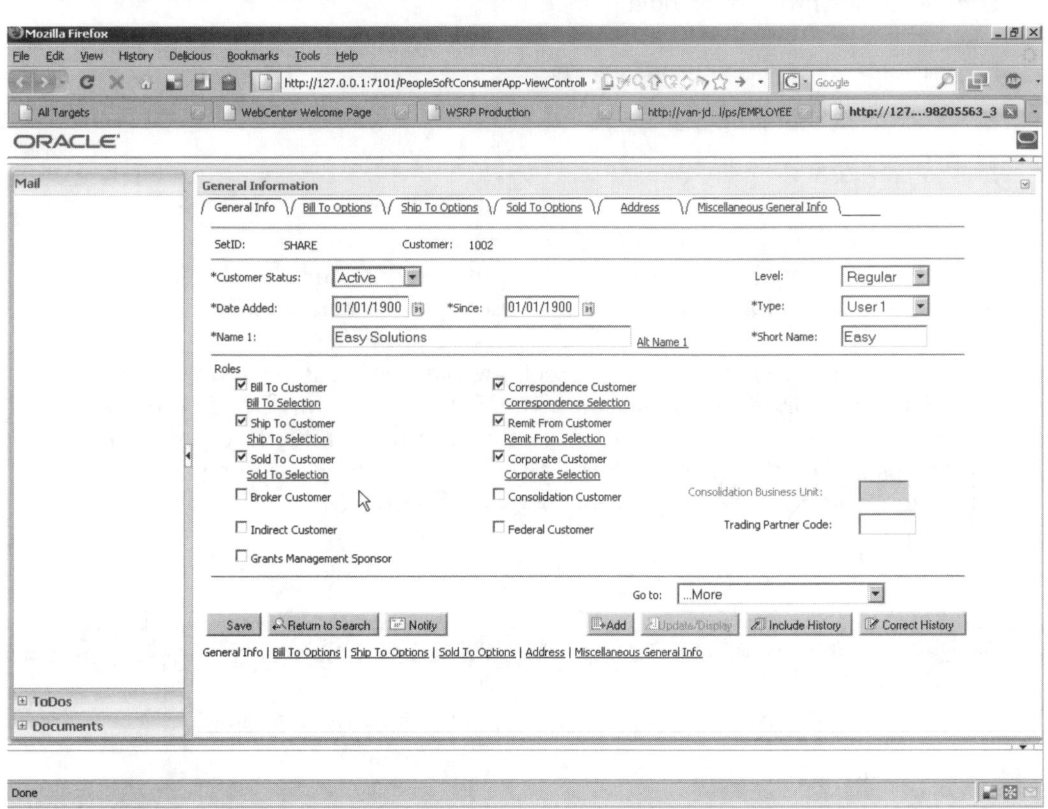

FIGURE 20-4 *Portlet executing inside the Oracle WebCenter application*

Oracle JD Edwards Enterprise One Portal Solution

For quite a while, JD Edwards Enterprise One has leveraged portal interoperability standards such as JSR 168 or JPDK to allow integration of JD Edwards functionality into enterprise portals. With Tools 8.98, this foundation was extended by the support for WSRP, providing a modernized framework for portal integration.

Enterprise One provides prebuilt portlets in:

- customer relationship management
- supplier relationship management
- human resource management

These portlets are part of Enterprise One and can be downloaded from JD Edwards as an electronic software update. They then either can be deployed to portal servers such as Oracle Portal or can be used in an Oracle WebCenter application.

Oracle JD Edwards Enterprise One portlets are built on the foundation of the JD Edwards Enterprise One Tools architecture. The JD Edwards Forms Design Aid is an integrated tool assisting in the creation of any JD Edwards user interface, including HTML screens and portlets (Figure 20-5). This enables you to use existing skills in case there is a need for extending existing portlet functionality.

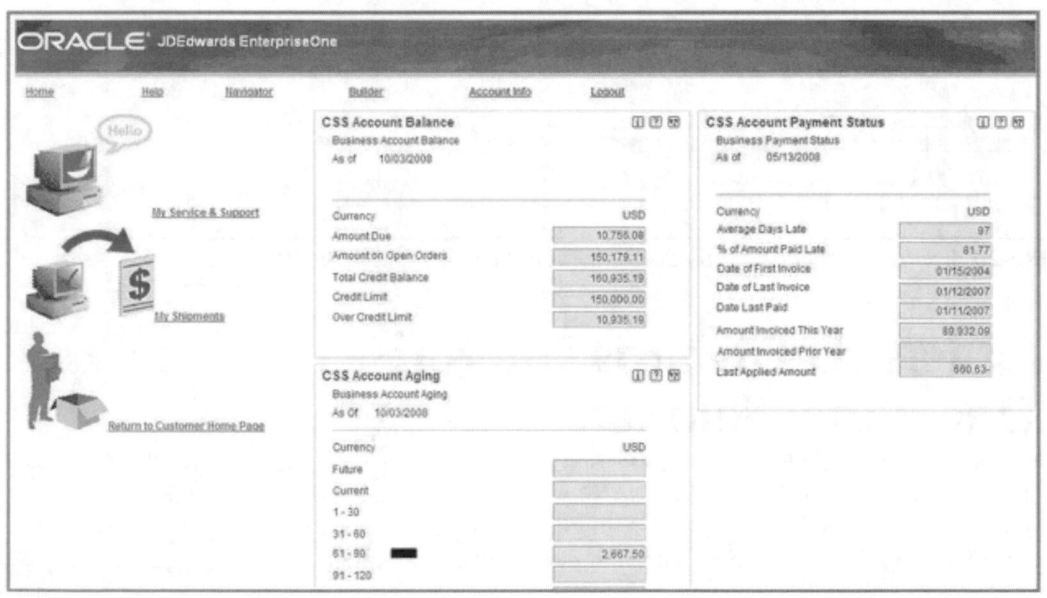

FIGURE 20-5 *JD Edwards portlets*

A Different Approach—Oracle Siebel Applications

The Oracle Siebel integration suite is taking a slightly different approach. Rather than providing portlets, Siebel applications allow you to expose their functionality via SOAP web services. This approach is partly triggered by the architecture of Siebel applications. While not pure SOA, the applications are service oriented, separating the user interface from the actual business logic, so exposing those services via standard SOAP was an easy thing to do.

Obviously this has advantages and disadvantages, mainly for the user interface. In fact, the disadvantage, compared with the portlet approach, can also be considered an advantage.

From the perspective of cost, using the services and creating your own user interaction elements is, obviously, more costly than simply using prebuilt portlets. In some cases, where there are no portlets, it is the only way to integrate, however.

While portlets are easy to use and fast to integrate, they are reusable components that cannot be customized all the way, which can lead to UI inconsistencies within your application. A service-based approach, on the other hand, only exposes the input and return values, and the presentation to the user can be customized to your liking. Any integration would therefore integrate 100 percent into your application, but at the same time require more work, as the complete user interaction needs to be created from scratch. Concepts such as ADF task flows can, however, provide reusability of those UI layers across applications.

Creating a so-called Siebel Inbound web service is an administrative task (Figure 20-6) that maps business operations to a service name; you can choose what protocol, in our case HTTP, you want to use. Also information, such as the authentication required, can be configured there.

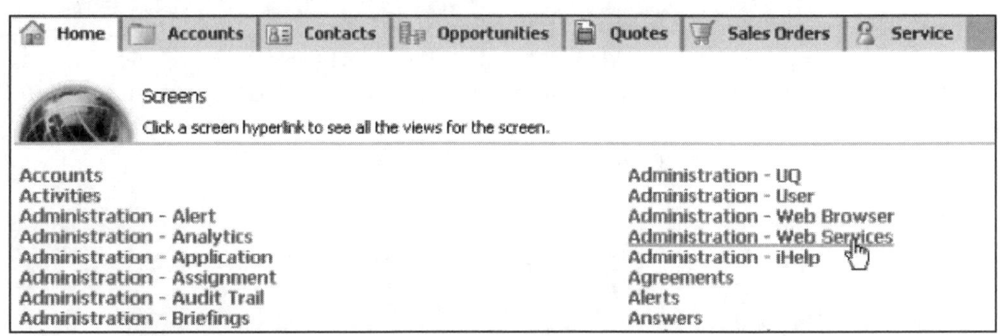

FIGURE 20-6 *Creating a Siebel web service*

```
  <?xml version="1.0" encoding="UTF-8" ?>
- <definitions xmlns="http://schemas.xmlsoap.org/wsdl/" xmlns:xsdLocal0="http://www.siebel.com/xml/Acco
    xmlns:soap="http://schemas.xmlsoap.org/wsdl/soap/" targetNamespace="http://siebel.com/fmw"
    xmlns:soapenc="http://schemas.xmlsoap.org/soap/encoding/" xmlns:xsd="http://www.w3.org/2001/XMl
    xmlns:tns="http://siebel.com/fmw">
  - <types>
    - <xsd:schema elementFormDefault="qualified" xmlns:xsdLocal0="http://www.siebel.com/xml/Account%20Ir
        attributeFormDefault="unqualified" targetNamespace="http://www.siebel.com/xml/Account%20Interfa(
        xmlns:xsd="http://www.w3.org/2001/XMLSchema">
      - <xsd:annotation>
          <xsd:documentation>Copyright (C) 2001-2004 Siebel Systems, Inc. All rights reserved. Siebel XSD
            Generation</xsd:documentation>
        </xsd:annotation>
        <xsd:element name="ListOfAccountInterface" type="xsdLocal0:ListOfAccountInterface" />
      - <xsd:complexType name="ListOfAccountInterfaceTopElmt">
        - <xsd:sequence>
            <xsd:element name="ListOfAccountInterface" maxOccurs="1" minOccurs="1"
              type="xsdLocal0:ListOfAccountInterface" />
          </xsd:sequence>
        </xsd:complexType>
      - <xsd:complexType name="ListOfAccountInterface">
        - <xsd:sequence>
            <xsd:element name="Account" maxOccurs="unbounded" minOccurs="0" type="xsdLocal0:Account" />
          </xsd:sequence>
        </xsd:complexType>
      - <xsd:complexType name="Account">
        - <xsd:sequence>
            <xsd:element name="AccountId" maxOccurs="1" minOccurs="0" type="xsdLocal0:string30" />
            <xsd:element name="AccountStatus" maxOccurs="1" minOccurs="0" type="xsdLocal0:string24" />
            <xsd:element name="Alias" maxOccurs="1" minOccurs="0" type="xsdLocal0:string50" />
            <xsd:element name="AssignmentAreaCode" maxOccurs="1" minOccurs="0" type="xsdLocal0:string5" />
            <xsd:element name="AssignmentCountryCode" maxOccurs="1" minOccurs="0" type="xsdLocal0:string5
            <xsd:element name="CompetitorFlag" maxOccurs="1" minOccurs="0" type="xsd:string" />
            <xsd:element name="CreditAutoApprovalLimit" maxOccurs="1" minOccurs="0" type="xsd:string" />
            <xsd:element name="CreditStatusDate" maxOccurs="1" minOccurs="0" type="xsd:string" />
            <xsd:element name="CurrencyCode" maxOccurs="1" minOccurs="0" type="xsdLocal0:string15" />
            <xsd:element name="DUNSNumber" maxOccurs="1" minOccurs="0" type="xsdLocal0:string15" />
            <xsd:element name="DomesticUltimateDUNS" maxOccurs="1" minOccurs="0" type="xsdLocal0:string15
            <xsd:element name="NumberofEmployees" maxOccurs="1" minOccurs="0" type="xsd:string" />
            <xsd:element name="Expertise" maxOccurs="1" minOccurs="0" type="xsdLocal0:string30" />
            <xsd:element name="GlobalUltimateDUNS" maxOccurs="1" minOccurs="0" type="xsdLocal0:string15" />
            <xsd:element name="HomePage" maxOccurs="1" minOccurs="0" type="xsdLocal0:string100" />
            <xsd:element name="IntegrationId" maxOccurs="1" minOccurs="0" type="xsdLocal0:string30" />
```


FIGURE 20-7 *The generated WSDL file*

From there you would also generate the WSDL file (Figure 20-7) required to later create the components necessary to connect to that web service from your application.

In Oracle JDeveloper you can then simply create a web service data control based on this web service. Through simple drag-and-drop you can then create the necessary UI components to interact with the web service (Figure 20-8).

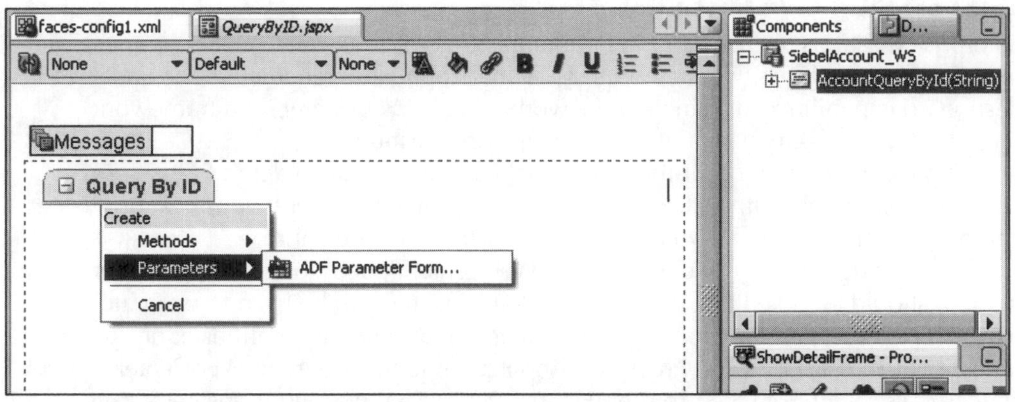

FIGURE 20-8 *Creating the UI component for the web service*

Usually, you create two pages, one for the query form, the other for the result table. The two pages are connected by an ADF page flow (Figure 20-9), while the Data Control framework takes care of keeping the query form and the result set in sync.

Because you are manually re-creating the user interaction layer, you can perfectly match its look and behavior to your application, the functionality of which you can seamlessly integrate with that of Siebel applications.

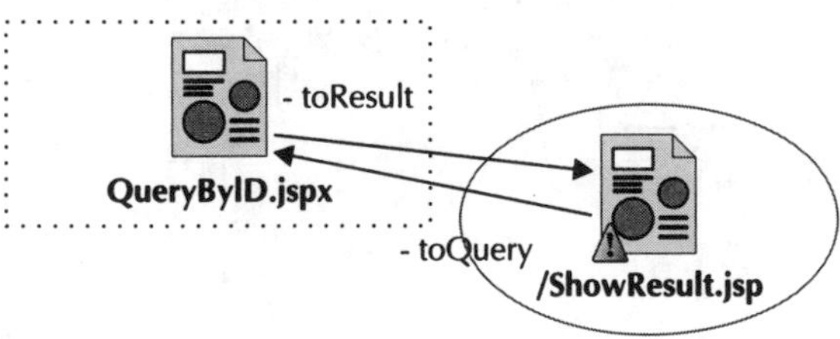

FIGURE 20-9 *Sample page flow diagram*

Putting It All Together

Enterprise mashups, the evolution of traditional enterprise portals, are becoming increasingly popular as they combine traditional application characteristics and dashboard capabilities in a single framework. Oracle WebCenter, as a framework, provides the necessary capabilities to create those mashups.

With the integration capabilities that applications such as Oracle's E-Business Suite, Siebel, PeopleSoft, or JDEdwards provide, Oracle WebCenter applications can provide the insight into your business that your users demand.

And although we do not cover Oracle WebCenter Spaces in any detail in this book, it should be noted that the same mechanisms that can be used to integrate enterprise application functionality into Oracle WebCenter applications at design time can also be used to add Enterprise Application functionality to WebCenter Spaces pages right from the browser (Figure 20-10). That way, your business users can create those mashups or composite applications themselves.

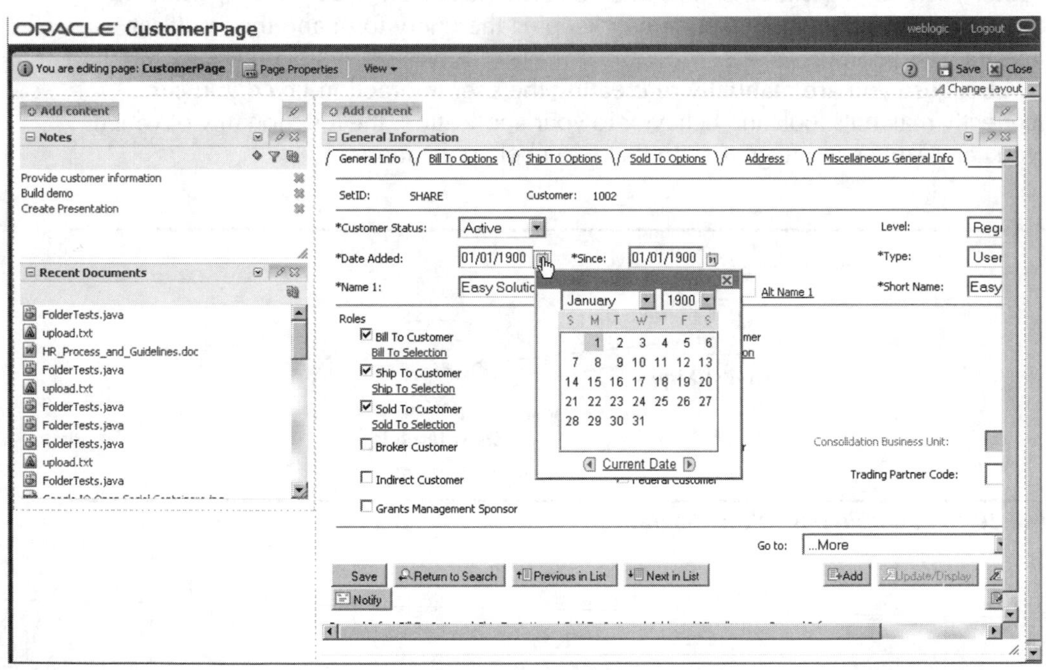

FIGURE 20-10 *PeopleSoft portlet running in a WebCenter Spaces page*

CHAPTER 21

Looking to the Future with WebCenter and Fusion Applications

The birth of Oracle WebCenter can be traced to a number of different driving factors, such as the evolution of browsers and web UI technologies, the development of standards in the Java and web services world, the emergence of visual declarative IDEs, and Web 2.0 trends in the consumer web. One particularly significant factor contributed to the architecting and building of the brand-new portal product and framework: Oracle WebCenter. After acquiring many of the enterprise application vendors in the marketplace (PeopleSoft, JD Edwards, and Siebel), Oracle realized that a traditional integrated application development and middleware technology stack didn't cut it anymore, and that there was a need for a more flexible and richer set of tools and services to build the next-generation enterprise applications, and thus developed Oracle Fusion Middleware. Oracle Fusion Middleware, of which Oracle WebCenter is a component, includes all the features we've discussed throughout this book: Oracle ADF, Oracle JDeveloper, SOA, and so on, and enables application developers to build true Enterprise 2.0 applications.

In developing Oracle Fusion Middleware, Oracle has also launched the development of Fusion Applications—Enterprise 2.0 applications built using Oracle Fusion Middleware. At the moment, Oracle Fusion Applications have not yet been released. However, these applications are intended to be rich, customizable applications based on modules that can be used in either enterprise applications or portals. WebCenter is a key tool for building these applications, as, for one, it was designed with Fusion Applications in mind, and two, it enables application developers to integrate so much of the run-time customization, Web 2.0, and collaboration features required by next-generation Enterprise 2.0 applications.

From a bird's-eye view, Fusion Applications are really custom WebCenter applications containing Web 2.0 services using JavaServer Faces component technology. Oracle's implementation of JavaServer Faces components, ADF Faces components, are built on top of MDS that enable full run-time customization. Fusion Applications fuel the Enterprise 2.0 revolution by taking these components and creating reusable modules. Application developers can take these modules and customize them for their own environments, or even extend their applications by creating new modules with Oracle Fusion Middleware.

While Oracle Fusion Applications have not yet been released, development is rapidly moving forward, and Oracle has announced several major areas where Oracle WebCenter is being used to build Fusion Applications, which we'll share with you in this chapter. Some of those areas are WebCenter Web 2.0 Services, search, customization (by way of Oracle Composer), and communities.

Keep in mind that the concepts described in this chapter are intended to outline the general product direction, and should not be relied on in making purchasing decisions.[1]

Modularized and Consistent User Interface

By taking advantage of the integrated development framework, Fusion Applications developers are building a well-defined page layout that looks and behaves consistently across all the Fusion Applications modules. You can find operations like navigation, search, preferences, and help in the same place in each module, and they always work the same way. The user interface shell, or UI shell, defines the fundamental outline of the pages.

Not only will the application show how you can leverage Oracle Fusion Middleware to build intuitive user interfaces, you will be able to extend these applications using Oracle Fusion Middleware to customize the application for your organization.

WebCenter Web 2.0 Services in Fusion Applications

The core functionality of Fusion Applications concerns transactional or dashboarding capabilities, which address the more common requirements for enterprise applications and portals. However, one cannot emphasize enough the value that rich, well-integrated, secure Web 2.0 services bring to applications. Let's take a look at a couple of design patterns that the Oracle Fusion Applications teams are considering.

One example of how Fusion Applications use Oracle WebCenter is tagging. The main objective of tagging is to simplify information classification and location. For example, Figure 21-1 shows an overview page of a sales opportunity for Laboratory Upgrade – XYZ Corp. Business users can assign keywords, or tags, to the opportunity, and can review the previously assigned tags as well.

[1] The content of this chapter outlines general product direction. It is intended for information purposes only, and may not be incorporated into any contract. It is not a commitment to deliver any material, code, or functionality, and should not be relied upon in making purchasing decisions. The development, release, and timing of any features or functionality described for Oracle's products remains at the sole discretion of Oracle.

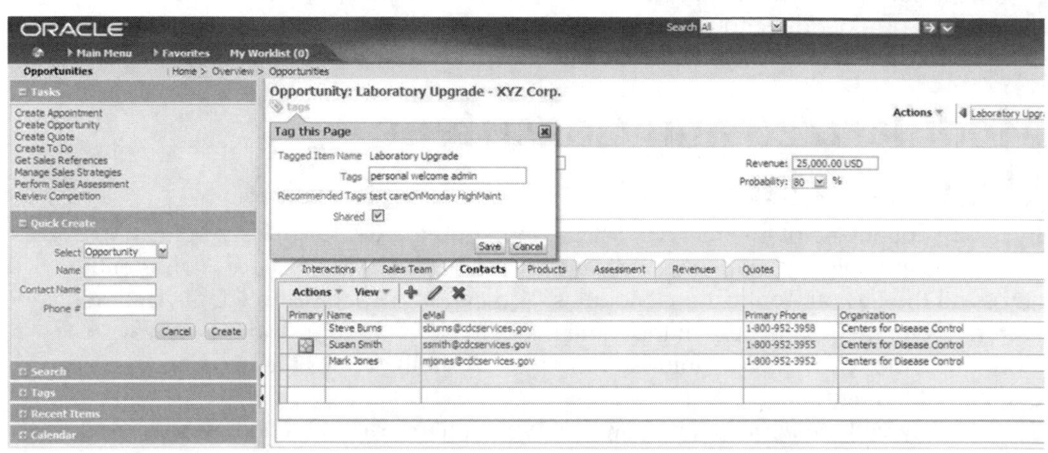

FIGURE 21-1 *Tagging a sales opportunity*

Not only do tags show up in simple search results, they also help users discover previously unknown relationships between their business objects. The main facilitator of this discovery is the Tag Center, shown in Figure 21-2. In addition to the tag cloud, the Tag Center features a number of ways to refine the result set, for example allowing you to specify additional tag keywords or the person who tagged the object.

Figure 21-3 shows an example of threaded discussions that are part of the projects module in Fusion Applications. In addition to high-level information, scheduling, and

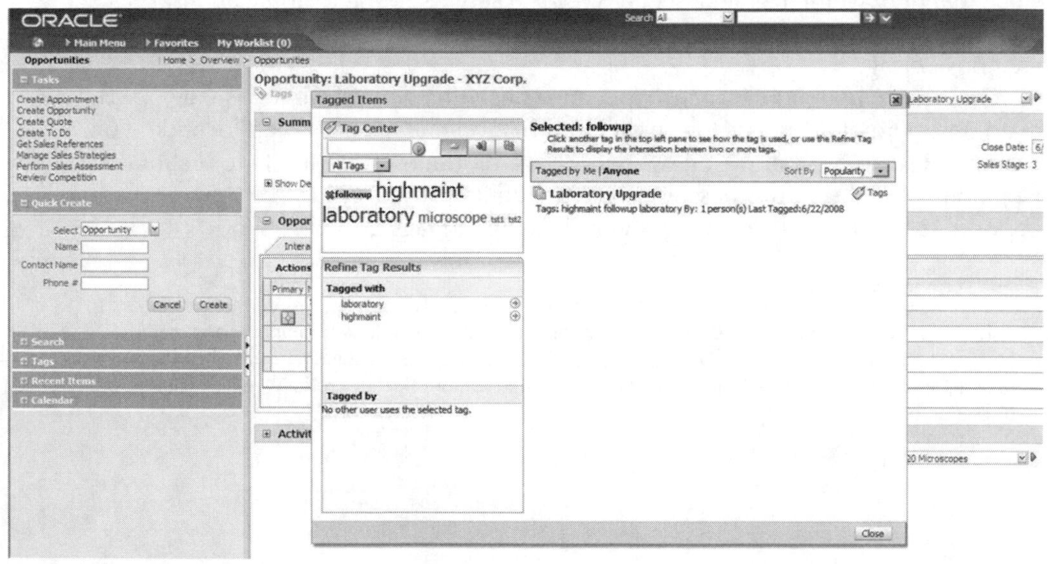

FIGURE 21-2 *Tag Center integrated with Fusion Applications*

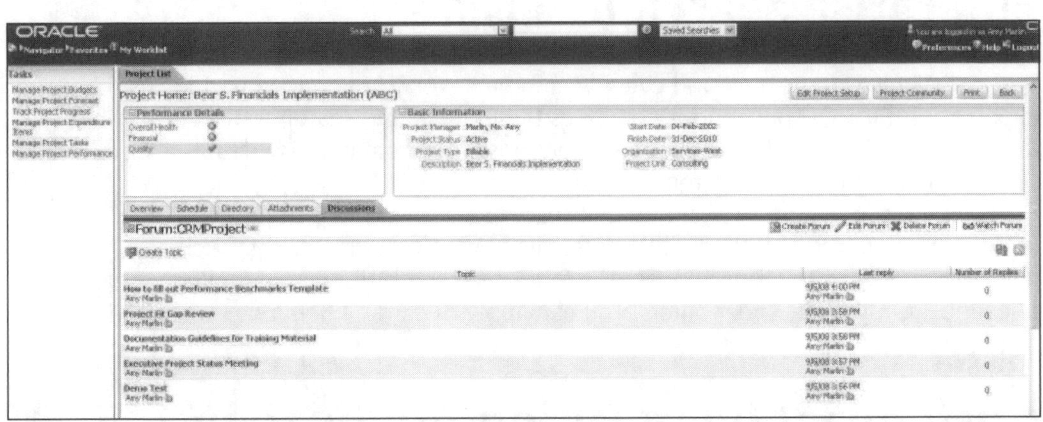

FIGURE 21-3 *Threaded discussions integrated with projects*

project-specific attachments, the page features threaded discussions, where project members can share information and discuss questions and issues.

Another example of how WebCenter services work with Fusion Applications is in the UI shell. Through UI shell icons, developers can let users have direct access to the groups of which they are members. Figure 21-4 shows how contacts are made instantaneously available to Fusion Applications users.

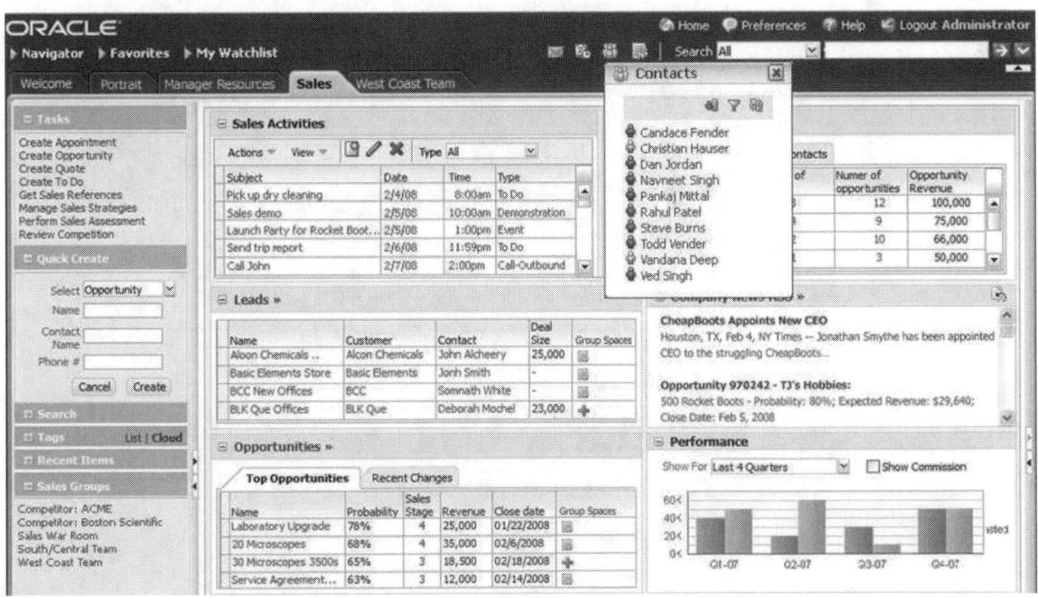

FIGURE 21-4 *Accessing contacts through the UI shell*

Enterprise Search in Fusion

It is critical for any business user to quickly find the information he or she needs. The WebCenter Framework and every WebCenter Web 2.0 Service provides search capabilities. Fusion Applications combines these integrated search tools with Oracle Secure Enterprise Search, enabling full, enterprise-, and database-wide full-text searches in an organized, customizable interface.

For example, Figure 21-5 shows that search results show up from a number of different sources, including all the integrated WebCenter resources, such as discussions, tags, and group spaces. The federated search results are ranked by relevance. On the left under Filters, you can apply dynamic filters on your search results.

Customization in Fusion Applications

Because the customization requirements of enterprise portals are very similar to those of enterprise applications, with Oracle WebCenter, Oracle chose a unique approach by leveraging the exact same infrastructure to store, manage, and expose

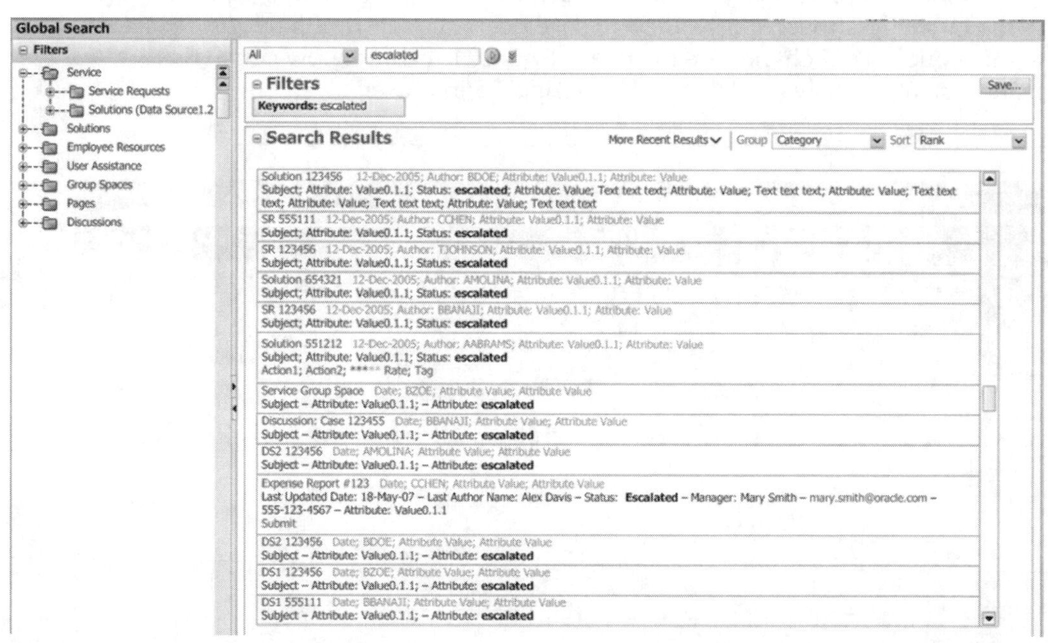

FIGURE 21-5 *Fusion global search integrated with WebCenter content*

customization capabilities in the two worlds. As part of the Oracle WebCenter Framework, Oracle Composer serves as the run-time customization UI, and Oracle Metadata Services (MDS) handles the storage of customization metadata.

Fusion Applications modules also enable developers to accommodate a broad array of customization requirements by using a dozen or more MDS customization layers. Developers can control each layer to finely tune the customization capabilities for each user. Developers can even use these layers to enable a whole range of customization actions at design time and run time.

Figure 21-6 shows a dialog that displays before a user invokes Oracle Composer in a Fusion Application at run time. The purpose of the dialog is to allow the user, typically with administrator privileges, to select the customization layer where the changes will be saved. This is just one example of a customization layer stored in MDS.

Figure 21-7 shows a Fusion Applications page in Edit mode, being edited with Oracle Composer.

It is important to note that Fusion Applications also places great importance on ensuring customizations are upgrade safe. That is, when a new version of Fusion Applications becomes available, you will be able to apply existing customization metadata to applications built with the new version.

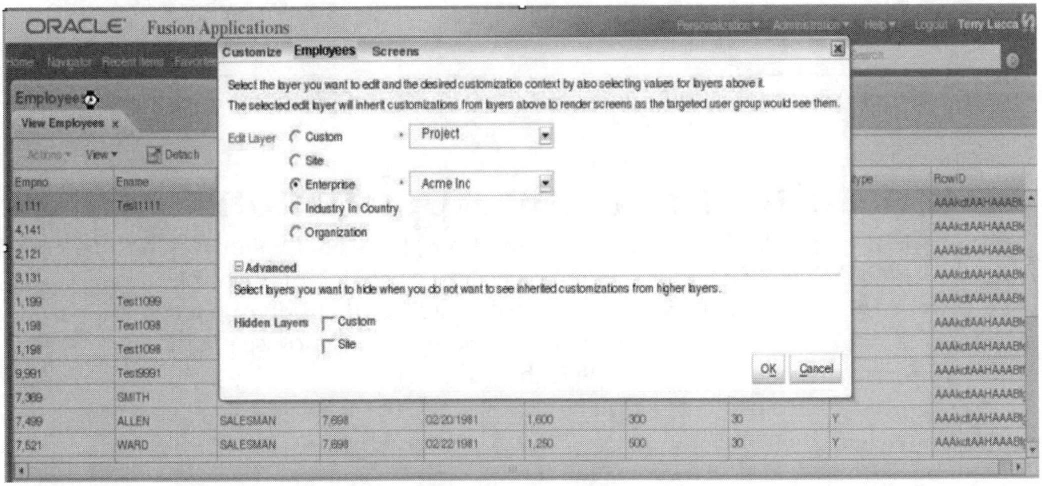

FIGURE 21-6 *Selecting the customization layer*

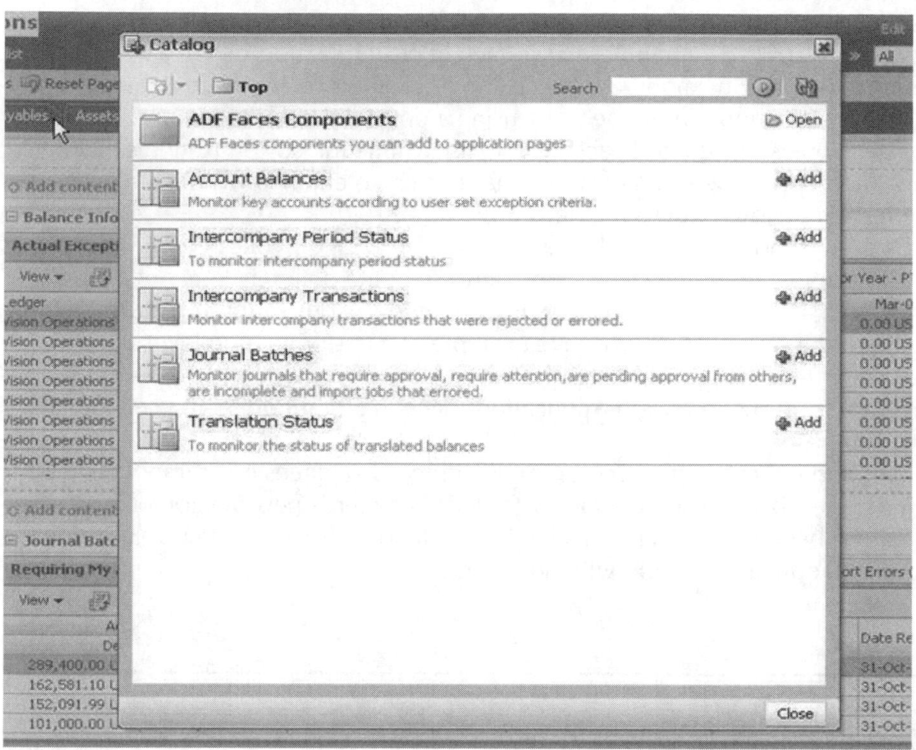

FIGURE 21-7 *Editing a Fusion Applications page with Oracle Composer*

Communities in Fusion Applications

While we do not cover WebCenter Spaces in this book, we want to point out that you can integrate WebCenter Spaces, including group spaces, with custom WebCenter applications. The integration between WebCenter Spaces and Fusion Applications is in the works too. WebCenter Spaces excels at providing an easy-to-use platform for business users to interact and collaborate with each other.

You can associate a dedicated group space with the business objects in Fusion Applications, which enables business users to collaborate in a single online community. Group spaces are beneficial in most cases where business users share a common goal. They can use collaborative services like discussions, documents, dynamically created pages, wikis, and blogs.

Users can also create group spaces as they need them. For example, a number of employees, or Fusion Applications users, may all be working with the same customer for different reasons. One of the users can quickly create a new group space and associate the group space with a custom relationship module. Then, all the users (and new users) who work with the customer can use the group space to communicate with each other and collaborate to share intelligence and foster their relationship with the customer.

Group spaces are tightly integrated into the Fusion Applications user interface, but are deployed and run separately by a WebCenter Spaces installation.

Figure 21-8 shows an example of linking group spaces to an opportunity business object. The UI allows you to navigate to a group space, associate an existing group space with the opportunity, or even create a new group space that will be associated with the opportunity.

Figure 21-9 demonstrates how group spaces are rendered in the UI of Fusion Applications.

You will also be able to embed Fusion Applications modules into Spaces applications by taking advantage of reusable components: task flows and portlets. You can expose task flows and portlets you create using Fusion Applications in WebCenter Spaces, which developers and users can then add to pages through Oracle Composer.

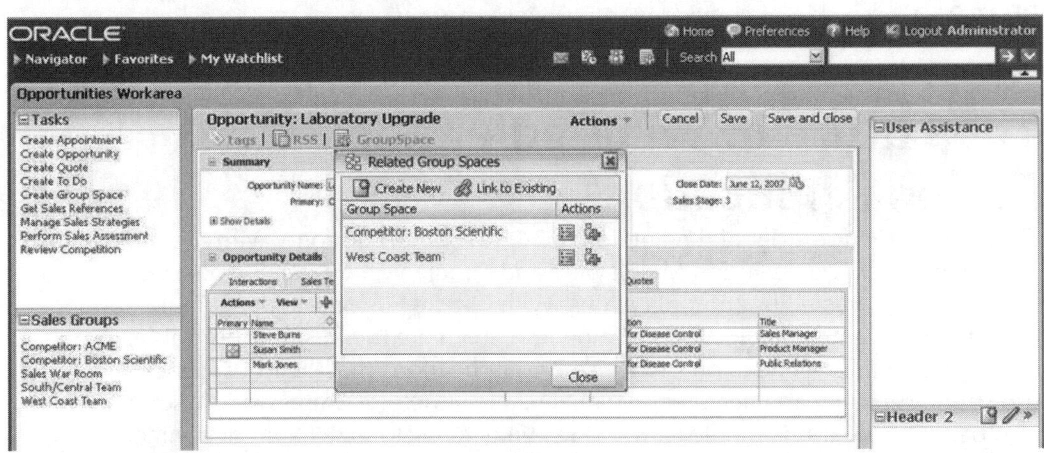

FIGURE 21-8 *Associating group spaces to Fusion Applications opportunities*

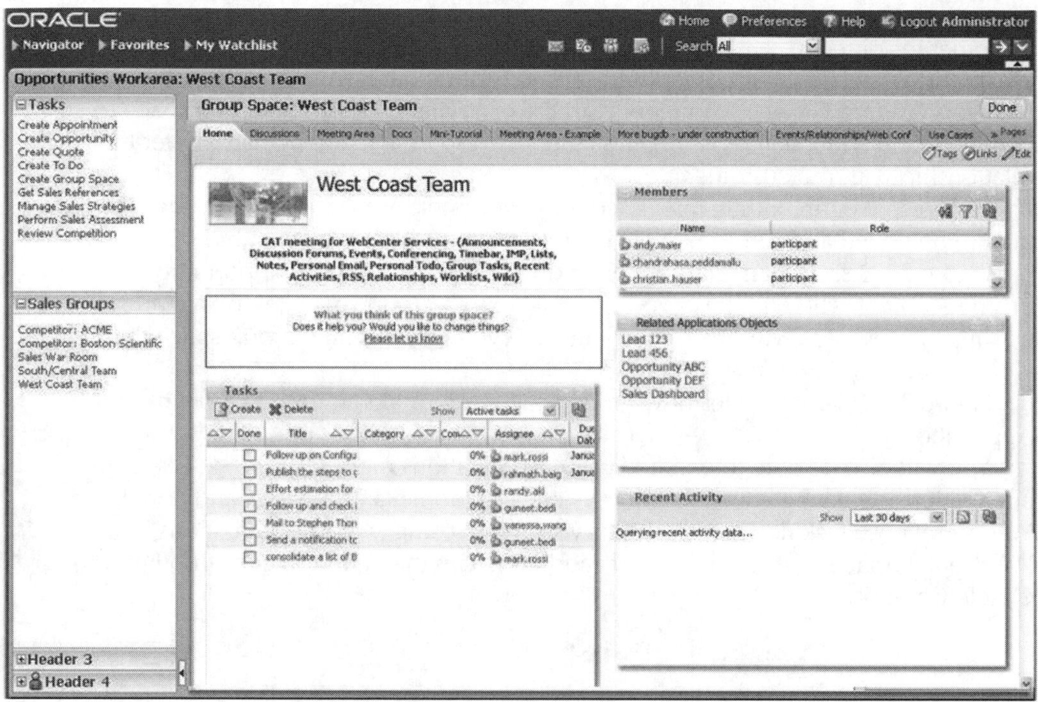

FIGURE 21-9 *Group spaces embedded into Fusion Applications*

The Future of WebCenter and Fusion Applications

Oracle is at the forefront of the Enterprise 2.0 revolution not only with the development of Oracle Fusion Middleware and Oracle WebCenter, but also with the emerging Oracle Fusion Applications. With Oracle Fusion Middleware, IT departments, namely application developers, can create the fully customizable, rich, complex next-generation Enterprise 2.0 applications that their businesses and users require, using an integrated, organized, and structured framework. Users will also benefit from this technology, with the ability to customize their environment specifically to their own needs, as well as to the needs of their collaborators.

With Oracle Fusion Applications, Oracle is striving toward enabling businesses, users, and application developers (or IT departments) to have the best of both worlds: off-the-shelf Enterprise 2.0 applications that can be fully customized for specific organizations with little start-up cost.

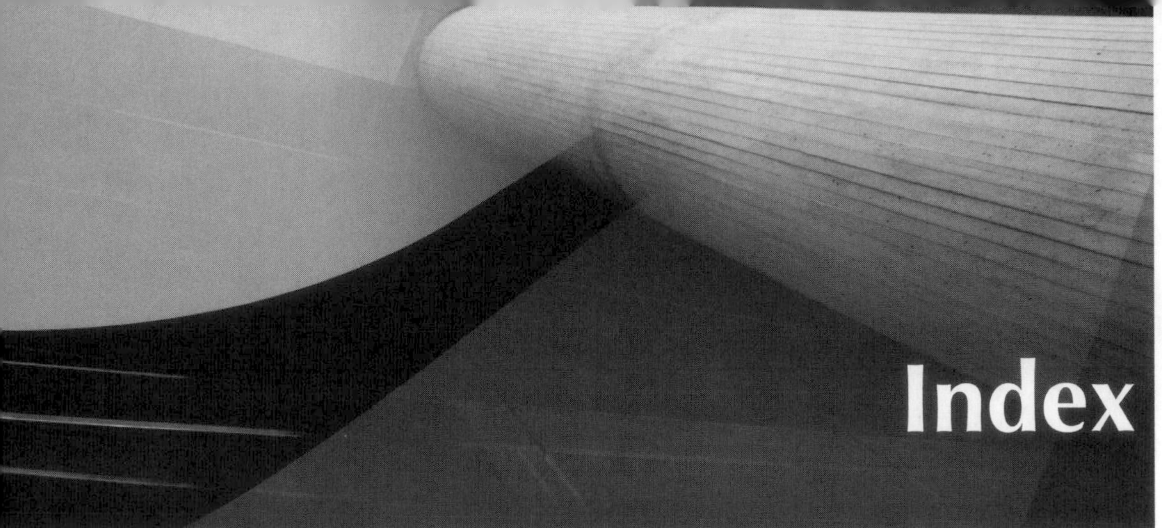

Index

A

B

D

E

F

G

H

I

N

O

Q

R

S

T

U

V

W

X

GET YOUR FREE SUBSCRIPTION TO *ORACLE MAGAZINE*

Oracle Magazine **is essential gear for today's information technology professionals.**
Stay informed and increase your productivity with every issue of *Oracle Magazine*.
Inside each free bimonthly issue you'll get:

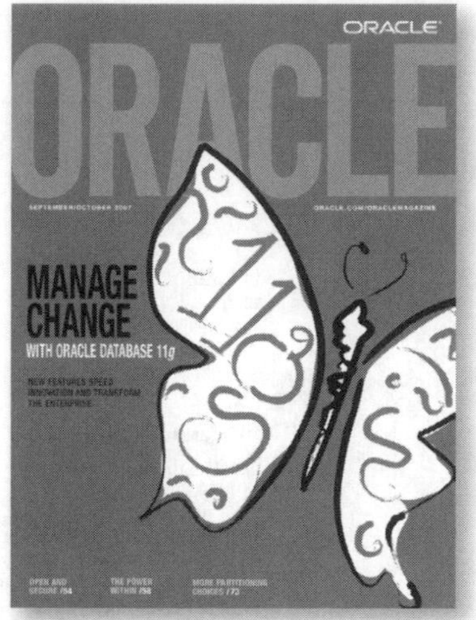

- Up-to-date information on Oracle Database, Oracle Application Server, Web development, enterprise grid computing, database technology, and business trends
- Third-party news and announcements
- Technical articles on Oracle and partner products, technologies, and operating environments
- Development and administration tips
- Real-world customer stories

If there are other Oracle users at your location who would like to receive their own subscription to *Oracle Magazine*, please photocopy this form and pass it along.

Three easy ways to subscribe:

① **Web**
Visit our Web site at **oracle.com/oraclemagazine**
You'll find a subscription form there, plus much more

② **Fax**
Complete the questionnaire on the back of this card and fax the questionnaire side only to **+1.847.763.9638**

③ **Mail**
Complete the questionnaire on the back of this card and mail it to **P.O. Box 1263, Skokie, IL 60076-8263**

ORACLE

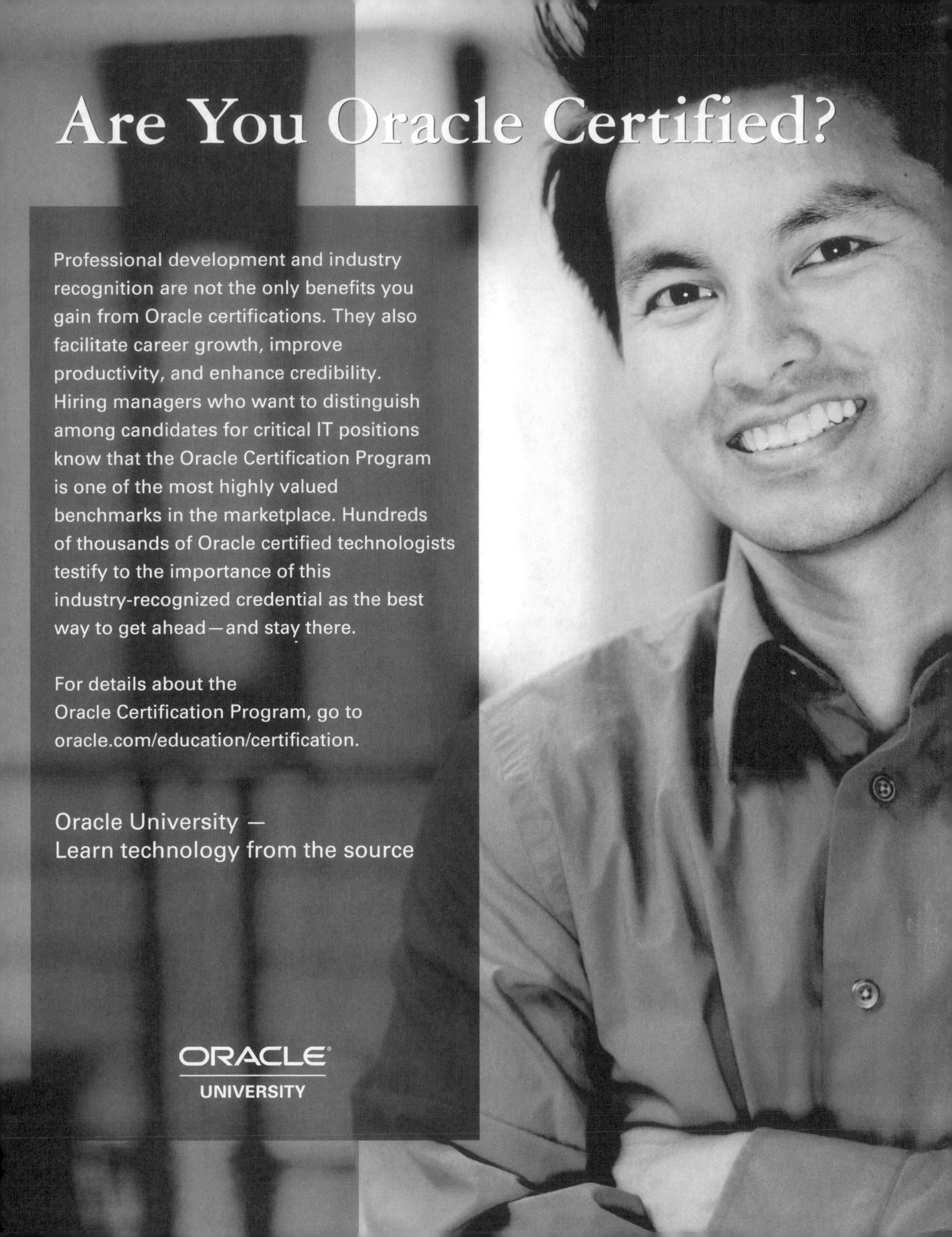
Are You Oracle Certified?
Professional development and industry recognition are not the only benefits you gain from Oracle certifications. They also facilitate career growth, improve productivity, and enhance credibility. Hiring managers who want to distinguish among candidates for critical IT positions know that the Oracle Certification Program is one of the most highly valued benchmarks in the marketplace. Hundreds of thousands of Oracle certified technologists testify to the importance of this industry-recognized credential as the best way to get ahead—and stay there.
For details about the Oracle Certification Program, go to oracle.com/education/certification.
Oracle University — Learn technology from the source
ORACLE
UNIVERSITY